Social Legislation of the
East India Company

Social Legislation of the East India Company

Public Justice versus Public Instruction

Nancy Gardner Cassels

Los Angeles | London | New Delhi
Singapore | Washington DC | Melbourne

Copyright © Nancy Gardner Cassels, 2010

All rights reserved. No part of this book may be reproduced or utilized in any form or by any means, electronic or mechanical, including photocopying, recording or by any information storage or retrieval system, without permission in writing from the publisher.

First published in 2010 by

SAGE Publications India Pvt Ltd
B1/I-1 Mohan Cooperative Industrial Area
Mathura Road, New Delhi 110 044, India
www.sagepub.in

SAGE Publications Ltd
2455 Teller Road
Thousand Oaks, California 91320, USA

SAGE Publications Inc
1 Oliver's Yard, 55 City Road
London EC1Y 1SP, United Kingdom

SAGE Publications Asia-Pacific Pte Ltd
3 Church Street
#10-04 Samsung Hub
Singapore 049483

Published by Vivek Mehra for SAGE Publications India Pvt Ltd, typeset in 10/12pt Adobe Garamond by Star Compugraphics Private Limited, Delhi.

Library of Congress Cataloging-in-Publication Data

Cassels, Nancy Gardner, 1936–

    Social legislation of the East India company : public justice versus public instruction/Nancy Gardner Cassels.

      p. cm.

    Includes bibliographical references and index.

    1. Social legislation—India—History—18th century. 2. Social legislation—India—History—19th century. 3. East India Company. I. Title.

KNS1208.C37   344.54—dc22   2010   2010040014

ISBN: 978-81-321-0515-2 (HB)

The SAGE Team: Qudsiya Ahmed, Pranab Jyoti Sarma, Nand Kumar Jha and Umesh Kashyap

To Alan

Contents

Acknowledgements   ix

Introduction   3
- Introduction of English Law amidst Indian Laws and Customs   5
- 'Venal Pandits' and *Shastra* Patronage   11
- Criminal Law   16
- Retreat from Codification   20

1. Law, Order and Power: Thagi, Dacoity and Sorcery   28
- Thagi and Dacoity   28
- Sorcery   71
- Murder of Children for the Sake of Their Ornaments   80
- Hook Swinging   82
- Conclusion   82

2. Law as a Weapon against Child Sacrifice, *Sati*, Female Infanticide and Meriah Sacrifice   86
- Child Sacrifice at Saugor Island   86
- *Sati*   88
- Female Infanticide   112
- Meriah Sacrifice and Female Infanticide among the Konds   140
- Conclusion   156

3. The Legal Rights of Coolies, Slaves and Emigrant Workers   165
- Coolie Labour   167
- Slavery   173
- Emigrant Labour   209
- Conclusion   234

4. **Civil Law and the Policy of Religious Toleration** — 245
   - Temple Management — 246
   - Religious Disabilities Removal Act, 1850 — 256
   - Remarriage of Hindu Widows — 272
   - Hindu Wills — 292
   - Adultery and Polygamy — 293

5. **Abkarry and Pilgrim Taxes: Excise as a Regulating Instrument** — 295
   - Opium Monopoly — 298
   - Pilgrim Tax — 319
   - Revenue or Regulation? — 336

6. **Public Instruction Begets Indian Agency, Free Press and Trial by Jury** — 338
   - Public Instruction — 339
   - Indian Agency — 354
   - Female Education — 360
   - Emergence of a Free Press — 364
   - Trial by Jury — 381
   - Judicial Oaths — 391

Conclusion: Social Legislation in the Arena of Public Instruction versus Public Justice — 395

Some Key Pieces of Social Legislation — 404
Glossary — 414
Bibliography — 421
Index — 439
About the Author — 448

Acknowledgements

This volume has been a work in progress for many years during which time many individuals and institutions have rendered support and assistance. Initially, during work on my doctoral dissertation at the University of Toronto, Professors Milton Israel and Narendra Wagle with the external approval of Professor Holden Furber at the University of Pennsylvania encouraged my study of the East India Company's (Co.) social legislation. This led to extensive research visits to Great Britain and India. An invaluable resource has been the British Library with its special collections in the India Office Library where staff generally were and remain very helpful and where I owe special debts of gratitude to Dr Richard Bingle, Martin Moir and Timothy Thomas. Other British archives important to my research were the Bentinck Papers at Nottingham University, Church Missionary Society Records at Birmingham University, Colonial Office Records and Cornwallis and Ellenborough Papers at the National Archives at Kew, Dalhousie and Baird of Elie papers at the National Archives of Scotland and the Dundas of Ochtertyre Muniments and Walker of Bowland Papers at the National Library of Scotland. Other important libraries in England are the Oxford Indian Institute Library and the Oxford Law Library where Ronald Richenburg helped me to disentangle some legal jargon. In India, the National Archives of India in New Delhi provided a central focus before visits to the Andhra Pradesh State Archives, the Bombay Record Office, the Bihar State Archives, the Tamil Nadu Archives, the Uttar Pradesh State Archives at Allahabad, Lucknow and Dehra Dun and the West Bengal State Archives. The Supreme Court Libraries in Calcutta and Chennai were also very hospitable. Research grants from the Social Sciences and Humanities Research Council of Canada and the Shastri Indo-Canadian Institute made visits to these archives possible. I do hope both these institutions will deem this return on their investment worthwhile. Footnotes and bibliography pay tribute to the multitude of scholars who have gone before me in investigating the context of the East India Co.'s social legislation. I owe a particular debt of gratitude to individual scholars who offered inspiration, encouragement and helpful criticism along the way. In this connection, I would like to mention Professor B.N. Pandey, prematurely and tragically deceased, Professor Peter J. Marshall, Professor Robert E. Frykenberg and Professor Geoffrey Oddie. Finally, I pay tribute to my husband, Alan, and daughters, Celia and Jennifer, who patiently kept the proverbial home fires burning during my lengthy research trips. Alan, in particular, as a well-known and published historian, has always set a high standard for me to emulate.

Photograph 1: 'Infanticide in India as Practised in the Temple of Ganesa'
Courtesy, Center for Study of the Life and Work of William Carey, D.D. (1761–1834)
William Carey University, Hattiesburg, Mississippi, USA.

Introduction

Trois degrés d'élévation du pôle renversent toute la jurisprudence, un méridien décide de la vérité. [Three degrees of latitude reverse the whole of jurisprudence, one meridian decides the truth.][1]

Although Pascal was pondering the fate of jurisprudence amidst contrasting cultures on opposite sides of the Pyrenees, his thoughts are remarkably apropos the development of Anglo-Indian law in British India during the late eighteenth and early nineteenth centuries. Depending on the perspective, be it that of a *pandit*, a *kazi*, a *vakeel*, a district magistrate, a puisne judge or a Chief Justice, the law could be the symptom or the cause of both order and disorder, both justice and injustice—not to mention illicit personal gain. The development of what came to be known as Anglo-Indian law was a tortuous process involving many contradictions in principle and practice. Whereas the English East India Company began in the seventeenth century in Bombay to build a system of jurisprudence which called for absolute respect for local custom and usage, by the nineteenth century its Government in Bengal had acquired sufficient confidence to attempt to influence some customs and usage through social legislation enforced by Company Courts. This was not a straightforward process. There were many twists and turns. Essentially, Company administrators, beginning with Warren Hastings, worked through the medium of Muslim criminal law in order to avoid confrontation over civil law. However, with the Caste Disabilities Removal Act of 1850, the Company dared to breach the barrier in Hindu civil law protecting the Hindu joint family from inheritance claims of religious converts. And, just before the end of its reign, the Company attempted in 1856 to legislate the right of the Hindu widow to remarry.

In order to come to terms with the enormous variety of circumstances and thought patterns which led the Company to enact legislation regarding some social issues but not others, it is necessary to be free of notions about

---

[1] Blaise Pascal, *Pensées #60*, Lafuma, ed. (Harmondsworth, 1966), p. 46.

4   *Social Legislation of the East India Company*

the 'colonial state'. Before historians of nineteenth-century India became swept up in the conspiracy theories of anti-elitist defenders of the subaltern ranks of Indian society or by the anti-Orientalist literary deconstructionist followers of Edward Said, Holden Furber issued a warning 'that the words "colony" and "colonial" were almost never used in Bengal or India, and the word "empire" seldom'.[2] As John Rogers has observed with respect to criminal justice, there were 'other processes in the British period (such as) the centralization of the state and the expansion of a market economy which were more important than the colonial nature of the state'.[3] Indeed, the new Cambridge Histories have effectively revealed the lively interaction between the highly developed commercial economy of late Mughal India and the maritime trading connections provided by the East India Co.[4] A focus upon the 'colonial state' can be misleading. For example, B. Cohn concludes in his 'Law and the Colonial State in India' that after the 1864 judicial reforms banished Hindu and Muslim law officers from the courts, Hindu law was transformed 'into a form of English case law...with English law as the law of India'.[5] This contrasts sharply with the view of Professor S. Venkataraman:

> Till 1864 it could have been said with regard to Hindu law that no voice was heard unless it came from the tomb. Thereafter it proved to be a living and growing system showing an amazing adaptability to modern conditions. This was mainly due to the impact of English law on the Hindu law.[6]

---

[2] Holden Furber, 'The Theme of Imperialism and Colonialism in Modern Historical Writing on India,' in C.H. Philips, ed., *Historians of India, Pakistan and Ceylon* (London, 1962), pp. 334, 337.

[3] John D. Rogers, 'The Historical Study of Crime in South Asia,' *Criminal Justice History* 7 (1986).

[4] See, for example, C.A. Bayly, *Indian Society and the Making of the British Empire—The New Cambridge History of India*, Part II-1 (Cambridge, 1988); P.J. Marshall, *Bengal: The British Bridgehead, Eastern India 1740–1828—The New Cambridge History of India*, Part II-2 (Cambridge, 1987); C.A. Bayly, *Rulers, Townsmen and Bazaars, North Indian Society in the Age of British Expansion, 1770–1870* (Cambridge, 1983); D.A. Washbrook, 'Progress and Problems: South Asian Economic and Social History c. 1720–1860,' *Modern Asian Studies*, Vol. 22, Part 1 (1988); all cited in Nancy G. Cassels, ed., *Orientalism, Evangelicalism and the Military Cantonment in Early Nineteenth-Century India—A Historiographical Overview* (Lewiston/Queenston/Lampeter, 1991), pp. 2–3.

[5] Bernard S. Cohn, 'Law and the Colonial State in India,' in June Starr and Jane F. Collier, eds, *History and Power in the Study of Law* (Ithaca, N.Y., 1989), pp. 150–51.

[6] S. Venkataraman, 'Influence of Common Law and Equity on the Personal Law of the Hindus,' *Revista del Instituto de Derecho Comparado (Barcelona)* Vols. 8–9 (1957): 178, cited by J.D.M. Derrett, *Religion, Law and the State in India* (London, 1968), p. 315.

If the historian is to determine as nearly as possible what actually happened when the East India Co. entered the arena of social reform, the pejorative imaginings of post-Marxist, post-structuralist literary and political critics must be laid to rest. Otherwise we must join with Wendy Doniger who, in order to prepare the way for her translation of *The Laws of Manu*, finds it necessary to declare that 'the time has come' for 'anti-anti-"Orientalism"'. Yet, although Doniger disengages herself from the anti-Orientalist view that any translation is necessarily a cultural rape, she protests that 'the most common translation of the title, "laws", skews it towards what the British hoped to make of it: a tool with which to rule the Hindoo.'[7]

Another standard charge levelled against the 'colonial state' is that in the British courts Hindu law and society fossilized. In a speech before the Lok Sabha on 21 May 1954, Jawaharlal Nehru declared that British rule had suppressed dynamic elements within Hindu society thereby making change possible only by legislation. J.D.M. Derrett insists that there was no complaint 'about the effects of fossilization'. Instead, 'what had bothered people was the distance between the personal law and the system by which they wanted to live'.[8]

Introduction of English Law amidst Indian Laws and Customs

Charters issued by Charles II to the East India Co. in 1661 and 1668 provided the earliest authorization for the Company to exercise judicial powers in its factory settlements in India. However, most authorities consider that the Charter of 1726 establishing a Mayor's Court in each of the three presidency towns, in fact, introduced British statute law into India for the first time.[9] Although not expressly stated, it has generally been understood

---

[7] Wendy Doniger and Brian K. Smith, trans., *The Laws of Manu* (London; New York, 1991), pp. xvii–xviii, xlix.

[8] J.D.M. Derrett, *op. cit.*, pp. 315–16; P.V. Kane, *History of Dharmasastra*, 2d ed. (Poona, 1973) III, pp. 820–24 and *Journal of the Bombay Royal Asiatic Society*, Vol. 6 (1925): 34–39.

[9] W.H. Morley, *An Analytical Digest of all the Reported Cases Decided in the Supreme Courts of Judicature in India, in the Courts of the Hon. East-India Company & on appeal from India, by Her Majesty in Council* (London, 1850) I, pp. xi, xxiii and George C. Rankin, *Background to Indian Law* (Cambridge, 1946), p. 1, cf. A.B. Keith, *Constitutional History of India 1600–1935* (London, 1937), p. 36. Keith dates the introduction of English law back to the establishment of the Court of Judicature in Bombay in 1672. Sir Erskine Perry ruled in 'Maclean v. Cristall' [1849] that 'the period when English law was introduced on this side of India...cannot be placed... later...than 1661'. E. Perry, *Cases Illustrative of Oriental Life* (London, 1853), p. 89.

that the terms of the Letters Patent of 1726 intended the Mayor's Courts and Courts of Quarter Sessions in Bombay, Madras and Calcutta to follow legal procedures based on English law. This enabled civil grants of probate and testamentary jurisdiction to be recognized by English courts and criminal indictments to be supported by petty and grand juries. Indians were only eligible to serve on juries if they were Christians, a restriction which lasted for another one hundred years.[10] The Mayor's Courts were essentially courts of the King of England with final appeal in substantial cases to the King in Council; the Court of Quarter Sessions consisted of the Governor and five senior members of Council who exercised the powers of English Justices of the Peace. The Letters Patent of 1726 also bestowed legislative power on the Governor and Council, provided that their regulations were not contrary to the laws of England and were confirmed by the Court of Directors. This was an important initiative, inasmuch as there had hitherto been no serious claim to legislative authority by any of the presidency governments.

The essential reason why the Mayor's Courts of 1727 are regarded as significant symbols of the introduction of English law is that they were established by royal authority, whereas earlier courts had been established by the second hand authority of the Company. The Mayor's Courts of 1727, royally endowed, were quick to establish their judicial independence. In 1730, the Company upheld the authority of the Mayor's Court in Bombay against the Governor's Council over issues of religion and caste. Similarly in Madras in 1736, the Mayor's Court sentenced two Indian merchants to prison for refusing to take oaths 'contrary to their Religion and the Rules of their Cast', and thereby provoked a near riot among Hindus followed by a reprimand from the Governor who released the merchants on parole. The Company responded by upholding the authority of the court while censuring its spirit.[11] The interaction between English statute law and the laws and customs of Hindus, Muslims, Parsees, Jains, Jews, Armenians, Portuguese, Konds, Bhils and other tribal peoples was truly the crucial issue in the development of Indian jurisprudence. Each presidency experimented with different methods of administering justice to Indian inhabitants of the Company and its adjacent territories.

As early as 1674, Governor Aungier of Bombay recommended that the authority of caste *panchayat*s to administer justice within their caste constituency be recognized. Under the impromptu system of justice inaugurated by

---

[10] Wynn's Jury Act [1826] 7 Geo IV c. 7 admitted non-Christian Indians to petty juries and 2&3 Wm IV c. 17 [1832] admitted non-Christian Indians to grand juries. See Chapter 6.

[11] H.D. Love, *Vestiges of Old Madras 1640–1800*, Vol. II (London, 1913), p. 276. A.B. Keith, *op. cit.*, pp. 45, 48.

the Company in Bombay in 1718, *chowghula*s,[12] headmen and *vereadores*[13]—who represented various castes and communities—were virtually empowered to act as an inferior court settling caste and communal disputes. Justices referred questions of indigenous law and custom to *chowghula*s, *kazi*s, caste headmen or even Hindu or Muslim merchants. Cases are on record of the Bombay Court reversing the orders of a *panchayat* for caste expulsion.[14]

In Bengal, the Company gained jurisdiction over Indians when it purchased the three villages of Sutanati, Govindpur and Calcutta and thereby acquired *zamindari* rights. A member of council regularly presided over a *Zamindari* Court administering both civil and criminal law. This court survived the establishment of the Mayor's Court in 1727, only to be divided into two courts in 1758 as a result of criticism of its claim to jurisdiction over disputes between Europeans and Indians of European descent. The two new courts were designated as criminal and civil courts, respectively. There was a third Cutcherry Court which reenforced the coercive powers of *zamindar*s in their capacity as collectors of revenue. These Courts were known to indulge in customary practices of flogging delinquents 'even unto death' and of allowing, against all traditions of English law, an interested party to act as judge and inflict punishment in his own cause.[15] These three *zamindari* courts in Bengal were unique among the three presidencies for their consistent capacity to administer justice within the Indian community.

In seventeenth-century Madras, the Company had assumed jurisdiction over Indians from the moment local petty chieftains conceded authority to the English government. Thus, in the 1680s it is recorded that the Company's government claimed powers of capital punishment over Indians, a power neither claimed nor exercised in Bombay or Calcutta; and in 1680 the Governor even dared to forbid a *sati*.[16] Nevertheless, in the first instance disputes among Indians were left to the Indian *adigar* or town governor to arbitrate according to custom at the choultry or town house. And in 1678, three justices were appointed to the Choultry Court with appeal in the form of a jury trial presided over by the Governor and Council. In 1727, the Company disapproved efforts by the Madras Council to supersede the

---

[12] Maratha word for assistant to a patil or village headman.
[13] Municipal officers who were a legacy of Portuguese rule.
[14] See, for example, Bandaree caste expulsion case reversed in Bombay Court of Justice Proceedings 4 November 1724, I.O.R., Bombay Proceedings P/416/99, fol. 29.
[15] W. Bolts, *Considerations on India Affairs* (London, 1772) I, pp. 80–81, 110–11n.
[16] M.P. Jain, *op. cit.*, pp. 30–31 and E. Thompson and G.T. Garratt, *Rise and Fulfilment of British Rule in India* (London, 1934), p. 49.

Choultry Courts which continued to exercise minor criminal jurisdiction until their abolition in 1800.

The clash in 1730 between the Mayor's Court and Governor's Council in Bombay over religious and caste issues was echoed in the Petition of Castes in 1731 to the Madras Government. The Company ruled that disputes among Indians should be settled according to local custom by themselves; if, however, Indians wished their dispute to be resolved in the English courts, then English law must apply. To quell these conflicts, the Charter of 1753 decreed that all suits between Indians were exempted from the jurisdiction of the English courts unless expressly submitted by both parties. W.H. Morley considered that this was the first reservation of their own laws and customs to Indians, although he claimed that this rule was ignored for all practical purposes in Bombay.[17] In Madras, the Choultry Court had such limited authority that there was no effective alternative to the Mayor's Court. Only in Bengal was the exemption of suits between Indians effective because the Zamindari Courts were already disposing of such cases.[18] As for the employment of Indians in any position of judicial authority, the prospects were bleak.[19] Nevertheless, the reservation to Indians of their own laws by the 1753 Charter was the first manifestation of the most consistent feature of Anglo-Indian law in its development up to the present day. To implement his instructions to 'stand forth as *diwan*', Warren Hastings proposed his celebrated plan for the Administration of Justice which was adopted in 1772 complete with the 23rd Rule:

> That in all suits regarding inheritance, marriage and caste and other religious usages or institutions, the laws of the Koran with respect to Mahomedans, and those of the Shaster with respect to Gentoos shall be invariably adhered to.

Empowered to make laws by Lord North's Regulating Act of 1773 [Sec. 36, 13 Geo III c. 63], Hastings' Council enacted the Bengal Government's first Judicial Regulation on 11 April 1780 incorporating the 23rd Rule word for word as Sec. 27.[20] The next year the Rules governing the Company's Sudder and Mofussil Adawlut courts were revised by Chief Justice Impey

---

[17] W.H. Morley, *op. cit.*, p. clxix; Justice Erskine Perry argued the reverse in 'Perozeboye v. Ardaseer Cursetjee' [1843] in E. Perry, *op. cit.*

[18] One volume of Bengal Zamindary Court Proceedings in 1766 is extant in the India Office Records, I.O.R., P/155/71.

[19] In 1692, the Co. alluded with disapproval to the fact that in 1690 as many as 8 of the 12 Madras aldermen were English. H.D. Love, *op. cit.*, I, p. 503.

[20] I.O.R., V/8/15, p. 133.

who added the word 'succession' to Hastings' list of reserved subjects.[21] Until recently Impey has been credited with the suggestion 'that in all cases within the jurisdiction of the Mofussil Dewannee Adawlut, for which no specific Directions are hereby given, the respective Judges thereof do act according to Justice, Equity and good Conscience'.[22] Meanwhile, in 1781 Hastings' amended list appeared in statute law as Sec. 17, 21 Geo III c. 70 and was applied subsequently to Madras and Bombay by Secs 12–13, 37 Geo III c. 142 [1797]. 21 Geo III c. 70 was a declaratory act passed to explain powers of the Supreme Court. Specifically, it gave civil jurisdiction to the Supreme Court over Indians resident in Calcutta with the exception of the reserved subjects on Hastings' list. Sec. 17, revised Hastings' list to include 'inheritance and succession to lands, rents and goods and all matters of contract and dealing between party and party', and to exclude 'marriage, caste and other religious usages'. Thus the Supreme Court was effectively limited to questions of inheritance and contract. Sec. 17 further introduced the law of the defendant stipulating that disputes between native inhabitants of Calcutta should be determined 'where only one of the parties shall be a Mahomedan or Gentoo, by the laws and usages of the defendant'. Sec. 18 protected family custom according to Hindu or Muslim law by concluding that 'acts done in consequence of the rule and law of caste' shall not 'be held and adjudged a crime, although the same may not be held justifiable by the laws of England'.

Constitutional authorities note that while Secs 17 and 18, 21 Geo III c. 70 entrench Hastings' list in statute law, it confuses the issue of where the Government intended to draw the line between English law and Indian laws. As pointed out by Rankin, according to 21 Geo III c. 70, within Calcutta the residual law was to be the law of England, not the formula of 'justice, equity and good conscience' of Bengal Judicial Regulation VI 1781. J.H. Harington stated emphatically in his *Analysis* that thoughts of 'substituting' for the provisions of Muslim Criminal law 'a new code of laws, founded on those of England...were not the sentiments of those who framed the Laws and Regulations comprised in the Bengal Code of 1793'.[23] As for 'Justice, equity and good conscience', J.D.M. Derrett traces the origins of the formula

---

[21] Beng. Judl. Reg. VI 1781 sec. 37, I.O.R., V/8/15, p. 168.

[22] Beng. Judl. Reg. VI 1781 sec. 60, I.O.R., V/8/15, p. 176; cf. G.C. Rankin, *op. cit.*, p. 2 and J.D.M. Derrett in J.N.D. Anderson, *op. cit.*, pp. 133–39.

[23] J.H. Harington, *An Elementary Analysis of the Laws and Regulations Enacted by the Governor General in Council at Fort William in Bengal, for the Civil Government of the British Territories under that Presidency* (Calcutta, 1808) 2nd Part, Sec. II, pp. 341–42.

to Roman law, thus allowing judges, in the absence of a clear Hindu or Muslim law, to draw upon a wide range of Roman Law, law of continental Europe and ultimately Natural Law. The provisions of the 1781 Judicial Regulation for judges to apply 'justice, equity and good conscience' were copied in subsequent Regulations and ultimately in Statute law.

Hastings' list was to undergo yet further permutations. It was reincarnated in the Cornwallis Code as Sec. 15 Beng. Reg. IV 1793. This regulation recites the complete list as published in Beng. Judl. Reg. VI 1781, rather than the 1781 Statute law's emphasis upon inheritance and contract, but refers simply to 'Mahomedan laws' and 'Hindoo Laws' instead of the 'Koran' and the 'Shaster'. This would appear to indicate a movement away from the focus on religious texts during Hastings' time. But there was little indication that there was any understanding of the complex variety of legal traditions current among Muslims and Hindus—not to mention Parsees, Jains, Jews and Armenians. The eighteenth-century conception of Indian law as religious law based on sacred books was to ignore, in the case of Islam, three sources of law in addition to the Koran, namely, tradition or *hadith*, consensus of the learned or *ijma* and analogical reasoning or *kiyas*. In addition, there were four schools of Sunni law; Shia law was practically ignored in Bengal until 1810. To focus on the *shastras* as the source of Hindu law was to ignore that Hindu law is rooted in custom. Indeed, custom also entrenched upon sacred Muslim law. Sec. 3 Beng. Reg. VIII 1795 extended Sec. 15 Beng. Reg. IV 1793 to Benares and the Upper Provinces, but added to it the law of the defendant. An echo of Sec. 17 of 21 Geo III c. 70, Sec. 3 Beng. Reg. VIII 1795 decreed that 'in cases in which the plaintiff shall be of a different religious persuasion from the defendant, the decision is to be regulated by the law of the religion of the latter'.[24] This rule became a bone of contention for Lord William Bentinck's judicial reforms. Sec. 8 Beng. Reg. VII 1832 turned the tables on the defendant by rescinding the clauses of Sec. 3 Beng. Reg. VIII 1795 cited above and reinstating Sec. XV Beng. Reg. IV 1793 pure and simple. Thus the law of the defendant was replaced by the formula 'justice, equity and good conscience'. At the same time, the Bengal Government was keen to ensure that an English law or rule would only be allowed to displace biased religious law if it happened to be an expression of the formula 'justice, equity and good conscience'.[25] Ironically, Beng. Reg. VII 1832

---

[24] I.O.R., V/8/16, p. 480.
[25] N.B. English law was not applied in 'Gopeekrist v. Gungapersaud' (1854) 6 M.I.A. 53, 75–76, and in 'Soorjemoney Dossee v. Denobundoo Mullick, etc.' (1857) 9 M.I.A. 549–56. In the latter case, the Privy Council emphasized the spirit of Hindu law.

served as the precursor of the Caste Disabilities Removal Act of 1850—an Act which, in protecting the property rights of Christian converts, threatened property customs of the Hindu joint family and thus violated the spirit evoked by Hastings' reserved list.

In Bombay where local custom or usage had been acknowledged by the courts since the time of Aungier's emphasis on the *panchayat*s, the law of the defendant was used as a wedge to open the door to local usage or custom. Sec. 14, Bom. Reg. IV 1799, unlike its Madras counterpart (Sec. 16, Mad. Reg. III 1802), did not follow the policy implied by Hastings' list as it was inscribed in Sec. 15, Beng. Reg. IV 1793 of the Cornwallis Code. It stipulated that all civil suits concerning property, marriage or caste were 'to be decided, as far as shall depend on the point of law, by that of the defendant' in the case of Hindus and Mussalmans; 'with respect to Portuguese and Parsee...defendants, the judge is to be guided by a view to equity...making due allowance for their respective customs'. 'But in all cases of succession to landed property, the Judge is...to ascertain...any general usage of the district where the disputed land is situated, or...any particular usage of the family of the defendant.' In addition, the law of the defendant applied in Bombay to criminal cases, as well as the civil suits covered by Hastings' list. Finally, Elphinstone's Code continued to honour the law of the defendant. Although custom, where ascertainable, was the primary rule on all subjects, Sec. 26 Bom. Reg. IV 1827 decreed that, failing statute law and usage of the country, the law of the defendant prevailed. In the absence of any specific law, the formula of 'justice, equity and good conscience' came into play.

'Venal Pandits' and *Shastra* Patronage

It is necessary to return once again to the Governor Generalship of Warren Hastings to discover some of the perceptions and misperceptions of attitudes and motives which bedevilled 'Orientalist' scholarship concerning the sources of Hindu and Muslim laws. It was the 'choices made and confirmed in 1772 and 1781' which established the framework for Anglo-Indian law as it is today. Hastings' 'Plan for the Administration of Justice' of 1772 was a response to the near breakdown of a justice system in the hands of Indians.[26]

---

[26] B.N. Pandey refers to the system for the administration of justice in Bengal at the time of the Company's acquisition of the *diwani* as 'inadequate, irregular and corrupt'. B.N. Pandey, *The Introduction of English Law into India* (London, 1967), p. 21.

The 'Plan' bestowed upon European judges, who admittedly lacked any legal training, responsibility for administering civil justice. However, the 'Plan' required these judges to consult *pandit*s and *maulvi*s hired by the courts to declaim the *Shastra* or Koran concerning the subjects on Hastings' curious list which singled out 'inheritance, marriage, caste and other religious usages or institutions'. Derrett explains Hastings' selection of subjects as being founded on advice that these topics were based on 'unseen motives' and therefore were not subject to argument. There was no tradition of case law until the establishment of the Supreme Court in Calcutta. Initially, there was no concern over the fact that *pandit*s delivered different *vyavastha*s or opinions and *kazi*s different *futwa*s or decisions in different courts or that the same *pandit*s and *kazi*s delivered inconsistent *vyavastha*s and *futwa*s. Such discrepancies became apparent only when the Supreme Court began to consult *pandit*s in the course of exercising its 1781 mandate to decide cases concerning 'inheritance, succession...and...matters of contract'. As the English practice of taking note of precedents played an increasing role in court decisions, the inconsistencies of the *pandit*s and *kazi*s became an increasing embarrassment.[27]

By the time of Governor General Cornwallis, corruption among the law officers of the courts had become legendary for Company servants. Chief Justice Impey remarked in the Patna Case: 'That they should be mean, weak, ignorant and corrupt, is not surprising, when the salary of the principal judge, the Cazi [*Kazi*], does not exceed ₹100 per month.'[28]

In order to train the *pandit*s and *kazi*s needed for the Company's courts, Hastings had supported the establishment of Sanskrit Colleges in Benares and Calcutta and the Muslim Madrassa at Calcutta. He encouraged the study of Muslim and Hindu laws. Under his sponsorship there appeared Charles Hamilton's translation of the *Hidayah*[29] and Nathaniel Brassey Halhed's translation of *Vivadarnave-setu* or 'Bridge Across the Ocean of Litigation'—better known after its linguistic journey through a Persian translation as *A Code of Gentoo Laws*, or, *Ordinations of the Pandits*. Hastings enjoyed a ready response from *pandit*s eager to serve the new *diwan* in Bengal, the English East India Co. A committee of 11 *pandit*s worked in Calcutta

---

[27] J.D.M. Derrett, *op. cit.*, pp. 231–79; n.b. P.V. Kane re 'Unseen Motives' in P.V. Kane, *op. cit.*, 2nd ed. (Poona: 1974) II, Part I, p. 437.

[28] Sir James Fitzjames Stephen, *The Story of Nuncomar and the Impeachment of Sir Elijah Impey* (London: 1885) II, p. 176.

[29] C. Hamilton, trans., *Hidayah* [Guide to Arabic Books of Law], I.O.L., MSS. Eur. D 34. The *Hidayah* was essentially a compilation of the four schools of Sunni Muslim law.

between May 1773 and February 1775 to compile a digest of Hindu law in accordance with Hastings' instructions.

The most quoted condemnation of Indian law officers is Chief Justice William Jones' remark in his letter to Cornwallis of 19 March 1788 that he 'could not with an easy conscience concur in a decision merely on the written opinion of native lawyers in any cause in which they could have the remotest interest in misleading the Court'.[30] It was in this letter that Jones proposed the compilation of a digest of Hindu and Muslim law concerning inheritance and contract. Derrett notes that this portion of Jones' letter to Cornwallis is 'gleefully' quoted nearly four decades later by Francis W. Macnaghten's 'extraordinary' preface to his *Considerations on the Hindoo Law*. Macnaghten continued Jones' linkage of the perceived venality of the *pandit*s with the need for 'an ascertainment of the law [as] a corrective of this evil'.[31] This suspicion of the *pandit*s was also fostered by F.W. Macnaghten's son, William Hay Macnaghten, whose Sudder Dewanny Adawlut Reports contained an account of a corrupt opinion delivered by 10 *pandit*s inspired by bribes.[32]

With the advantage of hindsight after the *pandit*s were dismissed from the courts altogether by Act XI 1864, judicious observers conceded that Jones and the Macnaghtens were unduly harsh in their assessment of the *pandit*s. In an attempt to make amends, Justice J.B. Norton remarked that 'We have abolished the Pandits, and ourselves kicked down one of the ladders by which we have climbed; for time was, when there was scarcely another source of law open to us to consult'.[33] Ironically, respect for the *pandit*s lingered only in the Privy Council. Dwarka Nath Mitter invoked the Privy Council ruling in the Ramnad Case, as he reflected sorrowfully that 'so long...as the opinion of the Pundit was invariably followed, the indigenous development of the law continued'.[34]

---

[30] William Jones to Lord Cornwallis, 19 March 1788, Calcutta, in Lord Teignmouth, *Memoirs of the Life, Writings and Correspondence of Sir William Jones*, Vol.I (London, 1804) p. 307.

[31] F.W. Macnaghten, *Considerations on the Hindoo Law as it is Current in Bengal* (Serampore, 1824), pp. x–xii.

[32] W.H. Macnaghten, *Reports of Cases Determined in the Sudder Dewanny Adalat*, new ed. Vol. I (Calcutta, 1827), p. 40; W.H. Macnaghten, *Principles and Precedents of Hindu Law*, Vol. I (Calcutta, 1828), p. iv. W.H. Macnaghten further stated that he had examined every opinion delivered in Bengal courts 1811–28, only to find that 'at least nine-tenths of the opinions were ascertained, on examination, to be erroneous, doubtful, unsupported by proof, or other-wise unfit for publication'. *Ibid.*, pp. xxiii–xxiv.

[33] J.B. Norton, Preface to *A Selection of Leading Cases on the Hindu Law of Inheritance*, Part 2 (Madras, 1871), p. v.

[34] 'Collector of Madura v. Moottoo Ramlinga Sathupathy' (1868) 12 M.I.A. 438–39; Dwarka Nath Mitter, *The Position of Women in Hindu Law* (Calcutta, 1913), pp. 27–29.

The reputation of the *pandit*s, tarnished or untarnished, is not the prime concern of J.D.M. Derrett. Derrett attributes the apparent rigidity of English courts in India and their inability to allow for custom or usage to some fundamental early misunderstandings about the variety of sources for Indian laws and about the very nature of the *shastra*s. These misunderstandings began with Sir William Jones. Behind the Digest of Hindu and Muslim Laws proposed by Jones was his romantic belief 'that Hindu law was immemorially old', 'that it was possible to fix it at any given moment without doing it any harm', 'that the conscientious opinions of the sastris [*pandit*s] could be made to assume a fixed form'—in short 'the need for certainty took precedence over...the science of jurisprudence'. Compounding the confusion in Derrett's view was 'the error perpetuated by Sir William Jones that Brahmins were priests'. Jones' plan for the Digest which was executed by the venerable compiler, Jagannatha Tarkapancanana, focused on *smrti* texts at the expense of supplementary treatises. Symptomatic of Jones' romanticized outlook was his translation of the *Manusmrti*, dismissed by Derrett as 'destined to have more effect on oriental studies in the West than it ever had on the administration of law in India'.[35]

The plan of the Digest drawn up by Jones for Jagannatha called for a selection of legal opinions usually identified with Mithila and Bengal, and later labelled by English scholars as the *Mitakshara* and *Dayabhaga* 'schools', on the subjects of Inheritance and Contracts. Jones respected Halhed's Code, 'as far as it goes a very excellent work', but he felt the section on contracts was too brief and superficial. In reality, Derrett considers that Halhed's Code 'maintained...a more practical air than Jones' *Manu*...could ever aspire to'.[36] Jagannatha, in the end, paid tribute to Halhed by entitling the Digest *Vivada-bhangarnava* or 'Ocean of Resolutions of Disputes', a variation on the original title for Halhed's *Code*. In implementing Jones' Plan, Jagannatha used techniques of *mimamsa* and *nyaya* to present every intellectually respectable opinion according to various degrees of approval but without stigmatizing any as wrong. To the western mind the result was a contradictory, inconclusive muddle.

The translator of Jagannatha's *Digest*, Henry Thomas Colebrooke, was dissatisfied with Jones' Plan and with Jagannatha's indiscriminate discussion

---

[35] J.D.M. Derrett, *op. cit.*, pp. 234–45, 249–50. Cf. the defence of Jones by G. Cannon, *The Life and Mind of Oriental Jones—Sir William Jones the Father of Modern Linguistics* (Cambridge, 1990), p. 287.

[36] Lord Teignmouth, *op. cit.*, I, p. 309; J.D.M. Derrett, *op. cit.*, p. 240.

of 'discordant opinions...leaving it uncertain whether any of the opinions stated by him do actually prevail, or which doctrine must now be in force and which obsolete'. In a letter to his brother, Colebrooke explained why it had been necessary to supersede Halhed's *Code* with the *Digest*. He asserted that the *Code* 'is not full enough to enable a magistrate to judge of the fidelity of the Hindu lawyer who gives him a law opinion'.[37] To improve on the *Digest*, Colebrooke attempted a conclusive study of inheritance which he deemed to be the most important branch of jurisprudence, constituting 'that part of any national system of laws, which is the most peculiar and distinct'. He continued the trend set by the *Digest* in dismissing any need for a compilation of criminal law on the grounds that 'mankind are in general agreed in regard to the nature of crimes'. He chose to translate the two treatises considered to be 'the standard authorities of (the) Hindu law of inheritance in (the) schools of Benares and Bengal'. One treatise by Jimutavahana was 'constantly cited' by Bengali *Dayabhaga* lawyers; the other was 'an extract from the still more celebrated Mitakshara'.[38] Ironically, it was Colebrooke's remarkable reputation as a scholar which virtually established his idea that 'jurisprudence is...to be taught and studied in schools'.[39] As explained by Ludo Rocher, this was an understandable mistake, given the current knowledge of Muslim 'schools' of law and the current demand for authoritative law books in the Company's courts. But the reduction of a lively, continually evolving Hindu legal tradition to 'schools of law' was to limit the ability of the Company's courts to deal with varying interpretations of Hindu *smriti*s or legal treatises for generations to come.[40] In the last half of the nineteenth century when *shastric* research enjoyed a renaissance, the translator of the important treatise on Maratha jurisprudence, the *Vyavahara Mayukha*, denounced the move away from the *Dharmasastra* as a living science: 'To say that the Mitakshara or any other similar treatise is decisive of Hindu law is in my opinion completely to ignore the history and growth of the Hindu law itself.'[41]

---

[37] Letter, Mirzapore, 21 June 1796 in T.E. Colebrooke, *Miscellaneous Essays by H.T. Colebrooke, with Life of the Author*, Vol. I (London, 1873; repr.), p. 84.

[38] H.T. Colebrooke, Preface to his translation of *Two Treatises on the Hindu Law of Inheritance* (Calcutta, 1810) in T.E. Colebrooke, *ibid.*, II, pp. 476–79.

[39] Cited in T. Strange, *Elements of Hindu Law*, Vol. 1, 1st ed. (London, 1825), p. 317.

[40] L. Rocher, 'Schools of Hindu Law' in J. Ensink and P. Gaeffke, eds, *India Maior* (Leiden, 1972), pp. 167–76. For a discussion of the schools of Muslim law, see R.K. Wilson, *An Introduction to the Study of Anglo-Muhammadan Law* (London, 1894).

[41] Mandlik, *Vyavahara Mayukha* (Bombay, 1880), p. lxx. J.D. Mayne also lamented that 'in Southern India it came to be accepted that Mitakshara was the last word that could be listened to on Hindu law'. J.D. Mayne, *Hindu Law and Usage*, 6th ed. (Madras, 1900), p. 44.

Criminal Law

In Hastings' instructions to 'stand forth as *diwan*', there lay a conscious decision to leave the administration of criminal justice or the *Nizamut* in the hands of the *Nizam* and his deputies. The Company assumed responsibility for criminal justice in 1790 when Governor General Cornwallis, after three years of consultations with judges and magistrates, declared the need to correct 'the shocking abuses and wretched administration of justice in the Foujdary department'. From 1790 until the enactment of Macaulay's Penal Code in 1860, the Company proclaimed Muslim criminal law to be the law of the land, except in Bombay where Hindu criminal law was reserved to Hindus. However, with each passing year in this period, the Islamic criminal law became more and more of a mere facade parallel with the political fiction that the Company governed as a vassal of the Mughal Emperor. Remarkable innovations were initiated by the Company with the result that a corpus of Anglo-Indian law emerged in the form of Company Regulations which were generally considered to be more humane than both the English criminal law of the day and the Islamic law. For authority to make these innovations, the Company drew upon the Muslim legal concept of *seeasut* (*siyasat*) and upon its constitutional position as defined by Lord North's Regulating Act.

Seeasut was a supplementary doctrine which vested in the 'Sultan' or the ruler a 'discretionary coercive authority...for the public good'. The discretionary realm of public justice defined by *seeasut* contrasts sharply with the realm of private justice that dominates Muslim criminal law and obstructs western concepts of egalitarian justice. The basic principles of Muslim criminal law are usually summarized with reference to the four standard punishments: *hadd* or defined punishment; *kisas* or retaliation; *diya* or blood money and *tazir* (*tusheer*), *acoobut*, *seeasut* or discretionary punishment.[42] *Hadd* is the most rigid punishment applied only to specific crimes. It prescribes stoning or scourging for *zina* or illicit intercourse; scourging for wine drinking and false accusation of illicit intercourse; amputation of one limb for theft and amputation of two limbs for highway robbery if unattended with murder—death for highway robbery attended with murder. However, *hadd* was more horrifying in the print of the Sharia or Muslim sacred law than in reality. Procedural obstructions meant that convictions were rare. Neither circumstantial nor written evidence was admitted. The only evidence accepted was the oral testimony of eye witnesses. But interested parties,

---

[42] J.H. Harington, *op. cit.*, 2nd Part, Sec. I, pp. 245–340.

women, slaves and non-Muslims were all barred as witnesses. A confession had to be made four times before a *Kazi* and could be retracted at any time. *Hadd* is also excluded if, in cases of theft and highway robbery, the criminal and the victim are relations. *Kisa*s or retaliation reflects the essence of the nomadic tribal Arabic society which spawned Islam. Inasmuch as Muslim criminal law distinguishes between crimes against God and crimes against man, it need only concern itself with the latter, since no human punishment is possible for the former.[43] According to Muslim law, crimes against man imply to the victim and his heirs all rights of punishment. *Kisa*s prescribes the death penalty for wilful murder and mutilation for serious maiming. Crucial to a sentence of capital punishment was the distinction in the Hanafi School of law in Bengal between intentional and nonintentional killing. The Hanafi school considered that intentional murder could only be committed with an instrument likely to cause death; otherwise, the cause of death was open to doubt. Where intention cannot be proved, *diya* or a fine of blood money is substituted for *kisa*s. Only the victim and his heirs can prosecute for *kisa*s, or commute the punishment to *diya*. If they do not prosecute, nothing happens. However, if the value of the life or limb taken by *Kisa*s is superior to that taken by the criminal, the victim or the heirs may not prosecute. Thus parents could murder their children or masters their slaves with impunity. *Tazir* or discretionary punishment is prescribed for a legion of offences not enumerated under *hadd* or *kisa*s. Sentences are left to the discretion of the judge on the understanding that they will be less rigorous than *hadd* or *kisa*s.

In Sec. 33 of his Judicial Regulation of 3 December 1790, Cornwallis contrived to substitute the intention of the criminal for the nature of the instrument of death as the criterion for murder. He cited Abu Hanafa's disciples 'Yusuf and Mahomed' as authorities for this revision of Hanafi doctrine.[44] Sec. 34 of the same regulation deprived the next of kin of their right to pardon a murderer. The Judicial Regulation of 10 October 1791 commuted the punishment of mutilation to imprisonment with seven years substituted for each limb. Another Judicial Regulation—that of 27 April 1792—decreed 'that the religious tenets of witnesses be no longer considered as a bar to the conviction or condemnation of a prisoner'. These regulations

---

[43] F.L. Beaufort, *A Digest of the Criminal Law of the Presidency of Fort William and Guide to all Criminal Authorities Therein* (Calcutta, 1849), p. 22.

[44] Berating modern scholars for their failure to go beyond eighteenth and nineteenth century British sources, J. Fisch notes that 'Mahomed' was in fact al-Saybani. J. Fisch, *op. cit.*, pp. 45–46, n.129.

were then all incorporated in the Cornwallis Code as part of Beng. Reg. IX 1793.[45] This was the beginning of a process which legal theorists of the late twentieth century and early twenty-first century have dubbed 'legal pluralism'. In the view of the Cambridge school of Indian history, this multiplication of legal authorities mitigated the cultural rupture caused by the Company's increased political dominance. In contrast, the subaltern school is derisive of any notion of a rule of law in a colonial society.[46]

In legislating these changes to the Islamic law, Cornwallis introduced the tactic of creating a legal fiction. The Judicial Regulation of 13 April 1792 provided for the state to prosecute cases of murder regardless of the wishes or even the existence of the heirs of the victim. The *futwa* was to be delivered hypothetically as if the heir of the murdered person had prosecuted or a non-Muslim witness had been Muslim. The case was then to be referred to the Nizamut Adawlut in Calcutta without sentence being passed in the provincial court. Thus the *futwa* was bypassed by means of a deliberate fiction. This technique was repeated over and over again in subsequent regulations, as for example, Beng. Regs. IV and XIV 1797, VIII 1799 and VIII 1801 regarding homicide cases where the judge disagreed with the *futwa*.[47]

As the Company became accustomed to its role in administering criminal justice, there was a steady tendency towards making the law more severe in the interest of efficient justice—all in the name of public justice. Before another 10 years had elapsed, it was evident that the use of *futwa*s based on legal fictions was but a step towards the practice of dispensing with the *futwa* altogether. Sec. 4 Beng. Reg. XVII 1817 empowered the Justices of the Nizamut Adawlut to override a *futwa* of acquittal.[48] It was another five years before the Justices of the Nizamut Adawlut were empowered by Secs 1 and 2 of Beng. Reg. IV 1822 to override a *futwa* of conviction.

Beng. Reg. XVII 1817 is usually remembered, not so much for its triumph over the *futwa* and Muslim restrictions on evidence, as for its withdrawal from Benares Brahmins of immunity from capital punishment. With Sec. XXIII of Beng. Reg. XVI 1795 and Secs VII and IX of Beng. Reg. XXI 1795,

---

[45] Secs 47, 50–56, 74–77 and 79, Beng. Reg. IX 1793, I.O.R., V/8/16, pp. 113–18.

[46] Rina Verma Williams and Lauren Benton make a strong case for perceiving the emergence of a 'politics of legal pluralism' involving 'multiple legal authorities' to produce an interaction between state centred law and local traditions or customs. See Rina Verma Williams, *Postcolonial Politics and Personal Laws* (Oxford, 2006), pp. 40–52; Lauren Benton, *Law and Colonial Cultures: Legal Regimes in World History, 1400–1900* (Cambridge, 2002), pp. 253–64. See also Ranajit Guha, *Dominance Without Hegemony: History and Power in Colonial India* (Harvard, 1997).

[47] Cf. G.C. Rankin, *op. cit.*, p. 173; also J. Fisch, *op. cit.*, p. 47.

[48] Sec. 4 Beng. Reg. XVII 1817, I.O.R., V/8/19.

Cornwallis had responded positively to the entreaties of the Resident of Benares, Jonathan Duncan, to respect the privilege of Benares Brahmins convicted of murder not to be liable to a death sentence.[49] Sec. 15 of Beng. Reg. XVII 1817 rescinded the relevant sections of Beng. Regs. XVI and XXI 1795 and called for magistrates 'to execute all sentences of death against brahmins', provided the execution did not take place on a 'spot of ground held sacred by the Hindoos'. The revolutionary force of this quasi-egalitarian move against Benares Brahmin privileges was echoed 10 years later by Wynn's Jury Act [7 Geo IV c. 37 (1826)] which admitted non-Christian Indians to Petit Juries. In response to the first invitation from the Bombay Recorder's Court to serve on a Petit Jury, a group of Hindus submitted a list of requests to protect their caste sensibilities. High on this list was the 'request that we be exempted from all Juries when a Brahmin is tried for a capital crime; it being our religious duty not to contribute to the death of any Brahmin'.[50]

Although the jury system was acknowledged to be 'alien to the feelings and customs of the country',[51] it was one of the advisory bodies which Beng. Reg. VI 1832 substituted for the law officers in criminal courts. It is Beng. Reg. VI 1832 which has generally been considered to have wielded the deathblow to Muslim criminal law as the effective law of the land. According to Beaufort, since the passing of Sec. 6, Beng. Reg. VI 1832 'the court now never call for a futwa' except in capital or special cases.[52] The *futwa* was not officially dispensed with in Madras until Act I 1840 absolved the Court of the Foujdary Adawlut from the necessity of consulting law officers for their *futwa*s. This was after a reference to the Law Commission which ruled in 1837 that the Madras Foujdary Adawlut was competent to decide cases based on Muslim law according to the revised Muslim criminal law contained in the Madras Code of Regulations and in recorded precedents.[53] Indeed, the criminal code as revised in Bengal had been virtually copied word for word in Madras with Mad. Regs. VII and VIII 1802 parallel to Beng. Reg. IX 1793. In Bombay, although the Muslim criminal law was not applied to Hindus, Bom. Regs. V 1799, III and VIII 1802 and II 1805 contained the

---

[49] J. Duncan, Resident at Benares, to the Earl of Cornwallis, Governor General, 14 January 1789, Bengal Revenue Proceedings, 4 February 1789, I.O.R., P/51/32, fol. 187.

[50] F. Dawtrey Drewitt, *Bombay in the Days of George IV—Memoirs of Sir Edward West* (London, New York, Bombay, Calcutta, 1907), pp. 249–51.

[51] George Campbell, *Modern India* (London, 1852), p. 473.

[52] F.L. Beaufort, *op. cit.*, p. 181. Cf. Rankin's assertion that 'Reg. VI 1832 marks the end of Muslim criminal law as the general law applicable to all persons'. G.C. Rankin, *op. cit*, p. 180.

[53] Letter, 30 May 1837, *Parliamentary Papers* (1842) XXX, p. 232.

amendments to Muslim law made in Bengal and repeated in Madras. As for Hindu criminal law, even Elphinstone, the champion of the rights of subject peoples in the only province to reserve Hindu law for Hindus, dismissed the 'absurdity' of the punishments prescribed. This could be attributed to the dominating characteristic of Hindu law whereby 'a greater distinction was made in the punishment on account of the caste of the criminal than the nature of the crime'.[54] Ultimately, Elphinstone promulgated a separate statutory code of law for Bombay. Bom. Reg. XIV 1827 was a self-contained penal code which set forth a schedule of punishments to fit specific crimes. Though a shadow of their former selves, the law officers and their *futwa*s remained in all three presidencies until they were abolished by Act XI 1864 as a result of the enactment of the Indian Penal Code in 1860 which did not require their services. Thus the decisive break with Muslim criminal law as the basis of Anglo-Indian jurisprudence came with post-Mutiny legislation 1860–64.

Retreat from Codification

The Elphinstone Code of 1827 represented the first attempt at codification in British India. The penal code contained in Bom. Reg. XIV 1827 was to earn the disdain of Macaulay's Law Commission for its rough classification of crimes and punishments. The Law Commission wrote to Lord Auckland that the penal law of 'the Bombay Presidency has over the penal law of the other Presidencies no superiority, except that of being digested'. In fact, in Bom. Reg. XIV 1827 'the principles according to which crimes ought to be classified and punishments apportioned have been less regarded than in the legislation of Bengal and Madras'. Indeed, Elphinstone had foreseen this criticism, but his Code reflected a vision different from Macaulay's. Macaulay's Law Commission stated unapologetically that 'no existing system has furnished us even with a groundwork'.[55] In total contrast, Elphinstone would never yield his own sense of the importance of stating a basic respect for Hindu and Muslim laws:

---

[54] Mountstuart Elphinstone, *Territories Conquered from the Paishwa—A Report* (New Delhi; Repr. 1973), p. 52.

[55] Law Commission to Lord Auckland, 14 October 1837, *Parliamentary Papers* (1837–38) XLI, pp. 465, 467.

The more I think of the plan for consulting the law officers as to the punishment for the offences specified in the penal regulation *the more difficult does it seem to me to reconcile the two objects—attention to the Mohummadan and Hindoo codes and the specification of offences*...[T]here is no foreseeing, I think, the difficulties that may occur in estimating the same crime in different codes.[56]

Actually, this last mentioned phenomenon had already become a reality. As just one example later given by the Law Commission in their observations to Lord Auckland:

In Bengal serious forgeries are punishable with imprisonment for double the term fixed for perjury [Beng. Reg. XVII 1817 s. ix]: in Bombay...perjury is punishable with imprisonment for a term double of the term fixed for the most aggravated forgeries [Bom. Reg. XIV 1827 s. xvi–xvii]: in Madras...the two offences are on exactly the same footing [Mad. Reg. VI 1811 s. III].[57]

Elphinstone derived inspiration for the codifying work of his Regulations Committee directly from the interest taken by Jeremy Bentham in framing a body of law for India.[58] Bentham's self-appointed apostle, James Mill, gave detailed plans for an Indian code in his *History of British India*. In an internal memo circulated among members of the Bengal Governor's Council, W.B. Bayley cited huge extracts from the fifth volume of Mill's *History* to justify a strategy for authorizing Europeans to formulate a Law Code with the assistance of Muslim and Hindu *pandit*s.[59] Bayley recommended a focus upon judicial procedure as a means of ascertaining customs defining native rights. He would have endorsed the observations of the Register of the Bengal Sudder Adawlut who rebuffed a proposal from the Madras Sudder Adawlut: 'the defending of rights...is not so much the object of the Regulations, as the prescribing of rules for the conduct of public officers in their transactions with persons possessing or claiming those rights'.[60] He looked forward to W.H. Macnaghten's forthcoming Sudder Adawlut Reports as a 'gradual

---

[56] 'Notes and Papers Regarding the Preparation of the Bombay Code of Regulations', in Elphinstone Papers, I.O.L., MSS Eur F88 Box 14 E 24.

[57] Law Commission to Lord Auckland, 14 October 1837, *op. cit.*, p. 466.

[58] Elphinstone to Edward Strachey, 21 April 1821, Camp at Sookaltteerit, in T.E. Colebrooke, *Life of the Honourable Mountstuart Elphinstone* (London, 1884) Vol. II, p. 125; M.P. Jain, *op. cit.*, p. 604.

[59] Memorandum by W.B. Bayley, n.d., and W.B. Bayley to John Adam, n.d., in Elphinstone Papers, *op. cit.*

[60] R. Clarke, Acting Register Sudder Adawlut to Government in Judicial Department, 27 July 1818, in 'Notes and Papers Regarding the Preparation of the Bombay Code of Regulations' in Elphinstone Papers, *op. cit.*

elucidation' of points of Law with a view to establishing principles that might be 'embodied in a Legislative Enactment'.[61]

Accordingly, Elphinstone became determined to produce a code worthy of Bentham—a code which would excel the limitations of the work of Jones and Colebrooke. In aid of this work Arthur Steele produced his exhaustive *Summary of Law and Custom* and Henry Borradaile compiled reports of Bombay Sudder Court decisions. With the support of such painstaking labour, Elphinstone's Regulations Committee drafted 27 regulations which were promulgated in 1827 as the Bombay Code. In keeping with Bombay traditions of sensitivity to local custom, Sec. 26 Bom. Reg. IV 1827 enshrined the law of the defendant and Sec. 21 Bom. Reg. II 1827 excluded caste questions from the jurisdiction of civil courts. Elphinstone had worked hard to follow his own advice.[62]

Sadly, despite his popularity and generally acknowledged competence as Governor, Elphinstone, in the last two years of his career, exacerbated petty quarrels with the Chief Justice of the Supreme Court, Sir Edward West.[63] These quarrels over the jurisdiction claimed by the Bombay Supreme Court outlived both protagonists to become something of a cause celebre. Finally, in 1829, the Privy Council overruled the efforts of Sir J.P. Grant, Sir Edward West's successor, to extend the Supreme Court's jurisdiction over *mofussil* courts.[64] Horrified by the unedifying spectacle of the two highest ranking English governing bodies heaping public calumny and slander on each other, Charles Metcalfe raised the alarm within the highest councils of the Bengal Government. His minute of 1829 calling for ultimate government control over the Supreme Court in each of the three presidencies opened vigorous debate among Judges of the Supreme Court in Calcutta. It is generally

---

[61] W.B. Bayley to Elphinstone, 25 August 1822, in Elphinstone Papers, *ibid.*

[62] Elphinstone to Edward Strachey, 21 April 1821, Camp at Sookaltteerit, in T.E. Colebrooke, *ibid.*, p. 125. Elphinstone had a favourite tale to tell of the dread with which the Company's courts of law were regarded early in the nineteenth century: During the progress of British conquests in the Northwest many of the inhabitants were encountered flying from the newly occupied territory. 'Is Lord Lake coming?' was the inquiry. 'No,' was the reply, 'the Adawlut is coming.' He referred to this story in his letter to E. Strachey, 10 March 1822, in T.E. Colebrooke, *ibid.*, p. 131.

[63] For Sir Edward West's view, see F. Dawtrey Drewitt, *op. cit.*; Drewitt's principal source is Lady West's Journal; otherwise he insists on a hypothesis that all the King's Judges were sorry victims of local Indian governments and of the Indian climate.

[64] Proceedings Before H.M.'s Most Honourable Privy Council in Relation to the Petition by Sir John Peter Grant, Knight, Only Surviving Justice of the Supreme Court of Judicature at Bombay, I.O.R., V/27/141/8; 1 *Knapps Reports*, p. 1.

acknowledged that this debate launched the movement for codification in the 1830s.⁶⁵

In the interest of finding a constructive use for the talents of Supreme Court Judges, Governor General Bentinck proposed that Justices should sit on the Governor's legislative council.⁶⁶ Some Justices preferred their existing powers of refusing registration of government regulations such as were exercised by the Bombay Supreme court in rejecting John Adam's Press Regulations. The Home Government steered a middle course with the 1833 Charter. 3 and 4 Will IV c. 85 introduced a Legal Member to the Governor General's Council in the person of T.B. Macaulay, created a Law Commission and decreed that the Company's Regulations were no longer required to be registered in any court of justice. Finally, Sec. 53 enunciated the Benthamite dream of codification. In his despatch of 10 December 1834, explaining the aims of the 1833 Charter, James Mill underlined the role of the new Law Commission in preparing 'a code of laws common (as far as may be) to the whole people of India'.⁶⁷ But it was Macaulay's words which were to become immortal: 'We do not mean that all the people of India should live under the same law; far from it...Our principle is simply—*uniformity where you can have it—diversity where you must have it—but in all cases certainty*.'⁶⁸[emphasis by author]

Codification in India in the early 1830s was the siren call of Benthamite liturgy. Macaulay and James Mill can be understood better in the English context of law reform than in the Indian context of codification. For Mill and Macaulay, India served as an experimental laboratory for testing schemes of good government and codification.⁶⁹ However, the Benthamite vision of codified Indian law projected by Sec. 53 of the 1833 Charter as explained

---

⁶⁵ Correspondence between the Governor General in Council and Judges of the Supreme Court as well as between Indian and Home authorities regarding the establishment of Legislative Councils for British India, New System of Courts of Justice and Formation of a Code of Laws from 1828, Appendix to Report on Affairs of the East India Co., *Parliamentary Papers* (1831) VI, pp. 465–655; Whitley Stokes, *The Anglo-Indian Codes* (Oxford, 1887), p. ii and G.C. Rankin, *op. cit.*, p. 20.

⁶⁶ Bentinck to Supreme Court, 14 July 1829, in C.H. Philips, ed., *The Correspondence of Lord William Cavendish Bentinck, Governor General of India 1828–1835* (Oxford, 1977) Vol. I, pp. 255–56, paras. #9 and #11.

⁶⁷ Para. 29, Public Despatch, No. 44 to Government of India, 10 December 1834, I.O.R., E/4/742, fol.

⁶⁸ Macaulay's speech on second reading of 3&4 Will IV c. 85, *Hansard* 3rd series XIX cols., p. 531–33.

⁶⁹ See Javed Majeed, *Ungoverned Imaginings—James Mill's 'The History of British India' and Orientalism* (Oxford, 1992).

by Macaulay and Mill was to fade away to nothing under the East India Company's regimen.

Macaulay did, indeed, proceed to India to undertake his Herculean labours as Legal Member on Bentinck's council. His greatest success was, without doubt, the draft Penal Code of 1837. It has received numerous tributes, not the least of which is the fact that, although it was not enacted until 1860 in a version revised by Barnes Peacock, it is still the Penal Code of India today.[70] But otherwise the Law Commission took two false steps, both of which had to be retracted. First, there was the proposal embedded in the 1833 Charter to codify Muslim and Hindu law. This simply did not happen. After the departure of Macaulay from India, the Law Commission steadily lost status and clout. Sec. 28 of the 1853 Charter authorized the appointment of a Law Commission for India based in England. This Commission produced a Report in 1855 which came to the conclusion that 'no portion either of the Mahomedan Law or of the Hindu Law ought to be enacted as such in any form by a British Legislature'.[71] The second false step of Macaulay's Law Commission was its efforts to establish English law as the *lex loci* throughout British India. At least, because the *Lex Loci* Report of 1840 was presented by the Law Commission soon after Macaulay's departure from India, it is generally considered that he knew of it. In this Report, the Law Commission argued that no legislative power was needed to introduce English law as a *lex loci*: 'if it be admitted that neither Hindu nor Mohamedan law can be considered as *lex loci*, then British India must…be considered with regard to all persons not Hindus nor Mohammedans as an uninhabited country colonized by British subjects'.

Such an unhistorical vantage point simply could not prevail against the more legitimate perception of the Company's historical beginnings as the Mughal Emperor's *diwan* of Bengal.[72] Abortive efforts to compile a digest of English law suitable to India were gradually abandoned as was the very idea of English law as a *lex loci*. Ironically, the enactment of the Caste Disabilities Removal Act of 1850 embodied Clauses from 10 to 12 of the draft '*Lex Loci*

---

[70] Twentieth-century critics have called for modification of the draconian punishments preserved from Macaulay's day. Cf. H.S. Gour, *The Penal Law of India—Being an Analytical, Critical and Expository Commentary on the Indian Penal Code*, 10th ed., Vol. I, revised by M.C. Desai, G. Kumar and R.B. Sethi (Allahabad, 1972–73), p. 390. Nevertheless, the authors remark that Macaulay foresaw this criticism in 'Note A' of his draft Penal Code.

[71] Cited by A.F.M. Abdur Rahman, *Institutes of Muslim Law—A Treatise on Personal Law According to the Hanafite School* (Calcutta, 1907), pp. ix–x.

[72] G.C. Rankin, *op. cit.*, pp. 29–30 and M.P. Jain, *op. cit.*, pp. 621–34; see also Sec. 9 Beng. Reg. VII 1832 which decreed that the provision for justice, equity and good conscience did not justify the introduction of English law, *supra* p. 24.

Act' and was therefore erroneously labelled by some as the '*Lex Loci* Act'. Insofar as the 1850 Act promoted principles of modern jurisprudence vis-à-vis traditions of inheritance among Hindu castes, it seemed to acknowledge the fact that a separate code of English law as a *lex loci* in India was not necessary. The 1855 Report of the second Law Commission surmounted the strident Benthamism of the 1830s and the reckless *lex loci* movement of the 1840s to call for codification of Anglo-Indian law. There was, however, a minority dissent which echoed the 1840 *Lex Loci* Report in calling for the immediate importation of English law as of 1726. The majority prevailed. However, their report merely dictated the policy of codification. It remained for a third Law Commission to begin the actual work of drafting the laws.

In post-1857 legislation Hastings' list of reserved subjects was preserved as a guideline for codification even after the merging of the Sudder Courts and Supreme Courts by the High Courts Act of 1861. However, the difference between the courts of the *mofussil* and the High Courts was preserved in the language of the new legislation. Hastings' principles as stated for the *mofussil* courts in sec. 15 Beng. Reg. IV 1793 appeared in the Civil Courts Acts and Hastings' principles as summarized by Edmund Burke for the Supreme Court in Calcutta in sec. 17 Geo III c. 70 1781 appeared in the Government of India Acts. Thus the rules for codification remained the same for the Crown and the Company.

The real boost for codification derived from the 1853 Charter's authorization for an enlarged Legislative Council in India, including two Judges.[73] In this way, Bentinck's suggestion of 1829 was finally acted upon. The presence of the Judges on the Council and Governor General Dalhousie's enthusiasm for the new legislative body resulted in a legislature far more independent than the Home Authorities either anticipated or approved. J.S. Mill expostulated: 'Will anyone pretend for a moment that Parliament, when it passed either the Act of 1833 or that of 1853, had any idea that it was taking away the control of the legislation of India from the Home Government?'[74]

Ultimately, Dalhousie's flamboyant legislative council was superseded by the more pedestrian Indian Council under the Viceroy. In the wake of the 1857 uprising, Codes of Civil and Criminal Procedure, as well as the Penal Code were enacted as law. In his defence of the Company in 1858, J.S. Mill argued that these laws would have come into existence much sooner but for the events of 1857–58. G.C. Rankin and M.P. Jain insist that, quite the

---

[73] Sec. 22, 16&17 Vic., c. 95.

[74] J.S. Mill, Minute, *Parliamentary Papers* (1876) LVI, p. 18. G.C. Rankin considered that the minute's terms of reference date it ca. 1856. G.C. Rankin, *op. cit.*, p. 68.

contrary, the 1857 disturbances precipitated the codes.[75] Either way, the fact remains that the East India Company never did muster the political will to enact the sweeping codes prepared by successive Law Commissions.

Although it retreated from the bold Benthamite aims of codification, the Company, nevertheless, enacted several individual regulations with the force of law which directly challenged specific aspects of Indian society. Some initiatives such as those against *sati*, thagi (thuggee) and dacoity are well known. Others such as the introduction of wills as legal instruments or the regulation of such practices as impressed labour or hook swinging are less well known. And then there were practices such as female infanticide or the murder of children for the sake of their ornaments which only prompted the Company to defer legislation, if not reject the idea of legislation altogether in favour of a course of public instruction. Indeed, Sec. 43 of the Company's 1813 Charter had provided the support for such instruction by requiring the Company to make a substantial investment in the education of its Indian subjects. In the case of female infanticide during the Company period, education was very much the preferred remedy. When it came to social legislation, as will be seen in the following chapters, the Company invoked the Islamic concept of *seeasut* or public justice to attack practices ranging from *sati* to slavery through the medium of criminal law. Thus Muslim and Hindu criminal law were modified almost beyond recognition. However, substantive civil laws such as the 1850 Caste Disabilities Removal Act or the 1856 Hindu Widow Remarriage Act were the exception. As will be seen below, the Company, almost subconsciously, evolved an *ad hoc* policy of enacting specific declaratory laws to make desirable modifications of Hindu and Muslim law; thus the wholesale importation of English law was rejected altogether. The work of more rigorous codification was left to the post-1857 Crown government and ultimately to the independent Government of India.

Interestingly, the dates which mark the tides of change in social legislation are not the same as the dates of military conquest and political domination. During the British Raj, enthusiasm for formal codification waxed and waned. Until the first Law Commission, significant alterations of the law were accomplished somewhat haphazardly by the Regulations. Apart from its draft Penal Code, the first Law Commission was generally considered a failure. The second and third Law Commissions presided over a period of intensive legislative activity from 1853 to 1870; the Report of the fourth

---

[75] J.S. Mill, 'Memorandum of the Improvements in the Administration of India during the last Thirty Years,' in J.S. Mill, *Writings on India*, ed. John M. Robson, Martin Moir and Zewahir Moir (Toronto, 1990), p. 114; cf. G.C. Rankin, *op. cit.*, p. 69 and M.P. Jain, *op. cit.*, p. 644.

Law Commission, despite its plea for continuous codification, marked the end of an era in the 1880s. Social legislation by a colonial government was repugnant to the nationalist movement of the late nineteenth and early twentieth centuries. Finally, as a record of its legislative independence, the Indian Parliament, by Act LVII of 1960, repealed all British statutes which had ever formed any part of Indian law.

1

Law, Order and Power: Thagi, Dacoity and Sorcery

Jiski Lathi Uski Bhains[1]

The ability to preserve law and order has historically determined the power of governments to rule effectively. For some regimes, responsibility for law and order becomes an obsession. Certainly, the British in India considered that law and order was perhaps the greatest gift of the British Raj to the subcontinent. The East India Company's reactions to the murderous disorder caused by thugs and dacoits, to the summary executions of alleged practitioners of sorcery, and to instances of children murdered for the sake of their ornaments, have provided twentieth and twenty-first century historians with data to substantiate the charge that the Company's policies on these issues were all based on considerations of power. However, a study of the Company's legislative response to these issues calls for a genuine concern for public justice to be weighed in the balance.

Thagi and Dacoity

With the advantage of hindsight, historians increasingly argue that the East India Company's policy regarding thugs and dacoits, although a necessary response to murder and theft, was essentially an exercise in the wielding of

---

[1] W. Taylor, Officiating Commissioner of Patna, used this Hindi saying to sum up the relationship between the civil power of the East India Company and its pugnacious subjects. Translated by Mr Taylor, 'Jiski' referred to the Company's Indian subjects who 'have the cudgel and therefore get the Buffalo'. This Hindi saying might be translated more generally as 'Whoever has the stick has the power'. W. Taylor, Officiating commissioner of Patna, to Secretary to Government of Bengal, 26 August 1855, B.S.A., P.C.O., Vol. 472.

power amidst the detritus of Mughal rule.² Most recent scholarship on the subject of thagi and dacoity in the early nineteenth century has focused on the question of the identity of accused thugs and dacoits with literary critics even dismissing their very existence as a phantom of colonial orientalist imagination.³ Historians have inevitably stumbled upon endless regional variations of the term '*thag*'. The first comprehensive report on the thugs compiled by Dr Robert C. Sherwood and published in *The Madras Literary Gazette* in 1816 identified the practitioners of the cult of thagi in five different languages.⁴ Twenty years later Mr D.F. Macleod, with the benefit of information from his thug informants traced thugs back 15 generations to Muslims settled amongst the Lodhee tribe and the 'roguish and vagabond Communities of Chouras (84 tribes) in the vicinity of Delhi'.⁵ Christopher Kenna distinguishes between the first individual thug captives who appeared in government records of 1810 as *manihar*s or low caste Muslim artesans and the captives yielded by the intensive campaign against thugs in

---

² *See* Stewart N. Gordon, 'Scarf and Sword: Thugs, Marauders, and State-formation in 18th Century Malwa,' *Indian Economic and Social History Review*, Vol. 6, No. 4 (1969): 403–29; Sandria B. Freitag, 'Collective Crime and Authority in North India,' in Anand A. Yang, ed., *Crime and Criminality in British India*, Association for Asian Studies Monograph No. XLII (Tucson, Arizona, 1985), pp. 140–63; Christopher Kenna, 'Rural Crime, Banditry and Colonial Control: Thugs, Dakaits and Bureaucratic Orientalism in India 1790–1863' (PhD Thesis, University of Sydney, Australia, 1986); Radhika Singha, 'Providential Circumstances: The Thuggee Campaign of the 1830s and Legal Innovation,' *Modern Asian Studies*, Vol. 27, No. 1 (1993): 83–146 and Kim Wagner, 'The Deconstructed Stranglers: A Reassessment of Thuggee,' *Modern Asian Studies*, Vol. 38, No. 4 (2004): 931–63.

³ Parama Roy, 'Discovering India, Imagining Thuggee,' *Yale Journal of Criticism*, Vol. 9, No. 1 (1996); Amal Chatterjee, *Representations of India, 1740–1840: The Creation of India in the Colonial Imagination* (London, 1998); Máire ní Fhlathúin, 'The Travels of M. De Thèvenot through the Thug Archive,' *Journal of the Royal Asiatic Society*, 3rd series, Vol. 2, No. 1 (2001). Kim Wagner deftly argues that 'by making the erroneous assumption that proving the Orientalist origin' of a 'constructed stereotype of thuggee also proves the non-existence of thuggee, Roy, Chatterjee and Fhlathúin have in reality thrown the baby out with the bath water'. Kim Wagner, *op. cit.*, p. 949.

⁴ Dr Robert C. Sherwood, 'Of the Murderers Called Phansigars,' Communicated by Col. McKenzie, N.A.I., Foreign Department, Political Consultations 21 January 1831 #34, fol. 1.

'The Phansigars or stranglers are thus designated from the Hindustani word *phansi*, a noose. In the more northern parts of India these murderers are called *thugs* signifying deceivers; in the Tamil language they are called *Ari Tulucar* or mussulman noosers; in Canarese *Tanti Calleru* implying thieves who use a wire or catgut noose and in Telegu *Warlu Wahndlu* or *Warlu Vayshay Wahndloo*, meaning people who use the noose.'

⁵ D.F. Macleod, Report on the Origin of Thagi, submitted to F.C. Smith, Agent to the Governor General in the Saugor and Nerbudda Territories, Jubulpore, Camp Lehore, 10 October 1834, India Political Proceedings 11 May 1835, No. 7, I.O.R., P/193/75.

the 1830s who were Ahirs, Lodhis, some Brahmins, but mostly Muslims. Kenna makes the point that whatever their background or disguise, the captured thugs told of practices which resembled those of tribes or low castes. After a comprehensive study of depositions of 65 thug prisoners recorded in the period 1810–50, Kenna concludes that there were a very few Brahmins and landholders at one end of the scale balanced by Chamars and beggars at the other end of the scale. The vast majority of thug prisoners represented the rural poor who supplemented with thagi their inadequate livelihood from agricultural labour, military service, peddling or religious mendicancy.[6] Stewart Gordon, in what has become a seminal analysis of thagi, points out that the thugs were but one of eleven different types of marauders identified by John Malcolm in late eighteenth-century Malwa. Gordon argues that the thugs were simply a 'small core of families, numbers of which had been murderers for several generations' who emerged during 'the severe dislocation of the last decade of the eighteenth century and especially after the British defeat of the Marathas in 1803'. Gordon's prime concern is to discount what he perceives to be conspiracy theories of Company administrators who 'played up these locally organized, small scale marauding groups' into a 'hideous' national religious fraternity.[7] Sandria Freitag embellishes Gordon's notion of a thagi mythology created by British administrators to argue that 'it is likely that the disappearance of thugs may have been at least partly a matter of nomenclature, with thugs after 1840 relabelled as dacoits—just as dacoits after 1870 were frequently recast as criminal tribes'.[8]

Whereas no one yet has been able to pinpoint the origin of the *thag* hereditary murderers,[9] studies of the prevalence of dacoity in the early

---

[6] Christopher Kenna, *op. cit.*, pp. 40, 272–80. In a tabular study of thag trials at Sagar and Jabalpur 1831–36, Kenna concludes that of 995 convicted prisoners, 31 per cent were Muslims, 30 per cent Lodhis and 7 per cent Brahmins. *Ibid.*, Appendix I, Table 1, pp. 309–10. Kenna observes further that the thug castes thus described 'made up the bulk of the rural population in northern and central India'. *Ibid.*, p. 279.

[7] Stewart N. Gordon, *op. cit.*, p. 428.

[8] Sandria B. Freitag, *op. cit.*, p. 186, n. 21.

[9] On the basis of the oral evidence of one of his thug prisoners, W.H. Sleeman speculated on the dispersal throughout India of thug families from a concentration of 'old…families' of thugs in the Sindouse pargana of Etawah. W.H. Sleeman, *Ramaseeana* (Calcutta, 1836), pp. 222–25. Christopher Kenna finds support for this idea in official reports dating as far back as 1812 and referring to 'a species of Robbers denominated by the Zumeendars who protect them and participate in their spoils, their Sipahees or Soldiers; by the rest of the world Thugs'. C. Kenna, *op. cit.*, pp. 177–93. Kim Wagner has actually identified the names of 318 families from Sindouse on a 1797 list of villagers who paid a 'Thug Tax' to the Maratha state. Kim Wagner, *op. cit.*, p. 951.

nineteenth century have yielded a rich harvest of explanations for the backgrounds of dacoits. The most tempting model for historians seeking to portray the typical dacoit is that of social revolutionary bandit heroes projected by Eric Hobsbawm:

> They are peasant outlaws whom the lord and state regard as criminals, but who remain within peasant society, and are considered by their people as heroes, as champions, avengers, fighters for justice, perhaps even leaders of liberation, and in any case as men to be admired, helped and supported.[10]

However, the professional Indian dacoits who terrorized the high roads and raided villages by night, but, between expeditions, toiled in the fields by day, rarely fit Hobsbawm's model of classical banditry based in a marginal rural society. Perhaps this is because the dacoits' ties with caste bound Indian village society are not really similar to the bonds between the Russian Cossacks or Bulgarian Haiduks or even the mythological Robin Hood and the feudal serf bound societies of mediaeval Europe.[11] Although predominantly of low caste, Indian dacoits were more an integral part of rural society than their rogue counterparts among the Russian Cossacks or Bulgarian Haiduks.[12] It was not unknown for high-caste Brahmins to provide intelligence of potential victims to dacoit gangs.[13]

In his study of dacoity at the beginning of the nineteenth century in Bengal, John R. McLane is doubtful of the relevance of Hobsbawm's model to Bengali dacoits. While lamenting the destruction of dacoit confessions in pre-1820 Company records, he is able to infer links between dacoity at the beginning of the nineteenth century and the unsettling effects which the Cornwallis reforms had on Indian society. Official lists of dacoits suggested that they came from the lowest castes. McLane suggests that dacoit leaders or *sirdar*s were former *chaukidar*s or village watchmen who had been deprived of employment as the Company resorted to the courts rather than physical coercion in the collection of rents and who had been driven from service lands by government resumptions and by the usurpation of the new patron

---

[10] Eric Hobsbawm, *Bandits* (Middlesex, 1972), p. 17.

[11] For a thorough analysis of Hobsbawm's bandits as social heroes who are totally inappropriate models for *thag*s in the Indian context, see Kim Wagner, 'Thuggee and Social Banditry Reconsidered,' *The Historical Journal* (June 2007): pp. 353–76.

[12] Hobsbawm, himself, excluded Indian dacoits from his model in his 'Social Banditry,' in Henry A. Landsberger, ed., *Rural Protest: Peasant Movements and Social Change* (London, 1974), p. 148.

[13] Deposition of Lukha Dacoit, 15 September 1840, N.A.I., Legislative Department, Law Proceedings, 2 September 1843, fol. 404.

landholding class created by the 1793 Permanent Settlement from the middle men of the eighteenth century. These new patrons, under the pressure of the Company's high revenue demand, willingly accommodated dacoit gangs, partly in response to threats and partly in response to the promise of a share of the loot. McLane puts forward a cogent argument that the Company failed to understand that its revenue and administrative reforms effectively eroded moral authority in the countryside by replacing the traditional paternalist authority of the old *zemindar*s with salaried police and new competitive revenue farmers.[14]

For F. Bruce Robinson, writing about the settlement of the Western Deccan in the Bombay Presidency after the Maratha wars, Hobsbawm's social bandits are a useful reference point. Dacoity was not acknowledged as such in the Bombay Presidency. Instead, the most worrisome plunderers took the form of armed bands living in narrow river valleys of the Western Ghats. Robinson observes that these armed bands fit Hobsbawm's vision of a marginal society, inasmuch as they 'occupied a position somewhere between the point where caste society breaks down and tribal society begins'.[15] They even rose to the challenge of social revolution as the Ramoosies seized Purhandar Taluk in 1824–27 and the Kolis staged a rebellion in 1829–30. By the 1840s, the Company changed its strategy of pacification. Instead of attempting to win the cooperation of the armed bands by granting their chiefs police powers and privileges, the Company began to pursue them as criminals. Thenceforward, the armed bands regarded themselves as a social force rather than a political force. Their aim was to obstruct the new oppressors introduced by the Company's government: 'money lenders, forest police, revenue peons and regular police enforcing new laws'.[16] This form of social banditry paralleled that of the Bengali dacoits.

David Arnold uses a remarkably similar argument for dacoity in mid nineteenth-century Madras. However, Arnold does not find Hobsbawm's 'social bandit' a particularly instructive model. Commenting on the tremendous diversity among dacoities, he notes the crime category of dacoity could include 'famine looting, the armed depredations of professional bandits and the raiding and feuding of faction gangs'. He accepts food prices as a

---

[14] John R. McLane, 'Bandits and Rebellion in Nineteenth-Century Western India,' in Anand A. Yang, ed., *Crime and Criminality in British India* (Tucson, Arizona, 1985), pp. 26–47; cf. 'Fifth Report from the Select Committee on the Affairs of the East India Company,' *Parliamentary Papers* (1812) Cmd. 377, p. 71 (hereafter cited as 'Fifth Report').

[15] F. Bruce Robinson, 'Bandits and Rebellion in Nineteenth Century Western India,' in Anand A. Yang, ed., *op. cit.*, p. 56.

[16] *Ibid.*, p. 60.

'natural barometer of crime' and argues persuasively that dacoities and other crimes were most frequent in the hot dry months prior to the monsoon when 'there was little work to be done in the fields, food reserves were low but prices high, and advantage could be taken of doors and windows left open from the heat or of villagers sleeping outdoors'.[17] Only when he enlarges his horizons to include bandits in the hill tracts does Arnold make a connection between dacoity and rebellion. Yet, for the Company period, he cautions against identifying these rebellions as protests of the poor: 'The 1840s witnessed the rebelliousness and the feuding of the elite, not the risings of the peasant masses'.[18]

Underlying the perception that the Company unwittingly destroyed the basis of moral authority in the countryside where it alienated or even dispossessed the natural leaders of the villages and large landed estates, there is a heated debate about the role of the state. Burton Stein has suggested the relevance to Indian history of Aidan Southall's African model of a 'Segmentary State'. This vision of numerous, similar, small units organized in a pyramidal fashion works well for the many 'little kingdoms' of South India and for the bandit kingdoms of the hill country.[19] Bruce Robinson finds the 'Segmentary State' a useful concept for explaining the independent spirit of the armed bands of the Deccan who occasionally staged a rebellion against the British power at the centre.[20] However, such a concept does not blend very well with Indian caste society. Bernard Cohn argues that the African model is ill suited to the evolution of Indian historical periods.[21] Anthropologists generally view the 'Segmentary State' as a 'transitory and unstable form moving toward the normative unitary condition'.[22] Robert E. Frykenberg advances the argument one step further by expressing strong misgivings about any European concept of a state in South India. In an effort to 'conceptualize both ever changing polities and processes', he emphasizes

---

[17] David Arnold, 'Crime and Crime Control in Madras, 1858–1947,' in Anand A. Yang, ed., *ibid.*, pp. 68–71.

[18] David Arnold, 'Rebellious Hillmen: The Gudem and Rampa Risings, 1839–1924,' in Ranajit Guha, ed., *Subaltern Studies I: Writings on South Asian History and Society* (Delhi, 1982), p. 107.

[19] Burton Stein, 'The Segmentary State in South Indian History,' in Richard G. Fox, ed., *Realm and Region in Traditional India* (Duke University Press, 1977), pp. 3–51.

[20] F. Bruce Robinson, *op. cit.*, pp. 59–60.

[21] Bernard S. Cohn, 'African Models and Indian Histories,' in Richard G. Fox, ed., *Realm and Region in Traditional India* (Duke University Press, 1977), pp. 90–113; Sandria B. Freitag, *op. cit.*, pp. 141–42 and n. 4, pp. 185–86.

[22] Burton Stein, *op. cit.*, p. 6.

the 'persistence and strength of political fragmentation, disaggregation and disintegration down to the village'.[23]

At some point it does become necessary to conceptualize the kaleidoscopic nature of social change. However, as far as the development of social legislation is concerned, speculation about the nature of the state is not necessarily helpful. Given the *Arthasastra*, it would seem impossible to deny the concept of statehood in India altogether. At the other end of the debate, it would seem that the Company's efforts to pass legislation valid for all of its Indian subjects leaves it open to the charge that it was trying to fit a unitary mantle over a plural, if not segmented, society. But it is possible to add an important caveat to the latter accusation by simply observing that a good law does not lend itself to manipulation by either the state or the ruling elite or the subaltern classes.

Chronology also plays a role which cannot be ignored. C.A. Bayly has opened a window on the political fluidity of the Gangetic plain of the late Mughal period when 'herdsmen and marauders' co-existed with settled local petty rulers. When the East India Company succeeded in establishing a 'land revenue-based state' with 'settled agriculture', nomadic marauders no longer had a base of operations.[24] A slightly different perspective is offered by one of those marauders, namely, *Poorun Phansigar*:

> It was before the establishment of tranquillity over the Country that...our excursions were neither carried to so great a distance as they have since been, nor were so lucrative or certain, for in those days travellers, particularly with much property seldom ventured to go from one place to another without being well escorted or in large parties and we feared the Pindaries and other mounted plunderers as much as other classes did.[25]

Sandria Freitag argues that in the period of nascent Company power when political power was fluid, marginal marauding groups could be integrated into sedentary discrete Indian society. As the trading company evolved

---

[23] Robert E. Frykenberg, '"Company Circari" in the Carnatic c. 1799–1859: The Inner Logic of Political Systems in India,' in Richard G. Fox, ed., *op. cit.*, p. 124; *see also* Robert E. Frykenberg, 'Traditional Processes of Power in South India: An Historical Analysis of Local Influence,' *Indian Economic and Social History Review*, Vol. 1 (1963): pp. 122–42.

[24] C.A. Bayly, *Rulers, Townsmen and Bazaars, North Indian Society in the Age of British Expansion, 1770–1870* (Cambridge, 1983), Introduction and Chapter 1.

[25] Deposition of *Poorun Phansigur*, enclosed in letter from Capt. W. Borthwick, Political Agent at Mehidpore, 26 July 1829, Political Proceedings 23 October 1829 and 4 August 1830, U.P.S.A. C.O.V. M.V.), Judicial Letters Issued and Received, Sl No. 2, Vol. 9, 2 February 1822–30 October 1847, fol. 67.

into a land revenue-based state, roving thugs and dacoits trying to establish themselves as petty rulers were viewed as a threat to the power of the British state. This historiographical concern with the role of the state, in the end, diverts attention away from the development of law and the judiciary to the exercise of administrative and police power.[26]

This point of view is increasingly easy to argue from the vantage point of clashes between the Nationalist Movement and the British Government of the late nineteenth and early twentieth centuries. But in the early nineteenth century, the East India Company was trying to come to terms with its perceived responsibility for law and order. Although its territorial domain was steadily increasing, it did not perceive itself as an overwhelming imperial power. The problems of thagi and dacoity provoked a legislative response which does raise some interesting questions about the balance struck by the Company between power and justice. The questions which the Company found most challenging involved legal definitions and litigation procedures.

Legal Definitions

The terms 'dacoity' and 'thagi' were forever being defined and redefined by the Company. Originally a Hindi word, 'dacoity' derives from 'dakaity' which John Beames' *Comparative Grammar* traced to the verb 'dakna', meaning 'to shout'; it may also have been connected with the Sanskrit 'dashta' or 'pressed together'.[27] The origin of the word 'thug' or 'thag' is even more obscure. Stewart Gordon informs us that 'thag' was a 'common eighteenth-century Hindi word meaning a cheat or trickster—anyone from the perennial practical joker to a sleight of hand artist or a coinage swindler'. The related verb translates 'to amaze'.[28] These classical definitions seem far removed from the definition which became operational in the Company's legislation regarding both dacoits and thugs, namely, their combination into or association with 'gangs'.

Beng. Reg. LIII 1803, the first Company law to deal comprehensively with dacoity as a crime, went to great lengths to avoid the term 'dacoity'. This

---

[26] Sandria B. Freitag, *op. cit.*, pp. 149, 160–61.

[27] John Beames, *Comparative Grammar of the Modern Aryan Languages of India (1872–79)*, 3 Volumes, cited in Col. Henry Yule and A.C. Burnell, *Hobson-Jobson—A glossary of Colloquial Anglo-Indian Words and Phrases, And of Kindred Terms, Etymological, Historical, Geographical and Discursive* (London, 1903), p. 290.

[28] Stewart N. Gordon, *op. cit.*, p. 408.

regulation, which was duplicated as the authority on the subject by Madras Reg. XV of the same year, referred to the term 'dacoity' only parenthetically. Sec. III cl. 1 designated as guilty of 'robbery by open violence':

> [...]any person or persons who shall, in the day or in the night, go forth with any offensive weapon, or in a gang with or without an offensive weapon with the criminal intent of committing robbery, and shall, by force or intimidation, rob, or attempt to rob...or shall attack by open violence...shall be deemed guilty of the crime of robbery by open violence (denominated in the Mahomedan law *suruca-i-kubra* and more commonly *shubkhoone*, or *dukaytee*).[29]

Beng. Reg. IX 1808 was the first Company law to boldly address the problem of apprehending 'Leaders of Gangs of Dacoits'. The crime of dacoity was identified as the 'Offence of Gang Robbery'.[30] The word 'dacoity' never appears in the Bombay series of Regulations.

In these early days of Company policy, there was confusion among district officers over the distinction between 'dacoits' and ordinary 'banditti'. In 1808, the Judge and Magistrate of Bundelkhund reported on 'the barbarous and savage state' of the inhabitants of Ramgurh. He attributed this circumstance to the exploitation which drove agricultural slave labourers to abscond into 'the fastnesses of the woods' where they turned to acts of 'theft and plunder' and became hardened 'banditti'.[31] According to a late nineteenth-century glossary, 'banditti' were 'persons put under a ban and outlawed' whereas 'dacoits' were 'thieves who go about the country in gangs'.[32]

As early as 1810, the government in Calcutta began to receive reports from Etawah district of 'a detestable race of monsters called thugs'. There were further reports concerning the thug families in the Sindouse pargana of Etawah district.[33] Then, Dr Sherwood's 1816 'Report of the Murderers called

---

[29] Sec. III Cl. 1 Beng. Reg LIII 1803, I.O.R., V/8/17; Madras Reg. XV 1803, I.O.R., V/8/26.

[30] Beng. Reg. IX 1808, I.O.R., V/8/18, p. 293; *see also* Madras Reg. XIII 1809, I.O.R., V/8/27.

[31] J. Richardson, Judge and Magistrate of Bundelkhund, to H.T. Colebrooke, J.H. Harington, J. Tombelle and T. Parr, Judges of the Sudder Dewanny Adawlut and Nizamut Adawlut, I.O.R., 23 March 1808, *Board's Collections*, Reg. 14078, F/4/578, fols 99–101.

[32] Rev. H. Percy Smith, ed., *Glossary of Terms and Phrases* (London, 1883), pp. 55, 155.

[33] Cited by C. Kenna, *op. cit.*, pp. 148, 177 and 179. Kenna speculates that the deposition of Gholam Hossyn, a 16-year-old manihar, forwarded from Mynpooree, Etawah to Calcutta on 19 March 1810, was 'perhaps the first appearance in government records of a thag confession'. *Ibid.*, p. 33.

Phansigars' fostered a general perception that alongside India's high roads lurked fraternities of murderers. Before the end of the second decade of the nineteenth century, the Superintendent of Police in the Western Provinces had demanded that restrictions in Sec. 10 Beng. Reg. VIII 1818 requiring a 'notorious' dacoit to give security before his release be applied to other suspected 'notorious Thugs and Highway Robbers'.[34] This was accomplished by Beng. Reg. III 1819.[35] Twenty years later the same procedure occurred in reverse as Sec. I Act XXX 1836 enacting that 'whoever shall be proved to have belonged...to any gang of Thugs...shall be punished with imprisonment for life...' was extended to apply to 'persons proved to have belonged to any gang of Dacoits...' by Sec. I Act XXIV 1843.[36]

In actual fact, it was Macaulay's Law Commission that decided what constituted a 'gang'. In Madras, a Foujdary Adawlut Circular Order had decreed in 1829 that 'any robbery by more than one individual is Gang Robbery'. When the judges of the Madras Sudder Court later asked the Law Commissioners to specify what number constituted a 'gang', the Commissioners replied that the number was established by the new Penal Code.[37] This Code as printed in Calcutta in 1837 decreed that a dacoity gang consisted of six persons; a more recent edition of the Code states that a dacoity gang consists of five or more persons and that, according to a 1973 court ruling, a 'conviction of less than five persons can be sustained'.[38]

Just as the numbers required to constitute a dacoity gang varied in different legal documents, so legal definitions of a thug were multifaceted. It is now a matter of legend that a young officer in the Bengal Army was so stunned by Dr Sherwood's report on the *phansigars* (stranglers) that he decided to dedicate the remainder of his career to the study and repression of the fraternities of murderers known variously as thugs, *phansigars*, *megpunnas* (child-stealers) and *dhutoorea*s or *meetawalla*s (poisoners). The latter poisoners

---

[34] W. Ewer, Superintendent of Police, Western Provinces, Report submitted to W.B. Bayley, Chief Secretary to Govt. at Fort William, 6 April 1819, I.O.R., Beng. Judicial Criminal Proceedings, 16 April 1819, No. 6.

[35] Beng. Reg. VIII 1818 for modifying some of the existing requisition of security for good behaviour;... (passed 28 August 1818) and Beng. Reg. III 1819 for extending provisions of Sec. X, Reg. VIII 1818 to Robbers not being Dukuyts or Gang Robbers (passed 16 April 1819) I.O.R., V/8/19.

[36] Act XXIV 1843 for the better prevention of the crime of Dacoity, I.O.R., V/8/33.

[37] N.A.I., Legislative Department A, Original Consultations 8 August 1836 containing extract from Proceedings of Foujdarry Adawlut, Fort St. George, 17 June 1836.

[38] N.A.I., *A Penal Code Prepared by the Indian Law Commission* (Calcutta, 1837), pp. 98–99; see also *The Indian Penal Code* (Lucknow, 1981), p. 97.

appeared in Sleeman's early reports on the thugs, compiled in central India.[39] They also featured in a list assembled by J.S. Mill in London of 'fraternities of professional murderers, closely allied to the Thugs':

> [...]in particular, the Meetawallas or poisoners in Bengal; a class in the Upper Provinces, who murder parents for the sake of obtaining possession of their children and certain classes of religious Mendicants in the Deccan, some of whom are proved to practice assassination in the manner of the Thugs.[40]

Yet, although the *dhutoorea*s or *meetawalla*s were well known both in central India and in the corridors of East India House as early as 1840, eight years later Lt. Col. Sleeman was unable to win support for his own draft Act to expand the definition of thug to include the poisoners alongside stranglers and child-stealers. He argued for a declaratory act including poisoners rather than an act of definition. He particularly objected to the phrase 'offence of robbery not amounting to dacoity' as a source of doubt and confusion which had already caused trials of poisoners to be suspended in Agra and Oude.[41] But, despite Sleeman's pleas backed by the likes of W. Dampier, the Superintendent of Police in the Lower Provinces, Act III 1848 was enacted precisely to clarify definitions. Furthermore, it defined a thug as 'a person... habitually associated with...others for the purpose of committing, by means...likely to cause death...the offence of child-stealing or the offence of Robbery not amounting to Dacoity'.[42] Sleeman's concern over the confusion caused by the reference to 'dacoity' was belatedly accommodated when the Penal Code essentially incorporated the definition of thug in Act III 1848 without any reference to 'dacoity'.[43]

---

[39] William Henry Sleeman, *Ramaseeana* (Calcutta, 1836); William Henry Sleeman, *Report on the Thug Gangs* (Calcutta, 1840); William Henry Sleeman, *Rambles and Recollections of an Indian Official* (first published 1844), ed. Vincent A. Smith (repr. Karachi, London, 1973).

[40] J.S. Mill, Political Despatch to India, 15 July 1840, No. 26, I.O.R., E/4/763, fol. 556. For confirmation of Mill's authorship of this despatch, in addition to his signature on the frontispiece, see M. Moir and John M. Robson, eds, *Writings on India by John Stuart Mill* (Toronto, 1990), Appendix A, p. 250.

[41] Sleeman's Draft Act, N.A.I., Legislative Department, Law Proceedings 26 February 1848, No. 29, fols 316–17; Lt. Col. W.H. Sleeman, Superintendent for Operations against Thuggee, to G.A. Bushby, Secretary to Government of India, Jhansi, 21 September 1847, No. 31, fols 318–19.

[42] Act III 1848 for removing doubts as to the meaning of the words 'Thug' and 'Thuggee', and the expression 'Murder by Thuggee', when used in the Acts of the Council of India, I.O.R., V/8/33.

[43] Cf. Sec. 310, *The Indian Penal Code* (Lucknow, 1981): 'Whoever...shall have been habitually associated with any other(s) for the purpose of committing robbery or child-stealing by means of or accompanied with murder, is a Thug.'

However, Sleeman's concern to bring the *dhutoorea* thugs within the jurisdiction of his department was only popular within the ranks of his own department and the police. Quite inexplicably and erroneously, for some months after the February 1848 enactment of Act III, Police Superintendent Dampier proclaimed his belief that 'the offence of administering Drugs is brought within the definition of Thuggee…by…Act III of 1848.[44] In actual fact, the Government of India persisted in its unwillingness to use the approver system of the Thagi and Dacoity Department against the *dhutoorea* thugs. One of Sleeman's colleagues and successors, Lt. Col. Hervey, raised the issue on behalf of the Department in 1865, 1868 and 1873, only to be rebuffed on all three occasions.[45]

Thus the legal definition of thug fell far short of the comprehensive definition including all varieties of thugs identified by William Sleeman, not to mention J.S. Mill. Later gazetteers identified even more varieties of violent gangs.[46] On the one hand, this confusion re-enforces Stewart N. Gordon's remark:

> The late nineteenth century official, the military officer and the twentieth century historian are surely to be forgiven if British officials at mid-nineteenth century contemporary to the Thug phenomenon could not figure out what a Thug was! The only people who seemed positive that they could tell a Thug when they saw one were from the Thagi and Dacoity Department.[47]

On the other hand, it belies the assumption, seemingly contained in Stewart Gordon's analysis, that Sleeman and his Department always had their way.

Col. Sleeman's efforts to extend the definition of 'dacoit' to include vagrants was more successful than his efforts to include poisoners in the definition of thug. Sleeman acknowledged before the Government of India that the Sudder Nizamut Adawlut had decreed in 1844 that penal provisions of Sec. 10 Beng. Reg. XXII of 1793 authorized magistrates to demand security

---

[44] W. Dampier, Superintendent of Police, Lower Provinces, to Major Riddell, Assistant General Superintendent for the Suppression of Dacoity and Thuggee, Patna, Garden Reach, 2 June 1848, B.S.A., Patna Commissioner's Office, Vol. 714, No. 1250; see also W. Dampier to F.J. Halliday, Secretary to Government of Bengal, Garden Reach, 6 March 1848, *ibid.*, No. 478.

[45] 'Papers Relating to the Crime of Robbery by Poisoning', N.A.I., India: Selection from the Records of the Government of Calcutta 1853–1911, No. 167.

[46] See for example, Robert Russell and Hira Lal, *Tribes and Castes of the Central Provinces of India* (London, 1916), p. 558; D.C.J. Ibbetson, *Outlines of Punjab Ethnography* (Calcutta, 1883), pp. 308–13.

[47] Stewart N. Gordon, *op. cit.*, p. 412.

for future good behaviour from vagrants and that Cl. 1 Sec. 8 Beng. Reg. VIII of 1818 empowered those officers to detain vagrants if such security was not furnished. However, he objected: 'These regulations are not in force in the Bombay and Madras presidencies; and political functionaries in Native States through which they are passing with their booty, when arrested, do not feel authorized to act upon them'. The Government of India accepted Sleeman's argument without questioning the implications of such an all embracing definition. And so Act XI 1848 subjected 'any wandering gang of persons associated for the purposes of theft or robbery, not being a gang of Thugs or Dacoits' to the same procedures and punishments as those outlined by Acts XXX 1836, XVIII 1837 and XVIII 1839 for thugs and Act XXIV 1843 for dacoits.[48]

Legal Procedure

The draconian measures against dacoits proposed in Art. 35 of Warren Hastings' 'Plan for a Judicial Establishment' are notorious. Hastings' idea of a triple punishment whereby convicted dacoits would be executed in their villages as a 'terror and example to others', their villages fined and their families made slaves of the state, was typical of the atavistic response of Company officialdom to the problem of dacoity. Exemplary punishment for dacoits, and eventually thugs, was a tactic favoured consistently by officers from Warren Hastings' time through to the era of the Thagi and Dacoity Department. However, summary justice for convicted dacoits Hastings-style did not receive the sanction of the Cornwallis Code.

Cornwallis himself proposed the more subtle remedy of instituting a system of approvers. His suggestion that dacoits be allowed 'to become witness against each other...care being always taken that no person be ever convicted on the sole testimony of accomplices, unless their Credit be supported by circumstances' unwittingly anticipated by 50 years legislation dealing with thagi and dacoity.[49] The Cornwallis Reforms specifically removed barbaric aspects of Muslim law involving punishment by mutilation and prosecution only by the victim or the victim's family. Prior to Judicial Regulation XXXIV 1791, and Beng. Reg. LIII 1803, offenders convicted of robbery

---

[48] Act XI 1848 for punishing wandering gangs of Thieves and Robbers, I.O.R., V/8/33.

[49] Minute by Governor General Cornwallis, *Bengal Revenue Consultations*, 3 December 1790, I.O.R., P/52/22, fols 224–25.

without murder according to Muslim law were to be punished by having two limbs amputated. Thus, in 1789, Jonathan Duncan, as Resident at Benares, presided over a court case in which the *maulvi* or law officer ruled that the defendant was 'deserving of losing his hand because he took the Bale from under the head of the traveller and carried it off'. Because the owner of the stolen property did not appear in court to prosecute, the defendant was 'not to have his hand cut off' but was 'deserving of greater punishment' at the discretion of the judge. Duncan took the opportunity to order the defendant to be imprisoned for one year and then released.[50] Dacoity had yet to be recognized as a problem meriting specific legislation. All that surfaced in the Cornwallis Regulations was the mild encouragement given by Judicial Reg. XLIV 1792 to magistrates to offer a reward of 10 *sicca* rupees for assistance in the apprehension of a dacoit to be paid upon said dacoit's conviction. Thus the Cornwallis Code both acknowledged that individual dacoits were beyond the reach of the Company's magistracy and assumed that gangs of dacoits could be dealt with effectively by its criminal justice system.

However, at the turn of the century, Governor General Wellesley discovered an alarming increase of gang robberies. One of his administration's most competent judges, Henry Strachey testified to a shift in the nature of the menace of dacoity:

> Dacoits do not now often assemble in large bodies and set the magistrate at defiance. They lie concealed, come about the court, intrigue with the lower officers or with the jailor, ascertain the probability of detection, conviction, and punishment, what sort of evidence may be requisite to disprove facts. In short the country is infested with robbers and villains who know how to elude the law.[51]

Wellesley's Government responded to the crisis with the comprehensive Beng. Reg. LIII of 1803 which aimed to stem the increase of violent raids on travellers and villagers by modifying the provisions in Muslim criminal law for punishing the 'heinous' crime of 'robbery by open violence'. This law was immediately duplicated by Madras Reg. XV of the same year, but no parallel measure directed specifically at dacoity was adopted by the Government of Bombay.

---

[50] Trial of Byjoo, Proceedings 7 September 1789, U.P.S.A., Duncan Records, C.O.V., Resident's Proceedings Basta #25, Register #22, fol. 53.
[51] Henry Strachey, Midnapore Zillah, to George Dowdeswell, Secretary to Government in Judicial Department, 30 January 1802, Appendix 10, 'Fifth Report', p. 533.

With Beng. Reg. LIII 1803 the Company aimed to build on the Cornwallis reforms in order to modify the provisions of Muslim criminal law which served to undermine in the courts the best efforts of the police to secure the apprehension and conviction of dacoits. The prime objective of Reg. LIII was to bring the crime of dacoity within the realm of public justice. The definition in Cl. 1 Sec. III of a generalized crime of 'robbery by open violence' is noted above as the foundation for the focus on 'gangs' in the Company's legal definitions. It was made necessary by the narrow focus in Muslim law on highway robbery. In Muslim law, the ultimate punishment of death was only applicable to crimes of robbery involving murder on the open highway 'at a distance from any inhabited place'. The Government reasoned that since this punishment represented the 'specific provision of hud (hadd)...by the right of God, being...exemplary punishment inflicted for the prevention of crime which is the end of public justice', it should be 'obviously applicable to all...crimes committed by open violence...whether on the highway, remote from or near to an inhabited place, or within a place inhabited or in any place whatever'.

Next, the Company tackled specific obstacles placed by Muslim law in the way of the actual punishment of convicted dacoits. The Regulation's preamble noted that for convicted offenders:

> ...specific punishment is barred by anyone of the band of robbers being under age, or a lunatic, or a relation within the prohibited degrees of the person robbed or murdered; or by the person robbed or murdered not being a fixed resident...; or...by one of the robbers having a joint interest in the property plundered, or such property not being considered in legal custody with respect to any one of the robbers, or lastly with regard to the separate punishment of each robber, if his share of the property taken shall not amount to ten dirms—somewhat less than three sicca rupees.

With such a litany of exceptions it was no wonder that so many convicted dacoits were released by the courts. Reg. LIII resorted to the tactic of creating a legal fiction. Cl. 4 Sec. II instructed the law officer, when a specific 'sentence of hud (hadd) is barred by some legal exception', to 'declare by a second futwa to what punishment the prisoner would have been liable under Mahomedan law...if the special exception...had not existed'. Moreover, Cl. 2 Sec. III boldly declared:

> Nor shall any of the circumstances noticed in the preamble of this Regulation as barring a sentence of hud (hadd) under the Mahomedan law...be hereafter allowed to operate against the punishment of persons convicted of...robbery by open violence...or of murder...or of an intent to rob.

Cl. 3 Sec. II endorsed yet another legal fiction in case the law officer should decide that, although insufficient legal evidence ruled out punishment by *hadd* or *kisa*s, the prisoner was liable to discretionary punishment (*tazir*, *acoobut* or *seeasut*) on grounds of 'strong presumptive proof'. In such a case the law officer was to declare by a second *futwa* 'to what specific punishment (of hud or kissas) the prisoner would have been liable under Mahomedan law, if he had been convicted by full legal evidence'. With such instructions Beng. Reg. LIII endeavoured to direct the Muslim law officers of the criminal courts away from their habitual 'consideration of the degree of proof against the party accused' to a more judicious concern for 'the degree of guilt and criminality of the act established against him'.

Sec. IV condemned to death leaders and members of gangs convicted of robbery with murder; those convicted of robbery with aggravated circumstances of maiming or setting fire to a dwelling but without murder were condemned to transportation for life and those convicted of robbery without aggravation to imprisonment with hard labour for 14 years. There was ample provision for mitigation of these prescribed punishments. And the Nizamut Adawlut was required to review cases from the courts of circuit involving capital cases, the Circuit Judges' disapproval of the law officers 'futwah', or the failure of the law officers of the Nizamut Adawlut to confirm conviction declared by law officers of the Courts of Circuit.[52]

While Beng. Reg. LIII 1803 cleared the way for magistrates and judges to deal more effectively with trials for gang robbery, the distrust of authority prevalent among the local population, combined with corruption among the police *darogah*s, left dacoits free to plunder without much fear of apprehension. W.C. Blaquiere's egregious spies or *goyenda*s were eloquent testimony to the need for extraordinary measures to bring apprehended dacoits before the magistrates in the districts around Calcutta, so that they could be committed for trial in the circuit courts. Although Blaquiere had his critics who accused the *goyenda*s of terrorizing the population with accusations of the innocent as well as the guilty, he won the approval and support of officialdom.[53] In the hill country of Ramgurh a magistrate and

---

[52] Governor General in Council, Bengal Regulation LIII for determining the punishment to be adjudged by criminal courts of judicature, in cases wherein a discretion is left by Mahomedan Law; for defining crime and punishment of robbery by open violence; and for declaring what convicts shall be hereafter liable to transportation, or to banishment; as well as punishment of such as may return from transportation, or escape from confinement, during the periods of their sentences, 21 July 1803, I.O.R., V/8/17, pp. 735–47.

[53] Dowdeswell, *Report on the General State of the Police of Bengal*, 29 September 1809, Appendix 12, 'Fifth Report', p. 617.

army officer operated a system of rewards and protection for informants in a successful campaign to apprehend the 'famous dacoit Fouj Roy'.[54] But the general difficulty of apprehending dacoits was acknowledged by Beng. Reg. IX 1808, the first Reg. specifically to use the term 'dacoits'. Sec. III Reg. IX 1808 boldly authorized magistrates to proclaim throughout the countryside by printed notice and by beat of drum the names of suspected dacoits. And if those suspects whose names were proclaimed failed to surrender at the appropriate cutcherry within two months, the proclaimed dacoit would be 'deemed guilty of the crime of which he stands accused and...be liable to be imprisoned and transported for life'. In addition, Sec. XI, while requiring 'all persons of whatever description...to afford every practicable assistance in the apprehension of such offenders', declared that if the proclaimed offender should be wounded or killed 'in consequence of his standing on his defence or flying, the person so wounding or slaying the criminal shall be deemed entirely guiltless'. This Regulation was duly duplicated by Madras Reg. XIII 1809 and the procedure of proclamation without specific reference to dacoity was sanctioned by Sec. XV Bom. Reg. III 1818 and Sec. III Bom. Reg. IX 1819.[55]

With open season thus declared on dacoits by Reg. IX 1808, the Government was optimistic about its prospects for success. Dowdeswell, in his 1809 police report, declared a 12-month campaign against dacoits in Nuddea District an outstanding success with the apprehension of several *sirdar* dacoits or leaders of dacoit gangs as far afield from Calcutta as Patna. But the tactics of both criminals and their Government prosecutors left the local population cowering in fear. Contemporary court cases recorded horrific scenes in which dacoits wrapped their victims in straw or in a blanket and then set them alight with their torches in order to extort information about the location of concealed property. Or, to gain revenge against an associate who had given evidence against them, they tied the hapless traitor to a stake and while threatening that they 'would teach him how to give evidence against them again', slashed his body with spears and swords.[56] On the side of the

---

[54] Correspondence between William Spedding, Acting Magistrate, Beerbohm, and E.S. Broughton, Commander of Ramgurh Battalion, B.S.A., C.N.C.O., Vol. 2, fols 13–14, 79–80, 147–48, 184–85 and 191.

[55] Governor General in Council, Bengal Regulation IX for apprehension of persons concerned in offence of gang-robbery, and especially the *sirdars* or leaders of gangs of dacoits, 4 Nov 1808, I.O.R., V/8/18, pp. 293–97; Madras Reg. XIII 1809, I.O.R., V/8/27; Bom. Reg. III 1818 and Bom. Reg. IX 1819, I.O.R., V/8/23.

[56] Jugnath Ghose v. Balram Sirdar et al., 16 September 1809 and Inhabitants of Gadpokheria v. Koraur Sirdar et al., 4 September 1809, cited in Dowdeswell, *op. cit.*, pp. 605–606.

Government, the secret of the successful campaign against dacoits in Nuddea District in 1808–09 was the collaboration of *goyenda*s or spies with *darogah*s or regular police. The *goyenda*s were customarily obtained from prisoners who had won acquittal in the courts, but who had been detained according to Cl. 6 Sec. II Beng. Reg. LIII 1803 on account of their reputation as bad characters until they could pay security for future good behaviour. With their knowledge of the habits and haunts of the principal dacoit gangs in their district, these prisoners were 'uniformly willing to engage as spies in the service of the magistrates'. The *goyenda*s denounced their prey to *gorinda*s or specially designated police *darogah*s who were a notorious 'pest to the country' on account of their insufficient salaries encouraging a general spirit of 'avarice and addiction to every species of extortion'.[57] Dowdeswell acknowledged the potential for abuse in the collusion of *goyenda*s and *gorinda*s as a necessary evil in the successful Nuddea campaign against dacoity, but insisted there was no other way to effectively curb dacoity.

Henry Strachey could not have disagreed more. He noted that in Nuddea District between 20 November 1808 and 31 May 1809, 2071 dacoits were imprisoned. After six months, 48 had died and 1477 had yet to be examined. Strachey concluded that 'the good done was purchased at the expense of too much evil'.[58] In the end, the population did not know whom to fear more, the dacoits or the magistrates armed with proclamations and *goyenda*s. In addition, apprehended dacoits learned how to mock the courts at the expense of innocent citizens. In 1815, the second Judge of the Moorshedabad Court of Circuit reported the fraudulent practise of dacoits summoning from 40 to 80 witnesses to attend the Courts of Circuit for months at a time at the expense of their reputations if they were *zamindar*s or of labour lost in the fields if they were *ryot*s. When said witnesses ultimately had the opportunity to declare that 'they never heard of, or saw' the offending dacoits 'before in their lives', the dacoits asserted 'with the most determined effrontery, that they were not the persons they meant but that their witnesses consisted of persons of the same names residing in the same villages'.[59]

---

[57] Dowdeswell, *op. cit.*, pp. 612, 615.

[58] 'H. Strachey's Answer to 13 Questions Circulated in 1813 among the Company's Judicial Servants Who Had Retired to England, 30 Dec. 1813', *Selection of Papers from the Records at the East-India House, Relating to the Revenue, Police and Civil and Criminal Justice under the Company's Government in India*, Vol. II (London, 1820), p. 70.

[59] Report of 2nd Judge of Moorshedabad Court of Circuit, Extract Bengal Judicial Criminal Consultations, Lower Provinces #33, 5 July 1815, I.O.R., *Board's Collections* F/4/578 Reg. 14078, fols 62–65.

The Nizamut Adawlut attempted to insert a corrective balance into the system. In the first instance, in 1811 the Court endeavoured to correct the miscarriage of justice which was the perceived result of a circular it issued on 31 May 1809 in the wake of the apparently successful campaign against dacoits in Nuddea District. The 1809 Circular directed magistrates to imitate the success of the magistrate of Nuddea *zillah* in 'assembling and explaining to...the zamindars...the consequences of any omission or neglect... either to assist the police officers or to deliver up notorious dacoits, vagrants or persons of bad or suspicious character' as required by Secs XI and XII of Reg. IX 1808. By 1811, the Government wished to modify the authority which magistrates, in accordance with their interpretation of the Nizamut Adawlut Circular of 1809, had invested in *zamindar*s to apprehend persons 'solely on suspicion of bad livelihood or on information of notoriety of bad character'. The Nizamut Adawlut Circular of 17 January 1811 instructed the magistrates to admit all such suspects to bail while investigating the truth of the suspicion against them.[60] In 1815, the Court ordered magistrates offering a reward for a proclaimed dacoit 'to shew the grounds and evidence on which the person or persons proposed to be proclaimed or for whose apprehension a reward is proposed'.[61]

In the meantime, well before the publication of Dr Sherwood's account of the *phansigar*s, the Nizamut Adawlut began to receive information about thugs. In Government v. Tuhowur Khan and two others, 12 July 1812, the prisoners were charged at the Etawah Sessions with being thugs after being apprehended on grounds of notorious bad character. The *futwa* of the law officer accepted the first prisoner's confession to a livelihood of 'murdering and robbing unwary passengers' alongside the testimony of two witnesses as grounds for conviction of being a thug liable to discretionary punishment by *Acoobut*. The Nizamut Adawlut, in the absence of any regulations on thagi, felt compelled to observe that the actual crime had been committed prior to the promulgation of Beng. Reg. VIII 1808 which had declared gang robbery without violence punishable with transportation for life. In addition, the Court was unconvinced of the truth of the prisoner's confession. Because, the prisoner was neither charged with nor convicted of a specific offence, the Nizamut Adawlut ordered that he be 'immediately discharged'.[62] Thirteen

---

[60] N.A. Circular Orders #53 and #80 in *Circular Orders Passed by the Nizamut Adawlut for the Lower and Western Provinces and Communicated to Criminal Authorities in Bengal and Agra Provinces by Registers of Those Courts from 1796 to 1844*, Part I (Calcutta, 1846) [hereafter cited as *Circular Orders*], pp. 20, 36–37.

[61] N.A. *Circular to Magistrates*, Fort William, 18 April 1815, B.S.A., P.C.O. Vol. 250A.

[62] 'Vakeel of Govt. v. Tuhowur Khan & two others', 12 July 1812, 1 N.A. Rep. 239.

years later the Court ruled that a trial for murder by thagi by the Sessions Court in Cawnpore was illegal because the crime was not committed in the district of Cawnpore.⁶³ With no specific thagi legislation to guide them, the Judges of Nizamut Adawlut could only fall back on the principles and provisions of dacoity legislation. Thus, in 1827, the Sudder Court assigned punishments of death and banishment to thug gang leaders and members respectively.⁶⁴

These sample court cases spanned two decades when the menace of thagi seemed to overtake the menace of dacoity. In Bengal, it is generally understood that there was a significant decrease in the number of cases of dacoity between 1815 and the 1840s. More specifically, Police Reports of 1827 and 1828 for the Patna Court of Circuit indicated that dacoity had 'become greatly mitigated in its character' and that its 'prevalence' had 'rather decreased'. Only a few exceptional cases of dacoity aggravated by murder persisted mostly in the hill country of Ramgurh.⁶⁵ In cases of both dacoity and thagi, there was consistent official objection to overly harsh or arrogant punishments. In 1824, the Home Government expressed horror over the idea reported by the Joint Magistrate at Shahjehanpore that 'it was customary when a thief was killed at a distance from the Sudder Station to send the head to the Magistrate'. The Court of Directors prohibited any future efforts to cut off the heads of dacoits as 'abhorrent to the spirit of a civilized Government'.⁶⁶ The Directors were to express similar disapproval of a slightly less ghoulish tactic authorized by a Sessions Judge in Bombay who ordered that convicted thugs were to be 'hung by the neck until they be severally dead and that their gallows be left standing'.⁶⁷ By the 1830s, the

---

⁶³ Chynsookh v. Umra Lodh and others, 18 May 1825, 2 N.A. Rep. 393. Whereas Radhika Singha argues that 'Islamic law as it was modified and actually applied in the Company's courts posed no very great obstacle to the trial of Thuggee and dacoity cases' in this period, in actual fact the Judges of the Sudder Court fought against the arbitrary disregard for rules of evidence and jurisdiction used against thugs. Radhika Singha, *op. cit.*, p. 195.

⁶⁴ Soodes & 22 others, 12 January 1827, 3 N.A., Rep. 1.

⁶⁵ John R. McLane, *op. cit.*, p. 44. Police Reports submitted by C.R. Barwell, Superintendent of Police, Lower Provinces, 29 December 1828 and 30 September 1829, B.S.A., P.C.O., Vol. 243A, fols 150–51, 192.

⁶⁶ Judicial Despatch to Bengal (Western Provinces) 28 April 1824, Para. 44, I.O.R., E/4/711, fol. 549. This practice persisted outside the Company's territories, as a Budduck Dacoit widow deposed in 1839: '…five heads were sent to Lucknow'. Capt. James Paton, *Collections on Thuggee and Dacoitee*, B.L., Add. MSS. 41300, fol. 358.

⁶⁷ Govt. v. Kumblee Wulud Hybutee & 5 others, 6 September 1830, in A.F. Bellasis, ed., *Reports of Criminal Cases Determined in the Court of Sudder Foujdaree Adawlut of Bombay*, Vol. I, 1827–46 (Bombay, 1849), p. 44.

Government was sufficiently alarmed by the growing numbers of travellers reported murdered on the roads of central India to sanction a highly focused, centralized campaign against thugs.

The campaign began with Government authorization of some extraordinary measures through the agency of the Thagi Department established by Governor General Bentinck in 1829 under his Agent in the Saugor and Nerbudda Territories, F.C. Smith. For example, the Government ordered that thugs who had been condemned to prison, only to be released later on security, should be 'branded with the Godna on some part of their body, not exposed to view, so that they may be recognized as Old Offenders should they again be apprehended'.[68] The process of 'branding with the Godna', often used as punishment for perjury, was a form of tattoo; the Company was ultimately to 'abolish wholly the practice' with Act II 1847. F.C. Smith, as the newly empowered Agent to the Governor General in the Saugor and Nerbudda Territories, was able to enlist the services of judicial and police officers countrywide. Thus, when Capt. William Sleeman, one of Smith's 'principal assistants', reported the capture in the Bombay Presidency of a notorious thug gang laden with plunder, the Bombay Government instructed the Political Commissioner of Guzerat and the Principal Collectors of Ahmedabad, Surat and Candeish to 'give their utmost attention' to any communication from Sleeman's mentor, F.C. Smith. In this particular case, extra assistance was needed to secure witnesses and evidence. Because the plunder consisted of gold and jewels carried by the thugs' victims from Surat to pay for opium in central India, it was sufficient to pay the cost of the trial; but, it was also sufficient to enmesh potential witnesses in silence.[69] In another instance the Bombay Government was willing to put pressure on the Guicowar of Baroda 'to apprehend and deliver up' a thug who, Capt. Sleeman claimed, had escaped into the sanctuary of the Guicowar's family.[70] Not only did the Thagi Department enjoy the legitimacy it derived from being a Government agency, but it also wielded considerable muscle in the

---

[68] Chief Secretary of Government in Political Department, submitted to Agent to Governor General in the Saugor and Nerbudda Territories, 4 August 1830, U.P.S.A., C.O.V. M.V., *Judicial Letters*, Issued and Received 2 February 1822–30 October 1847, Sl. No. 2, Vol. 9, fol. 78.

[69] W.H. Sleeman to F.C. Smith, Saugor, 11 July 1831; Bombay Government to F.C. Smith, 17 August 1831, Polit. Cons. 17 August 1831, #2131, Bombay Record Office (hereafter cited as B.R.O.), Political Department Vol. 24/409, fols 94–95, 118–27.

[70] Bombay Government to James Williams, 11 August 1832, Polit. Cons. 15 August 1832, #2862, B.R.O., Political Department Vol. 24/409, fols 329–30.

form of a Tomaun of Nujeebs[71] specially raised to aid Capt. Sleeman in his operations against thugs.

Bentinck's special measures against thagi won warm approval in London. On behalf of the Directors, John Stuart Mill undertook a careful appraisal of the Company's thagi policy in several despatches. Mill commended Bentinck's Government for 'vigorous measures' made necessary by the 'enormities of the Thugs ... mostly committed in our newly acquired possessions or in Territories of the Native Chiefs of Bundelcund, Malwa and Rajpootana'. However, Mill's commendation was not without criticism. He noted with disapproval that the only trial of thugs reported in Government despatches concerned thugs who had been imprisoned since 1823—nearly 10 years. It was clear that 'no explanation whatever' could excuse such a long delay. Mill mused further that 'the measures you have adopted in some instances of placing under restraint the wives and children of persons known or strongly suspected to be thugs, is one which ought to be very sparingly resorted to'. He applauded the tactic of sparing the life of the notorious thug, Feringeea, on condition that he confess all his 'acts of Thuggism' and name all his accomplices without any hope of 'ever being released from confinement'. And so, the system of thug approvers was sanctioned, with captured thugs providing a list of thugs still at large. However, he enjoined the judiciary in India not to convict 'upon the mere evidence of accomplices unless confirmed by circumstantial evidence'.[72]

This injunction against the conviction of anyone on the grounds of his reputation or association with a gang of thugs and without reference to a specific offence crystallized the essence of future debate. First, special thagi legislation was to endow the Thagi Department with special powers, later extended by special dacoity legislation to the Thagi and Dacoity Department. Then, for decades to come, bitter debate over the legitimacy of these special powers was to rage between judicial functionaries and the officers of the elite corps which served Sleeman after he was named 'General Superintendent of the Operations for the Suppression of Thuggee' in 1835

---

[71] Tomaun of Nujeebs refers to a Division of Infantry Soldiers. 'Tomaun' is a Mughal term referring to an army division of 10,000 soldiers; nujeebs were half-disciplined infantry soldiers under native Governments or militia under Brtish rule. For more details see, Hobson–Jobson, *A Glossary of Colloquial Anglo-Indian Words and Phrases, and of Kindred Terms, Etymological, Historical, Geographical and Discursive*, eds, Col. Henry Yule and A.C. Burnell (London, 1903), p. 290.

[72] Political Despatch to Bengal, 28 November 1832, I.O.R., E/4/735, fols. 1475–91. For confirmation of J.S. Mill's authorship, see Martin Moir and John M. Robson, *op. cit.*, Appendix A, p. 244.

and then 'Commissioner for the Suppression of Dacoity as well as Thuggee' in 1839.

In the person of John Stuart Mill, Sleeman enjoyed full official backing for his career as 'Superintendent of Operations against Thuggee'. In two successive despatches, Mill declared F.C. Smith 'whose judgement and ability framed the original system of measures' and Capt. Sleeman to be entitled to 'very high recommendation'. However, after surveying the success of the approver system devised by Smith and implemented by Sleeman, Mill was critical of thug trials in Hyderabad which, because of 'some inferiority in the conclusiveness of the proofs' released, on finding security, 42 persons found guilty of thagi. Mill lamented the widespread collusion of *zamindar*s and *Patel*s with thugs in the countryside.[73] With this criticism, Mill underlined the perceived need for yet more severe sentencing of thugs.

As if in answer to Mill's criticism, Act XXX 1836 introduced spectacular innovations in court procedure. In the first instance, under Sec. I, anyone who could be proved simply 'to have belonged...to any gang of Thugs' was liable to a sentence of life imprisonment with hard labour. According to Sec. II, any person so accused could be tried by any district court competent to try him even if the offence was committed outside its jurisdiction. And finally, Sec. III decreed that no *futwa* from any law officer was required in such trials. With this landmark piece of legislation, the Thagi Department could centralize its operations, requiring all apprehended thugs to be sent to its Superintendent or any of his Assistants for trial and imprisonment. And it circumvented the finer distinctions of both English and Muslim law. On the principle of guilt by association, it was possible to lock up any number of accused thugs without the expense and trouble of proving a specific offence. And without a *futwa*, the courts were free of the arcane provisions of Muslim law.

Somewhat ironically, given the Bombay Government's earlier support for the tactics of the Thagi Department, the most intense criticism of Act XXX 1836 came from the Judges of the Bombay Sudder Foujdary Adawlut. In the Judges' view, Act XXX was an insult to Governor Elphinstone's Bombay Code. They were outraged particularly by Sec. II Act XXX which they interpreted as providing that 'a Native Subject of this presidency may be sent to be tried by any Courts of the Bengal, Agra or Madras Presidencies...'. They argued that this provision effectively annulled Chap. I Bom. Reg. XI 1827

---

[73] Polit. Desp. to India, 16 April 1834, I.O.R., E/4/740, fol. 1120; Polit. Desp. to India, 12 August 1835, I.O.R., E/4/744, fols 989, 1010 and 1013. Cf. Martin Moir and John M. Robson, *op. cit.*, Appendix A, pp. 244, 246.

which was designed to protect the 'Subjects' of the Bombay Government 'from the violence, prejudice or injustice of foreign authorities'. The Judges speculated that under Sec. II Act XXX 1836, without the protection guaranteed by Chap. I Bom. Reg. XI 1827, the citizens of Bombay might be sent for trial at a distance away from their friends to be tried under unfamiliar laws 'in the presence of a public none of whom may be acquainted with their language or habits'.[74] W.H. Macnaghten answered this objection on behalf of Lord Auckland's Government with the argument:

> The Thugs are a race of vagrant offenders…Evidence sufficient for their conviction is seldom available at the place of their apprehension, and hence it becomes necessary to admit of a latitude in the conduct of their trials, not required in the case of ordinary offenders.[75]

The Judges took further offence over the apparent insult directed at Bombay Criminal Law by the promulgation of Act XXX. They pointed out that Bombay Criminal Law was different from that of the rest of British India, insofar as it did not 'acknowledge the Mahomedan Code either in Evidence or in punishment'. The Judges insisted that the Bombay law was 'most liberal and enlightened' containing 'nothing to prevent the conviction and punishment of the guilty' and containing nothing that can be dispensed with without causing 'injustice and oppression to the people'. To prove their point, they cited Cl. 2 Sec. XXXV Bom. Reg. XII 1827 as directly relevant to the Thagi Department's operation of the approver system with its declaration that 'evidence of an accomplice shall operate against a prisoner, only so far as it corroborates that of other witnesses or strengthens impressions produced by circumstances'. The Judges explained further that their observations were motivated in part by the fact that the 'Superintendent of Thuggee, and…his assistants, are likely from their previous professional employment having been Military, not to be fully versed in the requisites for the attainment of justice'.[76] Macnaghten remained unmoved by so many objections and observed simply that the only difference between the

---

[74] P.W. LeGeyt, Register Bombay Sudur Foujdaree Udalut, to J.P. Willoughby, Secretary to Government of Bombay, 30 December 1836, I.O.R., *Board's Collections* F/4/1760 # 72103, fol. 7.

[75] W.H. Macnaghten, Secretary to Government of India, to J.P. Willoughby, Secretary to Government of Bombay, 20 February 1837, I.O.R., *Board's Collections* F/4/1760 # 72103, fol. 12.

[76] P.W. LeGeyt to J.P. Willoughby, 30 December 1835, I.O.R., *Board's Collections* F/4/1760 # 72103, fols 8–10.

court procedure regarding thugs and that regarding other offenders was the elimination of the *futwa* 'and to this apparently there is no objection on the part of the Judges as the Mahomedan Code is stated by them not to be acknowledged at the Bombay Presidency'.[77] The Home Government supported the conclusion reached by Lord Auckland's Government, namely, that Act XXX 1836 was 'not liable to the objections urged against it' by the Bombay Sudder Court and that 'its provisions are well adapted to put down the atrocious offence of Thuggee'.[78]

That Act XXX 1836 was too simplified for the legal complexities of the different regions in India were to become apparent only too quickly. Its failure to mention the crime of 'murder by Thuggee' provoked the Judges of the Madras Sudder Foujdary Adawlut to demand further enabling legislation. Unlike their colleagues in Bombay, the Madras Judges did not object to the new thagi legislation on principle. They merely wished to overcome discrepancies between the new legislation and the Madras code. The Judges observed that 'on a charge of murder by Thuggee the mode of proceeding prescribed in Act XXX 1836' could be followed by neither the Courts of Circuit nor the Foujdary Adawlut because Madras Regulations required 'that a futwa shall be taken'.[79] Also, according to Clauses 1 and 3 of Sec. IX Madras Reg. X 1816, the crime of murder by thagi must be committed for trial by the 'Criminal Judge of the Zillah wherein the murder may have been committed'.[80] However, the Judges were disposed to remove the obstacle to the work of the Thagi Department posed by Criminal Judges as an intermediate authority. For authorization to circumvent the Regulations, they looked back to their own proceedings in 1807 in the wake of the Vellore Mutiny.[81] The Judges were merely arguing that fresh legislation was required to authorize the officers specially appointed for the suppression of thagi to bypass the criminal judges. Governor of Madras, John Elphinstone, agreed with

---

[77] W.H. Macnaghten to J.P. Willoughby, *op. cit.*

[78] Legislative Despatch to India, 21 August, 1839 #13, Para. 40, I.O.R., E/4/760, fol. 288.

[79] W. Douglas, Register Foujdaree Udalut, to Chief Secretary to Government, 20 February 1837, Judicial Consultations 14 March 1837 #8, Tamil Nadu Archives (hereafter cited as T.N.A.) Vol. 323A, fol. 1362; also in India Legislative Proceedings 19 June 1837 #5, I.O.R., P/206/89.

[80] W. Douglas, Register Foujdaree Udalut, to Chief Secretary to Government, *op. cit.*, fol. 1364; Madras Reg. X 1816, I.O.R., V/8/28.

[81] Extract Proceedings of the Foujdaree Udalut, 25 June 1833, Judicial Consultations 14 February 1837 #28, T.N.A.; also in India Legislative Proceedings 19 June 1837 #5, *op. cit.*

Law, Order and Power 53

the judges that it was 'desirable to avoid the interference of the criminal judge in thuggee cases', but he felt this could be done without legislation.[82] The case for further legislation was ultimately clinched by a query from Capt. F.C. Elwall, Assistant to the Superintendent of Operations for the Suppression of Thuggee concerning constraints in the Regulations. Capt. Elwall pointed out that Sec. XX Madras Reg. VIII 1802 did not allow for a conditional pardon to be allowed to a principal offender. And yet accomplices to the crime of murder by thagi were 'from the nature of the crime… strictly speaking principals in law'. The Judges again discovered grounds for exception to the rule in old records. In thagi cases tried in the Madras courts in 1814–16, thug accomplices had been granted a conditional pardon by the Governor in accordance with Sec. XX Madras Reg. VIII 1802; they also noted an instance reported in *Parliamentary Papers* of an accomplice being granted a pardon on the authority of Sec. III Beng. Reg. X 1824. However, the Judges, at the same time agreed with Capt. Elwall that the provisions of the Regulations for conditionally pardoning and consequently releasing from prison criminal accomplices 'could not be applied' to thug approvers who would 'immediately on release return to their old calling if they escaped being murdered by others of their profession'. The Judges also looked to English law for a helpful precedent since, according to Madras Reg. I 1818, evidence admissible in criminal trials by the Law of England was admissible in Madras Courts of Circuit. But English courts only admitted principals in murder to give evidence 'under an implied promise of pardon on condition of their making a full and fair confession'. The Judges finally concluded 'that neither the Regulations of this Government nor the rule observed in England can be applied to Thug approvers', and therefore fresh legislation was required. [83]

Governor Elphinstone ultimately recommended to the Governor General the Judges' Draft Act, Sec. I of which empowered magisterial officers in the Thagi Department to commit offenders to trial and Sec. II of which empowered the same officers to admit approvers and render their evidence

---

[82] W. Douglas, Register Foujdaree Udalut, to Chief Secretary to Government, *op. cit.*; Minute of Governor in Council, Judicial Consultations 14 March 1837 #11, Judicial Consultations 14 March 1837 #8, T.N.A., Vol. 323A, fol. 1362, fol. 1420 and I.O.R., *Board's Collections*, F/4/1760 # 72113, fol. 1.

[83] W. Douglas, Register Foujdaree Udalut, to Chief Secretary to Government, 10 March 1837, Judicial Consultations 14 March 1837 #9, T.N.A., Vol. 323A, fols 1365–69; also in I.O.R., India Legislative Proceedings, 19 June 1837 #5, *op. cit.*

valid.[84] Elphinstone further took the initiative to use the powers vested in him by Madras Reg. III 1827 to authorize the transfer of prisoners whenever 'it may be considered expedient to hold trials for Murder by Thuggee in any Court other than that within the jurisdiction of which the crime has been committed'.[85] Essentially, the Governor and the Madras Sudder Judges were arguing that the Madras Code had prepared the way for Act XXX 1836 very well; all that was needed was some enabling legislation to sanction the authority of the magistrates specially appointed in the Thagi Department.

The Supreme Government responded promptly to the suggestions from Madras by promulgating Acts XVIII and XIX in August, within six months of the initial proposal.[86] Sec. I of the Judges' Draft Act became Act XVIII empowering magisterial officers of the Thagi Department to commit to trial persons accused of both the crime of murder by thagi and that of belonging to a gang of thugs. Sec. II was edited in best Benthamite style by Law Member T.B. Macaulay before emerging as Act XIX. In the hands of Macaulay, the approver system which was the brainchild of F.C. Smith and William Sleeman attained full legitimacy by comparison with 'the old system of approvement' in England. Macaulay noted that the evolution of the old system in England into a 'much more simple and convenient mode of proceeding' could easily be replicated in India. This involved an informal offer of conditional pardon at the discretion of the magisterial officers of the Thagi Department without the specific authorization of special legislation. Macaulay devised what became Act XIX to validate the evidence given by a thug after his conviction and confinement on the basis of the confession which was the condition of his pardon. In a Benthamite frame of reference, Macaulay had succeeded in avoiding a 'separate Code of evidence for one particular crime'. Indeed, he had been 'unwilling to pass a law which would seem to imply that we are disposed to put up with worse evidence in cases of Thuggee than we think necessary...'. By decreeing in an Act applicable to all of India that 'no person shall, by reason of any conviction for any

---

[84] H. Chamier, Chief Secretary, to Government Fort St. George, to W.H. Macnaghten, Secretary to Government of India, Fort St. George, 18 March 1837, Judicial Diary 21 March 1827 #33, T.N.A., Vol. 323A, fol. 1517; quoted in Legislative Despatch from Government of India, 16 October 1837, I.O.R., *Board's Collections* F/4/1760 Register 72113, fol. 1.

[85] Minute by Governor in Council, 18 March 1837, Judicial Diary 21 March 1837 #32, T.N.A., Vol. 323A, fol. 1515.

[86] Act XVIII on Murder by Thuggee, and belonging to a Gang of Thugs, and Act XIX enacted 7 August 1837, I.O.R., V/8/31.

offence whatever, be incompetent to be a witness', Act XIX 1837 achieved Macaulay's objective of universality.[87]

In addition to his Benthamite triumph with Act XIX, Macaulay fulfilled the compromise envisioned by his colleague, H. Shakespeare. Shakespeare had noted the awkward constraints placed upon officers of the Thagi Department by the Regulations which contemplated a full pardon to accomplices in cases of murder. Thus, Sec. XX Madras Reg. VIII 1808 and Beng. Reg. X 1824 obstructed the magisterial officers of the Thagi Department who needed to detain the convicted thug approver on the basis of a partial pardon which offered him the mercy of exemption from capital punishment and transportation. Macaulay's draft for Act XIX provided the legal groundwork for Shakespeare's vision of a 'just...compromise with the Thug', whereby 'his life is spared, society is protected against his violence in future and his evidence is rendered instrumental to the general suppression of that crime for which his life was forfeited'.[88] The mode of proceeding for offering conditional or partial pardons to thug approvers was then set out in a detailed set of Instructions circulated by Government through the courts.[89] Thus, legitimacy was bestowed upon F.C. Smith's approver system which, by substituting conditional pardons for conviction by a magistrate, allowed officials of the Thagi Department to obtain 'additional information' from 'every gang seized'.[90]

The power so relished by Mr Smith was to prove a continual irritant to the Judges of the Sudder Foujdary Adawlut at Bombay. To the annoyance of the Supreme Government, the Sudder Judges at Bombay belatedly sent in hefty objections to Act XVIII and to the Instructions issued to Magistrates in explanation of Act XIX. The Supreme Government had circulated the drafts of the 1837 Acts to the Presidency Governments with a request for a report six weeks in advance of their enactment. The response of the Bombay

---

[87] Minute by Macaulay, n.d., I.O.R., *Board's Collections* F/4/1760 Register 72113, fols 106–109; also printed in C.D. Dharkar, ed., *Lord Macaulay's Legislative Minutes* (Oxford, 1946), pp. 246–47. N.B. pp. 128–29 where Dharkar traces Bentham's influence on Macaulay's thoughts to Bentham, *Works* Vol. IV, pp. 375–76. In line with his thoughts on universality, Macaulay recommended that Act XVIII 1837 be enacted as a separate law for the Madras Presidency only.

[88] Minute by H. Shakespeare, 20 April 1837, *India Legislative Proceedings*, 19 June 1837 #6, I.O.R., P/206/89.

[89] Nizamut Adawlut Circular Order No. 247, 22 September 1837, *Circular Orders*, Part I, pp. 288–90; also in Legislative Proceedings, 19 June 1937 #16, I.O.R., P/206/89.

[90] F.C. Smith, Agent to Governor General in Saugor and Nerbudda Territories, to Secretary to Government of India in Political Department, Jubbulpore, 17 April 1835, India Political Consultations 11 May 1835 #73, I.O.R., P/193/75, fol. 24.

Government arrived two months after the laws had been promulgated. The Bombay Judges continued the same line of argument pursued in their objections to Act XXX 1836. They stated again that the laws of the Bombay Code were 'adequate to meet the cases of Thuggee'; and, insofar as they perceived that the objective of Act XVIII was to 'enable Magistrates to commit persons, wherever the crime be perpetrated, to be tried at Jubbulpore', the citizens of Bombay were shorn of the protection and security guaranteed to them by Bombay laws. The Supreme Government answered this objection by stating that Act XVIII had been intended to apply primarily to the Madras Presidency where magisterial officers of the Thagi Department had not had the power of committing persons to trial. Moreover, as in 1836, the Supreme Government argued that 'with reference to the erratic habits of Thugs' it was necessary to empower Magistrates 'to commit Parties, wherever seized…to any tribunal…competent to try them…'

Regarding approvers and the validation of their evidence by Act XIX, the Bombay Judges observed that, by allowing the evidence of approvers to become the basis for both apprehension and conviction of the accused, such evidence would become 'an Engine for false accusation to an extent to endanger life, and effect extortion'. Specifically, the Bombay Judges objected that the Instructions issued to Magistrates in explanation of Act XIX 'were inconsistent with the provisions of Cl. 1 Sec. XXXV Bom. Reg. XII 1827'. This clause allowed that a pardon which 'shall not be liable to be disturbed' might be granted to an accomplice prior to giving evidence, but prescribed penalties should he 'withhold his evidence or give false testimony'. The Supreme Government answered that 'it was not proposed by those Instructions to offer pardon, but merely mercy to the accomplices admitted as approvers in trials for Thuggee'. But the Bombay Sudder Judges insisted that the words, 'such pardon shall not be liable to be disturbed', in Bom. Reg. XII 1827 rendered absolute the pardon offered to accomplices in order that they might give evidence in court. Thus 'a conditional pardon was altogether opposed to the spirit' of the Bombay Code, unless the law was altered. Insofar as the Judges did not believe the tactic of an absolute pardon always to have been successful, they favoured modification of the law to allow for conditional pardons to be granted in certain cases within 'the narrowest possible limits'. Accordingly, with Act XV 1838, the Supreme Government repealed Cl. 1 Sec. XXXV Bom. Reg. XII 1827.[91]

---

[91] Legislative Despatch from Government of India, 20 August 1838, in *Board's Collections*, I.O.R., F/4/1760 Register 72114, fols 1–7. Bom. Reg. XII 1827, I.O.R., V/8/24; Act XV 1838, I.O.R., V/8/31.

In the wake of the 1837–38 thagi legislation, Governor General Auckland was confronted with a proposal for yet another law to deal with the ambiguities of Act XXX 1836 regarding the distinction between the offence of murder by thagi and that of membership in a gang of thugs. Auckland balked at the thought of additional legislation specially directed at thagi. The prime source of confusion was Sec. III of Act XXX which dispensed with the *futwa* despite the custom of using *futwa*s in all capital cases. Auckland argued that, in cases involving a murder charge liable to capital sentence, he did not think it 'desirable to diminish the formality of the Trial by dispensing with the Futwa of a law officer...therefore...it would be better to leave the law as it stands.'[92] Mr Amos, a member of Auckland's Council, reflected that 'Act XXX 1836 was erroneously drawn and was intended to extend to trials for Murder by Thuggee'. However, he commented further that actual trials for murder by thagi outside the district where the offence was committed and without a *futwa*, although in accordance with Secs II and III of Act XXX 1836, were illegal, in virtue of the fact that they were not trials for simply being a member of a gang of thugs. Amos noted the proper use of a *futwa* in a recent decision by the Sudder Nizamut Adawlut, even though he suspected that 'in other parts of India it may still be the practise to try without the Futwa'.[93] Auckland persisted in his view that no further legislation was necessary; he challenged Amos' assertion that thugs had been convicted and executed illegally. Auckland doggedly insisted that all trials for the crime of murder by thagi were conducted not according to the 'easier process' of trials under Act XXX but with 'the strict observance of every prescribed formality'.[94]

The last of the Thagi Acts of the 1830s reflected the profound inefficiency of the Police, rooted in collusion between offenders and the police establishment at village level and in important *zamindari*s. Act XVIII 1839 simply decreed that persons accused of 'unlawfully receiving or buying property stolen or plundered by Thuggee' were subject to the trial procedures outlined by the Thagi Acts of 1836 and 1837.[95] The lamentable state of

---

[92] W.H. Macnaghten, Secretary to Government of India with Governor General, to T.H. Maddock, Officiating Secretary to Government of India, Simla, 6 September 1838, N.A.I., Legislative Department, Law Proceedings 15 October 1838 #1, fols 1–2.

[93] Minute by A. Amos, 1 October 1838, N.A.I., Legislative Department, Law Proceedings 15 October 1838 #2, fol. 4; Minute by A. Amos, 8 October 1838, N.A.I., Legislative Department, Law Proceedings 8 October 1838 #23, fol. 341. Cf. Govt. v. Kishore Sein and Others, 26 June 1838, 5 N.A. Rep. 89.

[94] Minute by Governor General Auckland, 17 September 1838, N.A.I., Legislative Department, Law Proceedings 8 October 1838 #22, fols 387–88.

[95] Act XVIII 1839 on Trials for Thuggee, I.O.R., V/8/31.

the police establishment and the total lack of any sense of community responsibility in the *mofussil* were brought to the attention of Government by a magistrate in Nellore District in 1836. Not only did thugs find it easy to recruit collaborators among *zamindar*s and village *chaukidar*s, but also criminal offenders of all types found little resistance to their activities in village communities. Magistrate T.V. Stonehouse of Boochereddypollam noted that, although he was satisfied that the increase in crime statistics was largely due to the increasing accuracy of police reports, yet he had 'no doubt…that crimes are committed which are not reported by the Village Police to the District Head of Police, particularly in the Zemindaries, and never come to the knowledge of the Magistrate'. He explained to the Court of Circuit that in the rural *mofussil*, when robbers attack a village, villagers 'shut themselves up in their own houses…mud houses easy of access to any Burglar and of jungly retreats in every direction, which…baffle every exertion of the Magistracy for their detection'.[96] The Government of Madras responded to the Nellore Magistrate's complaints about 'the want of cooperation on the part of the Village Servants in the Police Divisions' of one particular *zamindari* with a threat to 'resume the Police' of that *zamindari*.[97]

Against a background of such general laxity, it is not surprising that dacoity began to flourish again. The Magistrate of Bihar wrote in 1837 of 'the great accumulation of work arising from the prevalence of Gang Robbery and other heinous offences…in this District'.[98] The pressure of business on the circuit courts caused by an increase of dacoity ultimately caused the Supreme Government to acknowledge in 1843 that 'the crime of Dacoity…is still very prevalent in many parts of Bengal', and in December 1840 'to call the serious attention of the Government of Fort St. George to the numerous occurrences of dacoity'. In fact, regarding Madras, the Supreme Government expressed alarm that the 'evil' of dacoity had 'reached in the Presidency of Fort St. George a height which it has scarcely ever in the most unquiet times attained to in any other part of the British dominions in India'.[99] A member of the Governor's Council in Madras took exception to this charge. He observed that

---

[96] T.V. Stonehouse, Magistrate Boochereddypollam, to Register, Provincial Court of Circuit, Northern Division Masulipatam, 26 February 1836, A.P.S.A., Nellore District Records, Vol. 4117, fols 316–18.

[97] Minute Summarizing Proceedings, T.N.A., Judicial Consultations 9 March 1841, No. 17, Vol. 414B, fols 1497–98.

[98] W. Onslow, Officiating Magistrate Bihar, to T.R. Davidson, Commissioner of Circuit for Patna Division, Gyah, 28 August 1837, B.S.A., P.C.O., Vol. 276.

[99] F.J. Halliday, Junior Secretary to Government, to H. Chamier, Chief Secretary to Government of Fort St. George, 21 December 1840, Judicial Cons. 9 March 1841 #13, T.N.A., Vol. 414B, fols 1167–69.

'a considerable proportion of the robberies with aggravating circumstances are not of that description of crime which comes under the denomination of "decoity" such as is known in Bengal'.[100] A virtual chorus of magistrates lamented before Madras Courts of Circuit the 'insufficiency' of District police and 'inefficiency' of Village Police especially in the 'hot weather when the great body of the agricultural class having no regular employment are apt to betake themselves to robbery on the Highway or in Houses'. The crime of dacoity easily became entangled with other types of crime. Often cattle raids accompanied robberies 'in which grain for food was the object'. A magistrate in the Northern Circuit Court Division of Masulipatam noted some cases of cattle theft 'in which there was undoubtedly some connivance in the low country Villages, the carrying off of their cattle to the Hills being pleaded as an excuse for withholding the Revenue'.[101] The relationship between dacoity and food scarcity has been generally documented by gazetteers for all of India. David Arnold has charted the correlation between dacoity and food grain prices in Madras during the latter nineteenth century. By that time crimes 'formerly categorized as dacoities' came to be classified in the 'currently fashionable category of unlawful assemblies and riots'.[102] It was not only in Madras that the legal term 'dacoity' was embarrassed with practical difficulties. In Bombay in 1843 when the Supreme Government proposed further dacoity legislation, the Bombay Sudder Court Judges were unconcerned except to observe that 'the term "Dacoity" is one hardly known in any part of the Bombay Presidency'.[103] It would seem that the term 'dacoity' was the preference of Bengal administrators.

If the Governments of Bombay and Madras were unwilling or reluctant to contemplate gang robberies denominated as 'dacoity', the Government of the Northwestern Provinces (N.W.P.) was less inhibited. From the N.W.P. came drafts for two laws, both of which were promulgated by the Supreme Government in 1843. Act XVIII addressed questions of jurisdiction with its concern to provide 'better custody of persons convicted of Thuggee

---

[100] Minute by John Bird, 28 January 1841, Judicial Cons. 9 March 1841 #15, T.N.A., Vol. 414B, fols 1489–90.

[101] *Ibid.*; W. Lavic, Acting Magistrate, Cuddapah, to Register, Provincial Court of Circuit, Centre Division, 18 March 1840, Judicial Cons. 9 March 1841 #15, T.N.A., Vol. 414B, fol. 1325; G. Smith, Magistrate, Pottapoor, to Register, Provincial Court of Circuit, Northern Division, Masulipatam, Judicial Cons. 9 Mar. 1841 #26, T.N.A., Vol. 414B, fols 1246–47.

[102] David Arnold, *op. cit.*, pp. 68–71.

[103] W.H. Harrison, Register, Sudder Foujdarry Adawlut, to J.P. Willoughby, Secretary to Government of Bombay, 5 October 1843, N.A.I., Legislative Department, Law Proceedings 18 November 1843 #6, fol. 130.

and Dacoity' even if the crime and conviction occurred in the territories of Native Provinces outside the territories of British India. Act XXIV 'for the better prevention of the crime of Dacoity' assimilated thagi and dacoity legislation in line with suggestions originally submitted to the Government of the N.W.P. by Maj. Sleeman.

Act XVIII emerged from doubts concerning the legality of the decision of authorities in the state of Gwalior to send criminals convicted and sentenced in Gwalior to Agra to be imprisoned. In considering the draft for Act XVIII enabling East India Company jails to receive and detain prisoners from outside territories governed by the Company, A. Amos, member of the Governor General's Council, recognized that there were 'legal difficulties inasmuch as we might be punishing within our territories persons who never committed any offence within those territories and who were never our Subjects'. Yet he argued on behalf of Government that 'such difficulties must yield to the necessity of the case'.[104] As he presented his case for new legislation, Amos had to lean heavily on circumstances rather than principles. He noted that the Thagi Acts applied only to Company Courts and officers in Company territories. He even admitted that 'I have always thought that these acts were in excess of the powers of the Legislative Council'. In any event, the Thagi Acts were irrelevant because they 'do not touch the case in question'.[105]

Amos' draft act 'to render lawful the custody in our Jails of persons convicted of Thuggy, Dacoity...beyond the limits of the Jurisdiction of our own Courts' won the approval of the Legislative Council. The Council reasoned that 'if', according to the proviso in Amos' draft, 'criminals are tried and convicted before Courts in which our own officers preside with the sanction of the local Native Government there will be no objection to it'. However, the ultimate decision was left to Governor General Ellenborough who was in Allahabad. Ellenborough, a man of action, raised no objection and Amos' draft became Act XVIII 1843.[106] In actual fact this question of jurisdiction, insofar as it concerned subjects of the East India Company, had been addressed as long ago as 1805 by the Madras Sudder Court. On the question 'whether or not the Court of Circuit can try subjects of the Honourable Company's government for crimes committed on each other in

---

[104] Minute by A. Amos, 4 September 1842, N.A.I., Legislative Department, Law Proceedings, 3 February 1843 #24, fol. 344.

[105] Minute by A. Amos, 14 March 1843, N.A.I., Legislative Department, Law Proceedings, 3 February 1843 #22, fol. 342.

[106] Act XVIII for Better Custody of Persons Convicted of Thuggee and Dacoity, passed 9 September 1843, I.O.R., V/8/32.

territories not subject to the said Government', the Court reflected that 'the Mahomedan Criminal law is as much the Law of the English Government in India as the regulations themselves are', and that the 'Mahomedan Law extends to the persons committing the crime in what part of Hindustan soever the act is done'. And so, the Sudder Court ruled that 'all Subjects of the Honourable Company's Government who stand charged with crimes cognizable under the regulations be brought to trial before the Courts of Circuit without previous reference to ascertain the local jurisdiction in which the crime was committed'.[107]

The proposal to assimilate thagi legislation with dacoity legislation by extending Acts XXX 1836, XVIII and XIX 1837 and XVIII 1839 to Dacoity originated with Maj. Sleeman. Since his appointment in 1839 as Commissioner for the Suppression of Thuggee and Dacoity, Sleeman had become thoroughly frustrated over the difficulty of apprehending and convicting dacoits, numbers of whom, he was increasingly convinced, worked in systematic confederacies. Sleeman initially proposed to the N.W.P. Government that a law should be enacted 'declaring that all persons proved to belong to a tribe known to be robbers by profession should be liable to be convicted in the same manner as a man known to have been a thug altho' [sic] no distinct offence might be proved against him'.[108] As understood by one of Sleeman's great admirers, the Superintendent of Police for the Lower Provinces, W. Dampier, his proposal enjoyed the support of the Sudder Courts in both Allahabad and Calcutta. However, the N.W.P. Government was not entirely satisfied with Sleeman's ideas. In the process of consultation on the final draft act, they observed that approvers in the Thagi Department had been known to denounce 'as their relatives...innocent men...who had never participated in the crime'. The N.W.P. Government could see no reason why provision should not be made in the forthcoming law to the effect that 'one specific act of Thuggee or Dacoity should be established and adduced as evidence in support of the general crime'.[109] Of course, such an insistence upon proof of a specific offence was anathema to Sleeman

---

[107] Circular from T.B. Hurdis, Register Sudder Foujdaree Adawlet, Extract from procceedings of the Court of Sudder Foujdaree Adawlet, 17 December 1805, T.N.A., Madura District Records, Vol. 1192, fol. 225.

[108] Cited in, W. Dampier, Superintendent of Police, Lower Provinces, to F.J. Halliday, Secretary to Government of Bengal, Purneah, 21 November 1842, N.A.I., Legislative Department, Law Proceedings 2 September 1843 #1, fol. 386.

[109] R.N.C. Hamilton, Secretary to Government of the Northwest Provinces, to T.R. Davidson, Officiating Secretary to Government of India, Agra, 26 October 1843, N.A.I., Legislative Department, Law Proceedings 18 November 1843 #9, fol. 132.

and Dampier. In their experience it was impossible to secure evidence to convict highly professional gangs of dacoits on grounds of a specific offence. Dampier protested: 'It is clear that unless accidentally seized with the property obtained by them in particular Dacoities...they cannot now be prosecuted to conviction in our Courts'.[110]

In fact, Sleeman's desire to assimilate thagi and dacoity legislation was fuelled by his discovery of the Budduck dacoits. According to his prize Budduck prisoner, Lukha, the Budducks were Rajputs who escaped death at the hands of the Emperor Akbar to offer their services to the Nawab of Oude or to whomever else they could until, after two or three generations, in poverty and despair, some turned to robbery.[111] Lukha confessed to participation in 49 dacoities for all of which Sleeman was able to find corroborative evidence. The Lt. Governor of the N.W.P. encouraged Sleeman to publish a report on the Budducks, but this project was suspended by the Governor General until 'more progress had been made in the suppression of the crime'. In the meantime, W. Dampier discovered bands of Kechuk dacoits who appeared to resemble the Budducks in language and livelihood. The Bengal Government's willingness to print and distribute among magistrates and police officers Dampier's 'narratives' by Kechuk approvers encouraged Sleeman to bring forth his information on Budducks. Sleeman was very interested in Dampier's theory that the Kechuks and Budducks were members 'of the great robber family of the Bowreeas'. He wrote to Dampier that 'This class of offenders...can only be put down by being pursued to their homes as the Thugs were...by the same machinery of a subsidiary police'. But, even more important, he thought was the necessity for an 'Act declaring imprisonment for life'.[112]

It was the very severity of the measures which Sleeman and Dampier deemed necessary to apprehend and convict the professional Budducks and Kechuks which alarmed the N.W.P. Government. Echoing the sentiments of the Madras Government with respect to the universal category of 'Dacoity', the N.W.P. Government protested that 'in time of scarcity, the offence of Dacoity is of a very different complexion...and committed by a very

---

[110] W. Dampier, Superintendent of Police, Lower Provinces, to F.J. Halliday, Secretary to Government of Bengal, *op. cit.*, fol. 185.

[111] Deposition of Lukha, 15 September 1840, Khyrabad in Oude, N.A.I., Legislative Department, Law Proceedings, 2 September 1843, fol. 403.

[112] Maj. W.H. Sleeman, Superintendent of Measures for the Suppression of Thuggee, to W. Dampier, Superintendent of Police, Lower Provinces, Monghyr—Camp Punaree, 7 January 1843, N.A.I, Legislative Department, Law Proceedings, 2 September 1843, fol. 383.

different class of persons; these do not require to be dealt with in the same severe manner as the Budducks and other Professional Gangs'. However, the N.W.P. Government conceded that the draft Act extending thagi legislation to apply to dacoity was suitable for Budducks. In fact, they acknowledged that without such legislation 'it will be quite impossible to suppress the crime and render security to life and property'.[113]

The Government of Bengal prepared its arguments in support of Sleeman's draft Act carefully. They informed Dampier that the 'prevailing impression' was that 'as yet' there was 'no sufficient induction of facts to warrant a general measure of such severe tendency. But that such information as…in the case of Thuggee before the Thuggee laws were passed ought to be collected…' The Kechuk 'narratives' submitted by Dampier were commended as 'exactly of that kind'.[114] The Supreme Government, impressed by the arguments of the Government of Bengal, enacted Act XXIV which declared that anyone proved 'to have belonged to any gang of Dacoits' was liable to 'transportation for life' or lesser imprisonment, that persons accused of membership in a dacoit gang, of an act of dacoity or of receiving property stolen by dacoity might be committed and tried by any competent court and finally that no *futwa* be required.[115]

The assimilation of thagi and dacoity legislation represented the culmination of legislative authority for a high profile quasi-military campaign against thugs and dacoits. Thereafter there occurred something of a legislative retreat from official endorsement of extreme tactics. In fact, on the same day that the Legislative Council enacted Act XXIV 1843, they received a recommendation from W. Dampier 'to rescind those parts of Reg. IX of 1808 which relate to the proclaiming of a Dacoit'. Even such a hardened policeman as W. Dampier conceded that with the passing of Act XXIV 1843, Beng. Reg. IX 1808 'would not be necessary as it is in itself a most severe, altho' [*sic*] not an efficacious measure for the suppression of crime'.[116] Consequently, Act IV 1844 repealed Beng. Reg. IX 1808 which was deemed to have 'by

---

[113] R.N.C. Hamilton, Secretary to Government of Northwest Provinces, to T.R. Davidson, Officiating Secretary to Government of India, Agra, *op. cit.*, fol. 133.

[114] F.J. Halliday, secretary to Government of Bengal, to W. Dampier, Superintendent of Police, Lower Provinces, Fort William, 12 December 1842, N.A.I., Legislative Department, Law Proceedings, 2 September 1843 #1, fols 378–79.

[115] Act XXIV for the Better Prevention of the Crime of Dacoity, passed 18 November 1843, I.O.R. V/8/32.

[116] W. Dampier, Superintendent of Police, Lower Provinces, to F.J. Halliday, Secretary to Government of Bengal, Balligunge, 7 October 1843, N.A.I., Legislative Department, Law Proceedings 18 November 1843, fol. 131.

reason of...extreme severity, become nearly obsolete'. Within another three years Act II 1847 rescinded all sections of regulations in Bengal, Madras and Bombay which had authorized the practice of *godna* or the branding with an indelible mark of convicted offenders. The only legislation which might be regarded as increasing the severity of the campaign against thugs was Act X 1847 which required that convicted offenders sentenced to life imprisonment should also be sentenced to transportation for life.[117] Company officials had learned that, on account of the orthodox Hindu idea that those who travelled across the 'black water' lost caste, thugs feared transportation more than prison.

Judges and Magistrates versus Thagi and Dacoity Department

The repeal of earlier thug and dacoity laws emerged out of an atmosphere created by a steady undercurrent of protest and dismay from the Company's judicial service which took exception to the extraordinary powers granted to the Thagi and Dacoity Department. On the one hand, Sleeman's Department earned recognition as early as 1841 for a campaign against thugs which had been so successful as to make it 'possible to journey through the jungles and plains of India without danger of being strangled'.[118] On the other hand, as late as the 1850s, the judiciary continued to obstruct the operations of the Thagi and Dacoity Department. In Bombay, Capt. Hervey, after arresting dacoits of the vagrant tribe called *Khaikurrees*, complained of their acquittal in the courts despite their full confession. The problem lay with the Bombay Sudder Court which insisted that 'the evidence of approvers is not legally good and sufficient evidence of itself...unless corroborated by untainted evidence'. This was in complete contrast with the judicial practice in the N.W.P. and Bengal where 'the testimony of approvers is universally admitted by Session Judges and Sudder Courts as good and sufficient evidence for Conviction'. Ultimately, the Bombay Government supported Capt. Hervey's position and urged the Bombay Sudder Court to align its rules

---

[117] Act IV 1844 for repealing Reg. IX 1808 of the Bengal Code, (passed 2 March 1844) I.O.R. V/8/32; Act II 1847 to abolish the practice of branding and exposing Convicts (passed 27 January 1847) I.O.R. V/8/33; Act X 1847 for amending Act XXX 1836 (passed 19 June 1847) I.O.R. V/8/33.

[118] George Bruce, *The Stranglers—The Cult of Thuggee and its Overthrow in British India* (London, 1968), p. 215; see also J.S. Mill, 'Memorandum', *Parliamentary Papers* (1857–58) XLIII, p. 17.

with those of Agra and Calcutta by 'allowing the evidence of approvers to be received as good and sufficient evidence at the discretion of the Judge'.[119] Commenting on this scenario, Col. W.H. Sleeman reflected that the judicial authorities' distrust of approvers' evidence had been so strong when he began the campaign against thagi in 1830 that, had he depended on the courts, his campaign would have failed and 'every road in India would have continued to be lined with the dead bodies of murdered victims as they then were'.[120]

Indeed, Sleeman had never considered that the Company's courts were capable of coping with the menace of thagi and dacoity. To state the obvious, Sleeman was a military man whose career began with an Infantry cadetship in the Bengal army. For his competent service in the Nepalese War of 1814–16, he had been rewarded with an appointment in the Political Dept. as Junior Assistant to the Agent of the Governor General for the Sagar and Narbudda Territories. Thereafter his campaign against thugs and later dacoits was conducted under the auspices of the Political Department. The crowning achievement of his political career which had included a Residency at Gwalior was his appointment to the Residency at Lucknow in 1848. As Christopher Kenna astutely observes, 'operations against Thags were initially conducted in independent territories under the auspices of the Political Dept'. As Thagi officials 'made inroads' into Regulation provinces 'their style of judicial practice which relied heavily on approvers began to gain ascendancy over the powers of the Nizamat Adawlat'.[121]

That military tactics remained essential to the capture of thugs and dacoits was a self-evident truth. In the last decade of the Company's rule, Sam Wauchope of the Bengal Police recounted his own exploits against a notorious gang of river dacoits during the *Dussehra* vacation, when Calcutta office workers would travel by river to visit their families 'taking with them their earnings of which they are not unfrequently eased long before they reach their native villages'. Thanks to information from spies and informers, Wauchope learned of a daring dacoity planned on a 'Baboo and his servant' at 'Gulla Kata Nulla' or 'Cutthroat Canal'. Although Gopal Ghose, the notorious leader of the particular dacoit gang 'had been arrested by every Magistrate in that

---

[119] D.A. Blane and A. Bell, Judicial Dept., Government of Bombay, to Court of Directors, 16 September 1851, in N.A.I., Legislative Department A, Original Consultations, 10 March 1854 #39, fols 1–7.

[120] W.H. Sleeman to J.G. Lumsden, Secretary to Bombay Government, Judicial Department, 1 November 1850, Judicial Consultations 28 April 1851 #31, fol. 242, in N.A.I., Legislative Dept. A, Original Consultations 10 March 1854 #40.

[121] Christopher Kenna, *op. cit.*, p. 87; see also, Vincent A. Smith, 'Memoir of Maj.-Gen. Sir William Henry Sleeman K.C.B.', in W.H. Sleeman, ed., *Rambles and Recollections of an Indian Official*, pp. xxi–xxx.

part of Bengal, no one had been able to procure his conviction'. This was the result of effective bribes for court officials and intimidation of witnesses so that 'whenever Gopal was concerned in a Dacoitee the evidence against him invariably broke down'. However, during the *Dussehra* of 1850 Sam Wauchope caught Gopal in the act. He simply went to 'Gulla Kata Nulla' in the place of the intended victim and lay in wait for his assailants. After a skirmish worthy of Bollywood, Gopal and his gang were taken captive, 'brought to trial, convicted and transported'.[122]

While Wauchope considered the Company's courts to be obstructive, even corrupt, long after the enactment of the thagi and dacoity legislation of the 1830s and 1840s, members of the judiciary were equally frustrated. During the events of 1857–58, the argument came in a full circle back to Etawah district, the district of the Sindouse Thug families. The Magistrate of Etawah during the uprising was Allan Octavian Hume. After order was restored, Hume wrote a long letter to the Commissioner of Agra imploring Government to exempt Etawah from the operations of the Thagi and Dacoity Department. Hume alleged that innocent persons were accused by approvers who were coached to offer false confessions by corrupt subordinates of the Thagi and Dacoity Department. Maj. C. Hervey, having survived his skirmishes with the Bombay courts to become the Officiating Superintendent of the Thagi and Dacoity Department, refuted all of Hume's allegations to the satisfaction of the Governor General. Hume was obliged to receive an officer deputed by Hervey. At the same time, when he lamented a case involving the actual detention without trial of an approver for more than one year, the Governor General acknowledged that there were grounds for Hume's protestations. The Agra Commissioner adeptly summarized the case of approver Gunga Sing who, at the time of the Mutiny, was to be 'capitally punished for not denouncing his own nearest relations'. Not surprisingly, 'when the Mutiny broke out…he became an active and dangerous enemy'.[123]

---

[122] Sam Wauchope, 'An Adventure with Bengal Dacoits', n.d., in N.L.S., Dundas of Ochtertyre Muniments, Acc. 10654, fols 1–7.

[123] A.O. Hume, Magistrate of Etawah, to G.F. Harvey, Commissioner of Agra, 24 February 1859, I.O.R., N.W.P. Judicial Criminal Proceedings 15 April 1859, fols 312ff. The full text of this letter appears in S.R. Mehrotra and Edward C. Moulton, eds, *Selected Writings of Allan O. Hume, Vol. I—District Administration in North India, Rebellion and Reform* (Oxford, 2004). I am also indebted to Professor E.C. Moulton for bringing to my attention the report on the Thagi and Dacoity Department in Maj. C. Hervey to R. Simson, Under Secretary to Government, Jubbulpore, 29 October 1859, I.O.R., N.W.P. Judicial Criminal Proceedings, 18 January 1860, fols 304ff. and the summary of the Gunga Sing case in G. Harvey, Commissioner of Agra, to E.C. Bayley, Secretary to Government, 4 March 1859, I.O.R., N.W.P. Judicial Criminal Proceedings, 15 April 1859, fol. 311.

As demonstrated by the tale of Gunga Sing, some dacoits appeared as heroes of social protest. Inasmuch as dacoity contained an element of social crime, the officers of the Thagi and Dacoity Department failed to convict their elusive prey. They overextended their resources leaving their subordinates to manipulate the rules. By submerging themselves among the rural poor, many dacoits enjoyed the protection of their victims and their sponsors. The contrast between thugs and dacoits was striking. Thagi was an antisocial crime which terrorized the highways of the *mofussil*. While contemporary historians may reject Sleeman's vision of the thugs as a murdering cult, they cannot deny the role of ritual in Thug expeditions.[124] The Thug *Jemadar* Futteh Khan ingenuously declared: 'We never steal! What God gives us, He gives in Thugie. God is the giver, we never steal!'[125] Dacoits claimed no such divine inspiration. As summed up by Christopher Kenna, '"dakaity" implies a lower level of organization than "thagi"'.[126] I would argue further that, because dacoits did not trouble to separate themselves from their surroundings, they occasionally represented interests beyond their own personal gain. Thus there were attacks of apparent revenge on mahajans known for their extortionate usury. Kalinkar Datta has argued that in the case of the Santal Rebellion of 1855–57, such dacoities against rapacious Bengali and up-country mahajans and merchants were gradually redirected against 'the oppressive Naib Suzawals, the police and the courts then working under the Company Raj'.[127] An egregious present day example of this phenomenon is the 'Bandit Queen', Phoolan Devi, who announced a rights organization for women and the poor to be 'trained in the martial arts and travel India with bows and arrows to resist exploitation'.[128]

Perhaps the most remarkable contrast between thugs and dacoits was manifested in the process of their rehabilitation. The Victorians were especially proud of the recycled energies of thug approvers resident at the Jubbulpore School of Industry which was established in 1838. One of their handwoven carpets graced the Waterloo Room of Windsor Castle 150 years later.[129] John Stuart Mill boasted that 'the children of captured thugs have been taught several useful branches of manufacture'. As observed by Alan Ryan, 'the transformation of the Thuggees into useful tent-makers' was viewed by

---

[124] Cf. Christopher Kenna, *op. cit.*, chapter 9, especially p. 247.
[125] Paton MSS, *op. cit.*, fol. 23b.
[126] Christopher Kenna, *op. cit.*, p. 37.
[127] Kalinkar Datta, *The Santal Insurrection 1855–57* (Calcutta, 1940), pp. 5–10.
[128] Amit Roy, 'Rage of the Bandit Queen', *Sunday Telegraph*, 12 February 1995, p. 12.
[129] *See* illustration in David Annan, 'Thuggee', in Norman MacKenzie, ed., *Secret Societies* (New York, 1969), p. 81.

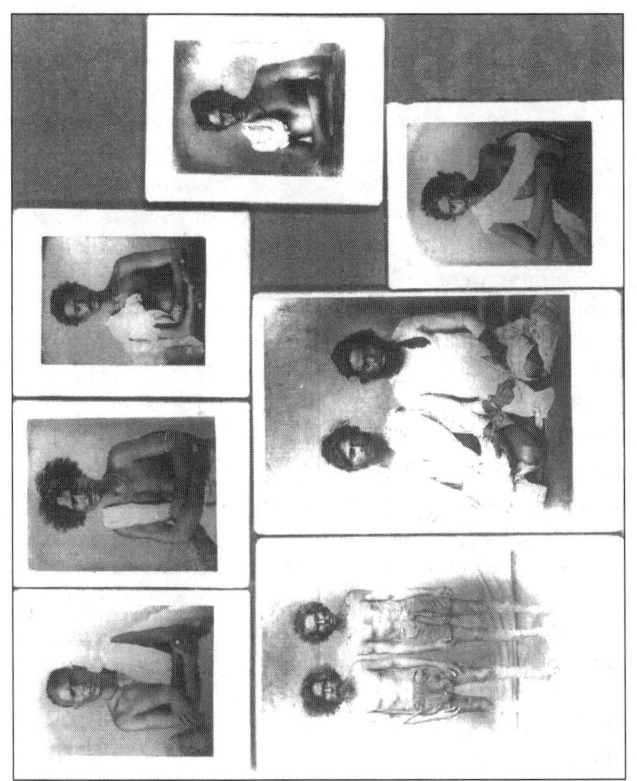

Photograph 2: Bengali Dacoits

From Dundas of Octertyre Muniments reproduced with kind permission of the Trustees of the National Library of Scotland.

J.S. Mill as 'one of the striking achievements of the East India Company's rule'. In the view of present day anti-Orientalists, this Benthamite success survives only as an example of official condescension and paternalism.[130] Whether a Benthamite success in line with modern ideas of prison reform *á la* Michel Foucault or an outrageous example of colonial condescension, the Jubbulpore School of Industry affords a sharp contrast with the Salikram settlement for Budduck dacoits. Salikram was a grant of land set aside in Etawah district to afford Budduck dacoit approvers 'the means of honest subsistence in a position where the surveillance of the District police could be maintained without difficulty and effectually prevent any attempt at a return to their old habits of depredation'.[131] In fact, at the beginning of this experiment in redirecting Budducks to agricultural pursuits, Col. W.H. Sleeman 'never had any hopes' of its success. His assistant, Lt. Henry Ward, shared Sleeman's scepticism, while observing that the Budducks on the grant took 'much more kindly to Police duties' than to cultivation.[132] William Sleeman's nephew, James, who was also his successor, declared that 'as a race the Budhuks are energetic only in crime'.[133] With this last remark, Maj. James Sleeman both admits to the Company's inability to tame the Budducks and reveals the growing tendency of government officials to think in terms of criminal tribes and races. Such thinking ultimately led to the enactment of the Criminal Tribes Act of 1871 which used the campaign against the thugs as a model for resettling or removing 'any tribe, gang

---

[130] J.S. Mill, 'Memorandum,' *Parliamentary Papers* (1857–58) XLIII, p. 17; Alan Ryan, 'Utilitarianism and Bureaucracy: The Views of J.S. Mill' in Gillian Sutherland, ed., *Studies in the Growth of Nineteenth-century Government* (Totowa, New Jersey, 1972), p. 47; cf. Christopher Kenna, *op. cit.*, pp. 94–100, for other schemes of rehabilitation such as Capt. Paton's 'Little Thuggery' which settled wives of captured Thugs in the Lucknow jail and a treadmill devised by F.J. Shore, Sleeman's successor as General Superintendent of Operations for the Suppression of Thuggee.

[131] Maj. James Sleeman, General Superintendent of the Thuggee and Dacoity Dept., to W. Paterson, Magistrate of Goruckpore, Simla, 14 April 1856, U.P.S.A. C.O.G. M.G.1 Miscellaneous Letters Received from the Superintendent of the Thuggee and Dacoity Dept., Series V, Basta 116, fol. 89.

[132] Lt. Col. W.H. Sleeman, General Superintendent of the Thuggee and Dacoity Dept., to Lt. H. Ward, Assistant General Superintendent of the Thuggee and Dacoity Dept. at Azimghur, Jhansi, 8 September 1845; Lt. H. Ward, Assistant General Superintendent, to H.C. Tucker, Officiating Collector at Goruckpoor, Azimghur, 19 January 1846. U.P.S.A. C.O.G. M.G.1 Miscellaneous Letters Received from the Superintendent of the Thuggee and Dacoity Dept., Series V, Basta 116, fols 45, 50.

[133] Maj. James Sleeman, General Superintendent of the Thuggee and Dacoity Dept., to W. Paterson, Magistrate of Goruckpoor, Simla, *op. cit.*

or class of persons' designated by local governments a 'criminal tribe'.[134] And so, ironically, after the Company disappeared from the scene, the Raj reverted to draconian measures similar to the proclamation system which the Company had adopted against dacoits in the early nineteenth century, only to renounce it by mid-century.

Whereas J.S. Mill talked of the eliminination of the thugs by 1840, it is generally considered that 'gradual extermination of the "Thags"' continued until 1860 when the Thagi and Dacoity Department ceased to operate in British India.[135] In the same year, Macaulay's Penal Code was finally enacted and the thug gained a kind of immortality by appearing in Sec. 310 which defined him as being 'associated with...others for the purpose of committing robbery or child-stealing by means of or accompanied with murder'. Sec. 311 decrees that the thug is punishable with life imprisonment. Perhaps the Penal Code reflected the suspicion expressed later by the Raj historian Vincent A. Smith: 'In India it is never safe to assume that any ancient practice has been suppressed...'.[136] Yet the fact that Secs 310–11 have not been rescinded by the Government of independent India undercuts any thoughts that the thugs were merely a figment of the imperial British imagination. On the other hand, dacoity has been an ongoing concern. As remarked by an archival expert on the Thagi and Dacoity Department, during the nationalist struggle 'some of the dacoit gangs of Bengal were organized by revolutionaries'.[137] Dacoity is defined by Sec. 391 of the Penal Code as a group of 'five or more persons (who) conjointly commit or attempt to commit a robbery...'. Secs 395–99 decree punishment for different varieties of dacoity and Sec. 400 decrees that membership in a dacoit gang incurs the punishment of life imprisonment or 'rigorous imprisonment' for up to 10 years. With the Penal Code both the Imperial Raj and the Government of India endorsed the legislative initiatives of the East India Company on the subject of thagi and dacoity.

---

[134] Anand A. Yang, 'Dangerous Castes and Tribes: The Criminal Tribes Act and the Magahiya Doms of Northeast India' in Anand A. Yang, ed., *Crime and Criminality in British India* (Tuscan Arizona: University of Arizona Press, 1985), p. 9.

[135] Thereafter the Department operated in the Princely States under the umbrella of the Foreign Department until it was abolished altogether in 1904. Its expertise in the business of gathering intelligence regarding organized crime was transferred to a new Central Criminal Intelligence Department. *Guide to the Records in the National Archives of India,* Part II (New Delhi, 1977), p. 84.

[136] W.H. Sleeman, *Rambles and Recollections of an Indian Official* (first published 1844), ed. Vincent A. Smith (repr. Karachi, London, 1973), p. 90.

[137] Doonger Singh, 'Source Material on Thagi and Dacoity Practices in India (1829–1902),' N.A.I., p. 2.

Sorcery

The practice of witchcraft in British India posed a challenge to the ability of the Company Raj to keep law and order, especially in frontier regions inhabited by primitive tribes. Sometimes an act of alleged sorcery provoked an entire village to take the law into its own hands. The resulting murders were not only offensive to ideas of due process which underlay the Company's court system, but they could become the focus of rural disturbance.

Witchcraft was usually associated with primitive tribes or an impoverished population isolated either geographically or socially. P.O. Bodding, who in the late nineteenth century undertook personal instruction in witchcraft as part of his effort to make close contact with witches among the Santals, observed that Santal women became witches because they were excluded from public worship. Only Santal men could perform sacrifices to appease the *bonga*s or supernatural spirits central to Santal religion. These *bonga*s were understood to wield powers, usually negative or evil, which operated through the forces of nature or possessed certain human beings and animals. Bodding noted mysterious meetings of Santal witches on Sunday nights which were dark because they were closest to a new moon. He suggested that these meetings could be interpreted as a 'form of female worship, having its real background in the inferior social status of the women'. As witches, these women ruled over an 'esoteric domain closed to men' and induced fear of what was conceived to be their ability to inflict disease and death through evil magic. Santal men responded with their own neutralizing magic performed by *ojha*s and *jan*s who specialized in identifying witches and curing disease attributed to witchcraft. Bodding asserted that 'all Jans (the man who knows)…are unmitigated scoundrels, who through spies get all necessary information respecting the sick and the suspected, so as to be able to denounce anyone they like'.[138]

Contemporary journalists and anthropologists continue to report the practice of witchcraft. Sohaila Kapur of the *Times of India* sees rituals of witchcraft in western India as 'the primitive imitation of nature'. G.M. Carstairs has noticed that a report from southern India by Scarlett Epstein reveals that in a Mysore village accused witches are absolved of all personal blame because

---

[138] P.O. Bodding, 'Taboo Customs amongst the Santals', *Journal of the Asiatic Society of Bengal* (1898): 67, cited by L.S.S. O'Malley in *Bengal District Gazetteers—Santal Parganas* (Calcutta, 1910), p. 125. See also, P.O. Bodding, O. Solberg, eds, *Witchcraft among the Santals* (Oslo, 1940), p. 257.

their actions are attributed to the influence of an alien spirit. Thus in this southern region 'accusations of witchcraft could be openly made and acted upon'. By way of contrast, Carstairs notes that 'in north India the witch is perceived as being both dangerous and quick to take revenge if she is accused of practising black magic'. For this reason village informants were reluctant to discuss with him their fear of witches. However, by the end of his stay in the village of Sujarupa, not far from Delhi, Carstairs was convinced that 'every village in this area harboured at least one witch...This was also true of Fatehpura and still more so of the Bhils of Kotra Bhomat'.[139]

The first instance of sorcery to impinge upon the conscience of the ruling East India Company occurred in 1792 in the district of Ramgurh where three men of the Sutar caste or tribe were indicted for the murder of five women for the practice of witchcraft. Sir John Shore, describing the incident 15 years later, referred to the Sutar both as 'a wild and unlettered tribe' and as simply a 'cast'. The prisoners confidently asserted that a tribal assembly had investigated and proved the charge of sorcery, called for the witches to be put to death and 'no complaint was ever preferred on this account to the ruling power'. In accordance with Muslim law, the prosecutors of the murderers were related to the five victims and, conveniently, they declared that 'they had no charge to prefer against the prisoners, being satisfied that their relatives had really practised sorcery'. They had been convinced by three forms of trial by ordeal devised to identify witches. In one trial branches of the Saul tree were marked with the names of all the women in the village over the age of 12 years and then planted in water for four and a half hours; those branches that withered were regarded as proof that the person whose name was attached practised witchcraft. A second trial involved wrapping portions of rice in cloths marked with the names of the village women and placing the same in a nest of white ants; the ants' consumption of the rice in some of the bags was considered proof of witchcraft against the women whose names were fixed to those bags. In the third trial a ceremony was performed at night with lighted lamps and water in cups made of leaves into which mustard seed and oil were poured a drop at a time, coinciding with the pronunciation of the name of each woman in the village; the appearance of any woman's shadow on the water during the ceremony condemned her to death for being a witch. The villagers unanimously asserted that the five murdered women had been proved witches by all three trials.[140] In response to these

---

[139] Sohaila Kapur, *Witchcraft in Western India* (Bombay, 1983), p. vi; G.M. Carstairs, *Death of a Witch—A Village in North India 1950–1981* (London, 1983), p. 129.

[140] Sir John Shore, 'On Some Extraordinary Facts, Customs and Practices of the Hindus', *Asiatic Researches* IV (1795), pp. 343–45.

cruel murders, the Cornwallis Government issued a proclamation to the effect that 'if any person(s) of the Sutar caste shall...put any person to death on the ground of him or her being versed in or practising sorcery...such person... shall be held guilty of murder and be invariably punished accordingly'. This proclamation was dutifully enacted into law by the government of Sir John Shore as Sec. VI Beng. Reg. IV 1797, part of a Regulation devised to modify practices of Muslim criminal law. And curiously, this Regulation, complete with its specific reference to the 'Sutar caste', was transferred verbatim into the codes of Madras, the Ceded Provinces and Bombay. In truth, it didn't appear in the Bombay code until 1812 and within another eight years, the Bombay government had revised the wording to exclude the reference to the 'Sutar caste'. Eventually the Elphinstone Code improved the wording by simply stating the essential principle that 'the belief that sorcery was practised by the deceased shall not be admitted as a justifiable cause for putting him or her to death'.[141]

Subsequent accounts of the practice of witchcraft in the records of the East India Company often confused massive witch hunts with civil disturbance in recently annexed territory or with protest against the Company's recent revenue settlement. The regions most fertile for sorcery were Ramgurh district in the Bengal presidency containing the primitive tribes of Chota Nagpur, the impoverished Northern Konkan ceded to the Bombay Government by the Peshwa and, in the Madras presidency, the Malabar Coast featuring the persecuted *pariar* slave castes. In Chota Nagpur in 1819, G. French, Magistrate of Ramgurh, initially attributed arson and murder in the town of Tamar to the Raja of Tamar's determination to collect revenue from villages which French, himself, had assigned to local *jagirdar*s two years earlier. Only after receiving fresh intelligence and reexamining his prisoners did he decide that 'the disturbances in Tamar certainly appear to have originated in the superstition of some of the inhabitants in supposing that...drought was occasioned by sorcery'. The fresh intelligence consisted of *arzee*s gathered by Maj. Roughsedge, Commander of the Ramgurh Corps. Two captive 'Insurgents' recounted in their *arzee*s that boys aged 7–12 were deputed to shoot arrows at a mark 'for the purpose of ascertaining the authors of the drought'. On the calling of the name 'Tribookum Mankee', the mark was hit. A party of ca. 200 then 'proceeded (*sic*) to Poorna Nughur for the

---

[141] Sec. VI Beng. Reg. IV 1797, I.O.R. V/8/17 p. 32; Sec. XXXIV Madras Reg. VII 1802, V/8/26; Sec. XXXIV Ced. Prov. Reg. 1803, V/8/17 p. 388; Sec. XVIII Bom. Reg. VIII 1812, V/8/22, rescinded by Sec. II and reenacted by Sec. XXV Bom. Reg. VII 1820, V/8/23 and Cl. 2 Sec. XXVI 1827 Bom. Code Reg. XIV, V/8/24.

express purpose of seizing Tirbhoonan (sic) Mankee and detaining him in confinement until it should rain'. But Tribookum Mankee drew up a defence party and successfully resisted his attackers, although his wife and son were killed in the affray. A *jagirdar* in Tamar declared in his *arzee* that 'affairs are out of my control'. The Raja of Tamar in his *arzee* asserted that Mankee and his supporters had 'resisted the payment of their Malgozaree [which was] the cause of my defalcations of Revenue'. He appealed for government protection. The Company's response was to send a party of Sepoys to restore tranquillity. Magistrate French wryly reflected that, had the party attacking Poorna Nughur succeeded in capturing Tribookum Mankee they probably 'would have offered him up a sacrifice to their Gods'.[142]

That G. French should have been slow to detect the baleful influence of witchcraft on the Tamar outrages is surprising because in the previous year French had reported to Government his suspicion that the Raja of Chota Nagpur was responsible for the death of an alleged witch, her daughter, two male relatives and some slave girls. The Raja had attributed the death of his son by smallpox to the powers of the alleged witch. The magistrate's efforts to investigate these murders ran afoul of the 'religious adoration all ranks of people pay the Rajah'. He reported that 'some Villages were wholly deserted by the Inhabitants who fled into the neighbouring hills on seeing my Chuprassies or Servants'. In the face of such obstruction, French determined that 'altho' [sic] nothing like legal proof has been established against the Raja, not a doubt exists in my mind of his criminality and I have found it necessary to detain him'. He further asked for authorization to offer a reward of ₹100 for the apprehension of each of a half dozen other suspects to be paid on their conviction. However, the Home Authorities declined, fearing that 'the application of principles which from their…want of adaptation to local circumstances and the ideas of the people, may produce evil instead of good'.[143]

---

[142] G. French, Magistrate of Ramgurh, to Maj. E. Roughsedge Commanding the Ramgurh Corps, Hazareebaug, 8 October 1819, B.S.A., C.N.C.O., Vol. 14, fols 695–96; Arzees of Two Insurgents, a Jaghirdar in Tamar and the Rajah of Tamar, W.B.S.A., Judicial Criminal Proceedings 26 November 1819 #13, Vol. 408, fols 172–75 and G. French, Magistrate of Ramgurh, to W.B. Bayley, Chief secretary to Government in Judicial Department, Fort William, Ramgurh, 5 November 1819 #15, W.B.S.A., Judicial Criminal Procedings 26 November 1819 #15, Vol. 408, fols 182–86. Also available in I.O.R. Bengal Judicial Criminal Proceedings, 26 November 1819, P/133/71.

[143] G. French, Magistrate of Ramgurh, to W.B. Bayley, Secretary to Government in Judicial Department, 10 December 1818, Extract Beng. Judicial Criminal Proceeedings, 1 January 1819 #3, I.O.R., *Board's Collections* F/4/746 Reg. 20327, fols 5–6, 9; G. French to W.B. Bayley,

At the same time that alleged witches in Chota Nagpur were held responsible for drought and a child's death by smallpox, on the opposite side of India in the Northern Konkan alleged witches were put to death as the result of an epidemic of 'jerry merry' or Cholera Morbus. In this instance, the Home Authorities were particularly exercised over the Bombay Government's apparent eagerness to introduce Company Regulations into territories newly ceded to the Company by the Peshwa. The Directors' instructions concerning desirable leniency in the sentencing of witch murderers were delayed over an entire year to allow the Board of Control to express its disapproval of the Bombay Government's 'justification of the extension of the Bombay Regulations' to its newly acquired territory. At stake were three trials for the murders of five alleged witches by 82 villagers, all of whom were convicted and, with the exception of one accessory, sentenced to death by the Circuit Court at Surat on 21 January 1819. However, the Circuit Judge recommended that all but one of the prisoners be granted mercy. The exception was a village *Patel* who, after fortifying himself with liquor, had used his authority in the village to arrange for three alleged witches to be beaten to death. The Sudder Court honoured the Circuit Judge's recommendation, granting a free pardon to 81 of the prisoners and ordering the *Patel*, on account of his greater criminality, to be transported for life beyond the seas in order to set an example. The Bombay Government then issued a proclamation which explained that 'the practice of putting innocent people to death on account of supposed witchcraft or Sorcery...is entirely repugnant to the enlightened and humane principles of the British Laws'. Specifically, the proclamation cited Sec. XVIII Bom. Reg. VIII 1812, an exact copy of Sec. VI Beng. Reg. IV 1797, thereby repeating the tactic of the Cornwallis Government in Ramgurh district. The Home Authorities deemed the proclamation 'highly judicious'.[144]

However, the Home Authorities did suggest a remission of the remainder of the Patel's sentence, if the proclamation proved to be effective. They

---

6 April 1819, Extract Beng. Judicial Criminal Proceedings, 30 April 1819 #8, I.O.R., *Boards Collection* F/4/746 # 20327, fols 21, 31 and 34. Judicial Despatch to Bengal 20 October 1824, I.O.R., E/4/712, fols 657–58 citing Judicial Despatch to Bengal, 16 February 1817 E/4/689, fols 896–98.

[144] Previous Communication #409 for Judicial Despatch to Bombay, 22 October 1823, I.O.R., E/4/1043, fols 655–64; Proclamation by Governor of Bombay, Bombay Castle, 18 February 1819, *Board's Collections* F/4/638 # 17671, fols 47–50; John Bax, Register to Superior Tribunal, to H. Newnham, Acting Chief Secretary to Bombay Government, 15 February 1819, extract Bombay Judicial Consultations 15 February 1819, *Board's Collection* F/4/638 # 17671, fols 27, 42–43.

noted that the Circuit Judge had observed the 'effects of the late trials on the population of the Northern Concan' and 'the beneficial effects of the seasonable proclamations...issued by Mr Marriot, the Zillah Magistrate on this subject'.[145] Yet, five years later the same magistrate, Savill Marriott, was unable to support the optimism of the Circuit Judge. Marriott remarked that not even 'capital punishment in cases of this nature has...been attended by the wished for effect'. Marriott reflected that if the degree of punishment was intended to depend upon the 'actual turpitude of the persons committing the homicide', then murderers of witches should go unpunished. He explained his belief that 'the lamentably ignorant state of the offenders leads them to the conviction that so far from committing a crime when they kill a person accused of witchcraft, they are performing a laudable act by putting a demon out of the way of injuring themselves and others'. At the same time, he believed that laws must operate to 'prevent injury to Society'. He factored into the moral equation the consideration 'that under the Native Government those who were supposed to practice witchcraft were put to death not only by the constituted authorities of the Country but their murders by the populace were even connived at...by the Government'. Marriott could only hope for long term solutions in the form of education coupled with rigorous enforcement of the law. Therefore, he concluded that a 'prejudicial misconstruction might be placed upon the mitigation of the punishment awarded' to the Patel. The Bombay Government endorsed Marriott's sentiments and 'with much regret' were unable to act upon the 'merciful suggestion' of the Directors. The Government pointed out that since the case in question, 'no less than four murders have been committed in consequence of superstitious feelings'. Apart from 'the tenor of the laws, a steady execution of which it may be hoped will put an end to murders for supposed witchcraft...there remains the more important and the only radical cure, that of the intellectual improvement of the people'.[146]

In the Madras presidency magistrates confronted by the hysteria of alleged witchcraft periodically proposed that the Government enact a law outlawing the actual practice of sorcery. The Sudder Court in Madras rejected all thoughts of legislation as an answer to the phenomenon of sorcery,

---

[145] J. Sutherland, 3rd Judge of Circuit, to J. Bax, Register to Court of Superior Tribunal, Provincial Court of Circuit at Surat, 25 March 1819, extract Bombay Judicial Consultations 19 May 1819, I.O.R., *Board's Collections* F/4/638 # 17671, fol. 62.

[146] Savill Marriott, Magistrate of Tannah, to William Stubbs, 2nd Register to Sudder Foujdarry Adawlut, 17 June 1824, extract Bombay Judicial Consultations 18 August 1824, I.O.R., *Board's Collections* F/4/925 # 25944, fols 13–23 [also P/399/36, fols 4735–41]; Judicial Letter from Bombay, 29 November 1824, *Board's Collections* F/4/925 # 25944, fols 2–4.

calling instead for progress through education. The judges explained that a 'certain consequence of such an enactment would be to attract more public attention to the thing itself and to strengthen the belief in its reality and its influence on the mind of the people'. They believed that an 'increase and general diffusion of sound knowledge' was all that was required to weaken 'the belief in magical arts'.[147]

This pessimistic pronouncement concerning the effect of sorcery cases in the law courts on deluded believers in the practice of witchcraft reenforced the order issued by the Sudder Court a decade earlier 'declaring the practice of sorcery not punishable by law'. During the proceedings of the Foujdary Adawlut of 2 July 1817 the *Cazee-ool-Coozat* and *Mufti*s of the Court declared in their *futwa* 'that a confession of sorcery does not subject a person to punishment under the Mahummedan Law unless it shall appear that injury has ensued'. Further, it was decreed on the same occasion that 'the Courts of Criminal Judicature are virtually prohibited by Sec. XXXIV Reg. VII of 1802 from trying charges of Sorcery'. And so the Madras judges endorsed the incorporation into the Madras code of the judicious revision of Muslim criminal procedure by Sec. VI Beng. Reg. IV 1797. It was not necessary to address the practice of sorcery as a social issue. It was only necessary to make it absolutely clear that the Company's law courts would never regard the practice of sorcery as a justification for murder.

Nevertheless, a circuit judge, A.D. Campbell, was to raise the issue again during a trial for murder on account of sorcery in Malabar in 1834 when he challenged the Foujdary Adawlut Order of 2 July 1817 to the effect that sorcery was a 'crime not punishable by law'. Campbell raised the issue before his colleagues again in December 1835 and finally so persisted with his argument in a minute of 16 September 1836 that the Sudder Court decided to refer the question to the Madras Government which, in turn, referred it to the Law Commission. Several court cases in the Malabar jurisdiction had revealed 'the unhappy belief prevalent on the West Coast that the Pariar slaves there possess the power of Sorcery, and of thereby perpetrating murder in a manner not liable to discovery...and even...of conjuring the living Foetus from the Mother's Womb'. In trial #1 of the 2nd additional calendar of Malabar for the 2nd sessions of 1834, an 'intelligent Nair' witness avowed that after a woman from one of the houses of one of the prisoners

---

[147] G.I. Casamajor, Register to the Foujdarry Udalut, to Provincial Court of Circuit in Centre Division, 8 September 1828, I.O.R., *Board's Collections* F/4/1760 # 72102, fols 11–12.

died in labour, 'a shell of a nut of the Crab Tree' was found 'in her womb instead of a Child'. Another case was recalled from 1829 in which 'two of these wretched Pariar slaves' were induced to confess to the murder of a female 'although the earthen pot then found with a piece of Calf skin in the corpse, was of a size that rendered it impossible to credit its introduction during life and led to their acquittal'. And finally there was the case of the massacre of 15 *pariar*s in the Nilgiri Hills. Campbell recounted how:

> The whole population of the neighbourhood, with one accord, in the open face of day, have...in defiance of all law and public authority, proceeded in the most daring manner to attack whole Villages of these miserable Pariar Slaves whom...they inhumanly and promiscuously beat, with their hands tied behind their backs...drove them in a body in this bound state, into a river, immersed them in this helpless condition under water, so as nearly to produce suffocation, obliged their own children to rub sand into their parents' wounds; and driving the whole into banishment to a foreign territory, razed their paternal dwellings from their foundations, so that not a vestige remained of the persecuted race.[148]

Campbell urged that people who 'actually resort to these arts' should be punished by law. Reflecting the utilitarian mores of his day Campbell remarked that 'the Government to be useful must lower its laws to the condition of the governed though it cannot do much to raise and enlighten their minds'. Campbell further pointed out that in five similar cases in Bengal, not once did the Nizamut Adawlut invoke the extreme punishment of the law. And three of these five cases in which the Nizamut Adawlut refrained from capital punishment 'occurred all in the Zillah of Ramgurh, where the people are described as "rude, uncivilized beings" whose superstition is extreme'.[149]

Both the Madras Sudder Judges and the Madras Government disagreed with the basic premise of Campbell's argument. They continued to be convinced that such a legislative act, instead of checking the practice of

---

[148] Savill Marriott, Magistrate of Tannah, to William Stubbs, 2nd Register to Sudder Foujdarry Adawlut, 17 June 1824, extract Bombay Judicial Consultations 18 August 1824, I.O.R., *Board's Collections* F/4/925 # 25944, fols 13–23 [also P/399/36, fols 4735–41]; Judicial Letter from Bombay, 29 November 1824, *Board's Collections* F/4/925 # 25944, fols 2–4.

[149] Minute of Acting Judge A.D. Campbell, 16 September 1836, I.O.R., *Board's Collections* F/4/1760 # 72102, fols 12–22; *see also* Case of Sangan and Others 16 January 1836, *Foujdaree Udalut Reports Madras 1826–50*, I.O.R., V/22/610, pp. 77–81. The Bengal cases cited by Campbell were: I N.A. Rep. 318; II N.A. Rep. 56, 188 & 196 and III N.A. Rep. 102.

sorcery, would be more likely to lend credence to sorcery as an art. However, they referred the proposed legislation to Macaulay's Law Commission. The Law Commission supported the Madras Government and Sudder Judges. They deemed any legislative effort to outlaw the practice of sorcery inexpedient. They reasoned: 'When the people universally believe in the reality of sorcery, if the law punished persons who profess the art, the people must think that the law itself recognized the reality of the art'. The only way they could rationalize a law punishing sorcery was to conceive of a general law 'which should make penal either the occasional or the habitual practice of deception'. But they reasoned: 'When the belief in Sorcery is firm the people would hardly be brought to understand that the law punished only deception, and it would so do harm, and where the belief in Sorcery is not firm, such a law can seldom be required'.[150]

Thus in the rarefied environs of the Law Commission, theories about making deception generally penal distracted Macaulay and his Commissioners from the legislative precedent established by Sec. VI Beng. Reg. IV 1797 to disqualify sorcery as a justification for murder. Inasmuch as this Beng. Reg. was duplicated in Madras and Bombay, it was one of the few laws uniform in all three presidencies. And Macaulay's failure to acknowledge the improvement in the concise phraseology of the Elphinstone Code suggests that his judgement was unable to rise above the arrogant contempt in which he held the Elphinstone Code. Without any fresh legislative statement, some confusion prevailed in the courts. The Madras Foujdary Adawlut found it necessary to issue a circular order on 6 December 1841 reprimanding a sessions judge for sentencing a prisoner accused of sorcery to six months of prison with hard labour. The Sudder Court recalled its ruling of 2nd July 1817 barring any criminal judge from taking cognizance of a sorcery case 'unless the prisoner was guilty of some overt act tending to injure the prosecutor'. And the sessions judge was reminded of the *futwa* by the Muslim law officers of 1817 that 'confession of sorcery does not subject a person to punishment under Mohomedan law'.[151]

---

[150] J.P. Grant, Officiating Secretary to the Law Commission, to W.H. Macnaghten, Secretary to the Government of India, Indian Law Commission, 15 July 1837, N.A.I., Legislative Department, Law Proceedings, 14 August 1837 #13; see also, C.D. Dharkar, ed., *Lord Macaulay's Legislative Minutes* (Madras, 1946), pp. 137–38.

[151] Circular Order #147, 6 December 1841, Judicial Consultations 21 Decemebr 1841, T.N.A. Judicial Consultations Vol. 427, fols 5428–30.

Murder of Children for the Sake of their Ornaments

On the same day that the Law Commissioners rejected the proposal for a law prohibiting the practice of sorcery, they pronounced a negative verdict on another legislative proposal from Madras. This was an official proposal from the judges of the Madras Foujdary Adawlut in November 1835 to enact that the police be authorized to remove 'Gold and Silver Ornaments' seen adorning 'Native Children' wandering alone in the 'Streets or Bazars of towns and Villages'. The ornaments would then be returned to the parents of the child, but if the child were found again 'wandering alone' and so 'ornamented', the ornaments would be 'confiscated to the use of Government'.[152] The Madras Judges thought that such a law might forestall horrific instances of children murdered for the sake of the ornaments they were wearing. The Law Commission instinctively felt that 'the proposed law belongs to a class of laws against the expediency of which there are arguments of great weight'. By the utilitarian standards of their time, they argued that 'the vanity which leads an Indian parent to adorn his child with a gold bracelet is by no means a useless feeling'. They seriously suggested that it was 'feelings of this sort' that stimulated industry, promoted the arts and raised societies 'from barbarism to civilization'. The Commissioners suggested that a law such as that proposed by the Madras Sudder Court could only be justified by 'a case of very great peculiarity' such as popular resentment of a caste rule requiring children to wear ornaments. Without information concerning the nature of the custom and without precise statistics as to the extent of the resulting murders, the Law Commission deferred a final decision until it received the results of widespread enquiries.[153]

Judicial functionaries from all over India responded to the Law Commission's queries. A tabular statement of the results presented in October 1838 revealed that over a period of the most recent three years, there were a total of 255 murders of children for the sake of their ornaments; far fewer than anticipated. The majority of judges and magistrates indicated that a 'law of the Character proposed would be very unpopular'. It was generally

---

[152] Cited in, J.C.C. Sutherland, Secretary to Indian Law Commission, to T.H. Maddock, Officiating Secretary to the Government of India in the Legislative Department, Indian Law Commission, 5 October 1838, N.A.I., Legislative Department, Law Proceedings, 29 October 1838 #32, fol. 185.

[153] J.P. Grant, Officiating Secretary to the Law Commission, to W.H. Macnaghten, Secretary to the Government of India in the Legislative Department, Indian Law Commission, 25 July 1837, N.A.I., Legislative Department, Law Proceedings, 14 August 1837 #29.

agreed that the motive for decorating children with ornaments was parental vanity rather than religion so that such a law would not be 'obnoxious as interfering with any religious rite'. However, there was widespread fear that the law would lead to police abuse. Interestingly, several officers remarked that most of the victims were children from 'poor and middling' families. These lower classes would be offended by the proposed law; rich families were unconcerned. Perhaps this was because, as the Circuit Judge of Cuddalore in the Central Division of Madras suggested, there was 'no want of security felt by parents capable of keeping servants' to watch over their children. The Magistrate of Cuttack in Orissa agreed with the Law Commissioners that the practice of adorning children with ornaments 'should be encouraged rather than repressed'. The Acting Judge of Chicacole in the Northern Division of Madras asserted that 'the practice of using ornaments relieves distress in years of scarcity'. From the Law Commission's point of view, the most convincing response came from the Madras Sudder Court which changed its collective mind to 'agree with Public Officers that the Enactment would fail being in direct opposition to the feelings of the community'.[154]

With such overwhelming support the Law Commission reported to Governor General Auckland that they adhered 'to their original opinion'. However, the Commissioners acknowledged that 'several intelligent public functionaries' reported strong support for the law in their districts. More important for the Commissioners, however, were the numerous references by officials in the Western Provinces and Bengal to a Circular Order issued by the Nizamut Adawlut on 4 February 1818 'to dissuade parents from the practice of allowing their ornamented Children to go about unprotected'. The Magistrate in Agra and a Judge in Tirhoot reported that, in the wake of specific murders, they reissued this proclamation with tremendous effect. Noting comments of the Sessions Judge of Mynpuree concerning the 'utility of the public press…whereby information of Crimes committed is spread and preventive caution excited', the Commission recommended 'such periodical publication'.[155] Governor General Auckland wholeheartedly supported the arguments of the Law Commission and the governments of Bengal, Bombay,

---

[154] J.C.C. Sutherland to T.H. Maddock, *op. cit.*, fols. 185–87; Tabular Statement, N.A.I. Legislative Department, Law Proceedings, 29 October 1838 #33, fols 188–201.

[155] J.C.C. Sutherland, Secretary to Indian Law Commission, to T.H. Maddock, Officiating Secretary to the Government of India in the Legislative Department, Indian Law Commission, 5 October 1838, N.A.I., Legislative Department, Law Proceedings 29 October 1838 #32, fol. 187.

Agra and Madras which were directed 'in order to check the habit of Parents allowing children to go unprotected with ornaments on their persons'. Governments were 'to give the greatest publicity to every instance of murder occurring from this cause'.[156]

Hook Swinging

Hook swinging sporadically attracted the attention of East India Company officers in all three presidencies. The clamour surrounding a drugged, usually low caste, devotee swinging from a pole with hooks piercing the flesh of his or her back or, in some instances, the tendons of his or her legs, was a source of embarrassment for higher castes and a general public disturbance.[157] Official reaction ranged from prohibition by proclamation in Bombay to an appeal to landlords in Bengal to discourage the practice. It was left for the Imperial Raj, to first reject a proposal for legislation in 1865 and then finally settle for reliance upon the general provisions of Sec. 188 of the Penal Code and Sec. 144 of the Criminal Procedure Code in support of the discretionary authority of magistrates.[158] Thus, inasmuch as hook swinging was more a source of annoyance than a criminal offence, it inspired a mixture of educational appeals and executive prohibitions.

Conclusion

'*Poorun Phansigar*'s declaration that before the East India Company established 'tranquillity over the country' the excursions of his gang were both less lucrative and less ambitious than 'they have since been' was an unlooked for and unwanted testimony to the Company's Pax Indo-Britannica.

---

[156] T.H. Maddock, Secretary to Government of India, to H. Chamier, Chief Secretary to Government of Fort St. George, Fort William, 29 October 1838, N.A.I., Legislative Department, Law Proceedings, 29 October 1838 #34, fol. 204.

[157] It inspired countless exhibitions of self mortification as described in an account of the Calcutta Charak festival in 'Cruel Practices of the Hindus at the Charak Puja,' *Calcutta Christian Observer*, Article IV in No. 59 (April 1837), pp. 182–3.

[158] For a comprehensive survey of this issue, see Geoffrey A. Oddie, *Popular Religion, Elites and Reform: Hook-Swinging and its Prohibition in Colonial India, 1800–1894* (Delhi, Manohar, 1995).

Clearly, 'Poorun Phansigar' and his colleagues posed a threat to the ideal of law and order on which the Company prided itself. With the advantage of hindsight, it is possible to argue that this threat was overblown by the Thagi and Dacoity Department which was granted extraordinary judicial powers by the legislature. Certainly, the thagi and dacoity legislation provided an unfortunate model for later legislation against 'Criminal Tribes' and the allegedly successful campaign against the thugs has even been cited as a model for draconian police measures in the twentieth century—notably in the aftermath of the Chauri Chaura outrages. To be sure, the Thagi and Dacoity Department's eagerness to brand entire communities such as the Budducks or the Kechuks as criminal, paved the way for the practice during the period of high imperialism of identifying 'Criminal Tribes'. In his study of the 1871 Criminal Tribes Act, Anand A. Yang ably plots this path of progression from thagi to criminal tribes legislation. However, his conclusion that 'colonial...law served as an instrument as well as an ideology of control' recalls Edward Said's dismissal of law in his vision of 'Orientalism' wherein 'the Oriental is depicted as something one judges (as in a court of law)' or as 'something one disciplines (as in a school or prison)' thereby subject to 'dominating frameworks'.[159]

To dismiss law as the tool of empire is to ignore all legislative debate and juridical tradition. In the specific case of the Company's thagi and dacoity laws, the 'colonial' reference is problematical because India was never a colony, and, during the Company era, it was not yet the British Empire. More to the point, the thagi and dacoity laws were enacted against a background of intensive debate. Legal experts such as A. Amos and C.H. Cameron seriously questionned the government's legislative authority for the Thagi and Dacoity Acts. Initially J.S. Mill, and later the N.W.P. Government insisted that thugs and dacoits be convicted for a specific offence. William Sleeman only won exemption from this constraint by providing elaborate procedures for protecting the innocent. Macaulay invoked a standard of universality in his endorsement of Act XIX 1837 validating the evidence of approvers. Judicial functionaries from the Bombay Sudder Court in the 1830s and '40s to Allan Octavian Hume in the 1850s vigorously objected to the abuse perceived in the Thagi and Dacoity Department's operation of the approver system. The military personae of Col. W.H. Sleeman and Capts. Elwall, Hervey and J. Sleeman didn't always get their way in the Company's courts. Although the overwhelming effect of the thagi and dacoity legislation was the promotion of guilt by association, the other side of that particular concern was that

---

[159] Anand A. Yang, op. cit., p. 126; Edward W. Said, Orientalism (New York, 1979), p. 40.

successive generations of the Legislative Council brought dacoity into the realm of public justice, thereby freeing the courts from the tangled restrictions of Muslim law. The legislators went to great pains to maintain consistency and clarity. This was the inspiration behind the Penal Code produced by Macaulay's Law Commission. And the fact that the essence of these laws survive in the Penal Code more than 60 years after Independence is testimony to their staying power.

Any notion that the Company was obsessed with imposing the values of western civilization on its Indian subjects is flatly contradicted by the Law Commission's rejection of laws proposed to prohibit the practice of sorcery and that of parents adorning their children with ornaments, in order to prevent murders on both accounts. As for hook swinging, that practice never came before the Commission during the Company period. All concerned were essentially satisfied with the discretionary authority given to local magistrates to deal with the matter. However, sorcery and the murder of children for the sake of their ornaments engaged the Commission to a greater extent.

In the case of sorcery, the Company very early distinguished between the practice of the art of sorcery and criminal acts provoked by belief in and practice of said art. The law enacted by the Government of Sir John Shore only made penal the act of murder resulting from a belief in sorcery. Remarkably, this law which reeked of condescension for a primitive tribe, was reenacted verbatim in the other presidencies. Inasmuch as the problem occurred usually among primitive tribes or very low-born castes, the Home Authorities urged the Company's courts to mitigate their sentences of convicted offenders. It remained only for Governor Elphinstone, first to eliminate the condescending reference to a primitive tribe which didn't reside in Bombay anyway, and then to rephrase the penal law in the style of certainty and clarity which was to be later the trademark of Macaulay's Law Commission. But Macaulay was not prepared to concede that there was any merit in the Elphinstone Code and so the law prohibiting sorcery as a justification for murder did not survive. The judicial functionaries of Madras who wished to outlaw the art of sorcery were completely overruled. The Law Commission joined the Madras Government and Sudder Court in the argument that such a law would only serve to lend official credence to the belief in sorcery. In the course of debate among judicial functionaries in other presidencies, it was suggested that education rather than law was the appropriate answer to the problems created by a belief in and practice of sorcery.

On both subjects of sorcery and the murder of children for the sake of their ornaments, the Law Commission indulged in rather arcane

Benthamite reasoning. To make sorcery penal, the Commissioners contemplated a law outlawing general deception with a specific reference to sorcery. But they gave up the idea when they realized how difficult it would be to enforce such a law effectively against the practice of sorcery. Caught up in their own line of abstract reasoning, they altogether forgot about the rather practical provision in the Elphinstone Code. As for the proposal to prohibit parents from allowing their children to wander alone adorned with ornaments, the Commissioners actually defended the vanity of parents who wished to bedeck their children with gold and silver jewellery. They saw such parental vanity as a symbol of civilization which promoted industry and the arts. Inasmuch as the statistics for the murder of children for the sake of their ornaments were not overwhelming and judicial officers across the country generally declared the proposed law to be very unpopular, especially among the poor and low-born classes, the Law Commission rejected the idea. Even the Madras Sudder Court, which originally proposed the law, turned against the proposal. Because both of these proposed laws had the potential for causing disturbance among the poorer classes of the Company's subjects, it is possible to argue that the Law Commission proceeded either from cowardice or from an astute calculation of popular feeling. But such a charge is easily countered by the evidence of the Company's police actions against whole villages in Bombay, Malabar and Ramgurh district which indulged in witch hunts. The genuine preference of Macaulay's Law Commission was to enact no more laws than absolutely necessary and to keep whatever laws were enacted clear, concise and consistent.

It remains to be said that the Penal Code produced by the Law Commission was framed for a unitary state. At least, uniform laws for all of British India would seem to presume the existence of a unitary state. However, as is evident from the markedly different official attitudes towards the enforcement of the Company's laws in the tribal hills and the settled plains, it is clear the Company administrators throughout the ranks, from Directors in London to the most remote district officer, were well aware of different circumstances in different regions. The Penal Code merely presented a universal standard of justice against which judicial proceedings throughout British India might be measured. This still allowed for judicial discretion so that murder by a Santal on account of supposed witchcraft could be treated very differently from murder by a dacoit on a Ganges river boat in the dead of night.

2

Law as a Weapon against Child Sacrifice, *Sati*, Female Infanticide and Meriah Sacrifice

That woman who, on the death of her husband, ascends the same burning pile with him, is exalted to heaven,...shall dwell in a region of joy for as many years as there are hairs on the human body (35 million) [and] expiates the sins of three generations on the paternal and maternal side of that family to which she was given while a virgin.[1]

Child Sacrifice at Saugor Island

Variations on the theme of human sacrifice consecrated within and adjacent to the Company's Indian territories transfixed with horror the imaginations of Company servants. The first instance of a sacrifice to prompt an immediate legislative reaction was that which occurred during full moon festivals in November and January on Saugor Island at the mouth of the Ganges. As described by Nundram Pauray, a shopkeeper who went 'every year to Gunga Saugore to sell Corralls and Beads to the Pilgrims':

> Twice every year a number of people flock to Gunga Saugore...for the purpose of performing certain Religious ceremonies....They consecrate Human Victims to the Ganges, they generally offer old women, old men, boys and girls and infants, by throwing them into the water, and they are devoured by Sharks.[2]

---

[1] Mantra recited by Brahmin priests during ceremony for the *sati*. The mantra is found in the 'Angirassmrti', H.T. Colebrooke, trans., *Digest of Hindu Law*, Vol. 2 (London, 1801), p. 451.

[2] Information given by Nundram Pauray, 19 December 1801, *Baird of Elie Papers*, Scottish Record Office, GD 147/59/8/4.

The old men and women believed that 'if they were devoured by sharks they would go to Heaven'. But the children were victims of their own parents. In Nundaram's words: 'The Parents make a vow that if they get a certain number of Children they will offer one of them to the Ganges'.[3] It was the testimony of Charles Starling, a mate in the Pilot Service, which swayed the Calcutta magistrates to demand Government interference. Recalling his shore visit to Saugor Island from his schooner, this deponent testified that 'during the time he was in the boat going to the shore, (he) saw altogether eleven men, women and lads destroyed by the Sharks'.[4]

Shocked by the news of this practice, the Calcutta magistrates investigated further. They discovered that the custom of sacrificing children 'was confined to the people of the eastern districts' of Bengal; that it arose from vows made by parents 'apprehensive of not having issue' or fearful that their children might not survive disease and death; that the Island of Saugor was 'held to be peculiarly sacred from its being considered as the termination of the Ganges and as the junction of the river with the sea' and that the practice was 'little countenanced by the religious orders or by the great body of the people'. They concluded that, because the practice had been neither authorized by the Mogul Government nor sanctioned by the British Government and because 'the parties concerned are liable to be tried and punished under the established law', the governor general might put a stop to the sacrifice—at least of the children—by issuing a proclamation that 'any persons who may be parties to such sacrifice will be tried and punished for the offence according to the general laws and regulations'.[5] They explained that they had considered that a regulation for the prevention of such sacrifices was consistent with existing precedents such as Sec. 9 Reg. XXI 1795 which charged the Brahmins of Benares with homicide for killing their women and children as a form of *dhurna* or resistance to legal process.[6] But they decided that a proclamation 'would be sufficient'. However, G.H. Barlow, the vice president in Council,

---

[3] *Ibid.*

[4] Deposition of Charles Starling, a mate in the Pilot Service, before C.F. Martyn, Justice of the Peace for Calcutta, 19 December 1801, *ibid.*, GD 147/59/8/2; also Bengal Criminal Judicial Consultations 18 February 1802, No. 3, in *Parliamentary Papers* (1824) XXIII, Cmd. 426, Part IV, pp. 435-36.

[5] G. Dowdeswell, Charles F. Martyn, W.C. Blaquiere, A. Macklaw, E. Thornton, Calcutta Magistrates, to G.H. Barlow, Vice President in Council, 18 February 1802, Bengal Criminal Judicial Consultations 18 February 1802, No. 2, *Parliamentary Papers* (1824) XXIII, Cmd. 426, Part IV.

[6] Secs 9 and 11, Bengal Regulation XXI for preventing Brahmins in the Provinces of Benares from establishing Koorhs, wounding or killing their female relations or children or sitting Dhurna, (passed 27 March 1795), I.O.R., V/8/16, p. 520.

favoured a regulation and requested the judges of the Nizamut Adawlut to transmit to him a draft regulation for preventing the sacrifice of children at Saugor Island. Judges H.T. Colebrooke and J.H. Harington obliged and on 20 August 1802 Governor General Wellesley promulgated Reg. VI of 1802 'for preventing the sacrifice of children at Saugor and other places'.[7] No effort was made to interfere with the 'self-devotion of the aged and infirm in the Ganges', for, as the Calcutta magistrates observed, 'the practice prevails... generally and is considered by the Hindoos...instrumental to their happiness in a future state of existence'. Without offering any evidence, the magistrates concluded that the voluntary suicide of the old and infirm by drowning or submission to sharks in the Ganges was a 'practice rooted in the most remote antiquity and sanctioned by express tenets in their (Hindu) sacred books'.[8] As for the effectiveness of Reg. VI 1802, its enforcement quickly came to depend on the use of armed troops.[9] Yet, from the standpoint of the Sanskrit scholar, H.H. Wilson, nearly half a century later, the Government's successful suppression of the practice was aided principally by the 'cordial concurrence of the Brahmans', inasmuch as the practice 'was not only unprompted, but condemned by Hindu religion'.[10]

Sati

Whereas Governor General Wellesley was able to respond to reports of the involuntary sacrifice of children to sharks off Saugor Island with instant legislation, the controversy surrounding the *sati* was far more complex and prolonged. The debate began in the early centuries of Indian history as a

---

[7] Nizamut Adawlut, to His Excellency Richard Marquis Wellesley, Governor General, Bengal Criminal Judicial Consultations 20 August 1802, No. 18, I.O.R., P/128/61; Beng. Reg. VI 1802 for preventing the sacrifice of children at Saugor and other places (passed 20 August 1802) I.O.R., V/8/17, pp. 307–8.

[8] Calcutta magistrates, to G.H. Barlow, *op. cit.*

[9] The Calcutta magistrates requested a party of 50 sepoys, 'all Mahometans', to prevent sacrifices on the occasion of the bathing festival at Saugor Island at the time of the full moon in January 1803. C.F. Martyn and W.C. Blaquiere, Calcutta Magistrates, to G. Dowdeswell, Secretary to Government, Post Office, Calcutta, 3 January 1803, Bengal Criminal Judicial Consultations 6 January 1803, No. 2, *Parliamentary Papers* (1824) XXIII, Cmd. 426, Part IV, p. 138.

[10] H.H. Wilson, 'The Religious Festivals of the Hindus', *Journal of the Royal Asiatic Society*, Vol. IX (1846): 68, reprinted in *Works by the late Horace Hayman Wilson*, Vol. II (London, 1862), p. 167.

simple matter of various *smrti* authors declaring either for or against the act of a widow becoming a *sati*. In the early nineteenth century, East India Company magistrates, judges and missionaries joined the *pandit*s in the courts in a rigorous effort to determine whether or not Hindu scriptures sanctioned the sacrifice of the widow on her husband's funeral pyre. Finally, in the twentieth century, feminists and a psychologist joined the debate contributing concepts of colonial discourse and female agency.

A *sati* was, in both myth and fact, a woman who attained a considerable degree of sanctity by virtue of committing *sahamarana* or the act of voluntarily immolating herself on the funeral pile of her husband. Other ways for the *sati* to attain sanctity included the rite of *anumarana* or cremation without the husband's corpse and burial alive, a practice preferred among the Telegus. It was only during the decades of intense debate by Europeans over whether or not the *sati* should be prevented from fulfilling her vows that the deed became confused with the doer. In the records of the East India Company the deed was known as 'suttee'.

The controversy leading to the decision of Governor General William Bentinck to 'abolish suttee' through legislation is well known. Therefore, it is only necessary to highlight some features of the arguments which developed on both sides. One reason the Company was slow to take action was that at the turn of the century Henry Colebrooke thought he had discovered a scriptural basis for the *sati* as old as Rigveda X.18.7. Ironically, only some 25 years after Bentinck's much trumpeted decision to legislate the abolition of *sati* did the Sanskrit scholars H.H. Wilson and Max Müller decide that the last word of the Vedic text translated by Colebrooke had been fraudulently altered so that 'agneh' (fire) replaced 'agre' (dwelling). Thus 'arohantu yonim agre' or 'let them go up into the dwelling' had been fatally altered to read 'arohantu yonim agneh' or 'let them go up to the place of the fire'. After removing the word 'fire' from the seventh verse of Rigveda X.18, Wilson turned his attention to the eigth verse to confirm that this hymn, in fact, implored the widow to 'rise up,...(and) come to the world of living beings'. And, to reenforce the scholastic authority of his pronouncements, Wilson cited the Brahmin commentator Sayana and the *Grihya Sutra*.[11] In response,

---

[11] Horace Hayman Wilson, 'On the Supposed Vaidik Authority for the Burning of Hindu Widows and on the Funeral Ceremonies of the Hindus', *Journal of the Royal Asiatic Society*, Vol. XVI (1856): 202–4; cf. Henry T. Colebrooke, 'On the Duties of a Faithful Widow', *Asiatic Researches*, Vol. IV (1807), p. 207. For a thorough discussion of Colebrooke's mistake, see O.P. Kejariwal, *The Asiatic Society of Bengal and the Discovery of India's Past* (Delhi, 1988), pp. 78–79. Other scholars still insist that Colebrooke's essay was intended as an argument against *sati*. See David Kopf, *British Orientalism and the Bengal Renaissance* (Calcutta, 1969), p. 40.

the eminent spokesman for conservative Hindu orthodoxy, Radhakant Deb, insisted that the eighth verse was 'in fact, a Sahamarana Mantra'. He cited as his authority the author of the 'Sahamaranavidhi' who explained that the eighth verse of Rigveda X.18 was addressed to the *sati* lying on the funeral pile 'only to test her resolution, and to induce her to retire if she be not sufficiently firm in her purpose'.[12] In an attempt to lay this controversy to rest, Arvind Sharma points to yet another Vedic text, Atharvaveda XVIII.3.1, which indicates that the act of the widow lying down beside her departed husband was a duty, already archaic by Rigvedic times. Thus Sharma concludes that 'while it is clear that the custom of sati is alluded to in the Vedic verses, it is equally clear that it was not practised'.[13]

In his study of the 'Duties of a Faithful Widow' Colebrooke also cited legal texts which prescribed the option of *brahmacharya* or chaste living as an option to *sahamarana*. The 'Vishnusmrti' of ca. AD 100 was one of the earliest to discuss both the *sati* and *brahmacharya* options for the widow. For every writer such as Vatsyana, Bhasa, Kalidasa and Sudraha who, beginning around AD 400, began to popularize the ideal of the widow as a devoted *sati*, A.S. Altekar has been able to mention *smrti* writers and commentators such as Brhaspati, the author of the 'Agnipurana', Medhatithi, Virata and Devanabhatta whose viewpoints range from downgrading the custom of *sati* as a second alternative to positive prohibition. Particularly noteworthy was the seventh-century poet Bana, who vehemently insisted:

> To die after one's beloved is fruitless….It does no good whatsoever to the dead person….The person who has died goes to the place determined by his own Karman, the person who accompanies him on the funeral pyre goes to the hell reserved for those who are guilty of the sin of suicide.

Unfortunately, such sane advice was ignored and, beginning about AD 700, *smrti*s by Angiras, Harita and Parasara promised the *sati* virtual sainthood, joining her husband in heaven for 35 million years, having expiated all his sins and those of his family going back three generations.[14]

---

[12] Raja Radhakanta Deb to H.H. Wilson, Calcutta, 30 June 1858, *Journal of the Royal Asiatic Society*, Vol. XVII (1860): 216–17; reprinted in *Works of the late Horace Hayman Wilson*, op. cit., p. 303.

[13] Arvind Sharma, 'The Scriptural Sanction for Sati in Hinduism', in Arvind Sharma, ed., *Sati: Historical and Phenomenological Essays* (Delhi, 1988), pp. 34–38.

[14] A.S. Altekar, *The Position of Women in Hindu Civilization*, 3rd ed. (Delhi, 1962), pp. 122–26; Arvind Sharma, 'The Tradition of Indigenous Protest Against Sati' and 'The Scriptural Sanction for Sati in Hinduism', in Arvind Sharma, ed., *op. cit.*, pp. 15–17, 31–33; 'Angirassmrti', trans, H.T. Colebrooke, *Digest of Hindu Law, op. cit.*

From the perspective of the twenty-first century, the East India Company appears archaic in its concern during the early decades of the nineteenth century over whether or not the *sati* was backed by sacred scriptures. Indeed, under the magnifying glass of colonial discourse, nineteenth-century British judges and magistrates are deemed to have 'privileged brahmanic scriptures as the key to Indian society' and as the source of Hindu law at the expense of custom and law enforced by caste *sabha*s.[15] At the time, at least around 1815–18, there was speculation that the attention paid by Company officers to the practice had the ironic effect of encouraging it. The Baptist missionary J.C. Marshman had a theory that the increase was a result of 'the increasing luxury of the higher and middling classes…which makes many families needy and anxious to get rid, by any means, of the necessity of supporting their mothers or the widows of their relations'.[16] The psychologist, Ashis Nandy, supported by many post-Independence scholars, endorses Marshman's theory as part of his own analysis which attributes the plague of *sati*s in Bengal in the second decade of the nineteenth century to the anomie of the new and old elite of 'colonial' Calcutta. Nandy argues that 'Bengali Brahmans were not merely religious leaders and interpreters of texts, traditions and rites, but major landholders and financiers who were being increasingly co-opted by the colonial system'. They therefore mounted a 'desperate defence of the rite' of *sati* 'in order to defend their self-esteem and traditional identity'.[17] Feminist historians insist that both would-be reformers among Company officers and the Bengali *bhadralok* qualified for Foucauldian discourse theory which identifies their use of religious texts as an exercise 'in colonial control'. Lata Mani particularly objects to the 'violent fiction of sati as a dutiful act of religious volition' which induced would-be nineteenth-century reformers to cast the widow as victim instead of a 'subject in action, negotiating, capitulating, accommodating, resisting'.[18] Andrea Major challenges Mani's heavily politicized interpretation to insist that 'the encounter with sati in the early nineteenth century was as much about British identity as it was about constructing an image of India'.[19]

---

[15] Lata Mani, 'Contentious Traditions: The Debate on *Sati* in Colonial India', in Kumkum Sangari and Sudesh Vaid, eds., *Recasting Women—Essays in Colonial History* (New Delhi, 1989), p. 114.

[16] Cited in M.A. Laird, ed., *Bishop Heber in Northern India—Selections from Heber's Journal* (Cambridge, 1971), p. 56.

[17] Ashis Nandy, 'Sati: A Nineteenth Century Tale of Women, Violence and Protest', in Ashis Nandy, *At the Edge of Psychology: Essays in Politics and Culture* (Delhi, 1980), pp. 7–9.

[18] Lata Mani, *Contentious Traditions: The Debate on Sati in Colonial India* (Berkeley, 1998), pp. 196, 31.

[19] Andrea Major, *Pious Flames—European Encounters with Sati 1500–1830* (Oxford: 2006), p. 7.

A historical retrospective reveals that the custom of the sacrifice of the widow on the funeral pile of her husband was prevalent in ancient times among Gauls, Goths, Celts, Scythians and Aryans in their Indo-European period. It is argued by the legal scholar, Jörg Fisch, in his comprehensive and authoritative global history of the burning of widows, that the mostly occasional Indian practice of *sati* was a case of 'following into Death' rather than a human sacrifice.[20] In any case, from the time the Aryans surfaced in Indian history, the custom disappeared altogether for several centuries. There is no mention of it in the literature of the reformist Buddhists, nor is it mentioned by Kautilya or Manu or the early *smrti* authors such as Yajnavalkya. There are a few references to *sati* in the original 'Mahabharata' dating from 300 BC, but none in the 'Ramayana' until a late edition around the sixth century AD. The earliest historical record of a *sati* is provided by Greek historians in their accounts of the resistance of a particular warrior tribe to Alexander in the Punjab in the fourth century BC. During the early centuries of the Christian era the custom gradually became popular among Kshatriyas. By the tenth century Hindu literature, sacred and profane, had recognized the *sati* custom as a laudable option. However, the only evidence of a deep-rooted commitment to the practice appeared in Kashmir where it was recorded in Kalhana's 'Rajatarangini'. Outside Kashmir evidence of *sati* was sparse until about the fourteenth century when medieval commentaries extolling the *sati* began to exercise widespread influence, especially among the Kshatriya warrior classes. At first, as ascetic ideals promoted the custom, it was prohibited to Brahmin women. In fact, the 'Padmapurana' explicitly condemned anyone assisting a Brahmin widow to the funeral pile. However, unwilling to be outdistanced in the practice of self-denial by the Kshatriyas, a few Brahmin families began to endorse the custom around AD 1000. South Indian commentaries of the twelvth and fourteenth centuries revealed that not only had the practice spread to the south of India, but it also had become popular in the Brahmin community. Madhava, commenting on the 'Parasarasmrti', stipulated that the Brahmin widow was only allowed *sahamarana*. If she did not immediately sacrifice herself on her husband's funeral pyre, she did not have the option available to other castes of committing *anumarana* or sacrificing herself at a later date on a

---

[20] Jörg Fisch, *Immolating Women—A global History of Widow Burning from Ancient Times to the Present*, trans. from German by Rekha Kamath Ragan (Delhi, Permanent Black: 2005), p. 19. Significantly, in the case of India, Fisch even declines to use the word 'sati'. He explains that a human sacrifice promises benefits for an 'entire community, whereas the benefits of following the dead are limited to the circle of those who are also entitled to being accompanied.'

separate funeral pyre with a piece of her husband's clothing to symbolize his body. By the seventeenth and eighteenth centuries memorial stones commemorating *sati*s all over India recorded that women of all classes had performed the sacrifice.[21] It is not impossible that lower classes performing *sati* were motivated by the desire to Sanskritize or upgrade their caste standing. Certainly Gunther Sontheimer, in his study of the Gonds, came to the conclusion that '*sati* amongst tribals was confined to chieftains who were under the influence of 'Kshatriyazation' or 'Rajputization'.[22] Such a notion of negotiable social status fuels Ashis Nandy's condemnation of 'the virtual epidemic of *sati*s that occurred in eighteenth and nineteenth century Bengal' as an ancient rite corrupted by market forces. Reflecting upon the shallow values of Bengali babus subservient to the East India Company, Nandy observes that no monument 'exists in honor of any one of the thousands of women who committed *sati*' at that time.[23]

As the custom of *sati* became popular throughout India, there was an infinite variety of procedures. Detailed descriptions of the ritual for the *sati* occurred only in digests dating from the seventeenth century. In the Deccan, western India and Mysore there are descriptions of the *sati* being placed in a deep pit. The same procedure was adopted at Puri, the town of Jagannath Temple in Orissa. A contemporary observer, while commenting on the paucity of *sati*s at Puri, remarked that the rite took place

> on the sea shore...at a spot...called 'Swarga Dwara' or 'passage to heaven'....
> The infatuated widow lets herself down into a pit, at the bottom of which the dead body of the husband has been previously placed with lighted faggots above and beneath.[24]

A house of grass was constructed in Bombay presidency; in Gujarat and northern Uttar Pradesh the widow was tied to a pillar in a specially built wooden house of 12 square feet. In Bengal her feet were tied to posts in the ground.[25] The Telegus of Andhra preferred to bury their widows alive

---

[21] A.S. Altekar, *ibid.*, pp. 126–33 and P.V. Kane, *History of Dharmasastra*, Vol. II, Part I (Poona, 1941), pp. 626–27.

[22] Gunther D. Sontheimer, 'On the Memorials of the Dead in the Tribal Area of Central India', in S. Settar and G.D. Sontheimer, eds., *Memorial Stones: A Study of their Origin, Significance and Variety* (Manipal, 1982), p. 96.

[23] Ashis Nandy, 'Sati as Profit versus Sati as a Spectacle' in John Stratton Hawley, ed., *Sati—The Blessing and the Curse* (Oxford, 1994), p. 137.

[24] Andrew Stirling, *An Account Geographical, Statistical and Historical of Orissa Proper* (Cuttack, n.d.), p. 163.

[25] A.S. Altekar, *op. cit.*, p. 134.

rather than burn them. The Chronicle of Fernao Nuniz described how Telugu widows

> go with much pleasure to the pit, inside of which are made two seats of earth, one for him and one for her, and they place each one on his own seat and cover them in little by little till they are covered up; and so the wife dies with the husband.[26]

As it was very difficult to escape from such contrivances, it is not surprising that, first, medieval travellers, then Muslim rulers and finally the British mercantile rulers of the East India Company questioned the voluntary character of the rite. Akbar intervened to stop specific *satis* and it is a matter of legend that the English founder of Calcutta, Job Charnock, dramatically rescued a *sati* and then married her.

By the end of the eighteenth century, the practice of *sati* was well protected by the Cornwallis Code's guarantee to the Company's Indian subjects of the 'free exercise of their religion'.[27] In fact, in the midst of the first official reports of *sati*s to be sent to the Government in Bengal by district officers, Lord Cornwallis specifically disallowed a request from the Collector at Shahabad to dissuade a *sati*. Cornwallis' circumspection rested on the solid foundation of the promise enshrined in the 1772 pronouncement by Warren Hastings' Council that in the Company's courts suits regarding 'all religious usages and institutions' would be decided for Hindus according to Hindu law. It was later alleged by orthodox Brahmins that Warren Hastings personally deputed the Sanskrit scholar, Charles Wilkins, to enquire into the religious sanction for the practice of *sati* during a specially authorized visit to Benares. According to the Brahmins, the result of the enquiry 'satisfied' Warren Hastings 'as to the validity of the laws respecting suttees', and 'this opinion was...confirmed by Mr Jonathan Duncan...in Benares'.[28] In the background there was Halhed's *Code of Gentoo* Laws which bestowed on the successful *sati* the promise of residence in the very highest of the six spheres above the earth.[29] With so much testimony from various

---

[26] Cited by Robert Sewell, *A Forgotten Empire (Vijayanagar)* (London, 1900), p. 393.

[27] See Nancy G. Cassels, 'The "Compact" and the Pilgrim Tax: The Genesis of East India Company Social Policy', *Canadian Journal of History*, VII (1972): 37–49.

[28] 'Petition of the Hindoos against the Abolition of *Sati*' sent to Lord William Bentinck, 19 December 1829, in C.H. Philips, ed., *The Correspondence of Lord William Cavendish Bentinck, Governor General of India, 1828–1835*, Vol. I (Oxford, 1977), p. 368; Mary Lloyd speculates on the special role played by Charles Wilkins in her 'Sir Charles Wilkins 1749–1836', *India Office Library and Records Report for the Year 1978* (London, 1979), pp. 17–18.

[29] N.B. Halhed, *Code of Gentoo Laws* (London, 1776), p. xlvii.

Photograph 3: 'Immolation of a Hindoo Widow upon her Husband's Funeral Pile' (1820 engraving from author's collection)

*pandit*s as to the scriptural authority for the *sati*, the Company at the end of the eighteenth century resorted to the tactic of modifying the Muslim law of retaliation as being 'essentially repugnant to the principles of public justice'. Sec. 3 Beng. Reg. VIII 1799 decreed that 'it shall not justify any prisoner convicted of wilful homicide, that he or she was desired by the party slain to put him or her to death'. The Nizamut Adawlut prescribed the death penalty for such murderers in order 'to preserve the lives of many from the effects of passion or revenge'.[30] To be sure, this regulation was conceived out of a concern to undermine the absolute authority claimed by masters over slaves or parents over children, especially in the case of Benares Brahmins. But Sec. 3 was open to interpretation as legal authority for the punishment of those who aided or abetted a *sati*.

At the turn of the century, the practice of *sati* attracted the attention of Baptist missionary William Carey whose investigation of the subject in 1803 was assumed by his colleagues in Serampore to be a crucial initiative for Company policy.[31] It was certainly true that missionaries generally maintained fairly steady propaganda portraying the *sati* as a victim of pagan Hindu superstition. Some, such as William Johns, who published his *Collection of Facts and Opinions about the Burning of Widows* in 1816, were credited with great courage for raising a hue and cry against the Government policy of the day at risk of deportation. Others, such as James Peggs, whose pamphlets appeared at the height of the movement for abolition, claimed credit for the ultimate legislation in 1829. However, more courageous than missionaries who allegedly courted deportation was the Bengali reformer, Rammohun Roy, who, after protesting in vain against his own sister-in-law's decision to become a *sati*, endured ostracism and even threats of physical violence for his steadfast campaign against the practice of *sati*.

But Government policy concerning the *sati* truly began with Governor General Wellesley's authorization of an investigation of the facts. Buoyed by his apparent success in promulgating legislation against infanticide off the Island of Saugor, Lord Wellesley assigned the Sudder Dewanny Adawlut the task of deciding official government policy. The *pandit*s of the Sudder Dewanny Adawlut submitted to Government on 5 June 1805 a *Vyavastha*, stating:

---

[30] Sec. 3 Beng. Rev. VIII for certain Modifications of the Mahomedan Law in Cases of Murder (passed 10 October 1799), I.O.R., V/8/17, p. 138.

[31] John Clark Marshman, *The Life and Times of Carey, Marshman and Ward*, Vol. I (London, 1859), p. 222.

Every woman of the four Castes/Brahmin, Khetry, Byse and Soodur/is permitted to burn herself with the body of her husband, provided she has not infant children, nor is pregnant nor in a state of uncleanness, nor under the age of puberty, in any of which cases she is not allowed to burn herself with her husband. But a woman who has infant children, and can procure another person to undertake the charge of bringing them up, is permitted to burn. It is contrary to Law as well as to the usage of the country, to cause any woman to burn herself against her wish by administering drugs to stupefy or intoxicate her.[32]

With such a quasi endorsement of the custom, Lord Wellesley bequeathed the controversy to his successors. It was not until 1812 that Governor General Minto's Government ordered the Sudder Nizamut Adawlut to frame instructions to magistrates and police officers based on the 1805 *Vyavastha*. The Government directed that 'according to the principle of religious toleration', it should 'allow' the practice of *sati* 'in those cases in which it is countenanced by [the Hindoo] religion and...prevent it in others, in which it is by the same authority prohibited'.[33] And so, a distinction emerged between the voluntary *sati*, the saint, and the involuntary *sati*, the victim. But even when the police officers were attempting to prevent an illegal or involuntary *sati*, they were to demonstrate that 'it is not the intention of the Government to check or forbid any act authorized by the tenets of the Religion of the inhabitants of their Dominions'.[34] As observed by Benedicte Hjejle, this protracted decision in the name of religious toleration to allow the practice so long as it conformed to the rules of the *Shastra* was 'probably due to H.T. Colebrooke...who had...found the text in the Rig Veda' which he believed to be in support of the sacrifice.[35]

It transpired that the Government was severely shaken by the limited but dramatic success which followed the issuing of their instructions to Police *darogah*s in the form of the Nizamut Adawlut Circular Orders of

---

[32] Cited in J.H. Harington and John Fombelle, Nizamut Adawlut, to Vice President in Council 14 September 1814, U.P.S.A., *Pre-Mutiny Records*, Saharanpur Collectorate, Letters Received from Superior Courts (Nizamut Adawlut) January 1805–September 1828, Vol. 186, fol. 162.

[33] G. Dowdeswell, Secretary to Government, to W.H. Turnbull, Register of Nizamut Adawlut, Fort William, 5 December 1812, B.S.A., P.C.O., Letters from Nizamut Adawlut 24 September 1812–20 November 1816, Vol. 250 A.

[34] Nizamut Adawlut Draft of Directions to be issued by Magistrates to Police Darogahs, *ibid.*

[35] Benedicte Hjejle, 'The Social Policy of the East India Company with Regard to Sati, Slavery, Thagi and Infanticide, 1771–1852' (unpublished dissertation, Oxford, 1958), p. 16.

29 April 1813. Before the end of the calendar year the Magistrate of Burdwan reported the prevention of five sacrifices in his district, four of which were 'prohibited from burning on the sole ground of their having Infant Children'. Alarmed lest the Burdwan *darogahs*' construction of their Circular Orders trigger some kind of tumult, Government again called upon the *pandit*s of the Sudder Dewanny Adawlut, this time, for an authoritative pronouncement on the question of whether the restriction of the *Shastra* was 'confined to...Women having an Infant at the breast or whether it extends to other children'. The result was an elaborate *vyavastha* citing *Vrihaspati* to the effect that no woman with a child less than three years of age was permitted to become *sati*. However, the *pandit*s insisted that on the authority of Raghunanda, a mother could become *sati* if she could find someone else who would undertake to care for her infant children. These *vyavastha*s were the basis of further instructions issued to the Police *darogah*s in the form of Circular Orders from the Nizamut Adawlut on 4 January 1815 complete with a 'Form of Engagement' to be signed by anyone taking responsibility for the upbringing of the sati's infant children.[36]

The most remarkable aspect of the Nizamut Adawlut Circular Orders of 4 January 1815 was their insistence that a widow could withdraw from the flames at the last minute without incurring degradation and humiliation. This countered the belief popular in the early nineteenth century that after the widow had pronounced the *Sankalpa* or prayer which was the final part of the ritual leading to her ascent of the funeral pyre, she could not retreat from the flames except in total disgrace to herself and her family. This was inevitably the reason given for forcing the widow back into the flames and holding her down with dampened bamboos. Such action, according to the 'Instructions to Police' in 1815 converted a voluntary and therefore legal *sati* into an involuntary and therefore illegal *sati*. The authority for these 'Instructions' lay in yet another *vyavastha* of the *pandit*s of the Sudder Dewanny Adawlut who declared that 'if a woman after pronouncing the Sunkulp...has not courage to proceed to the funeral pile, she may recover

---

[36] J.H. Harington and John Fombelle to Vice President in Council, 14 September 1814, enclosing letter from Magistrate of Burdwan of 10 December 1813, all of which is included in W.H. Turnbull, Register, to R.F. Grindall, Magistrate, Northern Division of Saharanpur, Fort William, n.d. 1815, U.P.S.A., Pre Mutiny Records, Saharpur Collectorate, Letters received from Superior Courts (Nizamut Adawlut), January 1805 to September 1828, Vol. 186, fols 157, 159, 161 and 168; G. Dowdeswell, Chief Secretary to Government, to W.H. Turnbull, Register of Nizamut Adawlut, also enclosed in W.H. Turnbull to R.F. Grindall, U.P.S.A., Pre Mutiny Records, Saharpur Collectorate, Letters received from Superior Courts (Nizamut Adawlut), January 1805 to September 1828, Vol. 186, fols 171, 179.

her purity by undergoing a severe penance, and her relations may then associate with her'.[37]

Much to the chagrin of Government, during the years immediately after the 'Police Instructions' of 1815, *sati* statistics more than doubled with a heavy concentration in Bengal. The concentration of *sati*s near the centre of government has been explained by Ashis Nandy as a manifestation of colonial rule. Contemporary explanations emphasized the role played by an epidemic of Cholera Morbus, and by rigorous police reporting of the practice. The Nizamut Adawlut's report to Government in 1829 argued that the high number of *sati*s in Hooghly District was owing to 'its being traversed to such an extent by the waters of the Ganges and other streams considered holy by the Hindoos'. These rivers were the preferred sites for the cremation ceremonies of higher caste Hindus.[38]

Stung by the dramatic increase in *sati* statistics, the Nizamut Adawlut plunged into further investigation as part of an agonizing reappraisal of Government policy. A *vyavastha* from Mritunjoy, the *pandit* of the Supreme Court, emphasized that the rite of *anumarana* was prohibited to Brahmin widows according to a text cited in the *Mitakshara* and a Commentary on Yajnavalka. He observed that 'few...eminently virtuous women of former ages' sacrificed themselves, that *sati* was only 'frequent among modern women', and that 'not the slightest offence attaches either to the women who depart from their resolution, or to those who persuade them to relinquish their intention'.[39]

The Judges of the Sudder Court then drafted a 'Regulation for maintaining an observance of the Restrictions prescribed by the *Shastra* in the Burning of Hindoo Widows on the Funeral Piles of their Husbands'. The preamble boldly declared that 'the suicide in these cases (sahamarana and anoomarana) is not indeed a religious act, nor has it the sanction of Menu and other ancient legislators...' It was observed that because the Circular Orders of 1813 and 1815 had been 'partly frustrated' by the failure of families of determined satis to inform police, it was necessary to make such an offence punishable by law. The police must be informed of any forthcoming sati and they must attend that *sati*, 'careful that the widow is fully apprised of the liberty allowed

---

[37] *Ibid.*, fol. 185.

[38] Extract from proceedings of Nizamut Adawlut, 9 August 1829, Bengal Criminal Judicial Consultations 4 December 1829, Part I, No. 9, I.O.R., P/139/34, fols 481–83.

[39] 'Bewusta by Mrtoonjoy' in *Parliamentary Papers* (1821) XVIII, Cmd. 749, pp. 119–21, 125.

her by the *shastra* and of the encouragement given to a life of virtue and piety'. In enlarging and clarifying the restrictions of the *Shastra*, the Court stipulated that the competent *sati* must be over the age of 16 years, must not be pregnant or a mother with infant at the breast or child up to seven years of age unprovided for; Brahmin widows were prohibited *anumarana* and all *sati*s, whether commiting *sahamarana* or *anumarana* must sacrifice themselves immediately after or after learning of the death of their husbands. Section 12 of the proposed Regulation included the text of the *vyavastha* which had been part of the Circular Orders of 4 January 1815 declaring that the would-be *sati* may retreat from the flames even after pronouncing the *sankalpa*, and, after undergoing a severe penance, her relatives may associate with her. The second clause of Sec. 12 even proposed to punish relations who might insist on disgrace for the *sati* who changed her mind at the last moment. Bolder still was the provision in Sec. 15 aimed particularly at the wealthy families of Bengal who were required by the *Dayabhaga* to allow widows to inherit family property. Sec. 15 proclaimed simply that the 'property of illegal *sati*s goes to Government'.[40]

In the absence of Governor General Hastings who was away from Calcutta attending to the business of war, the Government rejected the Court's proposed regulation with an air of great caution. They particularly objected to Secs 12 and 15. In the first instance, they feared that 'it would not be practicable by any penal enactment to compel individuals to associate with others whom they (however erroneously) might consider to be degraded'. Latterly, they were horrified to speculate about the extent to which Government motives for the confiscation of property could be misunderstood. Instead of a regulation, Government proposed that fresh instructions to police officers and magistrates based on the draft regulation be promulgated by the Court in the form of new Circular Orders. The Court duly framed the Circular Orders as suggested by Government with the omission of Secs 12 and 15 from their original draft, and with the addition of a section specifically forbidding the practice among the Jogee tribe of burying their widows alive. The new Circular Orders produced by the Court according to the instructions of Government on 9 September 1817 were submitted to Governor General Hastings. From his camp at Bilahra Mow, Hastings promptly approved these new measures. However, Hastings was ultimately to explain to the Directors in London that owing to the steady

---

[40] Draft of Regulation prepared by Court of Nizamut Adawlut, Fort William, 25 June 1817, *ibid.*, pp. 126–31.

increase in *sati* statistics, it was considered to 'be inexpedient to promulgate the circular orders prepared in the year 1817'.[41]

For his stance on the issue of *sati* Hastings nearly received a special encomium from Radhakant Deb. As recorded by Bishop Heber, a meeting convened by 'the Hindu gentlemen of Calcutta to vote an address of thanks to Lord Hastings on his leaving Bengal' rejected an amendment proposed by Radhakant Deb. Deb felt that 'Lord Hastings should be particularly thanked for the protection and encouragement which he had afforded to the ancient and orthodox practice of widows burning themselves'.[42] Counter to the attentions of Radhakant Deb was Rammohun Roy's dedication to the Marchioness of Hastings of his 1818 tract opposing *sati*. He dismissed the egregious Rigveda X.18.7, declaring that 'no one ever ventured to give it an interpretation as commanding widows to burn themselves on the pile and with the corpse of their husbands'.[43] The sharp divisions among leading Bengali intellectuals resulted in physical threats as well as verbal taunts being hurled at Rammohun Roy on account of his opposition to the *sati* custom. The ostracism of Rammohun was compounded by the tension in his relationship with his mother who, appalled by her son's criticism of the superstitions of the popular Hinduism of the day, undertook a pilgrimage to Jagannath Temple in order to redeem her son's soul.

With the stillbirth of the Nizamut Adawlut Circular Orders of 1817, the Company's policy regarding *sati* reached a stalemate which was to last for 10 years. Confusion reigned throughout the ranks of Company servants. For example, the Directors in London were vexed to discover that C.M. Lushington, Acting Magistrate at Combeconum, had been sufficiently emboldened by the knowledge that the Raja of Tanjore had discouraged the practice to fantasize that Governor General Cornwallis had abolished *sati* by proclamation in Bengal.[44] Judge V. Hale of the southern Concan,

---

[41] Circular Orders, 9 September 1817; W.B. Bayley, Secretary to Government, to Register of Nizamut Adawlut, Council Chamber, 9 September 1817; J. Adam, Secretary to Governor General, to W.B. Bayley, Secretary to Government in Judicial Department, Fort William, Camp Bilahra Mow, 19 October 1817; Political Letter from Governor General in Council to Court of Directors, 15 January 1820, *ibid.*, pp. 137–42, 144, 147 and 245.

[42] M.A. Laird, ed., *op. cit.*, p. 65.

[43] Rammohun Roy, 'A Second Conference between an Advocate for, and an Opponent of, the Practice of Burning Widows Alive', (Calcutta, 1820), in Jogendra Chunder Ghose, ed., *The English Works of Raja Ram Mohun Roy*, Vol. I (Calcutta, 1885), p. 351.

[44] Judicial Despatch to Fort St. George, 4 March 1818, I.O.R., E/4/920, fol. 752 and C.M. Lushington, Acting Magistrate Combeconum, to Secretary to Government in the Judicial Department, Fort St. George, Strdangy, 14 September 1813, I.O.R., *Board's Collections* F/4/522 #12457, fol. 12.

where the practice of *sati* had been prevalent under Maratha rule, reported that the former subjects of the Peshwa 'on becoming subject to British rule, voluntarily discontinued the practice on understanding that it was repugnant to British laws and only resumed it on finding that it was tolerated by the British Government'.[45] And then there was the ambiguous response of senior authorities to the harsh tactics pursued by H.M. Pigou as magistrate first in Jessore and then in Cuttack. In the latter instance the Commissioner of Cuttack severely reprimanded Pigou for ordering that parties to a *sati* be 'harrassed' by court summonses. Yet, the Judges of the Nizamut Adawlut observed that 'in the District of Jessore it may fairly be presumed that the system of severity pursued by...Mr Pigou...could not fail to be productive of considerable effect'.[46] And, Lord William Bentinck rhapsodized that 'in Jessore there were 30 Suttees in 1825, 16 in 1826, 3 in 1827 and in 1828 there were none. To no other cause can this be assigned than to a power beyond the law exercised by the Acting Magistrate'.[47]

In London a petition with 2,400 signatures representing gentry and clergy was presented to the House of Commons by the reformer, Thomas Buxton, urging abolition. This produced debate in parliament and in meetings at Leadenhall Street. But the Directors, partly on the advice of Judge J.H. Harington while he was home on leave, were determined to leave the decision to the Government in India. Thus in 1824, the Directors rejected paragraphs proposed for a despatch to Calcutta urging the Nizamut Adawlut to vest magistrates with increased discretionary powers to prevent the rite of *sati*.[48] Similarly, in 1827, the Board of Commissioners deleted from a draft despatch of the Directors the citation of a Resolution taken by the Court of Proprietors on 23 March recommending that the Government in India be instructed to interfere with the practice of *sati*.[49]

Without fresh instructions from London or legislation by the presidency governments in India, the only arena for action was the Nizamut Adawlut. In fact, J.H. Harington, upon his return to Calcutta, endorsed the idea of

---

[45] Despatch from Bombay, 6 May 1821, *Parliamentary Papers* (1823) XVII, Cmd. 466, p. 132.

[46] T. Pakenham, Commissioner of Cuttack, to H.M. Pigou, Magistrate of Cuttack, Commissioner's Office, 4 November 1828; Proceedings of Nizamut Adawlut 9 August 1829, Bengal Criminal Judicial Consultations, 4 December 1829, Part I, No. 9, I.O.R., P/139/34, fols 508, 484.

[47] Minute by William Bentinck, 8 November 1829, Bengal Criminal Judicial Consultations, 4 December 1829, Part I, No. 10, I.O.R., P/139/34, fol. 18 (572).

[48] Court of Directors meeting, 19 March 1824, *Parliamentary Papers* (1826–27) XX, Cmd. 354, p. 32.

[49] Judicial Despatch to Bengal, 25 July 1827, I.O.R., E/4/719, fols 1252–53.

a 'legal prohibition' of *sati*, or at the very least, the adoption of rules which would compel families of *sati*s to inform the police in time for them to take effective preventive action.[50] Meanwhile other judges on the Nizamut Adawlut began to express their frustration over the expectation that their rulings in *sati* cases might discourage the practice. In the particularly outrageous case of Government vs. Bhuraichee and others in 1821 wherein the hapless widow was forced back into the flames twice only to be beheaded upon her third escape attempt, Judge C. Smith refused to advocate either the death penalty or imprisonment for the accused accessories on the grounds that the 'suttee' was 'in the first instance voluntary. Facts of subsequent violence may be fabricated or exaggerated'.[51] In a later case, wherein the *vyavastha* of the Nizamut Adawlut *pandit*s expressly contradicted the *vyavastha* of the Sudder Dewanny Adawlut *pandit*s circulated as part of the Circular Orders of 4 January 1815 prohibiting *anumarana* to Brahmins, the fourth Judge W. Dorin remarked that 'it is in vain to think that the sentences of this court are to put a stop to suttee'.[52] In another case, C. Smith challenged the value of the Circular Order inasmuch as it had 'not yet [been] reduced into a printed Regulation…'. Smith asserted that 'it is quite obvious that a circular order can have no validity at all but as it confirms and enforces the existing law'.[53]

Judge Smith's refusal to use the Circular Orders of 1812 and 1815 to convict parties to a *sati* provoked radical critics of Company policy, such as the expelled journalist James Silk Buckingham, to write of judicial 'negligence'.[54] Smith's arguments as cited above in the case of Government vs. Bhuraichee and others have prompted a legal observer to comment from the distance of over 150 years that 'though the facts screamed that the *sati* was totally illegal…the most extraordinary and convoluted judgements' delivered a sentence which was neither the death penalty nor life imprisonment.[55] Yet, it was Judge Smith who was to propose that Sec. 3 Beng. Reg. VIII 1799

---

[50] Minute by J.H. Harington, 28 June 1823, *Parliamentary Papers* (1825) XXIV, Cmd. 518, pp. 8–18.

[51] C. Smith, Govt. v. Bhuraichee and others, 1st Sess. 1821, Zillah Gorruckpore, N.A. Rep. 2, pp. 92–93.

[52] W. Dorin, Government vs. Ramdut and Balgobind, 1st Sess. 1823, Zillah Juanpore, N.A. Rep. 2, pp. 274–75.

[53] C. Smith, Government vs. Surnam Tewarry, 1st Sess. 1823, Zillah Goruckpore, N.A. Rep. 2, p. 80.

[54] 'On the Burning of Hindoo Widows', *The Oriental Herald*, Vol. VIII, No. 25 (January 1826), p. 7.

[55] Vasudha Dhagamwar, 'Saint, Victim or Criminal' in *Seminar*, No. 342 (February 1988), p. 35.

should be enforced against *sati*s whether or not they were legal according to the *shastra*.⁵⁶ Indeed, it was possible to argue that all that was necessary was to enforce Sec. 3 Beng. Reg. VIII 1799 against *sati*; no special law was needed. The difficulty was that the Circular Orders issued by the Nizamut Adawlut had clouded the issue. By distinguishing between voluntary and involuntary *sati*s and by defining permissible conditions for a *sati* according to Hindu law, the Circular Orders seemed to imply that the *sati* custom required special attention. By causing confusion, the Circular Orders compounded the stalemate of Company policy. In London, the member who attempted to stir the Directors to action in March 1824 observed that the necessary laws for prohibiting *sati* were already in place.⁵⁷

It was to this atmosphere of frozen indecision that Governor General William Bentinck brought a sense of urgency, reporting:

> [T]he dreadful responsibility hanging over my happiness in this world and the next if as the Governor General of India I was to consent to the continuance of this practice for one moment longer, not than our security, but than the real happiness and permanent welfare of the Indian population rendered indispensable.⁵⁸

After extensive consultations with officers in the Company's army, with magistrates in the Company's judicial service, and with the judges of the Nizamut Adawlut, Bentinck discovered that fear of legislation against *sati* had largely disappeared from the English ruling classes in India. Indeed, F.J. Shore was to report a few years later that 'three out of four [of my countrymen] were...convinced that...the suttee might be abolished with perfect safety' and 'were anxious to see the promulgation of a law to this effect'.⁵⁹ However, Rammohun Roy, in conference with Lord William, was extremely apprehensive about the possibility that legislation against *sati*

---

⁵⁶ Minute of 2nd Judge C. Smith, 3 December 1824, *Parliamentary Papers* (1825) XXIV, Cmd. 518, p. 148.

⁵⁷ At a Court of Directors meeting 17 March 1824, *op. cit.*, pp. 3–4. N.B. Secs 15 and 16 Reg. VIII 1803 duplicated Secs 2 and 3 Beng. Reg. VIII 1799 for the Ceded Provinces; the same sections were also duplicated by Secs 15 and 16 Madras Reg. VIII 1802, whereas only Sec. 2 was duplicated in Sec. 6 Bom. Reg. III 1802, I.O.R., V/8/17; V/8/26 and V/8/22.

⁵⁸ William Bentinck to John Astell, 'Bentinck Papers' (Nottingham University, PwJf 2612, 12 January 1829).

⁵⁹ Frederick John Shore, *Notes on Indian Affairs*, Vol. II (London, 1837), pp. 217–18. For the long held view that the abolition of *sati* should be entirely credited to Lord Bentinck, see V.N. Datta, *Sati: A Historical, Social and Philosophical Enquiry into the Hindu Rite of Widow Burning* (Delhi, 1988).

would provoke fears that the English Government had abandoned its pledge to guarantee religious freedom to its Indian subjects. And, H.H. Wilson advised against any such legislation.[60]

Nevertheless, with the support of the Sudder Court and a majority of army and civilian officers, Governor General Bentinck introduced Beng. Reg. XVII on 4 December 1829. The new law declared that, inasmuch as 'the practice of suttee' was 'revolting to the feelings of human nature' and was 'no where enjoined by the religion of the Hindoos as an imperative duty', it was 'hereby declared illegal'. Sec. 4 cl. 2 further declared that 'all persons convicted of aiding and abetting in the sacrifice of a Hindoo Widow, by burning or burying alive, whether the sacrifice be voluntary on her part or not, shall be deemed guilty of culpable Homicide'.[61] With one stroke Beng. Reg. XVII 1829 cut through the equivocation of earlier Circular Orders to declare all *sati*s illegal regardless of circumstances and all parties assisting a sati guilty of culpable homicide. The only continuity with earlier policy occurred in Sec. V which declared that anyone who violated the rules of previous Circular Orders by 'using violence' or 'having assisted' a *sati* under the influence of intoxication or other involuntary circumstance was subject to the death penalty. Lesser offences were simply liable to punishment by fine or imprisonment. Circular Orders accompanying Beng. Reg. XVII, while cancelling their predecessors of 1812 and 1815, continued the theme of ultimate respect for the religious sentiments of potential Indian defendants. They instructed magistrates 'to abstain from using irons, handcuffs, or other unnecessary duress towards any persons apprehended under these rules' and to confine prisoners 'deemed not bailable…in the civil jail,…never in the criminal jail'. Furthermore the police *darogah*s were instructed 'to use all care and discretion in giving effect to these orders'.[62]

It is a matter of legend that the orthodox Bengali community, under the leadership of Radhakant Deb's Dharma Sabha, submitted a petition in protest against Regulation XVII which Bentinck forwarded to the Privy Council. Francis Bathie, the Supreme Court attorney who presented this petition to the Privy Council pointed out that the petition was based on 37 Geo. III c. 142 s. 12 which guaranteed that no act 'done in consequence of the rule of law or caste, so far as respects members of the same family only,

---

[60] Minute by Lord William Bentinck, 8 November 1829, *op. cit.*, fols 10–12 (564–66).

[61] Preamble, Sec. 2 and Sec. 4 cl. 2 Beng. Reg. XVII (passed 4 December 1829), I.O.R., V/8/21.

[62] Circular Orders No. 43, to the Several Magistrates and Joint Magistrates and Police Officers, 4 December 1829, pp. 177–79.

be deemed a crime, although the same may not be justifiable by the laws of England'.⁶³ Rammohun Roy gathered signatures in support of a counter-petition and travelled to London to testify before the Privy Council—a revolutionary gesture for his time, even though the East India Company's solicitor was prevailed upon not to 'put Rammohun in our appendix. It is not the case the Government acted on'.⁶⁴ For the feminist scholar, Lata Mani, the orthodox petition and Rammohun Roy's campaign against *sati* were the conservative and liberal parameters of colonial discourse, both of which were equally invalid because their focus on scripture rendered the widow, herself, a marginal figure.⁶⁵ However, the Privy Council, presiding over this liberal-conservative contest in 1832 without benefit of the idea of female agency, was able to dismiss the case of the Calcutta petition.⁶⁶

Meanwhile, the substance of Beng. Reg. XVII was reenacted in Madras and Bombay, although in Bombay the wording was much less forthright. No mention was made of the illegality of the *sati* custom. It was merely deemed necessary to rescind the part of the Elphinstone Code which had exempted persons 'assisting at rites of self-immolation, from the penalty of murder'. This was in keeping with the ideas of former Governor Mountstuart Elphinstone who had always been squeamish about the least interference with any custom remotely associated with Indian religions. However, Sec. 2, cl. 1 of Bom. Reg. XVI 1830 did declare persons assisting a *sati* guilty of culpable homicide.⁶⁷

Generally speaking, the new laws were accepted. There was no further protest. Only a handful of cases came before the courts. However, it was another 20 years before most of the princely states outlawed the practice. A most egregious case was that of Ranjit Singh who took with him to his flaming

---

⁶³ Case of appellants, I.O.R., L/L/13 (1030), Vol. 2, fol. 157.

⁶⁴ Rammohun Roy, 'A Few Remarks in Vindication of the Government of Bengal in Abolishing the Practice of Female Sacrifice, 14 January 1832' and Letter to Edward Lawford, Company Solicitor, from Mr Secretary Spankie, 16 January 1832, I.O.R., L/L/13 (1030), Vol. 3, fols 336–39, 342.

⁶⁵ Lata Mani, *Contentious Traditions: The Debate on Sati in Colonial India*, op. cit., p. 115.

⁶⁶ Case of Molla Rajnaram Roy Bahadur Zemindar and Others against Regulation 17 of 1829 prohibiting Sati, Privy Council Appeal, 1832, I.O.R. L/L/13 (1030), Vols. 1–3; East India Co., Statement Humbly Submitted on the Part of the Court of Directors of the East India Co. to His Majesty in Council in Support of the Bengal Regulation (passed on 4 December 1829), Declaring the Practice of Suttee Illegal and Punishable by the Criminal Courts; *Reasons for dismissing the Petition*, I.O.R. L/L/13 (1030), Vol. 3, pp. 213–18.

⁶⁷ Sec. 26, cl. 2 Bom. Reg. XIV 1827 was rescinded by Sec. 1 Bom. Reg. XVI (passed 29 May 1830), O.I.O.C., V/8/25; Madras Reg. I (passed 2 February 1830), I.O.R., V/8/28, was almost identical to Beng. Reg. XVII 1829.

funeral pyre four *ranee*s and seven slave girls.⁶⁸ As far as the development of the law was concerned, the most interesting case occurred in Bombay presidency. After a widow was prevented from committing *sati* at Poona, she simply removed herself to the neighbouring territory of a sympathetic Raja where she fulfilled her vows. The Bombay Government then proposed a law making 'the act of Suttee criminal in the Suttee'. The Government of India declined any further special legislation but referred the matter to the Law Commission in 1836.

By the time the Law Commission replied in 1837, Macaulay had drafted his Penal Code and considered that 'under a good construction of the Bombay law then existing, special legislation would be unnecessary'.⁶⁹ Sec. 298 of Macaulay's draft Penal Code defined 'voluntary culpable homicide by consent', giving as 'Illustration a': 'Z, a Hindoo Widow, consents to be burned with the corpse of her husband. A kindles pile. Here A has committed voluntary culpable homicide by consent.'⁷⁰ In 1846 the third Indian Law Commission speculated that Macaulay's distinction between 'voluntary culpable homicide' and 'voluntary culpable homicide by consent' was made out of regard for the practice of *sati*. Macaulay's Sec. 298 was ultimately incorporated in Exception 5 to Sec. 300 of the Indian Penal Code as enacted in 1860. As explained by Vasudha Dhagamvar: 'Voluntariness was all that mattered.'⁷¹ Jörg Fisch has discerned that *sati* was subsumed also under 'murder and homicide' in Secs 299 and 302–4, under 'abetment of suicide' in Secs 305–6, and under 'attempted suicide' in Sec. 309. Essentially he observes that there were 'no fundamental changes in the way the administration of justice dealt with *sati* after 1862'. Generally speaking, 'lenient sentences in sati cases in the lower courts were always set aside by higher courts'. Under British rule, it was unlikely that any major player in an instance of *sati* would suffer either the death penalty or transportation. However, after 1947, rulings of higher courts became more ambiguous because 'not all officials despised the custom'. In fact, in the wake of Independence, the debate between opponents and supporters of *sati* intensified. Finally, Fisch underlines the difficulty of the feminists' promotion of female agency.

---

⁶⁸ Khushwant Singh, *A History of the Sikhs*, Vol. I (Princeton, 1984), p. 289.

⁶⁹ This information is in the Index to the Law Commission Proceedings 1835–48, p. 218 at the National Archives of India. Unfortunately, the actual proceedings are reported lost by the archival staff.

⁷⁰ *A Penal Code Prepared by the Indian Law Commission and Published by Command of the Governor General of India in Council* (Repr. from Calcutta edition, London, 1838), p. 39 in Library of N.A.I.

⁷¹ Vasudha Dhagamvar, 'Saint Victim or Criminal', Seminar 352 (1988): 36–37.

If the widow is neither saint nor victim, but a conscious agent of her actions, then she must be a criminal. He noted the irony that the most committed of contemporary 'Indian opponents of *sati* portray the *sati* to a much greater extent as a helpless victim than did British officials in the nineteenth century, since they also dispute any kind of heroism'.[72]

Until 4 September 1987, Beng. Reg. XVII 1829 imperfectly subsumed under Sec. 300 of the Indian Penal Code, was broadly credited with bringing about an end to a very disturbing suicidal rite. This is not to say that there were not scattered manifestations of a surviving faith in the sanctity of the *sati*, especially in the princely states. The account of four *ranee*s and seven slave girls following Ranjit Singh to his funeral pile is legendary. But within another decade, Maharajah Golab Singh issued a proclamation from Lahore prohibiting *sati*, as well as infanticide and slavery in his dominions. Indeed, by December 1847, Governor General Hardinge was able to list 23 princes who had also taken measures to suppress the practice.[73] The princely states only slowly and separately came to heed the legislative example set in the presidencies until finally after 1847 the Indian Penal Code was extended to all of them. Yet, still, there were individuals who defied the law. Thus the Sanskrit scholar, A.S. Altekar, felt constrained to record, as late as 1946, the decision of 'his own sister Mrs. Indirabai Madhav Udgaonkar' to commit *sati* 'within 24 hours of her husband's death, in spite of the pressing entreaties of all her relations'.[74] However, more sensationally, on 4 September 1987, Roop Kanwar attracted local adulation and the attention of the world's press with her apparent resolution to burn herself with her husband's body. Legal experts declared that Sec. 306 of the Penal Code, which punishes the abetment of suicide with a fine and up to 10 years in prison, combined with Article 51A of the Constitution, which guarantees the dignity of women, provided sufficient authority for the state to deal with *sati*. However, the State Government of Rajasthan, under pressure for failing to implement a Rajasthan High Court directive to stop public celebrations after Roop Kanwar's death, hastily enacted the 'Rajasthan *Sati* (Prevention) Act No. 40

---

[72] Jörg Fisch, *op. cit.*, pp. 446–69, 360–61.

[73] Lt. Col. H.M. Lawrence, Agent of the Governor General to the Northwest Territories and Resident at Lahore, to H.M. Elliot, Secretary to Government of India with the Governor General, Lahore, 25 November 1847, N.A.I., Foreign Department, Political Consultations 24 December 1847, No. 172; Notification by order of the Governor General from...the Ganges off Monghyr, 2 December 1847, N.A.I., Foreign Department, Political Consultations 24 December 1847, No. 173; also in India Political and Foreign Proceedings, 24 December 1847, Nos. 172–73, I.O.R., P/198/6.

[74] A.S. Altekar, *op. cit.*, p. 137.

of 1987'.[75] The Central Government followed suit with 'The Commission of Sati (Prevention) Act No. 3 of 1988'.[76]

Much to the dismay of rational observers such as Vasudha Dhagamwar, neither the Rajasthan State Government nor the Central Lok Sabha invited or consulted outside expert opinions. In Dhagamwar's words: 'The Bill was produced from under the table and, hey presto, we had a brand new law'. In vain did she and others plead that

> involuntary *sati* was covered by the Indian Penal Code and was treated as murder. At the most we needed an amendment to S. 300 Exception 5 to declare that in no case of *sati* would the woman be regarded as having given her consent. Perhaps a separate legislation was needed to deal with the offences of glorification and exploitation, but the burning/burying alive of the woman should be treated as murder.[77]

A comparison of the 1987–88 Acts with Beng. Reg. XVII 1829 yields some remarkable findings. Most striking is the fact that the preambles of Beng. Reg. XVII 1829 and The Commission of Sati (Prevention) Act No. 3 of 1988, enacted more than 150 years apart, are identical. They both declare that the practice of suttee/*sati* is 'revolting to the feelings of human nature' and 'is nowhere enjoined by…religion…as an imperative duty'.[78] As remarked by Dhagamwar, 'electoral compulsion obviously exacts the same price as the needs of a colonial government'.[79] The legislation of both 1829 and 1987–88 declared all *sati*s to be illegal whether voluntary or involuntary. However, somewhat ironically, the Rajasthan State and Central Government legislation of 1987–88 carries to fruition the suggestion made by the Bombay Government in the mid-1830s that the 'act of suttee' should be made 'criminal in the suttee'. According to the Sati Acts of 1987–88, the *sati* is transformed from a saint to a criminal. If she survives her fiery ordeal, she is liable to punishment in Rajasthan of from one to five years' im-prisonment and a fine of ₹5,000–20,000 or, in the rest of India, a prison term of up to six months and/or an undetermined fine. This focus on the

---

[75] H.C. Upreti and Nandini Upreti, *The Myth of Sati* (Delhi, 1991), pp. 112–14.

[76] Both acts are printed in Sakuntala Narasimhan, *Sati—A Study of Widow Burning in India* (Delhi, 1990), pp. 168–83.

[77] Vasudha Dhagamwar, *op. cit.*, p. 37.

[78] Beng. Reg. XVII for declaring the practice of Suttee, or of burning or burying alive Widows of Hindoos, illegal, and punishable by the Criminal Courts (passed 4 December 1829), I.O.R., V/8/21. Cf. The 'Rajasthan Sati (Prevention) Act No. 40 of 1987' and 'The Commission of Sati (Prevention) Act No. 3 of 1988' in Sakuntala Narasimhan, *op. cit.*, Appendix, pp. 168–83.

[79] *Ibid.*, pp. 37–38.

sati removes a considerable onus from all those who may have assisted her. Under the Indian Penal Code, those who promoted an involuntary *sati* were guilty of culpable homicide; under the new laws, because all *sati*s are considered voluntary, those who assist are liable for punishment for 'abetment', not culpable homicide or murder. In actual fact, the punishment for abetment is death or life imprisonment, as well as a fine—the same punishment as that for murder. In practise, as has already been demonstrated in Deorala, such a stiff punishment is unlikely to be enforced. Sec. 16 of the Rajasthan Act further compounds the injury to the modern *sati* by shifting all the burden of proof on to her. The Central Government does not prosecute the surviving *sati* in the same prejudicial way. After the criminalization of the *sati*, the greatest innovation of the 1987–88 laws is the criminalization of the act of glorifying a *sati*, with punishment of a prison term of from one to seven years, accompanied by a fine of from ₹5,000 to 30,000. Although an effort to enforce this part of the new legislation has already run afoul of the Rajasthan High Court, such an attack on the ethos which sustains the *sati* is perhaps the most positive contribution of the Indian Lok Sabha. Certainly, it is a tactic which Bentinck, Macaulay and their contemporaries would never have dared to pursue.

Curiously, in the wake of the hysteria over the death of Roop Kanwar, Ashis Nandy insists that one must 'respect…the ideas of sati at the mythological level' before acquiring 'the right to criticize all individual instances of sati'. He thereby scolds the 'shallow, pompous progressives and feminists who believe that one ought only to immolate oneself for secular causes…'. He then distinguishes between the 'simple faith of the pilgrims who thronged Deorala after the *sati* and the actions of the main organizers of the event, who profited so greatly from it'.[80] It is not surprising, then, that one of these feminists responds by observing that Nandy has come full circle from his first denunciation of *sati* in the early nineteenth century as a colonial phenomenon to an appropriation of 'colonial assumptions about sati'. To Veena Talwar Oldenburg, Ashis Nandy appears to be 'presiding over the debate among the natives (traditionalists versus reformers) like a colonial officer'.[81] The ultimate irony for feminists Veena Talwar Oldenburg and Lata Mani is the fact that the legislation of 1987–88, by criminalizing

---

[80] Ashis Nandy, 'Sati as Profit versus Sati as a Spectacle', in John Stratton Hawley ed., *op. cit.*, pp. 136–37.

[81] Veena Talwar Oldenburg, 'The Continuing Invention of the Sati Tradition', in John Stratton Hawley, ed., *op.cit.*, pp. 169–70.

the *sati*, herself, implicitly bestows upon her the very female agency which was denied her by colonial discourse. Horrified by the Roop Kanwar case, Venna Oldenburg insists that, far from being the agent of her destiny, Roop Kanwar was the victim of murder. Oldenburg finally concedes that 'the question of agency is delicate, complex, even contradictory, and it certainly cannot be conceptualized as neatly as it has been in liberal feminist theories in the West'.[82]

Vasudha Dhagamwar, in her survey of the policy of the British Raj towards *sati*, gives highest marks to the ill-fated regulation drafted by the Nizamut Adawlut in 1817 and to Beng. Reg. XVII 1829. But, curiously, she introduces a caveat to the general view that Beng. Reg. XVII forbade the practice of *sati*. First, she argues unexceptionally that 'Reg. XVII 1829 made it far more difficult for a suttee to be committed in dubious circumstances than it had previously been'. But then she quibbles: 'More important it made people, most of whom had only heard of the Regulation, feel *mistakenly* that the government had prohibited suttee' [author's emphasis].[83] Surely the fact that Beng. Reg. XVII 1829 declared all *sati*s to be illegal and punishable in the criminal courts meant that the practice was prohibited. Given Dhagamwar's professional distaste as a law lecturer for unnecessary laws, it is strange that she fails to notice the perfectly adequate Sec. 3 of Beng. Reg. VIII 1799 which deprived the accused murderer of the defence that the deceased had requested his or her own death. Ultimately, Dhagamwar argues that 'all offences created by the new legislation [1987–88] are in fact covered by existing criminal codes' and the most that was needed was a 'clarificatory bill'. Yet by her own analysis the Indian Penal Code was disappointing in its inclusion of 'culpable homicide by consent' as an exception to Sec. 300. Logically, then, the legacy of Beng. Reg. XVII 1829 should reign supreme with its ringing declaration that all *sati*s are illegal. For the totally legalistic mind, even that Regulation should have been overshadowed and made redundant by the initial modification of Muslim criminal law in Sec. 3 Beng. Reg. VIII 1799, despite the fact that it was not *sati* specific. Overall, the saga of special *sati* legislation reveals that a good law, to be effective, must have the support of popular opinion.

---

[82] Veena Talwar Oldenburg, 'The Roop Kanwar Case: Feminist Responses', in John Stratton Hawley, ed., *op.cit.*, pp. 117–19, 124.

[83] Vasudha Dhagamwar, *Law, Power and Justice* (New Delhi, London: 1992), p. 65.

Female Infanticide

In the first instance, female infanticide was a much more straightforward issue for the East India Company than *sati*. There was no scriptural sanction for it. Quite the contrary, Jonathan Duncan, when he first grappled with the problem as Resident of Benares, was able to cite from the 'Bretim Bywunt Purana' the most horrendous of Hindu punishments for the murderer of a female:

> Let all the four casts of Brahmin, Khetry, Bys and Sooder, know that the killing of a woman is the greatest of crimes; and that the person guilty of such act, having gone into the nerk or hell called Kal Sooter, shall remain there without nourishment, and be gnawed by worms for as many years as there are hairs on the woman's body, and shall remain there always in pain and misery; and afterwards, being born again in the lesser casts, shall become a leper for the same number of years; and thereafter becoming of the cast of Sooder, shall be afflicted with the zukhma, or vomiting of blood. Being again born of that cast, he becomes the servant or valet of a brahmin, by which he becomes exonerated.[84]

This fact, combined with the circumstance that the custom was discovered amongst the manly Rajkumar Rajputs of Jaunpur, inspired Duncan with the confidence to negotiate engagements whereby individual Rajkumar heads of families renounced the practice. He set forth these engagements without the objections from Governor General Cornwallis which the Collector of Shahabad had encountered at about the same time, when he wanted to dissuade a *sati*. He went on to discover that other Rajput clans, such as the *Durgavansi*s and *Raghuvansi*s, also practised female infanticide.

It was Duncan's engagements with the Rajkumars which marked the beginning of the East India Company's policy towards infanticide. Governor General John Shore publicized the issue in *Asiatic Researches*[85] and enshrined Duncan's apparent success with the Rajkumars in legal history by calling

---

[84] Translation of Extract from 'Bretim Bywunt Pooran', U.P.S.A., Duncan Records in the Commissioner's Office of Varanasi (C.O.V.), Resident's Proceedings 23 December 1789, fol. 337; also printed in *Parliamentary Papers* (1824) XXIII, Cmd. 426, p. 7.

[85] John Shore, 'On Some Extraordinary Facts, Customs and Practices of the Hindus', *Asiatic Researches*, Vol. IV (1795).

for enforcement of the agreements in Sec. XIII, Beng. Reg. XXI 1795.[86] To be sure, most of Beng. Reg. XXI 1795 was designed to restrain Brahmins in the district of Benares from making suicidal or murderous threats involving their female relations as a means of resisting legal process. Inasmuch as Beng. Reg. XXI was enacted on the same day as Beng. Reg. XVI 1795, Sec. XXIII of which exempted Benares Brahmins from capital punishment, the female infanticide clause might be viewed as the Government's determination to exercise some form of control over these privileged castes. Certainly, the Company's district officers were appalled by the extreme social arrogance of Benares Brahmins who thought nothing of confronting an officer on an errand of official coercion with a *koorh* or circular enclosure confining an elderly woman committed to a fiery sacrifice. Another flagrant abuse of their rank was the Brahmins' habit of sitting 'Dhurna' or camping on a particular doorstep equipped with the means of committing suicide in order to embarrass the householder into payment of a debt or charitable donation. Having recognized the Benares Brahmins' claim to immunity from capital punishment with Sec. 23 Beng. Reg. XVI 1795, the Government under Sir John Shore enacted Beng. Reg. XXI to curtail the Brahmins' extravagant gestures of resisting legal process by establishing a *koorh* or extorting payment by sitting *dhurna*. In Sec. 13 of the same act, Government extended its authority to embrace Duncan's engagements with the Rajkumars by declaring that 'if any Rajkoomar shall designedly prove the cause of the death of his female child' he shall be liable to trial for murder. Sec. 13 Beng. Reg. XXI 1795 gained further legal clout with the enactment of Sec. 2 Beng. Reg. VIII 1799 which modified the Muslim law of retaliation that had hitherto shielded from the death sentence parents and grandparents convicted of murdering their children. Henceforward the Nizamut Adawlut was to sentence a convicted murderer to death regardless of his/her relationship to the victim 'as if the futwa of the law officers had declared him liable to Kissas' or retaliation.[87]

After thus having his policy of dissuading the Rajkumars from killing their infant daughters endorsed in law, Jonathan Duncan was posted to Bombay as

---

[86] Bengal Regulation XXI for Preventing Brahmins in Province of Benares Establishing Koorhs, Wounding or Killing Their Female Relations or Children, or Sitting Dhurna and for Preventing the Tribe of Raujekoomars in That Province Killing Their Female Children (passed 27 March 1795), I.O.R., V/8/16, pp. 514–22.

[87] Beng. Reg. VIII for certain Modifications of the Mahomedan Law in Cases of Murder; and to explain Parts of Reg. XXI 1795 and Reg. V 1797 in Cases of Dhurna (passed 10 October 1799), I.O.R., V/8/17, p. 138.

Governor. Although this might seem to be a just promotion, M.V. Kale has observed that at the time Duncan was assigned to Bombay, 'even the separate existence of the Bombay Presidency was in doubt'. It was possible that, as Kale concludes, 'a posting on the Bombay establishment was looked upon as some kind of punishment'.[88] Meanwhile, in the N.W.P., Duncan's infanticide policy appeared to be stillborn. As remarked by Lalita Panigrahi, 'for nearly 40 years after these regulations almost nothing was done in the North-Western Provinces...to further investigate or suppress the crime'.[89] Within five to 10 years of his arrival in Bombay, Governor Duncan was reliably informed, first by a servant of the Nawab of Surat and then by Gujra Bai, a lady of the royal family of Baroda, that female infanticide prevailed in parts of Kathiawad and Kutch.[90] On 27 May 1805 Duncan instructed the Resident of Baroda, Major Alexander Walker, to include in his campaign to pacify the Jahrejas of the Kathiawar peninsula an attempt to persuade the guilty parties to sign agreements similar to those signed by the Rajkumars when Duncan was Resident of Benares. Thus began Maj. Walker's herculean efforts to suppress female infanticide among the Jahrejas. Although the Company is generally credited with humanitarian motives in its opposition to female infanticide, for some historians its territorial ambitions in the Kathiawar Peninsula cloud the purity of its motives. It is possible to argue, as K. Pakrasi does, that 'female infanticide offered an easy entry to Col. Walker and his forces inside a territory which was still then outside (the) direct authority of (the) Government of Bombay'.[91]

To be sure, the campaign against female infanticide among the Jahrejas was preeminently the work of Alexander Walker. Nevertheless, Jonathan Duncan was virtually elevated to sainthood for his initiatives in the East India Company's infanticide policy. At the base of the marble monument to his memory in the Bombay Cathedral, two cherubs display a scroll with the

---

[88] M.V. Kale, 'Jonathan Duncan—Governor of Bombay (1795–1811)' (unpublished Ph.D. thesis, Wilson College, Bombay, 1982), p. ii.

[89] Lalita Panigrahi, *British Social Policy and Female Infanticide in India* (New Delhi, 1972), p. 18.

[90] Report from Kerpa Ram, Minister of the Nawab of Surat, received by Mr Duncan in 1800, 'Correspondence Relating to Hindoo Infanticide, Part II', *Parliamentary Papers* (1824) XXIII, Cmd. 426, p. 19; Gajrabai to Duncan, 8 February 1804, *ibid*. [also recorded in Walker of Bowland Papers, National Library of Scotland, MS 13651, fol. 31]. In Gujra Bai's words, referring to her caste in Kutch, 'the daughters are not brought up, but drowned immediately at their birth in a vessel filled with milk'.

[91] Kanti B. Pakrasi, *Female Infanticide in India* (Calcutta, 1970), p. 9. Cf. L. Panigrahi who considers the East India Co.'s infanticide policy to have been 'guided by purely philanthropic and humanitarian aims'. L. Panigrahi, *op. cit.*, p. 44.

inscription 'Infanticide Abolished in Benares and Kattywar'; a contemporary scholar of Indian mythology, Edward Moor, dedicated his work to Jonathan Duncan, proclaiming that 'to You and YOU solely, is humanity indebted for her triumph over unnatural enthusiasm, in the entire and voluntary abolition of that most extraordinary practice, INFANTICIDE'.[92] Such a noble tribute to Jonathan Duncan is doubly ironic principally because, before many years had passed, it became clear that infanticide had, in fact, been abolished in neither Benares nor Kathiawar. Secondly, there are no private papers to indicate that Duncan's concern for the victims of female infanticide went beyond a pragmatic expression of simple decency.[93] In contrast, the private papers of Alexander Walker reveal exhaustive efforts to eliminate infanticide among the Jahrejas during his active career in India, as well as an intensive lifelong interest in the Company's female infanticide policy.

Duncan's possibly superficial experience with the Rajkumars left him with the impression that they were men of honour and therefore could be trusted to fulfil the Engagements which he concluded with them.[94] Alexander Walker, in his comprehensive report of 15 March 1808 to Duncan, revealed considerable insight into the character of the Jahrejas, as the result of extensive dealings with them. Walker recounted how Jahreja Jehajee of Moorbee 'offered to accede to my wishes by preserving his daughters, provided I would reduce Mallia and restore the village of Harralla of which he had been deprived by the Guicowar Government'. Thus Walker thought he had discovered 'the selfish and mercenary motives that attached the Jahrejahs to Infanticide'. In stark contrast with Duncan's lofty assessment of the character of the Rajkumars, Walker concluded that 'as my intercourse and knowledge of the Jahrejahs increased, every circumstance tended to shew that they followed Infanticide from mean and interested motives only'.[95] Quite apart from his negotiations with the Jahrejas, Walker made a careful study of the phenomenon of infanticide in world history. In his Report to Duncan, Walker queried why 'none of the Governments who have acquired ascendancy in

---

[92] Edward Moor, *The Hindu Pantheon* (London, 1810), p. 414.

[93] V.A. Narain scarcely mentions Duncan's work regarding female infanticide in his thesis. Vishnu Anugrah Narain, *Jonathan Duncan and Varanasi* (Calcutta, 1959), pp. 176–77.

[94] J. Duncan to Governor General, 26 April 1789, 'Correspondence Relating to Female Infanticide, Part I', *Parliamentary Papers* (1824) XXIII, Paper 426, p. 5.

[95] Memorandum from A. Walker, to Jonathan Duncan, March 1808, NLS/WB, MS 13659, fol. 19; for Jahajee's offer, see Appendix 5 to Walker's Report, to Duncan, 15 March 1808, printed in 'Correspondence Relating to Hindoo Infanticide, Part II', *Parliamentary Papers* (1824) XXIII, Paper 426, p. 61.

India have ever been induced to attempt the abolition of Infanticide'.[96] He later discovered that Jehangir encountered a tribe of Muslim converts from Hinduism who were addicted to putting a 'secret period...to the existence of the Daughters the moment they were born'. And Walker referred to the 'Ackbull Nameh' as his source for a decree by Jehangir that anyone who should commit infanticide 'in future should be put to the torture'. But Walker speculated that 'it is not likely either from the fluctuating character of the Moghul Government or from the confusion into which it was soon afterwards thrown, that a mere measure of humanity would be long persevered in'.[97] Thus, against a backdrop of healthy scepticism, Walker concluded Engagements with the Jahrejas which were modelled on the Engagements which Duncan had negotiated with the Rajkumars.

Unfortunately, India was deprived of the services of both Walker and Duncan at about the same time—Walker, retiring to Scotland in 1812 after nine years as Resident at Baroda,[98] and Duncan, dying in office in 1811 after an unprecedented 16-year term as Governor. With the exception of Major J.R. Carnac who was one of Walker's successors as Resident at Baroda, the officers responsible for enforcing the Jahreja and Rajkumar Engagements were men of lesser talents than their predecessors. In Bengal, as early as 1816, 'it was known...that Beng. Reg. XXI of 1795 had failed to suppress the practice'.[99] The only case to come before the Nizamut Adawlut resulted in an acquittal on account of the fact that the accused was 'unacquainted with the Regulations of the English Government' because the Proclamation required by Sec. 11 Ced. Prov. Reg. III 1804 had never been published in his *pergunnah*.[100] Capt. Ballantine, Carnac's assistant at Baroda, reported on 20 June 1817 that he had managed to compile a register of female births which he claimed to be 'the first paper of (its) kind' with the disappointing result that the Jahrejas of the Kathiawar peninsula had only produced

---

[96] Para. 296 of Walker's Report, to Duncan, 15 March 1808, *ibid.*, p. 51.

[97] Notes to Paras 202 and 276 of Walker's Report of March 1808 NLS/WB interleaved between fols 15 and 16 and between fols 24 and 25; the note concerning Jehangir's edict later formed a 'P.S.' to Walker's letter to Joseph Dart, Secretary to Court of Directors, 27 August 1819, 'Correspondence Relating to Hindoo Infanticide, Part III', *Parliamentary Papers* (1824) XXIII, Paper 426, p. 128.

[98] According to the N.L.S./W.B., Walker was Resident at Baroda 1801–10; cf. C.E. Buckland who states in his *Dictionary of Indian Biography* (New York: repr. 1968), p. 439 that Walker was Resident at Baroda 1802–7.

[99] L. Panigrahi, *op. cit.*, pp. 44, 85–86.

[100] Vakeel of Government vs. Bussaween, 26 April 1810, N.A. Rep. 1, p. 209.

63 female offspring over the period of 10 years which had elapsed since Walker negotiated his Engagements. The current Bombay Government seized upon Ballantine's report to cast aspersions upon 'the success generally, but inaccurately, attributed to Col. Walker's influence and exertions'.[101] Major Carnac protested that 'the responsibility and blame cannot rest with Col. Walker, but with the Governor in Council of Bombay'.[102] The Governor in question was Sir Evan Nepean who was distracted from the cause of suppression of infanticide by a petty scandal.

Before Nepean's Government attempted to use Walker as a scapegoat for its failed infanticide policy, Walker had tried to stir the Home Government into action. He confided to B.S. Jones, Secretary to the Board of Control, that as early as 1815 he had 'endeavoured to rouse the apathy of the Court of Directors' but had 'received no answer'.[103] Jones replied sympathetically that he was surprised the Directors had not informed Walker that 'the attention of the Bombay Government had been called to the barbarous practice of infanticide' in a paragraph adopted in March 1816 'probably in consequence' of Walker's letter. Jones further remarked that Capt. Ballantine had proposed that 'Guzerattee Mehtas or Writers should be employed for the purpose of detecting infractions of the engagements on the part of the Jahrejah Chieftains'.[104]

Infuriated by Ballantine's claim to have compiled the first register of surviving Jahrejah daughters, Walker marvelled at the fact that Capt. Ballantine had actually served Walker as translator in the preparation of similar registers nine years earlier. Thus Walker remarked that 'I have still one of those lists in my possession in Capt. Ballantine's handwriting which contains the names of 32 Jahrejahs who had saved their female children in 1809'.[105] Then, after

---

[101] F. Warden, Chief Secretary to Government of Bombay, to Capt. J.R. Carnac, Resident at Baroda, 19 September 1817, Bombay Political Consultations 24 September 1817, 'Correspondence Relating to Hindoo Infanticide, Part III', *Parliamentary Papers* (1824) XXIII, Paper 426, p. 112. See also MS 13899 N.L.S./W.B., fol. 201.

[102] Minute, 18 October 1817 cited in J.R. Carnac, Resident at Baroda, to F. Warden, Chief Secretary to Government of Bombay, 4 October 1817, Bombay Political Consultations 22 October 1817, *Parliamentary Papers* (1824) XXIII, Paper 426, fols 209–11.

[103] A. Walker to B.S. Jones, Assistant Secretary to Board of Control, Bowland, 2 December 1816, N.L.S./W.B., MS 13722, fol. 78.

[104] B.S. Jones, Assistant Secretary to Board of Control, to A. Walker, India Board, 15 January 1817, N.L.S./W.B., MS 13722, fol. 93.

[105] Note by Walker on Capt. Ballantine's Report of 20 June 1817, N.L.S./W.B., MS 13899, fol. 187.

learning of the Bombay Government's ingratitude for his earlier service, Walker addressed a virtual sermon to the Directors to insist that female infants must be saved without recourse to the coercive methods proposed by Ballantine. Walker recalled that when he retired from India, he had suggested that the infanticide campaign should be the subject of an annual report and 'the object of continual care and solicitude'. He touched upon a raw nerve in the ranks of Company servants. He observed:

> It is scarcely to be expected that the Jahrejahs will seek our society without greater encouragement than it is the habit of our Countrymen generally speaking to afford to the Natives and we must therefore visit them in their Villages.

He commented on the advantages possessed by the Government in 1819 with its establishment of revenue collectors and political agents compared with the 'new and imperfect influence' of the government of his day. Drawing the line between coercion and friendly insistence, Walker opposed 'the idea of an expensive agency' and 'the employment of spies'. He speculated that 'if the intercourse was as frequent as I have recommended, many things would be casually learnt and little indeed could be concealed'.

For those Jahrejahs who cooperated, Walker recommended 'the present of an inferior Turban,...of a small Box, of a pair of Spectacles, or of any other trifling article [which] would be prized by them as a mark of honor and as a profitable acquisition'.[106]

In the spirit of constancy which characterized their lasting friendship, B.S. Jones reassured Walker that 'the insinuation that the want of success [in enforcing the infanticide engagements] was owing to a failure of your influence and exertions, shall not pass without the reprehension which it deserves'.[107] Now all depended on the 'zeal' of the Bombay Government, especially the 'vigour and energy' of the newly appointed Governor Mountstuart Elphinstone.[108] A few years later, Walker must have been disheartened when an old friend reported a conversation with Dewsee Soonderjee, son of the agent who assisted in the negotiation of the original Jahrejah Engagements. Soonderjee claimed to have overheard Elphinstone declare: 'If they choose to kill their children, let them'.

---

[106] A. Walker to Directors, 19 July 1819, N.L.S./W.B., MS 13724, fols 77A–82.
[107] B.S. Jones to A. Walker, 25 September 1819, N.L.S./W.B., MS 13724, fol. 120.
[108] A. Walker to B.S. Jones, 8 April 1829, N.L.S./W.B., MS 13725, fols 71–72.

Elphinstone's Infanticide Fund

Walker's confidant explained away the words quoted by Soonderjee as an indication that the Governor 'thought it impolitic to make [female infanticide] a cause of public contention'.[109] Elphinstone's stature as a statesman was such that scarcely anyone wished to challenge his judgement. Indeed, Elphinstone was extremely cautious in his wish to avoid at all costs interference with the private lives of his Indian subjects. In his Minute of 9 January 1821, he rejected out of hand a proposal from Ballantine to hire agents to spy on suspected families. He argued that 'such a measure would lead to so much intrusion into the most private and domestic proceedings of the superior casts/among whom alone infanticide prevails/...that I do not think the chance of success would compensate for the disaffection it would create'.[110] However, Elphinstone did insist on the Government's right to impose 'the fines authorized by Col. Walker's agreements'. He instructed the new Political Agent at Kattywar 'to throw all fines levied on chiefs for other offences as well as for infanticide...into a fund to be distributed in portions to the children so preserved'.[111] Three years later, Capt. Barnewall reported triumphantly that in the seven years since Capt. Ballantine recorded 63 surviving females, the number of Jahrejah daughters had 'more than doubled' to the number of 266. Perversely, Elphinstone chastised Barnewall for failing to report on his collection of fines. In his Minute of 25 March 1825, he ordered that all fines received since his earlier minute 'should now be formed into a fund and distributed'.[112] In later correspondence with Walker, by then the Governor of St. Helena, Maj. Barnewall noted the hypocrisy of the Company's attempt to claim the moral high ground with the Jahrejas,

---

[109] Lt. Col. Elwood, to A. Walker, The Beehive, Bombay, 23 August 1826, N.L.S./W.B., MS 13898, fols 103–4.

[110] Elphinstone Minute 9 January 1821, Bombay Political Consultations 21 February 1821, *Parliamentary Papers* (1824) XXIII, Paper 426, p. 116. According to the private papers of J.P. Willoughby, Political Agent in Kattywar, Elphinstone enjoyed the support of his subordinates; in disapproving Ballantine's proposals, Willoughby added his voice to those of Carnac, Walker and Elphinstone. He observed further that Ballantine's system would 'be open to so many abuses on the part of the informers'. *Willoughby Papers*, I.O.L., MSS Eur. E 293, Bundle 3.

[111] Elphinstone Minute 9 January 1821, *op. cit.* Elphinstone also encouraged his agent to use his authority as revenue collector to influence the Jahrejah Chiefs, granting remission to Chiefs who produced daughters and refusing remission to uncooperative Chiefs.

[112] Elphinstone Draft Minute 25 March 1825, I.O.L., MSS Eur. F 88, Box 13C, 14.

inasmuch as 'our relations with their Chiefs and especially our demands for tribute excite passions that materially weaken our influence'.[113]

In actual fact, Elphinstone's Infanticide Fund was to become the cornerstone of the Bombay Government's policy on infanticide. Although at first almost the entire fund, collected over four years in the amount of ₹40,233, was diverted to cover the cost of the military expedition sent by the Company to suppress the Kumaon rebellion, by 1840 the Fund had accumulated over a lakh of rupees.[114] Such a substantial accumulation reflected a certain paralysis of thought at the highest level of policy making. Elphinstone's successor as Governor, John Malcolm continued Elphinstone's mixed approach of avoiding intrusion into his subjects' private lives while cultivating the support and influence of their leaders, particularly, in the case of infanticide, the Jahreja Chiefs. Perhaps as a result of his military background, Malcolm favoured a system of rewards and punishments for key individuals. Thus he lectured an assembly of Jahreja Chiefs at Booj in March 1830 on the 'enormity of the crime' of infanticide and threatened that the 'East India Company' would 'dissolve all connection with a people who persisted in it'.[115]

Taking his cue from his illustrious superiors, J.P. Willoughby, first as Assistant Resident at Baroda and then as Political Agent in Kattywar, laid the groundwork for an aggressive anti-infanticide policy in the mid-1830s. In 1834 he completed an ambitious and meticulous census of Jahreja offspring. This revealed a modest rise in the female infant population from '0' in 1805 to 696 in 1834, but male children still outnumbered female children by a proportion of two to one. This evidence of continued infanticide provoked Willoughby to issue a Proclamation to all the Jahreja Chiefs during the closing months of 1834 with the blessing of the Bombay Government. In this Proclamation Willoughby reminded the Chiefs of the Engagements they had signed with Col. Walker. He described those Engagements as a

---

[113] Maj. R. Barnewall to A. Walker, Cape of Good Hope, 20 June 1827, N.L.S./W.B. MS 13898, fols 124–25.

[114] R. Barnewall, Political Agent in Kattywar, to Bombay Government, Rajcote, 7 June 1825, Bombay Political Consultations 6 July 1825, No. 43, in *Parliamentary Papers* (1828) XXIII, Cmd. 548, p. 17; Capt. G. Legrand Jacob, Acting Political Agent in Katteewar, to J.P. Willoughby, Officiating Chief Secretary to Government of Bombay, Rajcote, 23 October 1841, Bombay Political Consultations 17 August 1842, No. 4148, in *Parliamentary Papers* (1843) XXXV, Cmd. 613, p. 368.

[115] Col. Henry Pottinger, Resident in Cutch, to C.E. Trevelyan, Deputy Secretary to Government, Fort William, 31 August 1835, Enclosure in Bombay Political Letter, 20 February 1839, No. 5, in *Parliamentary Papers* (1843) XXXV, Cmd. 613, p. 217.

'compact' whereby the Government guaranteed the Chiefs protection for their possessions and privileges provided that the Chiefs ceased 'to disgrace humanity by destroying their own helpless offspring at the moment of its birth'. Penalties for breaking this compact could extend to 'trial for the heinous crime of 'child murder' before the High Court of Criminal Justice recently established in Kattywar' and forfeiture of property. Also informers were to be 'rewarded in proportion to the rank and consequence of the party convicted'. To counter these alarming threats, the Proclamation commended three specific Chiefs and 15 individual Jahrejas for their record of preserving a substantial number of daughters. In conjunction with the Proclamation, Willoughby recommended rewards of revenue remissions and presents to deserving Jahrejas.[116] True to his word, Willoughby saw to it that nearly ₹30,000 from the Infanticide Fund were distributed among the three meritorious Jahreja Chiefs. And also from the Infanticide Fund came rewards for informers in three infanticide convictions by the High Court in 1834–5. The most spectacular of these cases involved Suraji, Jahreja Chief of Rajkot. He incurred a fine of ₹12,000 and a warning that repetition of the offence would bring forfeiture of his estate. From the Government's point of view, as expressed by Willoughby's recommendation and approved by the Court of Directors, 'justice' was 'tempered with mercy'.[117] Thus the fine for the most inferior Jahreja in the three cases was limited to ₹100 and, with a true Benthamite preference for prevention of the crime rather than vindictive punishment, Governor Sir Robert Grant withdrew his proposal to disinherit any future sons born to Suraji without proper notification to the authorities. But, from the Jahrejas' point of view, as argued by Pakrasi, the open trial of Suraji, a Chief of high rank and wealth, was an affair of 'utter humiliation and disgrace'.[118]

In the midst of these proceedings Willoughby was promoted to serve as Chief Secretary to the Bombay Government. His successor in Kattywar, James Erskine, sharply criticized Willoughby's sudden enforcement of the

---

[116] J.P. Willoughby, Political Agent Katteewar, to C. Norris, Chief Secretary to Bombay Government, Rajcote, Enclosing Draft of Proclamation on subject of Female Infanticide in Katteewar, 24 September 1834, Bombay Political Consultations, 26 November 1834, in *Parliamentary Papers* (1843) XXXV, Cmd. 613, pp. 104, 106–8.

[117] J.P. Willoughby, Political Agent, Katteewar, to C. Norris, Chief Secretary to Government of Bombay, Porebunder, 12 April 1835, Bombay Political Consultations, 3 June 1835, in *Parliamentary Papers* (1843) XXXV, Cmd. 613, p. 151.

[118] K.B. Pakrasi, *op. cit.*, p. 93.

Jahrejas' Infanticide Engagements. He argued that the trial of Suraji had transformed the Rajkot Chief into a martyr among his people, while lack of Government protection for witnesses had resulted in the mysterious death of three out of five Rajkot informers. In fact, it was later proved that the principal informer in the Rajkot case was poisoned by Suraji's mother. She was later sent to prison by the Company's courts and the informer's family was compensated with ₹1,000 from the Infanticide Fund, some silver bangles and a 50 per cent remission of tribute. As the people resorted to ever more secretive ways to commit infanticide, it was hardly surprising that out of eight infanticide cases brought before the Court in 1836, there were no convictions. Erskine argued effectively that Willoughby's brutal measures were no answer to the deep rooted social causes of infanticide in the Jahreja community. He speculated that even Col. Walker had not anticipated 'what an enormous revolution the abolition of the practice would create in the Rajpoot community'. For, it was the fierce and irrational pride of Jahreja Chiefs that dictated ruinous wedding expenses for the impoverished and illiterate bulk of their tribe. This fact had been documented by Barnewall who predicted in his report of June 1825 that by 1837, 183 Jahreja daughters from the lowest rank would become eligible for marriage at a cost of nearly three lakhs of rupees. Conversely, the Government's willingness to use the Infanticide Fund to finance the marriages of needy Jarehjas indirectly encouraged 'a relaxed system of moral duty'. As Erskine sensibly queried, why could not the Government undercut the costly social pretensions of the Jahrejas by insisting that their Chiefs refuse to give their daughters in marriage to any tribe which refused to 'give them their daughters in return'.[119] To be sure, it was unlikely that the Company could so easily reverse the Jahrejas' historic degradation at the time of the Muslim conquest of Sind. Tainted by intermarriage with Muslims before their migration to Kutch and Kattywar, the Jahrejas had found that other Rajput clans would not accept their claim to high rank nor would they accept Jahreja daughters unaccompanied by impressive dowries.[120]

Ironically for Erskine, his voluminous despatch to the Bombay Government criticizing the coercive and sumptuary measures of Willoughby's Kattywar administration was received and answered by Willoughby himself.

---

[119] J. Erskine, Political Agent in Kattywar, to Chief Secretary, Bombay Government, Rajkote, 30 June 1837, Enclosure in Bombay Politcal Letter, 20 February 1839, No. 5, in *Parliamentary Papers* (1843) XXXV, Cmd. 613, pp. 197, 203–4, 209.

[120] James Tod, *Annals and Antiquities of Rajasthan* (New Delhi, repr. 1971) p. 507.

Of course, Willoughby was not pleased by Erskine's condemnation of 'almost every measure that has been adopted for the suppression of infanticide'. He either belittled Erskine's proposed tactics as 'auxiliary to those now in force' or, dismissed them totally as in the case of Erskine's proposal to grant the Jahrejas a two-year amnesty from all investigation in order to win their cooperation. However, on behalf of the Bombay Government, he warmly embraced Erskine's concluding emphasis on 'national education' as the only effective way for the Government to eradicate the crime. To illustrate his point, Erskine had noted that only eight or nine of the 28 Jahreja Chiefs to whom Willoughby had sent his Proclamation in 1834 could actually read it. The Bombay Government and the Court of Directors approved the policy shift in the direction of education but at the same time firmly endorsed Willoughby's system of investigation and punishment.[121]

Relative success of the Bombay policy concerning infanticide among the Jahrejas was apparent in the next major report on the subject by Erskine's successor, Capt. G. LeGrand Jacob. Capt. Jacob was able to report for the year 1840–41 the birth of 32 more girls than boys. However, he noted four cases of inferior Jahrejas who were acquitted of the charge of infanticide and objected to the harassment which necessarily attended the Government's investigations. He called for educational expenditure out of the Infanticide Fund with the suggestion that the Fund be the source of prizes for an essay contest on the subject of infanticide.[122] Willoughby, on behalf of the Bombay Government, endorsed the idea of an essay contest with the caveat that, given the absence of schools in Kattywar, the contest should be initiated among the scholars of the Native Education Society in Bombay, the prize essays being later printed and circulated in Kattywar. On 20 November 1844 it was announced that Shri Bhawoo Dajee, an Assistant Teacher in the Elphinstone Institution had won first prize for his essay entitled 'He who loves sin and

---

[121] Enclosures in Bombay Political Letter, 20 February 1839, No. 5, in *Parliamentary Papers* (1843) XXXV, Cmd. 613; Memo by J.P. Willoughby, Secretary to Bombay Government, 8 September 1838, p. 268; J. Erskine, Political Agent in Kattywar, to Secretary, Bombay Government, 30 June 1937, pp. 210–13; Minutes of Governor and Members of Council, 20 and 22 September 1838, pp. 286–87. See also Political Despatch to Bombay, 13 May 1840, *Parliamentary Papers* (1843) XXXV, Cmd. 613, p. 27.

[122] Capt. G. Legrand Jacob, Acting Political Agent in Katteewar, to J.P. Willoughby, Officiating Chief Secretary to Government of Bombay, Rajcote, 23 October 1841, Bombay Political Consultations 17 August 1842, No. 4148, in *Parliamentary Papers* (1843) XXXV, Cmd. 613, pp. 365–66, 368; Memorandum by J.P. Willoughby, Secretary to Government of Bombay, 1 June 1842, *Parliamentary Papers* (1843) XXXV, Cmd. 613, p. 395.

commits Infanticide shall be condemned to the Hell called "Tamisra"'.[123] Ultimately the Bombay Government approved the grant of a lakh of rupees from the Infanticide Fund for education. Meanwhile Jahreja Chiefs founded a Vernacular School in Rajkot.

The Company's Directors were so impressed by the evident success of the Bombay Government in dealing with Infanticide that they instructed other presidencies to learn what they could from the Bombay system.[124] However, district officers on the spot already knew that the degraded circumstances of the Jahrejas could not be compared with the demands of Bhats and Charans which escalated marriage expenses in Rajputana or with the rivalry among Rajkumar clans in the N.W.P. Nevertheless, L. Wilkinson, the Political Agent at Lehore, and Erskine in Kattywar were already comparing notes on the proposal for a conference of Jahreja chiefs on the subject of infanticide after a similar conference organized by Wilkinson among Rajput chiefs on 26 January 1836. Yet, Erskine observed that his predecessor 'Col. Barnewall...and many other able servants of Government' held the 'honest opinion...that [female infanticide] was not a safe subject to investigate and legislate upon'.[125]

Buttressing the Bombay Government's faith in education was the knowledge that the pretentious Jahrejas were but one of numerous Rajput clans, some of which had shown remarkable leadership on social issues such as female infanticide. Maharaja Beejee [Bukht] Singh had prohibited female infanticide in the mid-eighteenth century.[126] In fact, his decree served as a model for the 45th Article of the Jodhpur Code of Rules enacted in 1839 to regulate the fees of the Bhats and Charans or genealogical bards who were in the habit of charging extortionate sums for their services at weddings. Similarly, in Jaipur Maharajah Jey Singh had promulgated a law in 1731 prohibiting female infanticide and regulating marriage expenses so that they

---

[123] J.P. Willoughby, Chief Secretary to Bombay Government, to E.H. Townsend, Secretary to Government in the Revenue Department, Rev. G. Pigott, Secretary, Bombay Education Society, and C. Morehead, Secretary, Board of Education, 20 November 1844, Reprinted in K.B. Pakrasi, *op. cit.*, pp. 213–14.

[124] Para. 43, Political Despatch to Government of India, 16 May 1838, *Parliamentary Papers* (1843) XXXV, Cmd. 613, p. 5.

[125] J. Erskine, Political Agent in Kattywar, to Chief Secretary, Bombay Government, 30 June 1837, Bombay Political Consultations 20 February 1839, No. 5, in *Parliamentary Papers* (1843) XXXV, Cmd. 613, p. 198.

[126] Extract Notes by Lt. Col. Sutherland in the Joudpore Code of Rules, 3 January 1841, Enclosure in India Political Letter 12 August 1841, No. 43, in *Parliamentary Papers* (1843) XXXV, Cmd. 613, p. 57.

did not exceed one year's income from the estate of the bride's father.[127] This was the basis of a proclamation issued in 1844 by the Jaipur Council of Regency limiting marriage expenses by requiring the father of the bridegroom to pay 'a tythe' of the produce of his estate. And, in an effort to prevent Bhats and Charans from exploiting marriages outside their home territories, the Jaipur Council decreed that 'the father of the bride shall feed for one day all the Charans etc. of his own country who may attend the ceremony'.[128] The Governor General's political agents in Rajputana thus had the gratifying experience of gaining the cooperation of prominent Rajput rulers. What was particularly objectionable about the Bhats and Charans was their extortionate methods whereby they would resort to self mutilation—or even human sacrifice—reminiscent of the Brahmins' practice of *dhurna* in Benares. It was said that in Marwar there were more deaths by this means than by *sati*s.[129]

The Presidency Governments, the Supreme Government and the Home Government in London were in debt to the experience of district officers. It was increasingly apparent that there was no one-uniform procedure which could be followed across India in order to eliminate female infanticide. The Political Agent in Kathiawar, after reading reports from Rajputana about the limitation of gifts to Bhats and Charans, objected to the establishment of 'any scale of gifts to Bhats and Charans, as it would…lead to endless disputes, and entail expenditure on the Rajpoots which no future change could diminish.[130] Even Governor General William Bentinck, admitted that, if the practice of *sati* prevailed 'in the upper instead of the lower provinces, in the midst of a bold and manly people, I might speak with less confidence upon the question of safety'.[131] Thus, Bentinck followed in the footsteps

---

[127] J. Ludlow, Political Agent Jyepoor, to Lt. Col. J. Sutherland, Agent of the Governor General for the States of Rajpootana, 30 October 1847, India Political and Foreign Proceedings, 20 November 1847, No. 78, I.O.R., P/198/4.

[128] Memo furnished by the Council of Regency of Jypoor to Political Agent, 12 April 1844, India Political and Foreign Proceedings, 30 November 1844, No. 153, I.O.R., P/196/64.

[129] H.H. Greathed, Political Agent Jodhpoor, to Lt. Col. J. Sutherland, Agent of the Governor General for the States of Rajpootana, 11 September 1847, India Political and Foreign Proceedings, 24 December 1847, No. 144, I.O.R., P/198/6, cited in L. Panigrahi, *op. cit.*, pp. 70–71.

[130] A. Malet, Political Agent in Kathiawar, to J.P. Willoughby, Chief Secretary to Government of Bombay, 14 November 1845, N.A.I., Foreign Political Consultations, 11 April 1846, No. 26, fols 9–10.

[131] Minute on Sati, 8 November 1829, in C.H. Philips, ed., *The Correspondence of Lord William Bentinck, Governor General of India 1828–1835* (Oxford, 1977), p. 339.

of Elphinstone and Malcolm in leaving the issue to education and in confining his actions to commendation of individual leaders who came to his notice on account of their opposition to infanticide. He wrote personally to congratulate the Maharana of Udaipur, and his deputy in Agra, C.T. Metcalfe, wrote similar letters to the Raja of Bundi and the Raj Rana of Kotah.[132] There were occasional breakthroughs, as when Governor General Auckland, not known for his bold initiatives in social policy, personally encouraged the Political Agent in Jodhpur to investigate the matter. The unexpected result was the discovery of Maharaja Beejee [Bukht] Singh's prohibition of female infanticide in Marwar.[133]

Bold initiatives which included proposals of fresh legislation against infanticide were summarily rejected by the India Law Commission. In 1837 both F.J. Shore and the Government of Madras suggested a new enactment on the subject of infanticide. The Law Commission rejected these proposals in Macaulayesque style with the abrupt comment: 'This is a subject which belongs to the Penal Code'.[134]

Coercive Policies in the Northwestern Provinces

Meanwhile, in the N.W.P. where Jonathan Duncan had first confronted the proud infanticidal Rajkumars, the difficulties of district officers trying to enforce Sec. 11 Ceded Provinces Reg. III 1804 produced a pressure cooker of frustration. After decades of a paralysis of will at the highest levels of Government to enforce anti-infanticide legislation, the evangelically oriented Magistrate of Azimgurh, James Thomason, resolved to revive Government interest in the problem. He studied the records and discovered

---

[132] W. Bentinck to Maharana of Udaipur; C.T. Metcalfe to Rajah of Boondee and Raj Rana of Kotah, 28 January 1834, Bengal Political Proceedings 23 January 1834, Nos. 22–24, I.O.R., P/127/9.

[133] J. Sutherland, Agent of the Governor General for the States of Rajpootana, to J.C. Melville, Secretary, East India House, Cape Town, Cape of Good Hope, 28 June 1845, India Political and Foreign Proceedings 26 December 1846, No. 367, I.O.R., P/197/50, cited in L. Panigrahi, *op. cit.*, p. 71. L. Panigrahi credits Auckland with greater imagination in the area of social reform than I do.

[134] J.P. Grant, Officiating Secretary, Indian Law Commission, to R.D. Mangles, Officiating Secretary to Government in the Legislative Department, 30 March 1838, N.A.I., Legislative Department, Law Proceedings, Consultation 5 November 1838, No. 10. Also in India Legislative Proceedings 5 November 1838, No. 10, I.O.R., P/206/96. See also Letter from Chief Secretary to Government of Fort St. George, 14 April 1837, India Legislative Proceedings, 15 May 1837, Nos. 1–2, I.O.R., P/206/88.

that the last officer to address the issue was Mr Cracroft, Magistrate of Jaunpur. In 1817 when Governor General Hastings had drawn attention to the ineffectual Infanticide legislation, Cracroft 'used the most vigorous and energetic measures for the detection and punishment of the offence'. Hastings' Government, stymied by the conviction that further legislation was inexpedient, nevertheless rebuked Cracroft for his attempt at 'forcible suppression of this practice'.[135] Magistrates were expected to confront offenders in the courts. But Thomason observed that Cracroft's measures had entirely failed because 'the crime arises out of their Social State, and a Police is powerless for the correction of this'.[136] In the Deogaon *pergunnah* of Azimgurh, Thomason embarked upon a strategy of 'moral influence' among the Bais Rajputs. As described by a colleague, Thomason was 'ably seconded by the Tehseeldar', Meer Muksood Ally, who secured the cooperation of the *zamindars*. Intimately acquainted 'with many of them', Ally 'would…have been informed had the newborn infants come to an untimely end'.[137] However, the revered Meer Muksood Ally of Azimgurh, was unable to win the cooperation of infanticidal Rajputs in Jaunpur, prompting the Magistrate there to require the registration of all female births with the police.

By the time Thomason had become Lt. Governor of the N.W.P., he found himself at odds with officers who felt it necessary to resort to coercive measures. Thus when the Joint Magistrate of Mainpuri directed the Chouhan Rajputs of his district to send the bodies of female infants to the Civil Surgeon for examination, Thomason objected and suspended the order. He argued that such a command would 'defeat its own end' and 'supply a fresh reason for the concealment of the birth of a female child'.[138]

The Court of Directors approved Thomason's decision.[139] But frustration continued. In Etawah District the officiating Magistrate E.H.C. Monckton

---

[135] W.B. Bayley, Secretary to Bengal Government, to Magistrate of Jaunpore, 25 November 1817, Bengal Judicial Criminal Proceedings (W.P.), 25 November 1817, No. 18, I.O.R., P/133/17.

[136] J. Thomason, Magistrate, Azimgurh Zillah, to F. Currie, Commissioner of Circuit, 5th Division, Camp Alhow, 12 February 1836, U.P.S.A. Lucknow, C.O.V., Benares Judicial Files, Female Infanticide I, Basta 132, Vol. 4, fol. 29.

[137] H.C. Tucker, Acting Magistrate, Azimgurh, to E.P. Smith, Officiating Commissioner, 5th Division, Ghazeepoor, 27 June 1838, U.P.S.A. Lucknow, C.O.V., B.J.F., Fem. Infant. I, fol. 36.

[138] J. Thornton, Secretary to Government, N.W.P., to F.H. Robinson, Commissioner, Agra Division, Agra, 16 October 1844, U.P.S.A. Lucknow, B.J.F., Fem. Infant. I, fol. 44.

[139] Despatch, 19 January 1848, U.P.S.A. Lucknow, C.O.V., Benares Judicial Files, Female Infanticide I, Basta 132, Vol. 4, fol. 47.

managed, on the one hand, to convene successfully a *panchayat* of Thakurs which agreed on 11 September 1849 to expel from their caste anyone who committed infanticide as well as those who attempted to evade the issue by sending their wives out of the state for the actual birth. On the other hand, he organized a system of espionage using female Government officers with the ultimate end of making the surviving daughters wards of Government and of sending all infant corpses to the Sudder Station with the midwife. Monckton's coercive orders were immediately rescinded by his superior, Commissioner F.H. Robinson, who remarked that 'if the child lived the family would be degraded by being [*sic*] brought up by the "Feringees"'. Also such an approach would be 'siezed upon by the many agitators who maintain that Government are only waiting for an opportunity...for forcible conversion of the people to Christianity'.[140] Thomason supported Robinson's judgement that Monckton had 'acted judiciously in assembling a Punchayet' but had 'erred' in attempting to organize 'a system of inquisition which would have been oppressive'. Thomason reflected that 'legislation on this subject must be ineffectual as long as it is opposed by the custom of the tribe'.[141] Thomason's ideas were most successfully implemented by Charles Raikes who, as Magistrate at Mainpuri, organized in November 1851 a meeting of all the Chouhan Chiefs and the Raja in order to curtail marriage expenses according to Chouhan rank. A second meeting was convened in December of Rajputs from surrounding districts. The atmosphere rivalled that of a princely durbar with favourable press notices in *The Agra Messenger* and with the net result of a resolution signed by 360 Chiefs and village headmen.[142]

But Lt. Governor Thomason was not able to impose his influence universally. In his police report of 27 April 1852, the Magistrate of Agra, M.R. Gubbins, recorded remarkable success over a period of just seven

---

[140] F.H. Robinson, Commissioner, Agra Division, to J. Thornton, Secretary to Government, N.W.P., Agra, 11 October 1849, U.P.S.A. Lucknow, C.O.V., Benares Judicial Files, Female Infanticide I, Basta 132, Vol. 4, fols 50–51; Robinson personally rebuked Monckton in a letter dated 23 July 1849, U.P.S.A. Lucknow, C.O.V., Benares Judicial Files, Female Infanticide I, Basta 132, Vol. 4, fol. 54; for a translation of the proceedings of the *panchayat* held at Etawah 11 September 1849, see U.P.S.A. Lucknow, C.O.V., Benares Judicial Files, Female Infanticide I, Basta 132, Vol. 4, fols 62–65.

[141] J. Thornton, Secretary to Government, N.W.P., to Officiating Commissioner, Agra Division, Agra, 7 December 1849, U.P.S.A. Lucknow, C.O.V., Benares Judicial Files, Female Infanticide I, Basta 132, Vol. 4, fol. 66.

[142] C. Raikes, Magistrate, Mainpuri, to W.H. Tyler, Commissioner, Agra, Mainpuri, 17 November 1851; *The Agra Messenger*, 22 November and 13 December 1851 and W.H. Tyler, Commissioner, Agra, to E. Thornton, Secretary to Government, N.W.P., 20 December 1851, I.O.R., *Board's Collections*, F/4/2537, #147526.

months in the Thakur Villages of Thannah Bah Pinnahut as the result of a system of rigorous registration and surveillance. In 'suspected' villages, headmen and *chaukidars* were required to report every pregnancy by the fifth month, to prevent if possible the removal of a woman to another village for her confinement, to record every female birth and in the case of the death of a female child, 'to forward the body for the Examination of the Civil Surgeon'. Gubbins remarked further that he had notified the Thakurs in his district of the meeting convened by Raikes at Mainpuri and that most had attended. However, he remained unimpressed by the 'Vernacular Resolutions against excessive expenditure at Marriages and in favour of resisting the exactions of the Bhats'. He reported 'the opinion generally entertained that the very parties who signed the pledge are little likely to be bound by it'.[143] Thomason could not help but acknowledge the 'considerable effect' of the 'stringent measures adopted by Mr Gubbins'. Yet he questioned 'whether Mr Gubbins is acting prudently in…looking only to the restrictive and coercive measures of his powerful police, for its direct prevention'.[144]

At first, the contrasting methods of Raikes and Gubbins appeared to produce excellent results. Thus the Raja of Neemrana, the 'head of all the Chowhan Rajpoots in the Doab', promised to 'cause the Chowhans of my Province to sign an agreement'.[145]

Yet within a very few years, district officers began to suspect that the practice of female infanticide was flourishing. In 1854 the Commissioner of Benares reported his evening stroll through a village 'where in the Rugbuns families there were only 5 girls to 90 boys'.[146] The officiating joint magistrate of Jaunpur noted huge numerical discrepancies between male and female births despite the efforts 'made many years ago by…Mr Thomason when

---

[143] Extract from Police Report of M.R. Gubbins, Magistrate of Agra, 27 April 1852, U.P.S.A. Lucknow, B.J.F., Fem. Infant. I, fols 91–93.

[144] S.E. Marston, Tehsildar of Bah Pinnahut, to M.R. Gubbins, Collector and Magistrate of Agra, 27 April 1852, Pinnahut, U.P.S.A. Lucknow, C.O.V., Benares Judicial Files, Female Infanticide I, Basta 132, Vol. 4, fol. 96; extract, W. Muir, Secretary to Government, N.W.P., to W.H. Tyler, Commissioner of Agra, 21 August 1852, U.P.S.A. Lucknow, C.O.V., Benares Judicial Files, Female Infanticide I, Basta 132, Vol. 4, fol. 101.

[145] William Muir, Secretary to Government N.W.P., to Agent of the Governor General for Rajpootana, Agra, 11 June 1852, U.P.S.A. Lucknow, C.O.V., Benares Judicial Files, Female Infanticide I, Basta 132, Vol. 4, fols 80–81; Purport of Letter from Raja of Neemrana to Agent of the Governor General for Rajpootana, 10 September 1852, U.P.S.A. Lucknow, C.O.V., Benares Judicial Files, Female Infanticide I, Basta 132, Vol. 4, fol. 107.

[146] Circular No. 59, H.C. Tucker, Commissioner of Benares, 5th Division, to Each Magistrate in the 5th Division, Camp Syepoor, 10 November 1854, U.P.S.A. Lucknow, C.O.V., Benares Judicial Files, Female Infanticide I, Basta 132, Vol. 4, fol. 150.

Magistrate of Azimgurh through his subordinate Muksood Ali Khan, Tehsildar of Deogaon'.[147]

The magistrates of the infanticidal districts of the N.W.P. were the same magistrates who had been granted extraordinary powers of committing accused thugs before the courts. Although M.R. Gubbins was able to boast of 'effecting [the] conviction by the Court of Nizamut Adawlut' of 'Suddakoor...the first in which an inhabitant of Bah Pinnahut has ever been punished for this crime, since the accession of the British rule', his experience was an exception to the rule.[148] Not only were very few infanticide cases ever brought to trial but also those that were committed for trial usually ended in an acquittal. Even in the case of M.R. Gubbins' boast, the Sudder Judge objected in principle to the order issued by Gubbins in the Thannah of Pinnahut for the registration of every pregnancy. Judge A.W. Begbie declared such an order to be 'unwarranted by any law'.[149] District officers began to seethe in frustration over the mixed signals which they received from their superiors.

Even Governor General Dalhousie indulged in obfuscation when he expressed his 'opinion that anything like open supervision or secret espionage on the part of the police should be avoided as likely to lead to extortion and oppression'. Nevertheless, Dalhousie urged that Government 'condemnation of this horrible crime...be openly proclaimed and enforced by denunciation of certain punishment upon those who are convicted of offending'.[150] In this instance, Dalhousie was specifically addressing his chosen officers in the Punjab. He was concerned to avoid any system of espionage. He was keen to combine the coercive practice of proclamation and punishment for the guilty, in the style of Willoughby of Bombay, with rewards and honours for the innocent. He also supported C. Raikes who, as Commissioner of Lahore, proposed the meeting of infanticidal chiefs, be they Rajput or Khatra, which was held at Amritsar on 31 October 1853 and

---

[147] S.N. Martin, Officiating Joint Magistrate, Jaunpoor, to C.T. Le Bas, Magistrate of Jaunpoor, 7 February 1855, *ibid.*, fol. 146.

[148] M.R. Gubbins, Magistrate, Agra, 'Memorandum on the Practise of Female Infanticide among the Rajpoot Tribes in Zillah Agra', 23 January 1854 and 'Agra Police Report for 1852, No. 20, 18 March 1853', in *Selections from the Records of Government, North-Western Provinces*, Vol. 2, I.O.R., V/23/124 No. 1812, 3rd ed. (Repr. of Vol. 3, Part 15, Art. 16, No. 1708), Fiche No. 2783, pp. 38, 29; cf. Government vs. Mussumat Sadakour (5 November 1852), N.W.P. N.A. Rep. 2 Part 2, I.O.R., V/22/657, pp. 1463–66.

[149] Government v. Mussumat Sadakour, *ibid.*, p. 1466.

[150] Minute by Gov. General Dalhousie, 8 August 1853, I.O.R., *Board's Collections*, F/4/2564 #151171, fol. 72.

was hailed as an enormous success with multiple agreements for limiting marriage expenses and regulating intercaste weddings. M.G. Campbell, the Officiating Magistrate of Azimgurh, remarked on the essential 'incompatibility' of these various tactics. Campbell argued strongly for an infanticide policy using both compulsion and persuasion. While he was convinced that the Rajput chiefs must be induced to be 'content with equal marriages when they have not the means of purchasing higher rank', he insisted, at the same time, that 'till we have some means of proving by the evidence required by our law...that a certain child was born and murdered by certain persons,...the denunciation of certain punishment must be nugatory'.[151]

The Magistrate of Jaunpur forcefully backed Campbell's suggestion that Government appoint an officer especially responsible for the suppression of Infanticide. C.T. Le Bas, as the committing officer in the case of Govt. vs. Lulloo tried before the Sessions Judge in December 1854, exploded with frustration over the fact that the Jury first convicted the accused on the basis of a full confession and then acquitted him because the body was never found so that 'there was no legal proof that the child had been alive'. The Sessions Judge had dissented from the Jury but he argued that because the accused was a Rajkumar, his act of pouring the poisonous milk of the Mudar plant into the infant's mouth should be seen more as a 'social custom' than a 'crime'. When the case was referred to the N.W.P. Nizamut Adawlut, one of the Judges supported the Sessions Judge's recommendation of a very light sentence of five years' imprisonment. But Judge Begbie recalled Sec. 13 Beng. Reg. XXI 1795 and Sec. 11 Ced. Prov. Reg. III 1804 in support of his argument that 'the prisoner and his tribe...cannot...plead, in the face of laws promulgated 50 and 60 years ago, that ample warning has not been given, of the determination of the legislature to visit with the severest penalties offences of this nature'. Begbie proposed a sentence 'only short of death'—namely, 'imprisonment for life in transportation'. The third Sudder Judge effected a compromise sentence of 10 years with the argument that 'penal measures, to be repressive, cannot wholly disregard the opinions and feelings of the people...marked in this case by the acquittal pronounced by a jury of 2 Mosulmans and 1 Hindoo in the face of a clear confession'.[152] C.T. Le Bas, the infuriated and frustrated magistrate, averred:

---

[151] M.G. Campbell, Officiating Magistrate Azimgurh, to H.C. Tucker, Superintendent of Police, 5th Division, Benares, Azimgurh, 7 October 1854, U.P.S.A. Lucknow, B.J.F., Fem. Infant. I, U.P.S.A. Lucknow, C.O.V., Benares Judicial Files, Female Infanticide I, Basta 132, Vol. 4, fols 133–34.

[152] Govt. v. Lulloo (2 February 1855), N.W.P. N.A. Rep. 5, Part I, I.O.R., V/22/664, pp. 135–40.

If two or three commissioners were appointed for the N.W.P. and armed with ample powers, such as were entrusted to the Commissioners for the Suppression of Thuggee, in five or six years the practice of female infanticide would be eradicated. If ever there was a case for exceptional legislation this is one.[153]

Draft Legislation in Northwestern Provinces

In September 1855 as an apparent response to the frustration expressed by Magistrates Campbell and Le Bas, Lt. Governor Colvin appointed W.R. Moore Special Commissioner for Investigating the Extent of Female Infanticide in Benares Division. As Infanticide Commissioner, Moore was invested with the full powers of a Joint Magistrate and he was expected to 'suggest practical means in discriminating cases of infanticide from death of mere illness…or accident'.[154] When Moore embarked upon his assignment, he immediately requested the 'power of punishment…for Infanticide Rajputs' who fraudulently substituted 'girls of other castes' for their own daughters.[155] While assessing the alleged success of the preventive measures promoted by Thomason, Moore came to the conclusion that the infanticidal Rajput clans lacked the moral fortitude to abandon their 'addiction to ancient usage' and were in need of extensive and intensive police surveillance. He recommended that police *thana*s be established within a mile of every village at a ratio of one policeman per 50 married Rajput families. A midwife on fixed salary was to assist the police by staying in the house of confinement for a few days after the female births and then by returning for daily visits to aid the police officer in making daily reports of the children's health. To undermine deliberate deception by fathers,

---

[153] C.T. Le Bas, Magistrate, Jaunpoor, to H.C. Tucker, Commissioner, 5th Division, Benares, Jaunpoor, 26 February 1855, U.P.S.A. Lucknow, B.J.F., Fem. Infant. I, U.P.S.A. Lucknow, C.O.V., Benares Judicial Files, Female Infanticide I, Basta 132, Vol. 4, fols 140–42.

[154] William Muir, Secretary to Government of N.W.P., to H.C. Tucker, Commissioner 5th Division Benares, Nynee Tal, 22 September 1855, U.P.S.A., C.O.V., B.J.F., Fem. Infant. I, fols 199–200; William Muir, Secretary to Government of N.W.P., to W.R. Moore, Camp, 8 December 1855, U.P.S.A. Lucknow, C.O.V., Benares Judicial Files, Female Infanticide I, Basta 132, Vol. 4, fol. 231.

[155] H.C. Tucker, Commissioner of Benares, 5th Division, to William Muir, Secretary to Government of N.W.P., Camp, 30 November 1855, U.P.S.A., C.O.V., B.J.F., Fem. Infant. I, fol. 225.

Moore urged that fathers 'should be made responsible...It being proved...that the child has met with a violent death, that fact shall be sufficient for the conviction of the father'.[156]

With only three convictions for female infanticide in the Company's courts over the last 20 years, Moore argued that more stringent legislation was necessary to replace the current inadequate laws. But Moore proposed that the new law need only be applied to villages designated as 'suspect' by a careful census of Rajput children under the age of six. Moore further proposed to distinguish between villages which were merely 'suspected' of the crime of female infanticide because the percentage of female births fell below a prescribed rate of 35 per cent of total births and 'blood-red' villages where female births were less than 10 per cent of the total. Whereas all these villages would be taxed to support a special police force, in 'blood-red' villages fathers would be held responsible for reporting and safeguarding mother and child after seven months of pregnancy. Moore's superior, Commissioner H.C. Tucker, received the report and enthusiastically forwarded it to the Lt. Governor of the N.W.P. In Tucker's view the most important conclusion to be drawn from Moore's extensive study was that 'the new law should...constitute "Female Infanticide" a distinct offence in the same manner as Act XXIV of 1843 constituted having belonged to a Gang of Decoits a distinct offence'. He further suggested that female infanticide be defined as 'the "suspicious decease" of a female infant in a community of Rajpoots, among whom from their being registered as "suspect" or "blood-red" there was *prima facie* reason to assume that female infanticide prevailed'. Finally, he called for the crime of female infanticide to be considered a 'misdemeanour punishable with imprisonment with hard labour' no more than seven years. All that would be necessary for a conviction would be proof that the accused belonged to a 'suspect' or 'blood-red' community and that he was discovered amidst suspicious circumstances such as failure to notify the police of the birth or the attempt to conceal the infant's corpse. In true

---

[156] W.R. Moore, Infanticide Commissioner, to H.C. Tucker, Commissioner of Benares, Mirzapoor, 5th Division, 28 April 1856, U.P.S.A., C.O.V., B.J.F., Female Infanticide II, Basta 132, Vol. 5, Paras 93 (fol. 64), 123 (fol. 68), 146 (fol. 70), 230–35 and 238 (fols 80–81), 255 (fol. 83) and 265, (fol. 84). See also 'Papers on the subject of Mr W.R. Moore's Investigation and Report Regarding Female Infanticide in the Benares Division', *Selections from the Records of Government, North-Western Provinces*, I.O.R., V/23/120, No. 1757, pp. 21–22, 26, 29, 41–42, 44–45 and 47. [Unfortunately, these papers are only available in a fragile hard copy; they were omitted from the relevant I.D.C. microfiche copy.]

Benthamite fashion, Tucker declaimed: 'Certainty of punishment is more desirable than severity'.[157]

Lt. Governor Colvin could not accept the definition of female infanticide as 'suspicious decease of a female child'. Thus he opposed the attempt to treat female infanticide as a separate offence similar to the offence of belonging to a gang of dacoits or thugs. However, he did advocate that 'if the killing of any female child should be established...the father or resident head of the family...shall be held liable...even although the direct order or instigation of the murder should not be proveable against him'.[158] He then instructed the N.W.P. Nizamut Adawlut to draft special legislation for the suppression of female infanticide.

Of the four judges of the N.W.P. Nizamut Adawlut, two—Henry Unwin and Charles Raikes—were veteran magistrates of Mainpuri. It was Unwin who first discovered that the Chauhan Rajputs of his district were addicted to female infanticide when he conducted a survey of the population preparatory to a revision of the land revenue settlement in the wake of the devastating famine of 1838. As we have seen above, the coercive measures which Unwin favoured were discouraged by Lt. Governor Thomason. Raikes, on the other hand, in his vigorous pursuit of preventive measures, had avowed a greater faith in personal influence than in law. He had declared: 'When a government of mere law comes in, when *codes* instead of *men* are to rule India, the sooner the English are off to their ships the better'.[159]

Nevertheless, Raikes collaborated with Unwin to prepare a draft law in accordance with the N.W.P. Government's instructions. They incorporated most of Moore's suggestions—coercive and preventive—while taking note of Lt. Governor Colvin's views. Apart from his disapproval of the designation of female infanticide as a 'distinct offence', Colvin had endorsed Moore's plans for a special police establishment paid for by infanticidal villages and had indicated a willingness to overcome his own doubts and consider the idea that magistrates might promote *panchayat*s to regulate marriage expenses.[160]

---

[157] H.C. Tucker, Commissioner of Benares, 5th Division, to Secretary to Government of N.W.P., Benares, 3 May 1856, N.W.P. Criminal Judicial Proceedings 25 August 1856, No. 402, I.O.R., P/234/25.

[158] C.B. Thornhill, Officiating Secretary to Government, N.W.P., to Register of N.W.P. Nizamut Adawlut, Nynee Tal, 25 August 1856, N.W.P. Criminal Judicial Proceedings 25 August 1856, No. 409, *ibid.*

[159] C. Raikes, Magistrate, to W.H. Tyler, Commissioner Agra, Mainpuri, 17 November 1851, I.O.R., *Board's Collections*, F/4/2537, #147526; also cited in J.W. Kaye, *The Administration of the East India Company*. (Allahabad, Repr. 1966), p. 581.

[160] In fact, in his original instructions to the Infanticide Commissioner, the Lt. Governor had recommended just such a special police. C.B. Thornhill, Officiating Secretary to Government

The other two Judges—Henry B. Harington and A.W. Begbie—were veterans of Sudder Court infanticide cases most of which had resulted in acquittals. They were both on leave while Raikes and Unwin were preparing the Draft Act. Nevertheless, Lt. Governor Colvin thought the legislation so important that he insisted on receiving their opinions before submitting the Draft Law to the Legislative Council. The Judges were unanimous in their support for special legislation and for Secs IV–VI of the Draft Act which made the head of the family responsible for reporting births and deaths of all girls under the age of six years under penalty of a 200-rupee fine or imprisonment up to six months. Other punishable offences were the concealment of the corpse of a female infant and refusal to produce a girl under six years of age whose birth had been registered. However, Harington and Begbie had some fundamental criticisms of the Draft Act and offered contrasting suggestions. Begbie was the only Judge to urge the appointment of a special police establishment. However, he agreed with the others in their opposition to the levying of a tax on infanticidal villages in support of such an establishment. Harington suggested that any extra police needed could be funded by infanticide fines. While Harington and Begbie supported in principal the Draft Act's requirement that suspected clans register all births and deaths, Harington argued that the registration procedure should be made universal in order to avoid the 'invidious character' of legislation for particular clans.

The greatest disagreement occurred over proposed measures of enforcement. Secs VIII and IX of the Draft Act provided in cases of child murder for the father to be committed on a charge of 'wilful neglect' or 'privity to murder' subject upon conviction to imprisonment up to five years. Harington advocated instead that the burden of proof be shifted absolutely to the father, so that he would be required to prove that the child had died a natural death subject to punishment upon conviction of imprisonment up to seven years. Perhaps in proposing such an extreme extra-judicial tactic, Harington was expressing remorse over the doctrine which he had put forward in a recent Sudder case. In Byjnath Sing vs. Government on 25 June 1855, Harington argued that the male heads of a family could not be held responsible for the death of an infant in their household, because some other

---

of N.W.P., to Register of N.W.P. Nizamut Adawlut, Nynee Tal, 25 August 1856, in *Selections from the Records of Government, North-Western Provinces*, I.O.R., V/23/120, No. 1757, p. 112; cf. Report by W.R. Moore, Infanticide Commissioner, to H.C. Tucker, Commissioner of Benares, 5th Division, 28 April 1856, Paras 233, 240–41 and 305–8, U.P.S.A., Lucknow, C.O.V., B.J.F., Female Infanticide II, Basta 132, Vol. 5.

member of the household may have committed the crime.[161] Begbie opposed any such rules, preferring to leave the marshalling of evidence to the discretion of the committing officer. Begbie also thought imprisonment up to two years was sufficient punishment. Parallel with Harington's volte-face, it would seem that Begbie underwent a change of heart after he ruled in Government vs. Lulloo in 1855 that only by 'punishing severely in every instance of successful prosecution' could the Company hope 'to check, if we cannot altogether repress' the practice of infanticide. As for Moore's suggestion that the Rajput chiefs should be encouraged to form *panchayat*s for the purpose of regulating marriage expenses and that magistrates be empowered to enforce these resolutions, the Judges could agree that *panchayat*s might be encouraged but they reflected the Lt. Governor's doubts on the matter by their refusal to require magistrates to enforce the awards.[162]

Penal Code and Preparation of Act VIII, 1870

Before the Government could take action on the Draft Act, the infanticidal districts of the N.W.P. were swept up in the rebellious events of 1857. Unlike the Rajput chiefs in Punjab who remained loyal to the East India Company, the infanticidal clans in Etawah, Mainpuri and Azimgurh districts participated in the uprising and some were later punished by the confiscation of their estates. W.R. Moore was killed in action at Mirzapur. In the wake of the destruction and disruption of the events of 1857, chaos prevailed. Although Lord Canning was determined to restore the rule of law and, in the case of infanticide, secure the 'utter suppression of the abomination', a Capt. Burnes remarked on the reality that 'after the Mutiny nothing was done for a long time'.[163] However, M.R. Gubbins was one of the Judges of the N.W.P. Nizamut Adawlut when it was asked by the Viceroy in December 1858 to investigate the question. The Judges simply recommended the enactment of the act drafted by their predecessors in September 1856,

---

[161] This decision was particularly lamented by C.T. Le Bas, Magistrate of Jaunpoor, to H.C. Tucker, Commissioner of Benares, 5th Division, Jaunpoor Magistracy, 3 July 1855, U.P.S.A., C.O.V., B.J.F., Fem. Infant. I, fol. 163; cf. Byjnath Singh and Rampershad Singh vs. Government (25 June 1855), N.W.P. N.A. Rep. 5 Part I, I.O.R., V/22/664, pp. 984–85.

[162] H.W. Dashwood, Register, N.W.P. Nizamut Adawlut, to C.B. Thornhill, Officiating Secretary to the Government of the N.W.P., Agra, 24 September 1856, *Selections from the Records of Government, North-Western Provinces*, I.O.R., V/23/120, No. 1757, pp. 117–18.

[163] Lord Canning's statement cited by L. Panigrahi, *op. cit.*, p. 125; Burne's 'Note on Female Infanticide', U.P.S.A. Lucknow, Police Dept. File #710, Box No. 4, Cover No. 2.

either as a separate law or as part of the Penal Code.[164] Given the difficulties of reestablishing order in the N.W.P., legislative initiative on the subject of female infanticide fell by default to the Central Government. As a result, years of study and experimentation with preventive and coercive measures were encapsulated in Secs 315 and 317–18 of the Penal Code as finally enacted in 1860. Disappointingly, these very limited sections of the Penal Code merely prescribed prison sentences of at most 10 years for 'Exposure of Infants and Concealment of Births'. There was an 'Explanation' equating death by exposure with culpable homicide but Sec. 318 simply assigned a prison term of two years with or without fine for the act of 'Concealment of birth by secret disposal of dead body'.[165] However, Act XVII 1862 repealed Beng. Reg. XXI 1795 and Beng. Reg. VII 1804. The Penal Code applied a uniform standard of criminal justice throughout the Indian subcontinent. As the East India Company gave way to the Imperial Raj, infanticide legislation derived from Jonathan Duncan's experience with the Rajkumars gave way to a certain, simplified and generalized penal law.

In the N.W.P. the Penal Code seemed inadequate. The Lt. Governor lobbied the Central Government for a special law in accordance with the Draft Act of 1856 but with the addition of provision for a special police force supported by a tax on the villages which needed surveillance.[166] When the Government of India followed up this initiative by circulating among all the provincial governments the idea of special infanticide legislation, the response was lacklustre. The Governments of Bengal, Madras, the Straits Settlements, British Burma, Hyderabad and Mysore—all declared that the practice was nonexistent. Even the Government of Bombay feigned a lack of interest, claiming that the practice had been eliminated despite fresh evidence to the contrary among the lowly Koonbee caste in Gujarat. The Agent for the Governor General in Rajputana pointed out that the Rajput chiefs could not be bound by legislation passed by the Government of India and, in addition, individual Chiefs insisted that they had the problem under control. The same was true of Punjab, although R. Montgomery, the Lt. Governor, who had his first experience with infanticide as magistrate of Allahabad, urged the Central Government to enact legislation on a matter of such 'Imperial importance'.

---

[164] H.W. Dashwood, Register N.W.P. Nizamut Adawlut, to E.C. Bayley, Officiating Secretary to Government of N.W.P., Allahabad, 14 April 1859, I.O.R., N.W.P. Judicial Criminal Proceedings 29 April 1859, No. 523, I.O.R., P/234/56.

[165] Penal Code, *op. cit.*, pp. 78–80.

[166] G. Couper, to E.C. Bayley, 16 October 1862, India Legislative Proceedings, 4 March 1863, No. 1, I.O.R., P/208/8, p. 128.

Only the Chief Commissioner of Oudh commented on the N.W.P. Draft Act. He dismissed Judge Harington's idea of laying the burden of proof of innocence upon the fathers of deceased infants with the argument that fathers could do this easily simply by commanding the support of household members. He backed a special police force and urged the promotion of a scheme to lower marriage expenses. This generally lukewarm endorsement by the provinces of the idea of special infanticide legislation would seem to encourage the Viceroy, Lord John Lawrence's own preference for reform by education rather than legislation.[167] Nevertheless, he referred the matter back to the N.W.P. With reports that infanticide had revived throughout Etawah, Agra, Mainpuri, Saharanpur and Benares districts, the Lt. Governor of the N.W.P. could only persist in requesting the legislation.[168] The issue was finally forced upon the Government of India by a horrific report from R.T. Hobart, the Joint Magistrate of Basti. Hobart demonstrated that, since W.R. Moore's Report, infanticide had actually increased, ostensibly because the suspected clans had become impoverished as the result of the Government's confiscation of their lands as punishment for participation in the Mutiny of 1857.[169] Lord Lawrence suggested that Government could return the confiscated lands on condition that the clans concerned abandon the practice. But the lands had already been dispersed. It was generally agreed that 'legislative interference is urgently called for to suppress this barbarous practice which...is as prevalent as it was twelve years ago'.[170] Lord Lawrence had no option but to agree to authorize special legislation for the suppression of female infanticide.

The task of drafting the special legislation fell to John Strachey, a member of the Viceroy's Council. Strachey had already given considerable thought to such a bill in an earlier incarnation as Chief Commissioner of Oudh. In 1867 when asked to prepare a report on the subject, he prepared

---

[167] India Legislative Proceedings, October 1865, Nos. 10–26, I.O.R., P/208/11, pp. 1026–51.

[168] R. Simson, Secretary to Government of N.W.P., to E.C. Bayley, Secretary to Government of India, 13 November 1865, Allahabad, India Legislative Proceedings 4 January 1868, No. 1, I.O.R., P/436/55, p. 1.

[169] Para. 7, 'Report on the prevalence of female infanticide in Bustee', No. 1, Art. 10, by R.T. Hobart, Deputy Collector, Bustee, to F.S. Wigram, Collector and Magistrate, Bustee, 18 June 1868, India Legislative Proceedings 5 December 1868, No. 3, *Selections from the Records of Government, North-Western Provinces*, 2nd Series, I.O.R., V/23/128, No. 1825, Fiche 2807–8, p. 235.

[170] A. Shakespear, Commissioner of Benares, to R. Simson, Secretary to Government, N.W.P., Benares, 2 July 1868, *Selections from the Records of the Government, North-Western Provinces*, 2nd Series, I.O.R., V/23/128, No. 1825, Fiche 2807, p. 233.

instead a draft bill which was circulated among various governments.[171] As Strachey, himself explained, his draft bill was 'very similar to one prepared by the Agra Sadr Court in 1856'. It devolved powers to local governments, giving them the authority, in John Strachey's words, 'to frame rules, first to prevent extravagant expenditure on marriages and secondly to abrogate the custom...by introducing a system of registration of births and deaths in places tainted with the crime and a system of periodical inspection and enumeration of children'.[172] The Bill was referred to a Select Committee of the Legislative Council which included Strachey, Fitzjames Stephen and the Maharajah of Jaipur. The Select Committee endorsed the essential provisions—all outlined in Sec. 2 of the Act wherein local governments were to conduct a census of births, marriages and deaths among clans or districts specially notified as being subject to this special legislation. They might further raise a special police force, decide how to meet the expense of such a force, and were authorized to limit marriage expenses among persons specially notified as above. The Select Committee expanded these powers further to allow local governments, in cases of neglect of a female child, not only to remove the child from the person responsible, but also to order that person 'to make a monthly allowance for the maintenance of the child at [a] monthly rate not exceeding 50 rupees'. Finally, an Act for the Prevention of the Murder of Female Infants became law as Act VIII enacted on 4 April 1870.[173] The simple-minded Beng. Reg. XXI 1795 was now replaced by a flexible law open to the complications of the multifaceted nature of the crime. Thus the Committee formed in the N.W.P. to frame rules in accordance with the Act were able to implement the suggestions put forward by Tucker and Moore 15 years earlier, distinguishing between proclaimed villages 'where the proportion of girls to the non-adult population is under 25 percent' and those 'where the proportion of girls to the child population is above 25 percent'. M.R. Gubbins' tactics were resurrected in 'more guilty' villages where midwives were required to report pregnancies and fathers were made personally responsible to see that such reports were made. This was within the dictates of Sec. 2 Act VIII 1870. However, of the rules for implementing Sec. 2, Rule 26, which required the forwarding of female infant corpses to the civil surgeon in villages where the percentage of

---

[171] E.C. Bayley, Secretary to Government of India, to various Governments 4 January 1868, India Legislative Proceedings 4 January 1868, No. 14, I.O.R., P/436/55, p. 47.

[172] John Strachey, 'Statement of Objects and Reasons', 14 January 1870, India Legislative Proceedings 4 April 1870, No. 7, I.O.R., P/436/57, p. 10.

[173] Report of the Select Committee on the Bill for the Prevention of Female Infanticide, 10 March 1870 and Sec. VI, Act VIII 1870, India Legislative Proceedings 4 April 1870, Nos. 8, 10 and 42, I.O.R., P/436/57, pp. 10–14; see also I.O.R., V/8/42, p. 83.

girls was under 25 per cent, touched upon a longstanding bone of contention. Ultimately, the Infanticide Committee of the Government of the N.W.P. disallowed this rule. Infant corpses could only be forwarded on the strength of an executive order from the Lt. Governor.[174]

Somewhat curiously, the Home Authorities in London acclaimed the new legislation with special praise for the leadership of the Bombay Government in the suppression of female infanticide.[175] Despite the intensive discussions and dramatic confrontations in the N.W.P., the Bombay Government's educational measures of the 1830s and '40s dominated official memories. Perhaps this phenomenon reflects a preference for the 'compact' ideal of Col. Walker's engagements, which served as the foundation stone for Bombay Government policy, to the coercive procedures undertaken in the N.W.P. Certainly, all efforts among district officers in the N.W.P. to equate female infanticide with dacoity as a 'distinct offense', and to create a department for the suppression of female infanticide in the image of the Thagi and Dacoity Department were summarily rejected at the viceregal level. At the same time, Viceroy Mayo regarded Act VIII of 1870 as a veritable crown of achievement for Government social policy 'on a par with the abolition of suttee, thuggee, and other practices...which I believe has tended more than anything else to vindicate the justice and wisdom of our rule'.[176]

Meriah Sacrifice and Female Infanticide among the Konds

The rite of human sacrifice and the female infanticide practised by the Dravidian Konds in malarial jungles on the remote and inaccessible table

---

[174] Appendix B, 'Proposed Rules for the Suppression of Infanticide under Sec. 2 Act VIII 1870', Rules 6–10, 26; Proceedings of Infanticide Committee 27 September 1870; and Appendix C, C.A. Elliott, Secretary to Government of N.W.P., Azimgurh, to Officiating Secretary to Government of India (Home Dept.), 14 December 1870; see N.W.P. Judicial Criminal Proceedings 21 January 1871, Nos. 221–22, I.O.R., P/92, pp. 401–3, 421 and 424.

[175] Minute in Legislative Department preceding Legislative Despatch to India, 19 May 1870, I.O.R., L/P&J/3/1225, fol. 91.

[176] Viceroy's Minute, 4 April 1870, India Legislative Proceedings, 4 April 1870, No. 5, I.O.R., P/436/57, p. 9. For an analysis of the failings of Act VIII and the eventual abandonment in 1912 of its prescribed procedures in Rajput districts, see Malavika Kasturi, 'Crime and Law in India: British Policy and the Female Infanticide Act of 1870', *Indian Journal of Gender Studies* (1994) I, No. 2.

land of the Eastern Ghats elicited a very cautious response from Company officialdom. The Kond ritual of Meriah sacrifice only came to the attention of the British government as a result of the Goomsur Wars of 1835–37. As explained by George E. Russell, deputed by the Madras Board of Revenue as Special Commissioner to Ganjam District and its surrounding hills, the region designated as 'Khondistan' by Europeans spanned the two presidencies of Bengal and Madras. Only in Madras were these remote *zamindaries* 'subject to the Courts and general regulations in common with the inhabitants of the Carnatic'. Thus, when the Goomsur *zamindar* consistently defaulted on his tribute payments, the Collector of Ganjam District called in the Company's troops from Madras. By way of contrast, Russell pointed out that the remote *zamindaries* of Cuttack district in the Bengal presidency were 'expressly exempted from the operation of the general regulations' and 'their tribute a mere peppercorn compared with that paid by ours, default from want of means[,] impossible'.[177] To remove these inequities, Russell recommended that the Tributary Rajas of Ganjam and Vizagapatam Districts in the Madras presidency, be 'exempted from the jurisdiction of the ordinary Courts, and placed exclusively under the Collector of the district' empowered to try civil and criminal cases subject only to appeal to the Sudder and Foujdary Adawlut without reference to Mahomedan law.[178] The Government of India ultimately responded to this request by enacting Act XXIV of 1839 effectively exempting these *zamindaries* from the 'operation of Rules for the Administration of Civil and Criminal Justice as well as those for the collection of Revenue'.[179]

It was during the chase of the fugitive Raja of Goomsur and his heirs into the hills that Russell encountered the Konds and, as recorded later by the anthropologist E.T. Dalton, made

> the astounding discovery that we included amongst our fellow subjects a whole people who practised human sacrifice and female infanticide on a scale and with a cruelty which had never been surpassed by the most savage of nations.[180]

Henry Ricketts, the Commissioner of Cuttack, upon learning from Russell of the Kond system of sacrifice, ventured into the neighbouring territory of

---

[177] Russell Report, 11 May 1837, Madras Board of Revenue Proceedings 14 December 1837, I.O.R., P/301/13, fol. 16265.
[178] *Ibid.*, fol. 16274.
[179] Act XXIV for the Administration of Justice and Collection of Revenue in certain parts of the Districts of Ganjam and Vizagapatam, passed 2 October, 1839, I.O.R., V/8/31.
[180] Edward T. Dalton, *Descriptive Ethnology of Bengal* (Calcutta, 1872), p. 285.

Boad in Bengal and, after promising the Kond chiefs to abstain from the use of force, rescued 24 intended Meriah 'victims'.[181] Russell's Report of 11 May 1837 to the Madras Board of Revenue is generally credited with setting the tone of official policy regarding the Konds. Though horrified by the discovery of cruel, savage rites practised within the Company's jurisdiction, Russell opined that any effort to legislate against such a custom would be totally 'abortive'. He recommended instead the improvement of 'our intercourse with the tribes nearest to us with the view to civilize and enlighten them...using our moral influence rather than our power.'[182]

The principal reason for the Company's caution concerning, first, Meriah sacrifice and then, female infanticide, among the Konds was the realization that both practices were an integral part of Kond religion. The ritual of human sacrifice was demanded by the Earth Goddess, Tari, as her food in return for teaching man the arts of agriculture, hunting and war. Several villages combined to form a community for the period of three years which was the typical period of time required for the sacrifice. Every household shared the blood or flesh of the Meriah to offer as food to the earth at times of planting, harvest or for protection against ill health or ill fortune. There were five Kond districts among the Hill *zamindaries* which scorned the ritual of human sacrifice. They understood Tari to be subordinate to the supreme creator god, Bura. Sadly, they regarded female infanticide to be the divine command of Bura who was so appalled by the moral and physical evil wrought by his female consort and own creation, Tari, that he advised the ancestors of the Konds 'to bring up only as many females as they could restrain from producing evil to society'.

The first account of Kond customs to be published appeared in the *Madras Journal of Literature and Science* in July 1837.[183] The description of Meriah sacrifice was based on documents furnished by J.A.R. Stevenson, the Collector who launched the Goomsur Wars by calling in troops from Madras to occupy Goomsurtown and arrest its recalcitrant Raja. Stevenson's description had also provided the data for Russell's Report of 11 May 1837. With the benefit of several additional accounts of Meriah sacrifice by Company officers, later

---

[181] Report from Henry Ricketts, Commissioner and Superintendent of Tributary Mehals in Cuttack, 23 February 1837, Bengal Criminal Judicial Consultations 14 March 1837, No. 125, I.O.R., P/141/9.

[182] Russell Report, 11 May 1837, *op. cit.*, fols 16291–92.

[183] Rev. W. Taylor, 'On the Language, Manners and Rites of the Khonds or Khoi Jati of the Goomsur Mountains from documents furnished by J.A.R. Stevenson, Commissioner in Goomsur and W.G. Maxwell M.D.', *Madras Journal of Literature and Science*, Vol. VI, July 1837, pp. 17–46.

anthropologists have commented upon a misunderstanding of the Meriah as victim, which was intrinsic to European observation of the customs of the Dravidian Konds. Edward Dalton speculated that the word 'Meriah' derived from an aboriginal word 'Miri' meaning 'mediator or go-between'. Dalton concluded that the Meriah was 'perhaps...the messenger or mediator between man and the deity'.[184] J.G. Frazer observed further that 'the custom cannot be explained as merely a propitiatory sacrifice'. The individual Meriah was only acceptable for sacrifice if he or she had been purchased or else born a Meriah. Meriahs were nurtured for years in Kond villages in preparation for their ultimate sacrifice as 'consecrated beings'. He noted that 'the flesh and ashes of the victims were believed to be endowed with a magical or physical power of fertilising the land...his blood causing the redness of the turmeric and his tears producing rain'. He thus concluded that 'a direct or intrinsic power of making the crops to grow' was ascribed to the Meriah 'quite independent of the indirect efficacy which it might have as an offering to secure the good-will of the deity'. This belied the 'later view of the Meriah as a victim rather than a god' which 'perhaps...received undue emphasis from European writers'.[185]

Very broadly speaking, the Meriah rite took place annually in ever recurring three-year cycles involving continually shifting combinations of villages. As described by Barbara Boal, who worked as a missionary among the Konds in the 1950s, the Meriah sacrifice provided a ritual means of forging communities from fiercely independent migrant Dravidian clans which had, in their early history, retreated from the Aryan invasion of the fertile coastal plains. The ritual focused on three days. During the first day there was extensive drinking and dancing accompanying the lesser sacrifice of animals. On the second day, the Meriah fasted, although he or she was allowed liquor. The Meriah's host family dressed the Meriah for a parade through the village to a Meriah Grove of sacred trees near the village. The Meriah was then chained to a stake by a priest, anointed with oil and turmeric paste and adorned with flowers. Wooden clappers carved in the shape of peacocks accompanied the chanting of the Meriah Song. During the night the priest probed the earth for the softest spot. The deepest probe was considered the location designated by the Goddess Tari for a hole to receive the sacrificial blood. On the third day, to comply with the rule that the Meriah must neither be bound nor show any resistance, the bones of the arms and

---

[184] Edward T. Dalton, *op. cit.*, p. 29.
[185] J.G. Frazer, *The Golden Bough—A Study in Comparative Religion* (London, 1890), pp. 385, 389.

legs were broken. The priest, the village headman and the stand-in for the Meriah then engaged in a dialogue exculpating the villagers from all guilt, as they promised the Meriah ultimate divinity. At noon amidst frenzied drumming the priest initiated the sacrifice by wounding the Meriah with an axe. Then drunken heads of households cut strips of flesh from the Meriah while proclaiming: 'We bought you with a price! No sin rests on us!' The Meriah's blood dripped into the prepared hole. Each participant carried his parcel of flesh back to his home to bury it in his fields. Then all participants observed a three-day period of mourning while the next day, the priest cremated the Meriah's remains. After the period of mourning, a buffalo was slaughtered for a funeral feast for all participants. A buffalo was given to the Pan or low-caste agent from the plains who sold the Meriah to the Konds and the rite was completed one year later with the sacrifice of a pig.[186]

The nefarious trade plied by the Pans who kidnapped, as often as they bought, children whom they then sold to the Konds as Meriahs was an object of intense disgust for the British. But it was a fact that the Pans also served as a means of communication between the Konds and the British. As explained by the Agent to the Governor in Ganjam, R.A. Bannerman, the Pans played a vital role weaving cloth for the Konds and bartering 'various Hill products...for salt and other articles' in the plains. 'More intelligent than the Konds', they also served as the Konds' 'spokesmen'.[187]

Unfortunately, the Oriya language of the Pans was of Sanskritic origin and bore no resemblance to the Dravidian Kui language of the Konds.

In addition to the language barrier and the inaccessibility of the malarial homeland of the Konds, the British faced the disadvantage that they attempted to forge an acquaintance against a backdrop of war and devastation. In the jungle, a thousand miles from their headquarters in Madras,

---

[186] This is based on the most complete compilation of data on the Meriah rite available. *See* Barbara M. Boal, *The Konds* (Warminster, England, 1982), pp. 53–55, 107–23 and Felix Padel, *The Sacrifice of Human Being: British Rule and the Khonds of Orissa* (New Delhi, O.U.P.: 1995). Crispin Bates dismisses the sacrifice as a figment of the colonial imagination on the grounds that the British never found human bones when they visited shrines where the sacrifice was supposed to have taken place. Given the act of cremation, it is difficult to understand how any bones could have remained. See Crispin Bates, *Subalterns and Raj-South Asia since 1600* (Routledge, 2007), p. 50; and Crispin Bates, 'Human Sacrifice in Colonial Central India: Myth, Agency and Representation', in *Beyond Representation: Constructions of Identity in Colonial and Postcolonial India* (New Delhi, O.U.P.: 2006).

[187] R.A. Bannerman, Agent to Governor in Ganjam, to W. Douglas, Register, Foujdaree Udalut, Ganjam, 25 May 1841, Madras Judicial Consultations 3 August 1841, No. 1, I.O.R., P/326/10, fol. 3144.

facing disease and a people bewildered by their appearance, British troops resorted to horrific slash and burn tactics. A typical report from camp detailed the surrounding of a village with the result that 10 Konds were killed and many wounded by the bayonets of sepoys who 'took a good many prisoners and burnt the village and drove about 200 head of cattle'.[188] Even the *Calcutta Review,* imbued with the civilizing mission of the Company Raj, acknowledged that such 'horrible devastation' was 'a rough way of forming a first acquaintance'.[189]

It was also impossible for the British to know that the delinquent Raja whom they pursued into the hills operated a traditional hospitality pact with the Konds which commanded a resistance to all efforts at bribery or forceful penetration. Lt. Samuel Macpherson, one of the first East India Company officers to live among the Konds, was later to discover that 'hospitality is regarded as one of the first duties…"For the safety of a guest", say the Konds, "life and honour are pledged, he is to be considered before a child"'.[190] In a similar vein, Barbara Boal observes that the 'right relationship between man and the deity demands and involves right relationship with all one's fellowmen'. Commenting upon the survival of the Governor's Agent after his dramatic rescue of a Meriah in mid-ritual, she concludes that the Konds' insistence upon 'non-quarrelling relationships throughout the Meriah festivities' probably explained 'why Mr Bannerman and his large military force were not wiped out by the great company of drunken Konds gathered for the final-day ritual of their Meriah sacrifice, in the wildly remote village of Sikeraguda'. All that was required was that a substitute victim be found to replace the escapee. Indeed, it was duly reported that 'in a very few days another woman had been sacrificed in the place of the victim' rescued by Bannerman. Barbara Boal concludes with the disarming insight: 'So both Konds and British pursued their own policies in mutual incomprehension'.[191]

Perhaps nothing was more symbolic of this mutual incomprehension than the abortive trial in December 1837 of Yenuty Bimu for kidnapping Letchena in Purlah Kinnedy and selling him to a Kond Chief in Chinna

---

[188] Cited by Felix Padel, *op. cit.,* p. 46. Padel gives a graphic account of the Goomsur wars in chapter 2.

[189] Article I: 'Goomsur: The Late War There—The Khonds or Hill Tribes', *Calcutta Review,* Vol. V, No. IX (January–March 1846), p. 21n.

[190] *Lieut. Macpherson's Report upon the Khonds of the Districts of Ganjam and Cuttack* (Calcutta, 1842), p. 50.

[191] Barbara Boal, *op. cit.,* p. 57.

Kinnedy for sacrifice. Yenuty Bimu was, in the first instance, acquitted before the Northern Circuit Court on the grounds of insufficient evidence. Evidence of two witnesses was rejected because they were 'apprehenders'; Yenuty Bimu's own confession was set aside because, though delivered in the Oriya language, it was transcribed in Telegu so that the prisoner 'could not be supposed to verify by his mark, the contents which were thoroughly foreign to him'; and finally his wife's evidence as a witness to the kidnapping was rejected because under Muslim law 'husband and wife cannot be witnesses against each other'. The Government, in authorizing a new trial for Yenuty Bimu, instructed Mr Bannerman, the Magistrate of Ganjam, 'to procure all available evidence'. Bannerman protested that it was virtually 'impossible under existing circumstances to bring these uncivilized and barbarous men before the Court of Circuit as witnesses, more particularly, as those best acquainted with the facts, are themselves deeply implicated in the criminal transaction'. Also, he warned that among the Hill Chiefs, who were 'totally ignorant of everything relating to our Courts and Judicial forms of proceeding, a summons to appear as a witness before the Court of Circuit would not fail to excite much alarm and disgust'. All that survived this futile exercise was the Circuit Court's decision, subsequently endorsed by the Court of Directors in London, that 'the inhabitants of the low countries who provided the means of carrying on the horrible practice, from the most sordid motives, and not the Khonds in their present state of ignorance and barbarism, were the proper objects of judicial pursuit'.[192]

These 'inhabitants of the low countries' were, in fact, members of the Pan caste. Bannerman was able to prosecute successfully two members of this caste for kidnapping two youths and then selling them to the Konds as Meriahs for the paltry sums of three and five rupees. However, Bannerman, himself, argued that 'to inflict a severe punishment...for the sake of Example would be almost wholly nugatory as the fact of the punishment could not be brought to the knowledge of those who are likely to commit such offences'. The case was reviewed by the Sudder Court and the Madras Government, both of which essentially agreed with Bannerman. Governor Elphinstone opined that, much as he would like to impose the punishment of transportation for life on 'all parties connected in this unnatural traffick...it would tend to defeat...our main object which is to reclaim and civilize the wild tribes,

---

[192] Article II: 'The First Series of Government Measures for the Abolition of Human Sacrifice among the Khonds', *Calcutta Review*, Vol. VI, No. XI (July–December 1846), pp. 54–55; Revenue Despatch to Madras, 21 November 1838, I.O.R., L/E/3/679, fols 568–71.

by gaining their confidence and by promoting and fostering the intercourse between them and us by every possible means'.[193] Furthermore, the Sudder Judges explicitly disagreed with Bannerman's proposal that the rules according to Act XXIV 1839, which was enacted in order to expedite the prosecution of kidnappers of Meriah victims, needed to be modified to allow for corporal punishment on the spot.[194]

Arbitrary measures were distinctly out of favour among the higher echelons of Government. Indeed, the Governments of Madras and Bengal, Governor General Auckland and ultimately the Company's Directors in London, were unanimous in their rejection of any kind of military or even quasi-military solution to the problem. When Commissioner of Cuttack Henry Ricketts, after rescuing 24 intended Meriahs from the Kond districts of Bengal, suggested 'sending a strong party once a year from Cuttack to march through the country from end to end, with an Officer authorized to punish immediately by death…any person proved guilty of the crime', he met with a cautious refusal by the Government of Bengal, if only out of concern for the cost of such an expedition. On a higher level, Governor General Auckland was cited for his view that 'the working of a moral change among the people by the progress of general instruction and consequent civilization can alone eradicate from among them the inclination to indulge in rites so horrible'.[195] The Court of Directors cited the sentiments of Auckland and the earlier Russell Report as proof of 'the inexpediency of attempting the sudden suppression of these horrible rites by force'.[196]

However, throughout the Company's campaign against Meriah sacrifice, almost every officer, whether of the military, judicial or political service, felt the ultimate necessity of confronting the Konds with a show of force. A Lieutenant Hill of the Survey Department in Ganjam foresaw 'that Military force' would only result in 'an enormous slaughter, at a great expense on the part of the State, without the prospect of an entire and final abandonment

---

[193] R.A. Bannerman, Agent to Governor in Ganjam, to W. Douglas, Register, Foujdaree Udalut, Ganjam, 25 May 1841, and Minute by Governor John Elphinstone, 20 July 1841, Madras Judicial Consultations 3 August 1841, Nos 1 and 2, I.O.R., P/326/10, fols 3145, 3169–70.

[194] Government vs. Cahkra and Riga, 5 July 1841, T.N. F.U. Rep. I, I.O.R., V/22/610, pp. 183–84.

[195] Henry Ricketts, Commissioner and Superintendent of Tributary Mehals in Cuttack, to R.D. Mangles, Secretary to Government of Bengal, 23 February 1837 and R.D. Mangles, Secretary to Government of Bengal, to H. Ricketts, 14 March 1837, Bengal Criminal Judicial Consultations 14 March 1837, Nos. 125 and 126, I.O.R., P/141/9.

[196] Revenue Despatch to Madras, 21 November 1838, *op. cit.*, fols 559–60.

of the custom by the Khonds'. Yet, after ranking the Konds 'on the very lowest verge of civilization', immune to persuasion by outsiders, Lt. Hill found it difficult to believe in the power of 'persuasion *alone*'. He invoked the example currently set by the Thagi Department in the exertion of 'a strong and almost arbitrary power...by local authorities'. Lt. Hill reasoned: 'if murderers by trade cannot be persuaded to abandon their calling, can we hope that *persuasion* will have more effect on men who murder *solely* on the principle of making a *necessary* offering to their god?'[197] Although Lt. Hill's recommendation for an Agency for the suppression of Meriah Sacrifice similar to the Thagi Department was echoed by some of his fellow officers in the field, it fell upon the deaf ears of his more distant superiors. In fact, the Madras Government enjoyed total support from the Court of Directors in their belief that 'the barbarous practises of the Natives of the hills...[would] certainly become extinct under a more extended intercourse with the more civilized inhabitants of the low country'. This intercourse was to involve the building of roads 'through the hills from the Company's into the Hyderabad and Nagpore territories', the development of market fairs so that the Konds might procure their coveted 'salt, salt fish, brass utensils, scarlet woollen[s], red blankets, and all but the coarsest kinds of cotton manufacture' which they had been in the habit of seizing from their lowland neighbours either by 'rapine or exchange', and the Madras Government's proposal that 'every inducement...be held out to the Khonds to enter...[the public Service]... either as Peons or in whatever capacity they may be found useful'.[198] This policy became official in a Resolution of the Supreme Government which authorized the appointment of a special officer who would improve relations and communications with the Hill Chiefs. However, this office, held first by Lieutenant John Campbell and later by Lieutenant Samuel

---

[197] Extract from Report from Lt. Hill, Officer attached to Survey Department in Ganjam, 'History of the Rise and Progress of the Operations for the Suppression of Human Sacrifice and Female Infanticide in the Hill Tracts of Orissa' in *Selections from the Records of the Government of India (Home Dept.)*, 2 July 1838, No. V, I.O.R., V/23-1, Fiche No. 7, pp. 23–24. Other officers who made the occasional wistful reference to the powers of Col. Sleeman's Thagi Department were Commissioner Richard Bannerman in his letter to the Government of Fort St. George, 6 February 1841, I.O.R., *Board's Collections* F/4/1954 No. 85227, fol. 139 and Lieutenant Samuel Macpherson in his 'Report on the Konds', 21 June 1841, I.O.R., *Board's Collections* F/4/1954 No. 85228, fols 337–45.

[198] Revenue Despatch to Madras, 21 November 1828, *op. cit.*, fols 571–72; Russell's Report of 12 August 1838, in Article II: 'The First Series of Government Measures for the Abolition of Human Sacrifice among the Konds', *Calcutta Review*, Vol. VI, No. XI (July–December 1846), pp. 47–48; Lt. Chamier, Chief Secretary to the Government of Madras, to President and Members of the Board of Revenue, 21 November 1837, Madras Board of Revenue Proceedings, 14 December 1837, I.O.R., P/301/13, fol. 16175.

Macpherson, was kept subordinate to the Governor's Agent in Ganjam, the Governor General's Agent at Sumbulpore, the Resident at Nagpore and the Commissioner at Cuttack. Furthermore, the officer was instructed that 'he should cautiously approach any inquisition into human sacrifices'. The Madras Government specifically warned Lt. Macpherson:

> Care…should be taken never to allude to it [human sacrifice] as a *Khond custom*, but as a custom prevalent among barbarous tribes in every part of the world, repudiated by all civilized beings, and equally contrary to the law of God and man.[199]

When Lieut. Campbell was seconded to duty in the Chinese Opium War, Lieut. Samuel Macpherson was assigned the unenviable task of improving the Company's relations with the Konds in the capacity of assistant to Commissioner Bannerman of Ganjam. Macpherson was one of the few officers who dared to buck the tide of cynicism which engulfed his colleagues and led them to despair of bringing any influence to bear upon the Konds by virtue of moral suasion only. Ultimately, Macpherson won paeans of praise from the Government and successive generations of historians for his painstaking efforts to win the cooperation of Kond leaders and to collect information and gain insight into Kond customs.[200] Macpherson decided to begin his campaign in Goomsur where he had the advantage of contacts with Konds who had some understanding of the Oriya language and some appreciation of the British presence. However, he faced many disadvantages, not least of which was the treachery of the Hindu Samo Bisaye, the former patriarch of the Hodzoghoro Kond clans and agent of Kond affairs for the Goomsur *zamindar*. Samo Bisaye was unwittingly raised to a position of supreme authority over Goomsur Konds as Dora Bisaye, with the added title of Bahadoor Bakshee, by G.E. Russell. At the time, Samo enjoyed the full confidence of Russell, Collector J.A.R. Stevenson and Lt. John Campbell, Macpherson's predecessor as assistant to the Commissioner.[201] But Samo committed all his energy to the exploitation of the Meriah customs, deceiving

---

[199] Letter from Government of India, 3 May 1841, and Extract from Orders of the Madras Government, 27 July 1841, appointing Lt. Macpherson as Assistant to the Governor's Agent in Ganjam, in *Selections from the Records of the Government of India, op. cit.*, pp. 37, 39.

[200] N.B. Lieut. Macpherson, *Report upon the Khonds of the Districts of Ganjam and Cuttack* (Calcutta, 1842), pp. 86–87; admirers of Macpherson's work ranged from Alexander Duff, the Calcutta missionary identified by Barbara Boal as the anonymous author of several articles in praise of Macpherson in the *Calcutta Review* over a period of two years, and the official historian for the East India Co., John William Kaye, *op. cit.*, p. 496 to Barbara M. Boal, *op. cit.*, pp. 58–59.

[201] Russell's Report, 11 May 1837, *op. cit.*, fol. 16257.

Commissioner Bannerman, in order to encourage the rite, on the one hand, and then, on the other hand, exacting bribes and presents from the Kond participants. Further problems for Macpherson were caused by the fact that his hands were tied by the Government's lame instructions to refrain even from broaching the subject of Meriah sacrifice in conversation with Kond chiefs and by his subordinate position under the Commissioners of two separate presidencies. Aware that any success among the Goomsur Konds in prohibiting human sacrifice could easily be undermined by the importation of sacrificial human flesh from the territory of the Boad Konds across the border in Bengal, Macpherson appealed to the Madras Government for the effective unification of the Kond districts in the two presidencies by removing the Konds in Madras from the cognizance of the Foujdary Adawlut. Governor Elphinstone of Madras enthusiastically endorsed Macpherson's idea. But Elphinstone's minute and the resolution of his council lay fallow in Calcutta in the wake of the disasters overwhelming the Company in Afghanistan.

Meanwhile, Macpherson acted on the realization that the Hindu *zamindar*s had long intervened to foster feuds among the Kond clans. He perceived that, whereas the Kond patriarchs could maintain order within their clans, there was a desperate need for justice to be administered between clans, in accordance as much as was possible with Kond traditions. In Macpherson's own words: 'The law of compensation for wrongs, as it exists between Branches of a Tribe, was to be substituted for the usage of retaliation'. Macpherson referred disputes to Kond councils whenever possible, 'making it plain that I was there not to supercede the existing methods and instruments of justice but to strengthen them for good, and to supply their defects'.[202] With the help of two Indian assistants, one of whom spoke the Kui language, Macpherson won a pledge from a group of 12 clans or *Baro Muta* to substitute for Meriahs 'buffaloes, monkeys etc. with all the ceremonies usual on occasions of human sacrifice' in return for the administration of justice in the manner of the Company's courts in the plains and for permission 'to denounce the Government to their gods upon all occasions as the cause of the relinquishment of their ancient worship'.[203] As Macpherson and his assistants settled thousands of complaints, another group of 18 clans or *Atharo Muta*,

---

[202] S.C. Macpherson to R. Bannerman, 12 April 1843, I.O.R., *Board's Collections*, F/4/2083, No. 96448, fols 26–36.

[203] William Macpherson, ed., *Memorials of Service in India from the Correspondence of the Late Major Samuiel Charters Macpherson, C.B. Political Agent at Gwalior During the Mutiny, and Formerly Employed in the Suppression of Human Sacrifices in Orissa* (London, 1865), pp. 179–80.

with the exception of territories neighbouring Samo Bisaye's Hodzoghoro home, made the same pledge. In the next season, there were only five Meriah sacrifices among these tribes and they were all in areas under Samo Bisaye's influence. Samo even persuaded the guileless Konds that his authority was superior to that of Macpherson's and that Commissioner Bannerman had authorized the sacrifice of six more Meriahs. Macpherson summed up his frustration: 'Bannerman...is afraid to do anything...I have no power to act...It is a part of the only instructions I ever received that I am not to speak of the human sacrifice as a Khond rite!'[204]

Encouraged by his success in resolving 136 cases among the traditionally hostile clans of the *Baro* and *Atharo Muta*s, Macpherson also prosecuted Pan procurers of Meriahs only to find that replacements were easily obtained from Cuttack district in Bengal. In his report of 22 April 1843, Macpherson argued for uniting the Kond districts of Madras and Bengal under one authority.[205] Little did Macpherson realize the extent of Commissioner Bannerman's apathy. While Macpherson faced humiliation before the Kond chiefs by Samo Bisaye, his report lay unattended for six months on Bannerman's desk. Whether sick or jealous or both, Bannerman failed to forward Macpherson's request to Madras until Macpherson filed a second report to force the issue and finally win authority from the Government of Madras to discipline Samo Bisaye. Meanwhile, some Kond chiefs had broken their pledges. But, upon the revelation of Samo's deceit, a council of chiefs demanded that the Government also punish the delinquent chiefs. Indeed, Macpherson was deeply impressed by the personal integrity of the Kond people, having in his deliberations failed to encounter 'a single instance of bad faith in the suitors, or of falsehood in the witnesses, save occasionally on the part of Panwas of the borders'.[206] Macpherson summed up his successes and frustrations in his Report of 8 May 1844 which reminded the Government of Madras that no action had been taken on building a proposed road, that his Indian assistants deserved special recognition, that authority was needed to ban Samo Bisaye and key family members from Kond country altogether and, most important, that there was a pressing need for the unification of the Hill *zamindarie*s. The Governor of Madras, the Marquis of Tweeddale, acted promptly to authorize the banishment of Samo Bisaye, medals for Macpherson's assistants and to forward Macpherson's report to

---

[204] *Ibid.*, p. 185.
[205] Extract from Macpherson Report, 22 April 1843, *Selections from the Records of the Government of India, op. cit.,* p. 63.
[206] Article I: 'The Khonds—Abolition of Human Sacrifice and Female Infanticide', *Calcutta Review*, Vol. X, No. XX (July–December 1848), p. 277.

the Government of India. However, the Marquis Tweeddale did not share Macpherson's sympathetic approach to the Konds. He urged instead 'the introduction of law and regulations more in accordance with the Government in the Madras Presidency'.[207]

Though stymied by Government inaction on the issue of Meriah sacrifice, Macpherson conceived a remarkably effective ploy against the reality of female infanticide among Konds in a tract of five districts. In the years 1843–44 infanticidal clans requested the same administration of justice which Macpherson had dispensed among the Goomsur clans. This was all part of a process of negotiation which began with Macpherson's decision to give 53 of his Kond Meriah wards as wives to chiefs of infanticidal tribes to help with their problem of a shortage of wives. By thus winning considerable esteem from these clans, Macpherson was able to compile statistics of female births in half of the districts concerned. These efforts at first attracted criticism from the Madras Government but ultimately won the approval of Macpherson's superiors even to the point of a special commendation from the Directors.[208] The Directors later approved Macpherson's longstanding request for the combination of Kond districts in Madras and Bengal under the single authority of an Agent for Kond affairs. By the time the Directors' approval arrived in India, Macpherson had moved to Calcutta to seek medical attention and to provide information to the legislators. For a change, he enjoyed the wholehearted support of the current Governor General, Lord Hardinge.[209] Finally, in September 1845, Act XXI created a Governor General's agent for the suppression of Meriah Sacrifice.[210] In November, Macpherson was appointed to that agency. The Kond districts in Cuttack, the Southwest Frontier, Ganjam and Vizagapatam were united in one jurisdiction under Macpherson, subject only to instruction from the Government of India with judicial powers subject to appeal to the Sudder Courts.

---

[207] George Tweeddale, Minute, 20 October 1843, I.O.R., *Board's Collections* F/4/2083 No. 96448, fols 100–102, 117.

[208] William Macpherson, ed., *Memorials of Service in India, op. cit.*, pp. 194, 223–25; Resolution in Revenue Department, Fort St. George, 12 March 1844, and Extract from Madras Revenue Consultations, 1 October 1844, No. 4, I.O.R. *Board's Collections* F/4/2083 #96448, fols 175–78, 379–81; Revenue Despatch to Madras, 2 April 1845, No. 3, I.O.R. E/4/963, fols 616–17.

[209] Henry Hardinge to Walter (Hardinge), Calcutta, 2 June 1845, in Rawa Satinder Singh, ed., *The Letters of the First Viscount Hardinge of Lahore to Lady Hardinge and Sir Walter and Lady James 1844–1847*, Royal Historical Society, Camden Fourth series, Vol. 32 (London, 1986), p. 83.

[210] Act XXI respecting the appointment and powers of Agents for the suppression of Meriah Sacrifices in the Hill Tracts of Orissa (passed 13 September 1845) I.O.R., V/8/32.

Ironically, scarcely had Macpherson won the authority to administer a uniform system of justice among Kond clans in Madras and Bengal than he ran afoul of the intrigues of the Raja of Boad. After discovering that the Raja had developed a strategy of neutralizing British interference by handing over a selection of 25 Meriahs, a precedent set in the days of Commissioner Henry Ricketts, Macpherson appealed directly to the Kond Chiefs. Much to Macpherson's astonishment, these Chiefs turned in 170 Meriahs and then reversed their decision, demanded a return of the Meriahs and confronted Macpherson's Camp with an armed mob. The ensuing rebellion was based on rumours that Macpherson had been authorized by the British Government to assess Kond lands for taxes, to subject the Kond people to forced labour and to punish Kond Chiefs for past sacrifices. Ultimately, Macpherson restored the 170 Meriahs to the Raja of Boad for safekeeping and then set about quelling the Boad rebellion, which had spread to Goomsur as a result of the machinations of some of Samo Bisaye's relatives. Then, unluckily for Macpherson, a totally unrelated rebellion sprang from Angul district, on the opposite bank of the Mahanadi River from Boad. This disturbance concerned claims by relatives and discredited cronies of the dispossessed Goomsur *zamindar* who had been languishing in jail since 1836. Though Macpherson doused this fire as well, exaggerated tales of rebellion had reached Calcutta and the Government of India ordered the Madras Government to send an experienced officer to the scene with instructions to take charge of the Meriah Agency if, in his opinion, the rebellion had spun out of control. It is now a matter of legend that a credulous General Dyce of the Madras army absorbed all the malicious gossip that could be mustered by a disgraced *tehsildar* who had been dismissed by Commissioner Bannerman and had actually connived at the rebellion based in Angul. On the basis of this misinformation, General Dyce levelled serious charges against Macpherson, and thus forced his dismissal. At Capt. Macpherson's request, an inquiry was launched by the Government of India, led by the able civil servant J.P. Grant. Grant's study completely and triumphantly vindicated Macpherson's reputation, leading the Directors to acknowledge that 'searching investigation…has elicited nothing to support the sweeping condemnation…placed on record by General Dyce'.[211] However, the damage had been done to Macpherson's career as Governor General's Agent for the suppression of human sacrifices in the hill tracts of Ganjam and Orissa. Lt. Col. John Campbell had been

---

[211] Revenue Despatch to Government of India, 25 September 1850, No. 10, I.O.R., E/4/806, fols 781–82.

appointed Agent in his place. J.P. Grant's exoneration of Macpherson buttressed by Governor General Dalhousie's subsequent personal apology had no impact upon Lt. Col. Campbell who spent the rest of his life publicizing his own success as Meriah Agent, while attempting to cast a shadow over Macpherson's considerable accomplishments.[212]

Bitter personality clashes and bureaucratic snafus aside, the tale of the Kond Agency has attracted the attention of post modern historians and anthropologists. By far, the most straightforward account is the narrative by Barbara Boal. A missionary who lived among the Konds in the 1950s, Barbara Boal understandably relies heavily on the missionary press, particularly the *Calcutta Review*. But with her own experience of the Kond people and customs, she is able to verify the information and insights provided by Macpherson's studies almost 150 years earlier. Edith Brandstadter, by way of contrast, views the confrontation between British and Kond cultures through a prism of colonial exploitation. While correctly observing that the Government's policy initially floundered in failed litigation in the Company's courts, she makes a gigantic leap of logic over the years when Macpherson was successfully winning the trust of Goomsur Kond chiefs, while his superiors in Calcutta were distracted by events on the northwestern frontier. She then concludes that the aim of Government policy was to undermine tribal life through a process of 'Hinduization'.[213]

Most perceptive of post-modern scholars is Felix Padel. He asserts a basic premise that, whereas the outside world views human sacrifice as 'savage' or 'barbaric', Meriah sacrifice was a 'practice that at least affirms that a human life is something sacred and of great value'. He argues that Western society, in its efforts to 'civilize' tribal societies, indulge in a 'cruelty and inhumanity' that sacrifices 'the essence of what it means to be human'. Padel demonstrates how colonial soldier-administrators, missionaries and anthropologists, as well as contemporary development economists representing the World Bank at the behest of the Indian government, indulge in negative stereotypes in order to plan for social change. British rule introduced the 'modern conception of law as something that is very precisely defined but keeps changing according to a belief in "development", as well as the decisions of a remote group of

---

[212] John Campbell began by responding to the eulogies of Macpherson in the *Calcutta Review*. His *Narrative of Operations in the Hill Tracts of Orissa for the Suppression of Human Sacrifices and Female Infanticide* (London, 1861) was answered by William Macpherson's edition of Samuel C. Macpherson's correspondence under the title *Memorials of Service in India, op. cit.*

[213] Edith S. Brandstadter, 'Human Sacrifice and British-Kond Relations, 1759–1862', in Anand A. Yang, ed., *Crime and Criminality in British India* (Tucson, Arizona, 1985), p. 107, pp. 102–103.

people in power'. This is entirely alien to the 'custom sanctified by tradition' which constituted the dharma law upheld by Hindu Rajahs ruling the Kond peoples. Even today, local officials play upon 'the older conception of law as something that stays constant but is imprecisely defined' so that everything depends upon the whim of an official. Padel makes the poignant observation: 'a family can lose its land with the stroke of an offended official's pen'.[214]

Of course, at the root of post-modern obsessions with colonial exploitation is the East India Company's reliance upon military force. As noted above, the Government officially, and all district officers working among the Konds, unofficially, disavowed the use of military force to suppress Meriah sacrifice. However, it is also true that every officer, including Capt. Macpherson, felt impelled upon occasion to make a show of force, as during the Boad rebellion when Kond advisers urged Macpherson to destroy all the rebel villages. There remained only the sharp contrast between the efforts of Macpherson and his assistants to understand Kond language and culture, and the assertion of Capt. Campbell, after his return from the Opium War, that the Konds 'like all savages, and I might add, all Orientals, require to be dealt with much more of the *fortitur in re* than the *suavitur in modo*'.[215] On the foundation of this reality, the anthropologist, F.G. Bailey, builds his interpretative model of 'manipulated change'. Bailey argues that the distinction between Campbell's brutal frontal attack on Kond society and Macpherson's finesse as a mediator among feuding Kond clans is immaterial because both represent the East India Company which posed as an independent political structure rival to the Kond tribes. In depicting Campbell as a virtual terrorist who, when the Kond warriors vanished into the jungle, would 'hang the aged and infirm who could not run fast enough' and then 'burn the crops and houses', Bailey ignores the early phase of Campbell's career in the late 1830s when he rebutted colleagues who proposed such tactics. Conversely, he describes Macpherson's adroit manoeuvres among feuding Kond chiefs as a tactic for undermining clan solidarity. Having thus simplified the roles of Campbell, the terrorist, and Macpherson, the infiltrator, Bailey then employs them as instruments of manipulated change in a fascinating diagram which pits political structure against tribal environment.[216]

---

[214] Felix Padel, *op. cit.*, pp. vii, 239 and 294–95.
[215] John Campbell, *op. cit.*, pp. 108–9.
[216] F.G. Bailey, *Stratagems and Spoils—A Social Anthropology of Politics* (Oxford, 1969), pp. 186–87, 211–14. Cf. Edith Brandstadter who finds Bailey's characterization of Campbell and Macpherson 'curiously misleading'. E. Brandstadter, *op. cit.*, p. 101.

According to a report in 1854 by Lt. Col. Campbell, 1,260 Meriahs had been rescued and provided with old age pensions, settlement as *ryots*, adoption or schools.[217] By legislating a special jurisdiction for the Kond clans, the Company had enabled dedicated officers to distract Kond chiefs from their internal feuds and focus their attention upon a way of life which did not require human sacrifice. By 1850 schools were established which later became effective institutions. Because the first schools were founded by officers of the Kond Agency, they might be seen as an extension of the Agency's influence. But the subsequent success of Christian missions among first the Pans, and later the Konds, is a separate story. The Konds most effectively give their own version of the way in which the Company came to participate in their religious sacrifices. They simply revised their Meriah legend so that they could explain to the Earth Goddess: 'It was Kiomal and Mokmal [Campbell and Macpherson] who told us to give you buffaloes. It was not our fault; let the sin rest upon them'.[218]

Conclusion

Standing back from the fray, it is possible to make a few general observations. When Company officials encountered customs offensive to western sensibilities, they were instructed to avoid all interference, especially it if was determined that religious sanction supported the custom in question. In theory, the Company's willingness to legislate against specific social practices stood in reverse proportion to the degree of religious support claimed in any particular case. But, in the final analysis, the momentum for any legislative initiative depended upon the Company's assessment of its ability to implement or enforce its laws. The ideal for social legislation bequeathed by T.B. Macaulay in his Penal Code was certain reasonable punishment for criminal conduct. Macaulay disapproved of lengthy sermons in the form of preambles introducing rambling legislation based on theory. He was merely concerned to define a hard core of criminal conduct amidst customs

---

[217] Report by Lt. Col. Campbell, *Selections from Records of the Government of India*, 9 February 1854, No. V, *op. cit.*, pp. 135–36; see also K. Lahiri who sets the number of rescued Meriahs at 1506 in his 'Meriah Sacrifices', *Calcutta Review*, 3rd Series, CXXVI, No. 1 (January 1953), pp. 29–30.

[218] Verrier Elwin, *Tribal Myths of Orissa* (Bombay, 1954), p. 547.

and traditions which allowed one segment of society to exploit or torment another.

In the case of the Company's first venture into the arena of barbarous social custom—that of casting children to the sharks off Saugor Island in the mouth of the sacred Ganges River—there was a straightforward confrontation with a folk custom performed in isolation without any scriptural sanction or even support from the Brahmin priestly classes. The Company had already summoned courage to charge Benares Brahmins with homicide for killing women and children as a form of *dhurna*. Thus, Wellesley's Government was sufficiently confident to opt for full-fledged legislation in the form of Beng. Reg. VI of 1802 prohibiting the sacrifice of children to the sharks at Saugor.

The case of *sati* was much more difficult for the Company in the face of conclusions by such distinguished Sanskrit scholars as Charles Wilkins, N.B. Halhed and H.T. Colebrooke that the *sati*, indeed, enjoyed scriptural sanction. Against the backdrop of the Cornwallis Code's guarantee to all the Company's subjects of the 'free exercise of their religion', the only leverage available to the Company's courts against the mortification of *sati* was provided by Sec. 3 Beng. Reg. VIII 1799. Through this law the Company tried to make judicial process available to the *sati* by removing the protection granted to those who aided or abetted a *sati* by the Muslim law of retaliation. However, the act of the *sati* was not specified and this legal authority for punishing those who assisted a *sati* remained obscure for decades. Governors-General Wellesley, Minto and Hastings deferred to the Sudder Courts. The Sudder Dewanny Adawlut was instructed to study the issue and the Sudder Nizamut Adawlut was requested to issue procedural instructions to police *darogah*s for cases of *sati*. Inasmuch as the Chief Judge of the Dewanny Adawlut was H.T. Colebrooke, who thought he had discovered a scriptural basis for *sati* in Rigveda X.18.7, the Court's instructions implied Government approval of the rite by distinguishing between what constituted a voluntary or legal *sati* and what constituted an involuntary or illegal *sati*. The dramatic increase in the number of *satis* in the wake of the Court's instructions was an embarrassment for the Company compounded by the fact that this increase centred in Bengal near the seat of government in Calcutta. This embarrassment, hailed by the modern scholar, Ashis Nandy, as a manifestation of colonial rule, produced a stalemate during the Governor Generalship of Lord Hastings, Earl of Moira. Hastings retreated from bold advances preposed by his Sudder Court against *sati*, much to the joy of the orthodox leader, Radhakant Deb, and the dismay of the reformer, Rammohun Roy.

The presidency governments and the home government in London left the initiative in the hands of the Sudder Nizamut Adawlut. During the 1820s, despite the belief of the Chief Judge, J.H. Harington, that a 'legal prohibition' of *sati* was expedient, the Court failed over and over again to convict accused accessories, even those accessories who had clearly violated the Court's own rules. Judge C. Smith's abortive efforts to persuade his colleagues to apply Sec. 3 Beng. Reg. VIII 1799 against satis left the Company in a seemingly endless stalemate. It remained for Lord William Bentinck to make the pragmatic decision to defy the status quo and promulgate Beng. Reg. XVII on 4 December 1829 declaring all *sati*s illegal, regardless of the circumstances and those aiding or abetting a *sati* 'guilty of culpable homicide'. Bentinck's moral courage is noteworthy, given the fact that the scriptural sanction for the *sati* was not unequivocally discredited for another 25 years when H.H. Wilson and Max Müller proved that H.T. Colebrooke's translation had been based on a fraudulent text. Ironically, while Radhakant Deb contested and Rammohun Roy defended the new legislation before the Privy Council in London, it was Bentinck's law member of council, T.B. Macaulay, who clouded the issue by exempting those assisting a *sati* from the punishment for murder by declaring the *sati*'s act 'voluntary culpable homicide by consent'. Macaulay's Benthamite focus on the Penal Code did serve to rationalize the Law Commission's rejection of the Bombay Government's proposal to expand Bentinck's legislation to make 'the act of Suttee criminal in the Suttee'. His draft of a *sati* exemption ultimately emerged in the Indian Penal Code enacted in 1860 as Exception 5 to Sec. 300, with the elimination of 'voluntary' the only modification.

Despite a lingering addiction to the rite among the proud and manly Rajputs, the British Raj and its historians have generally credited Bentinck and the East India Company with the abolition of *sati*.[219] Perversely, 40 years after Indian Independence, the controversy erupted all over again among the same proud and manly Rajputs, with Roop Kanwar's dramatic action and instant legislative responses by the Rajasthan State and Central Governments. The identical preambles of Beng. Reg. XVII 1829 and the Sati Act No. 3 of 1988 underline the constancy of faith in law as a signpost distinguishing

---

[219] V.N. Datta perpetuates this view, whereas Jörg Fisch argues that Beng. Reg. XVII 1829 was 'not so much a great humanitarian achievement, as a late acknowledgement of a failed policy', in Jörg Fisch, *op. cit.*, p. 364. For a deconstruction of the adulation of Bentinck, see Nancy G. Cassels, 'Bentinck: Humanitarian and Imperialist—the Abolition of Suttee', *The Journal of British Studies*, Vol. V, No. 1 (November, 1965), pp. 77–87.

what is acceptable or legal from what is unacceptable or illegal in society. The Bombay Government's proposal in the mid-1830s to make the 'act of Suttee criminal in the Suttee' actually became law almost overnight in the legislatures of the Rajasthan State and Central Governments of 1987–88. That legislators of independent India have acted more impulsively and interfered further with private mores than the legislators of the Company Raj ever dared, is a sobering thought, indeed. Professor Dhagamwar paid an enormous tribute to Macaulay's vision with her statement that all the offences in the legislation of 1987–88 were already covered by the Indian Penal Code so that the most that was needed in the aftermath of Roop Kanwar's immolation was an 'amendment to S.300 Exception 5 to declare that in no case of sati would the woman be regarded as having given her consent'. She allowed only that 'perhaps' a new law was needed to make the glorification and exploitation of the *sati* criminal offences.

The very nature of the practice of female infanticide negated any thoughts of legislation parallel with Beng. Reg. XVII 1829 for the abolition of *sati*. Whereas the flaming funeral pile of the sati was a bold public act, it was almost impossible to obtain evidence of the murder of a female infant in the seclusion of a private household. Nonetheless, legislation against female infanticide shared the same putative legislative base as *sati* legislation in the form of Beng. Reg. VIII 1799, Sec. 2 of which modified the Muslim law of retaliation in order to expose to the death sentence parents and grandparents convicted of murdering their children. In the case of female infanticide, there was also an apparent legislative head start in Sec. 13 of Beng. Reg. XXI of 1795 enacted to enforce Jonathan Duncan's engagements with the Rajkumars, and reenacted as Sec. 11 Ced. Prov. Reg. III 1894. However, from the vantage point of the East India Company as legislator, the advantage of a lack of scriptural sanction for the practice of female infanticide was offset by complex motivating factors ranging from marriage costs to the interrelated social status of different Rajput clans.

As Col. Walker ruefully observed when he surveyed the failure of the Bombay Government to enforce his engagements with the Jahrejas of Kathiawar, an effective policy against female infanticide depended upon a free flowing social intercourse between rulers and ruled which was pretty well nonexistent in the *mofussil*. Walker's zeal for reform was further frustrated by Gov. Mounstuart Elphinstone's reluctance to interfere in the private affairs of the upper castes of his Indian subjects. Elphinstone placed his faith in the civilizing effect of the company's reign of law and order. His neutral contribution to the infanticide policy based on Col. Walker's Engagements was an Infanticide Fund. This fund, composed of fines collected from infanticidal chiefs who reneged on their Engagements was to be distributed to families who had preserved their daughters. However, the fund was not dispensed as planned, being diverted to cover the cost of a military expedition in the first instance, and then being allowed to accumulate a huge surplus by the year 1840.

Governors and Governors-General alike kept the issue of female infanticide at arm's length. An aggressive anti-infanticide policy undertaken by J.P. Willoughby as Political Agent in Kathiawar seemed, at first, to be successful with rewards from the Infanticide Fund for meritorious Jahreja chiefs and informers who helped to secure three infanticide convictions by the Bombay High Court in 1834–35. But this success quickly turned sour, as the most prominent Chief to be convicted became a martyr among his own people at the Company's expense and some informers were murdered. District officers came to the conclusion that female infanticide 'was not a safe subject to investigate and legislate upon'. Instead, they shifted their anti-infanticide policy towards education with grants from the Infanticide Fund for essay contests in schools. This hostility among Bombay officers towards any idea of legislation on the subject of infanticide was reenforced by the Law Commission in Calcutta which rejected proposals for fresh infanticide legislation.

Meanwhile, district officers in Rajputana and the N.W.P. had discovered that female infanticide was flourishing even among descendants of the Rajputs who had originally signed Engagements with Jonathan Duncan renouncing the practice. In the N.W.P. and Rajputana, Company officials tended to disagree over whether a coercive or educational strategy was more effective. The culmination of the educational approach was a number of *panchayat*s or *durbar*s of infanticidal chiefs who gathered to agree to change their ways. The ultimate coercive tactics involved espionage and inspection of infant corpses by the Civil Surgeon. The higher levels of government disapproved coercive tactics.

But the magistrates of the N.W.P. were the same magistrates who had been granted special powers by the Thagi and Dacoity Department to commit thugs before the courts. When these magistrates witnessed infanticide cases which ended over and over again in acquittal for lack of evidence, they exploded in frustration. One C.T. Le Bas, Magistrate of Jaunpur, called for the appointment of special commissioners entrusted with the same powers as the Commissioners for the suppression of thagi. The frustration of these magistrates was destined to continue, for they were denied special powers. However, they may have been gratified by the appointment of W.R. Moore as Special commissioner for Investigating the Extent of Female Infanticide in Benares Division with the full powers of a Joint Magistrate. Finding that the infanticidal Rajput clans were addicted to their murderous habits, Moore called for intensive police surveillance and a new law which would designate 'suspected' villages in accordance with a census of Rajput children under six years of age. In forwarding Moore's report to the Lt. Governor, Commissioner H.C. Tucker recommended also that the new law should 'constitute "Female Infanticide" a distinct offence in the same manner as Act XXIV of 1843 constituted having belonged to a Gang of Dacoits a distinct offence'. Lt. Gov. Colvin could not accept the designation of female infanticide as a 'distinct offence', but he did instruct the Nizamut Adawlut of the N.W.P. to draft a new law for the suppression of female infanticide. Colvin encouraged the Judges to implement Moore's suggestions that a special police establishment be created at the expense of infanticidal villages and that *panchayat*s be promoted to regulate marriage expenses.

The saga of this fresh legislative initiative in the N.W.P. was brutally interrupted by the rebellion of 1857. Unlike Rajput chiefs in Punjab who remained loyal to the East India Company, the infanticidal clans of the N.W.P. participated in the uprising and some were later punished by the confiscation of their estates. W.R. Moore, himself, was killed in action. Inasmuch as the infanticidal districts of the N.W.P. were also the scene of the destruction of 1857, any legislative initiative on the subject of female infanticide fell by default into the hands of the Central Government. The immediate result was the replacement of Sec. 13 Beng. Reg. XXI of 1795 with the simplified Secs 315 and 317–18 of the Penal Code enacted in 1860. Though limited, the Penal Code at least prescribed certain punishment for the 'exposure of infants and concealment of births'. From the perspective of Calcutta, the simplified and generalized penal law appeared a useful answer to the problem of female infanticide among the Rajputs. But in the N.W.P., the Penal Code was quickly judged to be inadequate. Almost immediately, the Lt. Governor of the N.W.P. began to lobby the Central Government for a special infanticide law along the lines of the Draft Act of 1856. When the Central Government surveyed the other presidencies and even some princely states as to the need for a new infanticide law, the response was overwhelmingly negative. It took an alarming report from R.T. Hobart, Joint Magistrate of Basti district, to force the issue. Hobart asserted that infanticide had, in fact, increased since the time of W.R. Moore, ostensibly as a result of the poverty caused by the Government's confiscation of lands as punishment for participation in the 1857 uprising. The viceregal response was necessarily a call for special legislation for the suppression of female infanticide.

John Strachey, the member of council assigned to draft the new law, adopted the 1856 draft of the Agra Sudder Court as his model. Act VIII for the Prevention of the Murder of Female Infants became law on 4 April 1870. Finally, the simple minded Sec. 13 Beng. Reg. XXI 1795 was succeeded by a flexible law open to the complexity of the multi-faceted nature of the crime. The flexibility derived from Sec. 2 which transferred to local governments responsibility for taking a thorough census of clans designated as being subject to this special legislation. If necessary, these local governments were authorized to raise a special police force, devise means of paying for it and limit marriage expenses among the specially designated clans. The Committee formed in the N.W.P. to frame rules in accordance with Act VIII, in effect, implemented the suggestions advanced by W.R. Moore. In Rule 26 there was even an effort to resurrect the tactics of M.R. Gubbins in requiring infant corpses to be forwarded to the Civil Surgeon. But, the Infanticide Committee ultimately disallowed this rule.

Although Act VIII of 1870 was enacted during the viceroyalty of Lord Mayo, it, nevertheless, must be understood to be the work of district officers under the East India Company culminating in the 1856 draft of the Agra Sudder Court and then deferred by the events of 1857. Beginning with Viceroy Mayo, high-ranking officers of the British Raj were anxious to regard Act VIII 1870 as an indication that female infanticide had been successfully suppressed. Sadly, the practice has become endemic in the twentieth century, spread far beyond the control of a handful of Rajput clans. If legislation were to be considered an answer to the infanticide which plagues India today, Act VIII 1870 would need to be radically revised in order to incorporate pressures in Indian society that are far more complex than the fierce pride which divided Rajput clans in the days of the East India Company.

The rites of Meriah sacrifice and female infanticide among the Kond tribes raised some new questions for Company officialdom. For a start, a legislative response was never a considered option as it had been in all the cases cited above. Because the Konds lived beyond or, at least, barely within reach of the East India Company's regulations, there was not much point in trying to dictate new mores by passing a regulation or legislative act. The real point of debate concerned the degree to which military force should be used. And, the legislation that was enacted addressed the need to establish a special agency with special powers in a geographical area newly designated to accommodate all the Konds. As in the case of female infanticide in the N.W.P., there were requests for authority modelled after the Thagi Department. But also, as in the case of the N.W.P., these requests were denied.

Just as effective action against female infanticide in the Regulation provinces depended upon social interaction and familiarity between the Company's officers and the offending clans, so did effective action against infanticide among the Konds. Because the Konds lived in remote jungle, across difficult terrain, accessible only in winter when malaria was not quite such a deadly threat and because the Konds' initial contact with the British occurred during the Goomsur Wars, there was little opportunity for social interaction. However, Capt. Macpherson developed an effective procedure for adjudicating feuds among the tribes. The reputation among Kond chiefs achieved by Capt. Macpherson for his administration of justice was extraordinary. Macpherson relied as much as possible upon Kond traditions so as not to force an alien system of law upon these tribal peoples. Indeed, Macpherson was rewarded by the discovery that the Konds operated to a much higher standard of personal integrity than could be found in the Company's courts on the plains. It was by winning the trust of Kond chiefs through his function as a quasi-judicial arbiter that Macpherson managed to negotiate the substitution of the buffalo for the Meriah among sacrificing tribes and the acceptance of Meriah wards as brides by repentant, formerly infanticidal chiefs.

As with *sati* and female infanticide in the Regulation provinces, initially efforts were made to work through the courts. But, all such efforts were quickly rendered abortive by the difficulties of translating the Dravidian Kui language and of obtaining evidence among a people who were totally unfamiliar with and contemptuous of the Company's court system. Any effort at prosecution was necessarily restricted to the Hindu Pans or procurers of Meriahs on the plains. There are other points of comparison between the Company's campaign against *sati* and that against Meriah sacrifice. Whereas there was some question of scriptural sanction for the sacrifice of the *sati*, there was no doubt of the religious base for the sacrifice of the Meriah. Just as the Company's legislators and administrators transformed the *sati* from a saint into a victim, so the Company's officers transformed the Meriah from a divinity into a victim. However, because the Meriah was beyond the reach of direct legislation, the Company finally decided to create a special agency with full magisterial powers under the careful supervision of the Sudder Courts. The Agent for the suppression of Meriah Sacrifice never had the independent authority won by Col. Sleeman for his superintendents for the suppression of thagi. However, legislation was useful in creating a jurisdiction for making uniform policy among the Konds. This policy involved sufficient interaction between the Company's officers and the Kond chiefs to produce the result that the Konds requested and received permission to denounce before their gods the British Government for ending the sacrifice of the Meriah. This, in the final analysis, was a matter neither of law nor military force, but rather an understanding between peoples of alien cultures and values. *Sati* and female infanticide, at least in the Regulation provinces, became subjects of law ultimately enshrined in the Penal Code, with special legislation enacted subsequently in response to apparent need. Meriah sacrifice and female infanticide among the Konds were subjects of negotiations between the Company's officers and proud Kond chiefs.

3

The Legal Rights of Coolies, Slaves and Emigrant Workers

The Chermar has in reality but few 'rights', and fewer 'benefits' and indeed differs very little in this respect from the other farm stock of their master. The ox and the Chermar are both fed and housed up to their value for work but very little beyond it.[1]

Slave labour, bonded labour and hired labour have been integral features of the Indian economy since historical records began. However, the terminology for different types of labour and labour conditions varied from region to region and even from district to district within regions. For example, in Malabar the labourers classified as slaves by British administrators were considered by high-caste landowners to be simply low-caste Chermars (Chamars) destined for labour in the fields. Labourers pressed to serve as Hill Porters between Almora and the plains were known as Khuseeas.[2] In Bihar 'ploughing, sowing, weeding and irrigation on which success in agriculture must greatly depend [were] effected by the "Moosher" or labourer, who [resembled] a Slave in every respect except that of being at liberty to reside where he [pleased]'.[3] In south Bihar agricultural labourers known as Kamias were linked with *malik*s or landlords for a lifetime of labour, living a restricted lifestyle with

---

[1] Criticism of the Law Commission's Report on Slavery by E.B. Thomas, Judge, Malabar, to Register, Foujdaree Udalut of Ft. St. George, 24 August 1842, Extract from Proceedings of the Sudr Udalut, 12 September 1842, Consultations 18 November 1842, No. 11, N.A.I., Legislative Department A, fol. 41.

[2] R.T. Glynn, Commissioner at Almorah, to George W. Traill, Commissioner at Kumaon, Almorah, 6 July 1822, U.P.S.A., C.O.K., Lucknow, Miscellaneous Letters Received by Commissioner at Kumaon, fols 209–10.

[3] Report by John Thurston Reade, Assistant to the Commissioner on Deputation, to J. Dunsmure, Acting Secretary to Board of Commissioners on deputation in Bihar, 17 November 1819, B.S.A., P.C.O., p. 88.

wages for days worked and assistance in times of need.[4] In Ramgurh in Chota Nagpur the term *soukeea* was used indiscriminately to indicate both the state of slavery and the person of the slave. However, in Chota Nagpur generally the term *sawuck* was more common. A *sawuck* was a labourer who executed a deed called a *sawuck puttna* according to which, in return for a loan 'amounting from 8 to 12 rupees', he became his creditor's 'bondsman for life'. Such a *sawuck* was guaranteed food, clothing and payment of marriage expenses as part of his bondage. It was also possible to be a *chota Sawuck* in bondage 'for a specified time' or until the loan was repaid with interest. A 'chota Sawuck' could expect 'an allowance for a maund of rice per mensem and one rupee...on the occasion of the cold season to purchase some warm clothing'. Or, a person could agree to 'hire himself for field labour' in return for 'six rupees a year and twelve maunds of rice'.[5]

Whatever the terminology, the East India Company was consistent in its reluctance to tamper with the relationship between master and servant. However, by the end of the eighteenth century, there was legal recognition for the slave's right to protection from criminal abuse by his master and for the cooly's right to protection from forced labour. Ultimately, European disapproval of slavery spurred heated debate—mostly among Europeans—until finally slavery was the subject of legislation by the Indian Government in 1843. Legislation guaranteeing the cooly a fair contract with appropriate wages developed parallel with the campaign for ostensible, legal abolition of slavery.

Nevertheless, the plight of the ill paid and exploited cooly only became an urgent matter of policy for the Indian Government in the 1830s when the Colonial Office joined with the Indian Government to raise a hue and cry over the perceived exploitation of Indian labourers emigrating to the sugar plantations of Mauritius and the West Indies. This emigrant labour which became the subject of numerous protective laws has been condemned as the 'New Slavery'.[6] And, more recently post-colonial historians have discarded the framework of 'New Slavery' in favour of a more complex analysis of the management of Indian subaltern labourers. Clare Anderson, in particular,

---

[4] Gyan Prakash, *Bonded Histories: Genealogies of Labor Servitude in Colonial India* (Cambridge, 1990), p. 1.

[5] Report by Mr Heatly, Collector, cited in Andrew Drummond (Surgeon), *Statistical Account of the Hazaribagh Division of the Political Agency South West Frontier*, 1775, I.O.R., India Office Reference Map Collection, X/1318, pp. 38–40.

[6] Hugh Tinker, *A New System of Slavery: The Export of Indian Labour Overseas 1830–1920* (New York, 1974).

has observed many similarities in ways of managing both convict or forced labourers and indentured or 'unfree' plantation labourers.[7] Although officers of the East India Company endeavoured to bestow legal rights upon those labourers they perceived as slaves or *coolies*, no effort was made to tamper with an established relationship between master and servant. This allowed the evils of bonded labour to endure throughout the nineteenth and twentieth centuries. The East India Company's primary concern was to create a level playing field in the market for Indian labour. Privately negotiated contracts such as the *sawuck puttna* which bonded labourers for a lifetime were regarded as beyond the jurisdiction of the Company's law courts. Whether or not they were protected by legislation giving them rights in a court of law, slaves, coolies and bonded labourers consistently suffered from their low status in Indian society. The illiterate slave was unlikely to claim his legal rights; the emigrant cooly labourer, saved from colonial exploitation abroad, was returned to the very poverty and lack of opportunity which had driven him to emigrate in the first place; desperate poverty had perpetuated the misery of bonded labour, one legacy of which is the present day curse of child labour. Nonetheless, the East India Company's efforts to save slave and cooly labour from criminal oppression is a compelling story of a European government attempting to graft European values and legal rights onto Indian traditions and customs.

Cooly Labour

The Collector of Coimbatore who remarked that 'slaves are on the whole better treated by their masters than the common class of free labourers'[8] touched upon a raw sore of the Indian body politic. The lowest classes and castes of Indian society who performed intensive seasonal agricultural labour or services to the army or to the imperial court were commonly ill paid and ill treated. Traditionally, the concept of 'naukee' or, service at the courts of the great Indian emperors conveyed dignity and honour. But service translated into hired cooly labour from the bottom rungs of Indian society conveyed contempt and degradation. The origin of the word 'cooly' is confused by the

---

[7] Clare Anderson, 'Rethinking Indian Indentured Labour in the Nineteenth Century' (a paper from the 20th European Conference on Modern South Asian Studies, Manchester, July, 2008).

[8] Collectors' answers paraphrased by A.D. Campbell to Hill, Board of Revenue Proceedings, 25 November 1819, *Parliamentary Papers* (1828) XXIV, Cmd. 125, p. 899.

existence of an Indian hill tribe known as Koli, by the fact that hill coolies were most prominent among the coolies and, finally by the existence of the term in both Chinese and Portuguese. After surveying numerous etymological sources for the word 'cooly', Hugh Tinker comes to the reasonable conclusion that 'the term...was used to describe those at the lowest level of the industrial labour market'.[9]

The aspect of cooly labour which most offended British sensibilities was the practice of *begaree* or pressed labour. This practice was ultimately defined by the 1827 Elphinstone Code in Bombay as:

> Compelling a person to serve as porter or guide by means of personal violence, as blows, or such treatment as produces corporal pain or injury: or by means of violence to property, as seizing or injuring any article belonging to him or in his occupation; or by means of threats expressed in words, or conveyed by conduct denoting an intention to inflict some injury to person or property apparently in the power of the culprit to effect.[10]

In the very earliest stages of the promulgation of the Cornwallis Code, Judicial Regulation XXV of 1790 forbid military officers and travellers from sending 'sepoys or Lascars into the villages for the purpose of procuring any sort of provisions or of pressing Coolies and Dandees'.[11] Shortly thereafter Sec. LXIX Reg. XXII of 1795 gave legal recognition to a prohibition issued in Benares three years earlier against 'begaree or the practice of individuals seizing and compulsively exacting service from artificers, masons and other workmen or servants'.[12] Confronted by the need to ferry large detachments of troops and their equipment through its territory, the East India Company enacted Bengal Regulation XI in 1806 to enable commanding officers in transit across the country to apply to local police for assistance in procuring the necessary 'coolies, boatmen, carts or bullocks'. Extending the prohibition enacted earlier in Benares to the entire Bengal presidency,

---

[9] Hugh Tinker, *op. cit.*, p. 43.

[10] Clause 2, Section XVII, Bombay Regulation XII for the Establishment of a system of Police throughout the zillas subordinate to Bombay; (passed 1 January 1827), I.O.R., V/8/24.

[11] Judicial Regulation XXV, Notification Prohibiting the use of the Uniform of the Company's Sepoys and Lascars by other Persons (issued 26 May 1790), I.O.R., V/8/15, pp. 218–19. *Dandee*s were boatmen who plied the Ganges.

[12] Regulation XXII for preserving the Record of the principal Rules regarding the Administration of Justice and Police in the Province of Benares passed between 1781 and the period of the abolition of the office of the Resident in 1795; and for determining what Part of those Rules are to be considered still in Force (passed 27 March 1795), I.O.R., V/8/16, pp. 543.

Sec. VIII Beng. Reg. XI 1806 forbid police officers 'under pain of dismission from office…to compel any persons not accustomed to act as bearers, coolies or boatmen to serve on such occasions'. Sec. VIII further enjoined police officers to ensure that 'proper compensation' was paid to the coolies and 'a just price' paid for provisions supplied.[13] Thus from the start, the Company was concerned, not with the lowly status of the cooly, but with the ideal of creating a level playing field so that 'proper compensation' and 'a just price' were paid for labour and supplies.

By the turn of the century in Madras, the Government required Collectors to complete a 'Table' in the languages of their respective districts and in English of the 'rates of cooly hire from Village to Village and Station to Station' calculated by each Collector in the 'Current Coin of his District'. The Collectors were further instructed 'to obviate any just cause of complaint, on the part of the Coolies from detention on the road' by distinguishing in their lists of rates between 'Coolies despatched with loads for any of the specified stations and daily hire for Coolies proceeding in company with Detachments or Travellers "till they are relieved"'. When the Coolies were discharged, they were to be 'further paid the same daily hire to compensate them for their Journey back without loads to the Station from which they were taken, calculating at the rate of 30 Miles per diem'. If coolies deserted before reaching the destination for which they had been hired, the Collectors had to find replacements. However, the Madras Government issued 'express orders…that pressing of Coolies…be as much as possible avoided'.[14]

Although the Madras Government's disapproval of the practice of pressed labour had been generally proclaimed in a Military General Order dated 10 December 1794,[15] there was no legislation on the subject in Madras until Clause 5 Section IX of Madras Regulation III 1810 reproduced almost word for word the prohibition first issued in Bengal by Judicial Reg. XXV of 1790. Sec. VIII of the same Madras Regulation had already reiterated the guarantee in Sec. VIII of Beng. Reg. XI 1806 of 'proper compensation for

---

[13] Bengal Regulation XI for facilitating the Progress of Detachments of Troops through the Company's Territories; for affording any requisite Assistance to Persons travelling through those Territories; and for extending rules…to the whole of the Company's Provinces subject to the immediate Government of the Presidency of Fort William; (passed on 3 July 1806), I.O.R., V/8/18, pp. 195–96.

[14] 'Draft of the Proposed Regulations for Coolies' enclosed in H.B. Travers, Secretary to Board of Revenue, to Collector of Tanjore, Fort St. George, 9 January 1801, T.N.A., Tanjore District Records, Vol. 3178, fols 11–14.

[15] *Ibid.*, fols 6, 9.

bearers, coolies, boatmen, carts or bullocks…and a just price for provisions'.[16] Insofar as Madras Reg. III of 1810 summarized the legislation concerning the rights of coolies in Bengal, it was only to be expected that the Bombay Government would follow suit which, indeed, it did by enacting a carbon copy of Madras Reg. III in Bombay Regulation VII of 1814.[17] Interestingly, the careful plans, reported in Tanjore in the 1790s, for 'Tables' of rates of cooly hire to be tabulated in each district, did not surface as an integral part of the official regulations until 1816 when Col. Munro and his fellow commissioners delivered their plans for reform of the Madras judicial system. Sec. LIII Madras Regulation XI of 1816, in pursuit of the objective stated in the preamble as a 'system of Police founded chiefly upon the ancient usages of the country', authorized magistrates 'to determine the rates of hire to be paid in their respective districts by travellers to palankeen bearers, coolies and boatmen' and to publicize these rates in a 'table authenticated by the signature of the Magistrate'.[18] Within two years the Bombay Government picked up the Madras initiative and reproduced the principles and tactics of Madras Reg. XI of 1816 in the preamble and Sec. LII of Bombay Regulation IV of 1818.[19]

Despite these efforts to legislate a code of fair practices for cooly hire, there was abundant evidence of abuse and oppression. Colourful testimony of such abuse came from Henry Russell, the Resident of Hyderabad, who reported on the behaviour of travellers and troops crossing the Nizam's non-Regulation territory from the Regulation provinces of Bengal and Madras. He recollected that 'a gentleman lately travelling here from Calcutta, found, on his arrival at a Village within the Nizam's frontier, that it had been entirely deserted by its inhabitants; and learnt that they had fled to avoid being pressed as Coolies'.[20] Within months of Russell's testimony, Governor General Hastings enacted

---

[16] Madras Regulation III for facilitating the progress of detachments of troops through the Company's territories; for affording any requisite assistance to persons travelling through the territories; (passed 6 November 1810), I.O.R., V/8/27.

[17] Bombay Regulation VII for facilitating the progress of detachments of troops through the Company's territories; for affording any requisite assistance to persons travelling through the territories;…(passed 17 August 1814), I.O.R., V/8/22.

[18] Madras Regulation XI for the establishment of a General System of Police Throughout the Territories Subject to the Government of Fort St. George (passed 13 September 1816), I.O.R., V/8/28.

[19] Bombay Regulation IV for the Establishment of a general system of Police throughout the territories subject to the Government of Bombay (passed 10 June 1818), I.O.R., V/8/23.

[20] H. Russell, Resident of Hyderabad, to C.T. Metcalfe, Secretary to Government of Fort William, Hyderabad, 25 July 1819, Bengal Political Consultations, 4 September 1819, No. 22, I.O.R., *Board's Collections*, F/4/773, fols 5–6.

Bengal Regulation III of 1820 which deplored the apparent sanction given by Beng. Reg. XI 1806 to the 'highly injurious practice, which prevails, of forcibly pressing certain classes of inhabitants of towns and villages under the denomination of *begarees* or coolies, for the purpose of carrying baggage or other loads from stage to stage or village to village'. Sec. II of Beng. Reg. III 1820 rescinded 'such part of the provisions of Reg. XI 1806 as authorize Collectors...or Magistrates...to give their official aid in procuring coolies' for travellers and troop detachments on the march. Within a very few years, the lack of precision in this reference to Beng. Reg. XI 1806 was to become useful to the Company faced with a continuing need for the services of cooly labour. However, Sec III of Beng. Reg. III 1820 declared unequivocally that

> the practice of pressing or compelling individuals, whether under the denomination of coolies, begarees or any other denomination, to carry burthens either for the public service or for the convenience of private individuals is hereby positively prohibited.[21]

Within five years of the legislation of this prohibition, the Company's concern for its ability to provide for its troops in transit across British territory appeared to overshadow the issue of pressed or forced labour. Without any mention of the prohibition against forced labour, Bengal Regulation VI of 1825 called for strict enforcement of Sec. III Beng. Reg. XI 1806 which made it incumbent upon all landholders to answer their district Collector's call for supplies and preparations for the 'march of troops' across their lands. Reg. VI 1825 referred to Cl. 2, Sec. III Beng. Reg. XI 1806 in order to emphasize the furnishing of supplies 'at current bazaar prices' and the preparation of 'boats, temporary bridges, or otherwise, for enabling Troops to cross Rivers, or Nullahs, intersecting their march'. No effort was made to discount the provision in Cl. 1, Sec. III, Reg. XI 1806 declaring it to be the 'duty of such native officers to provide troops with whatever bearers, coolies, boatmen, carts and bullocks may be indispensably necessary to enable the troops to prosecute their route'.[22]

It remained only for Secs XVII and XVIII of Reg. XII of the Elphinstone Code in Bombay to incorporate the cumulative substance of every regulation

---

[21] Bengal Regulation III for rescinding some of the provisions of Beng. Reg. XI 1806 and for preventing the practice of pressing coolies or *begarees* (passed on 24 March 1820), I.O.R., V/8/20.

[22] Cl. 2, Sec. III, Beng. Reg. XI 1806, *op. cit.*; Bengal Regulation VI for rendering more effectual Rules in force, relative to supplies and preparations for Troops, proceeding through British Territory (passed 4 April 1825), I.O.R., V/8/20.

enacted on the subject of pressed labour by the Government of Fort William since Sec. LXIX Reg. XXII 1795. True to the spirit of the Elphinstone Code, Bom. Reg. XII 1827 provided the full definition of 'pressed labour' cited above as well as a detailed format of graded fines or prison terms—all under ₹ 40 commutable to eight days in prison—for those who defied the law with acts of violence. The Bengal Regulations had spoken of punishment only in general terms, the most specific reference being the ceiling of 1000 Sa. ₹ set by Beng. Reg. VI 1825 for fines to be exacted from local officers who defaulted on their obligation to respond to their Collector's demand for labour or supplies.

With such an emphasis upon the obligation to supply cooly labour over and above the rights of the labourer, it is hardly surprising that in 1831 F.C. Smith, the Agent for the Governor General in the Saugor and Nerbudda Territories, voiced his suspicion that the 'salutary and humane provisions of Regulation III of 1820 forbidding the pressing of Coolies and Begaries have fallen into desuetude'. In an attempt to remedy the situation, Smith called upon the commanding officer of the Saugor Division of the Army to enforce 'the prohibition issued by Government (Reg. III of 1820) in the Marquis of Hastings's administration...(of) compulsory exaction of the service of individuals as porters or Coolies in aid of travellers or marching troops'. This was Smith's response to 'numerous complaints...made...by the Potails of Villages situated in the neighbourhood of the high roads...of the injury suffered by their Assamese and Cultivators from the practice of pressing Coolies and Begaries'. Yet, on a practical note, he recalled the 'rules of Regulation XI of 1806' as a 'standing Military Order' still valid except for the prohibition against forced labour legislated in Reg. III 1820. He then sent Circulars to his principal assistants advising them 'to make arrangements with the Potails of the Villages in the line of roads for them to furnish travellers with Coolies at a price to be settled by you after full enquiry into the usual price of labour and payable in advance'. After issuing these instructions, Smith reflected that 'I fear we have engaged in a task contrary to the habits and customs of the people and that we must therefore expect success to be gained solely by slow and almost imperceptible degrees'.[23]

---

[23] F.C. Smith, Agent to the Governor General in the Saugor and Nerbudda Territories, to H.T. Prinsep, Secretary to the Governor General in the Political Department, Headquarters, Camp Chindmarra, Nursingpoor district, 31 January 1831, I.O.R., *Board's Collections*, F/4/1382, No. 55136, fols 5–6; F. C. Smith, Agent of the Governor General in the Saugor and Nerbudda Territories, to Brig. General O'Hallaran, C.B., Commanding Saugor Division of the Army, Camp Nursingpoor, 28 January 1831, I.O.R., *Board's Collections*, F/4/1382, Reg. 55136, fol. 9.

The Legal Rights 173

The East India Company's willingness to accept limited objectives in its campaign against forced labour were perhaps best expressed in a letter from the Home Authorities to the Government in Bengal. They approved the proposal of a Lt. Ross in the hill country to substitute beasts of burden for hill porters. Yet, they issued the caveat that 'if it should be found impracticable to introduce the employment of Mules or other Beasts of Burthen, we hope that the Begaurs may eventually be induced by the certainty of a fair remuneration for their labours to volunteer their services in the performance of a necessary duty'.[24] Apparently, no amount of idealism could alter the fundamental demand for cooly labour in both European and Indian society.

Slavery[25]

Act V of 1843 by which the East India Company proclaimed slavery to be illegal within its Indian territories culminated 70 years of controversy. On one side of this 70-year debate were Company officials, many of very senior ranks, who argued that slavery in India was uniquely entangled with Muslim and Hindu law and custom; these Company servants were exponents of a traditionalism which guaranteed support for immemorial custom against any kind of Government interference. On the other side of the debate were Evangelicals within and without Parliament who, heady with the success of their campaign against the African slave trade and slavery in the West Indies, turned their attention towards the East Indies; they virtually forced the Board of Control to order the Court of Directors to demand, in turn, that the Government of India take legislative action against slavery in India.

Most latter-day historians agree that the debate on Indian slavery was conducted on distressingly superficial grounds. With the advantage of hindsight, twentieth-century historians were outraged by the view which prevailed among revenue collectors, legislative councillors and Law Commissioners that Indian slavery was exceedingly mild, totally unlike the oppressively evil slavery of the West Indian sugar plantations. Such remarks as W.W. Bird's statement before Governor General Auckland's legislative council that 'Slavery in India is little more than a name' provoked Benedicte

---

[24] Political Despatch to Bengal, 1 December 1819, I.O.R., E/4/697, fol. 775.
[25] The substance of this section appeared as 'Social Legislation under the Company Raj: The Abolition of Slavery—Act V 1843', in *South Asia—Journal of South Asian Studies*, New Series, Vol. XI, No. 1 (June 1988): 59–87.

Hjejle to declare that all the consultations of the legislative council reflected an abysmal ignorance of the 'real extent and nature of Indian slavery'.[26] Writing 30 years earlier than Hjejle and in a less controversial manner, D.R. Banaji nonetheless voiced dismay and suspicion over the insistence of a Law Commissioner that the Indian slave master had no power to extort productive labour from his slave.[27]

Insofar as the Company was consistently reluctant to abolish slavery outright, its officials, serving on administrative boards and consultative councils ranging from the Madras Board of Revenue to the Governor General's legislative council, focused on small points of law, four of which ultimately constituted Act V of 1843. The fact that most slave labour became bonded labour after the passing of Act V inspired one cynical observer to conclude that the Act was a 'calculated effort' to release a supply of cooly labour for coffee plantations, railroads and roads in the Nilgiris and indentured labour for the colonies.[28] The conventional wisdom among historians regarding the Company's slavery policy would appear to lie somewhere between this total cynicism and the view that the Company was simply reluctant to upset slave owning *mirasidars*. Contemporary research on colonial mentalities is inclined to regard the Company's law-making process as a colonial exercise. For example, Gyan Prakash attributes 'the general discourse framed by freedom and slavery' to a 'juridical notion of power' among 'colonial officials'. Yet, Prakash and another Bihar scholar, both observe that Act V 1843 made it impossible to perpetuate any form of bondage which smacked of a master–slave relationship.[29] Such an acknowledgment of the force of law rather undercuts the need to dismiss all British policies in India as a colonial exercise in projecting western notions of power relationships onto Indian society. The following historical narrative is intended to challenge both those historians who blandly accept Company policy dictums at face

---

[26] W.W. Bird, Minute 18 June 1841, India Legislative Proceedings, 6 September 1841, No. 11, I.O.R., P/207/17; Benedicte Hjejle, 'Slavery and Agricultural Bondage in South India in the Nineteenth Century', *The Scandinavian Economic History Review* XI (1967): 92–98.

[27] D.R. Banaji, *Slavery in British India* (Bombay, 1933), pp. 343–44.

[28] Manjari Dingwaney, 'Unredeemed Promises: The Law and Servitude' in Utsa Patnaik and Manjari Dingwaney, eds., *Chains of Servitude: Bondage and Slavery in India* (Madras, 1985), p. 313.

[29] Gyan Prakash, 'Bonded Labor in South Bihar: A Contestatory History', paper from the Conference on 'South Asia and World Capitalism', Tufts University, December 1986, pp. 14, 16–17; Jacques Pouchepadass, 'The Market for Agricultural Labour in Colonial North Bihar (1860–1920)', paper from the Ninth European Conference on Modern South Asian Studies, Heidelberg, July 1986.

The Legal Rights 175

value and the critics who give the Company little credit for grappling with the problem of slavery.

Numerous Company officials, in a genuine quest for justice for the Indian slave, went beyond legitimate concern for revenue and stability. There were Company servants at all levels motivated by a keen respect for the religion and social institutions of Hindus and Muslims. It was this traditionalism which inspired the Government of India to resist extreme pressure from England to take legislative action against Indian slavery—action which men on the spot deemed to be inappropriate. Indeed, this traditionalism had been enshrined as legal principle in regulations of the Warren Hastings administration and in the Cornwallis Code. Warren Hastings' Government undertook to protect the caste and property of its Hindu and Mahomedan subjects. In 1793 the Cornwallis Code guaranteed Hindus and Mahomedans that

> ... in suits regarding succession, inheritance, marriage, and caste, and all religious usages and institutions, the Mahomedan laws with respect to Mahomedans, and the Hindoo laws with regard to Hindoos, are to be considered as the general rules by which the Judges are to form their decisions.[30]

This principle was reiterated in the 1795 Act of Parliament 35 Geo III c. 155.

Insofar as Indian masters had established slaves to be their property and insofar as these property rights were defined by Hindu and Mahomedan law, successive Indian governments felt legally bound to show respect for such property claims. Indeed, on 12 April 1798, the Governor General in Council endorsed a ruling by the Calcutta Sudder Dewanny Adawlut that the spirit of the 1793 Regulation for observing Hindu and Mahomedan laws regarding property was 'applicable to cases of Slavery'.[31] Thus slavery became the law of the land in the Company's civil courts. However, within a year the Governor General's Council, with an eye to the 'ends of public justice', empowered the criminal courts to punish a master who murdered or abused his slave. After the enactment of Section II Bengal Regulation VIII 1799, the exemption provided by Muslim law from the punishment of death by *kisa*s or *seeasut* for the wilful murder of a slave by his master was no longer valid in the Company's courts.[32] This laid the foundation for reforming initiatives

---

[30] Section 15, Regulation IV, 1793, I.O.R., V/8/16, p. 36.
[31] W.H. Macnaghten, *Principles and Precedents of Hindu Law*, Vol. I (Calcutta, 1829), p. 113.
[32] Bengal Regulation VIII for certain Modifications of the Mahomedan Law in Cases of Murder; and to explain Parts of Reg XXI 1795 and Reg V 1797 in Cases of Dhurna (passed 10 October 1799), I.O.R., V/8/17, p. 138.

undertaken in the criminal courts by individual magistrates and judges who attempted to advance a progressive western view of the slave as a person with the same legal rights of protection from abuse as his master.

In Warren Hastings' time, scholarly Company officials attempted to translate Hindu and Muslim laws relating to slavery. N.B. Halhed, in his translation of Hindu laws, was able to list 15 classes of Hindu slaves.[33] At the bidding of Warren Hastings, himself, C. Hamilton undertook a translation of the *Hedaya* or *Guide to Arabic Books of Law*. Volume III 'The Book of Sales' set forward in no uncertain terms the rules governing the sale of slaves. Furthermore, until the enactment of Section II Bengal Regulation VIII 1799, these rules sanctioned the apparently unlimited authority of a master over his slave with the statement: 'The Law annexes no worthy punishment to the murder of a Slave by his Master...That is to say it is only subject to Expiation by Charity, Fasting or other religious penances'.[34] Despite the liberal authority accorded to a master over his slave by the *Hedaya*, Muslim law had a much more restricted view of slavery itself than did Hindu law. Instead of 15 classifications of slaves, the Muslim legal code acknowledged only one—that of the infidel taken captive during war.[35]

Because Muslim law had superseded Hindu law in the Company's criminal courts, it was possible for the Government of Warren Hastings to demonstrate respect for Muslim law and yet at the same time to take a stand against 'the practice of stealing children from their parents and selling them for slaves', a practice deplored by Muslim and Hindu law.[36] Regulations IX and X, recorded in the Bengal Revenue Consultations of 17 May 1774, decreed:

> That every Person who shall forcibly detain or Sell any Man, Woman or Child, as a Slave without a Cabowla or Deed attested in the usual Manner by the Cauzy of the place where the Slave was purchased by the Proprietor, or who

---

[33] N.B. Halhed, trans., *A Code of Gentoo Laws, or Ordinations of the Pundits from a Persian Translation, Made from the Original, Written in the Shanscrit Language* (London, 1776), pp. 156–57.

[34] C. Hamilton, trans., *Hedayah*, I.O.R., MSS Eur. D34, Vol. I, pp. 215–19.

[35] W.H. Macnaghten, *Principles and Precedents of Moohummudan Law* (Calcutta, 1825), p. 65.

[36] W.H. Macnaghten, *ibid.*, pp. 68, 313. Curiously, although Hindu pundits in Hastings' time denounced that practice, H.T. Colebrooke, generally considered an expert on Hindu law, declared that Hindu law recognized 'voluntary submission to slavery...as a pecuniary consideration...during a famine etc.' Paper written by Colebrooke in 1812, cited by J.H. Harington, *Elementary Analysis of the Laws and Regulations Enacted by the Governor General in Council at Fort William in Bengal, for the Civil Government of the British Territories under That Presidency* (Calcutta, 1805–17), p. 743n.

shall decoy away or steal any Children from their Families or places of Abode shall be punished as the Law to which he is Amenable shall direct...That from the 1st day of July 1774 no persons shall be allowed to buy or sell a Slave who is not such already by former legal purchase...

In fact, these regulations were an early attempt by the East India Company at 'abolishing the right of slavery altogether'.[37] However, it was evident that they were poorly enforced when, 10 years later, William Jones, in his capacity as Judge of the Supreme Court, declared before a grand jury: 'Hardly a man or woman exists in a corner of this populous town who hath not at least one slave child, either purchased at a trifling price or saved perhaps from a death that might have been fortunate'. He described boat loads of 'such children, coming down the river for open sale at Calcutta; ...the sale itself...a defiance of this Government'.[38]

One egregious exception to the general practice of non-enforcement involved a Danish sea captain. From the depths of his ignominy as a convicted slave trader, L. Horrebow appealed to Lord Cornwallis for mercy on grounds: that his disgrace was compounded by the fact that his family was of 'great consequence' in Denmark, his father 'having been one of the Judges of the High Court'; that he had been ignorant of English law, having been 'well acquainted with Merchants of the first Credit in England who openly and avowedly carry on a similar Traffick on the coast of Africa' and that slaves brought to him in a 'starving condition' in Chandernagore received 'humane treatment...from me' before they were delivered for sale in Colombo.[39] Unfortunately for the hapless Dane, his appeal was dated July 1789, the very moment when Lord Cornwallis resolved to crush the slave trade. Launching a string of initiatives taken by Company servants against Indian slavery in the form of official proclamations, Governor General Cornwallis declared on 22 July 1789:

---

[37] Regulations 9 and 10, Bengal Revenue Consultations 17 May 1774 #213; Minute recorded in Bengal Revenue Proceedings 17 May 1774 #213, I.O.R., P/49/46, fols 1484–85.

[38] Charge delivered by Sir William Jones, Judge of the Supreme Court of Calcutta, to the Grand Jury, June 1785, in 'Slavery in India: Correspondence of the Court of Directors and the Governments in India', *Parliamentary Papers* (1828) XXIV, Cmd.125, pp. 9–10. One Jeremiah Church cited the evidence of Sir William Jones when he complained to Lord Cornwallis of 'numbers of helpless creatures frequently exposed in the city to public auction, following a chair or a horse...', J. Church to Governor General Cornwallis, Calcutta, 30 January 1787, N.A., Cornwallis Papers, 30/11/13.

[39] L. Horrebow, to the Right Honourable Charles Earl Cornwallis, Governor General, July 1789, N.A., Cornwallis Papers, 30/11/31, fol. 216.

All and every Person or Persons, subject to the jurisdiction of the Supreme Court...who shall in future be concerned...in the practice of Purchasing or Collecting Natives of both Sexes, Children as well as Adult, for the purpose of exporting them for Sale as Slaves in different parts of India or elsewhere...shall be Prosecuted with the utmost rigour in the Supreme Court at the expence of the Company.[40]

The complexity of the Company's position was manifest in the fact that one very prominent official, Jonathan Duncan, is on record on both sides of the issue. In August 1789 as Resident of Benares, Duncan promulgated the Proclamation issued by Governor General Cornwallis. Yet, as will be demonstrated below, less than 10 years later, the same Jonathan Duncan, in his capacity as Governor of Bombay, authorized the overseer of the Company's plantation in Malabar to purchase low-caste Pullars as slaves. To be sure, Jonathan Duncan did not imagine himself to be the architect of the Company's policy on Indian slavery. Nevertheless, if he had regarded Cornwallis' proclamation as the cornerstone of Company policy, he could not have justified the purchase of slaves for the Company's use. Despite Duncan's dilemma, Cornwallis' proclamation served as a model for proclamations issued by the Madras Government in 1790 and, ironically, also by the commissioners of Malabar in 1792.[41] The Government of Bombay issued proclamations in 1805 and 1807 on the model of Cornwallis' prohibition of the slave trade and of customs duties levied on slaves.[42] Probably the most interesting proclamation was that issued in 1812 by Rani Lakshmi Bai, ruler of Travancore. The Rani was purportedly strongly influenced by the Company's Resident to declare that 'no person shall, for purposes of cultivation buy or sell...low caste people; and that no people of any other caste shall...buy or sell children of their own caste or pay toll to the Sirkar'.[43]

---

[40] Proclamation by order of Governor General in Council 22 July 1789, enclosed in J. White, Sub-Secretary, Bengal Government, to Jonathan Duncan, Resident at Benares, 22 July 1789, U.P.S.A., Allahabad, Duncan Records, [C.O.V.], Resident's Proceedings, Benares, Basta No. 25, Register No. 21, August 1789, fols 115–16.

[41] Fort St. George Public Consultations 6 March 1790, *Parliamentary Papers* (1828) XXIV, Cmd. 125, pp. 469–70; Bombay Commissioners' Regulations against the Slave Trade, Proceedings 9 October 1702, N.A.I., Foreign Department, Miscellaneous Records, Malabar Commissioners' Report, Vol. 56, Part II, p. 739.

[42] Cited in D.R. Banaji, *op. cit.*, p. 304.

[43] The full text of Rani Lakshmi Bai's Proclamation is printed in K.K. Kusuman, *Slavery in Travancore* (Trivandrum, 1973), p. 45.

Arguably the most effective proclamation was that issued independently of Bengal authorities by Charles Metcalfe, Resident at Delhi, on 4 September 1812. Initially, the Bengal Government objected to Metcalfe's efforts to go beyond Cornwallis' prohibition of 'the trade in Slaves by importation' to the 'emancipation of persons already in a State of Slavery'. But, they ultimately allowed his proclamation to remain unchanged. Years later, it was considered that Metcalfe had succeeded in abolishing not only the slave trade but also slavery itself.[44]

Of course, not much notice has been taken of Metcalfe's predecessor, Archibald Seton, who paved the way for Metcalfe's directives against slavery with bold actions of his own. Seton promulgated 'with the sanction and approbation of the King, a sort of bye law, of local operation, prohibiting in the Assigned Territories the sale of children under 12 years of age'. The provocation for this byelaw was 'that most cruel of thefts, the kidnapping children for the inhuman purpose of selling them as slaves'.[45] Seton's byelaw set the stage not only for Metcalfe's proclamation, but also for an appeal from the Sabah of Almora for 'officers of the British Government to put a stop to the traffic…in the sale of children who are collected in the hills, brought down into our Provinces by persons called Burdah Furrosh [slave merchants], by whom they are sold to subjects of our Government…and then conveyed…into the interior and disposed of as slaves'. The circuit court judge of Sarahanpur opined that, although some children may have been sold by desperately poor parents, 'numerous children are inveigled away, some secretly stolen and instances are not infrequent when they are forcibly carried off'. While referring the problem to Fort William, the circuit judge

---

[44] C.T. Metcalfe, Resident, Delhi, to N.B. Edmonstone, Chief Secretary to Government of Fort William, Delhi, 24 October 1812, enclosing translation of Proclamation issued at Delhi on 4 September 1812, extract from Political Proceedings 13 November 1812, W.B.S.A., Judicial Criminal Proceedings 19 December 1812, No. 48, fols 305–7; John Adam, Secretary to Government of Fort William, to C.T. Metcalfe, Resident at Delhi, Fort William, 13 November 1812, W.B.S.A., Judicial Criminal Proceedings, 19 December 1812, No. 48, fols 308–9. It was reported in 1839 that 'The Proclamation and all distinct recollection of its contents appear to have perished at Delhi. But in its place there subsists a belief that Sir C. Metcalfe abolished not the Sale of Slaves but Slavery itself'. C.H. Cameron, Minute submitted as an Appendix, to Indian Law Commission Report, 1 February 1839, I.O.R., *Board's Collections* F/4/1765 #72331, fol. 209.

[45] Archibald Seton, Resident at Delhi, to James Patton, Magistrate of Saharunpoor, Delhi, 4 May 1810. Allahabad, Miscellaneous Letters Received from Resident at Delhi November 1806–October 1812, U.P.S.A. Allahabad, Saharunpur District Records, Basta 23, Vol. 176, fol. 99.

called upon the magistrate of the district to issue a proclamation 'prohibiting the traffic'.[46] It is the opinion of one archivist that it was the complaint from the *Sabha* of Almora which prompted the Supreme Government to enact Bengal Regulation X on 6 August 1811 prohibiting the 'importation of slaves whether by land or by sea'.[47]

Bengal Regulation X 1811 reflected the determination of the Government in Calcutta to punish anyone convicted of importing slaves into the Company's territories with a minimum prison sentence of six months as well as a fine up to 200 rupees. The Government further undertook to return 'persons imported as slaves...to their friends and connexions in the country from which they may have been imported'.[48] Ironically Act 51 Geo III c. 23 declaring the practice of engaging in the slave trade a felony was also enacted in 1811. Although 51 Geo III c. 23 was enacted three months earlier than Bengal Regulation X 1811, its fifth section decreed that this legislation would not be operative in India until after 1 January 1812. Nevertheless, it was this Felony Act which was to become the cornerstone of legal debate and actual legislation concerning slavery in India for years to come. In reality, it represented the will of Parliament to prevent daring violations of its act of 47 Geo III c. 36 aimed at prohibiting the African slave trade in 1807. The expansive language of the preamble encouraged reform-minded Company servants to apply the law against the institution of slavery in India. It remained for legal experts to declare the intent of the law. As late as 1830, the Advocate General of Madras was called upon by the Court of Foujdary Adawlut to interpret 51 Geo III c. 23. He perceived in the preamble:

> ...some indication that the object was to put down the traffic which commonly passed by the appellation of the 'African Slave Trade' and that by...its prohibition of all removal of persons for the purpose of their being dealt with as slaves...was meant a traffic by sea.[49]

---

[46] Thomas Brooke, Judge of Court of Circuit, to George Oswald, Magistrate of Moradabad, 23 March 1811, U.P.S.A. Allahabad, *Letters Received from the Court of Circuit (1811–1812),* Saharunpur District Records, Basta 25, Vol. 191, fols 4, 7–8.

[47] Douglas Dewar, *Handbook of English Pre-Mutiny Records in the Government Record Rooms of the Upper Provinces of Agra and Oudh* (1920), p. 150.

[48] Regulation X for preventing the Importation of Slaves from foreign Countries and the Sale of such Slaves in the Territories immediately dependent on the Presidency of Fort William (passed 6 August 1811), I.O.R., V/8/18, pp. 460–61.

[49] George Norton, Advocate General, to Henry Chamier, Secretary to Government (forwarded to Judges of Foujdaree Udalut) 30 March 1830, A.P.S.A. Nellore District Records, Vol. 4174, fol. 386.

The Madras Advocate General could only follow the legal precedent set by the Government in Bengal in 1812 when it forwarded copies of the statute to the magistrates at seaports but not to magistrates in the interior because the Governor General in Council did not consider its provisions to be applicable to importation or removal of slaves by land.[50]

This distinction between slave trade by sea and slave trade over land was a decisive blow to those concerned with the human misery enshrined in Indian slavery. In 1817 the Government of Bombay questioned the Bengal Government as to the possibility of applying 'acts of Parliament for abolition of the slave trade to domestic slaves and the property of Individuals in them, such slavery being known and legalised under the Laws of both the Hindus and Moosulmans according to whose codes the Courts are bound to administer justice'. The Vice President in Council was quick to reply that, because Hindu and Mahomedan laws were protected by act of Parliament 35 Geo III c. 155,

> [t]he Native subjects of the British Government residing in the territories subordinate to the several Presidencies have in fact the same authority over their slaves...and the same property in them that they would have had if the act in question had never been passed.

All that was conceded was the authority of district and provincial courts to adjudicate disputes over property in slaves according to local laws. But in cases of applications by subjects of native states for restoration of slaves who had taken refuge in the Company's territory, the Supreme Government declared:

> A slave by entering the Company's territories does not become free nor can he who was lawful[l]y a slave emancipate himself by running away from one country where slavery is lawful to another where it is equally lawful...The property in the slave still continues in the master.[51]

In a lengthy minute dated 21 November 1818 concerning the status of legislation on the subject of slavery, Chief Judge J.H. Harington pondered the Government's Judicial Resolution of 9 September 1817, in order to clarify the apparent confusion over the degree to which 51 Geo III c. 23

---

[50] Cited in Resolution of Vice President in Council in Judicial Department, 9 September 1817 enclosed in H. Shakespeare, Secretary to Government of Bengal, to H. Chamier, Secretary to Government at Fort St. George, Fort William, 13 April 1830, A.P.S.A., Nellore District Records, Vol. 4174, fol. 609.

[51] *Ibid.*, fols 611–13.

overlapped Bengal Regulation X, 1811. Regarding 51 Geo III c. 23, he concluded that 'under the construction given to that statute by the resolution of Government under date the 9 September 1817, it must be considered to have superseded such parts of Regulation X 1811 as relate to the importation of slaves by sea' but, according to his judgement, provisions of Regulation X 1811 relating to the importation of slaves by land were still in force.[52] Because Regulation X 1811 was officially considered to be effective, the Supreme Government instructed the Governments of Madras and Bombay to enact similar legislation. Thus, Regulation II 1812 was enacted in Madras and Regulation I 1813 in Bombay. But neither could have had much impact since the Government of Madras found it necessary to enact Regulation II 1826 to enforce the Felony Act and the Bombay Government issued Regulation XIV as part of the Elphinstone Code in 1827 to the same purpose. These regulations merely attempted to control the slave trade, penalizing such transgressions as the sale of slave children with fines and imprisonment and providing a degree of magisterial control through registration or written permission. Homage was thus duly paid to 51 Geo III c. 23 but confusion reigned as a number of individual Company officers attempted to launch reforms that might actually benefit the slaves.

One of the earliest agitators against the institution of slavery was J. Richardson, Judge and Magistrate of Bundelkhund, who wrote to the judges of the Sudder Dewanny and Nizamut Adawlut in Calcutta in 1808 to argue at great length for the emancipation of slaves within the Company's territories. After asserting that 'there are Districts under the Company's Dominion wherein...the greatest part of the Cultivators and Labourers are Slaves', he avowed that this was the cause of 'the wild and uncultivated condition of the country and the barbarous and savage state of its Inhabitants'. He explained how misery drove slaves to abscond and then become Banditti:

> The increase of cultivation and abundance of Grain...makes no alteration in the miserable state of these unhappy wretches...A rag of the coarsest texture, scarcely sufficient to cover their nakedness and a scanty allowance of the most cheap and unpalatable food is their uniform portion. Sometimes ill usage forces them to abscond [from] their masters...If lucky enough to evade discovery they seek a retreat in the fastnesses of the woods and associate with men of similar circumstances. In daily...apprehension they cannot cultivate

---

[52] A.D. Campbell, Register to Foujdaree Udalut, to Secretary to Government in Judicial Department, Fort St. George, 27 February 1830, A.P.S.A., Hyderabad, Nellore District Records, Vol. 4174, fol. 380.

the soil, they cannot hire to service, dreading detection; they must live and by what means? The most obvious...are theft and plunder.[53]

The Court of Nizamut Adawlut, after questioning their own Muslim *muftis* and Hindu *pandits* concerning Muslim and Hindu slave law, invited Richardson to draft a Regulation for modifying existing laws. Richardson most humbly obliged with a draft Regulation based on Muslim law. He explained simply that 'the Mussulman law being the law by which we govern in cases of life and limb, surely it ought to be extended to personal freedom, for from personal freedom alone can life or limb, the first gifts of nature acquire their due value'.[54]

The Court never did submit Richardson's Regulation to the Governor General in Council, but his draft came to light when slavery issues were revived in 1816. A circuit court judge reported a 'very distressing practice', namely, 'the sale of children and even of men and women selling themselves in times of real distress...for a less sum than would purchase a Cat or a Dog'.[55] The Court suggested that Richardson's Regulation might provide a solution for this tragedy 'without hazard of any serious ill consequences'. They recommended two of Richardson's provisions, in particular. First, they saw no harm in allowing persons to sell themselves or their children in times of famine on a contractual basis without committing themselves or their descendants to eternal slavery. And, they favoured 'judicial emancipation of Slaves, on proof of any cruel maltreatment'.[56]

The Court freely admitted that 'the difficulty of the subject' prevented them from taking further action regarding Richardson's draft Regulation. Not surprisingly, two more years passed before the issue was raised again, this time by the noted Chief Judge of the Sudder Dewanny and Nizamut Adawlut, J.H. Harington. In his minute of 21 November 1818, Harington

---

[53] J. Richardson, Judge and Magistrate of Bundelkhund, to Judges of Sudder Dewanny and Nizamut Adawlut, Fort William, 23 March 1808, I.O.R., *Board's Collections* F/4/578 #14078, fols 99–101.

[54] W.B. Bayley, Register, Court of Nizamut Adawlut, to J. Richardson, Judge and Magistrate of Zillah Bundelcund, 29 March, I.O.R., *Board's Collections*, F/4/578 #14078, fols 154–55; J. Richardson, Judge and Magistrate of Bundelcund, to Judges of Sudder Dewanny and Nizamut Adawlut, 24 June 1809, I.O.R., *Board's Collections*, F/4/578 #14078, fol. 213.

[55] 2nd Judge of Moorshedabad Court of Circuit, Report, dated 5 July 1815 at close of 2nd Sessions of 1814, I.O.R., *Board's Collections*, F/4/578 #14078, fols 23–25.

[56] Resolutions of the Court of Nizamut Adawlut on the Report of the second Judge of the Moorshedabad Court of Circuit dated 5 July 1815 at close of 2nd Sessions of 1814, Proceedings of Nizamut Adawlut 11 January 1816, I.O.R., *Board's Collections*, F/4/578 #14078, fols 248–58.

analyzed Richardson's Draft and then proposed a Regulation of his own. Apparently motivated by similar traditionalist instincts, Harington and Richardson did not have any serious disagreements. Harington merely set aside Richardson's emphasis on Muslim law to argue that Hindus must be ruled by their own laws. He then expressed support for Richardson's idea of allowing the Hindu practice of voluntary slavery in times of famine on a limited contractual basis. In his own Regulation, Harington attempted to improve on Regulations passed at the turn of the century in order to authorize the Nizamut Adawlut to sentence the murderer of a slave to death.[57] The difficulty was that Mahomedan law officers persistently declared that the master who murdered his slave was not liable to suffer death. Therefore, Harington introduced the principle that anyone who committed a heinous offence against a slave would be liable to the same punishment he would incur if he had committed the offence against a free man. Ironically, although this last suggestion was to be enacted into law 25 years later, Harington's analysis and suggestions were ignored.

The Courts of Sudder Dewanny and Nizamut Adawlut delayed submitting Harington's proposed Regulation to Government until June 1823. W. Adam, member of Governor General Amherst's Council, strongly objected to any legislative interference with the institution of slavery. Adam argued that domestic slavery was so entangled with native customs that its sudden abolition would create disruption and well founded discontent. Taking his lead from Adam and from Colebrooke's 1812 paper on slavery, Governor General Amherst concluded that there was 'no statement of existing evils which render it incumbent on the Government to enter into the consideration of the state of slavery in India'.[58] Thus D.R. Banaji is able to remark:

> Consequently nothing was done in the matter and as far as the official documents go, that is up to the year 1843, we are in a position to say that both in law as well as in practice, slavery was in substance the same as when Richardson in 1808 first proposed to check and reform its abuses.[59]

---

[57] Secs II and III, Bengal Regulation VIII 1799; Secs XV and XVI Ceded Provinces Regulation VIII 1803, I.O.R., V/8/17, pp. 138, 394–95; Secs XV and XVI Madras Regulation VIII 1802, I.O.R., V/8/26 and Sec. VI Bombay Regulation III 1802, I.O.R., V/8/22.

[58] Observations in pencil by Mr Adam upon the proposed Regulation respecting slaves in 1823, W.B.S.A., Judicial Criminal Proceedings 29 December 1826, No. 15, Vol. 500, fol. 388; Governor General Amherst, Minute, 25 January 1826, Judicial Criminal Proceedings 29 December 1826, No. 18, W.B.S.A., Judicial Criminal Proceedings, 29 December 1826, No. 15, Vol. 500, fol. 398. For Colebrooke's paper, see n. 36 above.

[59] D.R. Banaji, *op. cit.*, pp. 258–67.

Agrestic Slavery in Madras and Kumaon

There were two distinct types of slavery in early nineteenth-century British India. Discussion so far of the development of Government policy towards slavery has focused on domestic slavery, principally in Bengal and Bombay. In the Madras presidency and some hill districts, most of the slave population consisted of Hindu slaves employed in agriculture and known as field slaves, agrestic slaves, or praedial slaves. Hindu law, according to H.T. Colebrooke, dictated that slaves were considered *adscripti glebae* and therefore sold and transferred with the land. Although in reality there was not a uniform practice of selling slaves with the land, certainly, according to Hindu law, no slaves enjoyed rights of property, much less the fruits of their labour.[60] Indeed, it is possible to cite the Code of Manu to the effect that 'three persons, a wife, a son and a slave are declared by the law to have in general no wealth exclusively their own; the wealth which they may earn is regularly acquired for the man to whom they belong'. A.D. Campbell, Secretary to the Madras Board of Revenue, remarked in 1819: 'The present state of Hindoo slaves appears to be nearly the same as it was defined and intended to be by the laws of Manu'.[61]

It is virtually impossible to trace decisively the origins of agrestic slavery in the south either to conquest or to voluntary bondage. Company servants and scholars therefore contented themselves with efforts to classify the slave castes of which the 'Pullars' or 'Poolyans' were the most numerous.[62] Whereas Colebrooke listed seven classes of Hindu slaves and Macnaghten listed fifteen, a Collector in Canara could list 12 classes of the Dher caste of slaves alone. The fabled history of the Dher slaves is perhaps the most apt proof of the difficulty of explaining the origins of the sudra slaves of the south. T.H. Baber, when he was a Magistrate in Canara, learned the mythology of the Dhers:

---

[60] H.T. Colebrooke, *A Digest of Hindu Law, Book II* (London, 1801), Chapter 4, Sec. 14; cf. n. 36 above.

[61] W.H. Macnaghten, *Principles and Precedents of Hindu Law*, II, *op. cit.*, p. 272; A.D. Campbell, Secretary to Board of Revenue, to Mr Hill, Secretary to Government of Fort St. George in Revenue Department, Board of Revenue Proceedings 25 November 1819, *Parliamentary Papers* (1828) XXIV, Cmd. 125, pp. 897–98.

[62] This slave caste also appears in Company records as 'Pooliars' and 'Pulayas'. Today 'Pulayan' is synonymous with 'Cheruman' or 'Cherumar'. A helpful discussion of the confusion which prevails in Company records over the terms 'Pulayan' and 'Cheruman' is provided by K. Saradamoni in her *Emergence of a Slave Caste: Pulayas of Kerala* (New Delhi, 1980), pp. 47–52.

> Parasu Rama was incarnated to destroy the Rajahs...then oppressing the earth. After twenty one different battles, he slew them all. To expiate which, it being a great sin to slay heroes...he went to Gokernum, and having there performed sacrifices and prostrated himself to Varuna, he made the ocean retire and thus created 160 Kadams of land. He then went and brought the Arya Brahmins of the sixty four grams and to induce them to remain he went in search of the wild people who inhabited the forests and mountains, collected them and presented them to the Brahmins as adiars, or slaves, since which period they have been considered as Jelm property equally with the soil itself.[63]

Whatever their origin, the agrestic slaves of the south were universally of low caste, and on the west coast they were usually untouchable to the point of being unapproachable. Because their presence or even the sight of them was considered a source of pollution, caste rules in Malabar 'prescribed that a slave of the castes of poolyan, waloovan and parian shall remain 72 paces from a Brahmin and from a Nair'. Typical of this region of rigid caste divisions is the following scenario:

> The lower servile classes, wherever they go, give notice of their coming by uttering a particular cry at every four or five paces; if the cry be answered by another uttered in like manner by a superior, giving warning that he is approaching, the slave instantly quits the road and retires.[64]

Undoubtedly, slavery was more deeply rooted in the soil and caste system of the southern districts of the Madras Presidency than in the northern districts of Bombay and Bengal Presidencies. Despite the Proclamations prohibiting the slave trade in Malabar and the Madras Presidency in the 1790s, the Company owned slaves on its own plantation in Malabar. Governor of Bombay Jonathan Duncan is on record in 1798 as having approved the plantation overseer's request for permission to purchase low-caste Pullars as slaves.[65] The Collector of Tanjore, at the turn of the century,

---

[63] T.H. Baber, Evidence, 2 April 1830, Report from Select Committee of House of Lords concerning the Affairs of the East India Company, *Parliamentary Papers* (1830) VI, Cmd. 646, p. 211.

[64] Indian Law Commission, 'Report from Indian Law Commissioners dated 15 January 1841', *Parliamentary Papers* (1841) XXVIII, Cmd. 262, p. 129.

[65] Jonathan Duncan, to President and Commissioners of Malabar, Bombay Castle, 31 July 1798, recorded under the heading 'Calicut August 1798', T.N.A., Malabar District Records, Vol. 1694; under the heading 'Calicut December 1798' is recorded a letter from Murdoch Brown, overseer of the Company's Randeterra plantation, explaining why it was necessary for him to acquire Pooliars. Without the benefit of Pooliar labour, the cost of hiring free labourers would force the plantation into debt.

The Legal Rights 187

gave notice that the Pullars and Pariars who had absconded from their masters 'to the prejudice of the Cultivation of the lands to which they immediately belong...are hereby peremptorily required to return immediately to their respective Villages'.[66] However, after the Felony Act and the licensing of missionaries in India by the 1813 Charter, slavery became difficult to justify, even in the south. Particularly conscience stricken was T.H. Baber, Magistrate and Judge in Canara and Malabar. Baber took independent action and made specific suggestions for improving slave conditions. In Canara he was credited with putting a stop to certain slave trading practices.[67] In Malabar, he submitted to the superior court his objections to the practice of selling the slaves of revenue defaulters. The Foujdary Adawlut declared itself incompetent to decide the question and referred it to the Governor who, in turn, instructed the Board of Revenue to conduct a study of the issue and report whether the practice should be allowed to continue, should be regulated or should be abolished.[68] This was the basis of the enquiries circulated in 1819 by the Madras Board of Revenue among Collectors to determine what power the *ryot* lawfully exercised over his slaves. The Collectors' replies generally painted a picture of a mutually beneficial master–slave relationship; thus, the Board decided against interfering with the rights of private property claimed by *ryot*s in their slaves. Nevertheless, the Board did wish to protect slaves from abuse. On 23 December 1819, orders were issued prohibiting Collectors from allowing the sale of slaves 'for arrears of revenue in Malabar where alone it has occurred'.[69] Benedicte Hjejle is dismissive of the Collectors' replies to the Board of Revenue on the grounds that the questions were very likely passed on to Indian slave owners.[70] However, in passing judgement on the Board's

---

[66] Advertisement announced by Alexander Grant, Collector, Caricaul, 6 July 1800, T.N.A., Tanjore District Records, Vol. 3254, fol. 41.

[67] T. Harris, Collector of Canara, to President and Members of Board of Revenue, Fort St. George, Mangalore, 10 July 1819, *Parliamentary Papers* (1828) XXIV, Cmd. 125, p. 843.

[68] T.H. Baber, Judge in Circuit, Tellicherry, to Register of Foujdary Adawlut, 31 December 1818, in Adoor K.K. Ramachandran Nair, *Slavery in Kerala* (Delhi, 1986), pp. 64–65. R. Anderson, Deputy Register, Foujdary Adawlut, to Secretary to Government in the Judicial Department, Fort St. George, 20 January 1819, I.O.R., *Board's Collections*, F/4/702 #19052, fol. 6; David Hill, Secretary to Government, to President and Members of Board of Revenue, Fort St. George, 28 April 1819, *Board's Collections*, F/4/702 #19052, fols 26–27.

[69] A.D. Campbell, Secretary to Board of Revenue, to Chief Secretary to Government, Fort St. George, 13 December 1819, I.O.R., Madras Board of Revenue Proceedings, P/277/32, fol. 428.

[70] She extends this criticism to condemn the work of Dharma Kumar and the Cambridge history school, generally, for its perception of slavery in nineteenth-century south India as one of 'mild bondage flourishing in Malabar and Kanara and only to a limited extent in Tamilnad'.

failure to act effectively, Hjejle does not take into account the Directors' ultimate instructions to the Madras Government to 'be extremely cautious in making any Regulations for defining the relations of Master and Slave'.[71]

Hjejle does not say whether or not she considers that outright emancipation was a viable option for the Madras Board of Revenue in 1819. Collector Vaughan of Malabar observed that 'in some respects chermars may be considered in more comfortable circumstances than any of the lower and poorer classes of natives', while in Coimbatore, the Collector asserted that 'the slaves are on the whole better treated by their masters than the common class of free labourers'.[72] Indeed, the one Collector whom Hjejle exempts from denunciation, C.M. Lushington of Trichinopoly, argued the case against emancipation. He asserted: 'To emancipate them (Pullars) entirely would be ruinous in its consequences both to the Revenue and the Puller: for emancipation in India would confer no rights beyond what the Puller at present enjoys'.[73]

To be sure, Lushington distinguished between the sudra Pullars as 'Creators of Revenue' and their Brahmin landlords or *mirasidar*s as 'Payers of Revenue'. Trichinopoly was one of the eastern Tamil districts where *mirasidar* rights were firmly established. Because the *mirasidar*s were 'prevented by the immutable laws of Cast (from) personally exercising the Offices of agriculture', they had a natural interest in treating their Pullars well. Conversely, the hydroculture of paddy cultivation made the services of Pullars vital to production. Lushington estimated that in the wet districts of Trichinopoly there were 10,000 Pullars compared to 600 in the dry districts. He explained that 'the Services they perform are chiefly confined to the irrigation of the land in its several Stages of Cultivation'. The *mirasidar*s were responsible for the subsistence of Pullars in sickness and in health; and they were obliged to meet all expenses of weddings, funerals and religious festivals. To clinch his point, Lushington reported:

Benedicte Hjejle, *op. cit.*, pp. 92–95; cf. Dharma Kumar, *Land and Caste in South India— Agricultural Labour in the Madras Presidency during the Nineteenth Century* (New Delhi, 1992), pp. 69–70 and Dharma Kumar, Tapan Raychaudhuri and Meghnad Desai, eds., *The Cambridge Economic History of India*, Vol. II, c. 1757–c. 1970 (Cambridge, 1983).

[71] Despatch to Fort St. George in the Judicial Department, 28 April 1824, I.O.R., E/4/929, fols 746–47.

[72] Collectors' answers paraphrased by A.D. Campbell to Hill, Board of Revenue Proceedings 25 November 1819, *Parliamentary Papers* (1828) XXIV, Cmd. 125, p. 899.

[73] C.M. Lushington, Collector, to President and Members of Board of Revenue, Fort St. George, Trichinopoly, 1 July 1819, T.N.A., Trichinopoly District Records, Vol. 3677, fol. 158; Lushington's Report is also published in *Parliamentary Papers* (1828) XXIV, Cmd. 125, pp. 838–41.

I have examined the Pullers...and asked them what course they would pursue if ill used. They replied they would seek other Masters at a distance who would treat them more kindly. In corroboration of this fact I have never received a complaint either in my fiscal or Magisterial capacity since my appointment to this district from a Puller against his Master.

Whether or not Lushington intended to admit that his duty as a magistrate was somewhat irrelevant in a society governed by custom, his argument here is quintessentially traditionalist. And, almost as if he wished to dissociate himself from the *mirasidar*s, he concluded his report by castigating them as 'an idle useless race born to consume the fruits of the earth'.[74]

The Collector of Tanjore, another eastern Tamil district where *mirasidar* privilege was entrenched, described slaves as 'Bondsmen' whose 'whole being' was founded upon a voluntary contract between themselves and the Brahmin *mirasidar*s. Unlike their Pullar counterparts in Trichinopoly, the Pullars and Pariars of Tanjore were sold independently of the land. The bondsman's rights were 'subsistence and protection for himself and family from his Master, with liberty to seek it elsewhere as a free agent if not found kind'. Furthermore, the bondsman had a 'house provided for him along with the others of his Cast to which a backyard of 80 Gomtahs rent free is attached'. In summary, the Collector reflected upon the relationship between master and bondsman:

> The disadvantage of the Bondsman is the power of being sold or transferred to other Masters and this I believe is not very frequent...The advantages are the more effectually securing subsistence and protection to themselves and families particularly in times of trouble or difficulty, than it is binding on Masters in general to bestow upon common labourers.[75]

It was on the west coast, particularly in Malabar, that slaves were usually attached to and sold with the land. A.D. Campbell, Secretary to the Board of Revenue, observed: 'The probability of being transferred with the land...gives them a sort of property in their huts and little spots of ground, which they can thus occupy without any fear of being turned out or transferred contrary to their interests, feelings and comfort'. This British predilection for finding

---

[74] C.M. Lushington, *ibid.*, fols 152–60.
[75] J. Hepburn, Collector of Tanjore, to President and Members of Board of Revenue, Fort St. George, Tanjore, 30 June 1819, T.N.A., Tanjore District Records, vol. 3284, fols 73–75; Hepburn's Report can also be found in *Parliamentary Papers* (1828) XXIV, Cmd. 125, pp. 837–38.

in property the key to all human happiness inspired a virtual oration on the plight of the propertyless slave:

> But because no immediate measures are urgently called for it does not follow that the most useful, the most laborious and one of the most numerous classes of our subjects in these territories should, from generation to generation, continue the hereditary bondsmen of their masters incapable of inheriting property of their own, deprived of that stimulus to industry which possession of property ever inspires...[76]

Such faith in property in the mind of a Company servant with traditionalist instincts could only lead to conflict over the role the Company should play if and when called upon to arbitrate the master–slave relationship. It was in Malabar on the west coast where slaves were 'absolute property, as much as the cattle upon a man's estate' that this conflict was most striking. T.H. Baber, 3rd Circuit Judge, felt keenly that the particularly miserable conditions among slaves in Malabar where 'there are upwards of 100,000 of them' cried out for legislative correction. He described 'their wretchedness. Small in stature, spare arms and legs, with large stomachs, in fact more like baboons than men'. He noted that landholders did not always live up to their obligations to the slaves: 'They do not subsist them [*sic*] as they ought to do. Often may they be seen in the wildest part of the forests and mountains, digging for wild yams for their very subsistence'.[77] This description contrasts markedly with Lushington's observation that 'in Malabar it would...appear that...the slaves are distinguishable by their diminutiveness. This subject holds out a fine subject for declamation, but...in Trichinopoly it is highly erroneous inasmuch as there is no class of people generally so Athletic or tall in stature as the Pullers'. He coupled Baber with Cicero as 'advocates of freedom who may think..."Mihi liver esse non videtur qui non aliquando Nihil agit" [I wouldn't consider him a free man who never has leisure]'.

Lushington's remarks together with the Tanjore Collector's comments concerning the relatively high level of subsistence guaranteed to the slaves by the *mirasidar*s create a rosy picture compared with that painted by Baber on the west coast. Also as Collectors, the observers of slavery in the Tamil districts of Trichinopoly and Tanjore frankly viewed revenue as their prime concern. Lushington unabashedly stated that 'so far as relates to the Revenue

---

[76] A.D. Campbell to Hill, Board of Revenue Proceedings, 25 November 1819, *Parliamentary Papers* (1828) XXIV, Cmd. 125, p. 899.

[77] T.H. Baber, Evidence, 2 April 1830, *op. cit., Parliamentary Papers* (1830) VI, Paper 646, pp. 210–11.

of this district (and I trust my opinion will not be supposed to extend further) the abolition of the Puller system would be attended with the most serious and ruinous consequences'.[78] Baber, as a Magistrate, had been in a position to learn about such barbarous practices as punishment by nose amputation. Privy to the sordid side of the slave's life, Baber resented officials who casually remarked 'that the slaves are protected', or 'that cruel treatment is punished', or 'that a court of justice requires a master to support his slave'. He singled out Collector Vaughan of Malabar, who claimed that Malabar slaves 'may be viewed in any light but that of an abject and horrid state of bondage'. Baber declared these facts to be 'erroneous'; he also objected vehemently to Lushington's Latin 'calumny'. He alleged he was morally offended by the fact that the Government, instead of defending Baber's reputation, simply printed Lushington's remark in full in the Government's proceedings.[79]

It is not surprising, then, that suggestions for improvements in slave conditions came from T.H. Baber. Unfortunately, after the Board of Revenue acknowledged his concerns by prohibiting the auction of slaves of revenue defaulters, no other action was taken against the sale of slaves in execution of decrees of court. However, 10 years later Baber won another victory with a sharp focus on the rights of slaves in the courts. Madras Regulation VI 1829 granted slaves the same right to prosecute and give evidence as free men.[80]

Nevertheless, by 1830 there was still no real change in the condition of slaves in the Madras presidency. Collector Vaughan had been right when he said that a declaration that slaves were no longer liable to be sold for revenue arrears was a 'drop in the ocean'.[81] The Board of Revenue had been constrained by its primary commitment to revenue from taking any other action in 1819. However, out of a sense of self-interest in maximizing the return from the industry of its subjects, it had made elaborate proposals for changes ranging from declaring slaves 'competent to possess and dispose of their own property' to providing that 'slaves shall have power to purchase their liberty at the price for which it was forfeited'. Yet these proposals were never considered further; they were 'merely ordered to be recorded'.[82]

---

[78] C.M. Lushington, *op. cit.*, fols 155, 157.

[79] Mr Vaughan, Collector of Malabar, to President and Members of Board of Revenue Fort St. George, 20 July 1819, *Parliamentary Papers* (1828) XXIV, Paper 125, p. 846; T.H. Baber, Answers to Questions Circulated by Commissioners for Affairs of India, 'Slavery in India', *Parliamentary Papers* (1834) XLIV, Cmd. 128, pp. 184–85, 195–96.

[80] Madras Regulation VI for modifying enactments contained in Sec. VIII Regulation I 1825 (passed 29 August 1829), I.O.R., V/8/28.

[81] Mr Vaughan, Collector of Malabar, to Board of Revenue, 20 July 1819, *op. cit.*

[82] A.D. Campbell, Answers to Questions Circulated by Commissioners for the Affairs of India, *Parliamentary Papers* (1834) XLIV, Cmd. 128, p. 216.

Baber testified that he only learned that the Board of Revenue had issued the orders prohibiting sales of slaves for revenue arrears after he returned to England and read about them in the 1828 *Parliamentary Papers*.[83] The only well-established law was the Felony Act and that merely applied to the slave trade by sea. In addition, it is alleged that as late as 1829 the highest criminal court in Madras did not even possess a copy of 51 Geo III c. 53; and extracts from the Act with translations into Persian and Arabic did not appear in Calcutta and in ports on the Persian Gulf until 1824.[84]

Areas outside the Madras presidency where agrestic slavery was prominent were located primarily in hill districts. As late as 1836, agricultural labourers in the terraced fields of the sub-Himalayan district of Kumaon were described as:

> [S]erfs or adscripti glebae under the denomination of *halee* by means of whom Brahmins and other principal landed proprietors who are restricted by the custom of the Country from personal labor in the fields cultivate as much of their land as practicable, and who are invariably Dooms or outcastes, belonging with their children and effects, to the lord of the soil, like the beasts or other stock upon it. The...field slaves...are boarded and lodged by their owners and receive moreover a *than* of cloth for a dress every six months, and a blanket every third year.[85]

An earlier Commissioner of Kumaon ascribed the bondage of agricultural labour in his district to the brutality of the Gurkhas' occupation of the region. F.J. Shore remarked: 'In Kumaon under the Gurkhas slaves were obtained by force, by plunder, by an uncle selling his nephews and nieces, an elder selling his younger brother...'[86] Before F.J. Shore, Commissioner G.W. Traill speculated on the origins of the system of slavery among aborigines of the area. He observed:

> This race of people, now reduced to about twenty families, wander in the rude freedom of savage life, along the line of Forests situated under the Eastern

---

[83] T.H. Baber, *ibid.*
[84] D.R. Banaji, *op. cit.*, pp. 293, 313.
[85] Morley Smith, Officiating Commissioner of Kumaon, to C. Macsween, Secretary to Government of Agra, Allahabad, Kumaon, 5 February 1836, Extract from Criminal Judicial Proceedings, North Western Provinces, 31 May 1836, No. 136, I.O.R., *Board's Collections*, F/4/1822 #75221, fols 12–13.
[86] F.J. Shore, Assistant Commissioner, Dehra Doon, to W.P. Okedea, Magistrate at Moradabad, 8 May 1828, U.P.S.A., Dehra Dun, General Letters Issued March 1828–December 1828, Vol. 38, fol. 64.

part of the Himalaya in this Province. In all probability the Outcastes or Dooms are in part descendant from them. This conjecture is founded chiefly on two circumstances; first, the great difference in the personal appearance of the Dooms from the other Inhabitants, many of the former having curly hair inclining to wool and being all extremely black; and secondly the almost universal state of hereditary slavery in which the Dooms are found here. With the origin of this Slavery even the proprietors are unacquainted—it may however easily be explained by supposing a part of the Aborigines to have been seized, and reduced to that condition.[87]

The Raja of Gurhwal, in 1835 court proceedings on behalf of one of his subjects who was trying to retrieve from Dehra Dun some runaway slaves, aptly described the age-old custom of agricultural slavery in the hill country surrounding Kumaon. He insisted that:

> [T]he purchase of slaves was formerly truly permitted...but that since the British Government conquered the country he has not permitted slaves to be sold in his territory for the purpose of being...carried away to other districts. That within his Territory individuals of the Dome caste are allowed to be transferred by sale from one master to another for the purpose of cultivation which was carried on solely by the Domes, there being no labourers of any other description obtainable as in the Plains, so that were this practice abolished cultivation would cease...That both Mr Shore and Mr Traill permitted the custom to be continued for the above reasons.[88]

The former Commissioner Traill, when queried about his sanction for this system of slavery, replied that the Raja was 'perfectly correct'. He noted that the custom whereby 'Brahmins of Kumaon will not cultivate the land and are obliged to purchase Domes for the purpose' had existed 'from time immemorial' and had 'not been prohibited by the British Government'.[89] However, Traill pointed out that the sale of widows had been forbidden as had the practice of husbands selling their own wives. Indeed, in 1823 when he was Commissioner of Kumaon, Traill had secured the approval of the Bengal Government to issue a proclamation prohibiting 'the practice of

---

[87] G. William Traill, Commissioner of Kumaon, 'Statistical Sketch of Kumaon', Part I, I.O.R., *Board's Collections*, F/4/1828 #21952, fols 97–99.
[88] Reply of Rajah Soodersun Sale to Political Agent's letter, Extract from Judicial Narrative, No. 5, dated 18 April 1837, I.O.R., *Board's Collections* F/4/1822 #75221, fol. 7; also in U.P.S.A., Dehra Dun, Pre-Mutiny Collectorate Records, Political Letters Issued 1829–42, Vol. 70, fols 135–37.
[89] Traill's Reply, 21 July 1835, Enclosure No. 11 in Political Agent's Letter, *ibid.*, fols 8–9; U.P.S.A., Dehra Dun, *ibid.*, fol. 137.

selling Wives and Widows by Husbands and their Heirs'.[90] Unfortunately, it is apparent that this proclamation had little effect. One hundred years later, a survey of the Kumaon Himalayas deduced that the 'position of the woman is greatly inferior...The cultivator here literally "needs a wife" to perform drudgery of the field'. The author of this 'Survey', S.D. Pant, concluded that 'the woman's legal disability is a corollary to her social inferiority'. He explained:

> The transition from the pastoral to the agricultural stage...seems to account for the low status of the woman. In the pastoral stage the woman was bought like an animal. When the hillman became an agriculturalist...the pastoral custom of purchasing brides enabled the hillman to procure as many extra hands as he could afford to keep...A woman has been likened to a worn-out shoe which can easily be replaced by another. The mortality, suicide and desertion figures illustrate her hard lot.[91]

What upset Company officials most about the 1835 court case concerning the Dome slaves who ran away from their new owner in Gurhwal was the evidence that 'prostitutes are upheld in the purchase of Females for the vilest purposes and in the case immediately referred to neither...the purchaser or...the seller are Bramans but Rajpoots, the natural cultivators of the soil in the Hills'.[92] In response to these allegations, the Government of Agra ordered a Report from the Officiating Commissioner of Kumaon, Morley Smith. Sadly, in his Report of February 1836, Smith deemed

> the purchase of slaves for agricultural purposes is still very common in this Province, and has never been prohibited by the Government...Young females are also bought from their parents by a class of prostitutes residing in the towns for the purpose of their profession. All such negotiations are accompanied by a 'Khut' or regular deed of sale.[93]

---

[90] Proposed Draft of a Proclamation to be issued in the Province of Kumaon for the prevention of the sale of Wives and Widows, extract Bengal Judicial Consultations 5 June 1823, No. 3, I.O.R., *Board's Collections* F/4/1158 #30396, fols 189–91.

[91] S.D. Pant, *The Social Economy of the Himalayans—Based on a Survey in the Kumaon Himalayas* (London, 1935), pp. 189–91.

[92] Lt. Col. F. Young, Political Agent, Dehra Doon, to T.T. Metcalfe, Agent to Governor of Agra, Delhi, 10 December 1835, Extract from Criminal Judicial Proceedings, North Western Provinces, 31 May 1836, No. 134, I.O.R., *Board's Collections* F/4/1822 #75221, fol. 4; also in U.P.S.A., Dehra Dun, Pre-Mutiny Collectorate Records, Political Letters Issued 1829–42, Vol. 70, fols 133–34.

[93] Morley Smith, Officiating Commissioner of Kumaon, to C. Macsween, Secretary to Government of Agra, Allahabad, Kumaon, 5 February 1836, Extract from Criminal Judicial Proceedings, North Western Provinces, 31 May 1836, No. 136, I.O.R., *Board's Collections* F/4/1822 #75221, fol. 13.

In the wake of Smith's 'Report', the Government ordered 'that in future no suits either for the restoration of Slaves or for the enforcement of Slavery shall be received in the Courts under the Commissioner in Kumaon'.[94] Thus Munsif Bhadev Joshi of Kumaon reported to the Law Commission: 'From the accession of the English Government till 1836, on proof, judgement passed in favour of owners against slaves. From 1836 their claims were not heard. Thus sale and purchase were stopped at once'.[95] The Home Government in London looked on with approval. Under extreme pressure from Parliament and the Board of Control to legislate against slavery in India, the Directors, with considerable self-satisfaction, proclaimed that 'the State of Slavery as it exists in this district will of course be disposed of together with the subject generally'.[96] Unfortunately, the most accurate appraisal of the situation was probably that of a *tehsildar* who testified before the Indian Law Commission that, although Mr Smith had reported on the subject of the sale of slaves and the Government had responded with a 'proclamation prohibiting the sale…with the connivance of Government, people still buy and sell; for without slaves persons of respectability could not transact their affairs…for hired labourers are not found in the hills'.[97]

Abolition of Slavery as the Law of the Land

The Kumaon *tehsildar*'s appearance before the Indian Law Commission advances the historical narrative of the development of slavery legislation by nearly 10 years. Because initiatives for the outright abolition of Indian slavery were to come from England, it is necessary to return to the appearance before Parliament at the beginning of the 1830's of Company servants who had returned home. Evidence given by T.H. Baber and A.D. Campbell to a Select Committee of the House of Lords in 1830 paved the way for the Charter of 1833. In the wake of the famous Act of 1833 which emancipated

---

[94] C. Macsween, Secretary to Lt. Governor of Northwestern Provinces, to Lt. Col. G.E. Gowan, Commissioner of Kumaon, Allahabad, 31 May 1836, *Ibid.*, fol. 21.

[95] Report of Bhadev Joshi, Munsiff of Zillah Kumaon, 8 October 1839, Return No. 6 of Public Officers respecting Slavery in the province of Kumaon, Appendix to Report of Indian Law Commission, 1 February 1839, N.A.I., Library, Appendix V, No. 6, p. 302.

[96] Despatch to India in Judicial Department, Northwest Provinces, 24 June 1840, I.O.R. E/4/763, fol. 136.

[97] Report of Khush Hal Singh Chhatri, Tehsildar of Kali Kamaon, Return No. 7 of Public Officers Respecting Slavery in Province of Kumaon, in Appendices to Report of Indian Law Commission, 1 February 1839, N.A.I., Library, Appendix V, No. 7, p. 303.

slaves in most British possessions, the evangelical President of the Board of Control, Charles Grant, attempted to insert into the new Charter a clause requiring that 'all rights over any persons by reason of such persons being in a state of slavery shall cease' by April 1837. But opposition from the Directors combined with members of both houses of Parliament defeated the measure in favour of section 88 of the Charter which simply directed the Governor General in Council to consider 'means of mitigating the State of Slavery as soon as such extinction shall be practicable and safe'.[98] The Directors eventually instructed the Government of India in a despatch dated 10 December 1834 as to the implementation of the Charter. They urged the Supreme Government to end slavery in India at the first safe moment; they suggested that 'the law should be made as severe against injuries done to a slave as if they were done to any other person'.[99]

Within another six months, the Indian Law Commission was formed under T.B. Macaulay in order to prepare a Criminal Code for all of British India. In their early deliberations the commissioners discovered that the existence of slavery made it important to decide how far the status of slavery affected the criminality of an act. Governor General Auckland immediately objected to the commissioners' plan to investigate slavery. However, he was overruled by the Court of Directors who called for a report as soon as possible. After hearing extensive evidence, the Law Commission recommended that in the Penal Code 'no act falling under the definition of an offence should be exempted from punishment because it is committed by a Master against a Slave'. This recommendation was applauded by the Home Authorities.[100] Macaulay proudly reported to his evangelical father that the new penal code would 'get rid indirectly of everything that can properly be called slavery in India'.[101] By endowing the slave with legal rights equal to those of his master in the Company's criminal courts, Macaulay considered that he had pulled the linchpin from the Indian master–slave relationship. This might be labelled a classic utilitarian approach. Certainly, the Indian Penal Code is a monument to Macaulay's genius in penetrating to the heart of any legal

---

[98] Cited in British and Foreign Anti-Slavery and Aborigines Protection Society, 'Memorial on Slavery in British India to the Right Hon. Lord Fitzgerald and Vesci, President, Board of Control', 6–8 February 1843, Rhodes House, Oxford, MSS Brit. Emp. S20 E2/19, fols 175–76. Act of Parliament 3 and 4 Will IV c. 85, section 88.

[99] Public Despatch to India, 10 December 1834, I.O.R., E/4/742, fol. 547.

[100] John Hobhouse, President, Board of Control, to Chairman and Deputy Chairman, Court of Directors, 17 September 1838, I.O.R., Letters from the Board E/2/40, fols 196–97.

[101] T.B. Macaulay to his father, Calcutta, 12 October 1836, G.O. Trevelyan, *The Life and Letters of Lord Macaulay* (London and New York, 1889), p. 329.

problem. He was determined to introduce as few new laws as possible. Thus, the very limited provision for protection of the Indian slave from criminal abuse necessarily reflected Macaulay's own view that slavery in India was a limited problem. However, the lasting effect of this one innovation in law would seem to transcend the utilitarian label. One hundred years later, D.R. Banaji hailed the penal code as the 'death-blow on slavery'.[102]

Indeed, only in the criminal courts was there room for the Company to challenge slavery as the law of the land in British India. There individual magistrates and judges could advance a progressive western view of the slave as an individual with legal rights to protection from abuse. For example, in 1836 C. Tucker, Commissioner of Patna, reported to the Law Commission that he had never received 'an application…by a slave for redress against his Master for Maltreatment on General principles of equity'. However, he alleged that if ever he did 'entertain such cases', he would 'proceed to their trial the same as if the applicant were a free man.'[103]

Commissioner Tucker's words ring a little hollow against the background of grisly Police Reports going back 10 years. In one case it was reported that 'a man killed a woman who was employed by him as a servant by strangulation, alleging as his reason that she had been guilty of Theft and then suspended the Corpse to a tree'. In another, the records alleged that 'a man who had not been paid his wages discontinued attending on his master…for which he received so violent a beating that he only survived it a few hours'. In both cases, all suspects were acquitted before the Court of Circuit.[104] Nevertheless, by the 1830s most magistrates testifying before the Law Commission were aware that they could provide legal protection for the slave from abuse at the hands of his or her master in the Company's criminal courts. Thus, the Magistrate of Benares reported that he had always considered 'Slaves…as much entitled to protection on complaints…of cruelty or hard usage by their Masters as any freeman'.

But just as they recognized their power to enforce criminal law, the same magistrates were aware that the civil law was another matter. And so, the same Magistrate of Benares admitted: 'Were I called upon to decide regarding either the persons or property of Slaves I should have no hesitation, however unwilling I might be to do it, in deciding in favour of Masters in cases

---

[102] D.R. Banaji, *op. cit.*, p. 336.
[103] C. Tucker, Commissioner, to J.F.M. Reid, Register to Court of Nizamut Adawlut, Fort William, Patna Division, 12 September 1836, B.S.A., P.C.O., Vol. 454, No. 42.
[104] 1827 Police Report of Superintendent of Police C.R. Barwell of Lower Provinces, B.S.A., P.C.O., Vol. 243A, fols 161, 166.

of clearly established slavery'.[105] Similarly, Commissioner Tucker declared: 'Magistrates were prohibited taking cognizance of cases involving the question of right to a Slave'.[106] Slavery had been established as the law of the land ever since the ruling by the Calcutta Sudder Dewanny Court in 1798 that insofar as rights of property in slaves were recognized by Hindu and Muslim law, they were valid in the Company's civil courts. The rights of Hindu and Muslim masters to property in their slaves remained untouched by 51 Geo III c. 23, Bengal Regulations X of 1811 and III of 1832, and parallel legislation in Madras and Bombay, all of which focused on the slave trade. There was no legislation which attempted to interfere with the relationship between master and slave.

Macaulay's Law Commission thus took its lead from the testimony of magistrates to attack slavery through the criminal courts. Since a traditionalist respect for Indian customs had become entrenched in the Company's civil law, the Commission, out of a utilitarian sense of expediency, proposed a new criminal law to protect the slave from abuse. On 1 February 1839 they submitted to the Supreme Government a Draft Act declaring that:

> Whoever assaults, imprisons or inflicts any bodily hurt upon any person being a slave under circumstances which would not have justified such assaulting, imprisoning or inflicting bodily hurt upon such person if such person had not been a Slave is liable to be punished by all Courts of Criminal Jurisdiction within the territories subject to the Government of the East India Company as he would be liable to be punished by such Courts if such person had not been a Slave.[107]

Remarkably, the Law Commission received little encouragement from Governor General Auckland. Although Auckland applauded Macaulay's Penal Code, he objected to later Law Commission proposals for legislation dealing with slavery. Auckland's continued objection to any further legislation would appear to be the result of the advice of his closest advisor and legal expert, W.H. Macnaghten. On the one hand, Macnaghten confided to Auckland that the 1798 Sudder Dewanny decision deserved to be overruled.

---

[105] D.B. Morrison, Magistrate, Benares, to H.B. Harington, Register to Sudder Dawanny and Nizamut Adawlut, Allahabad, 20 January 1836, U.P.S.A., Allahabad, C.O.V., Magistracy Varanasi, Judicial Letters Received 2 February 1822–30 October 1847, Serial No. 2, Vol. 9.

[106] C. Tucker, Commissioner, to J.F.M. Reid, Register to Court of Nizamut Adawlut, Fort William, Patna Division, 12 September 1836, *op. cit.*

[107] Draft Act of 1839, Report of Law Commissioners, 1 February 1839, I.O.R., *Board's Collections* F/4/1765 #72331, fol. 187.

He declared that he would 'remove from our Courts the opprobrium of being possibly compelled to decree even in a single case that one man shall be the slave of another'. But, on the other hand, he was emphatic in his advice that 'no Law should be passed against Slavery as such Law would be impolitic, cruel, alarming and inoperative for good'. Macnaghten's legal opinion was founded upon his conclusion that domestic slaves in India were 'comfortable' and that praedial slaves were not 'generally treated with cruelty'.[108] Although Auckland was prepared to admit that slavery perhaps existed in a 'more hideous form...in some...more distant districts' such as Assam or Malabar, he was generally complacent about the subject of Indian slavery. He remarked privately to J.C. Hobhouse, President of the Board of Control: 'We have but to assert that there is no slavery in India and in a very short time there will be none'.[109]

An appendix to the Law Commission's Report contained a minute by C.H. Cameron, one of the commissioners. Cameron wished to extend the Draft Act to include the master's power of moderate correction over a slave such as 'a Parent has in respect of a Child or Master in respect of a Scholar or an apprentice'. His argument seemed to be inspired by the same traditionalist sentiment that had characterized earlier reports by Collectors and Magistrates. He considered that slavery in India operated as an 'Indian Poor Law' and thereby contributed to the 'prevention of infanticide'. However, unlike the institutions of English pauperism or West Indian slavery, Indian slavery, according to Cameron, did not depend upon the extortion of productive labour from an unwilling labourer through the 'infliction of such punishment as English manners will not tolerate'. Because, he argued, particularly with respect to Bengal, slavery has existed for ages 'without any such power being vested in the Master as would enable him to extort productive labour...I believe that the power of parental correction which he possesses...may be taken from him without any real injury to his interests'. Curiously, Cameron's reason for taking away from the master his power of moderate correction of his slaves was 'the great liability of such a power to run into excess when it is exercised against adults'.[110] Most historians today take a jaundiced view of Cameron's mild picture of Indian slavery. Observing a slight inconsistency in Cameron's argument, D.R. Banaji concluded that

---

[108] W.H. Macnaghten to Auckland, 8 April 1837, ADD. MSS 36473, fols 106, 108–110.
[109] Auckland to Hobhouse, Calcutta, 21 March 1841, Broughton Papers, British Library, ADD. MSS 36474, fol. 467.
[110] Minute by C.H. Cameron, as an Appendix to the Report by Indian Law Commissioners, 1 February 1839, I.O.R., *Board's Collections* F/4/1765 #72331, fols 216–18, 222.

'Cameron ultimately based his reasoning for the suppression of the master's right of moderate correction not on the mild form of Indian slavery, but on the danger that such a right was always liable to be grossly abused'.[111] Be that as it may, Cameron's minute must be credited with some genuine insight concerning the tangled web of Indian slavery and Indian caste and custom. Certainly the suppression of the master's right of moderate correction became a focal point for debate during future sessions of the Law Commission and the Governor General's Council. Indeed, at almost the very moment that Cameron was writing his appendix, the Directors were drafting a despatch specifically asking the Law Commissioners to consider whether or not the master's power of moderate correction should be taken away.[112] Meanwhile, the Indian Government failed to approve the 1839 Draft Act and called for a new report. Caught between the desire to improve conditions of the slaves while at the same time protecting rights of the master in a bourgeois legal system, the Supreme Government garnered support from the Bombay and Madras Governments to doubt the expediency of the Draft Act and thus delay execution of the Directors' orders.

Pressure from the Home Authorities for action was unrelenting. A steady stream of petitions for the abolition of slavery in India poured into Parliament and the offices of Government ministers.[113] On 29 August 1838, the Court of Directors called attention to a notice standing on the order book of the House of Commons to the effect that the state of slavery in India was to be brought under consideration of the House. Indeed, the Directors were forced to put aside their own doubts expressed in a despatch dated 7 August 1839 which was mysteriously cancelled.[114] At that time they had recorded their agreement with Governor General Auckland's sentiments expressed in a minute of 6 May 1839: 'If the matter, however were wholly left to my discretion, I should very much prefer not to legislate at all for the purpose of regulating the conduct of Masters towards their Slaves. All

---

[111] D.R. Banaji, *op. cit.*, pp. 343–44.

[112] Legislative Despatch to India, 27 May 1839, cited in Indian Law Commission's Report, 1839–41, *Parliamentary Papers* (1841) XXVIII, Cmd. 262, 'Report from Indian Law Commissioners dated 15 January 1841', p. 284.

[113] Memorial of the Committee of the British and Foreign Anti-Slavery and Aborigines Protection Society to the Rt. Hon. Robert Peel, 10 September 1841, Rhodes House Library, Oxford, MSS British Empire S20 E2/19, fols 65–70; Petition to the Honourable the Commons of the United Kingdom of Great Britain from the Committee of the British and Foreign Anti-Slavery and Aborigines Protection Society, Rhodes House Library, Oxford, *ibid.*, fols 71–72.

[114] Legislative Despatch to India #457, 8 August 1839, PC 2489, Cancelled 31 July, I.O.R., Z/F/3/2.

such regulation implies a recognition of a State of Slavery'.[115] Less than a year later, a legislative despatch from Leadenhall Street demanded a report from the Law Commissioners and warned: 'Parliament and the Public are becoming impatient at the delay'.[116] Indeed, the Directors were never short of reminders from their mentors on the Board of Control. On 23 February 1841, John Hobhouse, President of the Board, wrote to the Chairman of the Court: 'You are doubtless aware of the extreme anxiety and impatience which is felt in Parliament for the promised Report from India on the subject of Slavery'.[117] He had already confessed to Auckland: 'What you tell me privately of your own opinion is very embarrassing; for, if you follow up that opinion, you will do nothing and the people here will not bear that'.[118] Hobhouse may have agreed with Auckland but all sense of an expedient regard for the reality of slavery in India had been overpowered by the Evangelical campaign in Parliament.

The Indian Law Commission Report on Slavery of 1841 has been declared by at least one historian as a 'confused and badly written document'.[119] After comprehensive and contradictory documentation, the Law Commissioners made 33 recommendations relating to contract labour, slave labour and bonded labour. They were all intended to mitigate the state of slavery in India. But the recommendations concerning contract labour merely sanctioned contracts limiting the freedom of individuals selling their labour for life. The recommendations concerning slaves aimed to regulate the system of slavery, checking abuses. And the recommendations concerning bondsmen simply regularized debt bondage. The 17 recommendations concerning slaves were the central concern of the Commission. Many of them, such as Recommendation 14 which suggested that no slave should be sold for revenue arrears merely reiterated regulations or government orders already enacted. The real bone of contention between the minority and majority of the commissioners was the issue of the power of moderate correction which the master possessed over his slave. On the one hand, the majority believed

---

[115] Minute by Lord Auckland, 6 May 1839, cited in Court to Board, 7 July 1842, I.O.R., Letters to the Board, E/2/17, fol. 203.

[116] Despatch to India in Legislative Department, 29 July 1840, I.O.R., E/4/763, fol. 643. It is of some interest that this one sentence is in a different handwriting from that of the rest of the despatch.

[117] Board to Court, 23 February 1841, I.O.R., Letters from the Board, E/2/41, fol. 184.

[118] Hobhouse to Auckland, 30 January 1841, Broughton Papers, I.O.R., MSS Eur. F/213/11, fol. 51.

[119] Hjejle, 'Slavery and Agricultural Bondage in South India in the Nineteenth Century', *op. cit.*, p. 368.

that the power should be left with the master for fear that otherwise field labourers would not be as productive as hired labourers and that any resulting emancipation would entail financial compensation. They also considered that the master was naturally under restraint because he could not discharge his slave without considerable loss. On the other hand, while disinclined to destroy the authority of the master, the majority did not recommend the interference of magistrates to compel slaves to perform their duties. They wished, then, to refrain from interfering either with the lawful status of slavery or with the lawful power of the master to punish and restrain. In sum, the Law Commissioners freely admitted that 'the more prudent course is not to add new provisions to the law which would be offensive and irritating and really injurious, so far as they should be operative, to the masters'. Instead, they wished 'to give efficiency to the existing law for the protection of slaves'.[120]

It is curious that the Law Commissioners' 1841 Report featured the views of the minority ahead of those of the majority. Perhaps this was because Governor General Auckland, in his much quoted minute of 6 May 1839, took the side of the minority whose views were ably represented in Cameron's minute cited above. Having been forced by the Home Authorities to shed his qualms over legislation, Auckland wished to pass a law 'declaring that any act which would be an offence if done to a freeman shall be equally an offence if done to a slave'. None of his Councillors agreed with him. W.W. Bird wished to enact a law declaring the entire extinction of slavery as a status in any form; A. Amos sided with Bird, while H.T. Prinsep wished to avoid legislation on slavery altogether and rely instead on the courts. Indeed, Prinsep was confident 'that if Negro slavery had never existed as a topic to be preached and declaimed upon in England and Europe…the customs and practices in respect to Slavery…in India would never have been regarded…worthy of a special direction of the Parliament'. However, he conceded that 'if the whole of India were…in the same condition as Malabar, I think I should have admitted the necessity of undermining the institutions of slavery…by positive laws'.[121] In such a state of disarray, the Government of India packed up the Law Commissioners' Report together with the legislative proceedings of the Governor General's Council and sent them to England.

---

[120] 'Report from Indian Law Commissioners dated 15 January 1841', *op. cit.*, pp. 494, 498.
[121] Minute by Governor General Auckland, 6 May 1841; Minute by W.W. Bird, 18 June 1841; and Minute by H.T. Prinsep, 31 July 1841, India Legislative Proceedings, 6 September 1841, Nos 6, 11 and 12, I.O.R., P/207/17.

In the meantime, A. Amos prepared a new Draft Act on 27 December 1841 which, after considerable discussion and disagreement, focused on four points.

1. That no slave should be sold for revenue arrears
2. That no magistrate would enforce rights arising out of slavery
3. That a slave would not be dispossessed of his property
4. That the sale of a minor's labour would be a penal offence

Prinsep wrote in the margin of Amos' Draft that he objected to the last measure because in times of famine the option of selling children for the sake of their survival was a long standing custom.[122] Auckland objected to the third section proclaiming a slave's right to any property he may possess. He saw this as counter to the 1798 Calcutta Sudder Court's ruling that the spirit of the 1793 Regulation for observing Hindu and Mahomedan laws with respect to property applied to cases of slavery. And, of course, he was adamant that 'it would not in my opinion be safe to give any legal power of punishment to Masters and that we can have no Security against their occasional bad character and excited passions other than that of withholding from them all the authority of personal coercion whatever'. Thus, Auckland protested against the omission of a clause declaring actions taken against slaves and freemen to be equal offences. He insisted that he would be 'very glad were it possible to avoid legislating upon this particular point at all…; but legislation on the Subject will probably be thought indispensable in England and I cannot believe that we shall be called upon to…give a legal Sanction to personal infliction by Masters'.[123]

Thus divided amongst themselves, the Government of India sent Amos' amended Draft Act to the Directors for their consideration. The Home Authorities eagerly perused the Law Commission's Report and Amos' Draft Act. The Directors' despatch in reply was fiercely debated by the Board of Control. The Board arbitrarily removed substantial paragraphs from the Court's despatch in which the Directors took pains to contrast the 'mitigated character' of Indian slavery with the abhorrent state slavery of the West Indies and to acknowledge that 'the leaning of all the Courts and officers of our Government is strongly in favour of the Slaves and against the privileges

---

[122] Drafts of an Act and Minutes of Council, I.O.R., *Board's Collections* F/4/1947 #84545; Amos' draft has comments pencilled in the margin by Prinsep.
[123] Minute of Governor General Auckland, 19 January 1842, I.O.R., *Board's Collections* F/4/1947 #84545.

of the master'.[124] The Courts' protests that these remarks were intended to satisfy 'Public feeling in England' fell on deaf ears.[125] Similarly struck from the Court's despatch were paragraphs in which the Directors took exception to the fourth section of Amos' Draft Act. They wished to argue that 'on the whole, looked upon as the alternative of extreme want and destitution... the practice [of selling the labour of children] is one which...it may not be improper to tolerate'.[126] The Board simply ruled that this sentiment was inconsistent with a previously stated 'conviction that one evil against which the Government of India would wish to provide was the sale of Children as Slaves'. The despatch which the Directors finally sent to India on 27 July 1842 approved the Draft Act as well as the provision proposed by Auckland 'that any act which would be a penal offence if done to a free man, shall be equally an offence if done to any person in any condition of dependence on a master'. And on a final note of sensitivity, the Directors gave generous discretionary authority to the Government of India.[127]

The Supreme Government, upon receiving the despatch, was uncharacteristically quick in taking action. Despite the Company's longstanding opposition to the practice of selling children into slavery in times of distress, they decided to omit the clause concerning the sale of children so as not to have the appearance of sanctioning a practice that was already illegal under Muslim law. This decision was possibly the result of Circular Order #111 authorized by the Madras Foujdary Adawlut in 1839 in order to promulgate the opinion of their Muslim law officers 'that at a time when scarcity does not prevail, the people of this Country are forbidden to sell their children, and that to do so renders them liable to Tazeer [discretionary punishment]'. When the Supreme Government requested an explanation of the 'Circumstances under which the issue of...Circular Order No. 111...was thought advisable', the Foujdary Adawlut recounted the numerous references and 'discordant opinions' which they had received on the subject. Going back as far as 1817, the Court recollected the outrage of the Magistrate of Vizagapatam over the *zillah* court ruling that parties to the sale of an infant aged only seven months were not liable to criminal prosecution. The magistrate protested that if the *zillah* court's ruling was correct, 'it was high time that the defect in the Law

---

[124] Paragraphs expunged 1 July 1842 from Legislative Despatch to India, 27 July 1842, No. 11, I.O.R., E/4/771, fols 330–34.

[125] Court to Board, 7 July 1842, I.O.R., Letters to the Board, E/2/17, fol. 204.

[126] Legislative Despatch to India, 27 July 1842, No. 11, I.O.R., E/4/771, fols 341–42.

[127] Board to Court, 20 June 1842, I.O.R., Letters from the Board, E/2/41, fols 400, 336–37, 342 and 344.

was rectified and that slave dealing was declared to be abolished in India'. The Foujdary Adawlut of the day supported the *zillah* judge with their ruling that the 'matter is connected with the religious usages and institutions of the Native Subjects...and is cognizable as a Civil action...and that the Magistrate is not authorized to take cognizance of the matter in question'. In the mid-1820s when the Collector of Tinnevelly called for a law prohibiting the prevalent custom of 'the sale and purchase of female children by dancing women for the avowed purpose of bringing them up to a life of immorality', the Provincial Court and Foujdary Adawlut disapproved of Government interference on the grounds that 'the sale of a child,...excepting under very particular circumstances, is punishable under Mahommedan law'. The Governor joined in the argument in a letter dated 13 January 1826 to urge 'Caution in Conducting any interference at all with the view of preventing parents or guardians from assigning Children in the customary modes to be brought up to the profession of dancing women'. Finally, in 1839 the Foujdary Adawlut noted that the *futwa* of its law officers to the effect that a mother selling her child was liable to *tazir* or discretionary punishment contradicted an 1819 *futwa* in the 'Records of this Court...declaratory of the non-liability to punishment of a party selling his or her Child'. Asked to explain their reasons for dissenting from the *futwa* of their predecessors, the law officers observed that 'it was accordant with the decisions recorded in the Books of Hanufah that at a time when scarcity does not prevail, the people of this Country are forbidden to sell their children...'. Even though the Supreme Government enacted a law in 1840 specifically disavowing the use of *futwa*s by the Madras Foujdary Adawlut, they were clearly impressed by these arguments. And so they declined to override the existing Muslim law on the subject of the sale of children.[128]

On 24 January 1843 a Draft Act was published in the *Government Gazette* including the first three points of Amos' Draft Act and Auckland's recommendation that 'any act which would be a penal offence if done to a free man shall be equally an offence if done to any person on the pretext of his being in a condition of slavery'. Within two months over 700 Hindu *zamindar*s from Sylhet and Backergunge districts in Bengal petitioned against the Draft Act. They argued that the new act ran counter to the guarantee in Bengal Regulations III and IV 1793 of native customs and usage. Another

---

[128] H. Davidson, Acting Register, Foujdaree Udalut, to Chief Secretary to Government, 19 November 1839, Judicial Consultations 3 December 1839, No. 3, T.N.A., Vol. 381B, fols 8857–63; Act I for regulating Procedure on Trials referred to the Court of Foujdaree Udalut at Madras (passed 27 January 1840), I.O.R., V/8/31.

700 Muslims from Sylhet protested that their slaves did not feel degraded.[129] But the Government paid no attention and enacted the January Draft Act as Act V on 7 April 1843. However, not until the Penal Code was enacted in 1860 did the buying and selling of slaves become a penal offence.[130] Inasmuch as slave trading rather than slavery, itself, became illegal, the Penal Code could be seen to be only an extension of the Felony Act of 1811.

The four provisions of Act V 1843 reflected the Company's encounter with the traditions surrounding slavery in India. The only dramatic change in Company policy was the last minute decision of the legislative council to drop from the Act the prohibition of the practice of selling children into slavery, in recognition of the fact that such sales outside of times of famine had always been illegal under Muslim law. Thus came to an end the Company's longstanding objection to sales of children which dated back to Sir William Jones' denunciation of the slave boats in Calcutta in 1785. Otherwise, the Company's experience in its courts of law provided a solid foundation for legislation. T.H. Baber's recommendation that the practice of selling slaves for revenue arrears be prohibited became Section I of Act V. Section II prohibiting the enforcement by a court or magistrate of the right of property in the person or services of another as a slave echoed the 1836 orders of the Government of Agra to the Commissioner of Kumaon. The 1817 Bengal ruling that a slave could not emancipate himself by absconding from a state where slavery was lawful into Company territory no longer obtained. Nor could slaves any longer be sold in execution of judicial decrees. This vindicated the Madras Foujdary Adawlut which, only six months earlier, had issued instructions to 'Judicial officers in the Provinces to refuse application for the sale of a Slave as moveable property apart from the Estate to which he belongs'.[131] The third provision that slaves could not be dispossessed of any property they may have acquired had no case history. But it did fulfil the vision in A.D. Campbell's 1819 revenue minute of

---

[129] Abstract Translation of a Bengalli Petition from the zemindars of Sylhet appealing against the Slavery Act/bearing about 680 signatures/23 February 1843; Abstract Translation of a Bengalli Petition from Mohamedan Inhabitants of Sylhet/bearing about 700 signatures/24 February 1843; and Translation of a Bengalli Petition from the Landholders of the district of Backergunge/bearing about 125 signatures/10 March 1843. India Legislative Proceedings 7 April 1843, Nos 13–15, I.O.R., P/207/27.

[130] Act V for declaring and amending the Law regarding the condition of Slavery within the Territories of the East India Company (passed on 7 April 1843), I.O.R., V/8/32; Secs 370–71, *Indian Penal Code*, Act XLV of 1860 (Lucknow, 1981), p. 91.

[131] Extract from Proceedings of the Sudr Udalut, 12 September 1842, N.A.I., Legislative Department A, Judicial Consltations 18 November 1842, No. 11, fol. 25.

slaves transformed into industrious labourers by the promise of property. And, finally, the last provision that penal offences done to slaves were to be treated as offences done to freemen was the culmination of a consistent effort by Company servants to protect the slave from abuse. Bengal Regulation VIII 1799 had modified the Muslim law which sheltered the master who murdered his slave; J. Richardson and J.H. Harington had recommended that cases involving personal freedom should fall within the jurisdiction of criminal courts where slaves were considered equal to freemen; Harington's Draft Regulation contained almost the same words as Section IV of Act V; the Law Commission's 1839 Draft Act reiterated the same principle and that principle then echoed through the minutes of Governor General Auckland's legislative council. However, this principle when articulated by Macaulay's Law Commission aimed to create the slave as an equal to the freeman in the Company's criminal courts; for Governor General Auckland it was somehow to be a means of taking away from the master his power of moderate correction over his slave. Macaulay's vision was more in line with the Home Government's determination to abolish slavery in India altogether than was Auckland's confusion and procrastination over his instructions from London calling for slavery legislation. Yet, to be fair to Auckland, the Home Government had always disapproved any effort on the part of the Indian Government to interfere with the relationship between master and slave in India. As to the significance of Act V 1843, the renowned Madras judge, T.L. Strange, observed:

> Act No. V 1843 deprives the master of power to exact the price of the slave, or to compel him to labour; as well as of the means of recovering possession of him, should he abscond…The Act would seem, moreover to have been the result of instructions from the Court of Directors for the entire abolition of slavery.[132]

Without the ultimatum from the Home Authorities, it is doubtful that Act V 1843 ever would have been enacted. Beginning with the 1774 Regulations of Warren Hastings' Government, there was a steady progression of measures taken by the Indian Government against slavery. That these regulations always had to be understood alongside Muslim and Hindu law was a fact appreciated by certain traditionalist Company officials who were sensitive to indigenous traditions. In this sense, it is possible to designate Sir William Jones, Governor General Cornwallis, J. Richardson, J.H. Harington,

---

[132] T.L. Strange, Sub-judge, to H.V. Conolly, Collector and Magistrate of Malabar, Calicut, 23 September 1843, T.N.A. Judicial Diary 23 April 1844, No. 7, Vol. 470A, fol. 1273.

T.H. Baber, A.D. Campbell, C.M. Lushington and C.H. Cameron as traditionalists. They had more than an orientalist knowledge of classic texts; they went to great lengths to understand local custom and behave appropriately. Macaulay's Law Commission was inspired by a utilitarian vision of efficient law. The 1839 Draft Act was a measure of expediency calculated to attack the practice of slave abuse and thereby fulfil Macaulay's prophecy of 'getting rid indirectly of everything that can properly be called slavery'. But ultimately, the final recommendations of the Law Commission, Auckland's legislative councillors and even the Court of Directors rested upon traditionalist concern for the continuity of Hindu and Muslim custom and laws.

It may be argued that the Company's administrators cared only for the landowners who paid their revenue. Certainly, the Madras Board of Revenue in 1819 was very reluctant to disturb the social order which provided the revenue; the members of the Law Commission and Auckland's Legislative Council worried about financial compensation which the government might owe to masters of slaves after their emancipation. However, the judiciary, as represented by the Penal Code and the minutes of J. Richardson, J.H. Harington and T.H. Baber, was keen to promote social justice, at least in criminal law. Judges and magistrates consistently made rulings and recommendations on behalf of the rights of individuals, whether slaves or freemen, in the context of their own customs and traditions.[133] Nonetheless, the anomalies of civil law eluded would-be reformers to the end, so that no attempt was ever made to challenge the existing property right claimed by a master in his slave. In this sense, the 'slave' in the eyes of the nineteenth-century libertarian transmogrified into the 'unfree' labourer depicted by post-colonial historians such as Gyan Prakash. Prakash argues that Act V 1843 was largely superficial because the 'unfreedom' that it ended had very little basis in the existing ties of dependence between 'master' and 'slave'. With respect to the Kamias of South Bihar, the state approved 'contracts providing for the Kamias' lifelong labour for the maliks...landlords and laborers ordered their relations as contracts founded on advances of loans'.

---

[133] There were actual instances of judicial emancipation of slaves. As early as 1805, Judges H.T. Colebrooke and J.H. Harington emancipated a female slave on grounds of maltreatment [Vakeel of Government v. Nujoom oon nisa, 5 September 1805, W.H. Macnaghten, ed., *Reports of Nizamut Adawlut* Vol. 1, (Calcutta, 1834), pp. 55–56]; and as late as 1835, Judge R.H. Rattray emancipated slaves who had ceased to require maintenance [Kirteenarain Deo and others vs. Gouree Sunkur Dutt, Respondent, 7 December 1835, Judges' Library, High Court, Calcutta, *The Indian Decisions (Old Series)*, Vol. VII *Sudder Dewanny Adawlut Reports, Bengal* (Madras, 1913), p. 705.]

And thus Kamias were liberated from slavery only to be 'reconstituted as bonded laborers'.[134]

Emigrant Labour

Emigrant labour was an issue which differed substantially from that of slavery in a legislative point of view. Whereas the question of slavery was vigorously agitated by Evangelicals before the English parliament which ultimately forced the Government of India to legislate Act V 1843, the fulcrum of political pressure and debate on the welfare of India's emigrant labourers lay in the Colonial Office. Although the Colonial Office was not free simply to dictate policy to the Government of India, it certainly held the upper hand. The role to be played by each of the parties to the debate— the Government of India, the Colonial Governments, the Colonial Office, Parliament and the Abolitionists—became clear in the mid-1830s when the issue was first agitated. With the abolition of slavery in the colonies of Mauritius and the West Indies in 1834, the colonial sugar planters looked to India for free immigrant labourers to replace their slaves. The Abolitionist, Lord Brougham, discovered an Order of Council of 12 July 1837 conceding the demands of 'some planters' in British Guiana to extend to five years the three-year period of apprenticeship for immigrant labourers sanctioned only four months earlier. He thereupon delivered an oration worthy of Cicero to Parliament. On 6 March 1838 he introduced in the House of Lords a Resolution condemning the Government for passing such an Order, the 'proposed object' and 'inevitable consequence' of which he 'compared...with everything that the history of the past has taught us of the slave trade'.[135] As planned by Lord Brougham, this set off a chain reaction beginning the very next day with the Duke of Wellington's denunciation of Acts V and XXXII, promulgated in 1837 by the Government of India, as totally inadequate for the protection of Indian labourers. Two months later, Lord Glenelg introduced into the House of Commons on behalf of the Colonial Office his 'Natives of India Protection Bill'. Two years later, the 1837 legislation of the Government of India was repealed and all emigration suspended. Outraged by the tortuous delays in Parliament, Lord Ellenborough confided to his

---

[134] Gyan Prakash, *op. cit.*, p. 222.
[135] Lord Brougham, 6 March 1838, *Hansard's Parliamentary Debates*, XLI, p. 417.

Journal that when Lord Brougham showed him his Resolution in advance of his speech before the House of Lords, Ellenborough confronted Lord Glenelg, then the Secretary of State for the Colonies, with the urgent need for legislation. When Lord Glenelg replied that he would bring in his bill 'very shortly', Ellenborough retorted that 'if what Lord Brougham had said and he had corroborated were true, *every hour of delay was an hour of permitted crime*'.[136] Ellenborough was convinced that the parliamentary process was hampered by earlier indulgences to West Indian planters. Such vested interests induced an attitude of caution even in the Duke of Wellington.

Two things became apparent during this initial legislative sparring among colonial governments, the Colonial Office, Parliament and the Government of India. First, although part of the reason for Lord Glenelg's delay in introducing his legislation was his need to consult with the East India Company's Board of Control, the problems of Indian immigration were first and foremost a matter of imperial legislation rather than legislation by the Indian Government. This was for the obvious reasons that only the Colonial Office could enforce legislative directives in the colonies and only imperial legislation could dictate conditions on the high seas. Second, as Lord Glenelg lost time in consultation with the East India Company's Home Authorities, parliamentary debate became both dilatory and inconclusive. Finally, the Government decided to abandon Glenelg's bill, while commanding the East India Company to instruct its government in India to ban all emigration of Indian labourers pending further inquiry.[137] The Government of India duly enacted Act XIV 1839 to repeal Acts V and XXXII 1837 and to prohibit the 'hiring of Natives for emigration, under penalty'.[138] As explained later by a knowledgeable officer of the Company: 'On the whole the history of the parliamentary discussion throws little light on the question of immigration. The combatants on both sides fought equally in the dark'.[139]

In actual fact, the Government of India, on the basis of information from its own officers as to the abuses endured by immigrant Indian labourers in Mauritius, had already decided to suspend emigration by executive order. T.C. Scott, a magistrate and collector of Balasore, had reported, after a medical sojourn in Mauritius in 1837, that the 'condition of the labourer

---

[136] Lord Ellenborough's Political Journal, 22 February 1838, N.A., Ellenborough Papers 30/12/28/6, fols 199, 206.
[137] Colonial Office to Board of Control, N.A., Colonial Office (hereafter C.O.) 111/161.
[138] Act XIV Emigration (passed 27 May 1839), I.O.R., V/8/31.
[139] J. Geoghegan, 'Note on Emigration from India' (Calcutta, 1873), I.O.R., V/27/820/1, pp. 9–10n.; also in *Parliamentary Papers* (1874) XLVII, Cmd. 314.

practically depends upon the individual character of his employer'. Whereas labourers whom he interviewed spoke very highly of one or two planters, 'others were mentioned in terms equally unfavourable with very rare exceptions'. Compounding the labourers' predicament was the fact that scarcely any of them understood their contracts. As relayed by Scott: 'They all stated they had left Calcutta under the impression they were going to the Company-ka-bustee (Company's village), the name by which the Mauritius is designated by the Agents in India'.[140]

In the face of the abortive parliamentary reaction to its proposals, the only policy initiative left to the Government in England before total prohibition was an Order in Council. By the Order in Council of 7 September 1838, all contracts of immigrant labourers were limited to one year and they had to be negotiated after the migrants' arrival in the colony. Intended as protection for the labourers against the machinations of unscrupulous recruiters in India, this Order was to rankle with planters who persisted in pushing for longer term contracts.

Mauritius

Meanwhile, official inquiries focused on Indian labourers in Mauritius. The Colonial Office appointed a Commission of Inquiry into the present Condition of Indian labourers in Mauritius, while the Government of India appointed a committee in Calcutta to enquire into abuses alleged to exist in the export of coolies. Obviously, the Colonial Office and the Government of India responded to very different mandates. The Colonial Office was responsible for the welfare of British Colonies. Thus, it attempted to balance the economic interests of the planters and their sugar estates against humanitarian concern for the welfare of plantation labourers, be they ex-slaves or imported Indian labourers. By contrast, the Government of India only concerned itself with the interests of emigrant labourers from India.

Yet, it was the Commission in Mauritius appointed by the Colonial Office which actually visited individual estates to interrogate both planters and labourers. Thus, ironically, these commissioners had a better opportunity to assess the condition of the labourers than the Calcutta Committee which necessarily operated from the distance of Calcutta, interviewing recruiting agents and Indians returning from Mauritius. Compounding the handicaps

---

[140] Report of T.C. Scott, magistrate and collector of Balasore, India Legislative Proceedings, 6 March 1837, No. 9, I.O.R., P/206/87.

of the Calcutta Committee was the fact that the early report of the Mauritius Commission was forwarded directly to London so that committee members in Calcutta did not have the benefit of its first hand evidence.[141]

Members of both inquiries were aware that Indian Acts V and XXXII 1837 stipulated that emigrants should acquire permits from a Government officer whose job it was to ensure the fairness of limited contracts and to provide for safe and healthy transport. They were also aware that whereas the planters in British Guiana had attempted, with the Order in Council of July 1837, to supersede limitations prescribed by a previous Order in Council, the planters in Mauritius had persuaded their government to promulgate two ordinances in November 1836 which were contrary to the spirit of Indian Acts V and XXXII of the next year. The Council of the late King William IV had immediately disallowed these ordinances on account of their 'provision for the especial protection of Masters and the subjugation of all laborers, especially those emigrated from India, to extraordinary and rigorous coercion'. Henceforth, disputes between masters and servants were brought under the cognizance of the public justice of regular Courts and Special Justices were substituted for the Civil Commissaries who had formerly represented the planter class on local tribunals.[142]

One of those Special Justices was C. Anderson who was to prove a thorn in the side of the Mauritius Commission. Anderson declined to sign an interim report by the commissioners who, after a tour of Port Louis, expressed the 'hope that in the plantations we may meet with as few exceptions to the general good treatment of the Indian labourers as have hitherto come under the observation of the committee'. Anderson, in a separate letter to G.F. Dick, the Colonial Secretary in Mauritius, protested that in the course of the Commission's investigations he 'had seen much which...merited reprobation'. He specifically mentioned that, although 'Indian labourers employed in this town [Port Louis] are generally fed, clothed and paid' in accordance with their agreements, they suffered from severe 'overwork,...

---

[141] Minute by J.P. Grant, 1 March 1841, India Public Proceedings 17 March 1841, No. 3, I.O.R., P/186/97; also in 'Copies of a Letter from the Secretary to the Government of India to the Committee Appointed to Inquire Respecting the Exportation of Hill Coolies 1 August 1838; of the Report Made by the Committee; with the Minutes of Evidence and Appendix; of Any Minute Recorded on that Report by Any Member of the Committee; of the Letters from the Government of India to the Court of Directors of the East India Company Dated 16 and 19 October 1840', *Parliamentary Papers* (1841) XVI, in continuation of Cmd. 45.

[142] Act V Bengal—Emigration Act To Prohibit Contracts for the Emigration of Natives, except under regulation (passed 1 May 1837); Act XXXII Emigration Act (passed 20 November 1837) I.O.R., V/8/31.

personal chastisement [and] lodging...too confined and disgustingly filthy'. Asked to elaborate upon his statements by Mr Dick, Anderson described at length a number of reprehensible scenes. He further speculated that some of the Commission's evidence was suspect. For example, with reference to 'personal chastisement', he noted as a 'matter of public notoriety', the estate of Messrs Worthington and Co. He remarked:

> Knowing as three of the members of the committee did, what takes place in Mr Worthington's estate, with reference to bodily correction, there was some surprise expressed that it had not been alluded to by Indians. I confess that I attributed this silence to intimidation.

Given the chance to refute Anderson's arguments, the commissioners contended that Anderson had exaggerated the exceptions to the general run of evidence. Interestingly, Anderson was sent to London in 1840 to plead the case of the Mauritius planters for renewed immigration.[143]

Another member of the Mauritius Commission, Thomy Hugon, suggested improved regulation of immigration proceedings. Hugon was a native of Mauritius, a former seafarer in the India–China trade, as well as a former indigo planter and a member of the Bengal Civil Service with a reputation for his knowledge and understanding of Indian traditions. In a Report dated 1839, he tried to reconcile the interests of the Mauritius planters with the rights of the Indian labourers. Essentially, he argued that there was much for planters to gain from the 'study of the character and habits of Indians' inasmuch as 'amongst Indians' properly understood 'the respect to the master, or as they expressively say "the man whose salt they eat" may be said almost to be a part of their religion'. However, Hugon observed that the planters of Mauritius faced certain inherent difficulties in coming to terms with their Indian labourers. Indeed, Hugon's remark that 'it is no severe reproach to the man who has possessed slaves to say, that he has despotic habits which he has to change entirely when he comes into contact with free men' is generally considered a classic. As part of his argument, Hugon noted that material

---

[143] C. Anderson, Superintending Special Magistrate, to G.F. Dick, Colonial Secretary, Special Magistrate's Office, Port Louis, 19 and 30 November 1838; C.M. Campbell, J. Villiers Forbes, T. Hugon, W. Bury to G.F. Dick, Colonial Secretary, Port Louis, 5 December 1838 in 'Copies of Despatches from Sir William Nicolay on the Subject of Free Labour in the Mauritius', *Parliamentary Papers* (1840) XXXVII, Cmd. 58, pp. 36–40; C. Anderson, to Lord John Russell, Stevens Hotel, Clifford Street, 1 May 1840 in 'Correspondence Addressed to the Secretary of State for the Colonial Department Relative to the Introduction of Indian Labourers into the Mauritius and the Report of the Commissioners of Inquiry into the Present Condition of Those Located in That Colony', *Parliamentary Papers* (1840) XXXVII, Cmd. 331, pp. 194–97.

advantages for labourers who had emigrated from Bengal to Mauritius were substantial. They could earn triple the wages available to them in Bengal; the food was more abundant and the climate more salubrious in Mauritius. Yet, Hugon argued that the Indians possessed 'an independence of Spirit which...would make them reject...conditions of bondage however great its material advantages'. Thus, he made several suggestions. There was a need for flexible contracts instead of the previous five-year contracts which could prevent the labourer from 'profiting by any rise in the price of labour' over time; savings banks might secure labourers' savings and give them access to credit so that they were not vulnerable to planters who tried to 'lead' their labourers 'into debt in order to extend their engagements'; interpreters were needed in the courts; a few labourers might be hired as police peons in order to escape the corruption endemic among the regular police and, finally, free postage would enable labourers to keep in contact with their families. With such changes the planters could establish 'the great respect (not the abjectness of the slave) of the servant to "the man whose salt he eats"'.[144]

Coincidentally, similar reforms were proposed by Supreme Court Judge J.P. Grant in his dissent to the concluding report of the Calcutta Committee. Grant called for protection of Indian labourers from corporal punishment and from any interference with their liberty out of working hours; he argued that the labourers had a right to public justice assisted by the provision of interpreters and cheap and accessible courts; he also called for shorter contracts; finally, he thought the rights of the Indian labourers might be ensured by a Colonial Protector. With such reforms, Grant felt confident that the slave culture of the Mauritian planters could not endure. His suggestions were intended as an antidote to evidence before the Calcutta Committee of men kept confined on some plantations 'like criminals or slaves' or an overseer's systematic use of rattans or mule whips to make the labourer 'work and feel and think like a slave'.[145]

The regulations proposed by J.P. Grant were essential to his vision of successful emigration of Indian labourers carefully protected from the abuses catalogued by the Calcutta Committee. The Committee's final report, signed by only three of its original six members, submitted a vast amount of evidence of overwhelming abuse in support of their argument that the prohibition of Act XIV 1839 should continue indefinitely unless a Government agency

---

[144] 'Report of T. Hugon of the Bengal Service upon the Subject of Indian Emigration to Mauritius', *Parliamentary Papers* (1840) XXXVII, Cmd. 331, pp. 186, 193. *See also* Hugh Tinker, *op. cit.*, pp. 18–19.

[145] Minute by J.P. Grant, 1 March 1841, *op. cit.*

for trade regulating the cooly trade were established at an admittedly prohibitive expense. The three signatories of the report were important members of the Calcutta community whose opinions could not be lightly disregarded. The chairman, Theodore Dickens, was an advocate of the Supreme Court and prominent public speaker; Russomoy Dutt was the first Indian to be appointed as a Judge of the Small Causes Court and a founder of Hindu College[146] and Rev. James Charles represented Evangelical reformers' concerns. Of the remaining three members, the army officer, Major Archer, retired to England before the completion of the report; W. Dowson, a merchant active in the export of coolies to Mauritius, defended the planters from the Committee's accusations; it remained for J.P. Grant to take a moderate position.

Grant did not disavow the evidence which he had assisted the Committee to collect. In some instances his condemnation was more severe than that of his colleagues. Thus Grant did not deny evidence that the Calcutta police colluded with the recruiting agents to harass coolies into emigrating against their will, while fleecing them of their cash advances at the same time; he went further to observe that the police were 'the least suited to be an efficient protector of Coolies' and that cash advances from the planters through their agents should be disallowed. He complained that his colleagues failed to 'distinguish…maladministration from the mass of evils they hold to be inherent in the Cooly trade'. However, he did admit to passionate disagreement with the Committee over the question 'whether the whole of the labouring population of the vast portion of Her Majesty's Territories entrusted to the Government of the East India Company ought to be as free as the rest of Her Majesty's Subjects in respect to the disposal of their labour and their right of going about or not'. He certainly did not agree with the Committee's conclusion that the only remedy for abuse was prohibition.

In fact, Grant managed to discredit some of the given evidence presented by the Committee in their final report. Objecting to the Committee's assertion that 'the result of the migration that has already taken place has been most disastrous to the families of those who have emigrated', Grant challenged the legitimacy of the evidence. The Committee members had taken to heart a memorandum furnished by a Mr Taylor to a Landholders' Society showing 'that the districts of Bancoorah and Maunbhoom have been burdened with a vagrant and mendicant population of paupers,' composed

---

[146] H. Tinker observes that during the entire nineteenth century, 'few if any Indians were appointed by the Indian Government to public commissions of inquiry'. H. Tinker, *op. cit.*, p. 66.

of the deserted families of '291 individuals and families inhabiting 113 villages'. Grant observed that 'for any one Man to have procured by personal inquiry...satisfactory evidence in all these cases would have occupied...more hours than most officers would give to an incidental application of this sort'. He concluded that 'Mr Taylor merely sent in to the Landholders' Society the answers he got to some circular order...by Thannah Mohurrirs or Zemindaree Darogahs. If so [the memo] is utterly worthless'. Further casting aspersions on Mr Taylor's credibility as author of these returns from two districts, Grant noted that the format used in the two districts was completely different and therefore could not have been prepared by one officer. Also he noted that the English translation of the returned coolies' interviews was not the work of an Englishman. This was evident in the sample: 'Said you will get pay at five per month, if you wish can come home yearly, five years you should remain there, afterwards remain or not as you please, but it is now two or three years not returned nor sent any money'. Finally, he argued that the spirit of the two returns was contradictory:

> I should guess that the Bancoorah Return was prepared by some Mohurrir desirous to please some person inimical to the system of labourers going from India to cultivate sugar elsewhere, whilst the Maunbhoom Return may have been prepared by some Thannah Officer who had made a good thing by presents or fees from arkoties conducting coolies past his thannah.[147]

As in the case of slavery, Governor General Auckland found it impossible to offer leadership on this issue. Indeed, Edward Thompson and Hugh Tinker have described Auckland as a 'dilettante whose administration has been more generally condemned than that of any other Governor General'.[148] In receipt of the Calcutta Committee's final report in mid-October 1840, Auckland simply forwarded it to the Home Authorities confiding to John Hobhouse that 'it seems to be preposterous that a prohibition should be imposed to the free emigration of labour'.[149] Yet, he dwelled upon his doubts about renewing emigration accompanied by effectual checks against abuse.

---

[147] Minute by J.P. Grant, 1 March 1841, *op. cit.*, paras 24, 25, 29, 31, 40, 43 and 102; cf. Report of T. Dickens, Rev. Charles and Russomoy Dutt, 14 October 1840, India Public Proceedings 4 November 1840, No. 16, para. 22 and note to para. 37, I.O.R., P/186/95. Also in *Parliamentary Papers* (1841) XVI, Cmd. 45.

[148] H. Tinker, *op. cit.*, p. 65; *see also* E. Thompson, 'Introduction' to Emily Eden, *Up the Country; Letters Written to Her Sister from the Upper Provinces of India* (London, 1937).

[149] Auckland, to Hobhouse, Barrackpore, October 18, Calcutta, October 19, 1840, Broughton Papers, British Library, ADD. MSS 36474, fol. 370.

Noting the huge demand for labour in the sugar islands, Auckland warned:

> ...when for the supply of thousands and thousands of Laborers to various remote settlements, the iniquitous craft of this great City finds its account in acting the crimp upon those who are simple and unguarded, I greatly fear that...no strictness of regulation and no vigilance on the part of the authorities would immediately prevent the infliction of grievous oppressions and deceits upon large numbers of persons helpless from their poverty and from their utter ignorance and inexperience.[150]

So forceful was Auckland's language in expressing his doubts over the renewal of the cooly trade that the egregious abolitionist, John Scoble, actually incorporated Auckland's words in a memorial to Lord Stanley which he prepared on behalf of the British and Foreign Anti-Slavery Society.[151] Auckland's repetitive use of the word 'crimp' reflected a significant problem in Calcutta which was to escalate in time. Crimps were recruiting agents who felt no shame in defrauding or entrapping ignorant and illiterate coolies with contracts they didn't understand to undertake an arduous sea voyage to an alien land they knew nothing about.[152]

To be fair to Auckland, when the slavery and emigration legislation was debated in India, he was distracted by the disastrous first Afghan War. Also, his Council divided very much along the same lines as it had over the issue of slavery. W.W. Bird, with little faith in the Government's ability to protect the 'native population from being taken involuntarily from their homes and their families', concluded that 'we are bound by all the obligations of justice and good faith to persevere in the prohibition'. H.T. Prinsep thought that 'prohibition...ought not to be maintained' so long as labourers were protected against abuse and prevented from going west of the Cape of Good Hope. And finally, A. Amos took a more forceful position. Recalling his previous dissents 'from the principles of Act XIV 1839,' Amos argued that evasions of

---

[150] Auckland, Minute in General Department on Exportation of Coolies, 22 April 1841, Broughton Papers, British Library, ADD. MSS 36474, fols 511, 513–14.

[151] Memorial of the Committee of the British Foreign Anti-Slavery Society, to the Rt. Hon. Lord Stanley, Secretary for the Colonies, with duplicate to the Rt. Hon. the Earl of Ripon, President, Board of Trade, 1842, British and Foreign Anti-Slavery and Aboriginal Protection Society Papers, Rhodes House, Oxford, Memorials E 2/19, fol. 104.

[152] According to John Simpson and Edmund Weiner, eds., *Oxford English Dictionary*, Vol. IV, 2nd ed. (Oxford, 1989), p. 22, 'a Crimp is an agent making it his business to procure seamen, soldiers, etc. by seducing, decoying, entrapping or impressing them. Of uncertain origin'.

total prohibition would 'be attended with more frightful consequences than any...likely to issue from legal emigration properly regulated'.[153]

In the meantime, the Chief Commissary in the Police Department in Port Louis produced evidence that a woman, Carpaye, had lured 49 coolies before a Mr Vinay of Pondicherry who recruited them to work for Carpaye's brother, a planter in the Black River District in Mauritius—all in violation of the prohibition of Act XIV 1839. Carpaye's agents then marched the coolies in gangs under cover of darkness to Cuddalore where they were put on board the ships 'Constance' and 'Marie Laurie' for Port Louis without benefit of appearing before any authorities who might have questioned their arrangements. Benefitting from the lax enforcement of the law, Mr Vinay was ultimately prosecuted in connection with four coolies on the basis of evidence provided by Carpaye; Vinay alleged that he merely provided passage money for the four, insisting 'that he did not embark them as Laborers'. He escaped with the lenient punishment of a fine of 400 rupees—only half of the maximum.[154]

In the face of deadlock in Calcutta and defiance of the law by unscrupulous planters in Mauritius, the Home Authorities seized the initiative. Already, Lord Ellenborough had been appointed Auckland's successor. Before leaving England to take up his responsibilities in India, Governor General Ellenborough submitted to Lord Stanley a list of conditions which he thought appropriate for controlling emigration to Mauritius. Ellenborough's proposals for Emigration Agents in India and Mauritius to supervise the engagement of immigrant labourers in India, for all emigrants to be declared debt free upon landing in Mauritius, for women to be encouraged to emigrate and for free return passages to be provided by the planters for their labourers at the end of their contracts—these ideas all met with Lord Stanley's approval. The Colonial Secretary only disagreed with Ellenborough's suggestion of a five-year contract; Stanley insisted that 'no contract can be entered into for a longer period than one year'. After all, that was the essential requirement

---

[153] Minute by W.W. Bird, 6 May 1841; Minute by H.T. Prinsep, 9 May 1841; Minute by A. Amos, 11 May 1841, in 'Copy of Any Papers Respecting the Exportation of Hill Coolies, Received from the Government of India', *Parliamentary Papers* (1841) III, Cmd. 43, pp. 10–12, 14–17.

[154] George F. Dick, Colonial Secretary, Mauritius, to Secretary of Government of Fort St. George, 9 August 1841; John Finness, Chief Commissary, Police Department, Port Louis, to George F. Dick, Colonial Secretary, 9 and 18 June 1841; Madras Public Proceedings 28 September 1841, No. 15, I.O.R., P/247/63, fols 3741–42, 3754–55 and 3792–93. *See also* Report by C.H. Hallett, Collector of South Arcot, 5 January 1843, Cuddalore, Madras Public Diary for January 1843, No. 28, I.O.R., P/248/3, fols 260–62.

of the Order in Council of 7 September 1838. And, when Stanley suggested that the Governor General be limited in his discretion to require that no more than one third of the immigrants be female, Ellenborough replied that 'one quarter would be enough'.[155] Presumably, the consultations between Lord Ellenborough and Lord Stanley then formed the basis for the Privy Council's Order of 15 January 1842 which set up a Schedule of 22 Rules to have the force of law in Mauritius 'in the event of any Law being made in British India authorizing the emigration to Mauritius of the Natives of India'. Lord Stanley, in a letter to the Board of Commissioners of the East India Co., while presupposing the repeal in India of Act XIV 1839 'so far as respects the island of Mauritius', emphasized that the Government of India must support the new rules with vigorous enforcement. The Court of Directors then forwarded the Order in Council to the Government of India with the warning that, if the prohibition against all emigration in Act XIV 1839 were to be repealed, it must be repealed only for Mauritius and the new law must implement the Schedule of 22 Rules so as to ensure the welfare of the labourers.[156]

Unlike his predecessor, Governor General Ellenborough assumed a decisive role. He supplied Amos with the Order in Council, his joint memoranda with Lord Stanley and the current imperial Passengers Act so that he might produce a Draft Act. Ellenborough then asked Amos to send the Draft Act to him at his Camp in Delhi, along with the relevant source materials, commenting that 'the matter is of so much importance that I should think it advisable to have them printed for our use'.[157] These very careful deliberations eventually produced Act XV 1842 repealing the prohibition of all emigration in Act XIV 1839 so far as Mauritius was concerned. Mauritius first had to supply evidence of good faith in the form of Ordinance ll 1842 which authorized the appointment of emigration agents in Calcutta, Madras and Bombay and recommended the selection of the egregious Special Magistrate C. Anderson

---

[155] Ellenborough's conditions for emigration to Mauritius; Lord Stanley's memo on them; Ellenborough's remarks on Lord Stanley, enclosed in A. Amos, Minute 29 May 1842, India Legislative Proceedings, 3 June 1842, No. 4, Revenue, Judicial and Legislative Committee Papers: Emigration—Indian Correspondence, I.O.R., L/P&J/1/88. Cf. Ida May Cumpston, *Indians Overseas in British Territories 1834–54* (London, 1953), pp. 63–64, n. 6.

[156] Lord Stanley, to Commissioners for Affairs of India, Downing Street, 27 January 1842, *Parliamentary Papers* (1842) XXX, Cmd. 26; Despatch from Court of Directors to Governor General In Council, 22 March 1842, *Parliamentary Papers* (1842) XXX, Cmd. 192.

[157] Ellenborough, to Hon. A. Amos, Allahabad, 22 May 1842, India Legislative Consultations 3 June 1842, No. 5, Revenue, Judicial and Legislative Committee Papers: Emigration—Indian Correspondence 1842–59, I.O.R., L/P&J/1/88.

to be appointed by the Government of India as Protector, a post which Lord Ellenborough considered to be of vital importance. The Colonial Secretary at Mauritius asserted that 'Mr Anderson...possesses...that moral courage which enables him unflinchingly to carry into effect his decisions whether affecting the Masters or the Men'. Such was Anderson's reputation for defending the interests of the labourers, that a group of Calcutta merchants attempted to block his appointment. But Ellenborough ignored their petition and acquiesced in Anderson's appointment.[158]

Meanwhile, in London abolitionists attempted to embarrass Lord Stanley by denouncing his high-handed action of issuing the Order in Council of 15 January 1842 before seeking the approval of Parliament in the form of a clause to be added to the Colonial Passengers Bill renewing the cooly trade between India and Mauritius. But the denunciations fell upon deaf ears in a poorly attended House of Commons which endorsed Stanley's action by a substantial majority. Although the inspiration for India Act XV 1842 clearly lay with the Privy Council's Order, I.M. Cumpston expertly argues: 'The passing by a substantial majority in a thin House of a motion defeated two years before suggests that the primary obstacle to approval of the traffic in 1840 had been the request of the East India Company for delay'.[159]

Whatever the machinations behind the enactment by the Government of India of Act XV 1842, the Schedule of Rules governing the cooly trade which was originally dictated by the Privy Council was to form the basis of all future legislation on the subject. As has been demonstrated above, the Governor of Mauritius was required to appoint emigration agents at each of the ports of embarkation in India and a protector of immigrants in Mauritius—all subject to the approval of the Government of India, but on a salary paid by the Government of Mauritius. These salaried agents were to take over from the police the job of ensuring that no intending emigrant was a victim of fraud or delusion. Crimps were liable to a fine up to 500 rupees or six months in prison. As specified by the Order in Council of 7 September 1838, no contract was to be negotiated until the labourer reached Mauritius.

---

[158] G.F. Dick, Colonial Secretary, Mauritius, to Secretary to Government of India, 20 August 1842, India Legislative Consultations 30 September 1842, No. 19; Seven Calcutta Merchants, to W.W. Bird, Deputy Governor of Bengal, India Legislative Consultations 30 September 1842, No. 23 and C.G. Mansel, Junior Secretary to Government of India with Governor General to F.J. Halliday, Officiating Secretary, to Government of India, Simla, 25 October 1842, India Legislative Consultations 2 December 1842, No. 16, *ibid.*

[159] I.M. Cumpston, *Indians Oversees in British Territories 1834–54* (London, 1953), 66–67. For a closely argued analysis of the parliamentary background of early Indian emigration legislation, see her chapters 1–2.

For 48 hours after arrival, the labourer was guaranteed provisions by the captain of the ship on which he had travelled; he was also declared to be debt free. The rest of the regulations concerned the paperwork necessary for keeping accurate registers of the emigrants and shipboard comforts. Every passenger was to be guaranteed sufficient space, water and provisions. To avoid overcrowding, every ship was required to weigh in at two tons per passenger. Every passenger was allotted 5 gallons of water in sweet condition, 7 pounds of varied foodstuffs per week and 12 superficial feet of space.[160]

The renewed emigration to Mauritius was so successful that by the end of 1843 all but 1,000 of the 30,000 labourers required to work the sugar plantations had been recruited. However, the sudden arrival of 29,000 Indians had worried the Mauritian Government with greatly increased expense. The Mauritian Government therefore despatched Anderson to the Government in Calcutta to suggest changes to the system. Anderson then proposed to the Government that, since the quota for labourers in Mauritius was nearly filled including a healthy increase in the number of women emigrants, emigration might in future be limited to the one port of Calcutta.

From the point of view of the Government of India, there were more serious problems with Act XV than the immediate need to curtail the numbers of intending emigrants. W.W. Bird listed a number of abuses which ensued from the fact that Act XV had failed to implement the intention of the Home Authorities that the Government of India should appoint a protector of emigrants at each port of embarkation in addition to the emigration agent nominated by the Government of Mauritius. Bird pointed out that:

> The Consequence has been that the business of Emigration instead of being conducted as intended solely by the officers of the two Governments has been left as formerly to the private peculation[161] of the Mauritius planters themselves who employ the Agency Houses of Calcutta to procure emigrants which Houses entertain Crimps and Duffadars to go into the interior and by false representations and other devices induce ignorant People to agree to emigrate, who are thus brought down to Calcutta deceived in many cases as to their

---

[160] Act XV for the regulating the Emigration of the Native Inhabitants of the Territories under the Government of the East India Company to the Island of Mauritius (passed 2 December 1842), I.O.R., V/8/32.

[161] Curiously, the word 'peculation' which appears in the documents transcribed both in the National Archives of India and the India Office Records becomes 'speculation' in the printed *Parliamentary Papers*. Although not quoting directly from Bird, I.M. Cumpston accepts the term 'speculation' in her account (I.M. Cumpston, *op. cit.*, p. 68). Both words make sense in the context, but 'peculation' would seem to be closer to Bird's incriminating inference.

ultimate destination and rendered insensible to any explanation made to them by the Government Agent when brought before him for certification.

And finally, regardless of the increased number of women who emigrated in 1843, Bird lamented the practice of 'enlisting native Prostitutes for Emigration'.[162]

The result of this assessment of Act XV 1842 was the enactment of Act XXI 1843 which limited all future emigration to the port of Calcutta and provided for the Governor General to appoint a Protector of Emigrants at Calcutta. The collector at Allahabad, Thomas Caird, was appointed Emigration Agent for Mauritius at Calcutta. Within a year, the Indian Government seemed intent on making a mockery of its own legislative deliberations; Thomas Caird so impressed the Indian Government with his competence that the Protector of Emigrant's duties were cancelled.[163] The *Friend of India* once described such legislative futility as a 'race...between abuses and legislation, in which legislation was always found to be in the rear'.[164]

Individual reputations were also to prove vulnerable to the realities of the cooly trade. During the first six months of 1844, six vessels carrying repatriate labourers from Mauritius back to Calcutta suffered very high mortality. For example, 44 of 149 passengers died aboard the *Watkins* which only had proper accommodation for 86 persons. There was a water shortage after the ship was becalmed for two weeks. When the Bengal authorities complained to the Colonial Secretary in Mauritius, they were told that the Mauritian authorities 'did not consider themselves bound' by the Order in Council of 1842 for the return voyage. And, Anderson counterattacked with his own complaint that he was grossly overworked. Yet, as Hugh Tinker remarks, 'for a humane man [Anderson's] replies were sometimes strangely indifferent

---

[162] C. Anderson, Acting Protector of Emigrants, to Governor General, Calcutta, 27 October 1843, N.A.I., Legislative Proceedings 28 October 1843, No. 46; Minute by W.W. Bird, 8 November 1843, N.A.I., Legislative Proceedings 11 November 1843, No. 3; also in Revenue, Judicial and Legislative Committee Papers: Emigration—Indian Correspondence 1842–59, I.O.R., L/P&J/1/88, and in 'Correspondence Relative to Emigration of Labourers to the West Indies and the Mauritius, from the West Coast of Africa, the East Indies and China', *Parliamentary Papers* (1844) XXXV, Cmd. 530.

[163] Colonial Land and Emigration Commissioners, to Stephen, 30 October 1844, P.R.O., C.O. 318/162, cited by I.M. Cumpston, *op. cit.*, p. 70.

[164] *Friend of India*, 3 August 1839, cited on title page of J. Scoble, Memorial of the Committee of the British Foreign Anti-Slavery Society to the Rt. Hon. Lord Stanley, Secretary for the Colonies, with duplicate to the Rt. Hon. the Earl of Ripon, President, Board of Trade, 1842, British and Foreign Anti-Slavery and Aboriginal Protection Society Papers, Rhodes House, Oxford, Memorials E 2/19, fol. 104.

to humanity'. Asked about the starving paupers, Anderson replied that they should not receive 'extraordinary indulgence in the way of food' as it 'might prove an inducement to misconduct'. And, of the 'emaciated appearance' of some returning labourers, Anderson countered that these were 'dissolute and abandoned' vagrants. But, Tinker refers back to the legal framework for the cooly trade for his main conclusion that 'the Order in Council and Act XV did not provide for the return voyages'.[165]

Nevertheless, generally speaking, it was considered that the 'new system of emigration' to Mauritius based on Act XV 1842 and Act XXI 1843 was a huge success. Governor Gomm of Mauritius was able to report by early 1846 that there was no dearth of labour for the plantations; wages were reasonable; the general health of the coolies good; there was a general decline in vagrancy and absenteeism among labourers and that by the end of 1846, 23 million pounds more of sugar had been shipped than had been exported over the corresponding part of 1845.[166]

West Indies

While the planters in Mauritius showed some signs of coming to terms with their Indian labourers, the planters in the West Indies, still facing the prohibition of Act XIV 1839, were becoming desperate for labour. Their predicament had been more dramatic than that of the Mauritius planters, ever since midnight of 31 July 1834 when the British Parliament's Act of Emancipation freed nearly three quarters of a million slaves in the British West Indies compared with just under 57,000 in Mauritius.[167] The freed slaves entered a six-year apprenticeship during which period they owed their employers approximately 40 hours of unpaid labour per week. But the African labourers, once given a taste of freedom, did not respond well to the process of transition to contract labour. After their term of apprenticeship expired, they tended to withdraw from plantation labour altogether. By 1850, Governor Barkly of British Guiana reported that 'negroes were settling more and more up creeks and rivers beyond the pale of civilization, generally relapsing into barbarism of the deepest dye'.[168]

---

[165] H. Tinker, *op. cit.*, pp. 79–80.
[166] Governor Gomm, to Earl Grey, 24 December 1846, *Parliamentary Papers* (1847–48) XLIV, Cmd. 61, cited by I.M. Cumpston, *op. cit.*, p. 113.
[167] Panchanan Saha, *Emigration of Indian Labour (1834–1900)* (Delhi, 1970), p. 6.
[168] Governor Barkly, to Earl Grey, 17 April 1850, *Parliamentary Papers* (1851) XXXIX, Cmd. 624.

As early as 1836, John Gladstone requested the Agency House of Gillanders & Co. in Calcutta to supply labourers for his estate in British Guiana. By 1839 the abolitionist, John Scoble, had visited British Guiana and reported that coolies were settled on several estates in 'wretched' and 'filthy' conditions. After the Government of India instituted executive and legislative prohibitions against the cooly trade in 1838–39, a clear distinction was drawn between Mauritius and the West Indies as destinations for Indian labourers. Governor General Auckland was willing to contemplate the renewal of emigration to Mauritius as a 'British settlement, easily accessible from India and open to our observation'; whereas he confided to Hobhouse at the Board of Control that he would 'not be sorry for any law or regulation' which the Home Authorities might 'send to us throwing impediments in the way of [the coolies'] transportation to the West Indies'.[169] And, H.T. Prinsep remarked that the reason he would restrict the renewal of emigration to areas east of the Cape of Good Hope was that there was 'no regular direct intercourse between India and the Royal colonies to the west'.[170]

With the relatively successful reintroduction of Indian labourers to Mauritius in the wake of Acts XV 1842 and XXI 1843, the Colonial Office in London indicated to the Board of Control a willingness to reconsider the ban on Indian emigration to the West Indies. Governor General Ellenborough gave his support to the idea and by the middle of 1844, the Government of India received authorization from the Home Authorities to repeal the prohibition of Act XIV 1839 insofar as it affected British Guiana, Trinidad and Jamaica. The Government of India responded by enacting Act XXI 1844 which allowed emigration of Indian labourers to these three islands from Calcutta, Madras and Bombay. The Schedule of Rules incorporated in Act XV 1842 was also annexed to the 1844 act. The Government of Madras promptly prescribed a code of rules parallel to those followed in Calcutta. No rules were prescribed in Bombay because there were no prospective emigrants from Bombay to the West Indies.[171] Back in London, the Directors warned the Colonial Office that they expected the labourers to be returned home on the expiry of their contracts under the same conditions as those prescribed by Act XV 1842 for the outward voyage.

---

[169] Auckland Minute, 22 April 1841, Broughton Papers, British Library, ADD. MSS 36474, fol. 515; Auckland, to Hobhouse, *ibid.*, ADD. MSS 36473, fol. 284.
[170] Minute by H.T. Prinsep, 9 May 1841, *op. cit.*, pp. 14–15.
[171] Act XXI for regulating Emigration of Native Inhabitants of the Territories under the Government of the East India Company to Jamaica, British Guiana and Trinidad (passed 16 November 1844), I.O.R., V/8/32. See also John Geoghegan, *op. cit.*, pp. 16–17.

The demand for Indian labourers, especially in the West Indies, was closely tied to the parliamentary fortunes of the sugar planters' claims for protection. While the 1844 Sugar Duties Bill granted West Indian sugar protection worth 10 shillings per hundredweight, the 1846 Sugar Duties Bill plunged the planters into their most feared nightmare with the admission of slave-grown sugar from Cuba, the Philippines and the Dutch East Indies. Whereas the prime object of this move was to reduce the price of sugar in England, the Government rationalized their acceptance of slave produced goods by insisting that 'the competition of free labour' was the way 'to beat slave labour and the slaveholder's capital...not...prohibitory duties'.[172]

Reeling from this blow, the planters were finally forced to focus their attention on maximizing their internal resources instead of constantly crying for external protection. I.M. Cumpston, in the midst of her very adept analysis of the sugar controversy, remarks that Lord Russell when he was Colonial Secretary, and Earl Grey, his successor in 1846, had found that such 'advice...in adverse circumstances ran counter to the intolerant and recalcitrant temper of the colonists' for whom 'it was a revolutionary attitude' to focus on 'the problem of the best application of their labour supply to an economical and planned cultivation of the land'.[173]

Indeed, the planters proved unable to manage a system of free labour. There were endless complaints about vagrancy among the Indian immigrants. In Trinidad, a stipendiary magistrate proposed regulations to confine labourers to the estates by issuing leave tickets and passes. The Colonial Secretary, Earl Grey, disallowed these regulations principally on account of the power they placed in the hands of the master. A minute by a Mr Taylor claimed that Grey's withdrawal of these regulations resulted in 'the breaking of engagements, insecurity of labour, vagrancy, loss on the part of the planters, disease, misery and starvation in many instances'.[174]

The abolitionist, John Scoble, branded these proposed regulations the 'new slave code of Trinidad'.[175] Hugh Tinker had an equally abrasive explanation for the vagrancy complaints. He asserted that 'the planters would not accept that Indians absented themselves from the plantation, because conditions were unbearable'. Instead they fantasized that 'Indians had an instinctive urge to wander'.[176]

---

[172] Memoranda on the Charges Brought Against the Home Government by Witnesses Before the Recent Committee on Sugar Duties, 1848, N.A., C.O. 318/179, p. 147; 27 July 1846, *Hansard's Parliamentary Debates* 3rd series LXXXVIII.
[173] I.M. Cumpston, *op. cit.*, p. 110.
[174] Minute by Mr. Taylor, N.A., C.O. 318/178.
[175] Cited by I.M. Cumpston, *op. cit.*, pp. 121–22.
[176] H. Tinker, *op. cit.*, pp. 195–56.

Nevertheless, the planters pleaded before a Select Committee in 1847–48 that the combination of the admission of slave-grown sugar with the expenses imposed upon them by immigration legislation and the lack of effective laws against vagrancy was ruining them. The Select Committee took pity on them and reported in favour of reinstating the 10 shilling per hundredweight protection for six years. However, the House of Commons argued that this would create high prices in England and extravagant wages in the West Indies; they would only admit to the postponement of equalization of sugar duties until 1854. This was incorporated in a new bill which, in effect, repealed the 1846 Sugar Duties Bill and offered the incentive to the sugar colonies of guaranteed interest on loans amounting to £500,000 to cover the expense of introducing free labour or improving the infrastructure of roads, railways, drainage, irrigation or other public works.[177]

Yet, dismal news kept coming. In 1847 Thomas Caird was censured as a result of numerous deaths on ships he had sent from Calcutta. There were accusations that the labourers were not carefully selected. Caird responded that the very best class of cooly, the Dhangur or hill cooly was strangely susceptible to cholera. In these circumstances of illness, vagrancy and death among the labourers combined with the planters' plea of financial ruin, Earl Grey informed the East India Company in February 1848 that 'it has become necessary to relinquish the idea of sending any more Coolies' to the West Indies. At the same time, Grey terminated Thomas Caird's appointment vis-à-vis the West Indies.[178]

In a retrospective analysis of 'the general failure of Cooly Immigration', Governor Harris lamented the lack of preparation and insufficient government supervision. At the same time, he cast aspersions on the poor quality of some of the immigrants. Thus, he proclaimed that 'there would always have been a numerous body of useless, idle and dissolute, consisting of the scourings of Calcutta and Madras'. Harris attributed general vagrancy, not to 'ill usage', but to the manipulation of unscrupulous sirdars who hired coolies from one estate to another and to the lack of government regulation. And so he described the resultant misery:

---

[177] 12 Vict. c. XCVII, *Parliamentary Papers* (1847–48) VI, Cmd. 497.

[178] Colonial Land and Emigration Commissioners, to Caird, 2 July 1847, P.R.O., C.O. 318/172; Earl Grey, to Caird, 17 January 1848, N.A., C.O. 318/176. Cited by I.M. Cumpston, *op. cit.*, pp. 116–18. Herman Merivale, Downing Street, to Board of Control, 14 February 1848, Revenue, Judicial and Legislative Committee Papers: Emigration—Home Correspondence 1845–56, I.O.R., L/P&J/1/84.

By being permitted to move about as they pleased, on pretence of seeking for work, they were attacked by fever and ague, and the sores in the feet to which they are particularly subject were neglected and became sometimes incurable; ill and lame, and with no home to go to, and generally deserted by their comrades, they had nothing for it but to lie down and die, unless found and picked up by police.[179]

In addition to Lord Harris' contention that the coolies were selected from the dregs of Indian society, there was a perception that the coolies from Madras were inferior to those from Calcutta. This claim was advanced with particular reference to British Guiana. Governor Light of British Guiana described the Madrasis as 'idle, sickly, beggarly [and] filthy in their food and habits'.[180] This image would follow naturally from a report by the Protector at Madras, Capt. Christopher Bidon, regarding the principal recruiting grounds in south India. Bidon concluded that untouchables were prominent among the main flow of recruits in the overpopulated Tamil districts; they eagerly responded to any offer of release from their bondage to the upper castes. Bidon speculated that 'Trinidad is more adapted than British Guiana to the Indian Constitution'. The British Guiana authorities considered 'that country as less adapted to the inhabitants of the Madras Presidency than to Natives of the Plains of Bengal.'[181] In another Report, the Immigration Agent General in British Guiana made a scathing assessment of 'the Madras Coolies', claiming that it was impossible to give 'credence to their statements'. He asserted:

> They are greedy of gain and lend out money at usurious rates of interest which frequently leads to the loss of capital. They steal one another's free ticket or sell their own. They rob one another of the Savings Banks Books, and having obtained such particulars as will enable them to complete the fraud, become Masters of the deposit...For a paltry consideration they bear false witness against each other.[182]

---

[179] Governor Lord Harris, to Earl Grey, Trinidad, 1 July 1848 in 'Copies or Extracts of any recent Correspondence between the Secretary of State and the Governors of the Sugar Growing Colonies as to the Distress now existing in those Colonies', *Parliamentary Papers* (1847–48) XLVI, Cmd. 749, pp. 327–28.
[180] Governor Light, to Earl Grey, 11 January 1848, N.A., C.O. 111/250.
[181] Cololnial Land and Emigration Office, to Herman Merivale, 5 January 1855, I.O.R., L/P&J/1/84; see also H. Tinker, *op. cit.*, p. 54.
[182] Report by T. Gardiner Austin, Immigration Agent General, British Guiana, 23 October 1856, concerning passengers on the 'Empress Eugenie', I.O.R., L/P&J/1/84.

By way of contrast with the coolies from Madras, the *dhangur*s or hill coolies from Chota Nagpur, southwest of Calcutta, won the highest praise. In an early official reference to them, they were described as 'hardened savages' who could not be prevailed upon to come anywhere near a European camp.[183] As stark poverty drove them to seek employment outside of their hill country, they gained a reputation for hard work and honesty. They were among the first labourers to emigrate to Mauritius. In one of the first reports on emigrant labour, they were deemed superior to their fellow labourers inasmuch as they 'had come to Calcutta in search of employment' and 'had entered into the speculation with perfect good will'.[184] Overall in Bengal, recruits for emigration came from a great variety of backgrounds. Indeed, George Grierson, reporting on emigration from Bengal in 1883, was keen to explode the 'popular fallacy...that only the lowest classes emigrate'. Of a sample of 1,200 recruits, Grierson was able to show that 'two thirds of the Hindus recruited belong to castes of higher and medium social position'.[185]

It is not surprising then that when the British Guiana authorities joined Trinidad in a bid for renewed emigrant labour, they asked for coolies only from Calcutta.[186] In an effort to overcome the Colonial Office's opposition to the renewal of immigration, both British Guiana and Trinidad passed a series of ordinances to provide for control of the coolies. Trinidad was first, with an ordinance proposing strict disciplinary laws as an antidote to vagrancy. Ordinance 3 1849 not only confined labourers to their estates with a system of passes and penalized absence from work with imprisonment, but it also called for five-year contracts with labourers introduced at public expense. Earl Grey disallowed this ordinance, but reluctantly conceded a three-year contract.[187] This compromise admitted the earlier British Guiana Ordinance 3 of 1848 and Mauritius Ordinance 3 of 1849, both of which called for three-year contracts. Thus, the provision for one-year contracts in the Order in Council of 7 September 1838 became a dead letter.

---

[183] Capt. Linnock, to Major Roughsedge, Political Agent, 28 April 1819, B.S.A., C.N.C.O., vol. 14, fol. 343.

[184] T.P. Woodcock, to Lord Auckland, Governor General of India, Bengal Club, Calcutta, 19 November 1836, India Public Proceedings 1 February 1837, No. 15, I.O.R., P/186/75.

[185] George A. Grierson, 'Report on Colonial Emigration from the Bengal Presidency' (Calcutta, 1883), I.O.R., V/27/820/35, pp. 35–36.

[186] Governor Barkly, to Earl Grey, 27 August 1850, *Parliamentary Papers* (1851) XXXIX, Cmd. 624.

[187] Governor Harris, to Earl Grey, 6 February 1849; and Earl Grey, to Governor Harris, 28 April and 15 December 1849, *Parliamentary Papers* (1850) XL, Cmd. 643, pp. 207–210, 233–37, 239–41 and 383–86; *see also* Earl Grey, to G.W. Anderson, Governor of Mauritius, 17 May 1849, *Parliamentary Papers* (1850) XXXIX, Cmd. 741, p. 303.

British Guiana went on to pass four ordinances calling for severe penalties for offences and deductions from the coolies' wages for accommodation, medical treatment and for their return passage. The Home Authorities of the East India Company disapproved of these ordinances, arguing that they compared poorly with similar ordinances in Mauritius. However, taking into account the higher wages in British Guiana, the Colonial Office was prepared to overrule the Company.[188] The same ordinances were forwarded to the Protectors at Calcutta and Madras. Meanwhile, there were grim reports from returned labourers. When only half the contingent of labourers landed in 1845–46 returned in 1851–52, there was concern for the survival of the others. General alarm increased as returnees complained of ill treatment and religious persecution. In addition, the Calcutta press reached a state of near hysteria as *The Englishman* reprinted an account of death and destitution in Trinidad and the *Friend of India* declared that the colonial authorities had betrayed Indian labourers into the hands of West Indian planters who had not forgotten their habits of slave driving.[189] On the other side of the coin, some labourers returned with substantial savings and reports of good treatment. It was also alleged that the new disciplinary laws in Trinidad were approved by Indian authorities. Ultimately the Government of India took a neutral stand. While confident that Mauritius would be the preferred choice of intending emigrants, the Indian authorities declared that they would make no attempt to deter emigrants who might choose the West Indies. Given that the negative Calcutta press was mostly in English with Bengali translation, it is perhaps not surprising that emigrants from the interior of Bengal responded to recruiters and 'by the end of 1852 traffic was steady and without check'.[190]

By 1854, ordinances in both British Guiana and Trinidad won an official stamp of approval from the Colonial Office, the Home Authorities of the East India Company and the Government of India. British Guiana Ordinance 7 1854 and Trinidad Ordinance 24 of the same year featured three-year contracts, penalties for absence from work and a contribution from the labourer towards the expense of his return passage which was deferred in

---

[188] Governor Barkly to Earl Grey, 27 August and 11 September 1850; Appendix I comparing Mauritius Ordinance 22 1847 with British Guiana Ordinance 21 1850 in *Parliamentary Papers* (1851) XXXIX, Cmd. 624. For the Colonial Office's position, see *Parliamentary Papers* (1852) XVIII, Cmd. 1499, Appendix 52.

[189] *Parliamentary Papers* (1852) XVIII, Cmd. 1499, p. 57; T. Caird, to Hawes, 8 February 1851 and White, to Capt. Rogers, 16 December 1850, *Parliamentary Papers* (1851) XXXIX.

[190] I.M. Cumpston, *op. cit.*, p. 158.

time long after the expiry of the original contract.[191] In effect, Governor General Dalhousie had conceded the demands of the planters in British Guiana and Trinidad for an industrial residence extended to a period of 10 years. In the wake of this official success of the larger West Indian colonies with colonial and East India Company authorities, permission for Indian emigration was extended to other destinations. Act XIII 1847 repealed Act XIV 1839 regarding Ceylon on the condition that the Ceylon Government did not forward immigrant labourers to other destinations. Curiously, at about the same time and despite the poor reputation of Madras immigrants, Act VIII 1847 superseded the restriction of the cooly trade to Calcutta in Act XXI 1843 by allowing Madras to appoint a Protector of Emigrants to Mauritius. Act XXXI 1855 opened emigration to Granada and St. Lucia under precisely the same terms as were applied to British Guiana, Trinidad and Jamaica by Act XXI 1844.[192] Jamaica, although it was initially classified with British Guiana and Trinidad by Act XXI 1844, lost all enthusiasm for the idea after excessive mortality among the labourers first landed in 1845. While benefitting theoretically from legislation in 1845 which extended the sailing season by a month between Madras and the West Indies, Jamaica did not agitate against the ban of 1848 and, in fact, did not resume immigration until 1859.[193] Given continued reports of misery, disease and death among the immigrants,[194] this general official success must be seen as a victory for the sugar planters, especially those in British Guiana and Trinidad who never relaxed their campaign against the legislated restrictions on the coolie trade.

Recriminations against Emigration Legislation

Throughout the contest between colonial governments and East India Company authorities over emigration legislation, Mauritius was regarded as

---

[191] *Parliamentary Papers* (1854) XXVIII, Cmd. 1833, Appendix II; *Parliamentary Papers* (1854–55) XVII, Cmd. 1953.

[192] Act XIII for repealing Act XIV 1839 as far as it relates to the Emigration of Natives of India to Ceylon (passed 21 August 1847), and Act VIII for rendering lawful the Emigration of Labourers from the Port of Madras in the Presidency of Fort St. George to Mauritius (passed 8 May 1847) I.O.R., V/8/33; Act XXXI relating to the Emigration of Native Labourers to the British Colonies of St. Lucia and Granada (passed 14 November 1855), I.O.R., V/8/35.

[193] Act XXV for regulating the time of sailing of Ships carrying Emigrants from Madras to Jamaica, British Guiana and Trinidad (passed 20 December 1845), I.O.R., V/8/32. See also George A. Grierson, *op. cit.*, p. 2 and I.M. Cumpston, *op. cit.*, p. 139.

[194] See F.J. Mouat, 'Report on the Mortality of Emigrant Coolies on the Voyages to the West Indies in 1856–57', India Public Proceedings, October 1858, I.O.R., P/188/57.

a positive model. And yet the planters of Mauritius were no less persistent in their demands than their West Indian brethren. In fact, with Act IV 1852, the Government of India yielded to pressures from both planter interests. On the strength of West Indian claims that the sailing season from Calcutta was inconvenient, Section 1 extended the season by one month to match the concession given to Madras by Act XXV 1845. Sections 4 and 5 opening Bombay for emigration to Mauritius finally completed the emasculation of Act XXI 1843. And, as a result of 'repeated and urgent remonstrances of the Mauritius Government', the Government of India 'reluctantly' conceded reduction of the minimum requirements of shipboard space according to Act XV 1842. The minimum height between decks was reduced from six feet to five feet six inches and the minimum amount of space per labourer was reduced from 12 superficial feet to 72 cubic feet.[195]

However, it was on the subject of return passages that the Mauritius Government forged a path which eventually was to lead to a cancellation of the free return passage altogether. This change reflected, in part, a transition from the immigrant labourers viewed as a transient work force to the immigrant labourers viewed as permanent settlers. As early as 1845, Governor Gomm argued that the immigrant labourer might be expected to make a contribution to his own return passage. In support of his argument, Governor Gomm cited T. Hugon's description of the anxiety of some immigrants over their not having been called upon 'for any contribution toward the cost of their passage and inferring from it that they might be subjected to some restrictive conditions affecting their freedom in the Colony'.[196] While Governor Gomm made this somewhat revolutionary suggestion, he nonetheless dissented from his Committee of Council over their extravagant demands for many more immigrants than the number fixed upon by the Mauritius and Indian Governments. A report in the Colonial Office noted Sir W. Gomm's dissent:

> He observes that the calculation in regard to Absentees, Deserters is much exaggerated and that they do not in reality exceed 18%—that the Crop then in progress, for which the Laboring Population was sufficient, was expected to exceed considerably the largest crop ever gathered in the days of Slavery—...that on well managed estates there was little or no desertion or absenteeism, and consequently no deficiency of laborers—that vagabondage

---

[195] Act IV to amend the law relating to emigrant vessels and the emigration of labourers (passed 16 January 1852) I.O.R., V/8/34. See also J. Geoghegan, *op. cit.*, p. 20.

[196] W.M. Gomm, to Lord Stanley, 30 September 1845, N.A.I., Legislative Proceedings 29 November 1845, No. 20.

had prevailed chiefly among the worthless Immigrants introduced under the lax system of 1844.[197]

Generally speaking, Governor Gomm has been credited with the pursuit of a 'policy of seeking Indians' welfare, almost alone, his efforts slighted by the Anti-Slavery Committee'.[198]

By 1850 the Report of the Commission on Immigration to Mauritius pronounced the 'free return passage objectionable, not only in a financial point of view, but still more so as militating against the permanent settlement of the island'. Governor Gomm's successor, Sir George Anderson, suggested instead that 'a small deduction...should be made from the wages of the immigrants in aid of the expences of return passage'. After Calcutta contracts began deducting one rupee per month for return passages, 'it was found that "as a fiscal measure it had been an utter failure, having during three years cost, in collecting, £2,900 more than it produced" besides giving temptation to vagrancy and idleness and causing penalties to be incurred by the frequent attempts made to avoid its payment'.[199] Thus, in 1852, the Government of India allowed Mauritius to withdraw the right of a free return passage, a right which J. Geoghegan observed had been 'made legally binding on the colony by Sec. 1, Act XV 1842'. However, when Governor Harris proposed that the precedent set for Mauritius should be followed in Trinidad, the Court of Directors demurred. The grant of return passage was retained in the West Indies, the expense being partly borne by deductions from immigrants' wages. British Guiana planters, when their demands for prolonged indentures were rejected, won the consent of the East India Company home authorities to the collection of monthly sums from immigrants who did not consent to a second contract after the expiry of their first. Thus, in 1853 Dalhousie's Government 'permitted the extension of the period of industrial residence in British Guiana and Trinidad from five to ten years'. By 1857, voluntary commutation of the right of a return passage in the form of either money or land or both was discussed in both London and Calcutta with an emphasis upon the 'voluntary character of the transaction' and with the assurance that the full implications of any new contract be explained to the labourer by a resident Protector of Immigrants. In 1858–59, ordinances to this effect were passed in Jamaica, Trinidad and British Guiana.[200]

---

[197] Report by W.C. Murdoch, 7 April 1846, N.A., C.O. 167/263.
[198] I.M. Cumpston, *op. cit.*, p. 166.
[199] D.W.D. Comins, *Note on the Abolition of Return Passages to East Indian Immigrants from the Colonies of Trinidad and British Guiana* (Calcutta, 1892), I.O.R., V/27/820/11, pp. 1–2.
[200] J. Geoghegan, *op. cit.*, pp. 17–18.

Essentially, when the East India Company came to the end of its reign, the issue of return passages was left unresolved. What was becoming increasingly clear was a growing trend towards settlement in the colonies. Speculating about the circumstances of the returned labourer, Surgeon Major D.W.D. Comins wrote from the vantage point of the end of the century:

> If he returns with money he is fleeced by the priests and his relatives and so long as it lasts they may endure him, but with little sympathy and only selfish interest. On either side there is no longer any real tie and becoming disgusted with the simple ways and stricter habits of his relatives and village, the returned immigrant makes his way to the larger towns, and from poverty or other causes soon finds it advisable to again emigrate to his former or some other colony.[201]

By 1854, Indian labourers were credited with restoring prosperity to Trinidad and Mauritius.[202] Statistics began to reflect this trend. By the end of the century, G.A. Grierson reported that one third of the population of British Guiana and Trinidad was of 'Indian extraction' and in Mauritius nearly 70 per cent of the population was of 'Indian extraction'.[203]

Running counter to this broad picture of success were very severe problems. The emancipation of slaves in the French colonies of Réunion and Bourbon gave rise to increased emigration from the French ports of Pondicherry, Karikal and Yanam in the Madras presidency. The Madras Government complained that labourers from the Company territories were 'crimped and kidnapped and shipped to French colonies in overcrowded vessels to become…little better than praedial slaves'. Madras requested protests at the level of national government. But the Government of India simply stressed the need for stricter enforcement of Act XIV 1839. The result was an endless number of convictions before Madras magistrates. When, in 1850, the Madras courts questioned the legality of these convictions, the Government of India decided to enact Act XXIV of 1852.[204] For the first time, Act XXIV precisely defined the meaning of 'crimp':

> Any person who by force or fraud, unlawfully detains in any place or decoys to any place any Native of India, with intent to force or prevail upon him to enter into any service, or contract for service to be performed out of the Territories under the Government of the East India Company into which

---

[201] D.W.D. Comins, *op. cit.*, pp. 11–12.
[202] I. M. Cumpston, *op. cit.*, pp. 163, 165.
[203] G.A. Grierson, *op. cit.*, p. 2.
[204] J. Geoghegan, *op. cit.*, pp. 21–22.

he was not minded to enter, without such force or fraud, or who by means of false imprisonment, intoxication, intimidation, force or fraud, causes any Native of India to enter into any service or contract for service, or who attempts, by force or fraud, or by any false promise, pretence or representation, to cause any Native of India to depart either by land or water from the Territories under the Government of the East India Company, is a crimp, and guilty of crimping.[205]

However, such a crimp was only liable to punishment by a fine up to 500 rupees or six months of imprisonment, the same lax punishment prescribed by Act XV 1842. When this act proved ineffective, the Madras Government was authorized to establish a Mauritius agent at Karikal. Even more pathetic was the fact that, just as the East India Company's reign came to an end, Mauritius produced Ordinance 30 of 1858 which enabled planters to recruit directly through their own Calcutta and Bombay agencies which blatantly used 'Sirdars or rather crimps' to round up workers for their estates.[206]

Finally, the Government of India was goaded into admitting that all was not as their legislation would have it appear. In the wake of massive mortality as a result of defective quarantine operations on the lazaretto island off Mauritius, Act XIX empowered the Governor General to suspend emigration to a particular place for 'specified reasons'. Within a month of promulgating the law, Governor General Canning suspended emigration to Mauritius, only to reinstate the system within another six months upon receiving information that the lazaretto had been greatly improved.[207]

Conclusion

Prior to the great debate on slavery, the abuse of cooly labour chiefly through the practice of *begaree* or impressment constituted the most provocative challenge to the British sense of fair play proclaimed by the Cornwallis Code. Indeed, as early as the 1790s, the prohibition of 'begaree or the practice of individuals seizing and compulsively exacting service from…workmen' or

---

[205] Act XXIV for amending and explaining Act XIV 1839 and for the better prevention of Crimping (passed 14 May 1852), I.O.R., V/8/34.

[206] H. Tinker, *op. cit.*, pp. 132–33.

[207] Act XIX to enable the Governor General of India in Council to suspend the operation of certain Acts relating to the Emigration of Native Labourers (received assent of Governor General 19 September 1856), I.O.R., V/8/35. See G.A. Grierson, *op. cit.*, p. 2.

coolies became an integral part of the Cornwallis Code, as well as an exemplary administrative regulation in the province of Benares. It remained for Beng. Reg. XI 1806 to expand on this prohibition in order to call for 'proper compensation' for cooly labour and a 'just price' for provisions supplied. In accordance with the aim of uniformity in the Regulation provinces, it was considered that this legislation enshrined the fundamental rights of cooly labourers and was therefore reenacted in the presidency of Madras in 1810 and in Bombay in 1814. In addition, the Madras presidency, although it was not the hothouse for the Cornwallis Code, could report efforts to tabulate fair rates of cooly hire going back to the 1790s in Tanjore. The Munro Regulations finally called upon district magistrates 'to determine the rates of hire to be paid in their respective districts by travellers to palankeen bearers, coolies and boatmen'. The Bombay government followed suit in 1818.

All too predictably, the cruel practices of forced labour did not simply die away as the result of a legislated ideal. Graphic reports of abuse such as that documented by Henry Russell in Hyderabad forced Governor General Hastings to revisit the issue with yet another Regulation. Beng. Reg. III of 1820 declared that *begaree* or the practice of pressing labour was prohibited. Regulation III even attempted to enhance Beng. Reg. XI 1806 by rescinding the obligation its Sec. 2 had laid on collectors and magistrates to procure coolies for travellers and troop detachments on the move. However Sec. 3 of Beng. Reg. XI 1806 remained intact with its requirement that landlords respond to the demand of district officers for supplies 'at current bazaar prices' and for 'temporary bridges' in aid of the march of troops across their lands. By 1825, it was deemed necessary to enact Beng. Reg. VI to ensure sufficient provisions and preparations for the transit of the Company's troops across British controlled territory. The fact that the practice of pressed labour had survived all legislated attempts at regulation was apparent when the Elphinstone Code of Bombay found it necessary in 1827 to summarize all preceding legislation in addition to a full and precise definition of the practice of *begaree*. Revealing the Company's priorities, punishment for those who defied the law consisted of a system of graded fines or prison terms—all under 40 rupees commutable to eight days in prison. In stark contrast, Beng. Rev. VI 1825 set a ceiling of 1,000 *sicca* rupees for fines to be levied on local officers and landowners who failed to answer the district officer's demand for labour and supplies. It is little wonder, then, that, as late as 1831, F.C. Smith, the same agent for the Governor General in the Saugor and Narbudda Territories who launched the Company's campaign against thugs, lamented that the 'salutary and humane provisions of Regulation III of 1820 forbidding the pressing of Coolies and Begaries have fallen into desuetude'. More to the point, it was evident that the East India Company was willing to accept very limited objectives in its campaign against forced labour and for fair hiring practices in the face of the practical needs of its troops in transit. Ultimately, efforts to protect cooly labourers from abuse were enshrined in Sec. 374 of the Indian Penal Code. In Macauley-esque style, the full definition given by the Elphinstone Code is abbreviated as 'Unlawful compulsory labour' with punishment for 'Whoever unlawfully compels any person to labour against the will of that person' of a fine or prison term up to one year.[208]

Unlike the rights of coolie labourers whose abuse occurred well away from the spotlight of policy debates by the Company's Home Authorities in London, the rights of slaves in India were subject to the considerable publicity rendered by Evangelical interests in the English parliament. In fact, the inspiration for the Evangelical parliamentary campaign derived from a morality defined outside India in opposition to the African slave trade. Furthermore, it can be credibly argued that up until India Act V 1843, the most crucial legislation concerning slavery in India was enacted by the English parliament. Unfortunately, the so-called 'Felony Act' of 1811 [51 Geo. III c. 23], which declared anyone engaging in the slave trade to be guilty of a felony, was to prove virtually irrelevant to the practice of slavery including slave trading within India. And, any interference with the abuse of slaves within India was emasculated by the law enacted during the time of Warren Hastings to protect Hindu and Muslim laws [35 Geo. III c. 155]. No wonder scholars such as Gyan Prakash and Jacques Pouchepadass have complained of the colonial mentality supporting a 'juridical notion of power' in the legal discourse framed by freedom and slavery.

Nevertheless, despite the fact that the essential dynamic driving the decision to enact India Act V 1843 was provided by the Evangelical parliamentary campaign in England, there was intense debate in India. Reform minded Company servants found that in the theatre of the Company's criminal courts they might win some rights for slaves as individuals; however, in the civil courts, they were unable to make any inroads into the master–slave relationship protected by the Company's boldly proclaimed respect for Muslim and Hindu law and custom. Indeed, whereas Warren Hastings' Government with its Regulations IX and X of 1774 attempted to outlaw the kidnapping of children into slavery, it promised to protect the caste and property of its Hindu and Muslim subjects. This promise became enshrined

---

[208] *The Indian Penal Code, 1860 (Act No. XLV of 1860), As Amended up to date by Act 38 of 1975* (Lucknow, 1981), pp. 91–92.

in Sec. 15 Beng. Reg. IV 1793 of the Cornwallis Code which guaranteed that the Company's courts would respect Hindu and Muslim laws 'in suits regarding succession, inheritance, marriage and caste, and all religious usages and institutions'. A mere five years later, in April 1798, the Calcutta Sudder Dewanny Adawlut ruled that insofar as Indian masters had established slaves to be their property and insofar as their property rights were defined by Hindu and Muslim law, the spirit of the Cornwallis Code guaranteeing respect for Hindu and Muslim laws regarding property was 'applicable to cases of Slavery'. And so, before the end of the eighteenth century, slavery had become the law of the land in the Company's civil courts.

But for those who wished to bestow upon the Indian slave basic human rights, the Governor General's Council provided an arena in the Company's criminal courts. Sec. 2 Beng. Reg. VIII 1799 boldly disallowed the exemption in Muslim law from punishment of death for the wilful murder of a slave by his master. This paved the way for individual magistrates to insist in the courts that a slave enjoyed the same legal right to protection from abuse as his master. The Magistrate of Bundelkhund, J. Richardson, attempted to extend the slave's right to protection from abuse of life and limb to personal freedom. The judges of the Nizamut Adawlut could not bring themselves to approve the modification of existing law proposed by Richardson to effect an ultimate goal of 'judicial emancipation of Slaves, on proof of... cruel maltreatment'. After nearly 10 years of stalled debate, Chief Justice J.H. Harington bolstered Richardson's arguments by proposing a Regulation to improve upon Sec. 2 Beng. Reg. VIII 1799. Noting that Muslim law officers in the Company's criminal courts persisted in declaring that the master who murdered his slave was not liable to suffer death, Harington put forward the principle that anyone who committed a heinous offence against a slave would be liable to the same punishment he would incur, had he committed the offence against a free man. However, even Harington's Regulation faced tactics of delay and government inaction until Governor General Amherst laid it to rest in 1826 with his opinion that there was 'no statement of existing evils which render it incumbent on the Government to enter into the consideration of the state of slavery in India'.

Despite the apparent stalemate over legal principle, there existed the loophole of executive initiative. Even before the promulgation of his eponymous code, Governor General Cornwallis decreed by proclamation in 1789 that any person subject to the jurisdiction of the Supreme Court who purchased individuals in order to export them for sale as slaves in different parts of India would be subject to rigorous prosecution. This prohibition of slave trading was echoed in proclamations issued subsequently by the

Madras and Bombay Governments, the Malabar Commissioners, the Rani of Travancore and, most notably, by Charles Metcalfe as Resident in Delhi in 1812. Metcalfe even succeeded in surpassing Cornwallis' prohibition of the slave trade by calling for 'the emancipation of persons already in a State of Slavery'. Although Metcalfe's rhetoric was impressive, it was the action of his predecessor, Archibold Seton, which set the stage for potentially more meaningful legislation. Seton's byelaw prohibiting the sale of children under 12 years of age gave the Sabah of Almora confidence to appeal to the British Government to stop the traffic in children brought down from the hills for sale to subjects of the East India Company as slaves.

It is quite probable that the Sabah of Almora's petition prodded the Governor General's Council to enact Beng. Reg. X 1811 in order to prohibit 'the importation of slaves whether by land or by sea'. Ironically, the promulgation of the Felony Act at almost the same time overshadowed the Bengal legislation. And, although Beng. Reg. X 1811 was reenacted in Madras in 1812 and Bombay in 1813, would-be reformers in the ranks of East India Company servants perused the language of the Felony Act in vain for encouragement to extend the parliamentary 'abolition of the slave trade to domestic slaves and the property of Individuals in them'. Also, senior officials in Calcutta were quick to point out that Hindu and Muslim law still enjoyed the protection of 35 Geo. III c. 155 and therefore the Indian master had lost none of his authority over his slave. Nor could slaves in native states achieve freedom by fleeing to Company territory. Slavery remained the law of the land in the civil courts. The 1798 decision of the Sudder Dewanny Adawlut supporting the master's claim to property in his slave remained untouched by both the Felony Act and Beng. Reg. X 1811 along with its various offspring. The only progress towards the bestowal of rights upon the Indian slave came as a result of Beng. Reg. VIII 1799 making masters liable to criminal punishment for criminal acts against their slaves. Executive proclamations, while they raised expectations, did not have the same force as law.

As the highest ranking Company officials procrastinated over the slavery issue, the battle for slaves' rights fell into the hands of district officers. The most successful district officers operated in areas where agrestic or praedial slavery prevailed, far from the domestic master–servant relationship which prevailed in Bengal. In Malabar, on the west coast of the Madras presidency, T.H. Baber reported starvation and nose amputations as some of the cruelties suffered by the outcaste slave population. Thus he recommended to the Madras Foujdary Adawlut in 1818 that the practice of selling the slaves of revenue defaulters be disallowed. However, although the Madras Board of Revenue was to honour this recommendation, Baber knew nothing of their orders prohibiting the auction of slaves for revenue arrears until he read about them in *Parliamentary Papers* after he returned to England 10 years later. This was partly due to the poor communications of the time and perhaps partly deliberate, inasmuch as some of Baber's colleagues in the Tamil wet paddy districts on the east coast criticized his views as extreme. Nonetheless, Baber persevered in his campaign on behalf of the lowly Pullars to win for them in Madras Reg. VI 1829 the same right to prosecute and give evidence in the Company's courts as free men.

Meanwhile, in the sub-Himalayan district of Kumaon, field slaves were required to cultivate the terraced fields in which the resident Brahmins were forbidden by custom to work. G. William Traill, Commissioner of Kumaon in the 1820s, reported that Brahmins had purchased the outcaste Domes to till their fields 'from time immemorial' and that this practice had 'not been prohibited by the British Government'. However, in 1823, Traill had secured the approval of the Bengal Government to forbid by proclamation the local 'practice of selling Wives and Widows by Husbands and their Heirs'. When an 1835 court case concerning runaway Dome slaves in Gurhwal turned up evidence that prostitutes engaged in the purchase of female slaves, the Government of Agra directed the current Commissioner Morley Smith to investigate. Smith concluded that females were indeed purchased by prostitutes as part of a trade in field slaves which had never been prohibited by Government. This prompted the Government of Agra to order that no court in Kumaon should entertain suits 'either for the restoration of slaves or for the enforcement of Slavery'. A contemporary *munsif* alleged that this order successfully stopped the sale of slaves. However, probably more credible was the testimony of a *tehsildar* who asserted before the Law Commission that, despite the Government prohibition, slaves continued to be bought and sold because there were no hired labourers in the hills to till the fields of high-caste landowners.

The example of bold initiatives by Company servants in the remote districts of Malabar and Kumaon made little impression upon the Supreme Government. It was the combination of Sec. 88 of the 1833 East India Company Charter and continual parliamentary pressure which goaded the Home Authorities in London to call first for information and then for legislation In India. However, the content of the law was left to the discretion of the Indian Government. For a start, the Court of Directors had to overrule the objections of Governor General Auckland in order to call for a report from Macaulay's Law Commission. The Law Commission then followed the lead provided by the testimony of magistrates who were confident that the slave could find in the Company's criminal courts protection from his master's abuse. Indeed, the Law Commission's Draft Act of 1839 which was rejected by Auckland's Government aimed to establish the slave as an equal to the free man in the Company's criminal courts. It would seem that Auckland feared that Macaulay's vision of equality between slave and freeman in the Company's criminal courts would contravene the law of the land even though it operated only in the Company's civil courts to guarantee the master's property right in his slave. This would have been in accord with advice from Auckland's esteemed colleague, W.H. Macnaghten. Macnaghten opined that, although the 1798 Sudder Dewanny Adawlut decision protecting the master's property right in his slave deserved to be overruled, there should be no law granting the slave his freedom. Given his rejection of the Law Commission's 1839 Draft Act, it is ironic that Auckland supported the minority in the Law Commission's 1841 Report, who argued that, although the master's property right in his slave should remain untouched, the master's power of moderate correction over his slave should be removed lest it lead to abuse. It followed logically, then, that Auckland ultimately came to champion the provision that a 'penal offence done to a freeman shall be equally an offence if done to any person...in a condition of slavery'. The wording of this clause echoed the earlier Law Commission Draft Act and J.H. Harington's proposed regulation. From the time of J. Richardson, protection from abuse was available to the slave in the Company's criminal courts, but not until Auckland's hand was forced by the Home Authorities was this right enshrined in legislation.

The Indian Government's decision to drop the prohibition of the practice of selling children into slavery from Act V because it was already illegal according to Muslim law reflected the Company's respect for Hindu and Muslim law going back to the time of Warren Hastings. The argument that in time of famine, the practice proved to be the salvation of huge numbers of children was a compelling one. And, although since the time of William Jones individual magistrates had attempted to interfere with this custom, the Madras courts, in particular, decided to support the opinion of their own law officers that 'at a time when scarcity does not prevail, the people of this Country are forbidden to sell their children'. In the eyes of contemporary Judge Strange, the other provisions of the act—which forbid the practice of selling slaves in execution of decrees of court or for revenue arrears, decreed that no magistrate enforce rights of property in the person or services of another as a slave, and which guaranteed the slave any property he might have acquired by his own industry—amounted to 'nothing less than a law of positive emancipation...the result of instructions from the Court of Directors for the entire abolition of slavery'. A more realistic assessment, perhaps, would admit that the illiterate slave was unlikely to learn of his rights; however, his master learned from experience in the Company's criminal courts that abuse of his slave was a penal offence and ultimately, as a result of Act V of 1843 as well as Secs 370 and 371 of the Indian Penal Code, the act of buying and selling slaves was subject to the penalty of fines and imprisonment.

Indian emigrant labour has increasingly come to be viewed, metaphorically speaking, as the bastard child of Indian slavery sired by the Company's criminal courts, Act V 1843, and the Indian Penal Code, all of which loosened the grip of the Indian slaveholder on his slave. As the sufferings of Indian slaves were laid bare by Evangelicals in the English parliament, the sufferings of Indian emigrant labourers consumed the attention of every layer of government ranging from the district to the Supreme Government in India to the East India Company Home Authorities and the Colonial Office in London, as well as the colonial governments of Mauritius, British Guiana and Trinidad, in particular. Legislative initiatives in both England and India proved abortive in the face of overwhelming evidence of the emigrant labourers' victimization. The Colonial Office in London and the Supreme Government in Calcutta decided almost simultaneously to ban all emigration. The prohibition promulgated by India Act XIV of 1839 admitted to ignorance in both London and Calcutta of the plight of the emigrants. More to the point, the prohibition was intended to give both governments time to collect information and to formulate a plan for protecting the emigrants.

As the Calcutta Committee reported voluminously on the hardships and outright exploitation endured by emigrants to Mauritius, Governor General Auckland was characteristically unable to provide leadership. To be sure, members of his Council were divided along the same lines as they were over the issue of slavery. Also, the respected Supreme Court Judge J.P. Grant dissented from the Calcutta Committee Report to argue that the ban on emigration should be rescinded alongside the enactment of reforms designed to guarantee to Indian labourers their right to public justice defended by the courts and the office of a Colonial Protector. In response, all Auckland could come up with were some memorable remarks concerning the iniquitous legacy of slavery in Mauritius. Thus it was left for the Colonial Office to seize the initiative on the basis of evidence collected by its Commission in Mauritius. Discussions between Lord Stanley and the newly appointed Governor General Ellenborough laid the groundwork for the Privy Council to issue an Order in January 1842 with a Schedule of 22 Rules to form the core of any legislation enacted in British India to reinstate the emigration of Indian labourers to Mauritius. And so, Governor General Ellenborough, arriving in India shortly thereafter, was able to take a decisive role in the promulgation of India Act XV 1842 which repealed the prohibition of 1839 affecting Mauritius and enacted the Privy Council's Rules to protect the emigrants from fraudulent crimps, assure them basic comforts on their voyage and guarantee them, with the assistance of emigration agents at ports of embarkation and a Protector in Mauritius, the freedom to negotiate their own contracts after their arrival at Port Louis.

The policy of renewed emigration to Mauritius proved so successful that the Colonial Office encouraged the East India Company's Board of Control in London to lift the ban on Indian emigration to the West Indies. The Indian Government responded with Act XXI 1844 which permitted emigration to British Guiana, Trinidad and Jamaica from Calcutta, Madras and Bombay, in accordance with the rules laid down by the Privy Council. Indeed, these 22 Rules were to provide the basis of all future legislation on the subject. However, whereas Mauritius planters were able to fill their labour quotas and keep their coolies healthy and compliant with their contracts, resulting in a sugar crop in 1846 which exceeded the previous year's export by 23 million pounds, West Indian planters proved unable to look after their free labourers. When in 1846 the English parliament decided to admit slave-grown sugar, the West Indian planters complained bitterly of financial ruin. Even when the Government repealed the 1846 Sugar Duties Bill and offered the West Indian colonies guaranteed interest on loans of £500,000 to cover the cost of introducing free labour, the planters proved unable to manage their new labourers. Overwhelming reports of illness, vagrancy and death among the workers finally forced Colonial Secretary Earl Grey to suspend the emigration of coolies from India to the West Indies. In their efforts to persuade the Colonial Office to lift this suspension, the colonial governments of British Guiana and Trinidad passed a series of ordinances to demonstrate that their planters were competent to preside over a free labour force. Despite the disapproval of the East India Company's Authorities, Earl Grey reluctantly agreed to a compromise favouring three-year contracts over Trinidad's demand for five-year contracts. This was in line with recent ordinances enacted in British Guiana and Mauritius.

Earl Grey's compromise not only surrendered the idea that contracts should be limited to one year as stipulated by the Order of Council of 7 September 1838, but it also essentially marked a shift in outlook as Indian labourers were increasingly regarded as settlers rather than immigrants. The Government of India had been opening emigration to Ceylon, Grenada and St. Lucia. And, beginning with Act IV 1852, the Indian Government made concessions to Mauritius planters demanding access for emigrants to more ports in India and a reduction in the shipboard space required by

Act XV 1842. The most significant concession was the Indian Government's 1852 decision to allow Mauritius to withdraw from the immigrant labourers the right of a free return passage. That this was a difficult decision was evident in the Court of Directors' refusal to extend the same privilege to the planters of Trinidad. That it was, in fact, as J. Geoghegan charged, a violation of Sec. 1 Act XV 1842 was never considered. The East India Company was under constant pressure from the planters. Before long in British Guiana, the Company, in return for agreement that an individual labourer's return passage could never be 'absolutely commuted', granted an increase in indentures to a term of 10 years. Finally, Act XIX of 1856 empowering the Governor General to suspend emigration to a particular location for particular reasons would appear to be a tacit admission by the Indian Government that, in the words of the *Friend of India*, its efforts to protect the emigrant Indian labourer amounted to a 'race between abuses and legislation, in which legislation was always found to be in the rear'. Not only did the planters of Mauritius and the West Indies circumvent and emasculate existing legislation to suit their own convenience, but also the Indian Government's effort to define and condemn the practice of crimping for once and for all with Act XXIV 1852 failed due to insufficient penalties. Just as the 'slaves' of south Bihar had been reconstituted as bonded labour by Act V 1843, legislation which failed to protect the interests of emigrant labour, in reality, left them in a limbo of 'unfreedom' as observed by Clare Anderson.

By the time of the demise of the East India Company, the story of Indian migrant labour was, in reality, just beginning. Grim reports from returned labourers of disease, maltreatment, death and even religious persecution had to be measured over the years against the unremitting demand from India's most impoverished citizens for the right to find work by emigrating, sometimes for a second or third time. Destinations multiplied to include Jamaica, which only renewed its interest in immigrant labour in 1859; St. Vincent; Grenada; Tobago; French and Dutch colonies in the West Indies; the Indian Ocean and Southeast Asia; Natal in East Africa; the tea plantations of Assam and the Nilgiris within India; the Straits Settlements in Malaya; British Borneo and the Fiji Islands in the Pacific Ocean. From this diaspora, prominent authors, jurists and statesmen were to emerge on the world stage. V.S. Naipaul, the novelist from Trinidad, and the three Luckhoo brothers, all Queen's Counsel whose grandfather was a plantation labourer in British Guiana, are remarkable examples. Lessons learned from the East India Company's efforts to regulate the immigration process through legislation were ultimately consolidated in Act XIII 1864. With this law, the Government of India replaced all previous immigration legislation except for relevant provisions of the Penal Code. Act XIII detailed a system for processing emigrants through carefully regulated depots at ports of exit under the watchful eye of a Protector empowered to overrule Emigration Agents at the slightest hint of fraud or exploitation. In the *mofussil*, district magistrates received the same power to oversee recruitment procedures. The issue of guaranteed return passages was revisited by introducing into a reenacted Act XIX 1856 a stipulation that the provision of a return passage be considered a condition, the violation of which empowered the Governor General to suspend emigration. Also, the Governor General was authorized to make rules ensuring medical care at depots and on board ships; likewise, shipboard conditions were specified to ensure a more generous supply of water than had been required previously and to underline the most recently legislated decisions concerning adequate shipboard space per emigrant.[209] The ideals of protection and control set forth in East India Company legislation culminated in a Public Despatch in 1875 which served as a Magna Carta proclaiming the rights of Indians in British colonies.[210] However, relentless reports of starvation, misery and death among immigrant labourers suggest that the price for the success of such descendants as V.S. Naipaul and the Luckhoo brothers was too high. Sadly, when immigration faltered in the early twentieth century, emigrants returned to the same lack of opportunity which their ancestors had fled. In the words of one of the Company's most stringent critics, this was 'a strange end to a strange story'.[211]

---

[209] Act XIII to consolidate and amend the laws relating to the Emigration of Native Laborers (passed by Governor General of India in Council 18 March 1864) I.O.R., V/8/39; for analysis of this important legislation, see J. Geoghegan, *op. cit.*, pp. 39–46.

[210] Public Despatch (Emigration) No. 39, March 24 1875, I.O.R., L/P&J/3/1052; Hugh Tinker compares this Despatch with Queen Victoria's Proclamation of 1858; H.S. Tinker, *op. cit.*, p. 254.

[211] H.S. Tinker, *ibid.*, p. 366.

4

Civil Law and the Policy of Religious Toleration

...your Memorialists will not conceal that from the moment that the proposed Act [Caste Disabilities Removal Act XXI 1850] becomes a part of the Law applicable to Hindoos [,] that confidence which they have hitherto felt in the paternal character of their British rulers, will be most materially shaken—no outbreak of course is to be dreaded, but the active spirit of fervent loyalty to their Sovereign and of pride in their Rulers, will be changed into sullen submission to their Will and obedience to their power;...[1]

The records of the East India Company are abundant with references to the Company's guarantee to its subjects in India of the 'free exercise of their religion'. Company officials were so focussed on an attitude of religious neutrality towards their Hindu and Muslim subjects that they are accused by scholars of Christian missiology of virtually supporting a Hindu state at the expense of others such as Armenians, Anglo-Indians and, especially, Christian converts.[2] The Company's position was often embarrassed by the heated emotions which inevitably accompanied confrontations between religions. Official policy can be effectively traced by looking at laws governing the Company's relations with Indian religious institutions and at intermittent bold pronouncements of policy.

---

[1] Memorial of the Hindoo Inhabitants of Bengal, Behar and Orissa to the Governor General of India in Council against the proposed Act for Altering the Hindoo Law of Inheritance (Calcutta, 1850), India Legislative Proceedings, 11 April 1850, No. 80, I.O.R., P/207/59. Original signed by Raja Radhakant Bahadoor [Deb] and 3,000 Hindoos, the Inhabitants of Bengal, Behar and Orissa, in Parchment Records, I.O.R., A/1/100, fols 1–3.

[2] Penelope Carson, 'The Company and the Cross', *The Indo-British Review*, Vol. XXI, No. 2 (1995).

Temple Management

Christian missiologists most often complain that the East India Company was entangled in the affairs of Indian religious institutions. This was, in fact, true. However, beginning with legislation in 1810, the Company explained that it undertook responsibility for temple revenues in order to ensure that 'considerable endowments...granted in land by...preceding Governments... and by individuals...be applied according to the real intent and will of the grantor'. The Government's concern was that some individuals in charge of such endowments were known to have appropriated the proceeds to their personal use.[3] Even before 1810, Company officials found themselves collecting tax from pilgrims at the egregious temple of Lord Jagannath in Orissa in order to protect the pilgrims 'from undue exactions' and to preserve 'order, tranquillity and regularity in the town of Jugunnauthporee'.[4]

However, the Company's highly publicized involvement in the affairs of Jagannath Temple in the Bengal presidency was minuscule when compared with the overwhelming involvement of Company officials in the affairs of Indian temples in the Madras presidency. In 1814, J. Wallace, Collector of Tanjore, reported that 993 temples received financial aid from the Madras government in the amount of 37,102 Star Pagodas each. Three hundred and forty five of these temples also drew revenue from endowments. Wallace recommended the creation of an 'establishment' to assist temple officials in the 'control of the Church receipts and expenditures'. He specifically suggested that, in the case of the 'Principal Churches', revenue should be received into and disbursed from

---

[3] Bengal Regulation XIX for the due appropriation of the rents and produce of lands granted for the support of mosques, Hindoo temples, colleges and other purposes; for the maintenance and repair of bridges, serays, kuttras and other public buildings and for the custody and disposal of nuzzool property or escheats (passed 14 december 1810) [v/8/18 p. 411]. Madras Regulation VII for due appropriation of the rents and produce of lands granted for the support of mosques, Hindu temples and colleges or other public purposes; for the maintenance and repair of bridges, choultries or chattrams and other public buildings and for the custody and disposal of escheats (passed 30 September 1817), Government of India, Legislative Department—*The Madras Code: Consisting of the Unrepealed Madras Regulations, Local Acts of the Governor General in Council in Force in Madras, and Acts of the Governor of Fort St. George in Council with Chronological Tables and Appendix Containing Notifications, Rules and Orders, Issued under Scheduled Districts Act, 1874 and Act XXIV 1839 for Certain Scheduled Districts Together With an Index*, Vol. I, 3rd ed. (Calcutta, 1902), pp. 68–71.

[4] Bengal Regulation IV for levying a tax from pilgrims resorting to the temple of Jugunnauth, and for the superintendence and management of the temple (passed 3 April 1806), I.O.R., V/8/18, pp. 169–73.

the 'public Treasury'. The government supported establishment would see that 'expenses whether for Ceremonies or Servants wages of each Church' be limited to 'a certain sum proportioned to its Revenues'. Furthermore, Wallace recommended that the Collector select a certain number of prominent citizens in his district to 'form a Panchayet for seeing the ceremonies at the different Churches properly conducted...and for examining and controling [sic] the accounts...kept by the Church Servants'.[5] The Madras Board of Revenue approved Wallace's suggestions and immediately proposed that the Office of Superintendent be financed in the amount of 203 pagodas per year from 'Merah and Mauniam funds' or the revenue from temple lands.[6] And so, Company officers were drawn into, not only the management of temple finances, but also the supervision of temple ceremonies and festivals.

The extent of the Company's supervision of temple resources was revealed by the registers which Wallace reported as crucial to the regulation of alienated lands and of claims on *mauniam* funds by charities and individuals other than religious institutions. According to Wallace, '25% of the whole lands of the Province are wholly or partly alienated' from state revenue collection; 'the consequent alienation of the Public Revenue' was computed at 'St. Pa. 1,58,306 or $6^{1/8}$% of the whole land Jumma of the Province'. A registry of *Sunnud*s for these lands enabled the government to prosecute individuals who could not supply legal proof of their right to manage the lands. In the case of claims on *mauniam* funds, claims in support of *chattram*s or other charities were found 'in many cases' to be 'a source of private emolument' for persons originally assigned the responsibility of managing the revenues. Claims by individuals were of a 'most intricate and perplexing nature'. Of more than 2,000 claims submitted, 'few...are supported by regular Deeds'. The amount of the allowances claimed was characterized by 'the same irregularity'. To bring some order into this situation, a register was begun in the Collector's cutcherry in 1808. Wallace requested an assistant in order to complete this register, remarking that 'it is highly necessary that [such a task] not be entrusted to a Native Servant'. The completed register would enable the government to classify claims in support of an 'arrangement...for regulating the amount and duration of allowances from the Fund, and applying to more useful purposes such proportions of it, as there may not

---

[5] J. Wallace, Collector of Tanjore, Report on Devastanum Management in Tanjore, to Madras Board of Revenue, 15 February 1814, Madras Board of Revenue Proceedings, 24 February 1814, I.O.R., P/291/1, fols 2649-51, 2654-56.

[6] Madras Board of Revenue Proceedings, 5 December 1814, I.O.R., P/291/25, fols 14,141, 14,442-45.

appear sufficient ground for continuing to the persons who have hitherto received it'.[7]

Beyond its involvement with the management of the financial affairs of prominent Indian temples, the Company actually adjudicated caste disputes in its courts. At the Siringham Pagoda in Trichinopoly district, quarrels between Vadagala and Tengala Brahmins were the subject of court appeals over three decades. In 1836 the magistrate reported that the Sudder Court had overruled an 1832 decision of the provincial court in the southern division in order to reinstate a decree issued by the Trichinopoly district court in 1808 in favour of the Tengalas. Inadvertently underlining the futility of trying to settle caste disputes rooted in temple traditions, the magistrate observed that, ever since the Sudder Adawlut ordered that the 1808 decree against the Vadagalas be enforced,

> the Vadagalas have not attempted openly to interfere with the Tengalas in the Exclusive rights Confirmed to them in the Siringham pagoda, but they lose no opportunity of offering every petty annoyance in their power towards their successful rivals; and to shew their determined hostility, they several Months ago secretly struck off the Tengala Teroanum from one of the gates of the Pagoda and substituted their own distinguishing mark in its place.[8]

Twenty years after Wallace's report, the Collector of Trichinopoly, in his report on *Devastanum* management, objected to the standard of government support set by Wallace for two temples on Seringum Island.[9] At about the same time, R. Nelson, a minor revenue officer in Tanjore, protested against the duty which fell upon his shoulders as a sub-collector in Tanjore to conscript coolies to draw the cars of the idols at great religious festivals. He observed that the grandest annual festival in Tanjore required 30,000 labourers and over the course of a year at least 50,000 workers were conscripted. Such a huge number of people could only be gathered from countryside up to thirty miles or three days' journey from the pagoda. In the year of Mr Nelson's report, the principal festivals of Manargoody and Trivalore occurred simultaneously with a harvest season afflicted by heavy monsoon rains. The net result was that much of the grain in the district

---

[7] J. Wallace, *op. cit.*, fols 2658–60, 2662–67.

[8] H.M. Blair, Magistrate of Trichinopoly, to Board of Revenue, 30 November 1836, Madras Judicial Proceedings 10 January 1837, No. 16, I.O.R., P/325/31, fols 225–26.

[9] Mr Dickinson, Collector of Trichinopoly, Proceedings Regarding Devastanum Report, 14 February 1828, Madras Board of Revenue Proceedings 25 June 1829, I.O.R., P/297/12, fols 6279–94; also T.N.A., Trichinopoly District Records, Vol. 4382, fols 257–79.

'remained for days immersed in the water for want of persons to remove it'. Mr Nelson particularly deplored the fact that native Christians were among the field labourers 'continually called upon...to assist in the celebration of a Worship they rationally view with disgust'. He observed that in the case of 'the body of Meerasidars who sustain the loss and the laborers who suffer the hardship...the one pays largely to be exempted from the demand, while the other does not hesitate to make his escape if there is a chance of doing so unobserved'. This resulted in the custom of sending for 'many more coolies than are actually necessary to move the Cars, in order to meet the diminution occasioned by these desertions on the road'. Nelson noted the precedent set by one of his predecessors who, in 1801, forbid the pressing of native Christians into the service of Hindu gods and who insisted upon a minimal standard of humane treatment for conscripted coolies. After 1801 *mirasidar*s were required to supply at least two Madras measures of paddy for the labourers whom they sent to the *tehsildar* who had demanded the labour. Considering that the daily hire of such a labourer was usually four measures of paddy, this requirement was actually below reasonable standards. Against this background of human misery, Nelson confessed to his superior that on an earlier posting as sub-collector at Ramnad, he had refused to enforce orders for conscripting coolies to draw temple cars.[10]

N.W. Kindersley, Nelson's superior, who was also apparently ignorant of the Company's regulations forbidding the forcible impressment of coolie labour, was shocked by Nelson's audacity in raising the subject. To his superiors on the Madras Board of Revenue, Kindersley recommended that Nelson's letter should be expunged from the public records; to Nelson, he sermonized:

> Slavery and the degradation of the lower Castes are undoubtedly contrary to the abstract principles of justice, yet both are tolerated by our Government in deference to the customs of the Country...But altho' every Christian and Man of sense must allow that in the sight of God the Pariar is equal to the Brahmin, what magistrate would hesitate to punish a Pariar who should venture into a Pagoda, even for the laudable purpose of saying his prayers.[11]

---

[10] R. Nelson, Sub-Collector of Tanjore, to N.W. Kindersley, Principal Collector at Tanjore, 10 October 1828, Negapatam, I.O.R., *Board's Collections*, F/4/1263,#50837A, fols 19–62; also in T.N.A., Tanjore District Records, Volume 4205, fols 183–99.

[11] N.W. Kindersley, Principal Collector at Tanjore, to R. Nelson, Sub-Collector at Tanjore, 11 November 1828, Vullum, I.O.R., *Board's Collections*, I.O.R., *Board's Collections*, F/4/1263, #50837A, fols 96–97.

The Madras Board of Revenue wholeheartedly supported Kindersley's confusion of Nelson's efforts to withdraw official support for the practice of pressing coolies to pull temple cars with the Company's policy of religious neutrality. At first, the Board was prepared to accept Kindersley's recommendation of removing Nelson's correspondence from the public record, but they reconsidered 'the dangerous tendency of the principles advocated by Mr Nelson' and thereby deemed it 'their duty to record their deepest disapprobation, not only of Mr Nelson's sentiments but of his conduct also'. The Board particularly condemned Nelson's initiative in Ramnad where he 'issued a Proclamation which virtually altered the mode of celebrating the festival at Rameswaran, a place of peculiar estimation and sanctity to all classes of Hindoos'.[12]

Interestingly, back in London, the Board of Control took issue with the censorious tones of Kindersley and the Madras Board of Revenue. While supporting the Revenue Board's 'bounden duty' to discipline subordinates who, without the permission of their superiors, authorized 'changes of practice or system', the Board of Control deemed it 'quite inadmissible' for the Revenue Board to caution Mr Nelson against 'a recurrence of…useless and uncalled for discussion'. The case attracted the attention of John Stuart Mill who insisted that the practice of pressed labour was a socioeconomic issue quite separate from religious concerns. He further argued that such a custom could not be 'considered as equivalent to law'. The Board endorsed Mill's distinction between 'immemorial custom' and 'law' but excised from the Directors' draft of a despatch to Madras Mill's insistence that the 'question [of pressed labour] is not a religious one'. The Board asked the Directors to forbid the practice of pressed labour in support of temple festivals amidst plentiful protestations of religious neutrality. The Directors compromised with a 'strong recommendation rather than…positive command' for the abolition of pressed labour.[13]

By 1840, sensitivity over the issue of religious neutrality had reached a peak. Evangelical interests in England had successfully pressured Parliament

---

[12] D. Eliott, Secretary to Board of Revenue, to N.W. Kindersley, Principal Collector at Tanjore, 11 December 1828, Fort St. George, I.O.R., *Board's Collections*, F/4/1263, #50837A, fols 126–27.

[13] Previous Communication 979, 30 November 1831, to Political Despatch to Madras, 1 February 1832, No. 2, I.O.R., L/P&S/6/281–89; Political Despatch to Madras, 1 February 1832, No. 2, I.O.R., E/4/941, fols 259–60. Cf. N.G. Cassels, 'Mill, Religion and Law in the Examiner's Office', in Martin I. Moir, Douglas M. Peers and Lynn Zastoupil, eds., *J.S. Mill's Encounter with India* (Toronto, 1999), p. 177.

to demand that the Company abolish its taxes on pilgrims and withdraw from its involvement with Jagannath Temple, in particular. In a legislative despatch dated 25 August 1841, the Directors demanded that Company officers withdraw 'from all interference in the management of Native religious Institutions'.[14] Within four years a report produced in the Madras presidency, where religious issues were most intense, outlined 'arrangements… for transferring to Native Administrators the charge of the religious institutions heretofore managed by European Officers of the Government'. D. Eliott, the author of this report, was the same Madras Board of Revenue clerk who had severely reprimanded Mr Nelson nearly 20 years earlier. In the midst of his account of assigning the responsibility for certain temples to individual *raja*s, *zamindar*s or temple *dhurmakurta* (officer), Eliott was able to report most remarkably on a successful transition at Tirupathi [Tripetty] Temple, the temple in the Madras Presidency usually equated in significance with Bengal presidency's Jagannath Temple. Administration of Tirupathi Temple was made over to a single much respected *Mohunt* or priest.[15] The Company's withdrawal from Tirupathi was perhaps less complicated than was the case at Jagannath Temple because revenue collection and administrative arrangements at the temple were never made subject to Company regulations. This, despite the Madras Board of Revenue's initial desire that 'all the arrangements relative to Tripetty Pagoda should be framed into a Regulation as has been done in Bengal with respect to the Juggernaut Pagoda'.[16]

Whereas the Company scrambled to end its involvement with such prominent Indian temples as Tirupathi and Jagannath, it was unable to make a clean break from all its obligations. In the case of Jagannath Temple, Act X 1840, although it abolished the Pilgrim Tax and transferred superintendence of the Temple to the Raja of Khoorda, it left unresolved the question of remaining British financial obligations to the temple. These obligations, variously interpreted as an 'historic pledge' of 'established donation' were the subject of messy debate throughout the remainder of

---

[14] Cited in G.A. Bushby, Secretary to Government of India, to J.F. Thomas, Chief Secretary to Government of Fort St. George, 20 September 1845, India Legislative Proceedings, 20 September 1845, No. 161, I.O.R., P/207/38.

[15] Report by D. Eliott upon Arrangements made in the Presidency of Madras for transferring to Native Administrators the charge of the religious institutions heretofore managed by Officers of the Government and upon the questions referred by the Government of Madras for the determination of the Governor General in Council, 1 March 1845, India Legislative Proceedings, 20 September 1845, No. 156, I.O.R., P/207/38.

[16] Madras Board of Revenue, to Collector of North Arcot, Fort St. George, T.N.A., North Arcot District Records, Bundle 18 (5).

the Company's existence.[17] Meanwhile, in the Madras presidency, as late as 1848, 'repeated complaints...were preferred by parties interested in (Native Religious) Institutions throughout the Country regarding the frauds practised by those entrusted with their management'. To provide for such plaints, the Madras Government had inserted in its Regulation VII of 1817 a Sec. XVI equating temple servants and trustees or managers with government servants in the revenue department in terms of their liability for 'punishment of fraud or embezzlement in Native servants...'. There was no such provision in the otherwise identical Bengal Regulation XIX of 1810.[18] The special circumstances in Madras continued to require the enforcement of Madras Regulation VII 1817. In answer to the complaints of 1848, the Madras Board of Revenue instructed its officers that, since Regulation VII 1817 had never been rescinded and its modification was still under consideration by the Government of India, the 'more pressing cases of complaint' were to be decided according to Sec. XVI Reg. VII 1817, but all officials were to 'be careful to refrain from interference unless where it is urgently and obviously demanded'. In fact, this special caution against unnecessary interference was in accord with directions from the Governor of Madras who assumed that Reg. VII 'will shortly be rescinded'.[19] Both Bengal Regulation XIX 1810 and Madras Regulation VII 1817 had been under consideration by the legislative council of the Government of India since 1845. But, they both lingered on in the law books until finally repealed by Act XX of 1863.[20]

As the government responded to pressure from Evangelical forces to dismantle its structural connection with Indian religious institutions, it

---

[17] Prabhat Mukherjee, *Pilgrim Tax and Temple Scandals—A Critical Study of the Important Jagannath Temple Records during British Rule*, ed. Nancy Gardner Cassels (Bangkok, 2000), pp. 130–45.

[18] Sec. XVI, Madras Regulation VII 1817, *op. cit.*, p. 71, and Bengal Regulation XIX 1810, *op. cit.*

[19] T. Pycroft, Secretary to Board of Revenue, to J.F. Thomas, Chief Secretary to Government, Revenue Board Office, Fort St. George, 19 June 1848, T.N.A., Tanjore District Records, Vol. 3440, fols 41, 43–45; Circular to all Collectors, 14 August 1848 and H.C. Montgomery, Chief Secretary to Government, to President and Members of the Board of Revenue, 17 July 1848, Madras Board of Revenue Proceedings, 14 August 1848, No. 762, I.O.R., P/308/2, fols 11564–66.

[20] G.A. Bushby, Secretary to Government of India, to F.J. Halliday, Secretary to Government of Bengal, 20 September 1845, India Legislative Proceedings, 20 September 1845, No. 160; G.A. Bushby, Secretary to Government of India, to J.F. Thomas, Chief Secretary to Government of Fort St. George, 20 September 1845, India Legislative Proceedings, 20 September 1845, No. 161, I.O.R. P/207/38; Act XX to enable the Government to divest itself of the management of religious endowments (passed 10 March 1863), I.O.R., V/8/39.

found itself under equal pressure from its Indian subjects to dissociate itself from Christian missionaries. The Company was besieged with complaints and counter complaints such as those reported in 1842 concerning 'Hindoo Ryots...Missionaries and Native Christians in Tinnevelly'. The Directors in London demurred for the moment with their conclusion: 'It appears that great animosity prevails betwixt the Hindoos and Native Christians, but that there is no just ground for the imputation thrown out by each of them that the other has enjoyed unfair advantage from the officers of Government'.[21]

Increasingly, senior Company officials were aware that wherever religious sensitivities were concerned, they were walking on a hot bed of coals. Ironically in Malabar, upon the communication of Act V 1843 to slaves and masters, the magistrate, H.V. Conolly, unleashed near hysteria among his superiors with his reference to the potential usefulness of native Christians. In response to government requests for suggestions for improving the situation of the slave caste of chermars in Malabar, Conolly observed that inasmuch as Act V 1843 was 'to all intents and purposes a Law for the abolition of slavery throughout the Company's territory', the government might concern itself with employment of the emancipated chermars on public works at the same rate as free labourers and with schools for their children. He concluded that the 'person best fitted to help with chermar schools [was a] Native Christian or Mopla or Muslim i.e. a person free from caste prejudice'. Conolly's essentially very practical suggestion attracted the attention of Madras Governor Lord Tweeddale. Tweeddale listed it alongside such activities as a collection in a prominent church for missionary purposes and the 'attendance of the Collector of Tinnevelly at the opening of a Mission Church in his District' as circumstances which might excite the religious passion of the Company's Indian subjects. The Directors agreed with Lord Tweeddale, warning that in instances of ostensibly private support for Christian missions, 'the personal conduct of an officer cannot be divested of official influence' especially in the districts of the *mofussil* where the 'inhabitants...look up to particular officers as the personification of public authority'. More specifically, with reference to Mr Conolly's suggestion, the Directors commended Conolly's reputation for good sense. However, they warned that 'nothing could have a more unfortunate tendency than that the injury which the higher classes may conceive that they have sustained from the abolition of slavery should be connected in their minds with the education of the emancipated slaves,

---

[21] Judicial Despatch, to Fort St. George, 2 November 1842, No. 16, I.O.R., E/4/958, fol. 857.

especially if that education should in any respect partake of a religious character'.[22]

During the decade of the 1840s, the presidency of Madras became something of a tinderbox of raw religious emotions. In 1845 an assault by non-Christians on Christian villages in Tinnevelly district resulted in the arrest of 100 Hindus, many of whom were convicted by a sessions judge. This conviction was immediately appealed to the Foujdary Adawlut which reversed the judgement and ordered prisoners to be released. At this point, Governor Tweeddale interceded to order a new trial. The new court reinstated the convictions of the sessions judge, albeit with milder punishments. What emerged out of this confusion was a series of alarms at senior levels of government over intemperate language recorded in the judicial proceedings. The Madras government drew particular attention to the *zillah* Judge's reference to 'Christian and Heathen'. The Home Authorities sought to improve on the Madras government's censure by proposing to remove the offending judge from his office, but the proposal was 'negatived' by a vote of 14 Directors to 7. However, the Directors did endorse Governor Tweeddale's cancellation of the appointment of another judge to the Madras Council on the grounds of his partiality toward Hindus and discrimination against Christian missionaries.[23] More to the point, the Directors expanded upon their views of inappropriate language:

> In particular our attention has been attracted to a circumstance entirely new to us: we mean the use of the term "Heathen", to signify the people of India. As applied to Hindoos, or to Hindoos and Mahomedans conjointly, it cannot but be felt as an opprobrious epithet. We consider it to be repugnant to

---

[22] H.V. Conolly, Collector and Magistrate, Malabar, to J.F. Thomas, Secretary to the Government of Fort St. George in the Judicial Department, Calicut, 23 September 1843, Judicial Diary, 23 April 1844, No. 7, T.N.A., Judicial Consultations, Vol. 470A, fols 1253–55; Minute by Lord Tweeddale, 4 October 1844, Madras Judicial Proceedings, 22 October 1844, No. 18, I.O.R., P/326/41, fols 4079–4100; Judicial Despatch, to Madras, 21 May1845, No. 11, I.O.R., E/4/963, fols 1050–52, 1056–57 and 1059.

[23] R.E. Frykenberg attributes heroic status to the judge in question, namely Malcolm Lewin. His argument rests partly on the grounds that in October 1846 approximately 12,000 Hindus signed a memorial endorsing Lewin as a defender of 'the Civil and Religious rights' of Hindus against their violation by missionaries. Lewin remained a thorn in the side of the Company for the rest of his career. R.E. Frykenberg, 'The Impact of Conversion and Social Reform upon Society in South India during the Late Company Period; Questions Concerning Hindu–Christian Encounters, With Special Reference to Tinnevelly', in C.H. Philips and M.D. Wainwright, eds., *Indian Society and the Beginnings of Modernization* (London, 1976), pp. 208–10.

that regard for the feelings of the people, which forms an essential part of genuine toleration.[24]

Within another six months, the authorities in London ordered the Government of India to 'intimate to the Lt. Governor of the North Western Provinces that we entirely disapprove...of the use of the term "Pagan" as applied to any class of our subjects'.[25]

In the meantime, the Directors decided that 'circumstances of recent occurrence' in India warranted a restatement of the Company's principle of religious toleration. An examination of the correspondence between the Board of Control and the Court of Directors over the resulting despatch to the Indian Government of 21 April 1847 reveals that those 'circumstances' involved the participation of Government officers in the proceedings of missionary societies. At the exhortation of the Board of Control, the Directors excised a reference to government officers active in missionary societies in order to emphasize the 'most important principle...of abstaining from all interference with the Religion of the Natives of India'.[26] Without the advantage of access to these records, the Company's official historian, John William Kaye, observed that the despatch was 'so vague and meaningless that there is reason to suspect that all pith and purpose were cut out of it, in its passage through Committee, Court and Canon Row, in a hopeless endeavour to reconcile a diversity of conflicting opinions'.[27] However, a minute by Governor General Hardinge and a subsequent despatch from London reveal that the Home Authorities were very deliberate in their emphasis upon general principle as opposed to detailed practical instructions. Hardinge simply remarked upon the larger scope of the April '47 despatch compared with orders dated 21 May 1845 sent to the Madras government. These orders distinguished between the vulnerability of district officers perceived by the local population as symbols of government authority and the relative independence of higher ranking individuals in sophisticated presidency towns. By 1847 the Company's directive had become a 'comprehensive prohibition' enjoining all Company servants 'to take no part whatever in Missionary proceedings'. However, in keeping with the cautious sentiments of Marquis

---

[24] Judicial Despatch, to Fort St. George, 20 January 1847, No. 1, I.O.R., E/4/967, fols 113–14, 146–47.

[25] Revenue Despatch, to India, 16 June 1847, No. 7, I.O.R., E/4/972, fol. 744.

[26] Judicial Despatch, to India, 21 April 1847, No. 3, I.O.R., E/4/791, fols 1222–25; cf. Board to Court, 15 April 1847, I.O.R., E/2/43.

[27] J.W. Kaye, *History of Christianity in India* (London, 1859), pp. 449–50.

Tweeddale which inspired the Directors' 1845 Madras Despatch in the first place, Governor General Hardinge won the support of his Council in deciding to refrain from publishing 'any general order prohibiting the interference of public Officers in religious matters'. Enforcement of the general principle of religious toleration was left in the hands of senior officers in the presidencies who might 'at any time refer to the Supreme Government for advice'. The Home Authorities were not in the least disappointed by this muted reaction, inasmuch as they agreed with the Indian government that publication of the April 1847 despatch 'might give rise to discussion on a subject on which it is particularly desirable that the public mind should not be excited'.[28] A later despatch in the Ecclesiastical Department to Madras underlined the primary concern of Company officialdom to distance itself from any connection or association with missionary efforts. Having sanctioned various measures ranging from the erection of churches at military stations to compensation to the Society for the Propagation of the Gospel for finding 'a site for another Church' after selling their Vepery Church to Government, the Home Authorities concluded: 'The measures sanctioned in this Despatch will finally disconnect your Government from all Missionary Churches'.[29]

Religious Disabilities Removal Act—1850

J.W. Kaye observed that 'whilst the Government were thus impressing upon their servants the duty of an absolute religious neutrality, they were themselves sanctioning measures which were by no means regarded in that light by the people'.[30]

Among the controversial measures listed by Kaye was Act XXI 1850, variously known as the Liberty of Conscience Bill, the Religious Disabilities Removal Act, the Inheritance Act, the Emancipation Act or the Freedom of Religion Act. Technically, all that Act XXI 1850 did was to extend to all the Company's Indian subjects the protection against loss of property already

---

[28] Minute by Governor General Hardinge, Simla, 13 July 1847, India Judicial Proceedings, 11 September 1847, No. 4, I.O.R., P/206/28; Home Department Judicial Despatch to Directors, 7 September 1847, No. 12, I.O.R., E/4/202 and Judicial Despatch, to India, 19 January 1848, No. 2, I.O.R., E/4/795, fol. 167.

[29] Ecclesiastical Despatch, to Fort St. George, 19 July 1848, No. 5, I.O.R., E/4/970, fols 637–42.

[30] J.W. Kaye, *op. cit.*, p. 455.

guaranteed by Sec. 9 Regulation VII 1832 of the Bengal Code to religious groups other than Hindus and Muslims. Sec. 9 Bengal Regulation VII 1832 had simply decreed:

> Whenever in any civil suit the parties to such suit may be of different persuasions...or when one or more of the parties to the suit shall not be either of the Mahommedan or Hindoo persuasions; the laws of those religions shall not be permitted to operate to deprive such party or parties of any property to which, but for the operation of such laws, they would have been entitled.[31]

At first, this simple statement of civil rights attracted little notice as an innocuous section of a regulation which proclaimed itself to be merely modifying an earlier regulation for extending the powers of Munsiffs and Sudder Ameens in the trial of civil suits. During discussions leading to the enactment of Act XXI 1850, Hindu memorialists were to exclaim in disbelief that they had been 'unable to discover one single instance in the course of the 17 years during which it [Sec. 9 Beng. Reg. VII 1832] is supposed to have been the law of the Land in which it has been acted upon by any Superior Court'. And so they regarded the evolution of Sec. 9 Beng. Reg. VII 1832 into Act XXI 1850 as a 'secret...attack...upon what they considered the Law under which they lived'.[32]

To explain how a law which the English East India Company conceived as a guarantee of civil liberties could become a 'secret attack' upon Hindu laws in the minds of its Hindu subjects, it is necessary to recall the effort by the Home Authorities to establish a *lex loci* in India. In the 1833 Charter the English parliament called for the establishment of a uniform judicial system which could be applied to all classes of the inhabitants of India 'due regard being had to the rights, feelings and peculiar usages of the people'.[33] The Law Commission was subsequently appointed and assigned the task of drafting such a substantive law or *lex loci*.

One of these Commissioners, C.H. Cameron, traced the precedents for the draft of a *lex loci* which, although prepared in 1841, was not brought forward for public discussion until 1845. The concept of 'Lex Loci' harked

---

[31] Sec. 9, Bengal Regulation VII for modifying certain of the Provisions of Regulation V 1831 and for providing Supplementary Rules to that Enactment (passed 16 October 1832) I.O.R., V/8/21.

[32] The Memorial of the Hindoo Inhabitants of Bengal, Bihar and Orissa to the Governor General of India in Council against the proposed Act for Altering the Hindoo Law of Inheritance, India Legislative Proceedings, 11 April 1850, No. 80, I.O.R., P/207/59.

[33] Charter Act 3&4, Wm IV, c. 85, sec. 53; p. 50.

back to the 'great philosophic Jurists of Rome' who 'devised a body of principles and distinctions for applying Equity and good Conscience to the complicated affairs of men'. The principles were subsequently elaborated by English lawyers in successive court cases and by statutes enacted by the English parliament. In response to objections raised by the north-western Sudder Court, he noted that the Law Commissioners' reasoning was entirely consistent with the decree in Sec. 17 Bengal Regulation II 1803 that 'In cases...for which no specific rule shall exist, the Judge shall act according to justice, equity and good conscience'.[34] In line with this reasoning, judges might decree it 'consistent with justice and good conscience to give to the suitor the Law of his own country, when not bound to give him Regulation Law'.

On the subject of Regulation Law, Cameron was very insistent that the *lex loci* 'so far from abolishing "Regulation Law"...does not repeal a single Regulation nor a single Provision of a Regulation. The Regulations are the Code of Procedure for the Mofussil Courts'. Speculating on who would be subject to the *lex loci* in India, Cameron emphasized the need for a positive description of excepted classes. According to his own definition, the excepted classes would include

(1) Hindoos and Mahomedans;
(2) all persons possessing any other than the Christian Religion in respect of marriage, divorce and adoption; and
(3) all Races and Peoples not known to have been seated in any other country than British India in respect of any Law or usage immemorially observed by them and now enforced by the Courts.

Cameron hastened to explain that this last category would apply to Buddhists, Jains, aboriginal tribes, the Mugs of Arakan and the Sikhs of the N.W.P. With respect to the Government's obligations to its Hindu and Mahomedan subjects, Cameron rather dangerously mused: 'Perhaps the Hindoos and Mahomedans ought only to be excepted in respect of so much of their Law as is now administered to them under the Statutes and the Regulations, and brought under the *lex loci* for the rest'. Such a statement in itself was enough to alarm the Indian population with the thought that their own laws could eventually be replaced with English Law. On

---

[34] Bengal Regulation II for establishing and defining the Jurisdiction of the Courts of Adawlut, or Courts of Judicature, for the Trial of Civil Suits in the first Instance, in the Provinces ceded by the Nawab Vizier to the Honourable the English East India Company (passed by Governor General in Council, 24 March 1803), I.O.R., V/8/17, p. 317.

the other hand, Sir Henry Maddock, the one member of Government who objected to the draft Lex Loci Act as it was brought forward in 1845, considered that it was impossible to implement the Home Authorities' vision of a uniform judicial system so long as the Hindu and Mahomedan population enjoyed the distinction of 'excepted classes'.[35] The cause of *lex loci* was destined to die a slow death for lack of interest and support among both English rulers and Indian subjects.

In the wake of his predecessors' failure to consider the Law Commission's report on *lex loci* and the 1841 Draft Act, Governor General Hardinge decided it was time to force the issue. Hardinge's only concern with the proposed digest of English law principles serving as *lex loci* as explained by C.H. Cameron was that it might bring with it 'technicalities and special pleading' which would be an intolerable burden in the *mofussil* courts. He deferred to his chief justice, Sir Lawrence Peel, who opined that there was no need to fear the introduction of 'difficulties' or 'technicalities'. Peel was confident that 'the digest...could be readily enacted and would not displace Regulation Law but would displace personal laws of all people except Hindoos and Mahomedans which as at present would remain inviolate'.

While the Council minutes and debates on the broad subject of *lex loci* were returned to the Home Authorities for their deliberation, Hardinge's Government extracted sections x, xi and xii from the draft Lex Loci Act[36] to constitute a separate enactment, dubbed the Liberty of Conscience Bill. This Bill was to extend Sec. 9 Bengal Regulation VII 1832 to all of India. Lord Hardinge traced the origins of Sec. 9 Beng. Reg. VII 1832 back to testimony by Sir Hyde East before the English parliament in 1830. Sir Hyde East had declared that 'no Native of India shall forfeit any rights of property or personal benefit on account of his profession of any particular faith or doctrine'. The Directors had taken up the subject in a despatch dated 2 February 1831 which, while asserting the Home Authorities' aversion to any connection between the 'powers of Government' and 'the conversion of the Natives', nonetheless declared that 'it would certainly be more consonant to the principle...of perfect religious equality, that no disabilities

---

[35] Minute by C.H. Cameron, 1 August 1845, India Legislative Proceedings, 2 August 1845, No. 35, I.O.R., P/207/36. Also in *Parliamentary Papers* (1847) XLIII, Cmd. 14, pp. 697–709.

[36] The Law Commission had initially inserted these clauses into their draft Lex Loci Act in order to 'afford a remedy for the grievances complained of in a missionary memorial presented to Government in May 1841 'as far at least as such an object can be properly connected with the other purposes of this Act'. Indian Law Commissioners, to Governor General, 22 May 1841, India Legislative Proceedings, 8 July 1842, No. 17, I.O.R., P/207/22.

should exist by Regulation on account of religious belief'.[37] The Directors had enquired of Lord Bentinck's government about the extent to which Christian converts were subject to loss of property and other civil rights. And, Governor General Bentinck's Council had replied with the promulgation of Sec. 9 Beng. Reg. VII 1832. Obscurely tucked away in a regulation concerned with the powers of Munsiffs and Sudder Ameens, Sec. 9 of Bengal Regulation VII 1832 had made absolutely no impact upon the Indian population. Thus the Draft Act was published in the *Government Gazette* on 29 January 1845 and in Indian newspapers.

Hardinge was also conscious of the contrast between his willingness to act and his predecessors' general lassitude concerning *lex loci*. He described Lord Auckland as a 'timid politician' and noted Lord Ellenborough's aversion to any thoughts of religious conversion of the 'black race'. For Hardinge, the Liberty of Conscience Bill was an adjunct to education in India. In a letter to his stepson, he enthused: 'The educated classes are already deistic, and this act will do more eventually for Christianity than all the missionary societies'.[38] Hardinge was in fact a devout Christian who, while he despised any form of forcible conversion, placed great faith in English education as the true instrument of conversion. In Hardinge's mind, the Liberty of Conscience Bill was a very necessary complement to the East India Company's educational institutions. As he summed up his own outlook:

> [I]t was the duty of the Government to give effect to a measure…which could rescue the Government of India from the inconsistency and cruelty of fostering and patronizing the Hindoo College and other public institutions for Native Education, whilst we refused to give protection to the pupils who [,] preferring truth to superstition [,] were liable to forfeit their property because they had changed their religion.

In a final flourish, he recalled a well-known quote from *The Reformer*: 'What is the consequence!…Have all the efforts of the Missionaries given a tithe of that shock to the superstitions of the people which has been given by the Hindoo College?'[39]

While Governor General Hardinge took great pains to distance himself from Christian missionaries in the advocacy of his Liberty of Conscience

---

[37] Public Despatch, to Bengal, 2 Februrary 1831, No. 8, I.O.R., E/4/731, fols 12–14, 26.

[38] *The Letters of the First Viscount Hardinge of Lahore to Lady Hardinge and Sir Walter and Lady James 1844–1847*, ed. Bawa Satinder Singh, Camden Fourth Series, Vol. 32 (London, Royal Historical Society, 1986), p. 84.

[39] Minute by Governor General Hardinge, 18 July 1845, India Legislative Proceedings, 2 August 1845, No. 32, I.O.R., P/207/36.

Bill, ultimately the pressure upon the Government to promulgate Act XXI 1850, which guaranteed all apostates from either the Hindu or Muslim religion their civil liberties, came from Christian missionaries and Christian converts. The Government of India justified their legislative action in 1850 by reporting the memorials which they received after sending all the papers concerning the draft Lex Loci Act back to the Home Authorities in 1845. There were petitions signed by Christian missionaries in Calcutta, by the Presbytery of Katywar representing the Presbyterian Church of Ireland, by missionaries of the Free Church of Scotland in Nagpore and by Christian ministers in Bombay—all querying the 'existing state of the law as it affects Native Christians in respect to Marriage, Divorce and Inheritance'.[40]

The petition which really forced the issue came in 1849 from the Bishop of Bombay. The Bishop recollected that weeks before the Hardinge Government published the draft Lex Loci Act in the *Government Gazette* on 29 January 1845, he had submitted to Governor General Hardinge a letter stating 'the painful circumstances in which Native converts to Christianity were placed from having no protection in their Civil Rights and immunities under the existing state of the Laws'. The letter had cited 'several cases...in which Converts had been deprived not only of property but some of Wives and Children in their conversion'. And finally, the letter had noted the converts' lack of success in their 'proceedings in the Native Courts for the recovery of their Rights' and their realization 'that the Law in this Presidency in its present state could protect them only from personal violence'. The Bishop then remarked upon the apparent success of Secs 8 and 9 of Beng. Reg. VII 1832 as protection for the 'Civil Rights' of Bengal Christian converts. He requested that the Legislative Council extend that regulation to the Bombay Presidency.

A reply from Calcutta in the Judicial Department declared that the Legislative Council was considering an Act which would 'meet all the objects' of the Bishop's letter and was 'intended to be general to all India'. This draft Lex Loci Act was referred to the Bombay Government for its consideration and was published in the *Bombay Government Gazette* at the end of February 1845. The Bishop noted that Secs x, xi and xii of this Draft Act operated on the *lex loci* principle that there ought to be a law for 'persons...who cannot be brought within any of the defined classes' of the population subject to the

---

[40] Legislative Despatch from India, 6 December 1850, No. 19, I.O.R., E/4/217; Letter from India, 6 November 1847, No. 32, I.O.R., E/4/203; Legislative Despatch from India, 22 January 1848, No. 5, I.O.R., E/4/204; Legislative Despatch from India, 10 October 1848, No. 28, I.O.R., E/4/207.

country's laws, and so provided protection for Christian converts. Sec. xii, in particular, recalled Sec. 9, Beng. Reg. VII 1832 with its decree that

> so much of the Hindoo and Mahomedan law as inflicts forfeiture of rights or property upon any party renouncing or who has been excluded from the communion of either of these Religions shall cease to be enforced as Law in the Courts of the East India Company.

In conclusion, the Bishop lamented that four years had passed since the publication of the draft Lex Loci Act without any legislative protection being 'extended to the Native Converts in Western India'. He chided the Government over the fact that these native converts were 'amongst the most faithful and attached to the Government' and yet 'are the only persons to whom the British Law does not extend its protection although exposed in their defenceless state to severe persecution directed under cover of the existing Laws'.[41]

As part of his argument concerning the effectiveness of Secs 8 and 9 Beng. Reg. VII 1832, the Bishop remarked that in the 17 years of its existence no appeals had reached the Sudder Dewanny Adawlut. On this point the Bishop was correct. Indeed, as noted above, memorialists opposed to XXI 1850 used the same argument. At the time of the debate over inheritance as a civil right guaranteed to Christian converts, only two cases were recorded as having been decided according to Secs 8 and 9 Beng. Reg. VII 1832. They were both reported in the law reports for Azimgurh *zillah* in the N.W.P. Both these cases involved a Muslim appellant's claim of preemption against new Hindu neighbours in a contiguous village. In both cases the judge ruled that the appellant was within his rights to make the claim, but that the claim itself was totally unreasonable. In the words of the judge:

> I look upon the practice of claiming the right of preemption in contiguous villages as vicious: nor do I see anything in this particular case, which, according to justice, equity or good conscience, should induce me to decree in favour of the defendant. The appeal is dismissed with costs.[42]

---

[41] Thomas Bishop of Bombay to Right Hon. Viscount Falkland, Governor in Council of Bombay, 28 March 1849, India Legislative Proceedings, 11 April 1850, No. 58, I.O.R., P/207/59.

[42] Case No. 67, Mukbool Allum, Appellant vs. Ajoodhee Singh and Bisshehur Juttee, Respondents, 29 February 1848; Case No. 68, Shah Mukbool Allum, Appellant vs. Sheonarain Singh and Hurchurn Juttee, Respondents, 29 February 1848, Law Reports from Zillah Azimgurh, I.O.R., V/22/675, pp. 102–4.

However, as far as the Sudder Dewanny Adawlut in Calcutta was concerned, the lack of previous rulings at the Sudder Court level did not mean that the case for Act XXI 1850 was cut and dry. On the one hand, the Justices reflected upon Hindu claims that 'inheritance is a right accruing only in consequence of benefit conferred by the heir through the means of ...ceremonies on the soul deceased'. Considering this argument, the Justices observed that 'a provision against forfeiture of rights could have no effect where the rights themselves could not be created'. On the other hand, they contended that inheritance was a substantive right, 'not one dependant upon the performance of any particular religious rites'. In support of this argument, they cited a note in W.H. Macnaghten's *Sudder Dewanny Adawlut Reports* which they attributed to H. Colebrooke. Colebrooke had cited Jagannath's *Digest* Book 5, v. 455 and 457 to prove that 'the mere act of celebrating the funeral rites [does not give] a title to the succession'. However, the Calcutta Justices remarked that Colebrooke's note did not declare conversely that the succession could devolve upon anyone not performing the funeral rites. The Justices concluded that 'there is undoubtedly upon Dicta of the Hindoo Law Books much room for argument on the point'. Therefore, in the absence of any previous judicial decision, the Court urged caution.[43]

Doubts also plagued Governor General Dalhousie's Council. J.E.D. Bethune, asked to prepare a preliminary draft protecting the civil rights of Christian converts, confessed, on his first attempt in May 1849, to 'some lingering doubt'. He acknowledged 'Hindoo notions' that a son's right to his father's property depended upon his performance of funeral rites 'from which the outcaste is necessarily excluded'. In a preamble to his preliminary draft, Bethune 'endeavoured to...give [the Act] the slightest possible appearance of interfering with the religious notions of the natives' and yet to call attention to an Act of Parliament during the reign of King William IV which enjoined the Governor General to protect 'the Native[s] of India from insult and outrage in their persons, religion[s], and opinions'. The best way to accomplish this, suggested Bethune, was to extend Secs 8 and 9 of Beng. Reg. VII 1832 to all India while repealing any regulations inconsistent with them.[44]

---

[43] B.J. Colvin, Register of Sudder Dewanny Adawlut, to J.P. Grant, Secretary to Government of Bengal, Fort William, 21 December 1849, India Legislative Proceedings, 11 April 1850, No. 75, I.O.R., P/207/59; W.H. Macnaghten, 'Note', in *Reports of Cases Determined in the Sudder Dewanny Adalat, Select Cases 1791–1811*, Vol. I, new ed. (Calcutta, 1827) I.O.R., V/22/407, p. 22.

[44] Minute by J.E.D. Bethune, 31 May 1849, India Legislative Proceedings, 11 April 1850, No. 59, I.O.R., P/207/59.

As soon as Bethune's Draft Act was published in the *Government Gazette* of 31 October 1849 and the *Fort St. George Government Gazette* of 16 November 1849, memorials of protest were presented to Governor General Dalhousie from the 'Hindoo Inhabitants of Bengal, Behar and Orissa' and from the 'Native Inhabitants of Madras'. Both memorials indignantly stated that the draft act violated the promise of Warren Hastings' Government enshrined in 21 Geo III c. 70, Sec. 17 'which guaranteed to Hindus their National Law of Inheritance'. Also cited were the Cornwallis Code promising to protect the East India Company's subjects in the 'free exercise of their religion', Sec. 53 of the 1833 Charter and proclamations concerning the 'free exercise of religion' in the wake of the annexation of Coorg in 1834 and of Punjab in 1847. To sum up their sense of betrayal, the Bengal memorialists described

> the pain and distress, with which they have read the proposed Act, as the first inroad upon the integrity of the Laws of which they have hitherto, since the Country has been under the protection and Government of Great Britain, felt secure.[45]

The Bengal memorialists' view of events leading to the draft act challenged English dreams of civil rights for Christian converts and of substantive law as a *lex loci*. They observed, in the first instance, that 'the Act speciously pretends to be a mere extension to the whole of British India of a Regulation of the Government of Bengal passed in 1832'. Then they 'conscientiously affirm' that until reference was made to Secs 8 and 9 Beng. Reg. VII 1832 in correspondence connected with the draft Lex Loci Act of 1845, 'your Memorialists were almost universally ignorant' of it and 'those few who were aware of its existence never imagined that it would receive the interpretation which is now given to it'.

On the crucial subject of the Hindu Law of Inheritance, the Bengal Memorial focused on arguments put forward by G.A. Bushby, Secretary to the Government of Bengal, in response to memorialists protesting the draft

---

[45] Memorial against the proposed Act for Altering the Hindoo Law of Inheritance signed by Raja Radhakant Bahadoor [Deb] and 3000 Hindoos, the Inhabitants of Bengal, Behar and Orissa, in Parchment Records, I.O.R., A/1/100, fols 1–3; Memorial of the Native Inhabitants of Madras, January 16, 1850, India Legislative Proceedings, 11 April 1850, No. 81, I.O.R., P/207/59. Regulation XI for removing certain Restrictions to the Operation of the Hindoo and Mahomedan laws, with regard to the Inheritance of landed Property, subject to the Payment of Revenue to Government (passed by Governor General in Council, 1 May 1793), I.O.R., V/8/16, pp. 129–31.

Lex Loci Act of 1845. Bushby had asserted that Hindus, by protesting against an English law extending civil rights to Christian converts, demonstrated fundamental intolerance. In response, the memorialists proclaimed the Hindu religion to be exceedingly tolerant. They emphasized that, in contrast with Christianity and Islam, Hinduism is not a proselytizing religion. Thus, the Hindu 'persecutes no one for differing in opinion with him, where he has the power to persecute...but his law indisputably says...to every Hindoo, "if you quit your father's religion you must quit your father's property, for you are thereby absolutely disqualified from performing those duties which attach to its inheritance"'.

To buttress their central argument concerning the essential duty of the Hindu heir to perform funeral rites for his ancestor, the memorialists advanced several supplementary arguments. First, they pointed out that a Hindu apostate would not be liable to forfeit any property 'self-acquired... from trade or otherwise'. All that was at stake was inherited property. Secondly, they emphasized the extent to which the proposed law would be an abomination for all Hindus. As the Hindu Law decrees that 'the right of succession depends exclusively upon the right to present the funeral oblations', it is only by this act that 'sons and near kinsmen' inherit the property 'because according to the belief of Hindoos, it is by such Acts that the father's spiritual bliss, and that of his Ancestors to the remotest degree, is secured, and by the tenets of the Hindoo Religion an Apostate from that faith cannot perform the obsequies'. For an apostate to perform these duties 'would be a desecration of the rite, an abomination which would, according to their belief, work for evil...'. In the words of the *Dayabhaga*, 'His [son's] connexion with the property is therefore the reward of his beneficial Acts. If he neglect them, how should he have his hire?' Furthermore, almost all Hindus of property bequeath a portion of their property to temples dedicated to their family deities; certainly, every Hindu without exception is 'bound by the most sacred precepts of their religion to maintain and uphold the worship of their family deities established by their ancestors, and which are to be seen in the house of the poorest Hindoo'. The memorialists reasoned that 'the Christian or Mahomedan convert would look with contempt upon the idols' which had formerly been the objects of his devotions. Not only were the family deities seen to be at risk in the hands of apostates, but also the Hindu family could not 'associate in anyway with a converted brother or relative' for fear of loss of caste. Thus, the convert could not even approach the family shrine without polluting it. And so, the memorialists speculated that, were the proposed law 'to become a portion of the law to which the Hindoos were compelled to submit', the convert's entrance to the temple, whether for the purpose of removing the idols, or insulting the religion of his forefathers, could not be resisted without incurring the risk of committing a trespass. It would be the only alternative—trespass, or submit to desecration of all which sincere Hindoos hold sacred and revere[46].

Thirdly, the memorialists slyly questioned the quality of the Christian convert's new faith: 'If the convert is so satisfied that the religion of his fathers is erroneous,...it would be a faith hardly worth the cost of deserting that of his fathers for...if he was prevented from adopting it by the lingering love he felt for the property apart from its duties'. Finally, the Bengal memorialists took refuge in the very specific decree in Secs 2 and 6 of Beng. Reg. XI 1793 to the effect that 'landed property' was 'to descend according to Mahomedan or Hindoo law' and that property transfers to whomever and in whatever manner were to be allowed 'provided [the] transfer be not repugnant to Hindoo or Mahomedan law'.[47]

If a regulation such as Beng. Reg. XI 1793 did not protect the Hindu family from losing property to an apostate and the general promise of religious toleration proffered by the governments of Warren Hastings and Lord Cornwallis were to prove hollow, the Bengal memorialists concluded in despair that

> from the moment that the proposed Act becomes a part of the Law applicable to Hindoos [,] that confidence which they have hitherto felt in the paternal character of their British rulers, will be most materially shaken—no outbreak, of course, is to be dreaded, but the active spirit of fervent loyalty to their Sovereign, and of pride in their Rulers, will be changed into sullen submission to their Will, and obedience to their power—the readiness which many of the Hindoo body have exhibited on various occasions to contribute largely and liberally to the objects promoted by the British born Subjects of Her Majesty, need not be expected, when they are told in reply to a remonstrance against a Law which has for its object to sap the foundations of their religion and cannot have any operation unless by the destruction of the Most sacred and cherished precepts which are enjoined by their *Shastres*, that they are intolerant[,] illiberal and unenlightened.[48]

The contrast between the position of Government as champion of the civil rights of Christian converts and its Hindu subjects as defenders of their

---

[46] *Ibid.*
[47] *Ibid.*
[48] *Ibid.*

religious laws could not have been more stark. The Bengal memorialists, in particular, considered themselves to be at least as loyal to the British government as the Bombay Bishop's native Christian converts. They were deeply suspicious that the Government was unduly influenced by Christian missionaries. They were justifiably outraged by the missionaries' determination to brand their religion as evil, even criminal. A memorial from approximately 400 European Christian and missionaries equated the proposed Inheritance Law with such 'humane measures' as the abolition of Suttee and the Suppression of Infanticide and Thuggee 'which they regarded...as pledges that the Government of India will not allow the perpetuation of *injustice* and *crime*, under the sanction of any religion'.[49] At least some members of Governor General Dalhousie's Council perceived the proposed act to signify more than a technical extension of Sec. 9, Beng. Reg. VII 1832. A. Dick declared: 'This Act differs essentially in Principle from Regulation VII 1832 Section 9. That did not in any way interfere with the religion of the Hindoos. This does. The law of inheritance of Hindoos is founded on their religion.'[50]

It was J.E.D. Bethune who was called upon to rationalize the proposed 'Inheritance Law', the very same J.E.D. Bethune who, less than a year earlier, had sympathized with the Hindu family of a Christian convert. In May 1849, Bethune doubted the justice of an English legislative council enacting a law which interfered with penalties imposed within Hindu families by Hindu religious law. By the end of March 1850, Bethune was ready to adopt the arguments marshalled by G.A. Bushby, Secretary to the Government of Bengal, in his 1845 answer to memorialists in Madras and Bengal protesting the draft Lex Loci Act. With sleight of hand, Bushby had deflected his argument away from the 1845 memorialists' objections to the draft Lex Loci Act in general, and to Sec. 12 in particular for its refusal to enforce any Muslim or Hindu law that inflicted forfeiture of property on apostates. In 1845, as in 1850, memorialists accused the Government of violating its own pledge of religious neutrality dating back to the guarantee in the Cornwallis Code of the 'free exercise of religion', and even further back to the specific assurance by Warren Hastings, preserved in 21 Geo III, c. 70, s. 17 and 18, that in Supreme Court cases involving inheritance, the

---

[49] Memorial from approximately 400 European Christians and Missionaries representing the Church Missionary Society, the Baptist Missionary Society, the Free Church Mission and the Free Church of Scotland, submitted 3 April 1850, India Legislative Proceedings, 11 April 1850, No. 85, I.O.R., P/207/59.

[50] Note by A. Dick, 15 November 1849, India Legislative Proceedings, 11 April 1850, No. 75, I.O.R., P/207/59.

laws and usages of Gentoos would be applied to Gentoos, while the laws and usages of Mahomedans would be applied to Mahomedans. Denying all such pledges, Bushby argued in 1845 that the principles guiding the Government of India called for equal protection of all religions as 'just and right'. With a deft historical reference, he noted that the British Government had delivered Hindus from the injustice suffered under Mahomedan rule of being forced to obey Mahomedan law which deprived Hindus of their Law of Inheritance. And in this spirit of justice, he argued that the East India Company had enacted Sec. 9 Beng. Reg. VII 1832 to prevent Hindus from using their Law of Inheritance to punish apostates. Furthermore, Bushby noted the authority granted the Indian Government by the 1833 Charter Act to change the law while maintaining respect for distinctions of caste, religion and usage. Considering that his own arguments were unanswerable, Bushby then lamented:

> [T]hat at a period when public opinion among a great part of the Hindoos has become in a high degree tolerant and enlightened, a memorial founded upon doctrines of so opposite a character should have been presented by a respectable portion of that community.[51]

In 1850, the memorialists protesting the onslaught of Act XXI observed that, after Bushby's official reply in 1845, 'the *Lex Loci* Act was no more heard of and fell to the ground, with the obnoxious clauses objected to by the Hindoos'. However, in a minute dated 26 March 1850, J.E.D. Bethune incorporated Bushby's arguments into his own. To overcome his doubts as expressed in 1849, Bethune referred to chapter II of Halhed's *Gentoo Laws* to observe that whereas 'it is undoubtedly true that the obligation to offer the funeral cake descends on the same line of heirs as the right of Inheritance...it is by way of penalty only, that the outcaste loses his inheritance'. To avoid a patronizing tone, he then cited English law going back to the time of King Edward I to prove that 'the incapacity to inherit arising out of excommunication' was also a characteristic of the Christian religion ultimately used against the 'popish recusant' during the reign of King James I. Bethune wryly observed:

> It is the policy of the professors of every claimant religion to convert as much as possible their spiritual armoury into a storehouse of weapons of offence

---

[51] G.A. Bushby, Secretary to Government of India, to Luchinee Narasa Chetty, Chairman of a meeting of Hindoo Inhabitants of Fort St. George, Fort William, 24 May 1845, India Legislative Proceedings, 2 August 1845, No. 5, I.O.R., P/207/36; also in Special Report of Indian Law Commissioners (1845), *Parliamentary Papers* (1847) XLIII, Cmd. 14, pp. 645, 648–49.

for securing objects of earthly advantage; in this respect the Christian and Hindu histories shew the same kind of device.[52]

By thus describing laws of inheritance as secular tools subject to abuse by claimant religions, Bethune absolved his own conscience of any guilt over religious interference. He declared any inheritance to be a secular matter subject only to regulation by the state. Then he proceeded to embellish Bushby's arguments. First, unlike Bushby's total denial of any pledge, Bethune's argument began with an acknowledgement that, subject to the promise given by Warren Hastings and enshrined in 21 Geo III c. 70 s. 17, 'there was more room of doubting whether it was in the power of the local legislature to make any regulation in any way affecting the laws of inheritance of Hindoos'. But then Bethune allowed that the 1833 Charter c. 85 s. 53 had scuttled this concern so that 'there is now no such restriction on the power of the Governor General in Council'. More specifically, he referred to the instructions given to the Law Commissioners in connection with their assignment of formulating a *lex loci*. The commissioners were cautioned to have 'due regard to the difference of Castes, difference of religion, and the manners and opinions prevailing among different races and different parts of the said territories'. Bethune was anxious to explain that 'due regard means as much regard as ought to be had, considering each case by itself'.

Finally, having distanced himself from Bushby's absolute denial of any pledge such as that contained in 21 Geo III c. 70 s. 17, Bethune announced his conclusion supported by the legislative authority bestowed upon the Indian Government by the 1833 Charter. First, he declared: 'This discussion is important only so far as upon it depends whether or not it is necessary to declare a new law of inheritance in our act. I think not'. Then he asserted:

> I take the high ground of the inherent and inalienable right of every Government to regulate the law of property, and to deprive any class of its subjects of the power of securing conformity to their own opinions by the infliction of penalties, which it belongs to the Government only to impose.[53]

Governor General Dalhousie was delighted by Bethune's carefully reasoned minute. He readily supported his councillor; indeed, he eagerly endorsed the argument 'that it is the duty of the state to keep in its own hand the right of regulating the succession to property'. However, despite the claim

---

[52] Minute by J.E.D. Bethune, 26 March 1850, India Legislative Proceedings, 11 April 1850, No. 83, I.O.R., P/207/59.

[53] *Ibid.*

of his biographer that' 'Act XXI was always regarded by Lord Dalhousie as the most important of those passed by him,'[54] Dalhousie's minute revealed either that his reading of Bethune's minute was very cursory or that he failed to understand the central thrust of Bethune's argument. Whereas Bethune had explicitly stated that there was no need for a substantive new law of inheritance, Dalhousie freely speculated:

> The Government of India will doubtless continue as heretofore to administer to Hindoos the general body of Hindoo law; but I conceive that the Government will not do its duty, if it leaves unchanged any portion of that law which inflicts personal injury on anyone by reason of his religious belief.

He then insouciantly concluded that in promulgating Act XXI 1850 he could 'see no semblance of interference with the religion of the Hindoos, nor any unauthorized interference with rights secured to them'.[55] Perhaps, Stephen Neill's assessment of Dalhousie's character correctly faults him for lacking 'the essential gift of imagination'. Neill observed that:

> Dalhousie supposed…he was doing no more than putting into effect a principle of natural law, in accordance with the policy of toleration to which the Government of the East India Company had unceasingly given assent. He was unaware, or had forgotten, that in Hindu society as in Rome, the family is a religious as well as a sociological entity. The Hindu father needs a son to light the flames on his funeral pyre, and to prepare the *sraddha* ceremonies which are needed to ensure his passage to a happy life in the other world.[56]

Most offensive to the orthodox Bengali community was the apparent arrogance of the Dalhousie government. Whereas, in 1845, G.A. Bushby answered the arguments raised by memorialists in Bengal and Madras, in 1850, Dalhousie's Legislative Council resolved all arguments internally without even acknowledging the memorial presented by Raja Radhakant Deb.

Six months after the minutes by Bethune and Dalhousie, councillor F. Currie, despite his conviction that Act XXI 1850 went 'much further than S. 9 Reg. VII 1832', approved Bethune's draft. And so, amidst confusion and disagreement to the very end Act XXI was enacted on 11 April 1850 to ensure that:

---

[54] Sir William Lee Warner, *The Life of the Marquis of Dalhousie K.T.*, Vol. I (London, 1904), pp. 297–98.

[55] Minute by Governor General Dalhousie, 9 April 1850, India Legislative Proceedings, 11 April 1850, No. 86, I.O.R., P/207/59.

[56] Stephen Neill, *A History of Christianity in India,* Vol. II, 1707–1858 (Cambridge, 1985), pp. 413–14.

So much of any law or usage now in force within the Territories subject to the Government of the East India Company, as inflicts on any person forfeiture of rights or property, or may be held in any way to impair or affect any right of inheritance by reason of his or her renouncing, or having been excluded from the communion of any religion, or being deprived of caste, shall cease to be enforced as Law in the Courts of the East India Company, and in the Courts established by Royal Charter within the said Territories.[57]

Thus, Governor General Dalhousie's Government demonstrated that, if it suited the Government, English law could supersede Hindu or Muslim law. Fortunately for future Indo–British relations, the engine of *lex loci* had already sputtered to an end. Hence, the implications of Act XXI which so worried the memorialists were never realized. Apart from J.E.D. Bethune, it cannot be said that any of the major participants in the controversy truly understood what was at stake.

Immediately after the promulgation of Act XXI 1850 a memorial submitted to the Court of Directors by Raja Radhakant Deb on behalf of 4,000 Bengali signatories prayed for the repeal of Act XXI and Sec. IX Beng. Reg. VII 1832.[58] However, Governor General Dalhousie was unmoved and Act XXI became the 'Law of the Land'. Ironically, Act XXI played a decisive role in a case argued before the Sudder Dewanny Adawlut of Bombay, the one Presidency which had preferred local usage and custom over Hindu and Muslim law. When a Brahmin convert to Christianity sued his wife for the possession of his son, he was accused of 'Mahapathuk' or the 'reviling of (one's own or another's) religion'. The principal Sudder Ameen, operating according to principles of justice, equity and good conscience according to Sec. XXVI of Bombay Reg. IV 1827, decreed in favour of the Brahmin. However, the *zillah* Judge, noting references to *Yudneowulkeo*, the Law Code of Manu and the *Bhagavad Gita*, reversed the decision. He simply ruled that according to 'Hindoo law...a Brahmin renouncing his religion, becomes an outcaste and thereby forfeits all his civil rights'. When appealed to the Sudder Dewanny Adawlut, the case was reviewed by Judge P.W. LeGeyt who noted:

---

[57] Act XXI for extending the principle of Sec. IX Regulation VII 1832 of the Bengal Code throughout the Territories subject to the Government of the East India Company (passed by Governor General in Council, 11 April 1850), I.O.R., V/8/33.

[58] Memorial 14 May 1850 enclosed in Legislative Despatch from India, 25 July 1851, No. 12, I.O.R., *Board's Collections*, F/4/2436, Reg. 133501; original in Parchment Records, I.O.R., A/1/100, fols 4–6; also in India Legislative Proceedings, 25 July 1851, Nos 6–8, I.O.R., P/207/67, and Report of Select Committee on Indian Territories, Appendix 7, *Parliamentary Papers* (1852–53) XXVII, Cmd. 426, pp. 429–32.

[T]hat since the decree appealed against was passed, Act XXI 1850 had become the law of the land, and clearly provides that any law or usage which inflicts on any person forfeiture of rights or property by reason of his or her renouncing any religion, or being deprived of caste, shall cease to be enforced as law.

He then referred the case to be tried before a full court which 'reversed the decree of the *zillah* Judge with costs on respondent'.[59]

Remarriage of Hindu Widows

Act XV enacted on 19 July 1856 to remove all legal obstacles in the way of the marriage of Hindu widows was a logical sequence to both Bengal Regulation XVII 1829 prohibiting *sati* and Act XXI 1850 removing the civil disabilities of Hindu apostates. Act XXI 1850 had prepared the way for enactment of civil legislation guaranteeing freedom of conscience. Bengal Regulation XVII 1829 had compounded the misery of twice-born Hindu widows by delivering the *sati* from the flames of her husband's funeral pyre into the misery of *brahmacharya* or absolute austerity. As described by a 'Hindoo gentleman of great knowledge', the respectable widow's

> manner of life is minutely prescribed. Not only must she see no man, she must also avoid every approach to ease, luxury or pleasure; she must neglect the care of her person; she must wear no ornaments; her hair must be shaved, or at least must be worn dishevelled; she must not see her face in a mirror, not use perfumes or flowers; she must not freely anoint her body, and her dress must be plain, coarse and dirty. The use of any kind of conveyance is prohibited, and she must not rest on a bed. Her food is limited as to quantity as well as quality. She must not take more than a single coarse meal a day and the betel leaf which terminates every repast in India, and is often substituted for a meal, is denied her. Besides other fasts, perhaps a dozen in the year, the Hindu widow is required to abstain absolutely from food and drink twice a month, one day and one night, during every bright and dark period of the

---

[59] Case No. 2627, Special Appellant Narayan Ramchunder vs. Luxmeebaee, his wife, Respondent—₹1,000, 21 February 1851, *Selected Decisions of the Court of Sudder Dewannee Adawlut of Bombay*, compiled by James Morris, 1st Assistant Registrar (Bombay, 1852), pp. 61–67, Tamil Nadu High Court Library. For discussion of the unique background of lawmaking in the Bombay Presidency, *see* 'Introduction' above, pp. 7, 21.

moon, on the 11th and 26th day of her age, from which fasts not even a severe sickness can give her a dispensation.[60]

Efforts leading to the enactment of Act XV had a very long history of frustration. At the turn of the fifteenth century, Raghanundana, a Bengali *pandit* and compiler of a respected *Digest of the Hindu Law*, attempted to remarry his own widowed daughter to no avail. In the mid-eighteenth century, Raja Rajbulbub of Dacca obtained a *vyavastha* from learned *pandit*s in favour of remarrying his widowed daughter—again, to no avail. There was one successful instance recorded by Sir Thomas Strange in his study of Hindu law whereby *pandit*s in Poona gave permission for a widow remarriage which was acted upon.[61] There was even an attempt by the Company, as early as 1804, to guarantee with legislation property rights as well as the right to remarry for wealthy widows of *jagirdar*s.[62] In the 1830s a Maratha Brahmin, son of the minister of the Raja of Nagpore, described some of the consequences of the custom of prohibiting widow remarriage. As summarized by Major Wilkinson, the Resident of Nagpore, who published the Brahmin's essay:

> The present prohibition against the second marriages of widows, especially… infant widows, is highly impolitic and unwise, because in the first place, it disappoints the palpable purpose of the Creator in having sent them into the world; secondly, because it inevitably leads to a great moral depravity and vice on the part of these widows; thirdly, because it inevitably causes a frightful amount of infanticide and abortions; fourthly, because the maintenance of these widows in an honorable and virtuous course of life causes a ceaseless, though fruitless, anxiety to their parents, and parents-in-law…; fifthly, because these widows [,] inevitably rendered corrupt and vicious themselves by the hard and unnatural laws operating on them, cannot be prevented from

---

[60] Cited by J.P. Grant in preparing the Legislative Council for the first reading of the Bill to remove all legal obstacles to the Marriage of Hindoo Widows, Proceedings of the Legislative Council, 17 November 1855, from *Printed Records and Published Debates of the Legislative Council of India* (Calcutta, 1856), N.A.S., Dalhousie Muniments, GD 45/6/216, pp. 4–5.

[61] Sir Thomas Strange, *Elements of Hindu Law; Referable to British Judicature in India*, Vol. I (London, 1825), p. 241; for another case of a Raja attempting to persuade *pandit*s at his court to give a *vyastha* permitting widow remarriage, see J.D.M. Derrett, *Religion, Law and the State in India* (London, 1968), p. 235.

[62] Sec. XII of Bengal Regulation I for the better Management of Invalid Jagheerdar Establishments (passed 23 February 1804), decreed: 'Widows being heiresses to jagheers of their husbands, shall be allowed to marry whom they please without forfeiture of their jagheers, which, after their death, shall devolve to their heirs at law'. I.O.R., V/8/18, p. 4.

corrupting and destroying the honor and virtue of all other females with whom they associate.[63]

In Bengal, such desperate circumstances as these described in Nagpore were compounded by the phenomenon of Kulinism whereby male Kulin Brahmins were encouraged by their superior status to contract multiple marriages for the sake of large marriage gratuities. As described by one critic of the polygamous Kulins: 'They have been known to marry more than a hundred wives each, and it is customary with them, immediately after going through the nuptial ceremonies and receiving their gratuities, to leave the houses of the girls they have married, never to see their faces more'.[64] It has been speculated that the noted Sanskritist reformer, Iswar Chandra Vidyasagar, who was to agitate in favour of widow remarriage in the mid-nineteenth century, was much affected by the scenes of the rural Bengal of his childhood. There he witnessed the reality that, as a result of 'polygamy wedded to the cruel practise of Kulinism' and the prohibition of *sati*, 'the number of widows grew alarmingly'. And, 'most of these widows were young'.[65]

Within a decade of the prohibition of *sati*, it occurred to the Law Commission in the midst of their deliberations over infanticide in the N.W.P. that 'much of this crime may be owing to the cruel law which prevents Hindoo Widows from contracting a second marriage'. The commissioners decided in June 1837 to enquire of the Sudder Courts of Calcutta, Allahabad, Madras and Bombay 'whether there would be any objections to a law which should authorize the re-marriage of Hindu Widows, within the Provinces subject to the jurisdiction of your Court'.[66] The responses opposed the thought of such a law with devastating unanimity. The judges of the Calcutta Sudder Court felt that such a law would violate 'the pledged faith of the Government' to respect the religious faith and customs of its Hindu subjects. The Calcutta court emphasized the Hindu scriptures or '*shastra*s which they understood 'distinctly declared...that the re-marriage of a Widow involves guilt and disgrace on earth, and exclusion from Heaven'. They further cited Colebrooke's *Digest of the Hindoo Law* to support their assertion that 'the

---

[63] Cited by J.P. Grant, *op. cit.*, p. 5.

[64] Petition of Maharajah of Burdwan against Hindoo Polygamy, Legislative Council Proceedings 28 June 1856, Proceedings of the Legislative Council of India, I.O.R., V/9/2, col. 417.

[65] Benoy Ghose, *Iswar Chandra Vidyasagar* (Delhi, 2nd repr., 1973), p. 63.

[66] J.P. Grant, Officiating Secretary to the Indian Law Commissioners, to the Register of the Sudder Courts of Calcutta, Allahabad, Madras and Bombay, Indian Law Commission, 30 June 1837, *Board's Collections*, I.O.R., F/4/2691, #189069, p. 32.

whole frame-work of the Hindoo law of Inheritance would be shaken or subverted'.[67] The Allahabad Sudder Court cited the Government's pledge to 'secure to all classes of its subjects the free exercise of their religion and to preserve to them in Civil matters the laws and customs which they hold most sacred'. The Court emphasized that the prohibition of widow remarriage in the N.W.P. was considered 'both a religious and moral obligation, which can never be violated without entailing indelible disgrace and loss of character both on the woman herself and all connected with her'. And, so they concluded that 'any enactment of the nature of that proposed, would be nearly, if not wholly inoperative, particularly as regards those for whose benefit it is chiefly intended, namely, the females of the higher classes'.[68] The Madras Sudder Court was even more emphatic in remarking upon the outrage which the proposed law would inspire among the 'bigoted' castes of the South. They cited Macnaghten's *Principles of Hindoo Law* to make the point that 'marriage among the Hindoos is not merely a civil contract—but a sacrament forming the last of the ceremonies prescribed to the three regenerate classes, and the only one for the Soodras'. Noting that the 'Hindoos of the Peninsula' were distinguished by their 'bigoted adherence to their religious observances and the most sensitive jealousy of any interference with the rules of caste', the judges warned against

> a legislative act of the Supreme Government, concerning the only sacrament of their religion in which the Soodras participate...They would look upon such an act as an attempt to confound them with the inferior and outcast tribes, who admit of second marriages by widows—and are thereby lowered in the opinion of the superior tribes, as degrading no less themselves, than the families of their deceased husbands, to whom, according to the notions of the higher tribes, the chastity of a widow should be consecrated.[69]

The judges of the Allahabad and Madras Sudder Courts were alert to the fact that throughout India 80 per cent of the Hindu population were oblivious of the prohibition against widow remarriage. The custom of prohibition was

---

[67] R. Macan, Officiating Register, Sudder Dewanny Adawlut, Calcutta, to J.P. Grant, Officiating Secretary to Indian Law Commissioners, Fort William, 24 July 1837, *Board's Collections*, I.O.R., F/4/2691, #189069, p. 33.

[68] H.B. Harington, Register, Sudder Dewanny Adawlut of the Norh Western Provinces, to J.P. Grant, Officiating Secretary to Indian Law Commissioners, Allahabad, 11 August 1837, *Board's Collections*, I.O.R., F/4/2691, #189069, p. 34.

[69] W. Douglas, Register, Sudder Court, Madras, to J.P. Grant, Secretary to the Indian Law Commissioners, Fort St. George, 31 July 1837, *Board's Collections*, I.O.R., F/4/2691, #189069, p. 35.

only operative among the twice-born upper castes and, in the exceptional circumstances of the south, among the *Sudra*s of the Madras presidency. The subject of the legislation proposed in 1855–56 was more a question of principle than reality.

Against this background, it is hardly surprising that the call for change came from the western educated Bengalis. The July 1842 issue of the *Bengal Spectator* put forward the Derozians' view that there was no basis for a legal objection to widow remarriage in the Hindu *shastra*s. Alumni of Hindu College combined with the Tattvabodhini Sabha under Debendranath Tagore and Ramaprasad Roy, the son of Rammohun Roy, to advance the cause of widow remarriage. But, they only succeeded in triggering a strong Orthodox reaction. It was in despair over these failed initiatives that the renowned Sanskrit scholar, Iswar Chandra Vidyasagar, was moved to tackle the problem.

Before engaging in practical manoeuvres, Vidyasagar made a thorough study of Sanskrit texts. His research determined that there was indeed a *sloka* in the *Parasara Samhita* which allowed for the marriage of Hindu widows under certain conditions. This text had been cited by earlier sages such as Bandhayana and Narada, and it had the support of the *Agnipurana*. More importantly, Vidyasagar noted that the 'Dharmas enjoined by Manu' which prohibited widow remarriage were not intended for the people living in the current age or Kali Yuga. Vidyasagar agreed that the first chapter of the *Dharmasastra of Manu* says, in effect, that 'the Dharmas which the people of prior Yugas practised cannot now be observed by the people of Kali Yuga, because human power decreases in every successive Yuga...' It was the first chapter of the *Parasara Samhita* which explained that 'the Dharmas enjoined by Manu are assigned to the Satya Yuga; those by Gotama, to the Treta; those by Sankha and Likhita to the Dvapara; and those by Parasara to the Kali Yuga'. Specifically, the *Nastry Mritry sloka* of the fourth chapter of the *Parasara Samhita* decreed:

> On receiving no tidings of a husband, on his demise, on his turning an ascetic, on his being found impotent or on his degradation—under any one of these five calamities it is canonical for women to take another husband. That woman, who on the decease of her husband observes the Brahmacarya...attains heaven after death. She who burns herself with her deceased husband resides in heaven for as many Kalas or thousands of years as there are hairs on the human body or thirty five millions.

Vidyasagar explained that, since the act of 'concremation' or *sati* had been abolished by government and 'in the Kali Yuga it has become extremely difficult for widows to pass their lives in the observance of Brahmacharya...it is for this reason that the Philanthropic Parasara has, in the first instance, prescribed marriage'. Armed by this scriptural authority, Vidyasagar felt able to face those critics who charged that he was 'influenced more by compassion towards the unfortunate widows of my country than by a firm belief in their remarriage being consonant to the Sastras'. He insisted that 'I did not take up my pen before I was fully convinced that the Sastras explicitly sanction [widow] remarriage'. He alleged that he could 'safely affirm, that in the whole range of our original *Smritis* there is not one single text which can establish anything to the contrary'.[70]

Thus convinced of the scriptural authority for his cause, Vidyasagar added his signature to those of nearly 1,000 petitioners submitting the draft of 'An Act to declare the lawfulness of the Marriage of Hindoo Widows'. Described by one of Dalhousie's councillors as 'one who, in reputation for learning, yielded to no Pundit in this city', Vidyasagar had no difficulty in obtaining access to individual members of Governor General Dalhousie's Legislative Council. And so it was that a 'Humble Petition' of 984 'Inhabitants of...Bengal' was presented to the Legislative Council on 6 October 1855 with the argument:

> That by long established custom the marriage of Widows among Hindoos is prohibited.
>
> That, in the opinion and firm belief of your Petitioners, this custom is not in accordance with the Shasters, or with a true interpretation of Hindoo Law.
>
> That your Petitioners are advised that by the Hindoo law, as at present administered and interpreted in the Courts of Her Majesty and the East India Company, such marriages are illegal, and the issue thereof would be deemed illegitimate...
>
> That, in the humble opinion of your Petitioners, it is the duty of the Legislature to remove all legal obstacles to the escape from a social evil of such magnitude...

Attached to the petition was the draft of a law, the first section of which was to survive almost word for word as Section 1 of Act XV passed on 19 July 1856. The petition, the language of which was slightly more eloquent than that of Act XV, declared: 'No marriage contracted between Hindoos, shall

---

[70] Iswarchandra Vidyasagar, *Marriage of Hindu Widows* (Calcutta, repr.: 1976), pp. i–ii, 3–4 and 7–8; cf. Benoy Ghose, *op. cit.*, pp. 62–63 and P.V. Kane, *History of Dharmasastra*, Vol. II, Part I (Poona, 1941), pp. 610–11.

be deemed invalid, or the issue thereof illegitimate, by reason of the woman having been previously married or betrothed to another person since deceased, any custom on interpretation to the contrary notwithstanding'.[71]

It is odd that recent scholarship has fixed on this section as 'directly contrary to orthodox, textual Hindu law', a fact which created 'the necessity for legislation'.[72] The most cursory examination of the legislative proceedings leading to the enactment of Act XV reveals that the councillors took no interest in pronouncing 'any opinion whatever as to what should be the proper interpretation of the Shasters'. Act XV was directed at the Civil Law. Citing such legal authorities as Sir Thomas Strange and W. Macnaghten, J.P. Grant, upon first reading of the proposed Bill declared that Vidyasagar's petition was correct in saying that 'our Courts would disallow the marriage of a Hindoo widow'. Grant insisted that the 'Legislative Council could not stand in the way of the removal of a Municipal Law enforcing upon unwilling people a prohibition which...was in the highest degree mischievous'.[73] As he succinctly stated:

> It is well known that, by Hindoo doctrine, a Hindoo widow who does not burn as a Suttee...is bound to a life of the most painful bodily mortification. Those who agree with the Petitioners allow the reputable alternative of re-marriage. Those who do not, allow of no reputable alternative. The law of our Courts allows no reputable alternative to either class.

The proposed Bill was not compulsory like Bengal Regulation XVII 1829 which abolished *sati*; it was permissive or enabling. As stated in the preamble, the Bill aimed to enable those Hindus who agreed with the Vidyasagar petitioners to act 'in accordance with the dictates of their own consciences'.[74] In the words of Barnes Peacock, a member of the Legislative Council on the occasion of the final debate before passing Act XV, 'The Bill would not prevent any Hindoo from acting according to his own belief that the

---

[71] Proceedings of the Legislative Council, 6 October 1855, *Board's Collections*, I.O.R., F/4/2691, Reg. 189069, pp. 3–16; cf. Sec. I, Act XV of 1856, Proceedings of the Legislative Council, 19 July 1856, *Board's Collections*, I.O.R., F/4/2691, #189069, p. 258.

[72] Lucy Carroll, 'Law, Custom and Statutory Social Reform: The Hindu Widows' Remarriage Act of 1856', in J. Krishnamurty, ed., *Women in Colonial India—Essays on Survival, Work and the State* (Delhi, 1999), p. 9.

[73] J.P. Grant upon the first reading of the Bill 'To Remove All Legal Obstacles to the Marriage of Hindoo Widows', Proceedings of the Legislative Council of India, 17 November 1855, I.O.R. V/9/1, Cols 783–85, 790.

[74] J.P. Grant, 'Statement of Objects and Reasons', Proceedings of the Legislative Council, 17 November 1855, *Board's Collections*, I.O.R., F/4/2691, Reg. 189069, pp. 29, 25.

Hindoo religion forbade the marriage of widows; but it would enable those who entertained a different belief to act upon it'.[75]

To the credit of the Vidyasagar petitioners, the preamble which they proposed suffered only further explanatory references to the Civil Law at the hands of the Legislative Council and the wording which they suggested for Section One was virtually unchanged. In their deliberations over the basic principle of the new legislation, the Council was undeterred by 28 petitions bearing 55,746 signatures addressed to Government against the law. One of these negative petitions was organized by Raja Radhakanta Deb of Shovabazar with 36,763 signatures to represent the orthodox Calcutta community. The Raja urged the Government 'not to interfere with Hindu social institutions by any form of legislation since such legislation would be calamitous to the petitioners' familial relations, social life and religious beliefs'.[76] The Council which formed a Select Committee to ponder 21 petitions signed by 5,191 individuals in favour of the new law and the 28 petitions against it, had no difficulty dismissing the objections of the orthodox community by emphasizing the enabling sentiments expressed in the Preamble. The Council consistently refused to enter into any arguments over the meaning of different *shastra*s. But, Section 2, as proposed by the Vidyasagar petitioners, on the subject of Hindu Inheritance Law, opened a veritable Pandora's Box. In the end, the Select Committee expanded the petitioners' proposed law containing two sections into a law with seven sections. Not all of the new sections pertained directly to inheritance; nor did all of the new sections constitute a response to the 28 negative petitions.

Sir James Colvile, in the course of seconding J.P. Grant's motion for the first reading of the Bill, commended the second section as proposed by the Vidyasagar petitioners. By providing that 'all rights and interests which any widow may have by Law in her deceased husband's estate, either by way of maintenance or inheritance, shall, upon her second marriage cease and determine, as if she had then died', the petitioners had attempted to preempt further litigation. As explained by Colvile, the 'canon of inheritance which made the wife the heiress of her husband when he died without sons' gave her the property only for a specific purpose.

---

[75] Mr Peacock on third reading and passing of the Bill, 'To Remove All Legal Obstacles to the Marriage of Hindoo Widows', Proceedings of the Legislative Council of India, 19 July 1856, I.O.R., V/9/2, Col. 456.

[76] Cited by Arabinda Podder in his 'Introduction' to Vidyasagar, *Marriage of Hindu Widows* (Calcutta, repr., 1976), p. xi.

> In fact, the law gave it to her not for her own benefit, but from the notion that her prayers and sacrifices, and the employment of his wealth in religious and charitable acts, would be beneficial to her deceased husband in another state of existence. If then this Bill had enabled her to carry into the arms of another man, or into another family, the property which she had so acquired, its opponents might reasonably have objected...that, contrary to Hindoo law and Hindoo feeling, it enabled the widow to enjoy her deceased husband's estate freed from the trusts and conditions upon which alone the law gave it to her.[77]

Such a conundrum had been at the heart of objections to Act XXI 1850. Indeed, Section 2 was to become the focus of the deliberations of the Select Committee assigned to report upon the proposed law. Curiously, the second part of Section 2, proposed by the petitioners to guarantee to the widow her *stridhan* or property acquired by herself, did not appear anywhere in the Select Committee's final Report.[78]

On 26 January 1856, J.P. Grant moved that the Bill be referred to a Select Committee consisting of himself, Sir James Colvile, Mr Eliott and Mr Le Geyt, the latter of whom had expressed great enthusiasm for such a law as the result of his experience among the Maratha peoples of Western India. Upon the occasion of the first reading of the Bill, he had observed:

> In Western India, the prohibition against the marriage of Hindu widows was principally confined to Brahmins, and those sects which chose to imitate the practices of that class. Amongst other classes, the prohibition was not strictly regarded, and he had heard it frequently asserted that the state of higher morality which prevailed amongst the inferior grades of the Hindoo community in that Presidency was fully accounted for by that fact.[79]

Such a conviction concerning the inherent moral purpose of the proposed law bolstered the Select Committee in its response to those negative petitioners who insisted that the prohibition of widow marriage was prescribed by Hindu law and was an essential custom for respectable widows.

---

[77] Sir James Colvile on the first reading of the Bill 'To Remove All Legal Obstacles to the Marriage of Hindoo Widows', Proceedings of the Legislative Council of India, 17 November 1855, I.O.R. V/9/1, Cols 794–95.

[78] The text of 'An Act to Declare the Lawfulness of the Marriage of Hindu Widows', proposed by the Vidyasagar petitioners appears in *Board's Collections*, I.O.R., F/4/2691, Reg. 189069, pp. 15–16.

[79] Mr Le Geyt on the first reading of the Bill 'To Remove All Legal Obstacles to the Marriage of Hindoo Widows', Proceedings of the Legislative Council of India, 17 November 1855, I.O.R. V/9/1, Col. 796.

In its final Report to Council on 31 May 1856, the Committee merely reiterated the argument proffered by J.P. Grant and Sir James Colvile upon the occasion of the Bill's first reading. Thus, it was insisted that the proposed Bill was a very practical, enabling Act which made no effort to take sides in arguments about religious texts and customs.

In answer to the complaint that the new law would 'extend the operation of Act XXI of 1850, which, it is contended, is an unjust law, to a new class of persons...to widows who do not change their religion', the Committee simply asserted that Act XXI had established a principle of liberty of conscience. The Committee then rephrased the petitioners' objections in the most outrageous terms, namely:

> If a Hindoo widow turns Mahomedan...she may contract a valid marriage and...her children by such marriage will be legitimate...if the same widow remains a Hindoo...it is contended that the law of the land ought to make her incapable of contracting a valid marriage, and that, if she marries, following the dictates of her own conscience, she ought to be treated by the law of the land as a prostitute, and her children ought to be disinherited.

The Committee simply commented: 'We do not consider this to be a tenable doctrine'.[80]

Questions about inheritance raised by Section 2 of the proposed Bill were much more perplexing for the Committee than those of broad principle. There were petitioners who argued that 'the law, though professing to be merely permissive, will be in fact "compulsory" in regard to those whose rights of succession will be interfered with when widows remarry'.[81] In its final Report, the Select Committee resolved the several complicated cases submitted as evidence by petitioners with the statement that 'the one answer to all these cases is, that no marriageable person in a line of succession, if he or she wishes to marry, ought to be barred from marrying, merely because other heirs may thereby be disappointed in their expectation of success'.[82]

However, one case did attract the Committee's attention. According to the Hindu canon, a childless widow-daughter is excluded from inheritance on the grounds that 'being incapable of having lawful issue, she cannot continue

---

[80] Report of the Select Committee on the Bill, 'To Remove All Legal Obstacles to the Marriage of Hindoo Widows', Proceedings of the Legislative Council, 31 May 1856, *Board's Collections*, I.O.R., F/4/2691 #189069, pp. 248, 251.

[81] Petition submitted by Raja Radhakant Bahadoor (Deb) with 36,763 signatures, 17 March 1856, *Board's Collections*, I.O.R., F/4/2691 #189069, pp. 157–61.

[82] *Ibid.*, p. 249.

her father's line'. The Committee was unimpressed by this 'arbitrary' rule which was 'not very agreeable to natural justice or reason'. Nevertheless, 'adverting to the very complicated rules by which the order of succession of daughters is regulated, and to the probability that a very large class of widows will be indisposed to avail themselves of this law', the Committee inserted a new Section into the proposed law. Section 3 of Act XV decreed that the Act did not render any childless widow capable of inheriting.

One objection which the Committee found easy to sideline concerned the widow who, petitioners alleged, would neglect a dying husband's injunction that she adopt a son to perpetuate the family name and instead would be 'induced by the desire of worldly enjoyment' to take a second husband. The Committee's response was, unwittingly, a foreboding of lawsuits to come. They answered that 'the power of re-marriage cannot operate in the way of an inducement to adopt an heir to her deceased husband, because she cuts herself off from all such inheritance by re-marriage'.[83]

Negative petitions were not the only source of criticism of the Bill. Supporters from within the ranks of Government and among the thinkers of Young Bengal raised a variety of questions. Sir Robert Hamilton, the Agent of the Governor General for Central India, drew the attention of the Committee to two matters. First, he raised the concern that it would be disruptive in Hindu society for a widow to retain guardianship of her infant children after a second marriage. The Committee promptly agreed that to give the widow 'the power of removing the children of her late husband from their own family...would be socially inexpedient, and indeed unjust'. They therefore equated the widow's interest in her children with her interest in her late husband's property as an interest which would 'cease and determine' upon a second marriage. Second, regarding the widow's interest in her late husband's property, Sir Robert submitted the proposition that 'a widow ought not to be allowed to retain property left to her by her deceased husband for life by a will made before the passing of this Act'. In as much as two Commissioners in the N.W.P. expressed the same concern, the Committee decided to extend the principle of the second Section to 'all rights and interests which any Widow may have in her deceased husband's property...by virtue of any will...conferring upon her a limited interest in such property without the power of alienating the same'. All these 'rights and interests' were to terminate upon the occasion of a second marriage. The Committee then proceeded to strike off the proviso in the Vidyasagar petitioners' second Section which had guaranteed to the widow any property or *stridhan* acquired

---

[83] *Ibid.*, pp. 250–51.

apart from her deceased husband's estate. Instead, a newly minted Section simply stated that, except for the interest in her deceased husband's estate as described in previous sections pertaining to property and the guardianship of children, 'the widow shall not, by reason of her second marriage, forfeit any property, or any right to which she would otherwise be entitled'. And so the original Vidyasagar petitioners' references to *stridhan* and to the will of her late husband were removed from the description of property guaranteed to the widow. In the light of future litigation, the Committee's statement with regard to Section 2 rings a bit hollow. The Committee asserted that 'in no case is the forfeiture intended to be a penalty, or to operate as a restriction on a second marriage.'[84]

The avant-garde Derozians objected to Section 2 even as originally proposed in the Vidyasagar petition. Interestingly, two out of their three arguments hinged upon Act XXI 1850:

> Were a Hindoo widow to become a Christian or Mahomedan, and then marry, her civil rights would, under the Lex Loci Act, remain the same as before her conversion and marriage. But if continuing to be a Hindu, she married, her civil rights would be curtailed. This cannot but be felt as a grievous hardship, inflicted on her for a *conscientious adherence to her own religion.*

> Were a Hindoo widow, who has by law an interest in any property, to know that she would lose that interest by marrying, in many cases she would be deterred from marrying, and in some cases she would lead an immoral life.

And finally, the Derozians observed that the 'Lex Loci Act' guaranteed the widow 'her interest in her deceased husband's property…even if she leads an immoral life'. By contrast, under Section 2 of the proposed Bill, she would forfeit her property interest and thereby suffer 'a grievous injustice'.

The Derozians also insisted that it was necessary for the Vidyasagar petitioners' Section I to 'lay down in detail what shall constitute valid widow marriage'. They then submitted a draft of a General Marriage Law 'of a permissive character…such as would secure the object of the proposed Bill, without being interpreted into a direct interference with the religious usage of the Hindoos, a construction which the proposed law appears to be liable to'.[85] Unfortunately for the Derozians, Vidyasagar was not interested in changes in the 'institutional pattern of Hindu Marriage' and the Select

---

[84] *Ibid.*, pp. 253, 258–59.

[85] Native Inhabitants of Bengal, Petition submitted on 15 January 1856, Proceedings of the Legislative Council, 2 February 1856, *Board's Collections*, I.O.R., F/4/2691 #189069, pp. 89–92.

Committee followed his lead. Only in the interest of 'greater security and the removal of all doubts' did the Committee add a provision which was to become Section VI of Act XV with the effect that ceremonies valid for a first marriage were to be considered valid for the marriage of a widow.[86]

During the final debate on the Bill on 12 July 1856, J.P. Grant proposed two amendments. Both were accepted by the Legislative Council as the result of an underlying preoccupation with the need to assuage the fears of the orthodox Hindu community. In both cases, the amendments seized upon language which was perceived to be arbitrary in the Bill as presented by the Select Committee. Universal prohibitions were modified to encourage the remarriage of widows, but the modifications were incorporated in elaborate verbiage clearly directed at the disapproving orthodox.

In the first instance, Grant wished to modify the Committee's 'absolute forfeiture of a widow's right of guardianship over her deceased husband's children on her re-marriage'. He proposed that the one-sentence decree concerning the widow's right of guardianship be removed from concerns over her interest in property in Section 2 and become the subject of a new Section 3. The effect of the new Section 3 was to guarantee to the widow guardianship over her children if she had been appointed guardian by the will of her deceased husband. As explained by Grant:

> Under the Bill the widow's right of guardianship would depend upon the same principle as her own right of inheritance...If a deceased husband had appointed his widow the guardian of his children, without qualification, that would be a case analogous to the case of a deceased husband having made his widow a legatee without qualification.[87]

After the Council agreed to the new Section 3, the Bill expanded to contain seven sections. One sentence in the Select Committee's Bill terminating the widow's guardianship over her children upon a second marriage became a monster paragraph forming a new section. Not only did the new section list all the relatives eligible to petition the Court to challenge the widow's right of guardianship, but it also listed guidelines for the Court in honouring these petitions unless the widow's rights were expressly protected by her deceased husband's will.[88] In addition, there was the consideration that all this emphasis upon a will was only valid in Bengal, because Hindu wills were

---

[86] Benoy Ghose, *op. cit.*, p. 71; Report of Select Committee..., 31 May 1856, *op. cit.*, p. 252.

[87] J.P. Grant, Proceedings of the Legislative Council of India, 12 July 1856, I.O.R., V/9/2, cols 438–39.

[88] Cf. Section 2 of 'Bill as amended by the Select Committee', *Board's Collections*, I.O.R., F/4/2691, Reg. 189069, p. 258.

Civil Law and Religious Toleration 285

not valid in other parts of India. In fact, the Judges of the Madras Sudder Court had raised this point as an objection before the Select Committee. But the Committee had ruled that in Bengal the provision for a will was 'indispensable'.[89]

The second amendment requested by Grant and approved by the Council touched upon the consent of a male relative required for a widow remarrying as a minor. Grant was concerned that Section VI of the Bill as presented by the Select Committee automatically invalidated the marriage contracted by a widow as a minor 'without the required consent of any of her male relatives'. Instead, he proposed what became Section VII of Act XV 1856. The only positive innovation was the provision that 'no such marriage shall be declared void after it has been consummated'. Thus Grant allowed for a couple who might cohabit for years raising children and grandchildren despite the lack of consent of a male relative. Very like the amendment contained in the new Section 3 about rights of guardianship, the new Section VII, before stating the modification allowing for the reality of consummation, listed at length all the male relations eligible to give consent for a minor to remarry and decreed a fine or prison term up to a year for 'all persons knowingly abetting a marriage made contrary to the provisions of this Section'.[90]

It should be remarked that neither of these issues so elaborately expanded upon in amendments were raised either by the Vidyasagar petitioners or the Derozians. Nonetheless, the members of the Legislative Council, having exhausted their consciences inventing and reinventing scenarios in order to appease orthodox opinion, reported the Bill. A week later, on 19 July 1856, Mr Barnes Peacock extolled the proposed Bill as a victory for liberty of conscience. Emphasizing the enabling character of the new law, he asserted that 'the Bill would not prevent any Hindoo from acting according to his own belief that the Hindoo religion forbade the marriage of widows; but it would enable those who entertained a different belief to act upon it'. Then, Grant's motion that the Bill be read a third time and passed was carried.[91]

Epilogue

When the historian comes to evaluate the impact of Act XV 1856, a feeling of tragic irony is overwhelming. In Bengal especially, Vidyasagar faced immense

---

[89] Final Report of Select Committee, *Ibid.*, pp. 247–55.
[90] J.P. Grant, Proceedings of the Legislative Council of India, 12 July 1856, I.O.R., V/9/2, Cols 442–43.
[91] Mr Peacock, Proceedings of the Legislative Council of India, 19 July 1856, I.O.R., V/9/2, Cols 454, 456 and 458.

disappointment. In the first instance, it must be acknowledged, as remarked by Amales Tripathi, that 'the Derozians never aimed at the general adoption of the practise by all Hindus'. After the enactment of Act XV, lower castes persisted in imitating the prohibitions decreed by the orthodox higher castes while the liberal, educated Bengalis began to be swept along with the tides of Hindu nationalism and Hindu revivalism. As observed by Gopal Haldar, the editor of Vidyasagar's Bengali writings, the rise of Hindu revivalism after 1870 'made reform through government legislation by alien rulers suspect, even undesirable and indirectly put a premium on orthodoxy and even on obscurantism'. In Bengal, Vidyasagar cut a lonely figure, dubbed by some as 'Don Quixote in a dhoti'. Even Debendranath Tagore and Ramprasad Roy retreated from the cause of widow remarriage. Promised funds in support of widow marriage ceremonies were not forthcoming. With the advantage of hindsight, Benoy Ghose attributed the dismal reality of widow remarriage in Bengal in the wake of Act XV to Vidyasagar's determination to accomplish radical reform of custom and yet preserve traditional ceremonies. Ghose remarked that 'the gap in the Act pointed out by the Derozians grew evident as the Act was translated into practise'. In 1872, most of the Derozians' suggestions were incorporated into a Civil Marriage Act. In the face of opportunistic polygamists who took advantage of the hapless widows to extract money from patrons of widow marriage, Vidyasagar used his own money to the extent of borrowing 50,000 rupees. Ultimately, he drafted a contract of agreement which parties to the marriage were compelled to sign. The Derozians were thus indirectly vindicated for their original criticisms of the proposals for Act XV.[92]

Part of the irony enveloping Act XV was the fact that positive leadership for the plight of Hindu widows finally came, not from Bengal, but from the Arya Samaj in the Punjab and the Prarthana Samaj in Maharashtra. Inspiration for the cause of widows came from Malabari, Justice Ranade and D.K. Karve—all from Maharashtra.[93] As concluded by Gopal Haldar, Vidyasagar was disgusted by 'the shameful indifference...of the bhadralok in general, and the low morality of the men who often contracted widow

---

[92] Amales Tripathi, *Vidyasagar—The Traditional Moderniser* (Calcutta, 1974), pp. 62, 64; Benoy Ghose, *op. cit.*, pp. 70–71 and Gopal Haldar, *Vidyasagar—A Reassessment* (New Delhi, 1972), pp. 48–49.

[93] For fascinating accounts of D.K. Karve's second marriage to a widow in Poona in 1893, see D.D. Karve, *The New Brahmans—Five Maharashtrian Families* (Berkeley, California, 1963), pp. 11–104.

remarriage in Bengal'.[94] From the vantage point of a century later, Asok Sen discerns that Vidyasagar as a 'traditional modernizer' was necessarily doomed to failure by the colonial context in which he operated. Although Vidyasagar, himself, 'was never involved in parasitic landlordism, expedient usury or predatory commerce', his 'untiring will for positive social action' was totally frustrated by the 'critical social void of the middle class in nineteenth century Bengal, its values and their necessary inanity'.[95] From a broader, post-colonial perspective, Partha Chatterjee argues cogently that in the latter decades of the nineteenth century, the 'women's question'—so much a focus of social reform during the Renaissance of the early part of the century—disappeared from the agenda of the nationalist movement. For the nationalist leaders, women in the home became 'the principal site for expressing the spiritual quality of the national culture' which rendered India 'superior to the West and hence undominated and sovereign'.[96]

The most bitter betrayal of hapless Hindu widows in the last decades of the nineteenth century and early decades of the twentieth was perpetrated by judges in the High Courts of Calcutta, Bombay and Madras. This was despite a Privy Council ruling in 1880 in support of the Hindu widow's right to her first husband's estate. In Moniram Kolita vs. Kerry Kolitany the widow defendant caused a stir subsequent to claiming lands in her deceased husband's estate by taking a paramour and having a child by him. The cousin of her deceased first husband, according to the Bengal *Dayabhaga*, was next in line after her as heir to these lands. This cousin filed the original suit in 1870 to recover the lands as ancestral lands to which he was entitled; he did not charge unchastity. As the case was appealed from Munsiff to Deputy Commissioner to the Calcutta High Court and finally to the Privy Council, two questions were formulated:

(1) Whether under Hindu law as administered in Bengal...a widow who has once inherited the estate of a deceased husband is liable to forfeit that estate by reason of unchastity
(2) Whether the forfeiture, if any, is barred by Act XXI 1850

There was extensive debate and reference to *Dayabhaga* texts cited by Dwarkanath Mitter, one of the minority judges on the Calcutta bench, urging

---

[94] Gopal Haldar, *op. cit.*, p. 49.
[95] Asok Sen, *Iswar Chandra Vidyasagar and his Elusive Milestones* (Calcutta, 1977), pp. 149–50, 165.
[96] Partha Chatterjee, *The Nation and Its Fragments* (Princeton, 1993), pp. 132, 126.

'the childless widow' to keep 'unsullied the bed of her lord' in order to 'enjoy with moderation the property until her death'. However, the justices of the Privy Council also considered 'the great mischief, uncertainty and confusion' among other heirs of her husband 'that might follow upon the affirmance of the doctrine that a widow's estate is forfeited for unchastity, particularly in the present constitution of Hindu society, and the relaxation of so many of the precepts relating to Hindu widows'. They ruled accordingly that 'under the Hindu law as administered in the Bengal school, a widow who has once inherited the estate of a deceased husband is not liable to forfeit that estate by reason of unchastity' and that it was not necessary to decide the second question because the widow defendant had 'never been degraded or deprived of caste'.[97]

However, the judges of the High Courts of Calcutta, Bombay and Madras paid little heed to the decree of the Privy Council. In her study of the case law in the wake of Act XV 1856, Lucy Carroll demonstrates beyond all doubt that these judges were determined to enforce the forfeiture of the deceased husband's estate for all Hindu widows upon remarriage as decreed by Section 2 of Act XV regardless of 'whether or not the validity of their marriage derived from the Act'. Particularly in Calcutta, judges were prone to insist that 'if Section 2 did not apply, the same forfeiture was enjoined by Hindu law'.[98] In the case of Matungini Gupta vs. Ram Rutton Roy, Justice Wilson insisted upon applying both Act XV 1856 and a text from *Vrihaspati* to the defendant even though as a widow, after inheriting her deceased husband's estate, she had converted to the Brahmo Samaj and remarried according to the provisions of the Civil Marriage Act of 1872. Justice Wilson and his colleagues were obsessed with the view of *Vrihaspati* that 'Of him whose wife is not deceased half the body survives. How then should another take his property while half his person is alive?' Wilson could not justify the thought of a widow retaining the estate of her first husband when she 'ceases to be the wife or half the body of her late husband and becomes the wife and half the body of another man'. This line of reasoning led the dissenting Justice Prinsep to exclaim in disbelief:

> We have...the anomaly that, although she may change her religion and cease to be a Hindu, so long as she remains a widow, she continues as a Hindu to hold her husband's estate, that she does not forfeit this by leading a notoriously unchaste life (Moniram v. Kolitani) but that if she remarries she forfeits,

---

[97] Moniram Kolita v. Kerry Kolitany, Privy Council (1880), Law Reports 7, Indian Appeals, pp. 115, 143–44, 147 and 153–54.

[98] Lucy Carroll, *op. cit.*, p. 5.

because she ceases to be a widow and because the conditions under which she retained her husband's estate as part of his body no longer exist.[99]

While Calcutta justices were hypnotized by the 'half-body' metaphor, dismissed by the dissenting Justice Prinsep as 'that legal fiction', in the case of Vithu vs. Govinda, Bombay High Court justices focused on the enacting language of Act XV. Apparently without benefit of access to the debates in the 1855–56 India Legislative Council, the justices concluded that they should ignore assertions in the preamble declaring the legislature's enabling intention of simply removing the disability afflicting high-caste widows prohibited from remarrying. Chief Justice Farran argued that the general language of Sections I and II extended 'to all Hindus alike whatever their caste or the interpretation of the Hindu law authorized by their caste may be'. It was a sad irony that Justice Ranade, himself the second husband of a Hindu widow and an advocate of widow remarriage as well as women's education, endorsed the Chief Justice's argument. Ruling that a widow of the Kunbi caste necessarily forfeited upon remarriage the estate of her first husband which she had claimed upon the death of her infant son, Ranade accepted the 'general words of the enacting clauses' of Act XV as beyond the control of the language of the preamble. Curiously, Ranade assumed that the 1856 Legislature had consulted Arthur Steele's *Law and Custom of Hindoo Castes Within the Dekhun*... where Steele had listed the Kunbi caste as one of 60 'in which when a widow performed Pat [a second marriage], her husband's relatives succeeded to her husband's estate' and had thereby come to the conclusion that forfeiture of property upon remarriage was a 'universal practice'. Noting that 'there is not a single caste mentioned in which any custom to the contrary prevailed', Ranade reasoned that 'this fact must have been present to the mind of the legislature, and explains the omission of all qualifying words' in Section 2. Ranade speculated further that the Legislative Council was ignorant of the fact that only the 'higher castes...numerically less than twenty percent of the population enforced the prohibition against widow remarriage'. This is how he explained the discrepancy between the enabling language of the preamble and the general prescriptive language of Sections II, III and VI regarding the remarried widow's forfeiture of her first husband's estate, guardianship of any children by her first husband and acceptable content of the second marriage ceremony.[100] Surprisingly, Lucy Carroll joins in similarly wild speculations. On the basis of the ceremonies

---

[99] Matungini Gupta v. Ram Rutton Roy (1891), ILR 19 Calcutta 289, pp. 292, 300.
[100] Vithu v. Govinda (1896), ILR 22 Bombay 321, pp. 326–27, 330–31.

prescribed in Section VI, she asserts that 'the legislators believed themselves to be writing on *tabula rasa*.[101] As shown in the above account of debates in the Legislative Council, nothing could be further from the truth. The Legislative Council enacted Sections II–IV, VI and VII in response to specific cases or objections raised by petitioners or government officers. Over and over again, the councillors insisted that they had no desire to take sides in religious debates. In any event, with the Bombay ruling in Vithu v. Govinda, the die was cast. And, the Madras High Court ultimately ruled that no plea of custom of nonforfeiture could prevail against 'an express statutory enactment to the contrary' such as Section 2 of Act XV 1856.[102]

There seemed little hope of sustaining in India the spirit behind the Privy Council decision in Kolita vs. Kolitany. Of all the High Courts, only the Allahabad High Court rose to this challenge. Beginning in 1889 with the case of Har Saran Das vs. Nandi,[103] the Allahabad High Court established a tradition elevating customary law over the statutory law linked with the Hindu law traditions of the presidency courts. The Allahabad tradition culminated in Bhola Umar vs. Kausilla in 1932. Chief Justice Suleiman took inspiration from the Privy Council's 1880 decision. He noted that the Privy Council interpreted Dayabhaga texts enjoining 'the childless widow' to keep 'unsullied the bed of her lord' and to persevere 'in religious observances' as 'conditions [which] concerned the right of succession to the estate and did not lay down conditions for its retention when once vested'. Chief Justice Suleiman refused to regard the Privy Council's ruling as a 'premium on unchastity' whereby the widow 'can retain the property so long as she remains notoriously unchaste but the moment she remarries she will forfeit it'. He reasoned:

> It is now well settled, according to the authoritative pronouncement made by the Privy Council upon an interpretation of the texts relating to the conditions attaching to inheritance by the Hindu widow, that she is not divested of her estate by living in unchastity. When open unchastity does not entail forfeiture, it would *prima facie* follow that a remarriage would not; for if according to strict Hindu law and orthodox Hindu religion a remarriage be invalid, it is then tantamount to unchastity. Further, the strict and orthodox Hindu law cannot logically be invoked, in order to furnish a rule of forfeiture on remarriage, applicable in the case of those castes which, in derogation of

---

[101] Lucy Carroll, *op. cit.*, pp. 5, 13.
[102] Gajapathi Naidu v. Jeevammal, AIR 1929 Madras, 765.
[103] Har Saran Das v. Nandi (1889), ILR 11 Allahabad, 330.

that strict and orthodox law, have recognized and permitted the remarriage of widows.

Thus the Allahabad High Court ruled that Act XV 1856 did not apply to castes which had allowed widow remarriage before 1856 and that, in order to deprive a remarried widow of the estate of her first husband to which she had already succeeded, a custom requiring such forfeiture must be proved. As for Section 2 of Act XV 1856, Chief Justice Suleiman helpfully speculated about the motivation of the 1855–56 Legislative Council. He simply noted that Section 2 was expressly provided out of the consideration 'that remarriage, where it is not allowed by custom, should not disturb the relations of the deceased husbands or their estate'. This was a far more accurate assessment of the rationale for Section 2 than that of Justices in the late nineteenth century such as Farran and Ranade of Bombay and Wilson of Calcutta or of more recent scholars such as Lucy Carroll. Perhaps Chief Justice Suleiman consulted the 1855–56 proceedings of the Legislative Council.[104]

Regardless of the humane ruling of the Allahabad High Court, the Sanskrit scholar, P.V. Kane, writing about the same time as Chief Justice Suleiman, remarked that 'owing to the sentiment of centuries, widow remarriage is still looked down upon and during more than eighty years since the Act was passed not many widows have taken advantage of it'.[105] Pressures of Sanskritization among lower castes and non-Hindu tribes combined with the forfeiture of property penalty levied by the presidency courts to leave the Hindu widow in a position of checkmate. Finally, exactly one hundred years after Act XV 1856 endeavoured to give the Hindu widow the right to remarry, the independent Government of India enacted Section 14 of the Hindu Succession Act which converted the limited-to-life estate of a Hindu female into an estate of which she was the full and absolute owner. To give Lucy Carroll the last word:

[I]n law the remarried Hindu widow, after a century of penalty and forfeiture, is no longer in a worse legal position than the widow who lived in 'notorious unchastity' but wisely did not permit her paramour to make her an honest (and property-less) woman.[106]

---

[104] Bhola Umar vs. Kausilla (1932), ILR 55 Allahabad 24, pp. 25, 45.
[105] P.V. Kane, *op. cit.*, p. 616. J.D.M. Derrett also remarked: 'It is of great interest that although enlightened Hindu sentiment was behind that statute (passed in 1856) even now, a century afterwards, the permission granted by it is rarely utilized and the religious prejudice against remarriage of widows has not diminished'. J.D.M. Derrett, *op. cit.*, p. 320.
[106] Lucy Carroll, *op. cit.*, p. 26.

Hindu Wills

As seen above, Hindu wills in Bengal played an important role in the stifling of Hindu widow remarriage. On a more fundamental level, the introduction of Hindu wills represented a clash between judicial and cultural traditions. On the face of it, a will was totally unnecessary in the traditional Hindu family. Indeed, the Privy Council declared in 1856 that 'in ancient Hindu law...testamentary instruments, in the sense applied by English lawyers to that expression, were unknown'. Furthermore, according to Thomas Strange, 'the Hindu language has no terms to express what we mean by a will'.[107] As explained by one legal scholar, a will by a Hindu

> is a rare, it may be said, almost an impossible occurrence. The orthodox Hindu contemplates the claims of his children and dependants as indefeasible; they, in turn, reverence as laws the authority and wishes of the ancestor. When, in contemplation of death, or when resolved to become morally dead to the world, the Hindu proprietor usually causes to be written a document in which he gives an account, more or less detailed, of his possessions and of his affairs, together with his injunctions to those who are to occupy his place in the community. The religious necessity of male posterity, care and protection of the entire family, observance of the family *sraddha*s and the accustomed ritual of worship...are primary considerations.[108]

Such Hindu custom was specifically protected by early legislation contained in Sec. 2 of Bengal Regulation V 1799 and defended by the Elphinstone Code.[109]

It is speculated that the first Hindu wills to be produced in courts were made by Calcutta residents 'possibly influenced in their action by the example of their Christian and Mahomedan fellow citizens'.[110] By the end of the Company period the Privy Council confidently declared that 'the ancient law has long since been relaxed and throughout Bengal a man who is the absolute owner of property may now dispose of it by will if he pleases'.[111]

---

[107] Nagalutchonee Ummal v. Gopoo Nadaraja Chetty (1856), 6 M.I.A., pp. 344–45.

[108] Montriou on 'Hindu Wills', cited by Arthur Philips and Sir Ernest John Trevelyan, *The Law Relating to Hindu Wills* (London, 1914), p. 3.

[109] Bengal Regulation V, 1799, I.O.R., V/8/17; Bombay Regulation IV, 'prescribing the forms of proceeding of the Courts of Law in Civil Suits and Appeals and Rules for trial of the same (passed by Governor in Council 1 Jan 1827), sec. 26, I.O.R., V/8/24.

[110] Arthur Philips and Sir Ernest John Trevelyan, *op. cit.*, p. 2.

[111] Nagalutchonee Ummal v. Gopoo Nadaraja Chetty (1856), 6 M.I.A., pp. 344–45.

And subsequently, the Hindu Wills Act of 1870 repealed sec. 2 of Bengal Regulation V 1799 'so far as it relates to executors of persons who are not Muhammadans, but are subject to the jurisdiction of District Courts' in Bengal.[112] Ten years later, sec. 154 of the Probate and Administration Act V 1881 provided rules for the probate of wills of Hindus, Jains, Sikhs and Buddhists throughout Bengal and in the towns of Madras and Bombay.

Inasmuch as testamentary powers were recognized as part of Hindu law, the courts, bound to apply Hindu law 'in matters relating to inheritance and succession', referred to the Hindu law of gifts in order to interpret Hindu wills with respect to the beneficiaries and the actual property transferred. Old prejudices and customs undermining the rights of women could interfere with the provisions of a will. Adoption was one means of displacing the heir of a testator. One case which went all the way to the Privy Council reflected 'the desire to exclude females, which...persisted in spite of their recognition as heirs'. The tactic challenged in Soorjeemoney Dossee Sreemutty v. Denobundhoo Mullick in 1857 was the prescription of successors in future generations. The testator had made an 'absolute gift of his real and personal estate to his five sons', and, 'in the event of any of the five sons dying without son or sons, there was a gift over to such of his sons or son's sons as should be alive'.[113]

Adultery and Polygamy

Two other issues which became the subject of legislative debate were adultery and abuses committed by Kulin Brahmins in connection with their privilege of polygamy. Both these issues were deemed to be too intricately entwined with caste custom to merit regulation enforceable in the Company's criminal courts. In instances of adultery, magistrates were aware of inequities in Hindu law which prescribed that a woman guilty of adultery with someone of inferior caste was 'to be eaten by Dogs, or burnt with faggots', whereas a man committing adultery with an unmarried girl of inferior caste, even if 'done by violence', was only subject to a 'small fine'.[114] In the 1830s Sudder

---

[112] Hindu Wills Act XXI of 1870, I.O.R., V/8/42.
[113] Soorjeemoney Dossee Sreemutty v. Denobundhoo Mullick (1857), 6 M.I.A., 516. Cf. Arthur Phillips and Sir Ernest John Trevelyan, *op. cit.*, pp. 5, 45, 118.
[114] Charles Grant, *Observations on the State of Society Among the Asiatic Subjects of Great Britain, Particularly with Respect to Morals; and on the Means of Improving It* (London: 1813), fol. 60.

Courts of the Lower and Western Provinces of Bengal became embroiled in controversy over whether magistrates of criminal courts were empowered 'to compel a married woman to return to her husband against her will'. It was concluded that such cases could only be heard in the civil courts according to Sec. 5 Bengal Regulation II 1803. At the same time, the Law Commissioners concluded that there were no grounds for making any provision in the Penal Code for punishment of adultery.[115]

On the subject of polygamy, more than 30 petitions signed by upwards of 10,000 high-caste Bengalis were presented to the Legislative Council in June 1856. Petitioners, who included the esteemed Sanskritist, Vidyasagar, recounted the horrific abuses committed by Kulin Brahmins whose high rank and privilege was essentially an aberration created by Raja Bullal Sen before the Muslim conquest. Whereas this comparatively modern innovation prohibited the superior Kulin Brahmins from marrying their daughters to Brahmins of inferior classes, inferior classes of Brahmins were willing to pay large sums of money in order to marry their daughters to the superior Kulins. Individual Kulins were 'known to marry more than a hundred wives each, and it is customary with them, immediately after going through the nuptial ceremonies and receiving their gratuities, to leave the houses of the girls they have married, never to see their faces more'. Concealed, forced abortions, sometimes resulting in the deaths of mother and child, were among the gruesome ramifications of this custom. Petitioners called for the Legislative Council to enforce the Hindu law against these irregularities. But the high status of the Kulins prevailed as the Council was distracted by the events of 1857 from any fresh legislative initiatives.[116]

---

[115] J.F.M. Reid, Register, Nizamut Adawlut, Fort William, to Register, Nizamut Adawlut, Western Provinces, 1 August 1831, Extract from Legislative Proceedings, 18 December 1837, I.O.R., *Board's Collections* F/4/1765 Reg. 72317, fol. 8; Circular from H.B. Harington, Officiating Register, Nizamut Adawlut, North Western Provinces, to the Several Criminal Authorities in the North Western Provinces, 20 January 1837, *Ibid.*, fol. 10; Legislative Despatch, to India, 15 May 1844, No. 10, I.O.R., E/4/778, fols 454–55.

[116] 'Petition from Maha Rajah of Burdwan against Hindoo Polygamy', India Legislative Proceedings, 28 June 1856, O.I.O.C., V/9/2, Cols 416–18.

5

Abkarry and Pilgrim Taxes: Excise as a Regulating Instrument

Excise is a hateful tax levied upon commodities and adjudged, not by the common judges of property, but wretches hired by those to whom Excise is paid.[1]

In 1790, Governor General Cornwallis became determined to reform the collection of the excise on intoxicating drugs and liquor, known in India as Abkarry.[2] Bengal Regulation XXXIII passed on 19 April 1790 resumed the collection of Abkarry from landholders and put it in the hands of Government 'for the purpose of reforming abuses in these collections and thereby affording benefit to the commerce of the country'.[3] Three years later, Bengal Regulation XXVII revised these rules in the wake of Governor General Cornwallis' decision that 'all duties, taxes and other collections coming under the denomination of sayer [excise]…be forthwith abolished' with the exception of the Pilgrim Tax levied at Gaya and other places and the Abkarry which, at that time, was defined as an excise on intoxicating liquors and drugs.[4]

---

[1] Definition of excise by Samuel Johnson in first edition of his Dictionary, cited by Chief Justice in the course of debate on Abkaree Revenue Bill, India Legislative Proceedings, 6 September 1856, I.O.R., V/9/2, Cols 551–52.

[2] 'Abkarry' is derived from the Persian word 'Abkari' meaning 'the business of distilling or selling (strong) waters, and hence elliptically the excise upon such business'. Henry Yule and A.C. Burnell, William Crooke, eds., *Hobson-Jobson—A Glossary of Anglo-Indian Colloquial Words and Phrases* (London, repr.: 1969), p. 2.

[3] Bengal Revenue Regulation XXXIII (passed by Governor General in Council on 19 April 1790), I.O.R., V/8/15.

[4] Bengal Regulation XXVII for re-enacting, with Alterations and Modifications, Rules passed by the Governor General in Council on 11 June and 28 July 1790 for the Resumption and Abolition of Sayer or internal Duties and Taxes, throughout Bengal, Behar and Orissa (passed by Governor General in Council on 1 May 1793), I.O.R., V/8/16, p. 251.

On the same day Bengal Regulation XXXIV reenacted rules passed since 1790 to prevent the 'illicit Manufacture and Vend' of intoxicating liquors and drugs. With these rules, the Cornwallis Government legitimized the Abkarry system as a government regulated process of farming the privilege of producing and selling 'spirituous liquors' and 'intoxicating drugs' to contractors who also managed sales through retail shopkeepers. It was explained in the preamble that such government control was made necessary by 'the immoderate use of spirituous liquors and intoxicating drugs having become prevalent amongst many of the lower orders of the people, from the very inconsiderable price at which they were manufactured and sold and the proceedings of the criminal courts in a great measure, ascribable to the want of proper restrictions on the manufacture and vend of such liquors and drugs'.[5]

Bengal Regulation VI of 1800 further refined the ever evolving Abkarry rules 'so as to render the Tax more conducive to the Purposes of Police'. Acknowledging that the tax had so far failed to 'operate as a sufficient check on the immoderate use' of intoxicating drugs and liquors, Sections XIX and XX called for 'enhancing the price to the consumer...without giving rise to clandestine manufacture and vend of articles liable to tax and without its operating as a virtual prohibition of the use of [the stills]'. Section XIX called for magistrates to be given 'a more immediate and efficient control over the conduct of the vendors, and to render the tax as much as possible conducive to the general purposes of police'. It was also decreed by Section XXV that the working of stills for the manufacture of spirituous liquors was prohibited in major cities such as Moorshedabad, Patna, Dacca and Benares because they were 'considered a public nuisance...occasioning a great degree of filth and an accumulation of putrid substances, highly prejudicial to the health of the inhabitants'. As a further refinement, Section VIII baldly declared *cherrus* and *muddut* (or *koppah*) to be noxious drugs, the use of which was 'always highly prejudicial and dangerous to health' and therefore Collectors were forbidden to issue licenses for the manufacture and sale of these substances. Any production or promotion of these drugs became a criminal offense.[6]

---

[5] Bengal Regulation XXXIV for reenacting with Modifications, the Rules passed on the 16 April 1790 and subsequent dates, for levying tax upon intoxicating liquors and drugs, and for preventing the illicit Manufacture and Vend of them (passed by Governor General in Council on 1 May 1793), I.O.R., V/8/16, p. 299.

[6] Bengal Regulation VI for defining the Tax to be levied on the Sale of intoxicating Drugs and Toddy; and for amending the existing Rules relative to the licensed Sale of these Articles, as well as Sale of spirituous liquors, generally, so as to render the Tax more conducive to the Purposes of Police (passed by Governor General in Council on 27 March 1800), I.O.R., V/8/17, pp. 169–79.

Interestingly, *cherrus*, described in Hunter's *Hindostanee Dictionary* as 'the exudation of the flowers of hemp, collected with the dew; and prepared for use as an intoxicating drug' was to be taken off the list of banned substances by Bengal Regulation VII of 1824 which decreed that *cherrus* was 'not as noxious as supposed—no more so than ganja'. In contrast, both *muddut* which was described as 'a composition of opium and paun leaves, formed into balls and smoked like tobacco' and *koppah* which was 'understood to be cloth steeped in an infusion of opium' remained proscribed.[7] It was the opium formed into balls for smoking which was in demand in the Chinese market.

As might be expected in the case of the continuous evolution of 'Rules', both Bengal Regulations XXXIV of 1793 and VI of 1800 were superseded by Bengal Regulation X 1813.[8] Regulation X consolidated all rules previously legislated to control the trade in intoxicating drugs and liquors. For the first time, *putchwye* was added to *taury* or *toddy* in a list of intoxicating substances, and opium was specifically mentioned as an intoxicating drug. *Taury* or the juice extracted from the Tar or Palm tree, from the *khajoor* or date tree, and, in southern India, from the *nariyul* or cocoanut tree could only be sold under license subject to tax regardless of whether it was in a fermented or unfermented state. *Putchwye* consisted of boiled rice which was mixed with various drugs and then fermented.[9] In the case of spirituous liquors, the Bengal Board of Revenue, together with the Revenue Commissioners, was 'to cause the highest rates of duty to be fixed which can be introduced, without giving rise to illicit manufacture and sale of spirits'. The same Revenue officers were to determine the rate of duty on *taury*, *putchwye* and intoxicating drugs including opium. *Cherrus, muddut* or *koppah* remained forbidden for their 'noxious quality'. As for opium, Collectors were to discourage its sale and consumption 'except for medicinal purposes'. Finally, Regulation X set forth an elaborate set of licensing forms. There was a license for vendors of liquor obtained from the Sudder distilleries established by Revenue Commissioners in principal towns; there was a form for a Pass authorizing daily delivery to

---

[7] Section XV, Bengal Regulation VII for explaining and amending certain parts of the Regulations respecting the manufacture and sale of Spirituous Liquors and Intoxicating Drugs, and for enacting certain Rules for the better security of Revenue derived from the exclusive manufacture and sale of Opium (passed by Governor General in Council on 25 March 1824), I.O.R., V/8/20. For definitions of drugs, see J.H. Harington, *op. cit.*, Third Part, p. 187n.

[8] Bengal Regulation X for reducing to one Regulation, with Alterations and Amendments, Regulations at present in force respecting the Manufacture and Sale of spirituous Liquors, intoxicating Drugs, Taury and Putchwye (passed by Governor General in Council on 21 August 1813), I.O.R., V/8/18, pp. 537–51.

[9] J.H. Harington, *op. cit.*, p. 177n.

the vendor of a certain number of gallons from the Sudder distillery; there was a license for persons 'authorized to manufacture and sell spirits…beyond the boundaries prescribed for the Sudder Distilleries'; there was a license for persons 'authorized to manufacture Spirits at one Place and to retail at another…beyond the Boundaries prescribed for the Sudder Distilleries' and there was a license for persons 'authorized to vend Taury, Putchwye and intoxicating drugs, including Opium'. Because enforcement powers vested in magistrates were rescinded by Section XXXII, all the licenses issued by the Collectors vested responsibility for public order in the licensee. Thus, every licensee undertook not to 'harbour robbers, thieves or riotous persons, but on the contrary, give information to the nearest Magistrate or police officer of any suspected persons who may resort to his shop'. A vendor of intoxicating drugs was also required to 'prevent gaming and disorder within his shop'.[10] Two decades later, the distinguished Company servant and, ultimately a Director, Henry St. George Tucker ruefully observed: 'The Abkar is always a person of very low caste; and it was heretofore held to be a pollution to any respectable Hindoo to enter his shop. Before the year 1790 few shops were tolerated in a Hindoo district'.[11]

Opium Monopoly

The fact that opium is not specifically mentioned as part of the Abkarry Mehal until Bengal Regulation X 1813 obscures the significance of the opium trade to the Company's revenues. Indeed, the Abkarry Mehal accounts for 1806–07 in the distant Ceded Provinces revealed revenues 'progressively increasing' by a sum of nearly 65,000 rupees in net collections for a grand total of over four lakhs.[12] Six years earlier, an increase of over 1¼ lakhs between the years 1800/1 and 1801/2 had been reported in the net collections of Abkarry revenue in the whole of the Bengal presidency. At the time, the Company's

---

[10] Bengal Regulation X 1813, *op. cit.*, Secs XIV–XVII and XXXII. The license for a vendor of intoxicating drugs actually represented a modification of the license form in Bengal Regulation VI 1800 which required the vendor to 'prevent to the utmost of his power, all drunkenness, gaming and disorder within his shop'. See Bengal Regulation VI 1800, *op. cit.*

[11] Henry St. George Tucker, John William Kaye, ed., *Memorials of Indian Government; Being a Selection from the papers of Henry St. George Tucker, Late Director of the East India Co.* (London, 1853), p. 487.

[12] Board of Revenue to Lord Minto, Governor General in Council, 14 August 1807, Bengal Revenue Proceedings, 28 August 1807, Nos 43–44, I.O.R., P/55/4.

Directors in London assumed a righteous stance. They declared that, if the 'excess' revenue arose from 'an increased consumption of the Articles' rather than 'an improved mode of Collection of the duties', they would 'regard it as a matter of regret, rather than of satisfaction'.[13]

Such twinges of conscience, barely reflected in the Regulations which held licensees responsible for public order, were almost nonexistent in abbreviated debate over the establishment of a Government monopoly of the opium trade. Reviewing trade statistics for the opium trade monopoly in Behar since the establishment of English influence by the Battle of Plassey, Warren Hastings' Revenue Council observed a healthy growth of trade from 800 to 1800 chests over two years, an increase in price paid to the *ryot* and protection of the *ryot* from any pressure to cultivate the poppy against his will. When Warren Hastings argued for the creation of a government monopoly of the opium trade, his prime concern was to resist the clamour of 'Adventurers allured by the profits of this Trade'. He made the briefest of references to a sense of moral constraint as part of his rebuttal to those who argued for competition and free trade. Thus, he stated categorically that opium was 'a pernicious Article of Luxury, which ought not to be permitted but for the purposes of Foreign Commerce only, and which the Wisdom of Government should carefully restrain from internal Consumption'. At the time Hastings was obviously unaware of the tragic consequences to the Chinese opium smoker of his skewed moral compass. He settled for the pragmatic argument that regulation of the monopoly was less hazardous than abolition. Indeed, He even remarked that 'the Subject is not of much importance in itself'.[14]

The consideration which clearly swayed the decision of the Revenue Council to create a Government monopoly was revenue. George Vansittart, a member of Council, reflected upon the inevitable disadvantages of free trade as far as the *ryot*s were concerned. He argued that the *ryot*s would 'dissipate' any money advanced with their contracts and thus

> be unable...to complete their Engagements;...Ryots would be seized and imprisoned...the produce would be diminished, moreover the Ryots would adulterate their Ophium to compensate for their deficiencies, and both these circumstances would materially injure this Country by having an immediate tendency to the destruction of an advantageous Branch of its foreign Commerce.

---

[13] Revenue Despatch, to Bengal, 28 August 1804, I.O.R., E/4/1656.
[14] Letter from Warren Hastings, to Council of Revenue, Revenue Proceedings, 15 October 1773, I.O.R., P/49/41, fols 3237–43.

And so the Council unanimously resolved that 'the trade could not be laid open at this Junction without being productive of evil consequences to the Ryots and to the country' and a Monopoly 'for the advantage of the Company' was preferable to a 'Clandestine' one for the 'Benefit of a Single Factory'.[15] That this was a financially astute decision was borne out by the fact that between 1773 and 1785, the date of Hastings' return to England, the opium trade produced revenue for the Company of £500,000. As argued by a twentieth-century apologist for the Company's opium policy, the Company's support of the opium monopoly at the expense of moral issues must be set in the context of the eighteenth century: 'Prohibition was never seriously considered, nor can we be surprised that it was not. To blame the Company for having refused to embark on such a course would be to impute to the eighteenth century a standard of social ethics utterly foreign to it'.[16]

Within a very few years of Hastings' departure, it became clear that the revenue from the export of Bengal opium to east Asian maritime powers was a mixed blessing. The Cornwallis Government received reports from numerous Collectors of opium *ryots* victimized by coercion and corruption. It was a matter of record that some contractors forced advances upon impoverished *ryots* who, when they were unable to deliver their promised produce, were driven to buy opium at the stipulated advance price from *ryots* who had a surplus. These *ryots* also faced pressure from contractors to increase the amount of land dedicated to the opium poppy. Cornwallis undertook to guarantee the *ryot* a fair price for his opium by a revised process which required the contractor to make his advances for cultivation of a certain parcel of land and then wait for the maturation of the crop before assessing the *ryot* for his produce. In this way, if there was crop failure, the opium *ryot* could not be held accountable for an initial abstract assessment. With new contracts, the terms of which were incorporated into Bengal Regulation XXXII 1793:

> It was the object of Government to prevent this source of public revenue operating as an oppression upon the Ryots, by depriving the contractors of the power of compelling any person to cultivate the poppy, and by insuring to those who might voluntarily enter into engagements for that purpose, the full price of the quantity of opium which they might deliver.[17]

---

[15] Minute by George Vansittart, 15 October 1773; Resolution of Government, 23 November 1773, Bengal Revenue Proceedings, 23 November 1773, I.O.R., P/49/42, fols 3642–44.

[16] David Edward Owen, *British Opium Policy in China and India* (New Haven, Connecticut; London; Oxford, 1934), p. 25.

[17] Bengal Regulation XXXII for enacting into a Regulation, the Terms of the Contracts concluded for the Provision of Opium on account of Government in the Provinces of Bengal, Behar and Orissa, from the 1 September to 31 August 1797, for preventing illicit Trade in that Article (passed by Governor General in Council, 1 May 1793), I.O.R., V/8/16, p. 286.

Photograph 4: 'The Stacking Room, Opium Factory at Patna, India' drawn by Walter S. Sherwill, *Illustrations of the mode of preparing the Indian opium intended for the Chinese market* (London: 1851). © The British Library Board. X850.

Although, as one scholar has remarked, 'coercion of the ryots was never sanctioned by the Bengal Government', Lord Cornwallis clearly felt that legislation for protection of the opium *ryot* from abuse was imperative.[18]

Ultimately, the Cornwallis Government decided to adopt an agency system for managing the trade in drugs. Sections XVIII and XX of Bengal Regulation XXXIV of 1793 required all manufacturers and vendors of drugs to be licensed; any manufacture or sale of drugs without a license was decreed to be illicit and subject to a fine equivalent to three times the annual assessed rate of tax. Within six months, the amount of the fine was dramatically reduced to three times the daily assessed rate, 'the penalty directed by Regulation XXXIV 1793...having been found excessive'.[19]

Overall, the Company's Directors enthusiastically supported the Abkarry system of replacing individual monopolies with government-regulated agency and a government-regulated tax. Thus, they instructed the Bombay Government to follow Bengal's example in using Abkarry tax to regulate revenue from the *arrack* liquor extracted from brab trees. In their explanation of why they found the system of farming out *arrack* revenues 'liable to objections of a very serious nature', the Directors repeated the high moral stance adopted for Bengal. They explained:

> The System of Farming out the revenues arising from any Article of consumption is objectionable as it establishes a monopoly in the hands of an Individual whose sole object being to derive the greatest possible benefit therefrom...such a consideration with an avaricious Farmer may lead to the exercise of acts of the most rapacious and oppressive tendency. But besides this objection...there is another which is particularly forcible against letting the Arrack Revenue to Farm, for while it is the Farmer's interest to extend the consumption of this Article, it ought to be the object of Government by a very prudent means, short of a general prohibition, to restrain it, with a view to the preservation of the morals and health of the lower class of the Inhabitants....[20]

---

[18] H.R.C. Wright, 'The Abolition by Cornwallis of the Forced Cultivation of Opium in Bihar', *Economic History Review*, 2nd series, Vol. xii, No. 1 (1959), pp. 112–19.

[19] Bengal Regulation LI for punishing Persons convicted of illegal Manufacture or Vend of intoxicating Liquors or Drugs, who may be unable to pay the Penalty prescribed in Regulation XXXIV 1793 (passed by Governor General in Council, 27 December 1793), I.O.R., V/8/16, p. 391.

[20] Revenue Despatch, to Bombay, 28 August 1804, I.O.R., E/4/1019, fols 639–43.

Governor Duncan of Bombay duly ordered the Collector of revenue from an *arrack* farm on Salsette Island to introduce the Abkarry system using the principles of the Bengal regulations as his guide.[21] At the same time as the Abkarry system inclusive of a monopoly over opium production was expanded throughout the three presidencies, Governor General Wellesley made rigorous efforts to protect the Company's monopoly over revenue from the export trade in opium. Since Warren Hastings' pragmatic distinction between profit from foreign commerce and revenue from internal consumption of the 'pernicious drug', hypocrisy prevailed at the highest level of the East Company's government. Elaborate rules were promulgated to prevent individuals from possessing more than two *tolah*s weight of opium bought from licensed vendors in the interior.[22] But, even more elaborate rules were devised to protect the Company's monopoly from competition. Lord Wellesley persuaded the Portuguese Governor of Goa in 1805 to forbid the export of opium from the Portuguese territory of Daman off the west coast of India, on the grounds that the 'introduction of Guzerat Opium' was a 'great deterrent' to the foreign trade.[23] Wellesley was concerned to suppress the production and exportation of opium from the princely states in Malwa. The Select Committee of the Supercargoes at Canton, who represented the Company's trading interests in China, was also concerned to put a stop to the influx of Malwa opium.

Succeeding generations struggled with the challenge presented both by unlicensed production and sale of opium within the presidency of Bengal and by the use of the Company's seaports for export of opium produced and sold outside the Company's Indian territories to the maritime powers of East Asia. The difficulties of the administration of Lord Moira were compounded

---

[21] Bombay Revenue Proceedings, 28 August 1807, I.O.R., P/366/57, fols 1208–09; Sec. LXIII Cl. 1 Bombay Regulation I for preserving a Record of the principal rules respecting Revenue in the Island of Salsette (passed by the Governor in Council on 24 February 1808), I.O.R., V/8/22. The Abkarry system was also introduced into Madras Presidency, at least with respect to spirituous liquors, by Madras Regulation I for restricting and regulating the Sale of Foreign Spirits and manufacture and sale of Country Arrack (passed by Governor in Council on 9 February 1808), I.O.R., V/8/27.

[22] Secs LIII–LXXVI, Bengal Regulation XIII for reducing into one Regulation with alterations and amendments, rules at present in force concerning the manufacture and sale of Opium (passed by Governor General in Council on 17 May 1816); Sec. III, Bengal Regulation XI for modifying certain parts of Regulation XIII 1816 (passed by Governor General in Council on 6 November 1818), raised this limit to 5 tolahs, I.O.R., V/8/19.

[23] Order from the Portuguese Governor of Goa, 26 June 1805, Extract from Political Proceedings, 11 July 1815, *Board's Collections*, I.O.R., F/4/518 # 12422, fol. 7.

when, in addition to the clandestine trade within and without Bengal, orders arrived from the Directors to clamp down on internal consumption. Consistent with their earlier pronouncements, the Directors disclaimed all interest in increased revenue in favour of restraining the use of 'this pernicious drug'. They argued for 'the principle…not to introduce the culture of the Poppy into any district where it has not hitherto obtained'. In line with this principle, the Directors disapproved a proposal submitted by an Opium Agent in Behar to establish a factory in the district of Monghyr because there was no evidence of poppy cultivation in Monghyr. Conversely, in approving the revival of poppy cultivation in Rungpore, 'where every endeavour to prevent the illicit cultivation of the Poppy is stated to have proved ineffectual', they reasoned, as did Warren Hastings almost 45 years earlier: 'The only object is…to substitute an allowed instead of an illegal proceeding…and to employ taxation less as an instrument of raising a Revenue than as a preservation of the health and morale of the Community'. Illicit producers of opium in Behar were branded as smugglers by the Opium Agent in Behar, as he estimated that 600–800 maunds were smuggled annually from the province and that in the district of Purnea up to 800 *bigha*s of land were illegally cultivated. The Agent in Benares added that considerable quantities of opium were clandestinely floated down the Ganges to Dacca and Chittagong. Inasmuch as opium from Behar and Benares had a reputation for high quality and a high price at the Calcutta auction sales, it was also the preferred commodity for export. The Company not only had to deal with smugglers, but they also had to confront unscrupulous merchants who attempted to pass off inferior quality opium produced in other parts of Bengal such as Rungpore as opium of Behar or Benares. Condemning the fraudulent mixture of inferior and superior quality opium which inevitably lowered the ultimate price, the Directors reasoned that

> it is our wish not to encourage the consumption of Opium, but rather to lessen the use, or…abuse of the drug and, for this end, as well as for the purpose of Revenue, to make the price to the Public, both in our own and in foreign dominions, as high as possible.[24]

These concerns were reflected in Bengal Regulation XIII of 1816, Section XXXIX of which decreed: 'All opium, except that which may have been

---

[24] Despatch, to Bengal in the Separate Department of Salt and Opium, 24 October 1817, I.O.R. E/4/692, fols 205–12, 215–18, 226–27 and 231–36.

manufactured on account of Government, or sold by their authority,...will be considered as contraband, and shall be liable to seizure and confiscation'. Section XL simply required that all 'persons wishing to export by sea opium, purchased at the Company's sales' must apply for a certificate from the Board of Trade to prove that the opium was 'so purchased.'[25] This certificate of purchase marked the end of the Company's efforts to regulate the opium trade. Regulations which dictated the terms of licenses issued by the Abkarry Mehal, the method of enforcement, the penalties for noncompliance—all came to an abrupt halt, as far as the opium trade was concerned, as soon as the opium passed through the Calcutta auction sales. The opium was carried away from Calcutta by the Country trade merchants who traded independent of the Company. The port of Bombay was officially closed to the opium trade. Bombay Regulation I of 1818 decreed a duty of ₹12 per Surat seer on all opium imported into Bombay unless it came from Bengal. Bombay Regulation II of 1820 refined the threatening clauses of Regulation I 1818, to declare all opium imported into Bombay contrary to the provisions of Regulation I of 1818 to be considered 'smuggled'.[26]

As far as the Company was concerned, smuggling and contraband trade was to be closely regulated and punished within India. However, the fact that the Chinese regarded the opium trade as contraband did not worry the Company for a moment. Officially, the Company respected Chinese imperial edicts which, beginning in 1729, prohibited the importation of opium from outside China and the smoking of opium within China. A gild of merchants known as Supercargoes represented the Company in its trade with a corresponding gild of Chinese merchants known as Hong merchants in Canton. Thus held at arm's length by the Imperial Chinese government in Peking, the Supercargoes struggled to find a way to finance the export of Chinese tea to satisfy an ever-increasing English demand. At first, the Company paid for the tea investment with large quantities of bullion. In the seventeenth and eighteenth centuries, the Company exported two to

---

[25] Bengal Regulation XIII 1816, *op. cit.*

[26] Bombay Regulation I for imposing a duty on all Opium made out of the limits of the territories immediately dependent upon the presidency of Fort William, imported or brought into any port or place within the limits of the territories dependent upon the presidency of Bombay (passed by Governor in Council on 2 January 1818); Bombay Regulation II for explaining Regulation I of 1818 and for more effectively preventing clandestine importation of Opium into the town and island of Bombay and into any port or place whatsoever within the authority of the Governor in Council or within the limits of any territories dependent on the Presidency of Bombay (passed by Governor in Council, 10 May 1820), I.O.R., V/8/23.

three times as much treasure in the form of Spanish dollars as commodities.[27] At the end of the eighteenth century, this imbalance was reversed when it was discovered that, whereas the Chinese had no interest in English woollens and textiles, they were enthusiastic consumers of cotton and opium from British India. By the beginning of the nineteenth century, the sudden increase of Indian imports into Canton reversed the flow of treasure so that in the years 1806–09, approximately $7 million were sent from China to India. This trade was almost entirely in the hands of private merchants known as Country Traders. These merchants plied a coastal trade between Indian ports and ports eastward through the Malay archipelago to China and Japan. As explained by Michael Greenberg, the Company was able to finance half of its tea investment with exports to China of English products and Indian cotton. But the proceeds from the Country Trade which were almost entirely in opium were sufficient to pay for the entire tea investment. The Company's Treasury in Canton received specie from the Country Traders whose imports from India surpassed their exports. In return, the Country Traders received Bills of Exchange marketable in Calcutta. In this way the Company contrived to 'confine itself to the production of opium in India and not to participate in its distribution in China'. Every Company ship bound for China was strictly prohibited from carrying opium ' "lest the Company be implicated" with the Chinese! By 1800 the East India Company had perfected the technique of growing opium in India and disowning it in China'.[28]

Early in the nineteenth century, the Company's monopoly of opium production was challenged by Portuguese willingness to ship inferior Malwa opium from Goa and Daman. This was despite the initial willingness of the Portuguese Governor of Goa to cooperate with Governor General Wellesley's attempts to prohibit such trade. As a result of the 1813 Charter which ended the Company's trade monopoly, private merchants engaged in smuggling Malwa opium. But the actual amounts carried to China were small. However, by 1817 the high price attained by Behar opium attracted large-scale merchants to a strategy of introducing the cheaper Malwa opium as a substitute.

William Jardine, working at the time for Magniac & Co. and James Matheson, on the eve of his appointment as Danish Consul in Canton,

---

[27] 1601–20: £548,090 in treasure; £292,286 in goods. 1710–59: £26,833,614 in treasure; £9,248,306 in goods. H.B. Morse, *The Chronicles of the East India Company Trading to China 1635–1834*, Vol. I (Cambridge, Massachusetts, Oxford, 1926), p. 8.

[28] Michael Greenberg, *British Trade—The Opening of China 1800–42* (Cambridge repr.: 1969), pp. 12–14, 109–10. The Company's fear of being 'implicated in the charge of illicit trade' was expressed in a report from the Canton Supercargoes, to the Governor General of India, 9 December 1798, cited by H.B. Morse, *op. cit.*, Vol. II, p. 316.

participated in a scheme to ship Malwa opium secretly to China from the Portuguese ports on the west coast of India, Goa and Daman. Although that particular venture failed, the Magniacs formed a Malwa syndicate with Bombay agents. Private traffic between Portuguese ports in India and Macao undermined the prohibition by Section IV of Bengal Regulation XIII of 1816 against the importation of opium from the Maratha territories of central India. The Government in Bengal appealed to the Home Authorities to intercede on its behalf with the Government of Portugal. The Directors declined to intervene and suggested instead that 'the superiority of Bengal Opium in point of quality over that manufactured in other parts of India will…insure to it a preference in the foreign market so long as this superiority is not much more than counterbalanced by the difference in price'. And the Directors observed further that if a reduction in the price of Bengal opium were necessary, 'the expediency of proportionately increasing the annual provision will…engage your attention'.[29]

Before expanding Bengal production to lower the price of Behar opium, the Company experimented with buying 4,000 chests of Malwa opium on the Company account and selling it by public auction to licensed agents in the same manner as the Calcutta Sales. This flooded the Chinese market, causing the price of Bengal opium to crash. At the same time, it resulted in increased consumption of the Malwa opium which improved in quality to produce a greater proportion of extract for smoking than the Bengal product. James Matheson reported in 1824 that Malwa 'has now become the favourite drug of the great mass of Chinese with the exception of the wealthy'. The Company abruptly stopped buying Malwa and, in the wake of Lord Moira's Maratha wars, they shifted to a policy of using their newly won authority over the princes of central India to impose restrictions on opium cultivation by their Malwa neighbours. Bombay Regulation XXI of 1827 enforced the penalty of 12 rupees per Surat seer imposed by Bombay Regulation XXI 1818, on all opium brought into Bombay harbour except that imported by Government or authorized by Government for foreign trade.[30] But Bombay agents of Canton opium merchants continued to use Portuguese ports. Finally, the Company decided to authorize trade in Malwa opium through Bombay regulated by transit passes which, in the first year

---

[29] Despatch, to Bengal in the Separate Department of Opium, 27 January 1819, I.O.R., E/4/695, fols 405–13.

[30] Bombay Regulation XXI for collecting customs on opium and other specified articles, and imposing restrictions on trade therein, made with the sanction of the Court of Directors and the approbation of the Board of Commissioners for the Affairs of India (passed by Governor in Council, 1 January 1827), I.O.R., V/8/24.

of operation, brought in revenue of £200,000.[31] As summed up by Michael Greenberg, the 'competition of Malwa' forced the Company away 'from its policy of restricted production and high prices into a policy of maximum production in both British India and the Native States'.[32] It had proved impossible to control smuggling operations by private traders on the high seas. These cunning smugglers played the Portuguese and British maritime authorities off against each other. And, their profitable commerce simply grew and grew.

Ironically, the fatal blow to the Company's monopoly of the China trade in opium came, not from the likes of Jardine and Matheson, but from the textile merchants of England's mill towns. A Manchester Town Hall Meeting in 1829 launched a massive campaign for full freedom of trade to China. Petitions to Parliament, newspaper ads and collaboration with the Liverpool East India and China Trade Association mushroomed into a lobbying campaign supported by free trade interests in Manchester, Liverpool, Glasgow, Leeds, Bristol, Birmingham as well as Calcutta. Parliament appointed a Select Committee in 1830 to investigate the problem. After hearing extensive testimony throughout 1831–32, the Committee reported in favour of ending the Company's external monopoly over trade with China. However, the Committee accepted the defence of the Company's internal opium monopoly advanced by the foremost political economist, James Mill who also happened to be a Company employee. Mill argued that the Company's opium was produced not for profit but for revenue and that the revenue derived by the Company from its opium monopoly caused 'no injury or hardship to any class of persons'. Following Mill's lead, the Committee concluded:

> In the present state of the revenue of India it does not appear advisable to abandon so important a source of Revenue; a duty upon Opium being a tax which falls principally upon the foreign consumer and which appears upon the whole less liable to objection than any other which could be substituted.[33]

---

[31] Bombay Regulation XX for relaxing the restrictive system in regard to the sale and purchase of Malwa opium, and allowing importation by a direct route under passes to be granted for a consideration (passed by Governor in Council 17 November 1830), I.O.R., V/8/25.

[32] Michael Greenberg, *op. cit.*, pp. 124–31.

[33] Brian Inglis, *The Opium War* (London, Auckland, Sydney, Toronto, 1976), pp. 85–86. Testimony of James Mill before the Select Committee on the Affairs of the East India Company, 28 June 1832, *Parliamentary Papers* (1831–32) VIII, Cmd. 734 III, p. 70; in their Report, the Select Committee admitted that the 'monopoly of opium in Bengal supplies Government with Revenue of Sa ₹84,59,425 or £981,293 per annum—the Duty thus imposed amounts to 301¾ per cent on the cost of the article', Report from Select Committee, *Parliamentary Papers* (1831–32) XI, Cmd. 735 III, p. 268.

Abkarry and Pilgrim Taxes   309

As the 1834 Act ending the Company's monopoly of trade to China[34] brought an end to its control over British merchants in Canton, the Country Traders burst free of all restraints. The firm of Jardine and Matheson had already experimented with extending contraband trade in opium as far north along the Chinese coast as Tientsin. The huge expansion of the opium trade produced a threefold increase in the revenue of the East India Company from 10 million rupees in 1832 to 30 million rupees in 1838. In 1836, $18 million from opium sales in China covered the investment of British merchants in $17 million worth of Chinese tea and silk.[35]

Opium Trade through Chinese Eyes

For Chinese authorities, the opium trade was more than an economic bonanza for foreign merchants. It was an intense moral issue. Between 1729, when the first imperial edict prohibited the sale of opium, and 1839, nearly fifty imperial edicts prohibited all aspects of the opium trade within China. These edicts produced laws calling for draconian punishments ranging from flogging and prolonged wearing of the *cangue* for addicts to dismissal from office, exile or execution for opium producers and corrupt officials. An imperial edict in 1796 prohibiting the importation of opium, in effect, declared opium to be contraband. Interestingly, the punitive focal point of these edicts was the people of China.[36]

It was assumed in the realm of Imperial China that all foreigners would play the role of barbarians bearing tribute to the Emperor who was the 'Son of Heaven'. All mercantile activity was regulated within this tributary system. Foreign merchants were kept at arms length in Canton, a depot of trade since the T'ang empire of the seventh century. Trade at other points along the Chinese coast waxed and waned in accordance with the degree to which the Imperial regime felt secure from pirates and/or traitors. In 1759 the Peking Court decided to restrict foreign trade to Canton out of a fear that 'the northern ports at Ningpo, Shanghai and Amoy, being more accessible from the ocean than Canton would have difficulty in controlling the movement of foreign ships, thus contributing to collusion between the

---

[34] Sec. 24, 4 Will IV c.93.
[35] Immanuel C.Y. Hsü, *The Rise of Modern China* (London, Toronto, New York, 1970), p. 219.
[36] Hsin-pao Chang, *Commissioner Lin and the Opium War* (Cambridge, Massachusetts, 1964), Appendix A and p. 17.

aliens and traitorous natives'.[37] In fact, China had no navy which could deal with coastal intruders. Maritime interests had been neglected ever since 1421 when the Ming dynasty, despite its far-flung glory achieved by naval supremacy, moved its capital further inland from Nanking to Peking. The Manchus of the Ch'ing dynasty, which acceded to power in 1644, relied upon concentric rings of authority based on Confucian values to keep order within their domain.

When the Company lost its monopoly over the China trade, the British government replaced the Company's supervisory Select Committee of Supercargoes with a Chief Superintendent of Trade in the person of Lord William Napier. The Confucian Chinese Viceroy and Governor of the combined provinces of Kwangtung and Kwangsi, which included Canton, thereby faced a new challenge. Lord William Napier had been appointed Chief Superintendent of Trade in 1834 by the Crown. His instructions were contradictory inasmuch as he was expected to reside in Canton in order to represent the interests of British merchants to Chinese authorities, while maintaining full respect for Chinese laws and customs. According to Chinese law, only merchants were admitted to Canton; a Crown official such as Lord Napier was expected to report his arrival in the form of a petition delivered by the Hong merchants to the Viceroy of the combined provinces of Kwangtung and Kwangsi, and then wait in Macao for instructions from Peking. When Lord Napier arrived on board a man-o'-war in Canton and attempted to deliver, not a petition, but a letter directly to the Viceroy, he caused consternation. Lord Napier's envoy was kept waiting for hours at the Chinese 'Petition Gate' only to have his letter refused. The Viceroy responded to the situation by chastising the Hong merchants for failing to prevent Lord Napier's officers from arriving in Canton without the red permit which he was expected to obtain from Chinese customs officers in Macao before entering the Celestial Regime. The British representative was identified as a 'Barbarian Eye' called Lord Napier. The ideographs which the Viceroy selected for Lord Napier's name translated as 'Laboriously Vile'.[38] With such an inauspicious beginning 'Laboriously Vile's' efforts to establish commercial relations between Chinese authorities and the British Government spiralled downwards into an abortive confrontation.

Exhorted by Jardine to pursue aggressive tactics against the Canton mandarins, Lord Napier only succeeded in provoking a stoppage of all trade

---

[37] Immanuel C.Y. Hsü, *op. cit.*, pp. 183–86.
[38] Maurice Collis, *Foreign Mud* (London, 1946), p. 133.

for British merchants in Canton, while the wily Viceroy managed to blockade two British frigates in the inner river so that they could neither advance nor retreat. Lord Napier, himself mortified and ill, retreated to Macao where he succumbed to a raging fever. The only winner in this abortive course of events was William Jardine whose ambition to challenge Chinese trade restrictions provoked the kinds of diplomatic insults and injury which were ultimately to escalate into a British show of force. And, unlike smaller-scale British merchants in Canton, the firm of Jardine and Matheson was unaffected by the trade stoppage because most of its ships were engaged in the contraband trade north of the Canton River along the China coast.

In the wake of what came to be known in Canton as the 'Napier fizzle', the Chinese strengthened strategic maritime defences and reminded foreigners of the rules which prohibited all but merchant vessels from approaching the inner river at Canton.[39] Meanwhile, against the background of continual growth in the opium trade, a legalization movement blossomed in Peking with the blessing of the Empress Hsiao-ch'uän. On 10 June 1836 one of her followers, Sub-Director of the Court of Sacrificial Worship Hsü Nai-chi, presented a memorial urging the legalization of opium. Hsü Nai-chi argued that, in the face of ineffective efforts at prohibition, Peking might as well, 'permit the barbarian merchants to import opium paying duty thereon as a medicine, and...require that, after having passed the custom house, it shall be delivered to the Hong merchants only in Exchange for merchandize, and that no money be paid for it'.[40]

A former criminal judge in Canton, Hsü had witnessed many cases of blackmail and extortion affecting law-abiding citizens. He argued that civil servants, scholars and soldiers should be forbidden to smoke, but opium smokers from more ordinary occupations could be ignored, as a decrease in population was not a concern. However, a barter system was important to check the drainage of silver.

Within less than four months, the Emperor Tao Kuang, who had some years earlier watched his own son and heir die from an opium addiction, received two counter memorials. Councillor Chu Tsun reminded the Emperor of the 'baneful influence of opium among his people, and, of crucial importance,

---

[39] As described by Hsin-pao Chang, 'The "Napier fizzle"...was a wedge that cut deeply into Anglo–Chinese relations. It made the character of the "barbarian" more unfathomable to the Chinese and doubled the British merchants' disdain and distrust of the Chinese.' Hsin-pao Chang, *op. cit.*, p. 62.

[40] Memorial from Hzu-Naetse to the Emperor proposing to legalize the importation of Opium, Enclosure No. 1 in Capt. Elliot to Viscount Palmerston, Macao, 2 February 1837, *Parliamentary Papers* (1840) XXXVI, Cmd. 223, p. 158.

among his troops'. He recalled the instance when troops were sent to fight Yao rebels in 1832 but 'in consequence of smoking opium,...few were fit or strong enough to take the field'. The other memorialist, Sub-Commissioner Hsü Ch'iu, argued that the laws of prohibition were undermined by traitorous Chinese. He singled out for censure the Hong merchants who set prices, the small boats known as 'fast crabs' which ferried the opium chests ashore from the opium clippers at anchor off the[41] coast and the officials who connived at the trade in response to bribes. The majority of officials in Peking supported Chu Tsun and Hsü Ch'iu. And so, the Emperor was swayed to issue an edict ordering Viceroy Teng of Kwangtung and Kwangsi to devise a plan for arresting Hong opium merchants, crews of 'fast crabs', soldiers, and police who accepted bribes. The Viceroy was determined to expel from Canton the nine most notorious foreign merchants of whom Jardine was foremost. What was most remarkable about the legalization movement was that, despite the fact that it was very short lived in Peking, English officials in Canton convinced themselves that legalization was the way of the future.[42]

The Viceroy had great difficulty in executing his mandate because the Chinese coast was too long to patrol and addiction had reached such a level in the population that it supported a rigorous trade with foreign ships anchored offshore. Nonetheless, within a year, Viceroy Teng destroyed all the 'fast crabs' and Chinese smuggling networks around Canton thereby causing a dramatic decline in the price of opium. By the end of 1838, 2,000 Chinese opium dealers and smokers were in prison; addicts were executed daily. Meanwhile, in Peking the Director of Court Ceremonial called for the execution of all addicts who failed to reform within a year. The Emperor referred this proposal to all the Governors General and high officials. Most thought such a course was too extreme. But Lin Tse-hsü, the Governor General of Hu Kwang endorsed a rigorous approach. The Emperor was impressed both by Lin's six-point plan targeting dealers and consumers, and by his successful programme in Hupeh and Hunan of confiscating 5,500 pipes and 12,000 ounces of opium. On 31 December 1838, Lin was appointed Imperial Commissioner charged with suppressing the Canton opium trade. Within four months of his arrival in Canton, Commissioner Lin imprisoned five times as many people and confiscated seven times as many pipes as Viceroy Teng had managed to do over three years. Lin's memorial

---

[41] Memorial from Councillor Choo-Tsun to the Emperor against the admission of Opium, October 1836, Enclosure No. 5 in Capt. Elliot to Viscount Palmerston, Macao, 2 February 1837, *Parliamentary Papers* (1840) XXXVI, Cmd. 223, pp. 168–73.

[42] Brian Inglis, *op. cit.*, p. 78; Hsin-pao Chang, *op. cit.*, pp. 85–92.

to the Emperor calling for total suppression of the opium trade warned: 'If we continue to pamper it, a few decades from now we shall not only be without soldiers to resist the enemy, but also in want of silver to provide an army. When I think of this, I cannot but tremble'. Lines from this memorial memorized by school children, inspired patriots for more than 100 years.[43]

A Confucian scholar and holder of the highest chin-shih degree, Commissioner Lin was eminently qualified to represent the Son of Heaven to foreign 'barbarians'. In the month of March, immediately following his arrival in Canton, Lin endorsed a letter to Queen Victoria and fearsome edicts to both Hong and foreign merchants. The letter to Queen Victoria was the first of two, neither of which ever reached the Queen. Referring to the 'poisonous article' of opium, Lin warned:

> What it is here forbidden to consume, your dependencies must be forbidden to manufacture, and what has already been manufactured Your Majesty must immediately search out and throw it to the bottom of the sea, and never again allow such a poison to exist in Heaven or on earth....On receiving this, Your Majesty will be so good as to report to me immediately on the steps that have been taken at each of your ports.[44]

Lin preferred tactics of moral suasion backed by Chinese law over the despatch of a naval force, which he didn't have, to offshore anchorages of foreign ships. He commanded the Hong merchants to enforce his order that the foreign merchants surrender all their opium under penalty of confiscation of property, and, in some cases, death. Foreigners were also required to sign a bond promising never to import opium into China again. When foreigners balked at signing a bond which ostensibly made an entire ship's crew liable to capital punishment in the Chinese tradition, Lin effectively confined them to their Canton factories without their numerous Chinese servants.

Captain Charles Elliot, the newly appointed Superintendent of British Trade, responded by proclaiming that all British merchants must surrender their opium supplies to him as property of the British government to be delivered to the Chinese government. In the face of a dead market created by Lin's punitive measures against Chinese dealers and addicts, the merchants were only too happy to see their opium cargo transformed into public property with guaranteed commercial value. Indeed, by early June the Bombay Chamber of Commerce sent a petition to the Queen in Council for

---

[43] Immanuel C.Y. Hsü, *op. cit.*, pp. 225–26; Hsin-pao Chang, *op. cit.*, pp. 96, 128.
[44] Arthur Waley, *The Opium War through Chinese Eyes* (London, 1958–60), pp. 30–31.

a cash advance against full compensation for the surrendered opium chests. Elliot, for his part, having guaranteed the merchants financial compensation, assumed that Lin would use the surrendered opium to create an indemnity fund. How wrong he was! Lin moved quickly to destroy the more than 20,000 chests delivered to him and then freed the merchants from their Canton confinement. At about the same time, a 39-article statute was promulgated in Peking inclusive of a decree that anyone caught smoking within the next 18 months was subject to death by strangling. One more article, added at Commissioner Lin's request, made foreigners who imported and sold opium subject to execution. Just as Elliot underestimated the determination of the Chinese to destroy the opium trade, Lin failed to perceive that the siege of Canton and the requirement of a bond were seen by the British as a threat to British property and lives. The opium trade for the Chinese official was an issue of contraband; for the British, it was a matter of property. As the British community withdrew to Macao, Elliot appealed to London to take action.[45]

While reports of the crisis at Canton travelled to England, an inflammatory incident occurred. The behaviour of drunken English sailors ashore at Kowloon, opposite Hong Kong, provoked a riot among Chinese villagers, one of whom was killed. Lin demanded the surrender of the culprit so that he could be executed in accordance with Chinese law. But, ever since the *Lady Hughes* affair in 1784, it had been British practise never to hand over an English criminal to the Chinese for trial; Elliot refused. And so, the stage was set for war. On 18 October 1839, Lord Palmerston, the British Foreign Minister, ordered an Expeditionary Force of 16 warships with additional transports for 4,000 soldiers to be sent to Canton by the Indian Government. Palmerston acted upon his own authority largely in response to lobbying from William Jardine who had returned to England with Lord Napier's widow early in 1839 to promote the commercial interests of the Canton merchants. The only formal declaration of war was issued by the Indian Government on 31 January 1840. Not until the arrival of the Expeditionary Force in June 1840, were the Chinese made aware that they were, indeed, at war. As the Expeditionary Force succeeded in blockading Chinese ports all the way from Canton to Tinghai at the mouth of the Yangtze, the Emperor became completely disillusioned with Commissioner Lin. In a rage, he stripped Lin of his rank and sent him into exile. The only communication between the two governments consisted of a letter from Palmerston addressed to

---

[45] Hsin-pao Chang, *op. cit.*, pp. 172, 189–91 and Appendix A; Immanuel C.Y. Hsü, *op. cit.*, pp. 228–31; Brian Inglis, *op. cit.*, p. 125 and Peter Ward Fay, *The Opium War 1840–1842* (Chapel Hill, North Carolina, 1975), p. 190.

the 'Minister of the Emperor'. Palmerston set forth for the Emperor the argument that, instead of attempting to destroy the opium trade by seizing the property and attacking the lives of foreigners, the Chinese should begin by disciplining themselves.

Palmerston instructed Elliot to secure an apology for insults to the British at Canton, an indemnity for the confiscated opium, the opening of ports north of Canton and the cession of an island as a base for British trade. However, when Elliot negotiated the abortive Chuenpi Convention with Commissioner Lin's successor, he was dismissed by Palmerston for accepting the 'lowest possible terms' in the form of an indemnity of $6 million which was too small and the cession of Hong Kong 'a barren island with hardly a house upon it' which was the wrong island. His Chinese counterpart was dismissed for granting any indemnity and for ceding any territory.[46] It was almost an exercise in shadow boxing between the Chinese Emperor, insistent upon commanding the obedience of the barbarians to orders for destruction of the opium trade, and the English merchants insistent upon persuading their government to send warships to defend and promote free trade.

In the end, the English imposed the terms of the Treaty of Nanking by overwhelming naval force. Four of the six terms of the treaty had been urged upon Palmerston by William Jardine as objectives of war. These were: a substantial indemnity for the confiscated opium, an end to the Hong monopoly of trade, the cession of Hong Kong and the opening of ports to British consuls and merchants. The treaty also called for diplomatic relations between China and Britain as equals and a fixed tariff. Later treaties with the United States and France added the principle of extraterritoriality and the most-favoured-nation clause. The principle of extraterritoriality granted recognition of foreign jurisdiction over foreign citizens and the most-favoured-nation clause extended all privileges of successive treaties to all of the treaty powers.

Epilogue

Whereas the Opium War is universally acclaimed for launching a process known as the 'Opening of China',[47] the Treaty of Nanking was the foundation

---

[46] Peter Ward Fay, *op. cit.*, p. 218; Hsin-pao Chang, *op. cit.*, pp. 192–95; Immanuel C.Y. Hsü, *op. cit.*, pp. 230–41.

[47] Immanuel C.Y. Hsü, *op. cit.*; Hsin-pao Chang, *op. cit.*; Michael Greenberg, *op. cit.* and Peter Ward Fay, *op. cit.*

stone of the unequal treaty system. It made no mention of the opium trade as an object for regulation. Despite Commissioner Lin's disruption of the trade at Canton, operators of the contraband trade such as Jardine and Matheson flourished. James Matheson instructed his ships' captains on how to operate in the vicinity of the men-o'-war of the Expeditionary Force. He was confident that the Expeditionary Force had 'no mode of raising money for the expenses of the war unless from the drug sales in China'.[48] Meanwhile, as the British were evacuated from Canton, first to Macao and then to Hong Kong, American merchants functioned as middle men. As soon as Capt. Elliot stopped the war in the Canton River with his abortive Chuenpi convention, trade resumed. The opium trade was as brisk as ever; 'from India came the relentless flow of chests'.[49] Elijah Impey, a Port Surgeon and Government Examiner of Opium, remarked in 1848:

> The continued and steady renovation of demand for [opium] since the conclusion of peace with China, which keeps up the necessity for increased cultivation, has rendered the income from it so large and significant—the difference being that between £590,000 collected in 1817 and £2,439,400 in 1844, that it is out of the power of the Company to abandon the trade, however much it might be wished on other grounds.[50]

Without so much as a hiccup, legislation in India continued to target abuses in the system for management of the Abkarry revenue. Act XXV of 1840 launched an experiment in some districts for transferring the authority for control of Abkarry revenue from Collectors to Commissioners subject to the control of the Board of Customs, Salt and Opium.[51] This legislative pattern of continually revising the structure of the Abkarry department, always under the rubric of protecting their Indian subjects from themselves continued in 1856 with a massive overhaul of Abkarry Regulations. Act XXI of 1856 repealed virtually all previous legislation in order to pronounce authoritatively on the system for collecting Abkarry revenue and penalizing abuses. Authority for collecting the revenue was returned to the Collectors

---

[48] Matheson, to Jamsetjee, 4 August 1840, *James Matheson Private Letter Books*, Vol. 5, quoted by Peter Ward Fay, *op. cit.*, p. 239.

[49] Peter Ward Fay, *op. cit.*, p. 284.

[50] Assistant Surgeon Impey, *Report on the Cultivation, Preparation and Adulteration of Malwa Opium* (Bombay, 1848), p. 18.

[51] Act XXV for the better protection of the Abkaree Revenue within the Presidency of Fort William in Bengal (passed by Governor General of India 28 December 1840), I.O.R., V/8/31.

with the proviso that the Government might appoint special Commissioners in certain districts such as Calcutta which had always been a special case. In general, most of the provisions of earlier regulations such as the rules governing licensees were maintained. The new emphasis focussed on detailed provisions regarding enforcement.[52] Once again, pious statements were uttered. Councillor Peacock ruminated over his reasons for declining to grant the Board of Revenue the power of sub-letting retail licenses—a power already exercised in the N.W.P. Peacock opposed such licenses because 'the effect would be to encourage rather than discourage the sale of country spirits to the natives'.[53]

Considering that Act XXI of 1856 was intended to be the definitive legislation on Abkarry, it is revealing that the very next year, the Legislative Council felt impelled to enact Act XIII. Act XIII of 1857 repealed the few regulations and segments of regulations left intact by Act XXI of 1856. These earlier pieces of legislation were either considered obsolete or they were concerned with the opium monopoly and the prevention of 'the illicit cultivation of the Poppy'. And so, the Company's opium monopoly was reinforced yet again.[54]

The substantial body of legislation concerning Abkarry revenue generally and opium production, in particular, is enduring testimony to its importance. Although there were scattered pronouncements of concern by Company and Government officials over the need to protect the morals of their Indian subjects, they appear meagre beside the enormous tide of legislation regulating the revenue. Opium merchants took their grievances to the courts, occasionally as far as the Supreme Courts in Calcutta and Bombay.[55] But, except for an earnest lament by Henry St. George Tucker over the departure from Cornwallis' effort to control production and protect the cultivator from exploitation, no official objections were raised to the steady increase of opium acreage in India. The opium trade carried by smugglers over the

---

[52] Act XXI to consolidate and amend the Law relating to the Abkaree Revenue in the Presidency of Fort William in Bengal (received assent of the Governor General, 22 November 1856), I.O.R., V/8/35.
[53] India Legislative Proceedings, 6 September 1856, I.O.R., V/9/2, Col. 559.
[54] Act XIII to consolidate and amend the law relating to the cultivation of the Poppy and the manufacture of Opium in the Presidency of Fort William in Bengal (received assent of the Governor General, 6 June 1857), I.O.R., V/8/35.
[55] 100 Opium Cases, 1847–52, Sir Erskine Perry, *Cases Illustrative of Oriental Life and the Application of English Law to India, Decided in H.M. Supreme Court in Bombay* (London, 1853), pp. 177ff.

sea from India to China and Malaya produced a revenue which neither the British Government nor the Company could refuse, all the while denying any moral responsibility for it. As stated by Brian Inglis: 'The effect of the Treaty of Nanking was to ensure that the best land would continue to be used to grow poppy; that more land would continue to be appropriated for that purpose; and that the price paid for opium would remain low'.[56]

The Indian cultivator, whether working for the agent of the Company's monopoly in Bengal or for agents of the Rajput princes who contracted to supply the drug in Malwa, received only bare subsistence.[57] According to the philosophy of political economy made fashionable by James Mill, Adam Smith, Ricardo and Malthus, there must be no interference in the process of demand and supply. Governments might interfere with slavery, as it denied the labourer the best price for his labour. But it was not their business to regulate trade. Just as Palmerston had argued in his letter to the 'Minister of the Emperor', the demand for opium in China was not the moral responsibility of foreign merchants. Furthermore, according to the theories advanced by Malthus and Ricardo, the cultivator had no right to more than a bare subsistence. If he earned more, it could be appropriated by the landlord as rent or by the state as land tax. And so, the Indian cultivator could assuage Malthusian concerns for preventing overpopulation where resources were scarce by starving to death. Similarly, in China, concern over opium addiction focussed on the scholars and soldiers of the professions; low-class addicts might as well be sacrificed at the Malthusian altar. The Company, and by extension the British Government, could not afford to look askance at the revenue of more than £2 million delivered by opium merchants. The Chinese government had not the naval resources to stop the trade in this noxious drug which came by sea from foreign lands. With a steady increase in opium production, it is hardly surprising that, in the wake of the next armed confrontation over questions of jurisdiction over foreigners in China, the Chinese decided to legalize the opium trade, after all. Chinese government officials had begun to appreciate that a substantial revenue could be raised from an import tax on the drug. The low-class Chinese addict was expendable.

---

[56] Henry St. George Tucker, cited by Brian Inglis, *op. cit.*, p. 187; *ibid.*, p. 103.

[57] Hugh Stark, in his testimony before the Select Committee on 14 February 1832, stated that the opium cultivator received a mere 3½ rupees for poppy juice per seer which weighed just under two pounds. This contrasted with value to the Company of the opium monopoly estimated at one million pounds per year. *Parliamentary Papers* (1831–32) XI, Cmd. 735 III, p. 18.

Pilgrim Tax

Pilgrim taxes collected by East India Company officers at various temples and religious festivals throughout India were a potent symbol of government involvement with Indian religion. In Bengal Presidency, pilgrim taxes were officially collected at Gaya in Behar, Allahabad in the Ceded Provinces and Jagannath Temple in Orissa. The most egregious example of the Pilgrim Tax as a cause célèbre was the revenue collected by Company officials in support of Jagannath Temple in Puri, Orissa—a veritable Jerusalem of the East. Historically, the tax had been collected by previous rulers in response to the universal devotion accorded to the god, Lord Jagannath, by all Hindu creeds, whether Vaishnavite, Saivite or Tantricist. The temple, originally built in the mid-twelfth century for the prominent deity, Purushottama of Puri, housed a trinity of Bhagavata deities by the thirteenth century. And, early in the fourteenth century, Purushottama came to be known as Jagannath. Mediaeval Muslim Sultans began to collect pilgrim taxes at prominent Hindu shrines and festivals as a compromise with Muslim orthodoxy which prohibited non-Muslim religious festivals. Because Muslim rule of India was the result of a war of conquest rather than a holy war, mediaeval Muslim dynasties instituted the Pilgrim Tax as a symbol of toleration of their idolatrous subjects whom they did not wish to antagonize.

Later, more confident Muslim rulers acted according to their individual whims. In 1563, the grand Emperor Akbar abolished the Pilgrim Tax as a gesture of toleration for all religions. Ironically, at just about the same time, a rebellious Sultan in Bengal sent an invasion force into Orissa to punish an ambitious Raja and to desecrate the image of Lord Jagannath. There ensued a struggle between Afghan and Muslim forces for control of Orissa. After 20 years of virtual Afghan rule, one of Akbar's noblemen reestablished Muslim rule. It was at this time that an Oryan prince, namely, the Raja of Khurda, installed new images in the Temple of Purushottama. The legitimacy of these images was based on Hindu legend which recorded a sacred log revealed to a mythological king in a dream; the log was split into four images by the Vulcan of Hindu gods. As explained by Andrew Stirling, Persian Secretary to the Bengal Government, these images consisted of:

> Sri Krishna of Jagannath distinguished by its black hue, Baldeo (Balbhadra), a form of Siva, of a white colour, Subhadra, the sister of these brothers of the colour of saffron, and a round staff or pillar with the chakra impressed on each end called Sudersan.

This latter image is assumed to have been of tribal origin.[58] For his prodigious act of restoration, the Khurda Raja won the adulation of the local population and recognition, authorized by Akbar, of himself as custodian of the temple. Akbar's successors vacillated between tolerance and intolerance. The temple was alternately attacked or renovated, the images removed and hidden by the priests or restored, according to the temple's fortunes. Under Aurangzeb, the most intolerant of the Muslim rulers, the Subahdar or Governor of Orissa spared the temple from destruction in order to receive substantial revenue from the Pilgrim Tax which was then levied as a punitive measure rather than as a symbol of toleration.

When the Marathas gained control of the temple as a result of their conquest of Orissa in the mid-eighteenth century, they took an ardent interest in temple affairs. After defaulting on a debt, the Raja of Khurda was forced to surrender the four districts which comprised his estate, one of which was the Purushottam Chattar, the home of Jagannath Temple. Although he remained as Temple Superintendent, he lost all real authority. Despite elaborate gifts to the temple of rent-free lands culminating in an endowment estate known as Sattais Hazari Mahal, the Marathas mismanaged temple affairs. As a result, they resorted to extortionate methods of collecting the Pilgrim Tax in their effort to meet temple expenses.[59]

The *sraddha* or funeral ceremonies at Gaya were sanctioned by the sacred Purana texts. Gayawal Brahmins were allowed to receive gifts from devotees performing *sraddha*. As described by Warren Hastings, the pilgrim routinely offered *pinda*s or rice balls to the spirits of his ancestors and *dutchna* or gifts to his *gayawal* in order to receive the *gayawal*'s supreme blessing or *soophal*:

> By the tenets of the Hindoo religion the performance of the Pilgrimage to Giah is an indispensable duty...This has raised the reputation of the Giawauls to such a height that the Hindoos pay from 1 Rupee to a lack according to their capacity for the pronouncing of the single word 'Soop-hul'.[60]

---

[58] Andrew Stirling, *An Account, Geographical, Statistical and Historical of Orissa Proper, or Cuttack* (1822) [title page missing], pp. 155–56; R. Geib, *Die Indradyumna Legende, Ein Beitrage zur Geschichte des Jagannâtha Kultes* (Wiesbaden, 1975) and A. Eschmann, 'The Vaisnava Typology of Hinduization and the Origin of Jagannatha' in A. Eschmann, H. Kulke, and G.C. Tripathi, eds., *The Cult of Jagannath and the Regional Tradition of Orissa* (New Delhi, 1978), p. 99.

[59] Nancy Gardner Cassels, *Religion and Pilgrim Tax under the Company Raj* (New Delhi, 1987), pp. 16–18, 21–25; *see also* 'Groeme's Report', Document Nine in Prabhat Mukherjee, *Pilgrim Tax and Temple Scandals—A Critical Study of the important Jagannath Temple Records during British Rule*, ed., Nancy Gardner Cassels (Bangkok, 2000), pp. 41, 37.

[60] 'Description of Gya Ceremonies—Memoranda for an History', *Warren Hastings Papers*, British Library, ADD MSS 29367, fol. 102.

In addition to the *dutchna* payable to the *gayawals*, pilgrims were subject to road duties at customs barriers erected by landholders and government officials along roads leading to Gaya. In 1784–85 Thomas Law, Collector at Gaya, reported to the East India Company that Muslim officials interfered with the pilgrims' *dutchna* and road duties in order to reap a profit. The Company then authorized the collector to collect the pilgrim taxes at Gaya as a branch of the Sayer or excise taxes. Law introduced a system of licenses for pilgrims available at a fixed rate. Continued abuses in the collection of Sayer duties by landlords induced Governor General Cornwallis to order on 28 July 1790 the abolition of 'all duties, taxes and collections coming under the denomination of Sayer...with the exception of...the duties levied on pilgrims at Gya [*sic*], and other places of pilgrimage...'. This order was incorporated into Sec. 4 Bengal Regulation XXVII 1793.[61]

At Allahabad, similar licensing procedures were undertaken to protect pilgrims from extortion. However, at the turn of the century, there was no legislation to regulate the religious fairs held annually at Allahabad. The Magh Mela, held most years during the months of January and February, and the much more important Kumbh Mela, held every twelfth year when the sun is in Aries and Jupiter is in Aquarius, are festivals inspired by the *Ramayana*. Rama's brother, Bharat, allegedly pursued Rama to the junction of the Ganges and Jumna Rivers. This junction was considered the 'Triveni' because it was also assumed to include a junction with a third river, the more mythological than real underground Saraswati; and the 'Triveni' was also known as *prayaga* or place of sacrifice. Brahma is alleged to have performed a horse sacrifice there as a token of his universal supremacy. The Emperor Akbar visited Prayag in 1575 and decided to build an imperial city named Ilahabas on the site of what is known today as Allahabad. Badaoni, a contemporary Muslim historian confirmed accounts by the seventh-century Chinese Buddhist pilgrim, Hiuen Tsang, that pilgrims would commit suicide by hurling themselves into the deep river waters from the tall *Atchybut* or undying fig tree in order to die at the sacred spot where the rivers join. The *pragwals* or local priests who regulate ceremonies at the *Triveni* allegedly implement instructions set forth in the *Matsya Purana*. However, legend asserts that *pragwals* originated with the dilemma faced by Akbar when the

---

[61] Sec. IV Rule for the Abolition of the Sayer, passed on 28 July 1790, Regulation XXVII for reenacting, with Alterations and Modifications, the Rules passed by the Governor General in Council on 11 June and 28 July 1790, and subsequent Dates, for the Resumption and Abolition of the Sayer, or internal Duties and Taxes, throughout Bengal, Behar and Orissa... (passed 1 May 1793), I.O.R., V/8/16, p. 251; cf. Nancy Gardner Cassels, *op. cit.*, pp. 18–20.

river continually destroyed the foundations of the fort he was trying to build. Akbar resolved his predicament by sacrificing a Brahmin whose descendants were then designated as *pragwals*.[62] Such *pragwals* presided over shaving and bathing ceremonies for a fee. They kept caste lists of their clients who attended the Magh Mela and Kumbh Mela fairs in order to bathe in the sacred waters. The East India Company provided police protection and assistance to pilgrims when the rivers rose close to Akbar's fort. The Company also required the Collector to issue licenses to pilgrims with cash penalties for any barber assisting an unlicensed pilgrim. This was the Company's informal method of protecting pilgrims from extortion at the hands of the *pragwals*.[63]

By the end of the first decade of the nineteenth century, pilgrim taxes at these three sites in the Bengal Presidency were all subject to regulation by legislation. Taxes at Gaya continued to be collected by the authority of Sec. 4 Beng. Reg. XXVII 1793. However, the process of tax collection at Jagannath Temple underwent intense scrutiny. At the outset of the British occupation of Cuttack district which contained Jagannath Temple, Governor General Wellesley gave explicit instructions to his officers. With reference to the Maratha practice of collecting revenue from the pilgrims, his orders stated

> that if those collections have ceased since the occupation of Juggernaut by the British Authority, the Governor General does not wish that those Collections should at present be renewed. If the Collections should not have ceased, they are to continue under the Superintendance and Controul [*sic*] of the Civil local Authority.[64]

In the meantime, temple expenses were met from general revenue by the Company, upon request, to the extent of 38,876 *sicca* rupees in 1803–4 and 34,080 *sicca* rupees in 1804–5.[65] The reality in Puri was that, of the four priests entrusted with temple management by the Marathas, one had absconded and the remaining three had been so lax in their administration

---

[62] H.R. Nevill, *Allahabad, District Gazetteers of the United Provinces of Agra and Oudh*, Vol. XXIII (Allahabad, 1911), pp. 67–68, 151–52, 156 and 166.

[63] Nancy Gardner Cassels, *op. cit.*, pp. 25–26.

[64] N.B. Edmonstone, Secretary to Government, to Lt. Col. Harcourt, J. Melvill and H. Ernst, Commissioners for the Affairs of Cuttack, 1 November 1803, Bengal Secret and Political Proceedings, 1 March 1804, No. 26, I.O.R., P/Ben/Sec/123; cf. Prabhat Mukherjee, *Pilgrim Tax and Temple Scandles, op. cit.*, Document Five, p. 24.

[65] Note by J.P. Grant, Secretary to Government, 19 November 1852, *Parliamentary Papers* (1857–58) XLII, Cmd. 71, p. 23; cf. Prabhat Mukherjee, *op. cit.*, Document 7e, p. 32.

of the temple that temple affairs were plagued by confusion, indiscipline, corruption and debt. This state of affairs was confirmed by a lengthy report commissioned by the Cuttack Board of Revenue from Collector Charles Groeme in March 1805. Groeme completed his massive report in a mere two months with the substantial assistance of one of the temple priests. Groeme recommended that the Raja of Khurda be restored to a position of authority over the temple. This, despite the fact that the Raja was already languishing in jail as the result of his efforts to assert his traditional rights to livestock from villages near Puri at the time of the *Rath Jatra* or Car Festival, the most well-known temple festival. Groeme also recommended the renewal of the Pilgrim Tax accompanied by a system of passes issued to pilgrims according to their social and economic status. The Bengal Government promptly enacted Regulation XII of 1805, Sec. 31 of which called for legislation to create a system for collecting the Pilgrim Tax that would provide good order and protect pilgrims from abuse. Sec. 30 referred to an 'established donation for the support of the temple of Jagannath', a matter which was to become the subject of intense controversy.[66]

In keeping with the provisions of Sec. 31 Beng. Reg. XII 1805, a Company officer was immediately appointed Collector of Pilgrim Tax. And within six months, the Governor in Council enacted Regulation IV 1806 based on a draft drawn up by the Commissioner of Cuttack in the wake of the Groeme Report. Pilgrim Tax was to be levied on two classes of pilgrims: the high-class *Lal Jatries* who were to pay 10 rupees if they came from the wealthy regions of the north or six rupees if they came from the poorer regions of the south; all others were to be charged two rupees. There was also a list of pilgrims to be exempt from tax on account of either their holy status or their poverty. The more controversial sections of Beng. Reg. IV 1806 concerned temple management. The temple was to be governed by an assembly of *pandit*s appointed by the Governor General in accordance with the recommendations of the Collector of Pilgrim Tax and the Cuttack Board of Revenue. And, these *pandit*s were to be liable for dismissal by the Governor General on proof of misconduct. Within two weeks of the enactment of Beng. Reg. IV 1806, the Governor General in Council felt impelled to enact Regulation V of 1806 in order to impose a penalty upon fraudulent impoverished pilgrims; the Collector of Pilgrim Tax had reported

---

[66] Bengal Regulation XII for the Settlement and Collection of the public Revenue in the *zillah* of Cuttack, including the Pergunnahs of Puttespore, Kummardichour, and Bograe, at present included in the *zillah* of Midnapore (passed by Vice President in Council, 5 September 1805), p. 135; cf. Prabhat Mukherjee, *op. cit.*, Document 18a, p. 109.

numerous *Lal Jatries* attempting to evade their tax through disguise as an inferior class.[67]

It is not surprising that prominent Evangelicals, Charles Grant and Edward Parry who chaired the Court of Directors in London were outraged by the apparent 'interference' in the affairs of Jagannath Temple legalized by Beng. Reg. IV 1806. However, the able statesman, Robert Dundas, in his capacity as President of the Board of Control, rejected totally the Directors' attempt to argue that 'the principle of "disbursing out of public treasury anything towards the support of the religious establishments, Hindoo or Mahomedan beyond what their own religious establishments furnish" is objectionable'. The Board of Control, in its official correspondence with the Directors, pointed out that 'the revenues by which that treasury is supplied are wholly derived from persons of those religious persuasions'. Finally, the Board incorporated the very words which Dundas had used in private correspondence with Grant and Parry to refute their evangelical arguments:

> The Company have virtually contracted an obligation before they draw a single Rupee of Revenue from the country to support and maintain on a proper footing and under proper regulations those Establishments which have immemorially been held in reverence and deemed sacred by their Native Subjects.[68]

Back in India, the evangelical Directors had unwitting allies in the Cuttack district officers who were exasperated by the duties of administering the Pilgrim Tax. James Hunter, the first Collector of Pilgrim Tax, was so frustrated by the continued incompetence of temple priests that he pleaded with the Government to restore the Raja of Khurda to a position of authority over the temple. At the same time, the Cuttack Board of Revenue received complaints from 'respectable Hindoos...that serious inconveniences have been experienced by the pilgrims...owing to the scrutiny which takes place' according to the requirements of Beng. Reg. IV 1806. This prompted

---

[67] Bengal Regulation IV for levying a Tax from Pilgrims resorting to the Temple of Jugunnauth, and for the Superintendence and Management of the Temple (passed by Governor General in Council 3 April 1806); Bengal Regulation V for preventing Persons from evading Payment of the Tax established by Regulation IV 1806 (passed by Governor General in Council 17 April 1806); I.O.R., V/8/18, pp. 169–74; cf. Prabhat Mukherjee, *op. cit.*, Document Ten, pp. 64–65; *see also* Nancy Gardner Cassels, *op. cit.*, pp. 39–49.

[68] G. Holford, Secretary to Board of Commissioners, to W. Ramsay, Secretary to Court of Directors, 4 March 1809, Letters from the Board to the East India Company, I.O.R., E/2/31, fols 141–42; cf. Prabhat Mukherjee, *Pilgrim Tax and Temple Scandals, op. cit.*, Documents Eleven and 11c, pp. 68–71.

Governor General Barlow to virtually suspend the collection of Pilgrim Tax until a new Regulation could be formulated.[69] George Webb, Hunter's successor as Collector of Pilgrim Tax, had been assigned the task of reporting upon the temple's endowments. After surveying the temple's assets and trimming its expenses, Webb came to the conclusion that the Company was obligated to meet all the annual expenses of the temple which he estimated at 56,000 rupees in round figures. In later years, this sum came to be associated with the 'established donation' guaranteed by Sec. 30 Beng. Reg. XII 1805. When asked by the Bengal Government to submit rules for more efficient collection of the Pilgrim Tax, Webb opined that the way to make the Tax more productive was to increase the privileges of the high-class *Lal Jatries*. Convinced of the impossibility of controlling fraud, he merely designed an elaborate system to ensure superior privileges to the top class of pilgrims. It was his idea to introduce intermediate classes of pilgrims with *Nim Lal Jatries* as a second class owing five rupees coming from the north and three rupees coming from the south. *Bhurrung*s, a holdover from the days of Maratha rule, were to form a third class paying two rupees uniformly. There was a fourth class of the poverty stricken and despised low castes who were prohibited temple entry. Finally, there was a fifth tax-exempt classification of religious mendicants including the likes of the Ganges water carrier and the prostrating pilgrim who lay down at every step in order to measure the way to Jagannath by the length of his body.[70]

Ultimately, Governor General Minto rationalized the competing criticisms and suggestions from Evangelicals and district officers with the pragmatic necessity of establishing a regime of good order in Puri. The result was Bengal Regulation IV of 1809 which rescinded Beng. Regs IV and V of 1806. The Cuttack Board of Revenue and the Court of Directors were appeased by the restoration of the Raja of Khurda as Superintendent of the 'Temple of Juggunnauth'. However, the concern of the Bengal Government and the Board of Commissioners in London to maintain a vestige of control was met by retaining in the hands of the Collector of Cuttack the right of appointing three senior priests. These priests, in turn, were charged with the duty of reporting to the Collector of Pilgrim Tax any deviation

---

[69] T. Graham, President of Cuttack Board of Revenue, Minute 30 June 1807, Bengal Revenue Proceedings, 2 July 1807, No. 12; G. Dowdeswell, Secretary to Government in the Revenue Department, to Cuttack Board of Revenue, 2 July 1807, Bengal Revenue Proceedings, 2 July 1807, No. 14, I.O.R., P/55/3.

[70] G. Webb, Collector of Cuttack, to H.T. Colebrooke, President and Members of the Board of Revenue, 7 March 1808, Bengal Revenue Proceedings, 8 April 1808, No. 18, I.O.R., P/55/11.

by the Raja from the 'recorded rules and institutions of the Temple'. The Collector of Pilgrim Tax would represent the case to the Governor General for 'final orders...if it should appear on inquiry that the interposition of Government is necessary for the restoration of good order, and the prevention of disputes and irregularities'. Acting further on Robert Dundas' pragmatic sense of responsibility for the protection of pilgrims from extortion and the preservation of order and tranquillity, Beng. Reg. IV of 1809 provided for continued collection of the Pilgrim Tax according to elaborate rules which greatly embellished the original provisions of the rescinded Regulations IV and V of 1806. In accordance with George Webb's suggestions, four classes of tax paying pilgrims were enumerated. Buller improved upon Webb's recommendation of enhancing the privileges of the high-class *Lal Jatries* by extending their period of access to the temple from 16 days to 30 days. The *Nim Lal Jatries* were to be allowed temple access for 10 days during the prominent *Rath Jatra*, but only 7 days at all other times. The *Bhurrung Jatries* were allowed temple access for five days during the *Rath Jatra* and four days at all other times. The fourth class of *punjtirthee*s were forbidden all temple access. Instead, they were allowed to visit five sacred sites in the company of a police peon or *batpeada*. For two rupees they could enter the town for a period of 16 days to perform religious ceremonies, again in the company of a peon from the Collector's Office. To obstruct fraud, the first three classes were issued with certificates and passes specifying the amount of tax paid and privileges obtained. Finally, there was a class of pilgrims exempt from the Tax according to George Webb's list of religious mendicants and residents of the 'holy land' immediately adjacent to Puri. The only perceived omission of Beng. Reg. IV 1809 was quickly rectified by the enactment of Beng. Reg. XI 1810 to ensure tax exempt status for native sepoys, officers on duty in Puri and native servants of European officers on duty in Puri. It was considered that the system of certificates and passes introduced by Beng. Reg. IV 1809 was just what was needed to check tax evasion. More importantly, especially in the eyes of the Company's Evangelical critics, the Company's brief experiment with direct administration of Jagannath Temple had come to an end.[71]

---

[71] Secs I–III, Bengal Regulation IV for rescinding regulations IV and V of 1806; and for Substituting Rules in lieu of those enacted in the said Regulations, for levying Duties from the Pilgrims resorting to Juggunnauth, and for the Superintendence and Management of the Affairs of the Temple (passed by the Governor General in Council 28 April 1809), I.O.R., V/8/18, pp. 314–15; cf. Prabhat Mukherjee, *op. cit.,* Document Twelve, pp. 73–75; Bengal Regulation XI for amending a Part of Regulation IV 1809, respecting the Temple of Juggunnauth (passed 27 April 1810), I.O.R., V/8/18, pp. 390–91.

After the collection of the Pilgrim Tax was established at Puri as official Company policy, the Governor General in Council enacted Bengal Regulation XVIII in 1810 to regulate the collection of Pilgrim Tax at Allahabad.[72] Rates of tax were assigned according to the pilgrims' mode of conveyance. The lowest rate of one rupee was charged a pilgrim travelling on foot; the highest rate of 20 rupees was reserved for a pilgrim travelling by elephant. A system of licenses and exemptions was introduced so that no one could be allowed ablutions at the sacred conflux of the Ganges and Jumna Rivers without a license or *maafee chittee* indicating exemption. All barbers attending ablution ceremonies were required to be registered with the Collector under penalty of a 50-rupee fine or three months' imprisonment.

There was no other legislation regulating pilgrim taxes in the other two presidencies, although the Madras Board of Revenue expressed an interest in having 'all the arrangements relating to Tripetty Pagoda...framed into a Regulation as has been done in Bengal with respect to the Juggernaut Pagoda'. The Tripetty (Tirupathi) Temple was a temple of huge significance in the south. Towards the end of the East India Company period, its revenue was calculated at more than twice that of Jagannath Temple.[73] Remarkably, in the case of the Madras Government which was so deeply involved with a multitude of smaller temples and festivals, it was decided not to interfere at Tirupathi. North Arcot district officers had worried about peculation of revenue from the Tirupathi Temple at least as much as the Cuttack district officers fretted over corruption within Jagannath Temple. The Collector of North Arcot had reported in 1810 that the 'Pagoda Bramins' were 'indolent, licentious and avaricious to an extreme' but that even the 'arbitrary Government of the Mahomedans' had hesitated to interfere out of 'respect to the religious feelings of the Hindoos'.[74]

Regardless of this perceived need for surveillance, no action was taken by the Madras Government comparable to the Bengal Government's legislation affecting Jagannath Temple. The Madras Board of Revenue decided that the Pilgrim Tax system at Jagannath was 'not perhaps applicable to Tripetty where the offerings...are entirely voluntary'.[75]

---

[72] Bengal Regulation XVIII for the Collection of the Duties on Pilgrims at Allahabad (passed by Governor General in Council 16 October 1810), I.O.R., V/8/18, pp. 409–11.

[73] 'Government Connection with Idolatry in India', *Calcutta Review* X (1852): p. 128; cf. Nancy Gardner Cassels, *op. cit.*, Appendix E, p. 164.

[74] H.S. Graeme, Collector of North Arcot, to Madras Board of Revenue, 30 April 1810, T.N.A., North Arcot District Records, Vol. 12, fol. 32.

[75] Madras Board of Revenue to Collector of North Arcot, Fort St. George, 2 June 1812, T.N.A., North Arcot District Records, Bundle 18(5), fols 236–38.

However, it might be deduced that the legislation regulating collection of the Pilgrim Tax at Puri and Allahabad inspired the Bengal Government to enact the even more ambitious Regulation XIX of 1810 vesting responsibility for 'all the lands granted for the support of Mosques, Hindoo temples...in the Board of Revenue and Board of Commissioners'. And, as seen above, this regulation was more or less duplicated by the Madras Government in Madras Regulation VII 1817. In addition, the Bengal Government became suspicious that there were pilgrims who were, in fact, a fictitious disguise for foreign intruders intent on criminal activity within the Company's territories. With this in mind Bengal Regulation III of 1821 enlarged powers already vested in police *darogah*s to apprehend all vagrants and suspicious persons so that they might 'detain all persons travelling in bodies through their jurisdictions...under circumstances leading to the suspicion that they have assumed a fictitious character'.[76]

One matter not resolved by Beng. Reg. IV 1809 was destined to be of lasting embarrassment to the Company; this was the question of fees demanded by Jagannath Temple servants known as *Purharee*s (*Pratihari*s) and *Pundah*s. The *Purharee*s or *Pratihari*s guarded the inner doors of the Temple; it was their responsibility to conduct pilgrims into the temple and present them to the deity. The *Pundah*s were the temple priests who had the exclusive right to perform temple ceremonies. By 1840, the number of these officers was variously estimated at between 400 and 500 *Purharee*s and between 2,000 and 4,000 *Pundah*s. The very first Collector of Pilgrim Tax noted the notorious reputation of these 'pilgrim hunters', so labelled by Company servants for their practice of sending emissaries throughout India in search of pilgrims. In response to Hunter's remark that 'the pilgrims will never be well treated by their conductors unless they receive a present from their own hands', Section 6 of Beng. Reg. IV 1806 honoured his suggestion that the 'Purharees and Pundahs...be entitled to receive...a fee from pilgrims according to a table of rates'. They were then prohibited from making demands for money, although they were allowed 'presents or gifts...voluntarily made'. Hunter then set the *Purharee*s' fees at 1.8 rupees for the *Rath Jatra* and 2.4 rupees on all other occasions. He assigned to the *Pundah*s one rupee for each *Lal Jatri* and two annas for each *Bhurrung Jatri*. However, Hunter's table of rates was confirmed neither by the Cuttack Board of Revenue nor by the Bengal Government; Beng. Reg. IV 1809 ignored

---

[76] Cl. 2, Sec. 7, Bengal Regulation III...for vesting Magistrates with certain powers in regard to persons travelling through, or assembling within their jurisdictions, under suspicious circumstances (passed 19 January 1821), I.O.R., V/8/20.

the *Purharees* and *Pundahs*; and, before long *Purharees* and *Pundahs* fell to squabbling over 'rosoom' fees levied from the pilgrims by the *Pundahs*. On 28 March 1814, the Sudder Dewanny Adawlut ruled in favour of the *Purharee* claims against the *Pundahs*. In face of this ruling by the Company's highest civil court, the Collector of Cuttack, William Trower, began to collect two rupees from each *Lal Jatri* and six annas from each *Bhurrung Jatri* to create a fund to be equally distributed among *Purharees* and *Pundahs* after the *Rath Jatra*. The Bengal Government improved upon this scheme in 1821 to demand an annual payment from the *Purharees* totalling 3,040 Company rupees. The Commissioner of Cuttack had discovered that the Marathas had set an historical precedent by levying a substantial sum from the *Purharees* 'in consideration of which' the *Purharees* 'were allowed to levy from the pilgrims a higher rate of fee than the Pundahs who being servants of the Temple were exempted from any similar demand'. Thus cosseted by the Company's courts and the Government's willingness to collect fees on their behalf beginning in 1816, the *Purharees* became increasingly convinced that they had a right to Government largesse. In 1839, the Commissioner of Cuttack recorded that the Government demand of 3,040 Company rupees from the *Purharees* was offset by fees of three rupees collected from *Lal Jatris* and six *annas* collected from *Bhurrung Jatris*.[77]

As it happened, the Commissioner of Cuttack in 1839 had been instructed to draft legislation to abolish the Pilgrim Tax and withdraw all government interference with Jagannath Temple. This was the culmination of two and a half decades of sometimes very acrimonious debate. For most of this period, all debate was quashed by what was essentially a casual comment of the Court of Directors penned in the margin of an 1814 draft Revenue Despatch to Bengal. Reacting to reports of profit in the Jagannath Temple accounts of 1810–11, the Directors remarked that they 'do not consider the tax on pilgrims as a source of Revenue but merely as a fund for keeping the temple in repair'.[78]

---

[77] James Hunter, Collector of Tax on Pilgrims at Juggernauth, to G. Dowdeswell, Secretary to Government in the Revenue Department, 7 March 1806, Bengal Revenue Consultations, 20 March 1806, No. 18, I.O.R., P/54/52; Sec. 6 Beng. Reg. IV 1806, Prabhat Mukherjee, *op. cit.*, Document Ten, p. 64; A.J.M. Mills, Commissioner of Cuttack, to Sudder Board of Revenue, 11 May 1839, N.A.I., Land Revenue Records, Revenue Department Proceedings, 21 October 1839, No. 30, fols 97–124; cf. Prabhat Mukherjee, *op. cit.*, Document Twenty-Two, pp. 127–28.

[78] Bengal Revenue Despatch, 28 October 1814, I.O.R., E/4/681, fol. 315.

Meanwhile, dissatisfaction simmered among district officers in Cuttack who challenged their superiors in the Bengal Government intent on preserving the status quo based on the Pilgrim Tax Regulations. After a variety of unsavoury incidents culminating in the death of pilgrims in a stampede at the 1813 *Rath Jatra*, the Collector of Cuttack proposed a new regulation in 1814 to restructure the procedure for collection of Pilgrim Tax and to curtail the authority of the Raja of Khurda. The collector's immediate superior took his proposed regulation one step further to call for abolition of the Pilgrim Tax altogether in order to attract the wealthier classes of pilgrims who might then spend more in the district. The Bengal Government categorically rejected all of these proposals in the name of preserving the spirit of Beng. Reg. IV 1809, which kept European supervision of temple affairs at arms length.[79] Shortly thereafter, the same district officers accused the Raja of Khurda of fomenting the 1817 rebellion of Paik mercenary foot soldiers from the Raja's former estate. But a Judge from the Calcutta Court of Circuit counter-charged Cuttack district officers with being overly meddlesome, and a Special Commissioner appointed to investigate the rebellion criticized the Revenue authorities for inflicting damaging over-assessment in Cuttack district amidst 'exactions of a corrupt and oppressive Police'.[80]

Even the distinguished jurist, J.H. Harington, could not penetrate the armour of complacency encompassing the Bengal Government. In 1827, with thoughts of discontinuing the Pilgrim Tax altogether, he recommended that the Court of Directors review the 'general question of levying a tax on Hindoo Pilgrims'. The Governor General's Council promptly rejected Harington's suggestion, bestowing ultimate authority upon the Directors' remarks in their 1814 Revenue Despatch that they did 'not consider the tax on pilgrims as a source of Revenue but merely as a fund for keeping the Temple in repair'. Interestingly, the Council compared the Pilgrim Tax to the Abkarry or tax on spirituous liquors:

> All the arguments in favor of taxing the use of ardent spirits and narcotic drugs or any other propensity of human nature which it is wished to discourage apply with equal force to keeping pilgrimages under regulation, and for that purpose maintaining the impositions levied on them.[81]

---

[79] Trower's Draft Regulation, 1814, Nancy Gardner Cassels, *op. cit.*, Appendix F, pp. 164–69; see also in Prabhat Mukherjee, *op. cit.*, Documents Fourteen, Fifteen and Sixteen, pp. 82–94.

[80] W. Ewer, Commissioner, Report for Enquiring into the General State of the District of Cuttack, 13 May 1818, Bengal Criminal Judicial Proceedings, 28 August 1818, No. 86, I.O.R., P/133/33, Paras 8 and 26; cf. Nancy Gardner Cassels, *op. cit.*, pp. 91–92.

[81] Council Resolution, 5 July 1827, Bengal Revenue Consutations, 5 July 1827, Nos 36 and 37, I.O.R., P/61/19.

Furthermore, Governor General Bentinck, noted for his reforms, was to declare the Pilgrim Tax 'just and expedient'.[82]

In 1832, the Cuttack Board of Revenue recommended that the Bengal Government abolish the Pilgrim Tax—all to no avail. In London, the same year, even such luminaries as James Mill testified before a Parliamentary Select Committee that the collection of a Pilgrim Tax was an appropriate aspect of the Company's declared policy of guaranteeing respect for the religion of its Indian subjects. It remained for the Company's Evangelical critics to turn the tide of events. The 1832 Parliamentary Select Committee did hear one bit of testimony to the effect that 'no ill consequence would arise from the discontinuance of such taxes as serve to establish an unnecessary connection between us and the idolatrous practices of our subjects'.[83] This was the voice of J.A. Dalzell who, earlier in his career as a Madras revenue officer, had aroused the ire of the Governor's Council by distributing Christian literature among the cultivators in his district.[84] But, the muscle in the Evangelical attack came from the younger Charles Grant who, from his position as President of the Board of Control, manipulated Company policy. He persuaded the Board that they should override all objections from the Court of Directors and demand the abolition of the Pilgrim Tax as well as all British interference in temple management. This was the substance of the very contentious Revenue Despatch No. 587 of 20 February 1833, dubbed a 'Christian epistle' by the Company's official historian, J.W. Kaye. Although they dutifully signed the Despatch, the Directors bridled at these orders which they considered to be 'impolitic' and 'at variance with the compact of the British Government with the people of India to secure to them the full observance of their religion and laws'. From the Directors' point of view, the only saving grace of Revenue Despatch No. 587 lay in paragraphs 58 and 59 allowing the local government full discretionary authority in its implementation.[85]

---

[82] Minute by J.H. Harington, 1 July 1827, and Council Resolution, 5 July 1827, Bengal Revenue Consutations, 5 July 1827, Nos 36 and 37, I.O.R., P/61/19; W. Bentinck, 'Minute to the Military Board about Roads through the Bengal Presidency', 25 March 1831, Nottingham University, Bentinck Papers, PwJf 2666.

[83] The Select Committee, Report on the Affairs of the East India Company, *Parliamentary Papers* (1831–32) XI, Cmd. 735, pp. 280–81, 331.

[84] Thomas Munro, Minute on Missionary Collectors, 15 Novembr 1822, T.N.A., Public Sundries, Vol. 129, fols 157–78.

[85] Bengal Revenue Despatch, No. 587, 20 February 1833, I.O.R., E/4/736; P. Auber, to T.B. Macaulay, 21 February 1833, Letters from the Company to the Board, I.O.R., E/2/12, fol. 57; C. Majoribanks and W. Wigram, Chairman and Deputy Chairman of the Court of Directors, to C. Grant, President of the Board of Control, 13 June 1833, Letters from the Company to the Board, I.O.R., E/2/12, fol. 226; cf. Nancy Gardner Cassels, *op. cit.*, pp. 106–11; and Prabhat Mukherjee, *op. cit.*, Document Seventeen, pp. 101–104.

As Bengal Revenue Despatch No. 587 arrived in Calcutta in the wake of the Bengal Government's decision to reject similar recommendations from Cuttack district officers, it is not surprising that the new Supreme Government of India reacted to these new orders with purposeful indifference. Demand for full implementation of Revenue Despatch No. 587 came from Madras. First, there was a memorial presented by the Anglican Bishop of Madras on 8 August 1836 objecting to Madras Reg. VII 1817 which, like its Bengal predecessor Reg. XIX 1810, involved Company servants in the management of pagodas and mosques. Also subject to objection was the 'practice of requiring British officers and troops to be present at Mohamedan and Idolatrous ceremonies.'[86] Then, this memorial attracted the support of the newly arrived Commander-in-Chief in Madras, Sir Peregrine Maitland, who had strong Evangelical sympathies. Nevertheless, it was censured by the Government of Madras. In the wake of this censure, enmity between the Governor of Madras and his Commander-in-Chief intensified over an order boldly issued by Sir Peregrine in an effort to enforce a General Order issued by his predecessor to keep all troops apart from any religious procession or ceremony. An outright clash between the Governor and his Evangelical Commander-in-Chief was averted by forwarding the memorial to Governor General Auckland in Calcutta and by the arrival of a new Governor of Madras, John Elphinstone. Auckland took an ambivalent course, scolding both the Governor for his censure and the Bishop for the offence which his memorial caused to 'the religious feelings of the inhabitants of this empire'.[87] Meanwhile, the proceedings of the Madras Government were noticed in Bombay. The Governor, who coincidentally was the brother of the younger Charles Grant, expressed an eagerness to publish the very General Order concerning the presence of Company servants at Indian religious ceremonies which had caused such a storm in Madras. Robert Grant wished to interfere with the participation of Company servants in such ceremonies as the *Daftar Puja*—or worship of public records—and the custom of consecrating a cocoanut in the River Tapti at Surat and in the River Nerbudda at Broach in celebration of the end of the monsoon. Governor General Auckland expressed his horror over this proposed interference in a remarkably eloquent minute. He relished the 'rare' opportunity for the Government to show 'sympathies...in unison with those of the people'. Thus he commended

---

[86] 'Memorial Praying for Equal Religious Toleration to all Subjects of the State', in *Friend of India* (3 November 1836).

[87] Earl of Auckland, to Bishop Corrie, 7 December 1836, Auckland Papers, Letter Books, Vol. I, B.L., ADD. MSS 37690, fol. 18.

Government involvement with the *Daftar Puja* in Surat as a 'popular holiday' despite its elements of 'superstition'. He concluded:

> Something of Paganism may be traced in our English Feasts of May day and Harvest Home—something druidical in the rites of Hallowe'en, more that is Catholic in the village mummeries of Christmas...To time and the gradual growth of knowledge I would trust much, and would deprecate in these matters all overstrained fastidiousness of feeling, and a sternness of action which must tend to create alarm and to alienate the people from the Government.[88]

Back in London, John Poynder, the Evangelical among the Company's Proprietors, was intent upon shaming his brother investors with the claim that the Company had netted a clear profit of £1,000,000 from the Pilgrim Tax. The Proprietors then goaded the Directors into sending a Revenue Despatch on 22 February 1837 calling at least for information in response to their previous 'Christian Epistle' despatch of 1833. However, when papers arrived in London containing reports of the Madras Memorial and of the agitation over the involvement of Company servants with religious ceremonies in Madras and Bombay, Auckland's sentiments as expressed in his Hallowe'en Minute fell on fertile ground among the Directors. In a fresh Despatch dated 18 October 1837, the Directors reversed their earlier orders of 20 February 1833 and 22 February 1837 with instructions

> that no customary salute or marks of respect to Native festivals be discontinued at any of the Presidencies; that no protection hitherto given be withdrawn; and that no change whatever be made, in any matter relating to the Native religion, except under the authority of the Supreme Government.[89]

Storm clouds quickly gathered amongst the Company's Evangelical critics within and without. In Madras, Sir Peregrine Maitland caused huge embarrassment to his superiors by resigning his post, ostensibly over the Bengal Revenue Despatch of 18 October 1837 which he dubbed the 'Go Slow' Despatch; in his wake, R. Nelson also resigned. He was the revenue officer who had earned the censure of his superiors on the Madras Board of Revenue by refusing to participate in the forcible recruitment of agricultural

---

[88] Minute by the Governor General, 1 April 1837, *Board's Collections*, I.O.R., F/4/1618 # 64968.
[89] Bengal Revenue Despatch, No. 475, 18 October 1837, I.O.R., E/4/752, fol. 1121; Bengal Revenue Despatch, No. 82, 22 February 1837, I.O.R., E/4/749, fols 764–76; J. Poynder, Speech before the Court of Proprietors, 21 December 1836, cited in *The Times* (London), 16 March 1837; cf. Nancy Gardner Cassels, *op. cit.*, pp. 111–23.

labourers to pull the *rath*s or idol cars during the *rath* festivals in his district. In London, the Archbishop of Canterbury, the Bishop of London and Charles Grant who had been elevated to the peerage as Lord Glenelg—all appeared before the House of Lords to castigate the Government of India for its failure to implement the orders of 20 February 1833. Sir John Cam Hobhouse, the current President of the Board of Control, responded to the growing hysteria with a promise before the House of Commons on 26 July 1838 that the Government of India would receive immediate orders to act upon the Despatch of 20 February 1833. And so, the Board of Control forced the Directors against their better judgement to send Revenue Despatch, No. 446, of 8 August 1838 commanding the Government of India to enforce the 'Christian Epistle'. In their original draft of Revenue Despatch No. 446, the Directors had made pointed reference to the Company's principle of religious toleration and to the discretionary authority of local governments. When the Board removed all such indirect language, the Directors actually disclaimed 'all responsibility for the instructions as they are presently framed which the Court have been directed to send out to India'.[90] Almost at the very same moment, Auckland expressed his frustration over Evangelical agitation in a private letter to Hobhouse. He exclaimed: 'You may as well abolish the gin tax to make men sober as the Pilgrim Tax to convert Hindoos to Christianity'.[91] However, when Auckland received Revenue Despatch No. 446 at his camp at Ludhiana whence he was preparing to launch the disastrous First Afghan War, he promptly took action. He abolished the Pilgrim Tax at Allahabad by executive fiat. He then submitted a plan of action for abolishing the tax at Gaya and at Jagannath Temple.

In the relative safety and calm of Calcutta, Auckland's Council endorsed the substance of Auckland's proposals. On 11 March 1839, they resolved

> wholly to relinquish the tax on pilgrims; to continue the yearly donation now given for support of the temple, for which the faith of government is pledged; to make over to the rajah of Khoorda and his successors the entire management of the temple; to retain the temple lands (*sattais hazaree mahal*) in the management of the revenue officers of government, accounting to the Superintendent of the temple for the net proceeds; to exact nothing from the

---

[90] Court to Board, 9 August 1838, Letters from the Company to the Board, I.O.R., E/2/15. India Revenue Draft, No. 446, approved by Court of Directors 25 July 1838, India and Bengal Despatches, I.O.R., E/4/756, fol. 361; India Revenue Draft No. 446 altered by Board 28 July 1838 and signed 8 August 1838, *ibid.*, fol. 362.

[91] George Eden, Earl of Auckland, to John Cam Hobhouse, Simla, 23 August 1838, Broughton Papers, B.L., ADD. MSS 36473, fols 316–17.

temple for the support of poor pilgrims or a poor hospital; and to institute at the charge of government, a government dispensary in the town of Pooree, for the relief of all persons who may apply to it.[92]

Having thus demonstrated their willingness to act, the Council deferred the question of a legislative enactment. It was at this point that A.J.M. Mills, the Commissioner of Cuttack, received a request for more information to which he responded with a draft law requiring the repeal of all regulations sanctioning 'duties from Pilgrims at Juggernath' but salvaging the very words of Cl. 1, Sec. 2, Beng. Reg. IV 1809 to vest in the Rajah of Khoorda 'the superintendence of the Temple of Juggernath, and its interior economy'. When the *purharees* panicked at the thought that the Government would no longer collect the Pilgrim Tax in their interests, they submitted petitions on 4 August 1838 and 7 May 1839 calling for protection. Mills responded by prohibiting in his draft law 'all duties, fees or gratuities at the gate of the temple or other places demanded for the benefit of individuals'. Mills hastened to explain:

> This declaration would make the abolition of the tax a popular measure; popular it will be to all but the pundahs and purharees and they are the last whose interest should be consulted....Indeed it is a well known fact that the pilgrims are in the habit of burying outside of the town, or leaving in the hands of the shopkeepers on the road, enough to take them home, so well do they know, that these extortioners will turn them out of the town, naked and pennyless.

As for any remaining financial obligation to the temple, Mills made it clear that the 'temple of Juggernath at Poree' was still subject to the provisions of Beng. Reg. XIX of 1810.[93]

Even after Mills' masterful analysis of the situation at Jagannath, Auckland remained opposed to any new legislation. However, distracted by his Afghan campaigns, he allowed his Council to prepare the way to abolish the Pilgrim Tax with legislation. In November 1839, the Council requested the Deputy Governor of Bengal to proceed with abolition of the tax at Gaya. This involved the remission to a local Raja of some of his estate taxes and the transfer to the government treasury monthly charges in

---

[92] Resolution of Government of India, 11 March 1839, N.A.I., Revenue Consultations, 11 March 1839.
[93] A.J.M. Mills, Commissioner of Cuttack, to Sudder Board of Revenue, 11 May 1839, N.A.I., Land Revenue Records, Revenue Department Proceedings, 21 October 1839, No. 30, fols 97–124; cf. Prabhat Mukherjee, *op. cit.*, Document Twenty-Two, pp. 124–29.

support of a hospital in Calcutta. Then, on 20 April 1840, the Governor General in Council enacted Act X to abolish the Pilgrim Tax at Allahabad, Gaya and Jagannath. This meant the repeal of Sec. 31 Beng. Reg. XII 1805, Beng. Regs IV and V 1806, Beng. Reg. IV 1809, Beng. Regs XI and XVIII 1810 and Sec. 4 of Beng. Reg. XXVII 1793. Cl. 1, Sec. 2 of Beng. Reg. IV 1809 was effectively reenacted to continue vesting in the Rajah of Khurda full responsibility for the management of affairs at Jagannath Temple.[94] The Government of India officially informed the Governments of Bombay and Madras that the 'general principle...that the administration of the affairs and funds of the native religious institutions shall be vested in individuals professing the faith to which the institutions belong' applied to all three presidencies. In Bombay, a secular minded Sir James Rivett Carnac had become Governor after the death of Robert Grant. Carnac promptly approved plans submitted by his subordinates to withdraw all government interference in temple affairs in their districts. By proceeding case by case, he avoided the need for a general legislative enactment. In contrast, Governor Elphinstone in Madras attempted a partial withdrawal of government involvement in the affairs of Madras temples. He readily relinquished the proceeds of the Pilgrim Tax at Tirupathi Temple, but he proposed that temple lands throughout the Madras presidency should remain under the supervision of the Madras Board of Revenue. It was left to the Supreme Government in Calcutta to rebuke Elphinstone for not making government withdrawal 'final and complete'.[95]

Revenue or Regulation?

Certainly, the abiding refrain in debates and legislation governing the collection of pilgrim taxes was a guarantee of respect for the religion of the Company's Hindu and Muslim subjects. This could scarcely have been otherwise inasmuch as pilgrim taxes were collected at temples and shrines which were potent religious symbols in a land where the importance of religion far exceeded that of secular government authority. Perhaps at Gaya

---

[94] Act X for abolition of certain Pilgrim Taxes, and for superintendence of Temple of Juggernath (passed 20 April 1840), I.O.R., V/8/31.
[95] F.J. Halliday, Junior Secretary, to the Government of India, to H. Chamier, Chief Secretary to the Government of Fort St. George, 10 August 1840, *Parliamentary Papers* (House of Lords) (1841) V, Paper 20.

and Allahabad, it was credible that the Company's prime motivation was to protect pilgrims from exploitation at the hands of *gayawals* and *pragwals*. But, at Jagannath Temple, the Company found itself challenging the authority of the local Raja. Under the fig leaf of preserving order among throngs of pilgrims, the Company became involved in temple administration. Ultimately, the local rebellion which officials attempted to blame on followers of the Raja was reliably attributed to overzealous revenue assessments. Terrible deaths by trampling among the hordes of pilgrims attending the *Rath jatra* fuelled a sense of righteous obligation among Company officials at the highest level to preserve and protect the temple from violence and fraud. It was difficult to deny the need for preservation of order amidst the disorder which was inevitable when pilgrims, many desperately poor and wretched, perhaps even in suspicious disguise, assembled in vast numbers from all over India for a religious festival. However, evangelical critics and sensible Company servants were persistent in noticing the steady accumulation of profit. Finally, a Proprietor of the Company was willing to assert that the Company netted a clear profit of £1 million from its pilgrim tax revenues. The Company could no longer maintain the validity of its claim that pilgrim taxes were collected only in order to keep Jagannath Temple in good repair and to protect pilgrims at Gaya and Allahabad from fraud and abuse by *gayawals* and pragwals. Act X 1840 did not end the Company's entanglement with India's religious institutions, but it did end excise as an instrument of control.

By way of contrast, discourse revolving around Abkarry revenue was unfettered by any connection with Indian religion. And, Abkarry revenue long outlasted the East India Company, itself. Late in the nineteenth century, the Indian Government continued to draw criticism for its willingness to draw revenue from impoverished addicts of liquor or drugs. As expressed by one critic, the Government's reliance upon excise income was 'rapidly spreading drunkenness among the people of Bengal in order to supply revenue to the Government'. Opium production in India steadily increased. The Chinese Government struggled to pay off its indemnity from the Opium War well into the twentieth century. The Treaty Powers expanded the unequal treaty system in order to force diplomatic relations upon China and extract increased indemnity. The scourge of opium penetrated ever more deeply into Chinese society.

6

Public Instruction Begets Indian Agency, Free Press and Trial by Jury

A sum of not less than one [lakh] of rupees in each year shall be set apart and applied to the revival and improvement of literature, and the encouragement of the learned natives of India, and for the introduction and promotion of a knowledge of the sciences among the inhabitants of the British territories in India.[1]

As the mantle of public administration fell upon the English East India Company in the wake of its conquests at the end of the eighteenth century, the Company found itself in confrontation with issues deeply embedded in the beliefs and customs of its Hindu and Muslim subjects. Warren Hastings, eager to 'stand forth as *diwan*', devised an administrative framework pointedly sympathetic to Hindu and Muslim religious sensibilities. He responded to a petition from Muslim scholars by supporting the Calcutta Madrassa and he guaranteed to Hindus and Muslims protection of their respective rights of caste, inheritance and succession in the Company's law courts. The East India Company then defined its initiatives in accord with values perceived to be in the interests of a general public. The pragmatic objective of Hastings' Madrassa was to secure a supply of well trained legal officers or *maulvi*s to give legal advice in the form of *futwa*s in the Company's courts. With the expansion of government support for more educational institutions, a system of public instruction evolved. An emergent press challenged official views of an Anglo-Indian public. And, by the 1830s the Company began to experiment with the introduction of juries in order to reach out to an Indian public beyond that controlled by Muslim munsiffs and *maulvi*s. Ultimately *futwa*s were declared to be unnecessary and Persian was replaced by English and vernaculars as the language of the courts.

---

[1] 53 Geo. III, c. 155, s. 43.

Public Instruction

With the 1813 Charter Act, the English Parliament decreed that the education of the East India Company's Hindu and Muslim subjects was the responsibility of the state. Thereafter, education policy became the most lasting and unresolved controversy in the Company's history. At least, officials preparing the 1854 Charter of Indian Education draft despatch observed that 'There is no Indian question upon which more had been written...since in 1813 £10,000 a year was set apart by Parliament for native education'.[2] Although the deadlock between Orientalists and Anglicists on the Committee of Public Instruction in Calcutta in the 1830s long served as a benchmark for Indian historians, it can be argued that it was faith in the indigenous system of village schools and regional centres of learning which was truly at the heart of the Company's efforts to develop an educational policy. It has been speculated, though not proven, that Governor General Minto's Minute of 1811 urging the 'fitness of incurring some additional expense with a view to the restoration of learning' was the inspiration for the educational clause of the 1813 Charter Act. Despite the fact that scarce public funds were available for education in England, the 1813 Charter decreed that the Company must 'set apart...not less than one *lakh* of rupees...for the encouragement of the learned natives of India'.[3] In their letter of instruction to the Governor General on how to implement the Charter requirements, the Company's Directors lavished praise upon 'the mode of instruction that from time immemorial has been practised' by village teachers in India. They credited this 'distinguished feature of internal polity' with withstanding 'the shock of revolution' and producing 'the general intelligence of the natives as scribes and accountants'. They made specific reference to the system which was the successful experiment of Dr Bell, a Madras chaplain at the Madras Male Orphan Asylum, and which was later introduced into English schools by the Quaker, Joseph Lancaster, in order to provide education for all. It was a system which made use of monitors to teach each other, using first sand, then leaves and finally paper for the most advanced students, to write letters and arithmetical sums. The Directors further called

---

[2] Wood Papers, British Library, I.O.L., MSS Eur. F78/12a, fol. 97.
[3] Minute by Lord Minto, 6 March 1811, in H. Sharp, ed., *Selections from Educational Records*, Part I, (New Delhi, repr, 1965), p. 19; cf. 53 Geo. III, c. 155, s. 43 in Lynn Zastoupil and Martin Moir, eds., *The Great Indian Education Debate—Documents Relating to the Orientalist–Anglicist Controversy, 1781–1843* (Richmond, Surrey, 1999), p. 91n.

for the three presidencies in India to make enquiries into the 'present state' of indigenous schools.[4]

With Maratha, Pindari and Nepalese wars intervening, nothing transpired in India for a full 10 years. When the Government in Bengal finally resolved to create the General Committee of Public Instruction (G.C.P.I.) in order to regulate the existing Calcutta Madrassa and Sanskrit College at Benares, they brought down upon their heads the wrath of the Home Authorities in the form of a hectoring despatch generally attributed to James Mill. Denouncing the plans of the Committee to engraft science onto 'mere Hindoo or mere Mahomedan literature' at the existing Colleges, Mill proclaimed that 'the great end should not have been to teach Hindoo learning, or Mahomedan learning, but useful learning'.[5] Insofar as this 'useful learning' particularly stressed the teaching of science, it was what David Arnold has labelled 'exemplary' of what 'the British saw…as…their "civilising mission", clear evidence of their own superiority over, and imperial responsibility for, a land they identified as superstitious and backward'.[6] But, while preaching 'utility', Mill cautioned against both the Anglicist insistence upon teaching through the medium of the English language and the Orientalist tactic of supporting education through the medium of the classical languages of Sanskrit and Persian or Arabic. He actually preferred an emphasis upon vernacular education. Ironically, it was James Mill's son, John Stuart Mill, who was to respond to the G.C.P.I.'s efforts to adapt their policies to this devastating criticism. The younger Mill, while endorsing his father's emphasis upon useful learning, pronounced his satisfaction with the Bengal Government's gradual approach and emphasized 'the importance of what may be done to spread useful knowledge among the natives, through the medium of books and oral instruction in their own languages'.[7] The G.C.P.I. continued to

---

[4] Paras 19–21, Public Despatch to Bengal, 3 June 1814 in Zastoupil and Moir, *ibid.*, pp. 95–96. This economical means of teaching 'without spoiling paper, pens or ink' was described first by a Roman soldier, Peter Della Valle, in 1623, 'Comparative view of Plans of Education in Publications of Dr Bell and Mr Lancaster', Article XV in *Quarterly Review*, Vol. VI, No. XI (August 1811). Unfortunately, Bell's system of 'mutual instruction' was ultimately condemned in 1839 as a 'vicious system leading to disastrous results'. See H. Sharp, *ibid.*, p. 23n.

[5] Para. 83, Revenue Despatch, to Bengal, 18 february 1824, in Zastoupil and Moir, *op. cit.*, p. 116.

[6] David Arnold, *Science, technology and Medicine in Colonial India* [*The New Cambridge History of India* III.5] (Cambridge, 2000), p. 15.

[7] Public Despatch, to Bengal, 29 September 1830, No. 39, I.O.R., E/4/729, fols 397–98. For confirmation of Mill's authorship of this despatch, *see* J.M. Robson, M. and Z. Moir, eds., *Writings on India by John Stuart Mill, Collected Works of John Stuart Mill*, Vol. XXX, (Toronto, 1990) Appendix A, p. 291 (No. 1562).

reiterate their faith in vernacular education even when Governor General Bentinck threw his entire weight behind Macaulay's chauvinistic dismissal of 'the whole native literature of India' as inferior to a 'single shelf of a good European library'. Accepting Macaulay's advice that the G.C.P.I. was not 'fettered' by the 1813 Charter in its use of funds, Bentinck's Council resolved as of 7 March 1835 that all public funds at the disposal of the Committee must be expended to support 'useful studies' in the English language at the expense of 'Oriental learning'.[8] The members of the G.C.P.I., nevertheless, proclaimed themselves 'deeply sensible of the importance of encouraging the cultivation of the vernacular languages'. They insisted that they did not consider that 'the order of the 7th of March precludes this'.[9]

Far away from the dramatic standoff within government councils and committees in Calcutta, the reality of existing educational practices and institutions in the *mofussil* was to prove an ephemeral—even kaleidoscopic—phenomenon which continually eluded well-meaning Company officials. Inspired individuals launched impressive educational experiments. In 1814 in Bengal, Rev. Robert May established a vernacular school at Chinsurah. Within a year he had 16 schools with 957 pupils and by 1818 there were 36 May schools with 3,000 pupils. Governor General Hastings supported the schools with monthly grants of ₹600 and an enthusiastic endorsement of May's plan to establish a School for Teachers in connection with his Central School. As described by Robert May, himself, 'youths' were 'received on probation…(to) perform alternately the duties of general Monitor in the Central School (and) visit the Village Schools by turns which occupies each boy three days in every month'. These schools were operated by the Bell—Lancastrian system of monitors supervising children carefully separated according to their current prowess. Thus the 'Children must sit in regular rows one before the other—those who write on sand first…on the palm leaves next, on Plaintain leaves, and…on Paper last of all'. Yet, while rejoicing in the apparent success of his schools, May acknowledged that there was opposition from 'old Teachers' and 'rich natives' who opened 'two other schools…with a design of breaking up my School'.[10]

---

[8] Zastoupil and Moir, *op. cit.*, pp. 165, 195.

[9] G.C.P.I. Manifesto, cited in John William Kaye, *The Administration of the East India Company* (Allahabad/Delhi, repr.: 1966), pp. 597–98. Kaye further emphasized that 'It must not be supposed that Lord Bentinck and his supporters ever contemplated the degradation of the vernacular. The blow which they struck was aimed not at the living but at the dead languages of the country'.

[10] Report by Robert May, 8 April 1816, Judicial Criminal Proceedings, 5 July 1816, No. 8, W.B.S.A., Judicial Criminal Proceedings, Vol. 364, fols 31, 34–35; Report by Robert May, 5 January 1816, Judicial Criminal Proceedings, 5 July 1816, No. 6, *ibid.*, fols 12, 19–20.

In 1815 on the opposite side of India, the Society for Promoting the Education of the Poor established schools in Bombay, Thana and Surat for both native and European boys. And, in the Southern Concan of Bombay Presidency a society formed 'for establishing and conducting schools'. European subscriptions aided by 'very liberal payments...made...by the Natives of that Province' prompted Mountstuart Elphinstone's government to make a donation of ₹1,000 plus an annual subscription of ₹500. This was endorsed by the Home Authorities.[11] And yet, as in Bengal, there was a sense of unease in governing circles over the less than total enthusiasm among their Indian subjects for English educational institutions. As observed by Elphinstone's nemesis on Council, Francis Warden: 'We should never lose sight of the suspicions and alarms which the natives long entertained of our views in promoting education, which they conceived were solely directed to their conversion'.[12] It is no wonder that Governor Elphinstone responded to the first report of the Bombay Native School Book and School Society with the curt injunction: 'The Governor in Council relies on you carefully adhering to the rules of your society, that Religion, whether Christian or Heathen should not be touched on in any of your schools or Publications'.[13]

Ironically, the missionaries with their zeal for Christianity, were not the cause of offence. In all three presidencies, there were numerous testimonials of enthusiasm for missionary schools despite their Christian curriculum.[14] Lasting offence was instead caused by earnest Company servants who, although they lived by the Company's code of religious neutrality, were contemptuous of existing indigenous schools. In the Council of Governor Elphinstone of Bombay, the prime champion of vernacular education, Mr Goodwin complained that in Village Schools outside Bombay:

---

[11] Para. 41, Public Despatch, from Bombay, 11 August 1824, O.I.O.C., E/4/1506; Public Despatch, to Bombay, 21 September 1825, I.O.R., E/4/1046, fols 242–43.

[12] 'Evidence given by Frances Warden before the Select Committee on the Affairs of the East India Company: Public and Miscellaneous', 30 April 1832, *Parliamentary Papers* (1831–32) IX, Cmd. 735 I, p. 278.

[13] Governor Elphinstone's reply to the First Report of the Bombay Native School Book and School Society, 10 March 1824, included in *First Report of the BNSBSS*, University of Bombay.

[14] William Adam, Report on the State of Education in Bengal (1835), pp. 34–36 cited by Bruce T. McCully, *English Education and the Origins of Indian Nationalism* (Gloucester, Massachusetts, repr., 1966), p. 43; R.V. Parulekar, ed., *Survey of Indigenous Education in the Presidency of Bombay (1820–1830)* (Bombay, repr.: 1951), p. xix and James Hough, Chaplain at Palamcottah, to Governor in Council Fort St. George, 29 December 1819, T.N.A., Tinnevelly District Records, Vol. 3576, fols 149–60.

> The instruction received...is almost exclusively confined to the more elementary parts of Education, which go into the business of shopkeeper...Without general instruction we can hardly expect...to impress into their minds ideas which will gradually subdue their superstitions and prejudices and contribute to their Elevation in the Scale of Civilization.[15]

Among the reports which resulted from official enquiries into the state of indigenous schools in the Bombay and Madras Presidencies in the early 1820s, two have emerged as classics. T.B. Jervis, writing from Rutnagheree in the southern Concan proclaimed the 'Native System' of education to be 'not only defective, but in many respects pernicious'. A.D. Campbell, writing from Bellary, remarked that 'every school boy can repeat verbatim a vast number of verses, of the meaning of which, he knows no more than the parrot that has been taught to utter certain words'. The Governor of Madras, Thomas Munro, summed up the reports from Madras collectors as exhibiting a 'low state of education'. And, 10 years later in Bengal, William Adam introduced his first report on indigenous schools with the statement:

> The teacher...exercises no moral influence on the character of his pupils. For the sake of pay he performs a menial service in the spirit of a menial. ...There is no text...used containing any moral truths, or liberal knowledge, so that education being limited entirely to accounts, tends rather to narrow the mind and confine its attention to sordid gain than to improve the heart and enlarge the understanding.[16]

And yet, Company officials at the highest level expressed total admiration for the 'internal polity' in India which supported village schools with charges on produce of the soil and endowments of land. In 1813, Thomas Munro had testified before Parliament that in some areas of the Madras Presidency 'there were schools established in every village'. And, in 1821, a member of Elphinstone's Council remarked upon the schools in nearly every village where

---

[15] Minute by Mr. Goodwin, 8 January 1825, B.R.O., General Department, Vol. 8/92, fols 369, 371.

[16] Lt. T.B. Jervis, employed in statistical survey of Southern Concan, to James Farish, Secretary to Government, 8 September 1824, Rutnagheree, B.R.O., General Department, Vol. 8/63 1824, cited in R.V. Parulekar, *op. cit.*, p. 5; A.D. Campbell, Collector of Bellary, to Board of Revenue, Fort St. George, 17 August 1823, TNA, Board of Revenue Proceedings, 25 September 1823, No. 32, Vol. 958 cited in H. Sharp, *op. cit.*, p. 68; T. Munro, Minute 10 March 1826, cited in Dharampal, *The Beautiful Tree—Indigenous Indian Education in the Eighteenth Century* (New Delhi, 1983), p. 249 and William Adam, Report on the State of Education in Bengal (1835), p. 9, cited in Dharampal, *op cit.*, p. 269.

> young natives are taught reading, writing and arithmetic, upon a system so economical, from a handful or two of grain, to perhaps a rupee per month to the schoolmaster;...and at the same time so simple and effectual that there is hardly a Cultivator or Petty dealer who is not competent to keep his own accounts with a degree of accuracy...beyond what we meet with amongst the lower orders in our country.[17]

Obviously, the Directors and senior Company officers were delighted by the thought that India had the most economical school system they had ever encountered—a system that was copied by Bell in Madras and Lancaster in England.

Sadly, these glowing impressions of a thriving indigenous school system were not supported by hard facts. Ten years after Munro's testimony, A.D. Campbell, the Collector in Bellary which was formerly the district assigned to Munro, reported: 'In many villages where formerly there were schools, there are now none'. He further declared that fewer than 7,000 of a population of one million attended school. The defects in indigenous schools listed by Campbell ranged from a lack of books and competent teachers to the fact that few parents could afford, on the one hand, to pay fees which escalated in increments of ¼ rupee per month according to the pupil's progress, and, on the other hand, to release their children from labour in the fields. Then he ascribed these defects to 'the general impoverishment of the country...by the introduction of our own European manufactures, in lieu of the Indian Cotton Fabrics. The removal of our troops from our own territories, to the distant frontiers of our newly subsidized allies...has affected the demand for grain' none of which has 'been alleviated by a less rigid enforcement of the revenue due to the state.'[18] This general picture was reenforced by J.A.R. Stevenson in the Dharwar district of the Bombay presidency:

> ...poverty is the great drawback, particularly amongst the cultivating classes. A Ryut must not only pay the School Master, but he must lose the labour of his child, which is valuable to him from the most tender age. A child of

---

[17] Para. 19, Public Despatch, to Bengal, 3 June 1814, Zastoupil and Moir, *op. cit.*, p. 95; Evidence of Thomas Munro before the Select Committee on the Affairs of the East India Company, 12 April 1813, *Parliamentary Papers* (1812–13) VII, [122] p. 131; Minute by G.L. Prendergast, n.d., 1821, Bombay Public Proceedings, 27 June 1821, O.I.O.C., P/345/63, fol. 1025, cited in R.V. Parulekar, *op. cit.*, p. xxi and in Fisher's Memoir, *Parliamentary Papers* (1831–32) IX, Cmd. 735-I, p. 468.

[18] Paras 17–19, A.D. Campbell, Collector of Bellary, to Board of Revenue, Fort St. George, 17 August 1823, TNA, Board of Revenue Proceedings, 25 September 1823, No. 32, Vol. 958, cited in Dharampal, *op. cit.*, pp. 182–83, but not cited in H. Sharp, *op. cit.*

six years tends the Cattle, and very soon after is able in many ways to assist in his Father's Farm—should this child be sent to school a Boy must be hired, at from two to three Pagodas per annum, besides his food and lodging. In my Talooks there are not now ten children the sons of Ryuts attending the Schools.[19]

In Bengal, William Adam reported that there were villages in the Thana Nattore with only two schools where there had been 10 or 11 in living memory.

Joseph Di Bona attributes this decline to the reduced landholdings of *zamindar*s forced thereby to curtail their patronage. Di Bona further speculates that the British, as they pushed further into the interior, introduced cash crops as an alternative to seizing possession of land. Two crops in particular, namely—indigo and opium—brought in enormous profits. But these profits were generated by trade with London and China. So, Di Bona concludes: 'The profits…flowed to Calcutta and England rather than to the local populace for support of local institutions'.[20] In a similar vein, Dharampal concludes that, although soft statistical data undercuts any definitive statement, it is more than likely that the golden era of village schools referenced by Munro, Prendergast and Adam was made possible by:

> [T]he sophisticated operative fiscal arrangement of the pre-British Indian polity, through which substantial proportions of revenue had long been assigned for the performance of a multiplicity of public purposes (and which seems to have stayed more or less intact through all the previous political turmoils).

He reasons that, if this assumption is valid, then 'it was the collapse of this arrangement through a total centralisation of revenue, as well as political structure that led to educational [decay] as also to decay in the economy'.[21]

Triumph of Downward Filtration Theory

Assuredly, the fragile network of indigenous schools was ill equipped to withstand the steadily increasing weight of a public system of education run

---

[19] J.A.R. Stevenson, Assist. Collector, to St. John Thackeray, Principal Collector and Political Agent, Ranebennur, Dharwar, 2 August 1824, in R.V. Parulekar, *op. cit.*, p. 144.

[20] Joseph Di Bona, ed., *One Teacher, One School—The Adam Reports on Indigenous Education in Nineteenth Century India* (New Delhi, 1983), pp. 4–5.

[21] Dharampal, *op. cit.*, p. 15.

by the state. Legislation launched elite institutions which came to dominate educational policy. Noting the success of these institutions, Bentinck's Law Member of Council, T.B. Macaulay, was ultimately to despair of the possibility of educating the masses and proposed instead a trickle down theory which came to be known as 'Downward Filtration'. Nothing was more ominous than the imperialist vision which inspired Governor General Wellesley to introduce legislation for the foundation of the College of Fort William on 4 May 1800, 'the first anniversary of the reduction of Seringapatam'. Indeed, Lord Wellesley considered the College 'a becoming public monument to commemorate the conquest of Mysore'. He regarded the Company's Civil Servants as 'officers of a powerful sovereign' who 'should be regularly instructed in the principles and system which constitute the foundation of that wise code of regulations and laws enacted... for the purpose of securing...the benefit of the ancient and established laws of this country...'[22] Wellesley's College, staffed by Orientalists in Calcutta, provoked the ire of the Directors by surprising them with a bill for £250,000 to cover its expenses. The Evangelical Chair of the Directors, Charles Grant, feared that 15-year-olds would be 'Indianized' in such a setting. Promptly Grant reacted with a plan for training all future Company Servants at the East India College, later known as Haileybury, so that the Company Civil Service would be 'a spearhead of cultural and Christian change'.[23] And so, the battle line between Orientalists and Anglicists was already drawn long before the era of Macaulay.

The Charter Act of 1813 legislated financial support for: '[T]he renewal and improvement of literature, the encouragement of the learned natives... promotion...of sciences...and that any schools...in...British territories in India...shall be governed by...regulations...made by the...Governor General in Council'.[24]

There are Indian scholars who praise the launch of this educational behemoth. Atmanand Misra asserts that 'the greatest achievement of the British period

---

[22] Bengal Regulation IX for the Foundation of a College at Ft William in Bengal and for better Instruction of Junior Civil Servants of the Honourable English East India Company in important Duties belonging to several arduous Stations to which said Junior Civil Servants may be respectively destined in the Administration of Justice, and in the general Government of the British Empire in India (passed 10 July 1800), I.O.R., V/8/17, pp. 203–7; Para. 80, Minute by Governor General Wellesley, 18 August 1800, cited by G.S.A. Ranking, 'A History of the College of Fort William in Bengal from 1801–1900', I.O.L. MSS Eur. B185, fol. 2.

[23] Andrew Hambling, *The East India College at Haileybury 1806–1867* (Haileybury, 2005), p. 10.

[24] 53 Geo III, c. 155, s. 43.

was the legislative provision for the appropriation of state revenues in financing education'.²⁵

But, while authorities in Calcutta insisted upon an increasingly centralized control of the Company's educational policy, the growing Anglicist–Orientalist quarrel distracted their attention away from the indigenous vernacular schools. Even the Chinsurah schools which were entrusted to the G.C.P.I. in 1824 after Rev. May's death suffered from inattention and steady deprivation of funds until they were finally superseded by the founding of the Hooghly College in 1836. As early as 1831, J. Thomason declared it unnecessary to expend funds 'in promoting lower branches of education'.²⁶

The battle on behalf of village vernacular schools was waged most vigorously in the Bombay presidency by Mountstuart Elphinstone, ineffectively in the Madras presidency and most effectively in the N.W.P. far from Calcutta. While Commissioner of the Deccan after his victory over the Peshwa, Elphinstone developed a determined loyalty to the Peshwa's educational charities involving lavish financial support of learned Brahmins in Poona. His respect for the deposed ruling classes was legendary. As Governor of Bombay, he took umbrage over criticism by the Directors of the Hindu College in Poona founded in October 1821. This criticism he rightly suspected originated with James Mill in keeping with his utilitarian denunciation of 'mere Hindoo learning'.²⁷ At odds with utilitarian disrespect for existing Indian learning, Elphinstone had set forth his own ambitious plan for extensive Government support of village schools in his fabled Minute of 13 December 1823.²⁸ He was insistent that the teaching of English and European science through the medium of English must be based on elementary education through the vernacular. He was certain that the 'demand for English existed only in or near Bombay and among the few

---

²⁵ Atmanand Misra, *The Financing of Indian Education* (London, 1967), p. 206.

²⁶ Minute by J. Thomason, 16 December 1831, W.B.S.A., G.C.P.I., Vol. 5, fol. 3. *See also* minutes by H. Shakespeare, H.H. Wilson and W.W. Bird, *ibid.*, fols 1–14 and D.P. Sinha, *The Educational Policy of the East India Company in Bengal to 1854* (Calcutta, 1964), p. 84.

²⁷ Para. 10, Public Despatch, from Bombay, 11 August 1824, I.O.R., E/4/506; this was Elphinstone's reply to the Public Despatch, to Bombay, 11 June 1823, I.O.R., E.4/1043 generally credited to Mill, although some of the wording may have been altered by the Board of Control. Cf. Kenneth Ballhatchet, *Social Policy and Social Change in Western India 1817–1830* (London, 1957), pp. 256–58.

²⁸ Minute by Mountstuart Elphinstone, 13 December 1823, Bombay General Proceedings, 10 March 1824, I.O.R., P/346/4, fols 670ff.

who thought it would help their business'.[29] As observed a century later by a Professor at Elphinstone College, Elphinstone respected Oriental learning for pragmatic reasons, not because he placed value on Oriental learning per se.[30]

At the heart of Elphinstone's support for vernacular schools was his concern to instruct civil servants—both European and Indian—in their revenue and judicial duties in the vernacular. It is alleged that when the Directors ordered the formulation of a plan for a College at Bombay, Elphinstone sent for the regulations of the College at Fort William, but these regulations made him 'doubt whether more good will not result from the education of the natives than that of the Europeans'.[31] After calling for Government establishment, control and financing of elementary village schools, Elphinstone insisted that the most important part of his grand plan of 1823 was the preparation of 'natives for public employment'. He acknowledged the likelihood that 'Natives' raised through education 'to an equality with ourselves' and thereby admitted to 'a share in their own Government' would ultimately demand 'their title to the whole'. But he warned that 'we are' unlikely to be 'more secure on any other plan'.[32] However, in focusing his plan for promoting employment on the upper castes, Elphinstone unabashedly emphasized his own concern to conciliate the former ruling classes. Thus he argued that 'education for low castes would only create a new class superior to the rest in useful knowledge, but hated and despised by the castes to whom these new attainments would always induce us to prefer them'.[33] Governor Elphinstone's successor, John Malcolm, defended Elphinstone's emphasis upon vernacular education and conciliation of the former ruling classes. In approving the Principal of the College at Poona's request for permission to reward students of distinction, he remarked: 'The College at Poona was established to conciliate the Natives by liberality.... It may perhaps be deemed more a Charitable than a useful institution, but if it tends to the popularity and good name of Government, it is politic to support it'.[34] Upon Elphinstone's retirement, the chiefs and princes of the

---

[29] Minute by Mountstuart Elphinstone, 21 June 1821, B.R.O., General Department, Vol. 44–48, 1821–23, fol. 19.

[30] A.L. Covernton, 'The Educational Policy of Mountstuart Elphinstone', *Journal of the Bombay Royal Asiatic Society*, New Series, Vol. II (1926): p. 63.

[31] *Ibid.*, p. 58.

[32] Minute by Mountstuart Elphinstone, 15 April 1825, B.R.O., General Department, Vol. 8/92, 1825, fol. 431.

[33] Cf. Kenneth Ballhatchet, *op. cit.*, p. 258.

[34] Minute by John Malcolm 1828, B.R.O., General Department, Vol. 15/168, 1828, fol. 13.

Deccan rewarded his loyalty with funds to endow three professorships in English language and European science. The Company matched these funds to endow the foundation of Elphinstone College. It was left to John Malcolm to fend off the efforts of some of his Council to undercut the vernacular curriculum in favour of English.

That Thomas Munro, Governor of Madras, is remembered in the company of Elphinstone and Malcolm as advocates of conciliation in the grand tradition of Warren Hastings is not surprising. Elphinstone clearly regarded Munro as his mentor, inasmuch as Munro had already embarked on many of the initiatives which Elphinstone was contemplating in the early 1820s. Indeed, he personally requested from Munro information on the Indian officers of the Madras Board of Revenue, as an 'arrangement that...opens a door to the employment of natives in high and efficient situations'.[35] Even before Munro's term as Governor, Madras Regulation V of 1817 had established qualifications in the rules of the College of Fort St. George for employing Hindus and Mahomedans as law officers and Vakeels in the Adawlut (court). Without a certificate from the college no one could be nominated for an appointment as a Vakeel or Pleader. Munro was to object to the extension of the college's authority to cover the appointment of District Munsifs. He felt that 'sound judgement and a knowledge of local habits and customs' were just as important as academic training in the Law and Regulations.[36] Nevertheless, the success of the system of public examinations and certificates at the Madras College prompted Governor General Amherst to recommend to the G.C.P.I. that rules should be framed to ensure that 'scholars and law students of superior...qualifications [received] a just preference for public employment'.[37] This exchange ultimately led to the enactment of Bengal Regulation XI 1826 which declared that successful candidates for law offices in the courts must possess a certificate awarded as the result of the two respected educational institutions in Calcutta—the Calcutta Madrassa or the Hindu College. In the final analysis, this regulation has been criticized as a hollow promise because no uniform standard was set for examinations and vacancies were insufficient. The central government succeeded in placing a premium on higher education while neglecting a viable system of elementary education. In the words of

---

[35] Mountstuart Elphinstone, to Thomas Munro, 27 October 1822, Munro Papers, I.O.L., MSS Eur. F151/63, fol. 35.
[36] Minute by Munro, n.d., W.B.S.A., Proceedings of G.C.P.I., Vol. 4, fol. 453.
[37] A. Stirling, Persian Secretary, to Government, to G.C.P.I., 30 March 1825, W.B.S.A., Proceedings of G.C.P.I., Vol. 3, fol. 278.

D.P. Sinha, this was like 'lavishing money on the roof and neglecting the foundation of a building'.[38]

Meanwhile, in Madras, Governor Munro attempted to launch a programme of substantial government support for village schools. The reports received by the Madras Board of Revenue in response to their circular of 25 July 1822 had emphasized that the 'general ignorance of the teachers' and 'the poverty of the people' were the prime causes of the 'low state of education' in Madras. Munro responded by endorsing the proposal of the Madras School Book Society for a school for teachers; then he proposed that Government 'establish in each collectorate two principal schools, one for Hindoos, and the other for Mahomedans; and that…the Hindoo schools might be augmented so as to give one to each tehsildary, or about 15 to each collectorate'. This would eventually result in 40 collectorate schools and 300 *tehsildary* schools. But Munro warned that progress would necessarily be slow, inasmuch as the extension of 'the instruction of the people' depended upon 'the improvement in the condition of the people rendering a larger portion of them more able to pay for it'.[39] These plans initially received the highest praise and total support from the Home Authorities. Then in a despatch attributed to John Stuart Mill they were totally discounted, partly as a result of ignoring Munro's efforts to adjust the numbers in the total of people receiving education. The Board of Revenue had concluded that, of a population of 12½ million only 1 in 67 received instruction. Munro estimated that this percentage figure was badly skewed by the fact that there were no returns from the collectors on the numbers taught at home. In the City of Madras alone, Munro estimated that approximately one third of the male population received education. Yet, Mill dismissed the 'imperfect state of Native education' and declared that 'little aid is to be expected from the instruments which already exist'. For Dharampal, this response to 'what had been reported to be functioning' was a betrayal reeking of smug ridicule. Of course, Mill's prime focus concerned the quality of instruction offered. He allowed that 'Braminical instruction in many parts of the Madras territories is not so entirely destitute of real information as…described by the Sub-Collector of Cuddapah'. Yet he cited the portion of the Cuddapah report in which G.M. Ogilvie, the Sub-Collector, remarked that persons holding the *Enam*s set apart for support of village instruction were 'quite content to be ignorant of the higher branches of Science; their

---

[38] Bengal Regulation XI for providing a succession of duly qualified Hindoo and Mahomedan Law Officers, in several Courts of Justice; and for enacting an additional Rule for Appointment of Vakeels in Zillah and City Courts (passed 4 August 1826). D.P. Sinha, *op. cit.*, pp. 84–87.

[39] Minute by Thomas Munro, 10 March 1826, Dharampal, *op. cit.*, pp. 249–51.

utmost ambition being confined to the distinction of foretelling a fortunate hour for reaping, or a lucky day for a marriage'. He ignored the portion of the report in which Ogilvie called attention to the instruction 'gratuitously afforded' among Bramins. Ogilvie had recounted the remarkable stories of impoverished young Bramins sent by their families distances up to 100 miles to a village where another Bramin afforded 'instruction without recompense' and the young student was supported by 'Alms' received 'daily (for years) at the door of every Bramin in the Village'. Ogilvie called for 'the liberal and fostering care of Government' to bring to perfection 'this benevolent Custom for the General spread of education amongst a class of persons whose poverty would otherwise be an insurmountable obstacle to advancement in knowledge'. But Mill's prime concern was that Munro's Collectorate and *Tehsildary* schools should advance the cause of 'useful knowledge'.[40]

Disappointing to everyone concerned was the paltry response to the efforts of the Committee of Public Instruction appointed by Munro to establish a teacher training school in Madras. In January 1827 only 10 candidates out of a potential 80 from the 40 collectorates actually attended the Government training school.[41] Taking no heed of Munro's cautionary advice that progress would inevitably be slow, John Stuart Mill penned a brutal despatch on behalf of the Directors condemning 'the measures for native education which have as yet been adopted or planned at your Presidency' as a failure. He demanded that the Central Training School be transformed into a 'Seminary for the instruction of the Natives generally in the higher branches of knowledge'. The institutions in Calcutta were held up as examples of 'a degree of success…(in) spreading useful knowledge among the Natives of India, and diffusing among them the ideas and sentiments prevalent in civilized Europe'.[42] Thus sounded the death knell for Munro's scheme of vernacular education for the masses, not long after the death of Munro, himself. Unwittingly, Mill, in pursuit of the grand mission of encouraging 'useful learning', had paved the way for Macaulay's Anglicist rhetoric and Bentinck's Government resolution of March 7 1835 endorsing funds for English education at the expense of Sanskrit colleges and Muslim *madrassa*s. Mill was actually horrified by this result and attempted to rescue

---

[40] Public Despatch, to Madras, 16 April 1828, I.O.R., E/4/935, fols 364, 384–84 and 395. *See also* Dharampal, *op. cit.*, pp. 40, 222–23.

[41] Fisher's Memoir, *Parliamentary Papers* (1831–32) IX, Cmd. 735-I, p. 463; Bruce T. McCully, *op. cit.*, pp. 33–37.

[42] Public Despatch, to Madras, 29 September 1830, No. 34, I.O.R., E/4/939 in Zastoupil and Moir, *op. cit.*, pp. 125–27. For confirmation of Mill's authorship, *see* J.M. Robson, M. and Z. Moir, eds., *op. cit.*, Appendix A, p. 293 (No. 1602).

vernacular education in general and the *Tehsildary* and Collectorate Schools of Madras in particular in his draft of a Despatch on behalf of the Directors which was quashed by Sir John Cam Hobhouse, president of the Board of Control.[43] He confided to H.H. Wilson: 'The Government in India in their recent conduct have gone directly in the teeth of all the instructions they have received from this country'.[44]

So stunned were the Home Authorities by the arbitrary actions of Bentinck and Macaulay that no instructions regarding the March 7 1835 Resolution were sent out to India for five years. Their despatch of 20 January 1841 endorsed Governor General Auckland's grand compromise in order to clear the smoke from fiery petitions of Muslims and Hindus who were alike infuriated by the prescribed suspension of funding of oriental colleges. However, it was another year before they addressed Auckland's rejection of William Adam's proposed plans for extensive government support of existing village schools. Then, while acknowledging Adam's conclusion in his Third Report that 'existing native Institutions are the fittest means to be employed for raising and improving the character of the people', they agreed with Auckland that the support and supervision of the education of approximately 35 million people in Bengal and Bihar spread over vast distances was daunting. However, whereas Auckland narrowed his focus to the provision of 'vernacular class books', the Home Authorities were more emphatic in their insistence that 'Government should do nothing to supersede [existing Native Institutions] but should rather endeavour to supply the means for making them more effectual'. They were impressed by Adam's report of 'gratuitous instruction in the vernacular languages...afforded by resident Natives from Motives of benevolence or piety'. They concluded that existing institutions 'merit much more attention and far greater encouragement than they have hitherto received'.[45]

Under the weight of so much controversy there were but flickering signs of life for education in India's villages. In Bengal, the G.C.P.I. doggedly pursued a scheme for developing *zillah* schools primarily with the financial support of local wealthy *zamindar*s and *sheristadar*s. With the exception of

---

[43] Final Draft of Public Despatch, to India, July–December 1836, I.O.R., L/P&J/1/92 in Zastoupil and Moir, *ibid.*, pp. 225–41. Interestingly, Hobhouse noted in the margins of Mill's draft that 'Perhaps the remarks on the Madras schools may be retained'.

[44] J.S. Mill, to H.H. Wilson, 5 January 1836, Wilson Papers, I.O.L., MSS Eur. E301/2, fol. 143.

[45] Para. 6, Minute by Governor General Auckland, 24 November 1839, I.O.R., Board's Collections F/4/1846, No. 77638; Public Despatch, to India, 23 February 1842, No. 3, I.O.R., E/4/769, fols 546–48.

Bihar, these schools generally proved a success, so much so that Auckland, ever mindful of centralized control, proposed to link them with new Central Colleges located in all the major cities of the presidency.[46] Meanwhile, in the N.W.P. newly separated from Bengal under a Lt. Governor at Agra, James Thomason was able to develop an independent educational policy radically different from the centralized model of Bengal where *zillah* schools were subject to supervision by Central Schools. In order to encourage the development of vernacular schools, Thomason closed 8 of the 14 colleges bequeathed to the N.W.P. by the G.C.P.I. in Calcutta. This system was ultimately lauded as the only lasting 'systematic scheme...for making the Indigenous schools of the country as useful as possible'.[47] These indigenous schools answered well the needs of an impoverished population scattered over great distances. Because the interior of the country was not a scene of bustling commerce as in Bengal, or for that matter the other two presidencies, the Anglo-Vernacular Colleges at Agra, Benares and Delhi failed to attract the landed aristocracy, especially the dethroned Muslim ruling classes. Instead, the colleges were filled with 'the lower ranks of society...the hangers-on of the Government offices,...the inferior shopkeepers or...sojourning Bengalis'.[48] Two other successful experiments in vernacular education were the work of Lancelot Wilkinson, Assistant Resident at Bhopal, and Brian Houghton Hodgson, Resident at Nepal. Dubbed 'neo-orientalists' by Christopher Bayly, both Wilkinson and Hodgson believed in working in both Indian and western traditions.[49] In his widely acclaimed experiment at Sehore in Bhopal, Wilkinson introduced modern science with the help of *pandit*s well read in medieval traditions of astronomy. And Hodgson worked tirelessly to disseminate western ideas through vernacular languages. Contemptuous of both the 'exclusive learning' of Brahmin scholars and the 'haughty' Anglicists, Hodgson insisted 'every step we make in the grand project of indigenating...the vivifying spirit of our sound knowledge...in India by

---

[46] Bruce T. McCully, *op. cit.*, pp. 82–83. On 29 January 1847, Collector T. Sandys reported to the Commissioner of Revenue at Patna that 'the Inhabitants of this district have not shown the slightest disposition towards establishing any vernacular schools'. B.S.A., P.C.O., Vol. 58, p. 106.

[47] Anonymous Summary of State Education, Wood Papers, I.O.L., MSS Eur. F78/12a.

[48] Bruce T. McCully, *op. cit.*, p. 100. For description of concern registered by Muslim ashraf in 1840s that if they entered into public debate with missionaries, they might jeopardize judicial employment, see Avril Powell, *Muslims and Missionaries in pre-Mutiny India* (London, 1993), pp. 179–87, cited by Radhika Singha, *A Despotism of Law—Crime & Justice in Early Colonial India* (Delhi, 1998), p. 308.

[49] C.A. Bayly, *Empire and Information—Intelligence Gathering and Social Communication in India, 1780–1870* (Cambridge, 1996), p. 259.

means of vernacularization will prove a bond of blessed union between ourselves and the mass of our subjects'. Hodgson submitted his letters to the *Friend of India* in tune with that paper's declaration that 'the stillness of death reigns in the wake of lack of action on Adam's Reports'.[50] Writing at the end of the nineteenth century, William Wilson Hunter acclaimed Hodgson's 1835 Letters 'On the Education of the People of India' as 'the basis of Indian Public Instruction', having 'relegated the wranglings of Anglicists and Orientalists to the somewhat comical place which they now occupy in Indian history'.[51] Recently Savithri Preetha Nair has drawn attention to the remarkable accomplishments of Raja Serfoji II of Tanjore who created his own 'centre of calculation' pursuing 'useful knowledge' in the spirit of the Western Enlightenment. An obvious polymath, Serfoji maintained his own centre of experiments on electricity and chemistry, collections of socialized natural history, drawings and specimens, and support for art and music—all far removed from any metropolitan centre with museums and lecture halls.[52]

Indian Agency

While determined advocates of vernacular education held their ground, the proponents of downward filtration received a boost from the growing Indian demand for Government jobs. Symptomatic of this growing clamour was a petition sent by 4,000 Bombay residents to Parliament calling for knowledge of English to be a requirement for all Indian candidates for office in the Company's service. In actual fact, the Home Authorities had been calling for increased Indian Agency, especially in the judicial service, over and over again. As far back as 1824, the Directors had insisted that 'native functionaries must be multiplied' in order 'to secure a prompt administration of justice to the natives of India'.[53] Governor General William Bentinck seized the initiative in 1831. For the civil judicial service, Bengal Regulation V authorized the appointment of Principal Sudder Ameens, a new superior

---

[50] B.H. Hodgson, *Preeminence of the Vernaculars; or the Anglicists Answered: Being Four Letters on the Education of the People of India,* 4th ed. (Serampore, 1847), pp. 4, 66.

[51] William Wilson Hunter, *Life of Brian Houghton Hodgson* (London, 1896), p. 311.

[52] Savithri Preetha Nair, 'Native Collecting and Natural Knowledge (1798–1832): Raja Serfoji II of Tanjore as a 'Centre of Calculation', *Journal of the Royal Asiatic Society* 3rd series, Vol. 15 part 3 (November 2005): pp. 279–302.

[53] John William Kaye, *op. cit.*, p. 349.

class of judicial officers who were ultimately to be empowered to try cases involving property to any amount subject to appeal to a European judge. And it significantly expanded the jurisdiction of the lower ranks of Munsifs and Sudder Ameens. For example, Munsifs or Vakeels were initially known as Commissioners who assisted European judges during the Cornwallis era and whose jurisdiction at that time was limited to cases involving property up to the amount of ₹50. Their jurisdiction was increased gradually over the years until Regulation V set the limit for their suits at ₹300. Of course, Regulation V is perhaps best known for opening the path of Indian Agency to Christian East Indians so that applicants for any judicial office could no longer be discriminated against 'on account of his religious belief or persuasion'. Although Regulation V allowed a magistrate to refer a criminal case to a Sudder Ameen or Principal Sudder Ameen solely for investigation,[54] it was not until 1843 that Act XV called for uncovenanted Indian agency in criminal cases. Act XV empowered the Bengal and Agra Governments to appoint uncovenanted deputy magistrates in any *zillah*.[55] James Thomason had played a prominent role in prompting this legislation and, having secured government authorization, he funneled students from his Anglo-Vernacular Colleges into uncovenanted offices. In the meantime, Thomason had also prompted Auckland's government to create a plan in response to a proposal from the General Committee for Education for 'raising a superior description of persons for the office of Moonsiff' in the N.W.P. and Bengal presidency. This plan reached out to potential candidates for subordinate judicial office according to ability perceived formally through examination by Divisional Committees or informally by *zillah* Judges.[56]

---

[54] Bengal Regulation V for extending the Powers of Moonsiffs and Sudder Ameens in the trial of Civil Suits; and for authorizing the Appointment of Principal Sudder Ameens at Zillah and City stations; for modifying the powers and duties of *zillah*, City and Provincial Courts in connection with those arrangements, and for enlarging the sphere of selection with regard to the Offices of Moonsiffs and Vakeels (passed by Governor General in Council, 1 November 1831), I.O.R., V/8/21. See Preamble, Sec. III; Sec. V, cl.2; Sec. XIII; Sec. XVII; and Sec. XVIII, cl. 6.

[55] Act XV for the more extensive employment of Uncovenanted Agency in the Judicial Department (passed by Governor General of India in Council 5 August 1843), I.O.R., V/8/32.

[56] J. Hawkins, Register, Court of Sudder Dewanny Adawlut, Circular #369, to Zillah and City Judges in Lower Provinces, 30 November 1838, India Legislative Proceedings, 22 June 1840, No. 1, I.O.R., P/207/10; J. Thomason, Secretary to Government of North West Provinces, to T.H. Maddock, Judicial Secretary to Government of India, 18 April 1840, *ibid.*, No. 3; and F.J. Halliday, Judicial Secretary to Government of India, to J. Thomason, Secretary to Government of North West Provinces, 22 June 1840, *ibid.*, No. 6.

The English Parliament lent impetus to the momentum of increased Indian agency by declaring in Clause 87 of the 1833 Charter that 'no Native shall by reason of his religion, place of birth, descent [or] color...be disabled from holding any place, office or employment'.[57] The Directors then attempted to interpret this clause so that it would allow expansion of the Indian work force while posing no threat to their patronage in the covenanted service. Thus, they reassured their Indian minions that the object of Section 87 was 'not to ascertain qualification but to remove disqualification'. A 'useful education' was to be the principle means of removing this 'disqualification'. By emphasizing the importance of education, the Directors cleverly removed the sting of any implication of existing prejudice amongst European Company servants against Indian Agency. Indeed, they remarked:

> So far as respects...natives of the whole blood...the purposes of the Legislators have, in a considerable degree, been anticipated....Even judicial duties of magnitude and importance are now confided to their hands...still a line of demarcation, to some extent in favour of the natives, to some extent in exclusion of them has been maintained.[58]

Certainly, by 1853 when J.W. Kaye penned his administrative history of the Company, it was possible to claim that 'the administration of civil justice is at present almost entirely in the hands of these native officers'.[59]

Indeed, the source of inspiration for the growth of Indian Agency came from educational institutions. At about the same time as the enactment of Clause 87, there was growing ferment in Calcutta surrounding the Anglo-Vernacular Hindu College which had been founded in 1817 by an Anglo-Indian committee led by Rammohun Roy and the English watchmaker, David Hare. By 1831, the very talented Anglo-Indian teacher, Henry Derozio, whose teachings had the effect of encouraging students to break with tradition and absorb all forms of useful learning, enraged the orthodox Indian managers of the College. In April 1831, they were so incensed by the godless attitudes and behaviour of many of Derozio's pupils that they arbitrarily dismissed him as 'the root of all evils and the cause of Public alarm'. Derozio lamented 'the intemperate spirit displayed against me by the native managers of the College' in correspondence with H.H. Wilson;

---

[57] Clause 87, 3 & 4 Will. IV, c. 85.
[58] Public Despatch, to India, 10 December 1834, I.O.R., E/4/742, fols 574, 586–87 and 577–78.
[59] John William Kaye, *op. cit.*, p. 425.

he might have found solace in the fact that many of his pupils were to lead the young men who came to be known as 'Young Bengal'.[60] They inspired the large number of Bengalis who flocked to study at the Medical College founded in Calcutta in 1835; they were eager to participate in dissections and to learn surgical techniques which were taboo for their castes. Despite the objections of orthodox Bengalis, the Hindu College flourished in the wake of Macaulay's Anglicist rant. And, when the Hooghly College was opened in Calcutta in 1836, it was overwhelmed with candidates.[61] The same ferment enveloped Elphinstone College and the newly established High School in Madras. And, in the N.W.P., far from the turmoil of the coastal Presidency cities, rather than the sons of the elite classes, the sons of the poor clamoured for education and jobs.

Governor General Hardinge responded to this enthusiasm with his Resolution of 10 October 1844 throwing open public office to educated Indians. He confided to his son: 'We can't afford European agency. We must have recourse to native assistance'.[62] Unfortunately, Hardinge's enthusiasm was doomed to criticism and failure. On the one hand, Brian Hodgson confessed 'the apprehension that this new class of functionaries may prove competent in *our* special acquirements only by losing all competency in *their own*'.[63] On the other hand, the Council of Education which had succeeded the G.C.P.I. in Calcutta in 1842 acted upon the Resolution by setting a rigid high standard in English examinations at the Central Colleges at the expense of those who had a 'moderate and practical knowledge of English, with a thorough command of the vernacular'. Gradually, appointments to the Government service were made independently of the Council's list of candidates and within 10 years an education officer declared that 'Hardinge's Resolution was a dead letter'.[64]

---

[60] Special Meeting of the Directors of Hindoo College, 23 April 1831, in Susobhan Chandra Sarkar, 'Extracts from the Proceedings of the Hindu College Committee relating to the dismissal of Henry Louis Vivian Derozio', *The Presidency College Magazine*, April 1859, Vol. 41, p. 3. Derozio, to Wilson, 25 April 1831, H.H. Wilson Papers, I.O.L., MSS Eur. E301/1, fol. 204.

[61] Bruce T. McCully, *op. cit.*, pp. 80–81.

[62] Warren Hardinge, to Walter, 2 June 1845, in Bawa Satinder Singh, ed., *The Letters of the First Viscount Hardinge of Lahore to Lady Hardinge and Sir Walter and Lady James 1844–47*, Vol. 32, London: Royal Historical Society—Camden Fourth Series, 1986, p. 85.

[63] B.H. Hodgson, *op. cit.*, p. 3.

[64] J.A. Richey, ed., *Selections from Educational Records, Part II 1840–1859* (New Delhi repr.: 1965), pp. 92, 68, cited by D.P. Sinha, *op. cit.*, pp. 279–80.

Indian Agency Trumps Downward Filtration

The Council's insistence upon maintaining tight control of access to government jobs finally undermined the idea of downward filtration. Their emphasis upon 'higher education' only served to provoke the Home Authorities to proclaim a new 'Magna Charta of English Education in India' otherwise known as the Wood Despatch of 19 July 1854. No longer could vernacular education be ignored. The vast number of Indian donors whom the Company had relied upon to fund their schools were part of what Christopher Bayly has dubbed the 'ecumene' or information order. It was the ecumene which had inspired the creation of the Hindu College in Calcutta, the Elphinstone College in Bombay, Pachaiyappa's Central Institution and the High School in Madras. But they also created *zillah* schools in Bengal, vernacular schools in Bombay and supported indigenous schools in Madras and the N.W.P. They weren't concerned about the distinctions between an oriental and anglicist curriculum. As foretold by Mountstuart Elphinstone, and even Macaulay, they wanted control of their destiny with access to government jobs. Sir Charles Wood actually consulted a vast number of advisers in the preparation of his Despatch. Parliament heard testimony from returned servants of the Company such as C.H. Cameron, F.J. Halliday and W.B. Bayley; missionaries J.C. Marshman and Alexander Duff; former Directors such as Charles Grant and scholars such as H.H. Wilson.[65] The final draft was shown to Sir Erskine Perry, J.C. Marshman, H.T. Prinsep and Macaulay, although Macaulay's ideas were mainly kept alive by C.E. Trevelyan who had considerable personal influence with Sir Charles Wood.[66] Thus, it was not surprising that the Despatch endorsed the longstanding educational objective of 'the diffusion of the improved arts, science, philosophy and literature of Europe' taught through the medium of 'the English language...where there is a demand for it'. But, it ordered that 'such instruction should always be combined with a careful attention to the study of the vernacular language of the district'. New centralized machinery replacing existing Councils of Education with Government Departments was to extend inspection down to indigenous schools. And these schools were to be increased through a system of grants-in-aid available to well-managed schools that provided a 'good secular education'.

---

[65] The Select Committee of the House of Commons (1853), Sixth Report, *Parliamentary Papers* (1852–53) XXIX, Cmd. 897; House of Lords, Second Report, *Parliamentary Papers* (1852–53) XXXII, Cmd. 627-I.

[66] Wood Papers, I.O.L., MSS Eur. F78/59 and F78/12a.

Grants-in-aid were to be the means of bringing under Government inspection the vast network of missionary schools which had dominated the *mofussil*. Universities were to be organized as examining bodies with affiliated institutions. There was an effort to revive Hardinge's Resolution of 10 October 1844 with instructions that, while lists of meritorious students were to give preference to those who had received a good education, 'in lower situations, a man who can read and write' was to be 'preferred to one who cannot, if he is equally eligible in other respects'. Thus was erected the scaffolding of a state system of education with indigenous vernacular schools at the base of a pyramid capped by Universities.[67] As B.T. McCully rejoiced: 'At last, the old fallacious policy of downward filtration was to be scrapped, while vernacular schools for the masses were to be encouraged on a large scale and their support secured by generous grants-in-aid from the Government'.[68]

Concern over the perception that the Christian religion might be promoted in government schools was a prominent feature of the exhaustive consultations leading to the final draft of the Wood Despatch. Successive drafts painstakingly removed any possible reference to connections between Government policy and Christianity. As an example, the second draft attributed the general public's 'high estimation' of 'the ability and integrity of native judges' partly to 'their adoption…of that high moral tone which pervades the literature of Christian Europe'. The final draft removed the word 'Christian'.[69] After his return to India as Governor of Madras, Trevelyan highlighted the importance of extreme caution regarding religious sensitivities in government policy. He wrote to Wood, then Secretary of State for India, to warn of the potential for insurrection which had been created by Governor Tweeddale's proposal to the Council of Education to introduce the Bible into Government schools. This had caused the mass resignation of natives from the Council followed by an angry Petition. Trevelyan believed that grants-in-aid were 'the only possible solution' whereby 'the Government confines itself to secular instruction, leaving the Private Patrons of the School to teach any religion they please'. Answering the criticism that 'the Grant-in-aid system is unequal to the education of the Masses', Trevelyan insisted that it was 'perfectly equal to the task *so far as the People have any ease, leisure*

---

[67] Paras 7, 14, 53 and 75, Public Despatch, to India, 19 July 1954, No. 49, I.O.R., E/4/826; J.A. Richey *op. cit.*, pp. 364–93.
[68] Bruce T. McCully, *op. cit.*, p. 141.
[69] Wood Papers, I.O.L., MSS Eur. F78/12a, fol. 85, F78/12b, fols 11–12; Para. 77, Public Despatch, to India, 19 July 1854, No. 49, I.O.R., E/4/826; J.A. Richey, *op.cit.*, p. 386.

and intelligence' without which no educational advantage was possible. He blamed the revenue system for obstructing the advance of education, noting that 'the Ryots of Madras and Bengal proper have enough to do in toiling for their subsistence and in deceiving or bribing the Tahsildar or Zamindar in order to retain some portion of their earnings'.[70] Commending the effort made by Wood to back away from Christianity as an important 'civilizing' influence while setting up the grants-in-aid, R.J. Moore concluded: 'The charter for education is probably the most eloquent expression of Britain's hopes for regenerating the society and economy of India to appear during the false dawn of an age of reform that preceded the mutiny'.[71]

Female Education

The grants-in-aid announced in the Wood Despatch were, indeed, designed to allow Government funds to support both missionary schools and female schools which, to a large extent, were the same thing.[72] This amounted to the first official effort to include female education as part of the state system of education in India. Missionary institutions beginning with the Serampore College and then the Church Missionary Society schools in Calcutta were the pioneers of female education. The education of girls had proved too sensitively entwined with the domestic arrangements of Indian families to allow for government interference. A proposal brought by Miss Cooke from the British and Foreign School Society to the Calcutta School Society was blocked by the native gentlemen on the appropriate committee. On 11 December 1821 the Calcutta School Society yielded responsibility for female education to the Church Missionary Society which promptly established eight schools enrolling 217 girls. From the very beginning, these schools enjoyed the support of the Marchioness of Hastings. By 1823 there were 22 schools with 400 girls. However, the challenge of educating girls was daunting. Mrs Wilson (the former Miss Cooke) complained of 'the great apathy' of the 'respectable natives', the 'sad hindrance' of early marriages and the 'bad effect upon the minds of the children' of holidays and *puja*s. There were countless incidents of children who were beaten in their homes,

---

[70] Trevelyan, to Wood, 28 July 1859, Wood Papers, I.O.L., MSS Eur. F78/59, Part 1, fols 15–16.

[71] R.J. Moore, *Sir Charles Wood's Indian Policy* (Manchester, 1966), p. 116.

[72] Paras 83 and 84, Despatch, to India, 19 July 1854, No. 49; J.A. Richey, *op. cit.*, pp. 388–89.

withdrawn forcefully from the schools or even abandoned because they were considered to have lost caste. Perhaps it was this widespread hostility which prompted Priscilla Chapman to remark: 'With reference to female education, it is impossible for government to interfere; neither can the means for improving the condition of the female population become the subject of legislation'.

From the missionaries' point of view, government instruction was 'shackled' by the pledge '*not to interfere with...religious opinions*'.[73]

From the Government's point of view, the missionaries' proselytizing zeal posed a grave danger. Thus Governor General Amherst's government rejected a request for ₹10,000 from the Ladies' Society for Native Female Education to purchase land for a new school, even though the Society had been formed in March 1824 with Lady Amherst as their patroness. The government argued that 'propagation of Christianity [was] one of its objects'. J.S. Mill, writing on behalf of the Directors, agreed with Lord Amherst's fears that the object of promoting Christianity 'might be pursued without due caution and forbearance'. But he hastened to add that 'no inference' should be drawn 'of any indisposition generally to the objects of the society'.[74] However, the Ladies' Society enjoyed the support of prominent Calcutta citizens such as Raja Radhakant Deb, Raja Baidyanath Roy, Raja Shibkrishna, Nilmoni Das and Kashinath Ghoshal who both attended examinations and contributed funds. Raja Radhakant Deb, one of the managers of the Hindu College who voted for Derozio's dismissal, commented very favourably upon the examinations of the girls educated by the Ladies' Society. And, Raja Baidyanath Roy contributed ₹20,000 towards the building of a Central Female School. In 1825 in the wake of the Society's approval of the establishment of a Central Female School, Mrs H. Ellerton rejoiced that not only had the number of schools increased to 30 and the number of children to 500, but also there was the gratification of 'having the children read the New Testament in their own tongue'.[75] The cornerstone of the Society's

---

[73] Calcutta School Society Resolution relating to Miss Cooke, 11 December 1821, C.M.S., CI1/017/16; cf. Priscilla Chapman, *Hindoo Female Education* (London, 1839), pp. 76–82, 89–90 and 66–67.

[74] Public Despatch, to Bengal, 13 December 1826, I.O.R., E/4/718, fols 451–55; cf. Nancy Gardner Cassels, 'John Stuart Mill, Religion and Law in the Examiner's Office', *op. cit.*, p. 177 and D.P. Sinha, *op. cit.*, p. 282.

[75] Resolution of Ladies' Society for Native Female Education in Calcutta and its Vicinity, 18 April 1825 for approving the establishment of the Central School; address by Mrs Hannah Ellerton, Secretary to the Ladies' Society for Native Female Education, 1 June 1825, C.M.S., CI1/017/5/6.

Central Female School was laid on 18 May 1826 in Cornwallis Square 'in the centre of the thickest and most respectable Hindu population'.[76] But the Ladies' Christian zeal did not escape the notice of Young Bengal. In their newspaper *The Reformer* on 19 December 1831 they made 'pointed reference to the excessive Christian zeal of the Ladies' Society which ran counter to the deep-seated social values of the Hindu Society'.[77] While, for the youths of Calcutta, emphasis upon Christianity explained a substantial drop in support of the Ladies' schools, for Priscilla Chapman what was at fault was 'one of the greatest prejudices of the Hindoos—the novelty no longer exists, and worldly gain, which may have been looked for, has not been found to result'.[78] Meanwhile, a second Ladies' Association for Native Female Education, which had also been founded in 1824 'to establish schools for native girls in those parts of Calcutta which could not be undertaken by the Ladies' Society' was discontinued in 1834. In contrast to the Ladies' Society's schools wherein approximately one third of the teachers were European, all of the teachers for the Ladies' Association were 'heathen'.[79] It is fair to assume that these teachers were Christian converts. Indian Christians stood at the lowest rank of the ecumene upon whom the English were dependent for support for their schools.

The highest ranks of the ecumene included the likes of Raja Baidyanath Roy, who, in addition to his gift of ₹20,000 to the Central Female School, contributed ₹50,000 to establish scholarships at the Hindu College. His gift added to ₹20,000 donated by each of Hurrynath Roy and Kalu Sumkur Ghosal, netted the Hindu College ₹90,000 or almost the equivalent of the 1813 Charter standard of one lakh.[80] But, when it came to educating their own female wards, respectable Brahmins, such as Prasanna Kumar Tagore, enlisted teachers at home. No schools for girls were established by Bengalis until the late 1840s. When Kali Krishna Mitra, Dr Nabim Krishna Mitra and Peary Charan attempted to found a school at Barasat in 1847, they were 'subjected to much insult and violent opposition'. However, they were supported by high-ranking officials, one of whom was John Elliot Drinkwater Bethune, the Law Member of Governor General Dalhousie's

---

[76] Priscilla Chapman, *op. cit.*, p. 86.

[77] Sri Kumar Acharya, *The Changing Pattern of Education in Early Nineteenth Century Bengal* (Calcutta, 1992), p. 228.

[78] Priscilla Chapman, *op. cit.*, p. 112.

[79] John Long, *Hand Book of Bengal Missions in Connexion with the Church of England together with an account of General Educational Efforts in North India* (London, 1848), p. 439.

[80] Peary Chand Mitra, *A Biographical Sketch of David Hare*, ed., Gouranga Gopal Sengupta (Calcutta, 1979), p. 16.

Council. Bethune launched his own experiment, founding his own school for girls on 7 May 1849 in the teeth of ridicule from the Christian community and 'bigoted opposition' of orthodox Hindus. By way of contrast, Raja Radhakant Deb supported Bethune, condemned the hysteria of his brethren as the 'vituperation of a malignant mind' and established his own school in his residence. The secret of Bethune's ultimate success was the support of the educated middle class. The foundation stone of his school was laid 6 November 1850. After Bethune's death the next year, Dalhousie took personal responsibility for the school defraying the cost of ₹700 per month, himself. And finally, the Directors endorsed the school.[81]

However, Government support was to prove ephemeral. Initially it was thought that not only did the Government support Bethune's school, but also that support for female education was entrenched in the Wood Despatch's provision for grants-in-aid to be available to girls' schools. Lt. Governor F.J. Halliday recruited the renowned principal of the Sanskrit College in Calcutta, Ishwar Chandra Vidyasagar to 'dispel the hostility of the upper classes with his Brahmin Pundit's image'. Wrongly assuming that he had Government support for female education in rural areas, Vidyasagar opened 43 schools for girls in the *mofussil*. Then came the ruling by the Home Authorities that forbade the Government of India to grant aid to schools in the *mofussil*, while allowing grants not exceeding ₹1000 per month for schools in the immediate area of Calcutta. Vidyasagar was only able to help nine of his 43 schools to survive as the result of his own herculean efforts.[82] Even the Bethune school was to founder for lack of support. However, in Bengal by the end of the nineteenth century, there emerged the remarkably well-educated *bhadramahila*. Over a thirty-year period after the end of Company rule, the number of girls' schools operated by Indians increased twentyfold. Thus freed from any fear of western influence, these schools functioned in Bengali because, as explained by Partha Chatterjee, 'the central place of the educated woman was still at home' and an English education 'might devalue and displace that central site where the social position of women was located'.[83]

---

[81] Sri Kumar Acharya, *op. cit.*, pp. 232–36.
[82] *Ibid.*, pp. 237–39.
[83] Partha Chatterjee, *op. cit.*, p. 128. For the remarkable story of the *bhadramahila*, see Meredith Borthwick, *The Changing Role of Women in Bengal 1849–1905* (Princeton, 1984) and Ghulam Murshid, *Reluctant Debutante: Response of Bengali Women to Modernization, 1849–1905* (Rajshahi, 1983).

In Madras and Bombay presidencies reports on female education had been sparse. In Bombay, particularly, the most that was revealed in the reports received in 1824 were occasional comments such as that by the Criminal Judge of the North Concan that 'native custom excludes females from the advantage of education'.[84] Moreover, in the Bombay Reports, unlike the reports of William Adam in Bengal and Thomas Munro in Madras, the 'existence of domestic or private instruction on a fairly extensive scale...[was] altogether ignored'.[85] Interestingly, in Madras there were two districts—Malabar and a *zamindari* of Vizagapatem—where roughly one-third of the children reported to be attending schools were girls. Otherwise, the number of girls attending school was small, although all castes were represented, particularly the low-caste 'dancing girls' or Temple *devadasi*s reported by the Collectors of Masulipatam, Madura, Tinnevelly and Coimbatore.[86] Thus, as in Bengal, the work of establishing schools for girls was done by missionaries. In Madras, a Ladies' Society for Native Female Education was proposed in 1829.[87] Indeed, it was generally acknowledged that 'the number of schools maintained by missionaries in South India considerably exceeded the aggregate of those in all other Presidencies put together'.[88]

Emergence of a Free Press

Governor General Charles Metcalfe's decision to enact Act XI of 1835[89] without consulting his employers in London, in order to repeal existing Regulations of press censorship has always been an iconic symbol of a free press in British India. What is not so well understood is that the East India Company's earlier policies of censorship had no basis in law. The only legal authority which the government possessed for regulating the press rested in English libel laws and the power given to the Company to deport an unruly subject by 53 Geo III c. 155 Sec. XXXVI. Thus Macaulay, who was

---

[84] Evantt Baillee, Criminal Judge of N. Conkan, 3 November 1824, B.R.O., General Dept., Vol. 8/92 1825, fol. 199.

[85] R.V. Parulekar, *A Source Book of the History of Education in the Bombay Presidency* (Bombay, 1945), p. xix.

[86] Dharampal, *op. cit.*, pp. 36–37.

[87] C.M.S. Archives, CI2/033/26.

[88] University of Madras, *History of Higher Education in South India*, Vol. I (Madras, 1957), p. 3; cf. J.A. Richey, *op. cit.*, pp. 49–50.

[89] Act XI (passed by Governor General in Council 3 August 1835), I.O.R., V/8/31.

assigned the task of drafting Act XI, accurately explained: 'The question before us is not whether the press shall be free, but whether being free, it shall be called free'.[90]

A centre of controversy in early-nineteenth-century India, the press inspired fear in the hearts of Calcutta Tories who kept faith in a despotic government supported by a strong army which might resort to mutiny if exposed to rumblings of discontent in a free press. For said Tories there really was no public beyond the Company's covenanted servants and its army. But, for liberal minded Whigs there was a vast public of Indian subjects, independent merchants and artisans on whose good opinion the Company's dominion depended. Furthermore, such enlightened thinkers as Rammohun Roy perceived the potential for the press to promote a 'diffusion of knowledge and consequent mental improvement'.[91] In following the debate over the pros and cons of a policy of censorship, it is possible to trace the steady evolution of the concept of a public from a limited group of subservient officials to a vibrant population eager to respond to new ideas. On the one hand, in the highest circles of government, the notable autocrat, John Adam, and the proconsul Governor of Madras, Thomas Munro, asserted a strong belief in the necessity for censorship. On the other hand, at least three Governors General—Wellesley, Hastings and Bentinck—found themselves on both sides of the issue. Finally, an increasingly educated Indian public demanded a free press.

Official British Public

Governor General Wellesley was the first to resort to a policy of press censorship. In truth, there was no lack of precedents for his action. In 1782 Warren Hastings first jailed and then seized the printing press of James Augustus Hicky for the malicious gossip which appeared in his *Bengal Gazette*. A decade later, Acting Governor General John Shore contrived to deport the editor of the *Bengal Journal* over his refusal to print an abject apology for publishing a false report of the death of Lord Cornwallis. The apology had initially been demanded by a French officer to whom the false report had been attributed. The hapless editor's real crime was the creation

---

[90] Minute by T.B. Macaulay, 16 April 1835, India Civil Judicial Proceedings, 18 May 1835, No. 1, I.O.R., P/205/64, fol. 2.

[91] Rammohun Roy, Memorial presented to the Supreme Court, 31 March 1823, I.O.L., MSS Eur. D611 #5.

of unnecessary friction with the French at a time when the Company was nervously attempting to consolidate its conquests. Explaining his actions to the president of the Board of Control, Governor General Sir John Shore declared: 'Our newspapers in Calcutta have, of late, assumed a licentiousness too dangerous to be permitted in this country'.[92]

When the Marquess of Wellesley succeeded Sir John Shore at the turn of the century, he was immediately plunged into war with the Company's inveterate enemy, Tipu Sultan of Mysore. At the same time, Napoleon's ambitions in the East were a subject of constant speculation within the ranks of the Company. There was concern that ill-founded rumours might provoke French-trained Indian troops to support the enemy. When the editor of another Calcutta newspaper, the *Asiatic Mirror*, speculated on the relative strengths of the European and Indian populations, Wellesley ordered his Commander-in-Chief: 'if you cannot tranquillize the editors of this and other mischievous publications, be so good as to suppress their papers by force, and send their persons to Europe'.[93] He then promptly proposed Regulations which established a Secretary of Government as Censor. These Regulations required routinely that editors and proprietors furnish the Government with their names and addresses; that every 'printer of a newspaper...print his name at the bottom of the paper; and that no papers be published on Sundays'. More controversially, they decreed that 'no Paper' was 'to be published at all until it shall have been previously inspected by the Secretary to Government' under penalty of 'immediate embarkation for Europe'. These Regulations were approved by Wellesley's Council on 13 May 1799, were extended to Madras and Bombay, and received the 'entire approbation' of the Court of Directors.[94] Somewhat stunned, though compliant with the new policy of censorship, the proprietor of the *Bengal Hurkaru* wrote in apparent dismay to the Government on 13 May 1799, the very day that the Regulations were promulgated. He simply stated that the printer's name had always appeared at the bottom of the paper. Then, since subscribers expected the paper early the next morning, he requested 'to be informed to whom and where it is to be sent for inspection'.[95]

---

[92] Sir John Shore, to Henry Dundas, 31 December 1794, cited by M. Chalapathi Rau, *The Press* (New Delhi, 1974), p. 15.

[93] Lord Wellesley, to H.E. Sir Alured Clarke, 17 April 1799, in R.R. Pearce, *Wellesley's Memoirs*, Vol. I (London, 1846), p. 278.

[94] Bengal Public Consultations, 13 May 1799, *in Board's Collections*, I.O.R. F/4/69 #1567A; *see also* Diary 29 June 1799 extracted from Fort St. George Consultations, in *Ibid.*; Public Despatch to Bengal, 26 March 1801, I.O.R., E/4/650, fol. 335.

[95] I.O.R., Home Miscellaneous Series 536a, fols 758–59.

As long as he remained in India, Wellesley was suspicious of the press and contemptuous of the public supporting it. He considered that existing printing presses 'serve only to maintain in needy indolence, a few European adventurers who are found unfit to engage in any creditable method of subsistence'.[96] In his eyes, the Indian press was the work of nonofficial European merchants, indigo planters and other outsiders who deliberately attempted to promote discontent within the ranks of the Company's military and civil service. They would thus expose the foibles of those in authority and publicize the grievances of those in the lower ranks. However, long after he left India, Wellesley evidently had second thoughts about his efforts to protect a small official public of Company servants from the criticism inherent in a free press. Almost forty years later, he ordered the editor of his official despatches to omit his despatch on the Indian press.[97]

Wellesley's successors, George Barlow and Lord Minto, continued the practice of warning editors to refrain from potential indiscretions. In 1807, the mood of Company officialdom so strongly favoured censorship that it supported Lord Minto in his altercations with the missionary press. The Vellore Mutiny of 1806 in the Madras presidency, which had resulted from the interference of Army dress regulations with caste traditions of turbans and unshorn hair, had led Lord Minto to conclude that mutiny was a probable result of intense missionary activity. He therefore admonished the missionaries at Serampore that their Evangelical pamphlets were offensive to the native population. Although the Evangelical Chair of the Court of Directors wished to criticize Minto for his interference with the missionary press, Henry Dundas, as President of the Board of Control intervened to warn missionaries that 'discretion and moderation in their language and actions…are indispensably requisite for those who are employed in prosecuting the laborious work of conversion'.[98] Meanwhile, the Governor of Madras, William Bentinck, smarting from blame for his failure to prevent the Vellore Mutiny, responded to an unfavourable press comment in a more draconian way. After a newspaper published an indiscreet attack upon his Government by a Supreme Court Judge, Bentinck decreed that no book

---

[96] Despatch on the Indian Press cited by Margarita Barns, *The Indian Press: A History of the Growth of Public Opinion in India* (London, 1940), p. 78.
[97] R.R. Pearce, *op. cit.*, Vol. I, p. 291.
[98] Para. 14 added by Henry Dundas to Board's Draft #45, 26 August 1808, Board's Drafts of Secret Letters and Despatches to India, I.O.R., L/P&S/5/541; for full discussion of the 1807 missionary crisis, see Nancy Gardner Cassels, 'The Serampore Missionary Crisis of 1807', in Joseph T. O'Connell, ed., *Bengal Vaisnavism, Orientalism, Society and the Arts* (Michigan State University, South Asia Series, Occasional Paper No. 35, Summer 1985), pp. 91–104.

or newspaper be published without Government consent. He explained: 'It is necessary in my opinion for the public safety that the Press in India should be kept under the most rigid control'.[99]

Before long, such rigorous censorship was also to be reenforced in Bengal. The East India Company's Charter of 1813 authorized the licensing of missionaries in India and required the Company to throw open its monopoly over Indian trade. This injection of missionaries and independent merchants into the country created the basis of a public opinion outside the ranks of the Company's covenanted service. The prospect of a flood of independent merchants and artisans horrified senior Company officials who could only imagine that the new immigrants would be agitators of the worst kind. Soon after his arrival in India, Lord Minto's successor, the Earl of Moira (later the Marquess of Hastings) took action to overcome all such fears. On 16 October 1813, he endorsed new rules requiring Calcutta presses to submit proof sheets of all publications for Government approval. It is somewhat ironic that Lord Hastings should echo Lord Bentinck with his orders for 'rigid control' of the press. Before very many years had passed, both Hastings and Bentinck became self-proclaimed supporters of a free press.

Anglo-Indian Public

The Company's policy regarding the press was not to continue along the smooth road of censorship and compliance. The 1813 Charter not only opened the door to missionaries and independent merchants, but it also allocated funds for the encouragement of education. This liberated the Company's non-conformist critics—British and Indian alike. Rev. James Bryce of St. Andrews' Kirk in Calcutta defied the despotic authority of Chief Secretary John Adam who performed the duties of Press Censor. An exemplary member of the Company's Tory senior establishment, Adam was to clash even more dramatically with James Silk Buckingham, the controversial editor of the *Calcutta Journal*. In Adam's view, Bryce and Buckingham were adventurers to be despised and repressed. They occupied the lowest rung in Calcutta's European society, in the shadow of the Company's elite military and civil service, beneath even the independent merchants and agency houses licensed by the Company. In addition to these rabble rousing newcomers,

---

[99] Minute by William Bentinck, 24 August 1807, Madras Public Proceedings, 22 September 1807, No. 1, I.O.R., P/243/23; G.G. Keble to Superintendent of Government Press, *Madras Gazette, Madras Courier* and *Madras Monthly Journal*, 1 September 1807, *Ibid.*

there was an Indian renaissance emerging to perplex Calcutta's Tories. In 1816 Gangadhar Bhattacharya established the first Indian-owned Bengali newspaper in Calcutta. And, in 1818, the Baptist missionaries launched a monthly Bengali magazine, the *Dig Darshan*, as well as a weekly Bengali paper, the *Samachar Darpan*. Initially, the authorities responded by relaxing press restrictions. Individual newspapers were given permission to publish on Sundays in contravention of Wellesley's Regulations. Many years later, William Butterworth Bayley, who acted as Press Censor during an absence of John Adam, explained: 'The duty of the Censor had been exercised in a manner which...had allowed to the editors sufficient scope for the useful discussion of questions of general or local interest'.[100]

However, the calm was soon shattered by Mr Heatly, the Anglo-Indian editor of the *Morning Post*. Mr Heatly persisted in publishing 'passages' deemed inexpedient by Bayley while declaring that 'as a Native of India he was liable to no legal penalty for refusing to comply with the injunctions of the Censor'.[101] Governor General Hastings recognized immediately that 'the Censorship did not rest upon Law, and that an Indian born Subject...might any day set Government at defiance on that head'.[102] Thus on 19 August 1818, Hastings replaced the censorship of Wellesley's Regulations with new rules for editors. The new rules abolished the office of Press Censor, thereby shifting responsibility for eliminating offensive material from a public official to individual editors. Editors were forbidden to publish 'animadversions on the...proceedings...of the Government of India' in England or in India, to offend native religious opinion or to print private scandal.[103] Hastings was fully aware that, while the Company retained the power 'to deport undeserving British subjects...the Government did not possess legal power to enforce any rules for the regulation or control of the Press so far as related to publications...Conducted by persons coming under the denomination of Natives'.[104] Nevertheless, Hastings was hailed by 500 residents of Madras for his 'liberal...gift...of freedom of discussion'. He dramatically proclaimed in response: '[L]et the triumph of our beloved Country in its awful contest with Tyrant-ridden France speak the value of a spirit to be found only in

---

[100] Minute by W.B. Bayley, 10 October 1822, Bengal Public Proceedings, 17 October 1822, No. 8, I.O.R., P/10/55.

[101] *Ibid.*

[102] Lord Hastings, Minute 7 October 1822, Bengal Public Proceedings, 17 October 1822, No. 6, I.O.R., P/10/55.

[103] Reported in Public Despatch from Bengal, 1 October 1818, I.O.R., E/4/100.

[104] W.B. Bayley, *op. cit.*

Men accustomed to indulge and express their honest sentiments'.[105] Yet, Hastings privately conceded that his removal of Press Censorship was an act of 'disguising conscious want of Power under the show of Lenity and Forbearance'.[106] Thus it is not surprising that in London the Despatch announcing the new rules attracted the criticism: 'They were passed by Resolutions of the Governor General in the same way as Lord Wellesley's Regulations. Neither I presume have any force of law, not being passed with the concurrence of the Supreme Court'.[107]

No one was more aware of the fragile legal base for the Company's efforts to regulate the Indian press than James Silk Buckingham. Easily the most colourful figure in the controversy over the Indian press, Buckingham was but a lowly ruffian adventurer in the eyes of the Calcutta Tory establishment. He arrived in Calcutta in June 1818 as captain of the *Humayoon Shah* with its cargo of Arabian horses for use in the Bengal army. But when he discovered that his next assignment was to take on a cargo of slaves in Africa, he resigned his command and remained in Calcutta. Noted for an independent spirit and considerable literary talent, he was approached by John Palmer, prominent banker and merchant prince, who proposed that Buckingham become the editor of a new journal which would represent the views of Calcutta's merchants. The *Calcutta Journal* made its debut on 2 October 1818, less than two months after the promulgation of Hastings' Regulations. John Palmer, as leader of the very small independent merchant class, represented Calcutta's middle class. John Adam, who considered the existence of a middle class essential to the safe operation of a free press, estimated the number of merchants outside the Company's official service at 300, not enough to warrant the privilege of free discussion.[108] It was estimated that there was a rabble of some 4,000 English fortune hunters in Calcutta. Buckingham boldly proclaimed that a free press was as much a right of these commoners as of the official and merchant classes. He further commended the journalistic enterprise of the Company's Indian subjects.

Buckingham's notoriety had an infinite number of manifestations. He sparred with the Rev. James Bryce of the *Asiatic Mirror*, each charging the other with violations of the Sabbath. Accusations and counter accusations

---

[105] Governor General Hastings, 'Answer to the Address from Madras Inhabitants', *Madras Government Gazette*, 12 August 1819, Home Miscellaneous Series, 536a, fols 770–71.

[106] Hastings, Minute 7 October 1822, *op. cit.*

[107] Marginalia in Public Despatch from Bengal, 1 October 1818, *op. cit.*

[108] John Adam, *A Statement of Facts Relative to the Removal from India of Mr Buckingham, Late Editor of the Calcutta Journal* (Calcutta, 1823), pp. 53ff., I.O.R., Home Miscellaneous Series 533/2.

developed into a running war until eventually the *Asiatic Mirror* died a natural death. He reported receiving a letter from Madras 'written on deep black edged mourning post...communicating as a piece of melancholy and afflicting intelligence the fact of Mr Elliott's being confirmed in the Government of that Presidency for three years longer!' When Governor Elliott asked the Bengal Government to punish Buckingham, the Government, for lack of a firm libel suit, sent a warning letter to which Buckingham replied most cordially. As remarked by Buckingham's biographer: 'This episode disclosed the policy both of the Government and of the editor. On the part of the former the policy was to reprimand but not to punish; with the latter it was to regret but not to comply'. Despite his penchant for mischief, Buckingham had a loyal friend in Lord Hastings. When John Adam won the support of the Governor General's Council for the deportation of Buckingham over the publication of a letter from a young officer denigrating the army's method of promotion, Hastings overruled his council. The hapless officer was deported instead. Hastings was inclined to joke about the suspicions nurtured by his councillors. On one occasion when Buckingham applied for permission to visit Agra and Delhi, Hastings replied that his Council would never agree unless Buckingham could guarantee that he would not set the Ganges on fire.[109]

And so, Buckingham pushed his luck to the limit. In the *Calcutta Journal* of 31 August 1822, he brashly, if correctly, asserted that:

[I]n point of fact and in point of Law the Restrictions of June 1818 are mere waste Paper. They have never been passed into a Regulation in the only legal manner in which Regulations can acquire the force of law by the sanction of the Supreme Court; and are of no more force or value than would be a Circular of the Governor General in Council, commanding us to give up our Residence for the accommodation of the King of Oudh, if he were to visit Calcutta, or to give up our beds to his seraglio, and our table to his Servants.[110]

However, with the coming of the new year, Buckingham's esteemed protector, Lord Hastings, departed for England. John Adam was acting Governor General pending the arrival of Lord Amherst. Thus the stage was set for Buckingham to cast his final insult. In the *Calcutta Journal* of 8 February 1823 he denigrated the appointment of the Rev. James Bryce as Clerk to the Committee of Stationery. Within a week, Adam secured the

---

[109] Ralph E. Turner, *James Silk Buckingham 1786–1855, A Social Biography* (London, 1934), pp. 121, 137 and 180.

[110] *Calcutta Journal*, 31 August 1822, Vol. IV, No. 209, p. 850, I.O.R., SM 155.

support of his Council in the decision to deport Buckingham. Only J.H. Harington expressed residual doubt as he 'acquiesced...conditionally on account of his imperfect knowledge of the previous Proceedings'. In their despatches to the Directors, the Government of Bengal reported their decision to deport Buckingham, announced the preparation of a byelaw for licensing printing offices and appealed to the Directors to obtain authorization from Parliament to provide the Bengal Government with 'more ample and efficient powers...to keep the Evil in check'.[111]

On 15 March 1823, the byelaw empowering the Government to license printing presses within the town of Calcutta in response to applications sworn on oath under penalty of a fine not exceeding 400 *sicca* rupees was submitted to the Supreme Court for its consideration. On this occasion counsel was heard on behalf of J.S. Buckingham who had already filed an affidavit stating the losses he had incurred by virtue of his loss of license. But the most remarkable testimony before the Court was that offered by prominent Calcutta Brahmins led by Rammohun Roy, the noted Bengali reformer. Roy was much admired by Buckingham who commended his enterprise when he took over the Bengali weekly *Sambud Kaumudi* in December 1821 and when he founded the Persian newspaper, the *Mirat-ul-Akbar* in April 1822. Rammohun Roy's petition before the Supreme Court has come to be known as the 'Areopagitica of the Indian Press'. Referring to the Licenses required for all publications based on applications sworn on oaths, Rammohun declared:

> Those Natives who are in more favourable circumstances and of respectable character, have such an invincible prejudice against making a voluntary affidavit, or undergoing the solemnities of an oath, that they will never think of establishing a publication which can only be supported by a series of oaths and affidavits abhorrent to their feelings and derogatory to their reputation amongst their countrymen.[112]

Yet, Rammohun's protest fell upon deaf ears. On 31 March Justice Frances MacNaghten overruled all objections to the law and it was duly registered by the Supreme Court on 4 April 1823 as Reg. III with the full force of law. Laconically he remarked: 'If we are to have a Free Constitution, which we

---

[111] Public Despatches from Bengal, 15 and 28 February 1823, cited in I.O.R., Home Miscellaneous Series 536a, fols 798–801.

[112] 'Memorial from Certain Native Inhabitants of Calcutta', presented to Supreme Court, 31 March 1823, I.O.L., MSS Eur. D611 No. 5, p. 6. R.E. Turner obliquely suggests that Buckingham was the real author of the 'Areopagitica', R.E. Turner, *op. cit.*, pp. 191–92.

have not, let a Free Press follow, not precede it'.[113] Both Rammohun Roy and Buckingham appealed to the Privy Council against the Adam Press Ordinance and both appeals were rejected.[114]

Indeed, Sir Frances MacNaghten enjoyed sober support from very distinguished quarters. One of the most well-known discourses against a free press in India is the minute written by Sir Thomas Munro on 12 April 1822 shortly after he became Governor of Madras. This enlightened creator of the *ryotwari* settlement spoke bluntly: 'I cannot view the question of a free press in this country without feeling that the tenure with which we hold our power, never has been and never can be the liberties of the people'. He insisted: 'There is no public in India to be guided or instructed by a free press'. European society was dominated by the Company's military and civil servants. And libel laws were not much use since the juries were composed of 'shopkeepers and mechanics', an insignificant class who did not mix with merchants and covenanted servants and therefore would 'never...find a libel in a newspaper against a public officer'. Munro was principally concerned with the effect of a free press on the army. Thus, he warned: 'We are trying an experiment never yet tried in the world—maintaining a foreign dominion by means of a native army, and teaching that army, through a free press, that they ought to expel us and deliver their country'.[115]

In protest against this official emhasis upon a policy of censorship, Rammohun Roy withdrew from active journalism. On 18 April 1823 he did not support the *Sambud Kaumudi*'s application for a license in accordance with the Adam Regulations and publication of *Mirat-ul-Akbar* ceased altogether. Company officialdom took little notice of this gesture. Indeed, Macnaghten had defended the Regulations as a means of controlling the Indian-owned press, which had enjoyed a certain immunity since Indians could not be deported and also Indian editors did not receive the prohibitory circulars which went the rounds of English editors. The Directors approved Adam's Regulations. Also, the Bombay Government promulgated press

---

[113] Decision of the Supreme Court delivered by Sir Frances MacNaghten, 31 March 1823, I.O.R., MSS Eur D611 No. 5, p. 15. In his speech MacNaghten noted that both Wellesley and Hastings had ignored the custom that a regulation remain in the hands of the Supreme Court for 20 days before it could be registered and become law.

[114] Margarita Barns, *op. cit.*, pp. 124–25. *Proceedings before His Majesty's Most Honourable Privy Council, in Relation to the Appeal by James Silk Buckingham Esq. against Certain Regulations of the Bengal Government on the subject of the Press* (London, 1825).

[115] Thomas Munro, 'Danger of a Free Press in India', 12 April 1822, in A.J. Arbuthnot, ed., *Major General Sir Thomas Munro Bart., K.C.B. Governor of Madras—Selections From His Minutes and Other Official Writings*, Vol. II (London, 1881), pp. 287–88, 291 and 294.

regulations similar to Adam's Ordinances. However, in 1825 these rules were not approved by the Bombay Supreme Court and thus could not be considered the law of the land. Ultimately, Bombay Regulation XXIV of the 1827 Elphinstone Code incorporated the spirit and letter of the 1823 Regulations. In the meantime, in a despatch to Bombay the Directors ordered Company servants not to have any connection with the press.[116]

A prominent Bengal councillor, Charles Theophilus Metcalfe, was later to protest these orders. He argued that the enactment of Bengal Regulation III 1823 requiring a License for the printing of all Newspapers left

> Proprietors and Editors...responsible for the contents[.]...[T]herefore on the supposition that the Press is already in some degree free,...the exclusion of the Company's Servants...the only class of persons who feel any interest in the Company's Government...from taking a share in the exercise of the power which that Engine wields appears to me to be the very reverse of expedient.[117]

Unlike the Tory officials in Calcutta, Metcalfe was an admirer of the growing Indian press. Despite the Adam Regulations and Rammohun Roy's withdrawal from the arena, there had been remarkable growth in the vernacular press. There was even room for controversy among Indian editors. Thus in 1822 the original editor of the *Sambad Kaumudi* departed from the liberal reform views of Rammohun Roy to join the orthodox Calcutta Brahmins in launching the *Samachar Chandrika*. Although Rammohun Roy, himself, had retreated from public view, his friends continued his work. During the administration of Governor General Amherst, six vernacular newspapers were in operation in addition to the Serampore publications. Lord Amherst, who had not emerged from among the Calcutta bureaucrats, took a lenient view of the Adam Regulations. After 1825, although the Adam Regulations remained in force and were extended to Bombay outside the jurisdiction of the Supreme Court, there were very few violations reported.

Amherst's successor, Lord William Bentinck, took an interest in the growing Indian press. Immediately upon his arrival in 1828, he ordered a survey of existing newspapers and he made a considerable reduction in postal charges for newspapers in Bengal. In Madras and Bombay postage

---

[116] Margarita Barns, *op. cit.*, pp. 158, 165. Bombay Regulation XXIV for restricting the establishment of printing presses and the circulation of printed books and papers (passed by Governor in Council on 1 Jan 1827).

[117] Minute by C.T. Metcalfe, 29 December 1828, Bengal Public Proceedings, 6 January 1829, D, I.O.R., P/12/42 and *Board's Collections* F/4/1185 #30766, fols 133–137.

rates for newspapers remained as much as 10 times heavier. He opined that, although he was wary of the 'great evil that might arise from an unrestricted liberty of the press', he had no quarrel with the fact that 'the Press at Calcutta and Bombay' enjoyed 'at least as much freedom as in England'. He noted that enlightened graduates of Hindu College had 'little influence upon the population within the City and none whatever on the rest of India'. He deemed them 'incapable of political mischief'.[118] Indeed, the report on the Indian press by his Persian Secretary had assured Bentinck: 'It is to be feared that the poverty of our native subjects beyond the limits of the Presidency, operates generally speaking nearly as forcibly as their want of curiosity to indispose them from affording encouragement to Native Newspapers'.[119]

However, in 1830 Governor General Bentinck was saddled with the task of implementing the Directors' unpopular 'Half-Bhatta' Order. By reducing the allowances of army officers, the Company hoped to effect economies that would eliminate the deficit left by the Burmese War during Lord Amherst's administration. The decision was already highly controversial. Bentinck, himself, deemed the Directors' order 'extremely unwise and inexpedient, fraught with mischief and unproductive of any good'. Nonetheless, haunted by his memories of the Vellore Mutiny for which he had been held responsible, Bentinck decided to prohibit discussion of the Court's orders in the press. He justified his decision by making a distinction between debate on a proposal and clamour against a decision already taken by supreme authority. W.B. Bayley, a supporter of the Adam Regulations and an obedient servant to Lord Amherst, was also Chief Secretary to Lord Bentinck. He gave the Governor General's decision unqualified support. The only member of Council to object was C.T. Metcalfe. After rehearsing the obvious argument that a free press 'has afforded a vent for the expression of the feelings which a most unpopular measure excited', Metcalfe challenged the arbitrary action of Government: 'If I could think it sound policy to shackle the Press I should prefer the steady operation of the censorship, or any fixed rule, to the occasional interference of the Government by its arbitrary will'.[120] Paradoxically, in his minute concerning the Half-Bhatta Order, Bentinck indicated that he wished to be remembered as a supporter of a free press. He asserted that 'the liberty of the press is a most useful engine in promoting the

---

[118] Minute by William Bentinck, 28 December 1828, Bengal Public Consultations, 6 January 1829, A, I.O.R., P/12/42 and *Board's Collections* F/4/1185, #30766, fols 114, 118–19. See also S. Natarajan, *A History of the Press in India* (Bombay, London, New York, 1962), p. 59.

[119] Report by A. Stirling, I.O.R., *Board's Collections*, F/4/1185 #30766, fols 129, 132.

[120] Minute by C.T. Metcalfe, 6 September 1830, Bengal Public Proceedings, 6 September 1830, No. 3, O.I.O.C., P/12/53.

good administration of the country'.[121] Perhaps the most accurate statement is that made by Bentinck, himself, in 1836 to the President of the Board of Control, John Cam Hobhouse, to the effect that he never could make up his mind on the subject of a free press.[122]

Widespread support for a free press was slow in coming. Differing views of the concept of the Company's public continued to cloud debate. The Governor of Bombay, Lord Clare, asked Bentinck: 'Who and what is the public in India to be enlightened by an unshackled press?' He further complained of the radical Calcutta press: 'It would be absurd to attempt to gag our press with the licence given to yours, but they shall not publish libels at Bombay with impunity so long as I am at the head of the government'.[123] Meanwhile in Madras, Governor Frederick Adam switched back and forth. At first he regretted his predecessor's removal of press censorship orders in Madras and submitted to Bentinck some draft regulations in imitation of Bengal Reg. III of 1823. Bentinck deferred consideration of the draft regulations until after the Law Commission met. After that, Governor Adam supported Calcutta journalists who banded together to petition Bentinck on 6 February 1835 for repeal of the Bengal Regulation and Ordinances of 1823. Bentinck's Chief Secretary ultimately replied that the Governor General was aware of 'the unsatisfactory state of the laws relating to the press' and trusts that a new system would shortly be devised.[124] The very next day, Bentinck resigned his office on account of ill health and departed for England, leaving C.T. Metcalfe as acting Governor General.

Metcalfe's policy towards the press was to earn him the appellation 'Liberator of the Indian Press'. Without further ado, Metcalfe instructed T.B. Macaulay, Legislative Member of his Council, to draft an Act that would apply to all of India. In Bengal and Agra, the 1823 Ordinances and Regulations were still in effect and in Bombay the Government enforced press regulations outside the jurisdiction of the Supreme Court. But in

---

[121] Minute by William Bentinck, 6 September 1830, No. 1, I.O.R., P/12/53; see also C.H. Philips, ed., *The Correspondence of Lord William Cavendish Bentinck, Governor General of India 1828–1835* (Oxford, 1977), pp. 504–5.

[122] This point is made by Bentinck's biographer, John Rosselli, although there is no conclusive footnote reference. John Rosselli, *Lord William Bentinck—The Making of a Liberal Imperialist 1774–1839* (London, 1974), p. 321.

[123] Lord Clare, to Bentinck, Dapooree, 25 July 1832, C.H. Philips, *op. cit.*, Vol. II, p. 858; Lord Clare, to Bentinck, Satara, 6 October 1832, *ibid.*, Vol. II, p. 915.

[124] Sir Frederick Adam, to Bentinck, Madras, 28 November 1832, C.H. Philips, *ibid.*, Vol. II, p. 953. Adam and others, Petition to the Indian Government, *Ibid.*, Vol. II, pp. 1415–20.

Madras there were no laws curbing the press. Macaulay aptly analyzed the Company's dilemma:

> The question before us is not whether the press shall be free, but whether, being free, it shall be called free....[Yet,] while the Editor of a newspaper at Calcutta must have a license from the Government, the Editor of a newspaper at Madras may excite his fellow subjects to the most criminal enterprises, or may destroy the peace and honor of private families with small risk of being convicted before any legal tribunal....The Act which I now propose is intended to remove both evils, and to establish a perfect uniformity in the laws regarding the press throughout the Indian Empire. Should it be adopted, every person who chooses will be at liberty to set up a newspaper without applying for a previous permission. But no person will be able to print or publish sedition or calumny without imminent risk of punishment.[125]

Metcalfe heartily endorsed the arguments advanced by Macaulay.[126] Two of the remaining three on Metcalfe's council expressed reservations concerning the proposed legislation. H.T. Prinsep muttered darkly that the growing 'native press' may become 'a giant to wrestle with' and 'may...set the whole population against us'. He quoted the head of the legal profession in England: 'When you have a free press on board of a man of war, then you may think of giving one to India'.[127] Col. W. Morison called for extra vigilance over the 'native press'. Only A. Ross was wholeheartedly in favour of Macaulay's draft.[128] But Metcalfe carefully replied: 'A Tenure dependent on attempts to suppress the Communication of public opinion could not be lasting; both because such a Tenure must be rotten and because such attempts must fail'.[129]

Before Macaulay's draft could be passed into law, Europeans and Indians alike gathered at a public meeting in Calcutta to proclaim Metcalfe 'Liberator of the Indian press'. Metcalfe responded with an eloquent manifesto asserting the necessity of a free press as an accessory to the Company's civilizing mission:

---

[125] Minute by T.B. Macaulay, 16 April 1835, India Civil Judicial Proceedings, 18 May 1835, No. 1, I.O.R., P/205/64, fols 2–4.

[126] Minute by Governor General, 17 April 1835, India Civil Judicial Proceedings, 18 May 1835, No. 2, *Ibid.*

[127] Minute by H.T. Prinsep, 17 April 1835, India Civil Judicial Proceedings, No. 3, *Ibid.*, fols 5–6.

[128] Minute by Col. W. Morison, 25 April 1835, India Civil Judicial Proceedings, No. 5, *Ibid.*, fols 8–9; Minute by A. Ross, n.d., India Civil Judicial Proceedings, No. 4, fol. 8.

[129] Minute by the Governor General, 27 April 1835, India Civil Judicial Proceedings, No. 6, *Ibid.*, fol. 10.

It cannot be that we are permitted by Divine authority to be here merely to collect the revenues of the country, pay the establishments necessary to keep possession, and get into debt to supply the deficiency. We are, doubtless, here for higher purposes, one of which is to pour the enlightened knowledge and civilization, the arts and sciences of Europe over the land, and thereby improve the condition of the people. Nothing surely is more likely to conduce to these ends than the liberty of the press.[130]

The ultimate tribute to Metcalfe came from his Calcutta public in the form of the building of a public library, later known as Metcalfe Hall on the banks of the Hughli 'in commemoration of the recognition of the freedom of the Indian Press under the Government of Sir C.T. Metcalfe'.[131]

Finally, on 3 August 1835 Act XI was passed by Metcalfe with the unanimous support of his Council. The Act repealed the Bengal Press Regulations and Ordinances of 1823, as well as the Bombay Press Regulations of 1825 and 1827. It required the printer and publisher of every periodical to appear before the local magistrate and declare his identity, the name of the periodical and the location of the printing press; it required the name of the printer and publisher to appear on any book or paper published within the Company's territories; it required everyone who owned a printing press to make a declaration to that effect; all these declarations were to be made under penalty of a ₹5,000 fine or a two-year jail term.[132]

All responses to Metcalfe's decision to liberate the press were not as jubilant as that of the citizens of Calcutta. Palpably disappointed, the Madras Government inquired if the Company's order of 30 December 1825 forbidding Company servants to have any connection with the press 'was intended to apply to all persons in the public employ or solely to covenanted and commissioned servants of the Company'.[133] The Government of India replied that the Order only applied to covenanted and commissioned Company servants.

Outright condemnation was yet to come. The Directors roundly denounced Act XI of 1835 as counter to:

---

[130] Cited in J.W. Kaye, *The Life and Correspondence of Charles Lord Metcalfe* (London, 1858), Vol. 2, p. 15.

[131] Printed appeal from the Committee formed for the erection of the Metcalfe Library, I.O.R., Home Miscellaneous Series 790, fols 397–99.

[132] Act XI (passed by Governor General in Council 3 August 1835), I.O.R., V/8/31.

[133] R. Clerk, Secretary to the Madras Government, to H.T. Prinsep, Secretary to Government, 10 November 1835, India Public Proceedings, 25 November 1835, Nos 8 and 9, I.O.R., P/186/69.

[T]he solemn decisions both of the Supreme Court at Calcutta and of His Majesty's Privy Council..., the recorded opinions of all preceding Governments of Bengal, Madras and Bombay, and...the carefully considered measures of Lord William Bentinck and Sir Frederick Adam for extending the Licensing Regulation to Madras.[134]

Adding insult to injury, they reprimanded Metcalfe for having no 'real grievance the redress of which might justify your proceeding'. They intimated further: 'You are in possession of our sentiments, and we shall not be sorry to find that by returning to the former system, you have rendered our interference unnecessary'. Much as the Directors would have liked to reverse Metcalfe's decision, they dared not interfere. They well knew that 'repeal of such a law...might be productive of mischievous results'.[135] They desperately hoped that either Metcalfe would have second thoughts or else his successor, the Earl of Auckland, would renounce the policy of a free press. Meanwhile, they consigned Metcalfe to the N.W.P. and passed over him in 1837 when a new Governor of Madras was appointed. Upon enquiry, Metcalfe learned that his freeing of the press was unforgiven.[136]

Though a conscientious plodder who knew little of India, Lord Auckland fully endorsed Metcalfe's liberation of the press. He maintained cordial relations with Metcalfe who had reluctantly accepted his demotion as Lt. Governor of the N.W.P. He requested a study of the press and ascertained that the Indian press was in a very healthy condition. By 1839 there were 26 European and 9 Indian newspapers in Calcutta; Bombay boasted 10 European and 4 Indian journals. There were 9 European journals in Madras and Delhi, Ludhiana, Moulmein, Agra and Serampore each claimed one newspaper. Auckland commended Act XI for providing a legal basis for the Company's policy towards the press. He observed that the 'Laws of England' had provided the only remedy 'against abuses of the Press in India' since before Wellesley's effort to introduce censorship. And when an Anglo-Indian editor proved that the Company's power of deportation was easily evaded, Lord Hastings made a 'merit of necessity' by removing censorship. The revival of censorship in Bengal under John Adam and the deportation of Buckingham merely underlined the futility of arbitrary rules. The Charter of 1833 deprived the Company of its power of deportation; the Adam Regulations were effectively shelved as 'no Government would wish or dare

---

[134] Legislative Despatch, to India, 1 February 1836, No. 1, I.O.R., E/4/746, fols 1066–67, 1070–71 and 1075–76.
[135] *Ibid.*
[136] Edward Thompson, *The Life of Charles, Lord Metcalfe* (London, 1937), p. 330.

to use' powers of enforcement. By contrast, the press in the presidencies of Bombay and Madras were 'absolutely unrestrained except by Common Law'. And so Auckland welcomed the substitution of 'legal' for 'arbitrary rules and restrictions' in Bengal and he commended Act XI for bringing the press in Madras and Bombay 'more immediately under the cognizance of Government and the Law'.[137] In addition to his successful defence of Act XI, Auckland supported the Government of Bombay in its insistence that the Directors revoke their 1825 'prohibition against the connection of our servants with the public newspapers'. On 21 April 1841 the Directors determined to 'concede the point in question'.[138]

Epilogue

The events of 1857 terminated the rule of the Company and dramatically interrupted the development of administrative policies. One historian imbued with nationalist sentiment proclaims: 'In no small measure was the Press later responsible for the breakout and development of the "First War of Indian Independence"'.[139] But most historians of nineteenth-century India consider the mutiny of 1857 to have been a sad and highly complex event. Freedom of the press was merely among the benefits of British rule which might be counted alongside the development of education, but which failed to offset oppressive revenue collection and religious offence. S. Natarajan observes that there was no truly significant connection between the growth of the Indian Press and the causes of the Mutiny.[140] It is certainly true that one of the first moves of Governor General Canning after the Mutiny was his decision to gag the press. But it is also true that the Canning Act of 1857 was an emergency measure valid for only one year. Ironically, the Metcalfe Act remains the basis of legislation affecting the Indian press even today. Although it was technically repealed by Act XXV of 1867, the 1867 Press Act retained the essence of Act XI 1835. Viceroy Lytton's Vernacular Press Act of 1878 was repealed within four years. The Press Act of 1867, although modified and revised by legislation in 1890, 1910 and 1931, still obtains today. As summed up by Milton Israel: 'From 1835 to 1947 and

---

[137] Auckland, Minute 8 August 1836, Auckland Minute Books, British Library, ADD. MSS 37709, fols 93–94.
[138] Political Despatch, to India, 21 April 1841, I.O.R., E/4/765, fols 1168–69.
[139] N.K. Murthy, *Indian Journalism—Origin, Growth and Development of Indian Journalism from Asoka to Nehru* (Mysore, 1966), p. 47.
[140] S. Natarajan, *op. cit.*, p. 68; see also Margarita Barns, *op. cit.*, p. 236.

beyond, the Adam Regulations and the Metcalfe Press Law provided the parameters for official action, legislation, and perspective on the issue of the freedom of the press'.[141]

Trial by Jury

The effort to increase Indian agency in the Company's courts by allowing Indian juries was essentially an experiment directed by the Home Authorities. In India juries had been used sporadically by the Governor and Council in Bombay as far back as 1672 and authorized for general use with the establishment of Mayor's Courts in the presidency towns by the Letters Patent of 1726. When the Supreme Courts replaced those courts in 1774, the practice continued with British subjects resident in the presidency towns eligible to sit on the juries. However, Indians and Anglo-Indians were excluded from the process. The attitudes of nineteenth-century Company officials ranged from the enthusiasm of Thomas Munro who envisioned a transformation of the court process with something resembling a *panchayat* to the pragmatism of Governor General William Bentinck who strove to please his masters in London by adopting the less imaginative provisions of the Elphinstone Code. Bengal Regulation VI of 1832 provided for judges in the Company's civil and criminal courts to avail themselves of the 'assistance of respectable natives' either in the form of a *panchayat* outside the court, or as assessors making observations on testimony within the court, or by 'employing them more nearly as a jury'. Both the provisions in the Bombay Code for something like a jury and Bengal Regulation VI of 1832 followed in the wake of Indian Jury Acts passed by the British Parliament.[142]

Certainly, the Company official with the most positive vision of the possibilities for juries in Indian courts was Thomas Munro. After experience in the administration of Mysore, Canara and districts south of the Tungabhadra, he speculated on the role trial by jury might play in checking the prevalence of perjury in the courts. Munro's 'trial by jury' was more a 'trial by panchayat'. Thus he stated: 'There can be no doubt that the trial by panchayet is as

---
[141] Milton Israel, *Communications and Power—Propaganda and the Press in the Indian Nationalist Struggle, 1920–1947* (Cambridge, 1994), p. 4.
[142] Bengal Regulation VI for enabling European Functionaries to avail themselves of the assistance of respectable Natives in the Administration of Civil or Criminal Justice, and for modifying or dispensing with Futwas by Mahomedan Law Officers in certain trials (passed by Governor General in Council 31 July 1832), O.I.O.C., V/8/21.

much the common law of India in civil matters, as that by jury is of England'. He remarked further: 'The native who has a good cause always applies for a panchayet; while he who has a bad one, seeks the decision of a Collector or a Judge, because he knows it is easier to deceive them'.[143] Munro was well aware of the fluid character of the *panchayat* with its inconsistencies and capricious verdicts, yet he observed that 'natives...hold it [the panchayat] in so much reverence that they say "When the jury sits, God is present"'.[144]

Munro's vision was re-enforced by contact with Sir Alexander Johnston, Chief Justice and President of Council in Ceylon. Since 1806, Johnston had been working on a plan for making all residents of Ceylon eligible to sit upon juries. After visiting Madras, where he was encouraged by Munro, Johnston finally submitted his plan in 1808. Then he returned to England to explain his idea to the Home Authorities with the result that all residents of Ceylon were eligible to sit on juries by 1811. Within another five years, Anglo-Indians were petitioning the Home Authorities for the right to sit on juries and Munro authorized Sir Alexander to encourage English ministers to extend the right to all residents of British India.

Ultimately, Johnston inspired the President of the Board of Control, C.W.W. Wynn, to introduce the Indian Jury Act which was passed by the British Parliament on 5 May 1826.[145] This Act extended eligibility for jury duty to Indians and Anglo Indians. However, out of concern, as Wynn was later to explain, for 'long established habits of corruption and venality' in Indian judicial proceedings, a sharp distinction was made between the 'Christian' Anglo-Indians and the 'native' Indians. Christian Anglo-Indians were eligible to sit on the Grand and Petty Juries in trials of both Christians and 'natives'. But 'natives' were excluded from Grand Juries and were only allowed to sit on Petty Juries if Christians were not on trial. This distinction was to prove incendiary in Bengal.

Meanwhile, Munro, by this time well established as Governor of Madras, took heart from Sir Alexander Johnston's reports of his consultation with Wynn. Ultimately, he was encouraged to act when two Circuit Judges spontaneously submitted a proposal for a Regulation declaring all citizens of the Madras Presidency eligible to sit on juries in criminal cases and issuing detailed instructions regarding the rights and responsibilities of jurors.

---

[143] Thomas Munro, 'Trial by Panchayat', 15 August 1807, in A.J. Arbuthnot, *op. cit.*, Vol. II, p. 4.

[144] Thomas Munro, 'General Remarks on the Judicial Administration and on the Police', 31 December 1824, *Ibid.*, Vol. II, p. 26.

[145] East Indies Juries Act, 7 Geo IV c. xxxvii.

Judges Newnham and Dacre of the Centre Provincial Court argued that: '[I]n a trial by Jury...the Innocent will be secure from falling victim to any unjust prosecution but the man really Criminal will find it more difficult to escape with emboldening impunity so the good of public justice will be realised...'[146]

Governor Munro wrote a vigorous minute in support of the Regulation, hailing the Judges' proposal as 'proof' that there had occurred a 'change of opinion' among Judges in the Presidency hitherto opposed to the very idea of trial by jury operating in Madras. Sadly, Munro died before he could convince his council of the wisdom of such legislation. His official successor, Stephen Rumbold Lushington, had already been appointed six months earlier, but was not to arrive in Madras for another four or five months. In the meantime, H.S. Graeme took the helm, and on 11 September the Madras Council enacted Regulation X.[147] Lushington arrived the next month and promptly took umbrage over the precipitate passage of Regulation X much to the chagrin, and ultimately outrage, of H.S. Graeme. Lushington objected on principle that the appropriate formalities of consulting all the Madras Judges as well as the Home Authorities had not been observed. Greatly to his satisfaction, a subsequent enquiry resulted in a negative verdict. Two of the three Sudder Adawlut judges and 10 of 12 Circuit Judges deemed the 'innovation as utterly unsuited to its purpose, as barren of all hope of improvement in the administration of Justice' and 'pregnant with temptations to Native Corruption'.[148] Lushington then suspended the operation of Regulation X.[149] Unfortunately, some of Lushington's remarks, such as his reference to Munro's support for the measure 'as one of those mistakes of the wise in life's last days', enraged Graeme who stirred controversy within the Council with numerous vituperative minutes. Lushington freely cast aspersions upon the character of Judges Newnham and Dacre declaring 'their entire unfitness for the legislative office they thought fit so irregularly

---

[146] Thomas Newnham and Joseph Dacre, 2nd and 3rd Judges of Centre Provincial Court, to the Hon. Maj. Gen. Sir Thomas Munro, Governor in Council, Fort St. George, Madras Judicial Proceedings, 3 July 1827, No. 3, extracted in *Board's Collections*, I.O.R., F/4/1008, fol. 82.

[147] Madras Regulation X for the gradual introduction of Trial by Jury into the Criminal Judicature of the Territories subject to the Presidency of Fort St. George (passed by Governor in Council 11 September 1827), I.O.R., V/8/28.

[148] Judicial Despatch, from Madras, 22 April 1828, Madras Judicial Proceedings, 22 April 1828, No. 1, I.O.R., P/324/325, fol. 1610. Also in *Board's Collections*, I.O.R., F/4/1007, fol. 3.

[149] Minute by President, 21 December 1827, Madras Judicial Proceedings, 21 December 1827, No. 7, extracted in *Board's Collections*, I.O.R., F/4/1008, fols 396–97.

to assume'.¹⁵⁰ Tempers boiled. The Court of Directors was left to soothe ruffled feathers. They paid tribute to the 'zeal and ability' of 'Public Servants' on both sides of the question. They then suggested that the experiment launched by the 1826 Jury Act allowing for 'Native Juries…in the Supreme Courts at the Presidencies' be allowed to run its course.¹⁵¹

This stalemate in the debate over the introduction of native juries into *mofussil* criminal courts was sustained, in part, by the speculation which prevailed among both opponents and proponents of the experiment as to a basic incompatibility between the caste and jury systems. In Madras, Lushington noted the difficulty of attempting to recreate the 'English notion of a Jury that every man shall be tried by his Peers'. He argued that this would require a Muslim jury for a Muslim defendant and a Hindu jury matching the caste of a Hindu defendant. Otherwise, he reasoned a defendant would be:

[E]ntirely acquitted by a Jury of Mahomedans giving a verdict according to their own Laws and Customs; slightly punished or entirely absolved by a Jury of Hindoos, if of high caste; and inevitably condemned to death by a Jury of Hindoos, if of low caste.¹⁵²

Graeme retorted in a counter minute that 'it was not intended that the native jury should be made to correspond with our English notion of a Jury'. Rather, Muslims and Hindus would 'join in the same jury' to be guided, not by complexities of Muslim or Hindu criminal law, but by 'plain common sense assisted by the advice of the Presiding Judge'.¹⁵³ However, concern over the possible incompatibility between castes and juries was apparent in the remarks of the only Madras Sudder Judge to favour the introduction of trial by jury into the *mofussil* courts. J. Cochrane, the second puisne judge of the Sudder Court, devised a scheme to avoid the indiscriminate formation of a jury. He proposed that, in the case of a defendant of the right- or left-hand caste, the jury should be composed of two jurors from each of these castes and the remaining eight should be chosen at the discretion of the Judge. A Hindu defendant of any other caste would be matched by two jurors of the same caste. And, in the case of a Muslim defendant, half the jury might be Muslim. Only the 'lowest orders such as Pariars, chucklers and Pullars'

---

¹⁵⁰ Minute by Lushington, 7 January 1828, in *Board's Collections*, I.O.R., F/4/1007, fols 25, 28–29.

¹⁵¹ Judicial Despatch, to Madras, 2 January 1829, I.O.R., E/4/936, fols 427–32.

¹⁵² Minute by Lushington, 7 January 1828, in *Board's Collections*, I.O.R., F/4/1008, fol. 41.

¹⁵³ Minute by H.S. Graeme, 29 January 1828, Madras Secret Proceedings, 22 April 1828, I.O.R., P/Sec/Mad/109, fol. 219.

should be excluded from jury duty.[154] Lushington jubilantly observed that the one senior judge favourable to the experiment of trial by jury was 'aware of the unconquerable feelings and prejudices of the People'. He then argued that a jury, according to Cochrane's scheme, 'would be nothing like a jury of equals'. Instead, criminal justice for the right- and left-hand castes who constituted seven-eighths of the population would be delivered into 'the hands of the Bramins, Jains and Musselmen...than which there would be nothing more odious to them or more pregnant with corruption and intrigue'.[155]

At the same time, Wynn's Jury Act was sparking enraged protests in Calcutta on rather different grounds. Leading the protests was Rammohun Roy who accused the Government in his *Sambud Kaumudi* not only of religious discrimination but also of an attempt at forceful conversion to Christianity. He wrote:

> The consequences of this new Act is [*sic*] that in matters where a man's life is at stake or where banishment, imprisonment and severe punishment are awarded, we, Hindoos and Mussalmans, must submit to the verdict of Christians...whereas we...shall have no power of judging them.[156]

He further attacked the motives of Government, observing that, despite the failure of Christian missionaries to attract 'a single true and sincere convert,...many persons, no longer able to bear the reproach brought upon them by this Parliamentary Act, will take shelter under the Christian faith'.[157] By November of 1826, Rammohun had organized a petition which threatened that 'if these disabilities were not removed in time, no Hindoo or Mohammedan inhabitant will willingly serve as a juror in any capacity'. And, much to the chagrin of Rammohun's rival Tory paper, the *John Bull*, which dismissed the petition as 'humbug', no Hindus or Muslims accepted jury duty.[158]

When Rammohun's petition was finally presented to the House of Commons on 5 June 1829, C.W.W. Wynn explained his reasons for the 'distinction now complained of'. He noted 'the little respect paid by the

---

[154] Response to Queries by J. Cochrane, 2nd puisne judge of Sudr and Foujdaree Udalut, 10 March 1828, Madras Judicial Proceedings, 22 April 1828, I.O.R., P/324/25, fols 1418–19.

[155] Minute by Lushington, 19 April, Madras Secret Consultations, 22 April 1828, No. 17, I.O.R., P/Sec/Mad/109, fol. 405.

[156] *Ibid.*

[157] Cited in Saumyendranath Tagore, *Rammohun Roy—His Role in Indian Renaissance* (Calcutta, 1975), pp. 80–81.

[158] *Ibid.*; see also B.N. Dasgupta, *The Life and Times of Rammohun Roy* (New Delhi, 1980), p. 311.

natives...to the sanction of an oath' as part of 'the long established habit of corruption and venality in judicial proceedings'. Wynn further explained that 'the measure was in a great degree an experimental one; and it was evidently easier, if it should succeed, to extend its effects than, in the contrary event, to curtail them'. He then declared his experiment a success and urged the House to declare 'all the subjects of Great Britain, without distinction of blood or colour,...eligible to every employment for which their abilities, education and habits may qualify them'.[159] The House, however, simply deferred the issue to forthcoming Company Charter renewal discussions which, indeed, produced the now well-known declaration against discrimination in employment of Indians in Clause 87 of the 1833 Charter.[160] In the meantime, however, two more petitions arrived from Bombay. These were presented to the House of Commons in September 1831.

It must be said that, compared with the rage of Rammohun's petition, the tone of the Bombay petition was one of entreaty. The petitioners described themselves as conquered subjects with 'no sentiments of hostility to the British' and 'no hopes but what arise from British institutions'.[161] News had reached Bombay of the agitation in Madras among numerous citizens who had objected to any obligations of jury duty. Elphinstone's Bombay Code had already authorized European judges to avail themselves of 'the assistance of respectable natives' in both civil and criminal courts either by reference to a *panchayat* or by inclusion as assessors or members of the Court, or 'by employing them more nearly as a jury'.[162] Elphinstone's successor, Governor John Malcolm, aspired to go beyond such a rudimentary authorization. He wanted to adopt the regulation inspired by Thomas Munro. But, upon hearing of the ructions in Madras, he deferred to the Home Authorities.[163] The Company's Board of Control actually responded by ordering the Directors to send a despatch to Bombay allowing Malcolm 'to try the experiment of trial by jury'.[164] One Commissioner made the qualifying remarks that this

---

[159] Proceedings of House of Commons, 5 June 1829, cited in B.N. Dasgupta, *Ibid.*, p. 315.

[160] Clause 87, 3&4 Will. IV, c. 85.

[161] *Ibid.*, p. 317.

[162] Bombay Regulation IV prescribing the forms of proceeding of the Courts of Law in Civil Suits and Appeals and Rules for trial of the same (passed by Governor in Council 1 January 1827), Chap. IV, Sec. XXIV, Cl. 1; *see also* Bombay Regulation XIII for defining the constitution of the Courts of Criminal Justice and functions and proceedings thereof (passed by GinC 1 January 1827), Chap. VI, Sec. XXXVIII, Cl. 5.

[163] Sir John Malcolm, to Lord Melville, Bombay, 18 June 1828, in C.H. Philips, ed., *op. cit.*, Vol. I, p. 44.

[164] J.G. Ravenshaw, to Bentinck, 20 June 1829, India House, C.H. Philips, *op.cit.*, p. 235.

experiment should be 'not in the *strict and rigid form* of a *jury*, but acting upon the spirit and principle of that institution'. He would neither require 'a mystic number' of 12 jurors nor a 'unanimous verdict'. Yet, he deemed the experiment to be 'the best means for the correction of…defects…found in the judicial system…[and] laws of a country which…is…more abstruse than the wildest hieroglyphics'.[165]

Indeed, the president of the Board of Control, Charles Grant, took the lead in responding to the petitions before Parliament by proposing a new Bill to repeal the discriminatory clause of Wynn's Jury Act. Grant had to face the pressure of a parliamentary committee of enquiry investigating the substance of the Bombay and Bengal petitions. It is speculated that he was heavily influenced by Rammohun Roy, himself, who had just arrived in England as the personal representative of the Mughal emperor. He also faced the furious opposition of the Court of Directors who were unwilling to yield authority for Indians to sit on Grand Juries and on Petty Juries during trials of Christians. In fact, it was Rammohun Roy who effectively answered the objections of the Directors. The Directors had objected that, in the event an Englishman was to be tried by 'Hindoo or Mussalman Jurors', there could be no 'community of feeling, interest or habitude…between such parties' as expected according to 'a principle of the Law of England'.[166] Rammohun replied that 'every Government' had the obligation to treat 'the various classes of its subjects…as one great family, without showing an invidious preference to any particular tribe or sect'. Indeed, Saumyendranath Tagore has speculated that Charles Grant's reply to the Directors bore 'interesting marks of similarity' with Rammohun's remarks.[167] Despite the Directors' vigorous opposition through the press and petitions to the House of Lords, Grant's India Justices and Juries Act was enacted on 12 June 1832.[168]

At about the same time, Governor General Bentinck's council enacted Bengal Regulation VI, Secs III and IV of which duplicated word for word the provisions for a jury trial in the Elphinstone Code.[169] As explained by Bentinck's

---

[165] Lord Ashley, to Bentinck, India Board, 24 June 1829, *Ibid.*, pp. 241–42.
[166] Court, to Board, 9 December 1831, I.O.R., E/2/11, fols 71–74.
[167] Rammohun Roy, 'Remarks in Answer to the Objections Raised by the Court of Directors against the Introduction of the Proposed Jury Bill of Mr Grant', in Saumyendranath Tagore, *op. cit.*, p. 84. See also B.N. Dasgupta, *op. cit.*, p. 319.
[168] India: Justices and Juries Act, 2&3 Will. IV, c. cxvii.
[169] Bengal Regulation VI for enabling European Functionaries to avail themselves of assistance of respectable Natives in the Administration of Civil or Criminal Justice, and for modifying or dispensing with Futwas by Mahomedan Law Officers in certain trials (passed by Governor General in Council 31 July 1832), I.O.R., V/8/21; cf. Bombay Regulations IV and XIII (1827), *op. cit.*

Judicial Secretary, W.H. Macnaghten, Bengal Regulation VI was in keeping with the Directors' reservations concerning the expediency of the institution of trial by jury in India. The Elphinstone Code and Bengal Regulation VI of 1832 tentatively authorized three possible ways for the Company's Courts to access the language skills and local expertise of Indians. The courts could refer to *panchayat*s outside the court, admit Indian assessors into court proceedings as observers 'particularly in the examination of witnesses' or employ them 'more nearly as a Jury'. As summarized by Macnaghten, Bentinck had reasoned that 'so long as there remains any doubt as to the propriety of formally and generally introducing the system of trial by jury, it will be better to refrain from enacting any more precise rules or attracting any more general attention to the subject'. Local functionaries were to be given 'latitude as to the mode of adopting it where they may approve the principle'.[170] Indeed, Bentinck, himself, rather surprisingly in the wake of the passion of Rammohun Roy's petition, clearly discounted any Indian interest in the English experiment of trial by jury. And so, he remarked: 'Whenever the natives have come forward upon any public question (as upon the...Jury regulation), they have been considered rather the puppets of the European part of the Society than the originators of those petitions'.[171] Such sentiments were supported by a long hostile article in the *Meerut Observer* reprinted in the *Asiatic Journal* which broke with its traditional admiration for 'that enlightened ex-Brahmin, Rammohun Roy' to lament:

> [T]he arguments evidently supplied by the Hindoo patriot, who has sacrificed truth and honesty in order to pander to his passion for theory, and assured Mr Grant that all India regretted the non-appearance of native grand jurors, while he must have known that such a statement was hardly true when predicated of even the enlightened population of the single city of Calcutta.[172]

Underlining the English origins of the jury 'experiment' was the hard reality in Cl. 5 of Beng. Reg. VI, Sec. III. which vested the final verdict 'exclusively' in the Judge. Radhika Singha observes with a note of sarcasm: 'The measure therefore seems to have reserved the status of a truly impartial

---

[170] Bengal Regulation VI, Sec. III, Cl. 1–4 (1832); W.H. Macnaghten, Judicial Secretary to Governor General to James Thomason, deputy secretary to government, in C.H. Philips, *op. cit.,* Vol. II, p. 758.

[171] Minute by Bentinck, 28 December 1828, Bengal Public Proceedings, 6 January 1829, *Board's Collections*, I.O.R., F/4/1185 #30746, fol. 119.

[172] Cited in J.K. Majumdar, *Raja Rammohun Roy and Progressive Movements in India—A Selection from Records 1775–1845* (Calcutta, 1941), p. 404.

agency for the British judge, placing Indian jurors in a position of tutelage till they could, if this was ever possible, rise above the particularist ties of caste and community'. For Singha, the colonial context of Indian Jury legislation destroys all possibility of developing a 'broader social investment in working the law'.[173] Yet, it must be remembered that Jury legislation in India began with Madras Regulation X of 1827, Sec. XXIX of which decreed that the verdict of the jury was to be considered final. Also, in an effort to atone for offence to the feelings of non-Muslims subject to trial and punishment under the Muslim Criminal Code, Sec. IV of Bengal Regulation VI of 1832, in line with Sec. XXXIII of Mad. Reg. X, declared the *futwa*s of Muslim Law officers to be unnecessary.

A Very English Institution

The difficulties of introducing jury trials into *mofussil* courts were impossible to deny. However, the arguments of some of the protagonists in the never ending debate were clearly self-serving. A contemporary pamphleteer put forward a case that Lushington was engaged in a personal and political vendetta against the policies of his predecessor, Thomas Munro.[174] Burton Stein qualifies this judgement with the suggestion that Lushington was merely a politician struggling to stamp his authority on the Madras Council.[175] Later, in the wake of Bentinck's Regulation VI of 1832, the rebel bureaucrat, F.J. Shore, reported that in his district of Furruckabad the introduction of trial by jury would only succeed if local law officers were co-opted into service. Voluntary attendance would reap certain failure, as 'particularly the Hindus dislike it from fear of being ill-spoken, or of being objects of revenge if they pronounce a man guilty, and I am sorry to say that...these apprehensions are not without grounds'.[176] By way of contrast, back in the Madras Presidency, Rám Ráz, Native Judge in Mysore, insisted in a

---

[173] Radhika Singha, *op. cit.*, pp. 301–2.

[174] *The Government of Madras under the Right Hon. Stephen Rumbold Lushington* (London, 1831), pp. 1–29. [Burton Stein speculates that the author might have been a 'John Sullivan,' but this information is not certain.]

[175] Burton Stein, *Thomas Munro—The Origins of the Colonial State and His Vision of Empire* (Oxford, 1989), p. 312.

[176] F.J. Shore, to Register of Sudder Dewanny and Nizamut Adalut, Allahabad, 30 December 1834, in answer to Circular Letter from Macnaghten dated 11 July,1834, I.O.R., Home Miscellaneous Series 790/6, fol. 207. Cf. Peter Penner and Richard Dale MacLean, eds, *The Rebel Bureaucrat—Frederick John Shore (1799–1837) as Critic of William Bentinck's India* (Delhi, 1983).

testimonial addressed to H.S. Graeme that Hindu jurors were not inhibited by 'religious scruples in finding a verdict against a Brahmin'.[177] However, both Rám Ráz and F.J. Shore agreed that the discretionary authority of a presiding Judge negated 'the instrumentality of a native jury', reducing it to 'invidious' subservience.[178] Revealingly, towards the end of his deposition, Shore admitted to a lack of enthusiasm for the institution of trial by jury 'in England or Calcutta'. He confessed that if he were to be arraigned, he would prefer 'a quorum of three judges...in preference to the nine tenths of the Juries who are commonly empanelled in England'.[179]

Finally, it is apparent that, apart from Munro's enduring faith in *panchayat*s as the Hindu equivalent of a jury and Malcolm's admiration for Munro's ideas, the introduction of trial by jury into criminal trials in the *mofussil* in each of the three presidencies was very much an experiment promoted by a few Englishmen against the better judgement of their colleagues in the judicial service. Almost as if to prove the point, after the enactment of the relevant regulations in Madras, Bombay and Bengal, James Mill's famous despatch of 10 December 1834 explaining the intent of the new Charter pronounced trial by jury in the Company's *mofussil* courts a very English initiative indeed. Although the Directors were negative on the subject, their mentors on the Board of Control eagerly supported the experiment in accordance with Clause 85 of the 1833 Charter which directed that laws should be made 'for the protection of the Natives from insult and outrage' as a result of the newly authorized English settlement in the interior.[180] This contrast in outlook is evident in correspondence between the Board and Court concerning the relevant paragraphs of Mill's despatch. The Directors persisted in registering their doubts 'as to the effect of employing jury Trial in India'.[181] The Board countered by emphasizing that the 'maxim is that justice is to be distributed to men of every race, creed and colour, according to its Essence'. Board members confessed to being 'partial to the employment of Natives as assessors to the Judges'. And, in urging consideration of the introduction of the 'use of Juries in Criminal Trials...into the Provinces', they stressed that 'the prospect of an increased number of Englishmen in the Interior...forms an additional reason' for endorsing the institution of juries. Yet, they were careful to caution against adherence to an English model of

---

[177] Rám Ráz, 'On the Introduction of Trial by Jury in the East India Company's Courts of Law', *Journal of the Royal Asiatic Society*, Vol. III (1836): p. 253.
[178] Rám Ráz, *ibid.*, p. 257; F.J. Shore, *op. cit.*, fols 210–11.
[179] F.J. Shore, *ibid.*, fols 216–17.
[180] Public Despatch, to India, 10 December 1834, No. 44, I.O.R., E/4/742, fol. 529.
[181] Court, to Board, 23 October 1834, I.O.R., E/2/13, fol. 157.

a twelve-man jury producing a unanimous opinion. Instead, they urged the government in India to 'seek for precedents in the ancient usages of India' and to adopt a 'system of Criminal judicature...with an especial regard to the advantage of the Natives, rather than of the New Settlers'.[182]

Judicial Oaths

Judicial oaths, whether oaths of office or oaths sworn by witnesses in court, were another import from English judicial tradition into the court system in India. The efforts in the Company's courts to accommodate Indian religious traditions by requiring Hindu witnesses to swear on Ganges Water and Muslim witnesses to swear on the Koran totally backfired. As remarked by Rammohun Roy in his 'Aeropagitica', 'Natives...of respectable character have...an invincible prejudice against making a voluntary affidavit or undergoing the solemnities of an oath'.[183] The Bengal Sudder Judges were aware of the problem. Lamenting the perjury prevalent in *mofussil* courts, they blamed the 'present forms' of oath for 'operating as impediments to the appearance of a more respectable class of witnesses than are now generally brought forward'.[184] Furthermore, the Judges noted that the courts' discretionary authority to excuse 'superior classes of witnesses' from oath taking had the effect of further discrediting the 'usual forms of making an oath'.

In response to the Bengal judges, the Legislative Department of the Government of India submitted to the Law Commission a draft Act 'to retain the substance of an Oath', but to do away with forms 'generally disliked and often strongly objected to' and to take away the courts' discretion to allow a witness, 'as a special favour and mark of distinction, to subscribe...a solemn declaration, which is not objected to'.[185] The Law Commission, as

---

[182] Board's Corrections to manuscript of Public Despatch, to India, 10 December 1834, No. 44, I.O.R., E/4/742, fols 532–34; cf. Board, to Court, 15 November 1834, I.O.R., E/2/38, fols 75–76.

[183] 'Memorial from Certain Native Inhabitants of Calcutta', presented to Supreme Court, 31 March 1823, I.O.L., MSS Eur D611 No. 5, p. 6.

[184] Cited in Minute by A. Amos, Legislative Proceedings, 24 February 1840, No. 9, I.O.R., P/207/9.

[185] J.P. Grant, Officiating Secretary to Government of India Legislative Department, to J.C.C. Sutherland, Secretary to Indian Law Commission, 18 November 1839, Legislative Proceedings, 18 November 1839, No. 8, I.O.R., P/207/6.

a result of their subsequent study of the issue, noted that whereas Bengal and Madras courts allowed 'for dispensing with oaths in certain cases', the Elphinstone Code in Bombay had preempted the issue by prescribing the text of a preliminary admonition in civil suits.[186] But, in no presidency was there any provision, at least in the criminal judicature, for punishment for perjury. In typical Macaulay-esque preference for certainty and uniformity, the Law Commission revised the Legislative Department's Draft Act to require in all three presidencies an 'affirmation' rather than a 'declaration' because 'in the Regulations "declaration" always means [a] written oath'. However, the Law Commissioners' revised Draft Act included the Bombay preliminary admonition as an acceptable form of affirmation. The Commissioners rejected any 'express punishment for refusal to make affirmation' because 'that was included in the power to punish for refusal to give evidence'. But, they did stipulate that 'false testimony' should be punished as 'perjury'. The Commissioners' proposed 'affirmation' was to 'avoid distinctions based on religion'. Revealing a predisposition to favour the English clientele of the Her Majesty's Courts in the presidency towns, the Commissioners proposed exempting those courts from the new Act. However, they did insist that the new affirmations would be extended to all judicial proceedings not already provided for by the provisions of previous legislation in 1837.[187]

In their final deliberations over what was to become Act V 1840, the Indian Government's Legislative Department took exception to some of the points made by the Law Commission. In a lengthy minute, Amos, the legal member of the Governor General's Council, specifically objected to the Commissioners' recommendation that witnesses be 'relieved...from affording any religious guarantee for their testimony'. He argued that 'taking away the religious character of judicial testimony...would be opposed to the principles of the English law of evidence'. He further argued that the Act should not be limited to 'Hindoos and Mahomedans or to native witnesses'. Rather, 'it should be extended to European witnesses even though the deposition is less

---

[186] The text read: 'Be careful that you tell to the Court the whole truth and nothing but the truth in the matters on which you are now to be examined, or otherwise you will be liable to punishment as a false witness'. Sec. XXXIV Cl. 1, Bombay Regulation IV prescribing the forms of proceeding of the Courts of Law in Civil Suits and Appeals and Rules for trial of the same (passed by Governor in Council, 1 January 1827).

[187] J.C.C. Sutherland, Secretary to Indian Law Commission, to J.P. Grant, Officiating Secretary to Government of India Legislative Department, 3 February 1840, India Legislative Proceedings, 24 February 1840, No. 7, I.O.R., P/207/9. Act XXI to empower Presidency Governments to dispense with any Oath, not being in a Judicial Proceeding (passed by Governor General of India in Council 25 September 1837), V/8/31.

solemn than heretofore'. Consistent with this effort to level barriers between Indian and European witnesses in the court room, he insisted that the Act apply to Her Majesty's courts in the presidency towns as well as the Company courts in the *mofussil*. Curiously, he was prepared to grant discretionary authority to judges in the *mofussil* courts, only if it seemed necessary after a period of time, whereas he felt that the Act should offer exceptions for Quakers and Moravians. As for the preliminary admonitions stipulated in the Elphinstone Code, Amos suggested that it would be 'inexpedient to interfere with prevailing practices beyond prescribing that any oath or declaration made should be in conformity with the Act'. And, with reference to punishment for perjury, he excelled the Law Commission's own Macaulay-esque style of brevity and certainty by rejecting their creation of a new offence in 'false testimony'.[188] To enable final agreement on a draft for Act V, W.W. Bird, Member of the Supreme Council, pointed out that both the Law Commission and Amos went too far with their willingness to extend discretion in the courts, 'the withdrawal of which had been considered necessary' in the first instance by the Bengal Sudder Judges. He stressed that the 'object originally proposed was merely to provide by Legislative Act, that no other form of adjuration should in any case be exacted from Hindoos and Mahomedans than that of a solemn declaration'.[189]

Ultimately, the text of Act V excised all mention of any form of discretionary authority except for that granted to presidency Governors by Act XXI 1837. It adopted the Law Commission's recommendation that earlier requirements of a written declaration be replaced by an oral affirmation. However, it endorsed most of the arguments set forth by Amos, the Commission's most prominent critic. Thus, it was accepted that the newly required affirmations should contain 'religious character'. It ignored the Commissioners' wish to include the text of the preliminary admonition prescribed for the Company's courts in Bombay, and omitted their reference to a new offence of 'false testimony' in addition to the Bengal Sudder Judges' definition of 'perjury' as 'false statement'. Only Amos's wish that the Act be extended to European witnesses in Her Majesty's courts was rejected.

---

[188] Amos, Minute n.d., India Legislative Proceedings, 24 February 1840, No. 9, I.O.R., P/207/9.

[189] W.W. Bird, Minute 24 February 1840, India Legislative Proceedings, 24 February 1840, No. 10, I.O.R., P/207/9. This effort to prescribe a secular oath was more a retreat from practices found objectionable by the Company's Hindu and Muslim subjects than an attempt to please Evangelical critics of the Company's entanglement with Hinduism and Islam, as suggested by Radhika Singha, *op. cit.*, p. 297.

394   *Social Legislation of the East India Company*

And so, Act V 1840 decreed that 'Hindoos and Mahometans' make the affirmation: 'I solemnly affirm, in the presence of Almighty God, that what I shall state shall be the truth, the whole truth and nothing but the truth'. 'False affirmations' were to be punishable as 'Perjury' and the 'procuring of false information' punishable as 'subornation of Perjury'. Finally, Act V exempted from its provisions any 'Declarations' made in Her Majesty's courts or made by presidency Governors as authorized by Act XXI 1837.[190]

---

[190] Act V concerning the Oaths and Declarations of Hindoos and Mahometans (passed by Governor General of India in Council 24 February 1840), I.O.R., V/8/31.

Conclusion

Social Legislation in the Arena of Public Instruction Versus Public Justice

My fundamental argument justifying study of East India Company's social legislation is that the Company's administration depended upon a foundation in Anglo-Indian law which had steadily evolved since the establishment of a Mayor's Court with civil jurisdiction and a Court of Quarter Sessions with criminal jurisdiction in Bombay, Madras and Calcutta by the Charter or Letters Patent of 1726. There were legal signposts controlling all of its social policies. Thus 21 Geo III c. 70 secs 17 and 18 incorporated Warren Hastings' guarantee of the personal and property rights of Hindus and Muslims. Cornwallis' decision to modify Muslim criminal law made it possible to prosecute offenders in the Company's courts who had formerly been shielded by social position and Sharia law. Finally, section 43 of the 1813 Charter required the Company to invest in the education of its Indian subjects. In telling the story of the emergence of some legal initiatives and the rejection of others, I admittedly have focused on the historical records preserved in archives. I have tried to accommodate deconstructionist views which illuminate the thought processes of Company officials but have declined to vaporize issues, which were clearly a very real concern in their time, as mere figments of a colonial imagination. In analyzing the development of social legislation, I note that it was inspired either by the ideal of public instruction or by that of public justice.

The convoluted evolution of a state system of education under the East India Company was achieved in the name of a system of public instruction geared to providing well-educated elite recruits to the Company's civil service. Although vernacular education was consistently proclaimed to be the foundation for this educational system, elite colleges and *madrassa*s became the focus of School and School Book Societies and Committees of Public Instruction. Sec. 87 of the 1833 Charter acknowledged the growing appetite among educated Indian youth for employment, a hunger identified by Mountstuart Elphinstone as early as 1823. It was anticipated that graduates of such institutions as the Hindu College, the Calcutta Madrassa, the Elphinstone College and the Madras High School would acquire through the medium of the English language 'useful knowledge' which they would then pass on to their poorer and lower class brethren either through indigenous schools or through their employment as deputy collectors or as *munsif*s in the courts. This process was ultimately declaimed by Macaulay as the 'downward filtration theory'.

In truth, the process of downward filtration had been enshrined in law as early as Madras Regulation V of 1817 which required certificates from the College of Fort St. George as qualifications for law officers in Madras courts; Bengal Regulation XI of 1826 required similar qualifications from the Calcutta Madrassa or Hindu College for law officers in Bengal's courts. Avenues of employment were controlled from the centre. Enrollment at the Hindu and Hooghly Colleges in Calcutta, Elphinstone College in Bombay, Pachaiyappa's Central Institution and High School in Madras escalated. Governor General Hardinge attempted to throw open-public office to educated Indians with his Resolution of 10 October 1844. In the meantime, indigenous schools in the *mofussil* were allowed to decay for lack of funding and support. Even Rev. May's famed Chinsurah schools faded away. Governor Munro's plans for collectorate schools were dismissed out of indifference. Governor General Auckland's scheme of *zillah* schools linked to Central Colleges fizzled for lack of funding. The determination of the Council of Education in Calcutta to control access to government jobs ultimately rendered Hardinge's Resolution a 'dead letter'.

The 1854 'Magna Charta of English Education in India' ultimately reasserted the importance of vernacular education. Grants-in-aid were to revive indigenous schools and breathe life into the relatively recent efforts to support female education. New universities at the apex of this state system of public instruction were to reward advanced students of the 'improved arts, science, philosophy and literature of Europe' with an eye 'always...to the study of the vernacular language of the district'. However, by the time of Wood's Despatch, the decay and decline of indigenous schools in the *mofussil* had proved irreversible, just as Vidyasagar was to be disappointed by the government's ephemeral support for female schools. It can only be a matter for speculation whether or not the stumbling beginnings of female education during the Company period spurred the spectacular growth of vernacular education for Bengali girls or *bhadramahila*s in the latter half of the nineteenth century.

The growth of education spawned a vigorous Anglo-Indian press which sufficiently worried the Government with criticism and reports of scandals to provoke official censorship. However, gradually the Company's government was forced to recognize that its policies of censorship had no basis in law. Its only recourse against a troublesome editor was the authority of deportation granted by 53 Geo III c. 155 Sec. XXXVI, and, of course, that was only if the editor was British. With the emergence of an Indian press, first Lord Hastings in 1818 and finally Governor General Metcalfe in 1835 proclaimed an end to press censorship. Although Metcalfe's Act XI of 1835 was resented by the Directors in London, it provided an enduring standard for future governments.

Almost equally contentious for the Company, if not so prominent an issue as a free press, was the effort to promote trial by jury in the *mofussil* courts. Ironically two of the most colourful supporters of jury trials were Governor of Madras, Thomas Munro, a vigorous opponent of a free press, and the eminent Bengali reformer, Rammohun Roy, the author of the 'Areopagitica of the Indian press'. Ultimately Jury Acts enacted by the English Parliament in 1826 and 1832 combined with Sec. III and IV of Bentinck's 1832 Regulation VI to endorse the use of juries as an option for judges in *mofussil* courts. However, the provision in Sec. III Bengal Reg. VI that final authority to determine verdicts rested with the European judge undermined the potential vitality of jury duty for the Company's Indian subjects. Perhaps the abrupt suspension of the 1827 Madras Reg. XI, the most positive and elaborate provision for jury trials inspired by Munro, reflected a fundamental incompatibility between jury trials and the customary procedures of caste *panchayat*s.

Further tinkering with court procedures, the Company attempted to contrive an oath acceptable to the respectable classes identified by Rammohun Roy in his *Areopagitica of the Indian Press* as having a total aversion to the swearing of any oath. Act V 1840 prescribed a simple oath with reference to 'Almighty God' in order to end the practices of swearing on water from the Ganges or on the Koran which had proved offensive. At most, this legislation accomplished a retreat from entanglement with Indian religious symbols; it could scarcely be expected to win over the respectable classes to appear in the Company's courts as witnesses or jurors.

Parallel with education as a means of implementing the Company's mission of spreading 'useful knowledge' among its Hindu and Muslim subjects was a system of justice whereby the Company's courts were to protect the interests of a general public. Governor General Cornwallis manipulated *futwa*s to define an arena of public justice with egalitarian values in contrast with the private retaliatory justice which characterized Muslim criminal law.

Prominent social issues demonstrated the tactics of this two-pronged assault on customs of the Indian body politic perceived by Company servants to be social ills. In general, legislation for issues which were determined to be too closely entwined with caste and custom or veiled in Hindu or Muslim households was deferred with a preference for an educational approach. Such issues were usually subject to civil law which the Company had regarded as sacrosanct since the time of Warren Hastings. Those customs which were already matters of criminal law became subjects of legislation.

Bengal Regulation VIII 1799, with its provision for fictional *futwas*, became a fulcrum for action against *sati* and slavery. However, in the case of emigrant labour, the Company was handcuffed by its shared jurisdiction with the Colonial Office. It could only agitate for principles of public justice. Ultimately, it was the Privy Council which initiated 22 rules to ensure the welfare of migrant labourers; these were then incorporated into legislation by the Company. Bengal Regulation LIII 1803 provided for fictional *futwas* which prepared the way for rigorous and arbitrary action against dacoits in order to bring them within the realm of public justice. Subsequent regulations elaborated upon techniques to assist law officers in the Company's courts to focus on the 'degree of proof against the party accused' rather than 'the degree of criminality of the act established against him'. These laws evolved into the even more arbitrary Act XXX 1836 which essentially authorized the arrest and trial of thagi suspects simply for being members of a gang. Issues for which education was decidedly preferred over legislation enforced in the Company's criminal courts were sorcery, the murder of children for the sake of their ornaments, adultery and polygamy. The issue of hook swinging was deferred for resolution by the imperial government after 1857. Educational initiatives competed with attempts to formulate legislation to curb the practice of female infanticide until the imperial government enacted Act VIII of 1870. In sum, a civilizing mission, which was never very clearly articulated outside missionary circles, lost its momentum mainly for the lack of meaningful involvement in a civil service thinly spread over a vast population. The economic depression of the 1830s undermined any funding in support of indigenous education, while the Company's revenue systems did nothing to alleviate the rural poverty which lay behind the practices of female infanticide, *sati* and slavery, inspired the activities of dacoits and thugs and aggravated the concealed abuses of adultery and polygamy. However, East India Company's social legislation which pinpointed criminal issues was assured an afterlife in the Indian Penal Code. The fact that, apart from the Penal Code and Act VIII of 1870, there was very little development of social legislation by the Imperial Government during the last half of the nineteenth century is really not surprising when one considers the outlook of the Indian nationalist movement. As the nationalist response to 'proposals for effecting social reform through the legislative enactments of the colonial state' is explained by Partha Chatterjee:

> Unlike the early reformers from Rammohun to Vidyasagar, nationalists of the late nineteenth century were...opposed to such proposals, for such a method of reform seemed to deny the ability of the nation to act for itself even in the...spiritual domain...where it...considered itself superior to the West. [This was the reason for] the refusal of nationalism to make the women's question an issue of negotiation with the colonial state.... [A]fter Independence, when the nation had acquired political sovereignty,...it became legitimate to embody the idea of reform in legislative enactments about marriage rules, property rights, suffrage, equal pay, equality of opportunity and so on.[1]

The Company did make two exceptional forays into the zone of civil law. In the first instance, Hastings' guarantee of the personal and property rights of Hindus and Muslims was implicitly challenged by Section 53 of the 1833 Charter which called upon the Indian Law Commission to establish a uniform judicial system which could be applied to all the inhabitants of India with due respect for custom and tradition. The Law Commission then recommended a substantive law or *lex loci*. Such a 'law of the place' would apply to all those such as Sikhs, Buddhists, Jains or Christian converts, who were neither governed by the personal law of Hindus and Muslims guaranteed by Hastings nor governed by the English law of the Supreme Courts in the three presidencies. The Commission's 1845 draft Lex Loci Law raised the alarm, especially among orthodox Bengalis, that Indian law could be replaced by English law. When Governer General Hardinge attempted to promote the cause of *lex loci*, he found it to be controversial among both the English and the Indian subjects of the Company. He then provoked a storm of protest when he transferred three sections from the Lex Loci Act into a new Religious Disabilities Removal Act. Particularly at issue was Section XII which, in Hardinge's view, simply extended to all of India the protection of civil liberties provided by the hitherto obscure Sec. 9 of Bengal Regulation VII 1832. This Bengal Regulation had guaranteed to apostates from the Hindu or Muslim religions the right to inherit property. In response, the Dharma Sabha led by Radhakant Deb amassed thousands of signatures to protest that it was an essential duty of Hindu heirs to perform funeral rites for the deceased. And that, according to Hindu law in the *Dayabhaga*, an

---

[1] Partha Chatterjee, *op. cit.*, pp. 132–33.

'apostate from the faith cannot perform the obsequies'. It did not improve the atmosphere of debate when Christian converts and missionaries countered that the proposed 'Inheritance Law' was a triumph over ignorance and an evil equivalent to the abolition of *sati* or thagi. In the end a stalemate emerged between the Government as champion of the civil rights of Christian converts and its Hindu subjects as defenders of their religious laws. Governor General Dalhousie's Council simply ignored all protests and, without enacting a new substantive law of inheritance, declared unenforceable existing laws inflicting forfeiture of personal and property rights on apostates. Although dreams of 'Lex Loci' had long since been abandoned, Act XXI 1850 effectively allowed English law to supersede Hindu law.

But, perhaps the boldest of all of the East India Company's pieces of social legislation was the 1856 Widow Remarriage Act XV. Unlike the compulsory Bengal Regulation XVII of 1829 which decreed the abolition of *sati*, Act XV was enabling legislation. It would not interfere with Hindus who believed their religion forbade widow remarriage, but it would no longer allow the Company's courts to enforce prohibition on individuals who nurtured a different belief. Ironically, Section II of Act XV, which was actually proposed by Vidyasagar, the champion of widow remarriage, respected Hindu law and custom that a widow's inheritance from her deceased husband and even her rights of guardianship over their children would be terminated by a second marriage. Bengali Derozians objected that this section violated the Lex Loci Act's guarantee of the widow's civil rights, deterring her from remarriage and perhaps leading her to an 'immoral life'. Section III of the Act reversed an earlier decree whereby a widow's remarriage would result in forfeiture of her right of guardianship over her deceased husband's children. Section III guaranteed the widow the right of guardianship provided she had been appointed guardian by her husband's Will.

Ironically, especially in Bengal, the only viable encouragement of widow remarriage came from a Privy Council ruling in 1880 to the effect that a widow could not forfeit the estate of her deceased husband 'by reason of unchastity'. Yet, High Courts in all three presidencies ruled that the prescriptive language of Sections II and III regarding forfeiture of the first husband's estate and guardianship of his children prevailed over the enabling language of the preamble. Only in 1932 did an Allahabad Judge attempt to elevate customary law above prescriptive statutory law. However, even at this point, 80 years after passage of Act XV, few widows had taken advantage of the Act's enabling clause. Finally, Section XIV of the 1956 Hindu Succession Act won for the Hindu widow recognition of her full and absolute rights of ownership of her first husband's estate.

It is speculated that Vidyasagar's herculean efforts to promote widow remarriage were undermined by the colonial context in which he operated. Also, his own adherence to the traditional belief that the estate of the widow's deceased husband was only available to her as a means of benefitting her husband's memory and soul condemned the widow to a life of unchastity. Her sole lifeline was the legal will of her husband, a document known only in Bengal.

Indeed, in 1856, the same year as the enactment of Act XV, the Privy Council noted that in Hindu law there was no concept of a testamentary instrument such as a will. Funeral customs were specifically protected by Section 2 Bengal Regulation V 1799. However, at the same time, the Privy Council observed that wills had become accepted as common practice, at least in Bengal. In 1870 the Hindu Wills Act repealed Section 2 Bengal Regulation V 1799 and, by 1881, rules for the probate of wills of Hindus and non-Hindus were extended to Madras and Bombay. In the courts, just as a will could legitimize a Hindu widow's claim to personal and property rights, it could also play a role in undermining old prejudices and efforts to exclude females as heirs.

There is the obvious contention by those who look at all administrative policy through the prism of the colonial state that East India Company's social legislation could only be enacted by a government sure of its economic foundations. Two prominent social issues during the period of Company rule were, in actual fact, sources of substantial excise revenue. In the first instance, the Pilgrim Tax was promoted in debates about religious policy as a guarantee of respect for the religion of the Company's Hindu and Muslim subjects. This could scarcely have been otherwise inasmuch as pilgrim taxes were collected at temples and shrines which were potent religious symbols in a land where the importance of religion far exceeded that of secular government authority. Perhaps at Gaya and Allahabad, it was credible that the Company's prime motivation was to protect pilgrims from exploitation at the hands of *gayawals* and *pragwals*. But, at Jagannath Temple, the Company found itself challenging the authority of the local Raja. Under the fig leaf of preserving order among throngs of pilgrims, the Company became involved in temple administration. Ultimately, the local rebellion which officials attempted to blame on followers of the Raja was reliably attributed to overzealous revenue assessments. Terrible deaths by trampling among the hordes of pilgrims attending the *Rath Jatra* fuelled a sense of righteous obligation among Company officials at the highest level to preserve and protect the temple from violence and fraud. It was difficult to deny the need for preservation of order amidst the disorder which was inevitable when pilgrims, many desperately poor and wretched and some in suspicious disguise, assembled in vast numbers from all over India for a religious festival. However, Evangelical critics and sensible Company servants were persistent in noticing the steady accumulation of profit. Finally, a proprietor of the Company was willing to assert that the Company netted a clear profit of £1 million from its pilgrim tax revenues. The Company could no longer maintain the validity of its claim that pilgrim taxes were collected only in order to keep Jagannath Temple in good repair and to protect pilgrims at Gaya and Allahabad from fraud and abuse by *gayawals* and *pragwals*. Act X 1840 did not end the Company's entanglement with India's religious institutions, but it did end excise as an instrument of control.

The second controversial source of excise revenue was the egregious Abkarry revenue. Of course, discourse revolving around Abkarry revenue was unfettered by any connection with Indian religion. And, Abkarry revenue long outlasted the East India Company, itself. Late in the nineteenth century, the Indian Government continued to draw criticism for its willingness to draw revenue from impoverished addicts of liquor or drugs. As expressed by one critic, the Government's reliance upon excise income was 'rapidly spreading drunkenness among the people of Bengal in order to supply revenue to the Government'. Opium production in India steadily increased. The Chinese Government struggled to pay off its indemnity from the Opium War well into the twentieth century. The Treaty Powers expanded the unequal treaty system in order to force diplomatic relations upon China and extract increased indemnity. The scourge of opium penetrated ever more deeply into Chinese society.

Such robust sources of revenue, upon which the East India Company relied to support its administration, underpin the vantage point of the twenty first century which outweighs all the reports and debates in the archives with assertions of the opportunism of the colonial state. It is important to issue the corrective that in the Company period the colonial state was not necessarily foreseen as 'either desirable or possible'. These are the words of contemporary scholar Gunnel Cederlöf, who in her study of customary rights to land and resources in the Nilgiri Hills, observes that analytical concepts embracing the colonial state may put 'blinkers…on an understanding of people's acts and perceptions which are unlikely to have been guided by the notion of a future colonial state at all'.[2] Or as explained by Rina Verma Williams:

---

[2] Gunnel Cederlöf, *Landscapes and the Law: Environmental Politics, Regional Histories, and Contests over Nature* (Hyderabad, 2008), p. 111.

'It was not necessary to demonstrate that the colonizers deliberately, consciously or even unconsciously intended to establish and extend imperial control via the introduction of western legal concepts and structures in order for this to have been the precise effect of their actions'.[3]

In the arena of public instruction and public justice, countless Company servants and Indian reformers worked to expand educational resources and information networks and in the Company's courts to guarantee the rights of women, slaves, migrant labourers and victims of crime. It is of some significance that landmark pieces of social legislation do not coincide with dates of military conquest. As noted by Lauren Benton this is at odds with Ranajit Guha's 'derision of the notion that the rule of law ever came to exist in colonial settings'. From the subaltern point of view, Guha is insistent that, instead of the rule of law, 'the state developed "dominance without hegemony"—a form of power that relied much more heavily on coercion than persuasion'.[4] It only remains to point out that, as was demonstrated in the case of *sati*, a good law can serve as a guarantor of public justice.

---

[3] Rina Verma Williams, *op. cit.*, p. 42.

[4] Lauren Benton, *op. cit.*, pp. 253–55; *see also* Ranajit Guha, *Dominance without Hegemony: History and Power in Colonial India* (Harvard, 1997).

Some Key Pieces of Social Legislation

Sec. XXXVI, 13 Geo III c. 63
[Lord North's Regulating Act Empowered Company to make laws]

East India Company
Legislation Executive
Proclamations

English Parliamentary
Legislation
Privy Council
Rulings

Penal Code
Act XLV, 1860

Criminal Law

Secs. XLVII, L–LVI, LXXIV–LXXVII, and LXXIX, Bengal Reg. IX, 1793
(Revision of Muslim Criminal Law)
(Duplicated by Madras Regs. VII and VIII, 1802; and Bom. Regs. V, 1799; III and VIII, 1802; and II, 1805)

Sec. IV, Bengal Reg. XVII 1817
(empowered Nizamat Adawlat to override futwa of acquittal)

Sec. II, Bengal Reg. IV, 1822
(empowered Nizamat Adawlat to override futwa of conviction)

Bombay Regulation XIV, 1827

Sec. III, Act XXX
(no futwa required in Thagi cases)

Act I, 1840
(disavowed futwas in Madras Foujdaree Udalut)

Child Sacrifice
Bengal Regulation VI, 1802

Female Infanticide
Sec. XIII, Bengal Regulation XXI, 1795

Sec. II, Bengal Regulation VIII, 1799
Sec. XV, Ced. Prov. Reg. VIII, 1803

Sec. XI, Ced. Prov. Reg. III, 1804

Rajput Initiatives:

Decree by Jodhpur Maharajah Beejee Bukht Singh (Mid-18th century)

Article 45 of Jodhpur Code of Rules, 1839

Proclamation by Jaipur Council of Regency, 1844

Act VIII 1870 Sections 315 and 317–18

Meriah Sacrifice
and
Female Infanticide among the Konds

Act XXIV 1839

Act XXI 1845
[created Governor General's Agency for Suppression of Meriah Sacrifice]

Resisting legal process with Koorh
Enforcing legal process with Dhurna

Sec. XXIII, Bengal Reg. XVI, 1795
Secs. VII, IX and XI, Bengal Reg. XXI, 1795
Bengal Reg. V, 1797
Secs. IX and X, Ced. Prov. Reg. III, 1804
Sec. XV, Bengal Reg. XVII, 1817
(rescinded Benares Brahmins' immunity from capital punishment as guaranteed by Bengal Regs. XVI and XXI, 1795)

Sati
Secs. II and III, Bengal Regulation VIII, 1799
    Secs. XV and XVI, Madras Reg. VIII, 1802
    Sec. 6, Bombay Reg. III, 1802
    Secs. XV and XVI, Ced. Prov. Reg. VIII, 1803

Circular Orders 1813 and 1815 defining punishable conditions

Sec. 26, Cl. 2, Bombay Regulation XIV. 1827
(rescinded by Sec. 1 Bombay Regulation XVI, 1830)

Bengal Regulation XVII, 1829
Madras Regulation I, 1830
Bombay Regulation XVI, 1830

Section 298
[became Exception 5, Section 300]

Governments of Rajasthan and India, 1987–88
The Rajasthan Sati (Prevention) Act No. 40, 1987

The Commission of Sati (Prevention) Act, No. 3, 1988

Rights of Slaves
Laws of Manu

Bengal Regulations IX and X, 1774
(forbid sale of children into slavery)

Cornwallis Proclamation, 1789
    Madras Government Proclamation, 1790
        Commissioners of Malabar Proclamation, 1792
        Bombay Government Proclamations, 1805 and 1807

Bengal Regulations III and IV, 1793
                            35 Geo III c. 155
Supreme Court ruling 1798 that
Sec. 15, Bengal Regulation IV, 1793 applied to cases
   of slavery

Sec. II, Bengal Regulation VIII, 1799
(ended exemption in Muslim law from punishment
for wilful murder of slave by master)

Bengal Regulation X, 1811   51 Geo III c.23
(prohibited importation of slaves by land or sea)   (declared slave trade a felony)
    Madras Regulation II, 1812
    Bombay Regulation I, 1813
    Madras Regulation II, 1826
    Bombay Regulation XIV, 1827

Metcalfe Proclamation 1812
Rani of Travancore's Proclamation 1812

Kumaon Proclamation 1823

Madras Regulation VI, 1829
(slaves given right to prosecute and give evidence)

Bengal Regulation III, 1832

                    Sec. 88, 3&4 Will IV c.85
                            Sections 367, 370–72

Act V, 1843   (Penal offences done to slaves to be treated as offences done to freemen)

Impressed Labour—begarees

Judicial Regulation XXV, 1790
    Cl. 5, Sec. IX, Madras Regulation III, 1810

Sec. LXIX, Bengal Regulation XXII, 1795

Sec. VIII, Bengal Regulation XI, 1806
    Sec. VIII, Madras Regulation III, 1810
    Bombay Regulation VII, 1814

Sec. LIII, Madras Regulation XI, 1816
    Sec. LII, Bombay Regulation IV, 1818

Sec. III, Bengal Regulation III, 1820
(prohibited practice of pressing labour)

Bengal Regulation VI, 1825
Secs. XVII and XVIII, Bombay Regulation XII, 1827
                            Section 374

Emigrant Labour

Acts V and XXXII, 1837
                     Order in Council, 7 Sept. 1838

Act XIV, 1839
(repealed Acts V & XXXII 1837 and banned further emigration)
                   Order in Council, 15 Jan. 1842
                          (22 Rules)

Act XV, 1842
(repealed Act XIV ban vis-à-vis Mauritius; incorporated Privy Council's 22 rules)

Act XXI, 1843
(limited emigration to port of Calcutta)

Act XXI, 1844
(repealed Act XIV ban vis-à-vis

British Guiana, Trinidad and Jamaica;
incorporated Privy Council's 22 Rules)

Act VIII, 1847 (allowed emigration from Madras)

Act XIII, 1847 (repealed Act XIV ban vis-à-vis Ceylon)

                                      Colonial Secretary suspends migration to
                                                    West Indies, Feb. 1848

Secs. IV and V, Act IV, 1852 (allowed emigration from Bombay)

Act XXIV, 1852 (attempt to punish crimps)

Act XXXI, 1855
(repealed Act XIV ban vis-à-vis
Granada and St. Lucia;
incorporated Privy Council's 22 Rules)

Act XIX, 1856 (empowered Governor General
to suspend emigration for 'specified reasons')
Act XIII, 1864 (consolidated all previous legislation)

Dacoity

Judicial Regulation XXXIV, 1791
(commuted sentences of mutilation into
 sentences of imprisonment)

Bengal Regulation LIII, 1803
(emphasized degree of guilt rather than degree of proof)
    Madras Regulation XV, 1803 (duplicate)
Bengal Regulation IX, 1808 (proclamation)
    Madras Regulation XIII, 1809 (duplicate)
    Sec. XV Bombay Regulation III, 1818
    Sec. III Bombay Regulation IX, 1819

Acts XVIII and XXIV, 1843
(assimilated Dacoity and Thagi)

Act IV, 1844
(repealed Bengal Regulation IX, 1808)

Act III, 1848
(definitions of 'Dacoit')   Sections 391, 395–99, 400, 402, and 412

Thagi

Sec. XX, Madras Regulation VIII, 1802
(conditional pardon)

Cl. 1, Sec. V, Bengal Regulation XIV, 1810
(authorized conditional pardon by Nizamut Adawlut
without reference to Governor General)

Sec. III, Bengal Regulation X, 1824

Cl. 2, Sec. XXV and Cl. 1, Sec. XXXV,
    Bombay Regulation XII, 1827

Act XXX, 1836

Sections 310–11

Acts XVIII and XIX, 1837
Act XV, 1838
(repealed Sec. XXXV, Bombay Regulation XII, 1827 to
allow for conditional pardon)

Act XVIII, 1839

Acts XVIII and XXIV, 1843
(assimilated Dacoity and Thagi)

Act IV, 1844
(repealed Bengal Regulation IX, 1808)

Act II, 1847
(forbid practice of branding [tatoos])

Act X, 1847
(sentences of life imprisonment converted
to transportation for life)

Sorcery

Sec. VI, Bengal Regulation IV, 1797
    Sec. XXXIV, Madras Regulation VII, 1802
    Sec. XXXIV, Ced. Prov. Regulation VII, 1803
    Sec. XVIII, Bombay Regulation VIII, 1812
        (Duplicates)
Sec. XXV, Bombay Regulation VII, 1820
    (Revised Bombay Regulation VIII, 1812)
Cl. 2, Sec. XXVI, Bombay Reg. XIV, 1827

CIVIL LAW

Adultery

Sec. V, Bengal Regulation II, 1803
(jurisdiction in civil courts over adultery claims)

Hindu Widow Remarriage

Sec. XII, Bengal Regulation I, 1804

Act XV, 1856 Hindu Widow Remarriage Act

Government of India

Hindu Marriage Act XVIII, 1955

Hindu Wills

Sec. II, Bengal Reg. V, 1799

Act XXI, 1870
(repealed Sec. II, Bengal Reg. V, 1799)

Religious Toleration

Secs. XVII and XVIII, 21 Geo III c. 70
Secs. XII and XIII, 37 Geo III c. 142

Sec. XV, Bengal Reg. IV, 1793
Sec. XIV, Bombay Reg. IV, 1799
(enshrined law of defendant)
Sec. XVI, Madras Reg. III, 1802
Secs. II and VI, Bengal Reg. XI, 1793
(inheritance according to Hindu/Muslim law)

Bengal Reg. XIX, 1810
(supervision of temple endowments)

Madras Regulation VII, 1817
(supervision of temple endowments)

Sec. XXVI, Bombay Reg. IV, 1827
(preserved law of defendant)

Sec. IX, Bengal Reg. VII, 1832
(replaced law of defendant with formula
'justice, equity and good conscience')

Sec. 53, 3&4 Will IV c. 85
(overruled Sec. XVII, 21 Geo III c. 70)

Act XXI, 1850 Religious Disabilities Removal Act
(civil rights for Hindu apostates)

Revenue/Social Reform

Pilgrim Tax

Bengal Regulation XXVII 1793
(abolition of sayer except for pilgrim tax)

Secs. 30 & 31 Bengal regulation XII, 1805
(authorized pilgrim tax at Jagannath)

>Bengal Regulation IV, 1806
>Bengal Regulation V, 1806

Bengal Regulation IV, 1809
(restored Raja of Khurda as 'Superintendent' at Jagannath Temple)

Bengal Regulation XVIII, 1810
(regulated pilgrim taxes at Allahabad)

Act X, 1840
(abolished Pilgrim Tax)

Abkarry/Opium

Bengal Revenue Regulation XXXIII, 1790
(Government resumes Abkarry collection)
Bengal Regulation XXVII, 1793
(Abolition of sayer)

Bengal Regulation XXXII, 1793

Bengal Regulation XXXIV, 1793
(Rules to reform abuses in Abkarry collection)
Bengal Regulation LI, 1793

Bengal Regulation VI, 1800
>Bombay Regulation I, 1808
>Madras Regulation I, 1808

Bengal Regulation X, 1813

Bengal Regulation XIII, 1816
(Consolidation of previous opium rules)
Bengal Regulation XI, 1818

Bombay Regulations I, 1818
(port of Bombay closed to opium trade)
Bombay Regulation II, 1820

Bengal Regulation VII, 1824

Bombay Regulation XXI, 1827

Bombay Regulation XX, 1830

Act XXV, 1840

Act XXI, 1856
(Consolidation of previous legislation)
Act XIII, 1857

LEGISLATION SUPPORTING CIVIL SERVICE

Education

Sec. 43, 53 Geo III c. 155

Bengal Regulation IX, 1800
(founded College of Fort William)
Bengal Government Resolution, March 7, 1835

Employment

Madras Reg. V, 1817

Bengal Reg. XI, 1826

Bengal Reg. V, 1831

Sec. 87, 3&4 Will IV c. 85

Act XV, 1843

Oaths

Bengal Regulation IV, 1793
(Oaths in civil courts)
Bengal Regulation L, 1803
(Oaths in criminal courts)
Act V, 1840
(oral affirmation)

Freedom of the Press

Sec. 36, 53 Geo III c. 155
(authority for deportation)

Act XI, 1835

Indian Juries

7 Geo IV c. 37
(Wynn's JuryAct)

Madras Reg. X, 1827 (suspended)

Chap. IV, Sec. XXIV, Cl. 1, Bombay Reg. IV, 1827

Chap. VI, Sec. XXXVIII, Cl. 5, Bombay Reg. XIII, 1827

2&3 Will IV, c. 17

(Indian Justices and Juries Act)

Secs. III and IV, Bengal Reg. VI, 1832

Sec. 87, 3&4 Will IV, c. 85

Imperial Raj

Act XI, 1864
[final abolition of pundits and futwas]

Government of India

Act LVII, 1960
[repealed all British statutes enmeshed in Indian law]

Glossary

Abkarry (*Abkari*)	Excise tax on liquor and drugs
Acoobut	Discretionary punishment, torture
Adawlut (Udalut)	Court
Adigar (Adhikar)	Holder of high office, superintendent, governor
Agrestic Slaves	Agricultural slaves
Ahir	Shepherd caste
Amin (Ameen)	Indian judicial or revenue officer
Anumarana	Immolation of Hindu widow without husband's corpse
Arrack	Intoxicating liquor
Arthasastra	Sacred text concerning worldly affairs, wealth
Aryan	Early invaders of north India
Arzee (*Arzi*)	Testimony, petition
Atchybut	Fig tree
Atharvaveda	Vedic verses
Babu	Bengali clerk
Bandar	Low-caste servant/slave
Batpeada	Police peon
Begah (Bigha)	Proportion of an acre variable according to locality
Begaree	Pressed labour
Bewusta (*Vyavastha*)	Legal opinion
Bhadralok	Bengali merchant class
Bhadramahila	Educated female equivalent of bhadralok
Bhats	Bards, heralds, chroniclers
Brahmacharya	Chaste living
Brahmin (Brahman)	Highest ranking caste charged with duty of expounding the Vedas
Budduks (Budducks)	Rajputs involved in dacoity
Burdah Furrosh	Slave merchants
Cangue	Form of pillory punishment with heavy wooden yoke enclosing neck and hands
Chakra	Wheel, anything circular

Glossary 415

Chamars (Chermars)	Low-caste leatherworkers, slave caste in Malabar
Charans	Bards, heralds, chroniclers in western India where their personal security is held sufficient for important engagements
Chaukidar	Village watchman
Cherrus	Noxious drug derived from flowers of hemp
Choultry	Town house
Chouras	84 tribes settled near Delhi
Chowghula	Maratha word for assistant to a village headman
Churuck Puja (Charak)	Bengali style of hook swinging held upon Sun entering Aries
Crabs	Small Chinese boats used to ferry opium
Crimp	Agent recruiting emigrant labourers by force or fraud
Curnam (*Karnam*)	Village accountant
Cutcherry (Kacheri)	Office
Dacoit(y) (Dakaiti)	Thieves preying upon victims in gangs
Dukaytee (*Suruca-i-kubra*)	Islamic legal term for robbery by open violence
Daftar	Office, public records
Darogah	Head of police station
Dayabhaga	Bengali school of inheritance law
Devastanum	Temple property
Dewanny Adawlut	Civil court
Dharma	Legal or moral duty according to caste
Dher	Low ranking caste of scavengers, agricultural slaves in Kanara
Dhurna	Resistance to legal process by acts ranging from self-mortification to suicidal or murderous threats
Dhutooreas (Meetawallas)	Poisoners
Diwan	Finance or chief minister
Diya	Punishment with fine of blood money
Doms	Untouchable sweeper caste
Dravidians	Brahminical tribes of Southern Peninsula
Duffadars	Police officer or commander of soldiers or labourers
Dussehra (Dasehra)	Popular festival in honour of goddess Durga

Dutchna	Gifts
Futwa (*Fatwa*)	Legal decision
Foujdary (Faujdari) Adawlut (Udalut)	Chief criminal court in Madras and Bombay presidencies
Ganja	Noxious drug from hemp plant
Gayawals	Brahmin conductors of pilgrims to and at Gaya
Ghats	Mountains, steps on river bank, landing places
Godna	Tattoo
Gomtah	Land measurement
Gorinda	Specially designated police darogah
Goyenda	Spy
Hadith	Islamic legal tradition
Hadd (*Hud*)	Statutory punishment in Muslim penal law for certain crimes
Halees	Low-caste agricultural slave labourers in Kumaon
Hanufah	School of Muslim law
Jagir	Assignment of land revenue from given tract of land
Jagirdar	Holder of any assignment of revenue
Jatra	Religious festival, pilgrimage
Jatri	Pilgrim
Kamia	Bonded labourer in south Bihar
Kazi (*Qazi*)	Legal advisers for courts in cases of Muslim law, public notaries in mofussil
Khuseea	Hill porter in Almorah
Kisas (*Kissaas*)	Punishment by retaliation claimed by aggrieved parties
Kiyas	Analogical reasoning in Islamic law
Kolis	Low-caste water bearers, fishermen
Koppah	Cloth steeped in infusion of opium
Kshatriya	Second ranking ruling caste of warriors
Kulins	Privileged Bengali brahmins
Kumbh	Sign of Aquarius
Lakhiraj	Rent-free land
Lakh (*Lack*)	One hundred thousand
Lodhis (Lodhees)	Caste in northwest provinces practising husbandry

Glossary 417

Maafee chittee	License
Madrassa	Muslim school
Magh	Jan.–Feb.: 10th month of Hindu year when Sun enters Capricorn and full moon is near the asterism Magha
Mahabharata	Hindu epic
Mahajan	Merchant, money lender
Mahal	Estate
Malgozaree	Government revenue assessment
Malik	Manager, attorney, cultivator with proprietary right in land in south Bihar
Manihars	Artisans, jewellers
Mantra	Verse or stanza of sacred text, prayer
Maulvi (Maulavi)	Islamic legal scholar
Mauniam funds	Revenue from temple lands
Megpunnas	Murderers who kidnap children
Mela	Religious festival, fair
Merah funds	Portion of crop given to holder of proprietary right in village lands
Meriah	Quasi-divine victim of Kond tribal sacrifice with power over agricultural fertility
Mimamsa	Hindu school of philosophy, form of logic
Mirasidars	Holders of hereditary lands
Mitakshara	School of law associated with Mithila
Mofussil	Rural interior
Mohurrir (Muharrir)	Clerk, scribe
Moonsiff (Munsif)	Subordinate civil judge of lowest rank
Moosher	Bonded labourer in Bihar
Mopla	Malabar Muslim
Muddut	Balls of opium and pan (betel) leaves for smoking
Mufti	Islamic legal scholar whose duty is to expound the law
Naib	Deputy
Nair	Ruling caste in south
Naukee (Naukari)	Service at Imperial Mughal court
Nizamut Adawlut	Chief criminal court in Bengal
Nyaya	Form of logic, judgement
Palankeen (Palanquin)	Covered litter for one
Panchayat	Court of arbitration

Pandit (Pundit, puncah)	Scholar, expert, learned Brahmin
Pariar (Pariah)	Low slave caste
Patil (Patel, Potail)	Village headman
Peon	Foot soldier, orderly, subordinate police or court officer
*Phansigar*s	Stranglers
Pindaries	Association of mounted marauders from Maharashtra
*Pinda*s	Rice balls offered at funeral ceremonies to deceased kin
*Pragwal*s	Brahmin conductors of pilgrim ceremonies at Allahabad melas
Prayaga	Place of sacrifice
Praedial slave	Agricultural slave
Puisne judge	Subordinate judge
Puja	Worship
Pullars	Low agricultural slave caste
*Pundah*s	Temple priests
Purana	Interpretation of sacred texts outlining ancient Hindu traditions and legends
Purharees (Pratiharis)	Temple servants
Putchwye	Intoxicating drug made from fermented rice
Puttna	Deed, contract
Qazi (*Kazi*)	Legal advisers for courts in cases of Muslim law, public notaries in mofussil
Ramayana	Hindu epic
Ramoosies	Semibarbarous people in Maharashtra, thieves by profession retained as village watchmen
Rath	Chariot
Rigveda	Earliest Vedic verses
Rosoom	Fee, perquisite, gratuity
Ryot	Cultivator
Sabha	Assembly of persons of rank
Sahamarana	Voluntary immolation of a Hindu widow with corpse of her husband
Samhita	Commentary on sacred text
Sankalpa	Prayer, vow
Sattais Hazari	Seventeen thousand
Sati (*Suttee*)	Immolation of a Hindu widow
Sawuck (*Sewak*)	Bonded labourer in Chota Nagpur

Glossary

Sayer	Excise tax
Seeasut (Siyasat)	Governing authority, discretionary punishment (basis for public justice)
Sharia (Shariat)	Islamic religious law
Shastra	Hindu sacred text
Shia	Islamic sect, followers of Muhammad's son-in-law
Sicca	Rupee identified by weight of silver contained
Sirdar	Leader
Sloka	Clause, verse
Smrti	Legal treatise, body of recorded or remembered law
Soophul	Supreme blessing
Sraddha	Funeral ceremonies
Stridhun	Property belonging to a woman
Sudder Adawlut	Superior court
Sudra	Fourth ranking servile caste
Sunni	Islamic sect, followers of traditions
Sunnuds	Title deeds
Suzawal (Sazawal)	Collector of revenue
Tahsildar (Tehsildar)	Revenue collector for tahsil, in Madras also police officer
Tazir (Tusheer)	Punishment inflicted at discretion of judge
Thag (Thug)	Cheating deceiver preying upon traveller(s) in gangs, committing ritual murder by strangling (thought by British to be hereditary fraternity)
Thagi (Thuggee)	Ritualized murder and theft on roads in the mofussil
Thakur	Person of rank or authority
Thana	Police district
Toddy (Taury)	Intoxicating drug extracted from palm, date or coconut trees
Tolah	Weight measurement of silver usually equivalent to weight of one *sicca* rupee
Udalut (Adawlut)	Court
Uttur-adhikari	Successor, heir
Vaisya	Third ranking merchant caste
Vakeel	Lawyer, pleader

Vedas	Ancient Hindu sacred texts
Vereadores	Municipal officers who were legacy of Portuguese rule
Vyavastha (Bewusta)	Legal opinion
Yuga	Era
Zamin	Earth, land, soil
Zamindar	Holder of revenue rights from zamin; became proprietor
Zamindari	Office or rights of a zamindar
Zillah	District
Zina	Illicit intercourse, adultery

Bibliography

Archives

Andhra Pradesh State Archives [A.P.S.A.]
    Nellore District Records
Bihar State Archives [B.S.A.]
    Chota Nagpur Commissioner's Office [C.N.C.O.]
    Patna Commissioner's Office [P.C.O.] Letters from Nizamut Adawlut
Birmingham University
    Church Missionary Society Archives [C.M.S.]
Bombay Record Office (B.R.O.)
    General Department
    Political Consultations
British Library [B.L.]—Manuscripts
    Additional Manuscripts [ADD. MSS.] 41300.
    Auckland Papers, Letter Books, Minute Books, ADD. MSS. 37690, 37709.
    Broughton Papers, ADD. MSS. 36473, 36474.
    Warren Hastings Papers, ADD. MSS. 29233.
British Library—India Office Sanskrit Manuscripts [I.O.L., San. MSS.]
    Eggeling's Catalogue of Sanskrit Manuscripts No. 1507
    San. F 258.
British Library—India Office European Manuscripts [I.O.L., MSS. Eur.]
    MSS. Eur. D611.
    Broughton Papers, MSS Eur. F213.
    Elphinstone Papers MSS. Eur. F88.
    C. Hamilton, trans. *Hidayah* [Guide to Arabic Books of Law], MSS. Eur. D 34.
    Munro Papers, MSS. Eur. F151.
    Ranking, G.S.A., 'A History of the College of Fort William in Bengal from 1801–1900', MSS. Eur. B185.
    Willoughby Papers MSS. Eur. E 293.
    Wilson Papers, I.O.R., MSS. Eur. E301.
    Wood Papers, British Library, MSS. Eur. F78
British Library—India Office Records [I.O.R.]
    Acts and Regulations [V/8 series]
    Factory Records, Bombay Vols. I, II
    Bengal Judicial Criminal, Political, Public, Revenue, Secret and Political Proceedings
    Bengal Zamindary Court Proceedings, 1766
    Board's Collections

Board's Drafts of Secret Letters and Despatches to India, [L/P&S/5 series]
Bombay Court of Justice Proceedings, 1724
Bombay General, Judicial, Revenue Proceedings
Despatches to and from Bengal, Bombay, Madras and India [E/4 series]
Home Miscellaneous Series, Vols. 49, 51, 533, 536a, 790
India Civil and Criminal Judicial, Legislative, Legislative Council, Political, Political and Foreign, Public Proceedings
Law Reports from Zillah Azimgurh [V/22 series]
Letters between Board of Control and Court of Directors [E/2]
Madras Board of Revenue, Judicial, Public, Proceedings
Madras Secret Consultations [P/Sec/Mad]
Nizamut Adawlut Reports [N.A. Rep.], Northwestern Provinces Nizamut Adawlut Reports [N.W.P. N.A.], Tamil Nadu Foujdaree Udalut Reports [T.N. F.U.]
Northwestern Provinces Judicial Criminal Proceedings
Original Correspondence #3930, #3910
Parchment Records [A/1/100]
Public Despatch (Emigration) No. 39, March 24, 1875, L/P&J/3/1052.
Previous Communications [L/P&S/6 series]
Privy Council Appeal (1832), L/L/13 (1030).
Revenue, Judicial and Legislative Committee Papers: Emigration—Home Correspondence 1845–56, L/P&J/1/84; Indian Correspondence, L/P&J/1/88.
Selections from the Records of the Government of India (Home Dept.) No. V [V/23 series]
Selections from the Records of Government, North-Western Provinces [V/23 series]

The National Archives, Kew [N.A.]
    Colonial Office [C.O.]
    Cornwallis Papers
    Ellenborough Papers

National Archives of India [N.A.I.]
    Guide to the Records in the National Archives of India (New Delhi, 1977).
    Foreign Department, Miscellaneous Records, Political Consultations
    Land Revenue Records, Revenue Department Proceedings
    Legislative Department, Law Proceedings
    Legislative Department A, Original Consultations
    Revenue Consultations
    Selection from the Records of the Government of Calcutta 1853–1911, No. 167, 'Papers Relating to the Crime of Robbery by Poisoning'.
    Singh, Doonger, 'Source Material on Thagi and Dacoity Practices in India (1829–1902)'.

National Archives of India Library
    Report of Indian Law Commission, 1 February 1839, Appendix V, Nos. 6 and 7.

National Archives of Scotland [N.A.S.]
    Baird of Elie Papers
    Dalhousie Muniments, GD 45/6/216

National Library of Scotland [N.L.S.]
    Dundas of Ochtertyre Muniments, Acc. 10654
    Walker of Bowland Papers [W.B.]

Nottingham University
    Bentinck Papers, PwJf 2612, 2666.

Rhodes House Library, Oxford

British and Foreign Anti-Slavery and Aboriginal Protection Society Papers MSS. Brit. Emp., Memorials, S20 E2/19
Tamil Nadu Archives [T.N.A.]
    Board of Revenue Proceedings
    Judicial Consultations, Diaries
    Madura District Records
    Malabar District Records
    North Arcot District Records
    Public Sundries
    Tanjore District Records
    Tinnevelly District Records
    Trichinopoly District Records
Uttar Pradesh State Archives [U.P.S.A.]
    Allahabad
        Commissioner's Office of Goruckpore, [C.O.G.]
        Records of the Magistrate of Goruckpore [M.G.]
        Commissioner's Office of Varanasi [C.O.V.]
            Benares Judicial Files, Female Infanticide I, II [C.O.V., B.J.F., Fem. Infant. I, II]
        Duncan Records
        Records of the Magistrate of Varanasi [M.V.]
        Pre-Mutiny Records, Saharanpur Collectorate, Letters Received from Superior Courts (Nizamut Adawlut)
        Saharanpur District Records
    Dehra Dun
        Pre-Mutiny Collectorate Records, General and Political Letters Issued
    Lucknow
        Commissioner's Office of Kumaon [C.O.K.]
        Miscellaneous Letters Received by Commissioner at Kumaon
    West Bengal State Archives [W.B.S.A.]
        General Committee of Public Instruction Proceedings [G.C.P.I.].
        Judicial Criminal Proceedings

Law Reports

All India Reporter [AIR 1929 Madras]
Bellasis, A.F., ed., *Reports of Criminal Cases Determined in the Court of Sudder Foujdaree Adawlut of Bombay*, Vol. I, 1827–46 (Bombay, 1849).
Foujdaree Udalut Reports Madras 1826–50, I.O.R., V/22/610.
*The Indian Decisions (Old Seri*es), Vol. VII, *Sudder Dewanny Adawlut Reports, Bengal* (Madras: 1913). [Judges' Library, High Court, Calcutta].
Indian Law Reports [ILR]
    Allahabad [ILR 11 and 55 Allahabad]
    Bombay [I.L.R. 22 Bombay]
    Calcutta [I.L.R. 19 Calcutta]

Indian Privy Council Appeals [Law Reports 7]
Knapps Reports
Macnaghten, W.H., *Reports of Cases Determined in the Sudder Dewanny Adalat*, new ed. (Calcutta: 1827).
Macnaghten, W.H., ed., *Reports of Nizamut Adawlut*. [Judges' Library, High Court, Calcutta].
Moore's Indian Appeals [1, 6, 9 and 12 M.I.A.]
Morris, James, 1st Assistant Registrar, compiler, *Selected Decisions of the Court of Sudder Dewannee Adawlut of Bombay*, (Bombay: 1852), Tamil Nadu High Court Library.
Perry, Sir Erskine, *Cases Illustrative of Oriental Life and the Application of English Law to India, decided in H.M. Supreme Court in Bombay* (London: 1853).

Printed Government Sources

Buckland, C.E., *Dictionary of Indian Biography* (New York, Repr. 1968).
Cheap, G.C., compiler, *Circular Orders Passed by the Nizamut Adawlut for the Lower and Western Provinces and Communicated to Criminal Authorities in Bengal and Agra Provinces by Registers of those Courts from 1796 to 1844* (Calcutta: Rushton & Co.,1846) [*Circular Orders*].
Comins, D.W.D., Note on the Abolition of Return Passages to East Indian Immigrants from the Colonies of Trinidad and British Guiana (Calcutta: 1892), I.O.R., V/27/820/11.
Dewar, Douglas, *Handbook of English Pre-Mutiny Records in the Government Record Rooms of the Upper Provinces of Agra and Oudh* (Allahabad: Government Press, United Provinces, 1920).
Drummond, Andrew (Surgeon), *Statistical Account of the Hazaribagh Division of the Political Agency South West Frontier*, I.O.R., India Office Reference Map Collection, X/1318.
Duncan, Jonathan, 'Observations on the Administration of Justice as Applicable to Malabar', in *Reports of a Joint Commission from Bengal and Bombay Appointed to Inspect into the State and Condition of the Province of Malabar, in the Years 1792 and 1793 with the Regulations thereon Established for the Administration of that Province* (Bombay: n.d.), Vol. III.
First Report of the Bombay Native School Book and School Society, University of Bombay.
Forrest, Sir George, *Selections from State Papers in the Bombay Secretariat, Home Series* (Bombay, 1887) I.
Geoghegan, J., 'Note on Emigration from India' (Calcutta, 1873), I.O.R., V/27/820/1.
Government of India, Legislative Department, *The Madras Code: Consisting of the Unrepealed Madras Regulations, Local Acts of the Governor General in Council in Force in Madras, and Acts of the Governor of Fort St. George in Council*, 3rd ed. (Calcutta, 1902).
Grant, Charles, 'Observations on the State of Society among the Asiatic Subjects of Great Britain Particularly with respect to Morals; and on the means of improving it. Written chiefly in the year 1792 (*Parliamentary Papers* (1812–13) X, Cmd. 282.
Grierson, George A., 'Report on Colonial Emigration from the Bengal Presidency' (Calcutta, 1883), I.O.R., V/27/820/35.
Hansard's Parliamentary Debates, 3rd series XIX, XLI, LXXXVIII.
'History of the Rise and Progress of the Operations for the Suppression of Human Sacrifice and Female Infanticide in the Hill Tracts of Orissa', in *Selections from the Records of the Government of India (Home Dept.)* No. V, I.O.R., V/23-1, Fiche No. 7.

Lieut. Macpherson's Report upon the Khonds of the Districts of Ganjam and Cuttack (Calcutta, 1842).
Nevill, H.R., *District Gazetteers of the United Provinces of Agra and Oudh* (Allahabad: Government Press, 1911).
O'Malley, L.S.S., *Bengal District Gazetteers—Santal Parganas* (Calcutta: Bengal Secretariat Book Depot, 1910).
Parliamentary Papers (1812) Cmd. 377 ['Fifth Report'].
Parliamentary Papers (1812–13) VII, Cmd. 122.
Parliamentary Papers (1812–13) X, Cmd. 282.
Parliamentary Papers (1821) XVIII, Cmd. 749.
Parliamentary Papers (1823) XVII, Cmd. 466.
Parliamentary Papers (1824) XXIII, Cmd. 426.
Parliamentary Papers (1825) XXIV, Cmd. 518.
Parliamentary Papers (1826–27) XX Cmd. 354.
Parliamentary Papers (1828) XXIII, Cmd. 548.
Parliamentary Papers (1828) XXIV, Cmd. 125.
Parliamentary Papers (1830) VI, Cmd. 646.
Parliamentary Papers (1831) VI.
Parliamentary Papers (1831–32) VIII, Cmd. 734 III.
Parliamentary Papers (1831–32) IX , Cmd. 735 I.
Parliamentary Papers (1831–32) XI, Cmd. 735 III.
Parliamentary Papers (1834) XLIV, Cmd. 128.
Parliamentary Papers (1837–38) XLI.
Parliamentary Papers (1840) XXXVI, Cmd. 223
Parliamentary Papers (1840), XXXVII, Cmd. 58 and 331.
Parliamentary Papers (1841) III, Cmd. 43.
Parliamentary Papers (House of Lords) (1841) V, Paper 20.
Parliamentary Papers (1841) XVI, Cmd. 45.
Parliamentary Papers (1841) XXVIII, Cmd. 262.
Parliamentary Papers (1842) XXX, Cmd. 26 and 192.
Parliamentary Papers (1843) XXXV, Cmd. 613.
Parliamentary Papers (1844) XXXV, Cmd. 530.
Parliamentary Papers (1847) XLIII, Cmd. 14.
Parliamentary Papers (1847–48) VI, Cmd. 749.
Parliamentary Papers (1847–48) XLIV, Cmd. 61.
Parliamentary Papers (1850) XL, Cmd. 643.
Parliamentary Papers (1851) XXXIX, Cmd. 624 and 741.
Parliamentary Papers (1852) XVIII, Cmd. 1499.
Parliamentary Papers (1852–53) XXVII, Cmd. 426.
Parliamentary Papers (1852–53) XXIX, Cmd. 897.
Parliamentary Papers (House of Lords) (1852–53) XXXII, Cmd. 627 I.
Parliamentary Papers (1854) XXVIII, Cmd. 1833.
Parliamentary Papers (1854–55) XVII, Cmd. 1953.
Parliamentary Papers (1857–58) XLII, Cmd. 71.
Parliamentary Papers (1857–58) XLIII.
Parliamentary Papers (1874) XLVII, Cmd. 314.
Parliamentary Papers (1876) LVI.
The Indian Penal Code–Act XLV of 1860 (Lucknow, 1981).

A Penal Code Prepared by the Indian Law Commission (Calcutta, 1837; 1838 Repr.) N.A.I.
Proceedings before His Majesty's Most Honourable Privy Council, in relation to the Appeal by James Silk Buckingham Esq. against certain Regulations of the Bengal Government on the subject of the Press (London: Cox and Baylis, 1825).
Proceedings Before H.M.'s Most Honourable Privy Council in relation to the Petition by Sir John Peter Grant, Knight, Only Surviving Justice of the Supreme Court of Judicature at Bombay, I.O.R., V/27/141/8.
Selection of Papers from the Records at the East-India House, relating to the Revenue, Police and Civil and Criminal Justice under the Company's Government in India (London, 1820), I.O.R.
Richey, J.A., ed., *Selections from Educational Records, Part II 1840–1859* (New Delhi, Repr. 1965).
Sharp, H., ed., *Selections from Educational Records, Part I* (New Delhi, repr 1965).

Periodicals

Asiatic Researches (1795) IV, (1807) IV (1820), XIII.
Calcutta Christian Observer (April 1837), No. 59.
Calcutta Journal (31 Aug. 1822) IV, No. 209.
Calcutta Review (1846) V, VI, (1848) X, (1852) X, (1953) 3rd series CXXVI.
Criminal Justice History
The Englishman
Economic History Review
Friend of India
The Historical Journal
Indian Economic and Social History Review
Indian Journal of Gender Studies (1994), Vol. I, No. 2.
The Indo-British Review
Journal of the Bombay Royal Asiatic Society (1925), Vol. 6.
Journal of British Studies
Journal of the Bombay Royal Asiatic Society (1926) New Series, II.
Journal of the Royal Asiatic Society (1836) III, (1846) IX, (1856) XVI, (1860) XVII, (2005), 3rd series XV.
Journal of the Royal Asiatic Society of Bengal (1898), 67.
Madras Journal of Literature and Science (July 1837), Vol. VI.
The Madras Literary Gazette
Modern Asian Studies.
The Oriental Herald (Jan. 1826), Vol. VIII, No. 25.
The Presidency College Magazine (April 1859) 41.
Quarterly Review (August 1811), Vol. VI, No. XI.
Revista del Instituto de Derecho Comparado (Barcelona) (1957) Vols. 8–9.
The Scandinavian Economic History Review, (1967), Vol. XI.
Seminar (Feb. 1988), No. 342.
The Sunday Telegraph
Times of India
The Times (London), 16 March 1837.
Yale Journal of Criticism (1996), Vol. 9, No. 1

Unpublished Papers

Anderson, Clare, 'Rethinking Indian Indentured Labour in the Nineteenth Century', a paper from the 20th European Conference on Modern South Asian Studies, Manchester, July, 2008.
Hjejle, Benedicte, 'The Social Policy of the East India Company with regard to Sati, Slavery, Thagi and Infanticide, 1771–1852', unpublished dissertation (Oxford: l958).
Kale, M.V., 'Jonathan Duncan—Governor of Bombay (1795–1811)', PhD thesis, Wilson College, Bombay, 1982.
Kenna, Christopher, 'Rural Crime, Banditry and Colonial Control: Thugs, Dakaits and Bureaucratic Orientalism in India 1790–1863' (Ph.D. Thesis, University of Sydney, Australia, 1986).
Pouchepadass, Jacques, 'The Market for Agricultural Labour in Colonial North Bihar (1860–1920)', a paper from the Ninth European Conference on Modern South Asian Studies, Heidelberg, July 1986.
Prakash, Gyan, 'Bonded Labor in South Bihar: A Contestatory History', a paper from the Conference, on 'South Asia and World Capitalism' at Tufts University, December 1986.

Secondary Sources

Acharya, Sri Kumar, *The Changing Pattern of Education in Early Nineteenth Century Bengal* (Calcutta: Punthi Pastak, 1992).
Altekar, A.S., *The Position of Women in Hindu Civilization*, 3rd ed. (Delhi: Motilal Banarsidass, 1962).
Annan, David, 'Thuggee', in Norman MacKenzie, ed., *Secret Societies* (New York: Holt, Rinehart and Winston, 1968).
Arbuthnot, A.J., ed., *Major General Sir Thomas Munro Bart., K.C.B. Governor of Madras—Selections From His Minutes and Other Official Writings* (London: Kegan Paul, 1881).
Arnold, David, 'Crime and Crime Control in Madras, 1858–1947', in Anand A. Yang, ed., *Crime and Criminality in British India*, Association for Asian Studies Monograph No. XLII (Tucson, Arizona: 1985).
Arnold, David, 'Rebellious Hillmen: The Gudem and Rampa Risings, 1839–1924', in Ranajit Guha, ed., *Subaltern Studies I: Writings on South Asian History and Society* (Delhi, Oxford: O.U.P.,1982).
Arnold, David, *Science, Technology and Medicine in Colonial India* [*The New Cambridge History of India* III.5] (Cambridge: Cambridge University Press, 2000).
Bailey, F.G., *Stratagems and Spoils—A Social Anthropology of Politics* (Oxford: Blackwell, 1969).
Ballhatchet, Kenneth, *Social Policy and Social Change in Western India 1817–1830* (London: O.U.P., 1957).
Banaji, D.R., *Slavery in British India* (Bombay: Taraporevala Sons & Co., 1933).
Barns, Margarita, *The Indian Press: A History of the Growth of Public Opinion in India* (London: Allen & Unwin, 1940).

Bates, Crispin, 'Human sacrifice in colonial central India: myth, agency and representation', in *Beyond Representation: constructions of identity in colonial and postcolonial India* (New Delhi, O.U.P., 2006).
Bates, Crispin, *Subalterns and Raj-South Asia Since 1600* (London: Routledge: 2007).
Bayly, C.A., *Rulers, Townsmen and Bazaars, North Indian Society in the Age of British Expansion, 1770–1870* (Cambridge: Cambridge University Press, 1983).
Bayly, C.A., *Empire and Information—Intelligence Gathering and Social Communication in India, 1780–1870* (Cambridge: Cambridge University Press, 1996).
Bayly, C.A., *Indian Society and the Making of the British Empire—The New Cambridge History of India*, Part II-1 (Cambridge: Cambridge University Press, 1988).
Beaufort, F.L., *A Digest of the Criminal Law of the Presidency of Fort William and Guide to all Criminal Authorities Therein* (Calcutta: R.C. Lepage & Co., 1849).
Bentham, Jeremy, *The Collected Works of Jeremy Bentham* (London: Athlone Press, 1968).
Benton, Lauren, *Law and Colonial Cultures: Legal Regimes in World History, 1400–1900* (Cambridge: Cambridge University Press, 2002).
Bolts, W., *Considerations on India Affairs* (London: J. Almon, P. Elmsly, and Brotherton and Sewell, 1772).
Bodding, P.O., 'Taboo Customs amongst the Santals', *Journal of the Asiatic Society of Bengal*, No. 67 (1898).
Bodding, P.O., Solberg, O., eds., *Witchcraft among the Santals* (Oslo: 1940).
Borthwick, Meredith, *The Changing Role of Women in Bengal 1849–1905* (Princeton: Princeton University Press, l984).
Brandstadter, Edith S., 'Human Sacrifice and British-Kond Relations, 1759–1862', in Anand A. Yang, ed., *Crime and Criminality in British India* (Tucson, Arizona: University of Arizona Press, l985).
Browne, S, *Laws Against Ingrossing, Forestalling, Regrating and Monopolizing* (London: W. Griffin, 1767).
Bruce, George, *The Stranglers—The Cult of Thuggee and its Overthrow in British India* (London: Longmans, 1968).
Campbell, George, *Modern India* (London: 1852).
Campbell, Maj. Gen. John, *Narrative of the Operations in the Hill Tracts of Orissa for the Suppression of Human Sacrifices and Female Infanticide* (London: Hurst & Blackett, 1861).
Cannon, G., *The Life and Mind of Oriental Jones—Sir William Jones the Father of Modern Linguistics* (Cambridge: Cambridge University Press, 1990).
Carroll, Lucy, 'Law, custom and statutory social reform: The Hindu Widows' Remarriage Act of 1856', in J. Krishnamurty, ed., *Women in Colonial India—Essays on Survival, Work and the State* (Delhi; Oxford: O.U.P., 1999).
Carson, Penelope, 'The Company and the Cross', *The Indo-British Review*, Vol. XXI, No. 2 (1995).
Carstairs, G.M., *Death of a Witch—A Village in North India 1950–1981* (London: Hutchinson, 1983).
Cassels, Nancy G., 'Bentinck: Humanitarian and Imperialist—The Abolition of Suttee', *The Journal of British Studies*, Vol. V, No. 1 (November, 1965).
Cassels, Nancy G., 'The 'Compact' and the Pilgrim Tax: The Genesis of East India Company Social Policy', *Canadian Journal of History*, Vol. VII (1972): 37–49.
Cassels, Nancy G., 'John Stuart Mill, Religion and Law in the Examiner's Office', in Martin I. Moir, Douglas M. Peers and Lynn Zastoupil, eds., *J.S. Mill's Encounter with India* (Toronto: Toronto University Press, 1999).

Cassels, Nancy G., ed., *Orientalism, Evangelicalism and the Military Cantonment in Early Nineteenth-Century India—A Historiographical Overview* (Queenston, Lampeter: E. Mellen, 1991).

Cassels, Nancy Gardner, *Religion and Pilgrim Tax Under the Company Raj* (New Delhi: Manohar, 1987).

Cassels, Nancy Gardner, 'The Serampore Missionary Crisis of 1807', in Joseph T. O'Connell, ed., *Bengal Vaisnavism, Orientalism, Society and the Arts* (Michigan State University, South Asia Series, Occasional Paper No. 35, Summer 1985).

Cassels, Nancy Gardner, 'Social Legislation under the Company Raj: The Abolition of Slavery— Act V 1843', in *South Asia—Journal of South Asian Studies*, New Series, Vol. XI, No. 1 (June 1988).

Cassels, Nancy Gardner, 'Some Archival Observations on an Evangelical Tract', in *The Indian Archives*, Vol. XXX, No. 1 (January–June, 1981).

Cederlöf, Gunnel, *Landscapes and the Law: Environmental Politics, Regional Histories, and Contests over Nature* (Hyderabad: 2008).

Chang, Hsin-pao, *Commissioner Lin and the Opium War* (Cambridge, Mass.: Harvard University Press, 1964).

Chapman, Priscilla, *Hindoo Female Education* (London: R.B. Seeley & W. Burnside, 1839).

Chatterjee, Amal, *Representations of India, 1740–1840: The Creation of India in the Colonial Imagination* (Basingstoke: Macmillan, 1998).

Chatterjee, Partha, *The Nation and Its Fragments* (Princeton: Princeton University Press, 1993).

Cohn, Bernard S., 'African Models and Indian Histories', in Richard G. Fox, ed., *Realm and Region in Traditional India* (Durham, North Carolina: Duke University Press: 1977).

Cohn, Bernard S., 'Law and the Colonial State in India', in June Starr and Jane F. Collier, *History and Power in the Study of Law* (Ithaca, N.Y.: Cornell University Press, 1989).

Colebrooke, Henry T., *Digest of Hindu Law* (London: 1801).

Colebrooke, Henry T., 'On the Duties of a Faithful Widow', *Asiatic Researches* (1807) IV.

Colebrooke, J.E., *Supplement to the Digest of the Regulations enacted for the Presidency of Bengal* (Calcutta: 1807).

Colebrooke, T.E., *Life of the Honourable Mountstuart Elphinstone* (London: John Murray, 1884).

Colebrooke, T.E., *Miscellaneous Essays by H.T. Colebrooke, with Life of the Author* (London: Trübner & Co., 1873; Repr.).

Collis, Maurice, *Foreign Mud* (London: Faber, 1946).

'Comparative view of Plans of Education in Publications of Dr. Bell and Mr. Lancaster' Article XV in *Quarterly Review*, VI, No. XI (August 1811).

Covernton, A.L., 'The Educational Policy of Mountstuart Elphinstone', *Journal of the Bombay Royal Asiatic Society*, New Series, Vol. II (1926).

'Cruel practices of the Hindus at the Charak Puja', *Calcutta Christian Observer*, Article IV in No. 59 (April 1837).

Cumpston, Ina Mary, *Indians Overseas in British Territories 1834–54* (London: O.U.P., 1953).

Dalton, Edward T., *Descriptive Ethnology of Bengal* (Calcutta: 1872).

Dasgupta, B.N., *The Life and Times of Rammohun Roy* (New Delhi: Ambika, 1980).

Datta, Kalinkar, *The Santal Insurrection 1855–57* (Calcutta: University of Calcutta, 1940).

Datta, V.N., *Sati: A Historical, Social and Philosophical Enquiry into the Hindu Rite of Widow Burning* (New Delhi: Manohar, 1988).

Derrett, J.D.M., 'Justice, Equity and Good Conscience,', in J.N.D. Anderson, ed., *Changing Law in Developing Countries* (London: George Allen & Unwin, 1963).
Derrett, J.D.M., *Religion, Law and the State in India* (London: Faber & Faber, 1968).
Dhagamwar, Vasudha, *Law, Power and Justice* (New Delhi; London: Sage Publications in Association with The Book Review Literary Trust, 1992).
Dhagamwar, Vasudha, 'Saint, Victim or Criminal', *Seminar*, No. 342 (Feb. 1988).
Dharampal, *The Beautiful Tree—Indigenous Indian Education in the Eighteenth Century* (New Delhi: Biblia Impex, 1983).
Dharkar, C.D., ed., *Lord Macaulay's Legislative Minutes* (Madras: O.U.P., 1946).
Di Bona, Joseph, ed., *One Teacher, One School—The Adam Reports on Indigenous Education in Nineteenth Century India* (New Delhi: Biblia Impex, 1983).
Dingwaney, Manjari, 'Unredeemed Promises: The Law and Servitude', in Utsa Patnaik and Manjari Dingwaney (eds.), *Chains of Servitude: Bondage and Slavery in India* (London: Sangam, 1985).
Dodwell, H.H., 'Imperial Legislation and the Superior Governments, 1818–1857', in *The Cambridge History of India*, Vol. VI (Cambridge: Cambridge University Press, 1932).
Doniger, Wendy and Brian K. Smith, trans., *The Laws of Manu* (London: Penguin, 1991).
Drewitt, F. Dawtrey, *Bombay in the Days of George IV—Memoirs of Sir Edward West* (London: Longmans, Green, Calcutta: 1907).
Eden, Emily, *Up the Country; Letters Written to her Sister from the Upper Provinces of India* (London: H. Milford, O.U.P., 1937).
Elphinstone, Mountstuart, *Territories Conquered From the Paishwa—A Report* (New Delhi: Oriental publishers, Repr. 1973).
Eschmann, A., Kulke, H. and Tripathi, G.C. (eds.), *The Cult of Jagannath and the Regional Tradition of Orissa* (New Delhi: Manohar, 1978).
Eschmann, A., 'The Vaisnava Typology of Hinduization and the Origin of Jagannatha', in A. Eschmann, H. Kulke, and G.C. Tripathi (eds.), *The Cult of Jagannath and the Regional Tradition of Orissa* (New Delhi: 1978).
Fawcett, C., *The First Century of British Justice in India* (Oxford: Clarendon Press, 1934).
Fay, Peter Ward, *The Opium War 1840–1842* (Chapel Hill, North Carolina: University of North Carolina Press, 1975).
Fhlathúin, Máire ní, 'The Travels of M. De Thèvenot through the Thug Archive', *Journal of the Royal Asiatic Society* (2001), 3rd series, Vol. 2, No. 1.
Fisch, J., *Cheap Lives and Dear Limbs—The British Transformation of the Bengal Criminal Law 1769–1817* (Wiesbaden: Franz Steiner Verlag, 1983).
Fisch, Jörg, *Immolating Women—A global History of Widow Burning from Ancient Times to the Present*, trans. from German by Rekha Kamath Ragan (New Delhi: Permanent Black, 2006).
Fox, Richard G., ed., *Realm and Region in Traditional India* (Durham, North Carolina: Duke University Press: 1977).
Frazer, J.G., *The Golden Bough—A Study in Comparative Religion* (London: Macmillan & Co., 1890).
Freitag, Sandria B., 'Collective Crime and Authority in North India', in Anand A. Yang, ed., *Crime and Criminality in British India*, Association for Asian Studies Monograph No. XLII (Tucson, Arizona: University of Arizona Press, 1985).
Frykenberg, Robert E., 'The Impact of Conversion and Social Reform upon Society in South India During the late Company Period; Questions Concerning Hindu–Christian Encounters, With Special Reference to Tinnevelly', in C.H. Philips and M.D. Wainwright,

eds., *Indian Society and the Beginnings of Modernization* (London: University of London School of Oriental and African Studies, 1976).
Frykenberg, Robert E., 'Traditional Processes of Power in South India: An Historical Analysis of Local Influence', *Indian Economic and Social History Review*, Vol.1 (1963).
Furber, Holden, 'The Theme of Imperialism and Colonialism in Modern Historical Writing on India,', in C.H. Philips, ed., *Historians of India, Pakistan and Ceylon* (London: O.U.P., 1961).
Geib, R., *Die Indradyumna Legende, Ein Beitrage zur Geschichte des Jagannātha Kultes* (Wiesbaden: 1975).
Ghose, Benoy, *Iswar Chandra Vidyasagar* (New Delhi: Publications Division, Ministry of Information and Broadcasting, Government of India, 2nd Repr. 1973).
Ghose, Jogendra Chunder, ed., *The English Works of Rajah Rammohun Roy* (Calcutta: E.C. Bose, 1885).
'Goomsur: the late War there—the Khonds or Hill Tribes', *Calcutta Review*, Vol. V, No. IX (January–March 1846).
'The First Series of Government Measures for the Abolition of Human Sacrifice among the Khonds', *Calcutta Review*, Vol. VI, No. XI (July–December 1846).
Gordon, Stewart N., 'Scarf and Sword: Thugs, Marauders, and State-formation in 18th Century Malwa', *Indian Economic and Social History Review*, Vol. 6, no. 4 (1969).
Gour, H.S., *The Penal Law of India—Being an Analytical, Critical and Expository Commentary on the Indian Penal Code* 10th ed. revised by M.C. Desai, G. Kumar, and R.B. Sethi (Allahabad: Law Publishers, 1982–84).
The Government of Madras under the Right Hon. Stephen Rumbold Lushington (London: 1831).
Greenberg, Michael, *British Trade—The Opening of China 1800–42* (Cambridge: Cambridge University Press, Repr. 1969).
Guha, Ranajit, *Dominance Without Hegemony: History and Power in Colonial India* (Cambridge, Mass.; London: Harvard University Press, 1997).
Haldar, Gopala, *Vidyasagar—A Reassessment* (New Delhi: People's Publishing House, 1972).
Halhed, N.B. (trans.), *A Code of Gentoo Laws, or Ordinations of the Pundits from a Persian Translation, made from the Original, written in the Shanscrit Language* (London: 1776).
Hambling, Andrew, *The East India College at Haileybury 1806–1867* (Haileybury: 2005).
Hamilton, Alexander, *A New Account of the East Indies* (Edinburgh: J. Mosman, 1727; Argonaut Press, 1930).
Harington, J.H., *An Elementary Analysis of the Laws and Regulations Enacted by the Governor General in Council at Fort William in Bengal, for the civil government of the British territories under that Presidency* (Calcutta: Honorable Company's Press, 1808).
Hjejle, Benedicte, 'Slavery and Agricultural Bondage in South India in the Nineteenth Century', *The Scandinavian Economic History Review*, Vol. XI (1967).
Hobsbawm, Eric, *Bandits* (Harmondsworth: Penguin, 1972).
Hobsbawm, Eric, 'Social Banditry', in Henry A. Landsberger, ed., *Rural Protest: Peasant Movements and Social Change* (London: Macmillan, 1973).
Hodgson, B.H., *Preeminence of the Vernaculars; or the Anglicists Answered: Being Four Letters on the Education of the People of India*, 4th ed. (Serampore: 1847).
Hsü, Immanuel C.Y., *The Rise of Modern China* (London, Toronto, New York: O.U.P., 1970).
Hunter, William Wilson, *Life of Brian Houghton Hodgson* (London: J. Murray, 1896).
Ibbetson, D.C.J., *Outlines of Punjab Ethnography* (Calcutta: 1883).

Ilbert, Sir Courtenay, *The Government of India* (Oxford: Clarendon Press, 1907).
Inglis, Brian, *The Opium War* (Sevenoaks: Hodder & Stoughton, 1976).
Israel, Milton, *Communications and Power—Propaganda and the Press in the Indian Nationalist Struggle, 1920–1947* (Cambridge: Cambridge University Press, 1994).
Jain, M.P., *Outlines of Indian Legal History*, 2nd ed. (Bombay: N.M. Tripathi, 1966).
Kane, P.V., *History of Dharmasastra* (Poona: Bhandarkar Oriental Research Institute, 2nd ed.1973).
Kapur, Sohaila, *Witchcraft in Western India* (Bombay: Orient Longman, 1983).
Kaye, John William, *The Administration of the East India Company* (London: R. Bentley, 1853; Allahabad Repr.: 1966).
Kasturi, Msalavika, 'Crime and Law in India: British Policy and the Female Infanticide Act of 1870', *Indian Journal of Gender Studies*, Vol.1, No. 2 (1994).
Kaye, John William, *Christianity in India: An Historical Narrative* (London: Smith, Elder, 1859).
Kaye, John William, *The Life and Correspondence of Charles Lord Metcalfe* (London: Smith, Elder, 1858).
Keith, A.B., *A Constitutional History of India 1600–1935* (London: Methuen & Co., 1936).
Kejariwal, O.P., *The Asiatic Society of Bengal and the Discovery of India's Past* (New Delhi: O.U.P., 1988).
Kenna, Christopher, 'Rural Crime, Banditry and Colonial Control: Thugs, Dakaits and Bureaucratic Orientalism in India 1790–1863' (PhD Thesis, University of Sydney, Australia, 1986).
'The Khonds—Abolition of Human Sacrifice and Female Infanticide', *Calcutta Review*, Vol. X, No. XX (July–December 1848).
Kopf, David, *British Orientalism and the Bengal Renaissance* (Calcutta: Firma K.L. Mukhopadhyay, 1969).
Kumar, Dharma, *Land and Caste in South India—Agricultural Labour in the Madras Presidency During the Nineteenth Century* (Cambridge: Cambridge University Press, 1965).
Kusuman, K.K., *Slavery in Travancore* (Trivandrum: Kerala Historical Society, 1973).
Lahiri, K., 'Meriah Sacrifices', *Calcutta Review*, 3rd Series, CXXVI, No. 1 (January 1953).
Laird, M.A., ed., *Bishop Heber in Northern India—Selections from Heber's Journal* (Cambridge: Cambridge University Press, 1971).
Laird, M.A., *Missionaries and Education in Bengal, 1793–1837* (Oxford: Clarendon Press, 1972).
Lloyd, Mary, 'Sir Charles Wilkins 1749–1836', *India Office Library and Records Report for the Year 1978* (London: British Library Reference Division Publications, 1979).
Long, James, *Hand Book of Bengal Missions in Connexion with the Church of England together with an Account of General Educational Efforts in North India* (London: 1848).
Love, H.D., *Vestiges of Old Madras 1640–1800* (London: John Murray, 1913).
Macnaghten, F.W., *Considerations on the Hindoo Law as it is Current in Bengal* (Serampore: Mission Press, 1824).
Macnaghten, W.H., *Principles and Precedents of Hindu Law* (Calcutta: Baptist Mission Press, 1828–1829).
Macnaghten, W.H., *Principles and Precedents of Moohummudan Law* (Calcutta: Church Mission Press, Mirzapore, 1825).
Macpherson, William, ed., *Memorials of Service in India from the Correspondence of the Late Major Samuel Charters Macpherson, C.B. Political Agent at Gwalior During the Mutiny, and Formerly Employed in the Suppression of Human Sacrifices in Orissa* (London: John Murray, 1865).

Majeed, Javed, *Ungoverned Imaginings—James Mill's 'The History of British India' and Orientalism* (Oxford: O.U.P., 1992).
Major, Andrea, *Pious Flames—European Encounters with Sati 1500–1830* (Oxford: 2006).
Majumdar, J.K., *Raja Rammohun Roy and Progressive Movements in India—A Selection from Records 1775–1845* (Calcutta: Art Press, 1941).
Mandlik, *Vyavahara Mayukha* (Bombay: Education Society Press, 1880).
Mani, Lata, 'Contentious Traditions: 'The Debate on *Sati* in Colonial India", in Kumkum Sangari and Sudesh Vaid, eds., *Recasting Women—Essays in Colonial History* (New Delhi: Kali for Women, 1989).
Mani, Lata, *Contentious Traditions—The Debate on Sati in Colonial India* (Berkeley; London: University of California Press, 1998).
Marshall, P.J., *Bengal: The British Bridgehead, Eastern India 1740–1828: The New Cambridge History of India*, Part II-2 (Cambridge: Cambridge University Press, 1987).
Marshall, P.J., ed., *The British Discovery of Hinduism in the Eighteenth Century* (London: Cambridge University Press, 1970).
Marshman, John Clark, *The Life and Times of Carey, Marshman and Ward* (London: Longman & Co., 1859).
Mayne, J.D., *A Treatise on Hindu Law and Usage*, 6th ed. (Madras: Higginbotham, 1900).
McCully, Bruce T., *English Education and the Origins of Indian Nationalism* (Gloucester, Mass.: P. Smith, Repr. 1966).
Mehrotra, S.R. and Moulton, Edward C., eds., *Selected Writings of Allan O. Hume*, Vol. I— *District Administration in North India, Rebellion and Reform* (New Delhi; Oxford: O.U.P., 2004).
McLane, John R., 'Bandits and Rebellion in Nineteenth-Century Western India', in Anand A. Yang, ed., *Crime and Criminality in British India*, Association for Asian Studies Monograph No. XLII (Tucson, Arizona: University of Arizona Press, 1985).
Misra, Atmanand, *The Financing of Indian Education* (London: Asia Publishing House, 1967).
Mitra, Peary Chand (Gouranga Gopal Sengupta, ed.), *A Biographical Sketch of David Hare* (Calcutta: Jijnasa, 1979).
Mitter, Dwarka Nath, *The Position of Women in Hindu Law* (Calcutta: 1913).
Moir, Martin I., Peers, Douglas M. and Zastoupil, Lynn, eds., *J.S. Mill's Encounter with India* (Toronto: Toronto University Press, 1999).
Moor, Edward, *The Hindu Pantheon* (London: 1810).
Moore, R.J., *Sir Charles Wood's Indian Policy* (Manchester: Manchester University Press, 1966).
Morley, W.H., *An Analytical Digest of all the Reported Cases decided in the Supreme Courts of Judicature in India, in the Courts of the Hon. East-India Company, & on appeal from India, by Her Majesty in Council* (London: 1850).
Morse, H.B., *The Chronicles of the East India Company Trading to China 1635–1834* (Cambridge, Mass.; Oxford: Clarendon Press, 1926).
Müller, F.M. Max, 'Biographical Essays', in *Collected Works* (London: 1910).
Mukherjee, Prabhat, *Pilgrim Tax and Temple Scandals—A Critical Study of the Important Jagannath Temple Records during British Rule*, ed., Nancy Gardner Cassels (Bangkok: Orchid Press, 2000).
Murshid, Ghulam, *Reluctant Debutante: Response of Bengali Women to Modernization, 1849–1905* (Rajshahi, Bangladesh: Rajshahi University Press, 1983).
Murthy, N.K., *Indian Journalism—Origin, Growth and Development of Indian Journalism from Asoka to Nehru* (Mysore: University of Mysore Press, 1966).

Nair, Savithri Preetha, 'Native Collecting and Natural Knowledge (1798–1832): Raja Serfoji II of Tanjore as a 'Centre of Calculation', *Journal of the Royal Asiatic Society* 3rd series, Vol. 15 Part 3 (Nov. 2005).

Nandy, Ashis, 'Sati: A Nineteenth Century Tale of Women, Violence and Protest', in Nandy, Ashis, *At the Edge of Psychology: Essays in Politics and Culture* (Delhi; Oxford: O.U.P., 1980).

Nandy, Ashis, 'Sati as Profit Versus Sati as a Spectacle', in Hawley, John Stratton, ed., *Sati— The Blessing and the Curse* (New York; Oxford: O.U.P., 1994).

Narain, Vishnu Anugrah, *Jonathan Duncan and Varanasi* (Calcutta: Mukhopadhyay, 1959).

Narasimhan, Sakuntala, *Sati—A Study of Widow Burning in India* (New Delhi: Viking, 1990).

Natarajan, S., *A History of the Press in India* (London; Bombay: Asia Publishing House, 1962).

Neill, Stephen, *A History of Christianity in India: 1707–1858* (Cambridge: Cambridge University Press, 1985).

Norton, J.B., *A Selection of Leading Cases on the Hindu Law of Inheritance*, Part 2 (Madras: C. D'Cruiz, 1871).

Oddie, Geoffrey A., *Popular Religion, Elites and Reform: Hook-Swinging and its Prohibition in Colonial India, 1800–1894* (Delhi: Manohar, 1995).

Oldenburg, Veena Talwar, 'The Continuing Invention of the Sati Tradition', in Hawley, John Stratton, ed., *Sati—The Blessing and the Curse*, (New York; Oxford: O.U.P., 1994).

Oldenburg, Veena Talwar, 'The Roop Kanwar Case: Feminist Responses', in Hawley, John Stratton, ed., *Sati—The Blessing and the Curse* (New York; Oxford: O.U.P., 1994).

'On the Burning of Hindoo Widows', *The Oriental Herald*, VIII, No. 25 (January 1826).

Owen, David Edward, *British Opium Policy in China and India* (New Haven, Conn.: Yale University Press, 1934).

Padel, Felix, *The Sacrifice of Human Being: British Rule and the Khonds of Orissa* (New Delhi: O.U.P.,1995).

Pakrasi, Kanti B., *Female Infanticide in India* (Calcutta: Editions Indian, 1970).

Pandey, B.N., *The Introduction of English Law into India* (London: Asia Publishing House, 1967).

Panigrahi, Lalita, *British Social Policy and Female Infanticide in India* (New Delhi: Munshiram Manoharlal, 1972).

Pant, S.D., *The Social Economy of the Himalayans—Based on a Survey in the Kumaon Himalayas* (London: G. Allen & Unwin, 1935).

Parulekar, R.V., ed., *Survey of Indigenous Education in the Presidency of Bombay (1820–1830)* (Bombay: Asia Publishing House, Repr. 1951).

Pascal, Blaise, *Pensées* #60, Lafuma ed., (Harmondsworth: Penguin, 1966).

Pearce, Robert Rouiere, *Memoirs and Correspondence of the most noble Richard Marquess Wellesley* (London: R. Bentley, 1846).

Penner, Peter and MacLean, Richard Dale, eds, *The Rebel Bureaucrat—Frederick John Shore (1799–1837) as Critic of William Bentinck's India* (Delhi: Chanakya Publications, 1983).

Perry, Sir Erskine, *Cases Illustrative of Oriental Life and the Application of English law to India, decided in H.M. Supreme Court in Bombay* (London: S. Sweet, 1853).

Philips, C.H., ed., *The Correspondence of Lord William Cavendish Bentinck, Governor General of India 1828–1835* (Oxford: O.U.P., 1977).

Phillips, Arthur, 2nd. ed. by Trevelyan, Sir Ernest John, *The Law Relating to Hindu Wills* (London: Thacker, Spink & Co., 1914).

Powell, Avril, *Muslims and Missionaries in pre-Mutiny India* (Richmond, Surrey: Curzon, 1993).
Prakash, Gyan, *Bonded Histories: Genealogies of Labor Servitude in Colonial India* (Cambridge: Cambridge University Press, 1990).
Rahman, A.F.M. Abdur, *Institutes of Muslim Law—A Treatise on Personal Law According to the Hanafite School* (Calcutta: 1907).
Ramachandran Nair, Adoor K.K., *Slavery in Kerala* (Delhi: Mittal Publications, 1986).
Rankin, George C., *Background to Indian Law* (Cambridge: University Press, 1946).
Rau, M. Chalapathi, *The Press* (New Delhi: National Book Trust, 1974).
Raychaudhuri, Tapan, Kumar, Dharma and Desai, Meghnad, eds., *The Cambridge Economic History of India*, Vol. II, c.1757–c.1970 (Cambridge: Cambridge University Press, 1983).
Ráz, Ram, 'On the Introduction of Trial by Jury in the East India Company's courts of Law', *Journal of the Royal Asiatic Society*, Vol. III (1836).
Richey, J.A., ed., *Selections from Educational Records*, Vol. II (Calcutta: Superintendent Government Printing India, 1922; New Delhi: Repr. for National Archives of India by Manager of Publications: 1965).
Robinson, F. Bruce, 'Bandits and Rebellion in Nineteenth Century Western India', in Anand A. Yang, ed., *Crime and Criminality in British India*, Association for Asian Studies Monograph No. XLII (Tucson, Arizona: University of Arizona Press, 1985).
Robson, John M., and Moir, Martin and Zawahir, eds., *Writings on India by John Stuart Mill* (Toronto: University of Toronto Press, 1990).
Rocher, L., 'Schools of Hindu Law', in J. Ensink and P. Gaeffke, eds., *India Maior* (Leiden: E.J. Brill, 1972).
Rosselli, John, *Lord William Bentinck—The Making of a Liberal Imperialist 1774–1839* (London: Chatto & Windus for Sussex University Press, 1974).
Roy, Parama, 'Discovering India, Imagining Thuggee', *Yale Journal of Criticism*, Vol. 9, No. 1 (1996).
Roy, Rammohun, 'A Second Conference between an Advocate for, and an Opponent of, the Practice of Burning Widows Alive' (Calcutta: 1820), in Jogendra Chunder Ghose, ed., *The English Works of Raja Ram Mohun Roy*, Vol. I (Calcutta: E.C. Bose, 1885).
Russell, Robert and Lal, Hira, *Tribes and Castes of the Central Provinces of India* (London: Macmillan & Co., 1916).
Ryan, Alan, 'Utilitarianism and bureaucracy: the views of J.S. Mill', in Gillian Sutherland, ed., *Studies in the Growth of Nineteenth-century Government* (London: Routledge and Kegan Paul, 1972).
Saha, Panchanan, *Emigration of Indian Labour (1834–1900)*, (Delhi: People's Publishing House, 1970).
Said, Edward W., *Orientalism* (New York: Pantheon Books, 1978).
Saradamoni, K., *Emergence of a Slave Caste: Pulayas of Kerala* (New Delhi: People's Publishing House, 1980).
Sen, Asok, *Iswar Chandra Vidyasagar and his Elusive Milestones* (Calcutta: Riddhi-India, 1977).
Sewell, Robert, *A Forgotten Empire (Vijayanagar)* (London: Swan Sonnenshein & Co., 1900).
Shakespear, J., 'Observations regarding Badhecks and Th'egs' *Asiatic Researches*, Vol. XIII (1820).
Sharma, Arvind, 'The Scriptural Sanction for Sati in Hinduism', in Arvind Sharma, ed., *Sati: Historical and Phenomenological Essays* (Delhi: Motilal Banarsidass, 1988).

Sharma, Arvind, 'The Tradition of Indigenous Protest Against Sati', in Arvind Sharma, ed., *Sati: Historical and Phenomenological Essays* (Delhi: Motilal Banarsidass, 1988).
Sharp, H., ed., *Selections from Educational Records*, Vol. I (Calcutta: Superintendent Government Printing India, 1920; New Delhi: Repr. for National Archives of India by Manager of Publications: 1965).
Sherwood, R., 'Of the murderers called P'hansigars', *Asiatic Researches*, Vol. XIII (1820).
Shore, John, Baron Teignmouth, *Memoirs of the Life, Writings and Correspondence of Sir William Jones* (London: John Hatchard, 1804).
Shore, Frederick John, *Notes on Indian Affairs* (London: John W. Parker, 1837).
Shore, Sir John, 'On Some Extraordinary Facts, Customs and Practices of the Hindus', *Asiatic Researches*, Vol. IV (1795).
Singh, Khushwant, *A History of the Sikhs* (Princeton: Princeton University Press; London; Oxford: O.U.P., Repr. 1984).
Singh, Rawa Satinder, ed., *The Letters of the First Viscount Hardinge of Lahore to Lady Hardinge and Sir Walter and Lady James 1844-1847*, Royal Historical Society, Camden Fourth series, Vol. 32 (London: Offices of the Royal Historical Society, 1986).
Singha, Radhika, *A Despotism of Law—Crime and Justice in Early Colonial India*, (Calcutta; Oxford: O.U.P., 1998).
Singha, Radhika, 'Providential Circumstances: The Thuggee Campaign of the 1830's and Legal Innovation', *Modern Asian Studies*, Vol. 27, No. 1 (1993).
Sinha, D.P., *The Educational Policy of the East India Company in Bengal to 1854* (Calcutta: Punthi Pustak, 1964).
Sleeman, William Henry, *Ramaseeana, or a Vocabulary of the Peculiar Language used by the Thugs, with an Introduction and Appendix, Descriptive of the System Pursued by that Fraternity and of the Measures which have been Adopted . . . for its Suppression* (Calcutta: G.H. Huttmann, 1836).
Sleeman, William Henry, *Rambles and Recollections of an Indian Official* (first published 1844), ed. by Vincent A. Smith (repr. Karachi; London: O.U.P., 1973).
Sleeman, William Henry, *Report on the Thug Gangs* (Calcutta: Bengal Military Orphan Press, 1840).
Smith, Rev. H. Percy, ed., *Glossary of Terms and Phrases* (London: Kegan Paul, Trench, 1883).
Sontheimer, Gunther D., 'On the Memorials of the Dead in the Tribal Area of Central India', in S. Settar and G.D. Sontheimer, eds., *Memorial Stones: A Study of their Origin, Significance and Variety* (Manipal: Manipal Power Press, 1982).
Steele, Arthur, *Summary of the Law and Custom of Hindoo Castes within the Dekhun Provinces Subject to the Presidency of Bombay, chiefly affecting civil suits etc.* (Bombay: 1827).
Stein, Burton 'The Segmentary State in South Indian History', in Richard G. Fox, ed., *Realm and Region in Traditional India* (Durham, North Carolina: Duke University Press, 1977).
Stein, Burton, 'State Formation and Economy Reconsidered', *Modern Asian Studies*, Vol. 19, Part 3 (1985).
Stein, Burton, *Thomas Munro—The Origins of the Colonial State and His Vision of Empire* (Delhi; Oxford: O.U.P., 1989).
Stephen, Sir James Fitzjames, *The Story of Nuncomar and the Impeachment of Sir Elijah Impey* (London: Macmillan & Co., 1885).
Stirling, Andrew, *An Account Geographical, Statistical and Historical of Orissa Proper* (1822).
Stokes, Whitley, *The Anglo-Indian Codes* (Oxford: Clarendon Press, 1887).
Strange, T., *Elements of Hindu Law; Referable to British Judicature in India*, 1st ed. (London: 1825).

Strange, T., *Hindu Law: Principally with Reference to such Portions of it as Concern the Administration of Justice, in the King's Courts, in India,* 2nd ed. (London: Parbury, Allen, 1830).

Tagore, Saumyendranath, *Rammohun Roy—His Role in Indian Renaissance* (Calcutta: Asiatic Society, 1975).

Shore, John, Baron Teignmouth, *Memoirs of the Life, Writings and Correspondence of Sir William Jones* (London: John Hatchard, 1804).

Thomas, Timothy N., *Indians Overseas: A Guide to Source Materials in the India Office Records for the Study of Indian Emigration 1830–1950* (London: British Library, 1985).

Thompson, Edward, *The Life of Charles, Lord Metcalfe* (London: Faber & Faber, 1937).

Thompson, E. And Garratt, G.T., *Rise and Fulfilment of British Rule in India* (London: Macmillan & Co., 1934).

Tinker, Hugh, *A New System of Slavery The Export of Indian Labour Overseas 1830–1920* (London: O.U.P. for the Institute of Race Relations, 1974).

Tod, James, *Annals and Antiquities of Rajasthan* (London: Routledge & Kegan Paul, Repr. 1972).

Trevelyan, G.O., *The Life and Letters of Lord Macaulay* (London: Longmans, Green & Co., 1889).

Tripathi, Amales, *Vidyasagar—The Traditional Moderniser* (Bombay: Orient Longman, 1974).

Tucker, Henry St. George, John William Kaye ed., *Memorials of Indian Government; Being a Selection from the Papers of Henry St. George Tucker, late Director of the East India Co.* (London: Bentley, 1853).

Turner, Ralph E., *James Silk Buckingham 1786–1855, A Social Biography* (London: Williams & Norgate, 1934).

University of Madras, *History of Higher Education in South India* (Madras and Bangalore: Associated Printers, Madras, 1957).

Upreti, Harish Chandra and Nandini, *The Myth of Sati* (Bombay: Himalaya Publishing House, 1991).

Vidyasagar, Iswarchandra, *Marriage of Hindu Widows*, repr. (Calcutta: K.P. Bagchi, 1976).

Venkataraman, S., 'Influence of Common Law and Equity on the Personal Law of the Hindus', *Revista del Instituto de Derecho Comparado* (Barcelona), Vols. 8–9 (1957).

Wagner, Kim, 'The Deconstructed Stranglers: A Reassessment of Thuggee', *Modern Asian Studies*, Vol. 38, No. 4 (2004).

Wagner, Kim, 'Thuggee and Social Banditry Reconsidered', *The Historical Journal*, Vol. 50, No. 2 (2007).

Waley, Arthur, *The Opium War Through Chinese Eyes* (London: George Allen & Unwin, 1958).

Warner, Sir William Lee, *The Life of the Marquis of Dalhousie K.T.* (London: Macmillan & Co., 1904).

Washbrook, D.A,, 'Progress and Problems: South Asian Economic and Social History, c. 1720–1860', *Modern Asian Studies*, Vol. 22, Part 1 (1988).

West, Sir Raymond and Majid, Syed H.R. Abdul, *A Digest of the Hindu Law of Inheritance, Partition, and Adoption Embodying the Replies of the Sastris* (London: Sweet and Maxwell Ltd., 1919), 4th ed. of Raymond West and Johann George Bühler, *A Digest of Hindu Law, from the Replies of the Shastris in the Several Courts of the Bombay Presidency* (Bombay: Education Society Press, 1867).

Williams, Rina Verma, *Postcolonial Politics and Personal Laws* (New Delhi; Oxford: O.U.P., 2006).

Wilson, H.H., 'The Religious Festivals of the Hindus', *Journal of the Royal Asiatic Society*, Vol. IX (1846).
Wilson, H.H., *Works by the late Horace Hayman Wilson* (London: Trûbner & Co., 1862).
Wilson, R.K., *An Introduction to the Study of Anglo-Muhammadan Law* (London: W. Thacker & Co., 1894).
Wright, H.R.C., 'The Abolition by Cornwallis of the Forced Cultivation of Opium in Bihar', *Economic History Review*, 2nd series, Vol. XII, No. 1 (1959).
Yang, Anand A., 'Dangerous Castes and Tribes: The Criminal Tribes Act and the Magahiya Doms of Northeast India', in Anand A. Yang, ed., *Crime and Criminality in British India*, Association for Asian Studies Monograph No. XLII (Tucson, Arizona: University of Arizona Press, 1985).
Yang, Anand A., ed., *Crime and Criminality in British India*, Association for Asian Studies Monograph No. XLII (Tucson, Arizona: University of Arizona Press, 1985).
Yule, Col. Henry and Burnell, A.C., *Hobson-Jobson—A Glossary of Colloquial Anglo-Indian Words and Phrases, And of Kindred Terms, Etymological, Historical, Geographical and Discursive* (London: Routledge & Kegan Paul, 1903, 1969 Repr.).
Zastoupil, Lynn and Moir, Martin, eds., *The Great Indian Education Debate—Documents Relating to the Orientalist-Anglicist Controversy, 1781–1843* (Richmond, Surrey: Curzon, 1999).

Index

Act X 1840, 119, 123, 143
Adhikari (Odhakaree, Odheecary), 53, 58, 72, 111, 111n.1, 113
Gooroomookh Das, 53, 113
Afghanistan, 122, 138
First Afghan War, 135, 136
Aksay (Ukhy) But, 49, 49n.30
Akuapada, 105
Akund Mehecap, 43, 43n.24
Allahabad, 68, 92, 94, 106
Alsurung, 54
Amil, 48
Amrit Monouhee, 60
Anoochuttree, 109, 131, 131n.3, 135
Ansur Ghar, 76
Arakan (Mug country), 46n.26
Aranee(s), 45
Arati, 43n.22
Archbold, W.A.J., 188
Armstrong, J.S., Collector of Puri, 30
Asan Mundeep, 76
Assan (Ashan, Ashwina), 49, 128, 128n.5
Assah(s), 45
Athara Nulla (Autara Nullah), 30, 37, 37n.2, 38, 46, 54–56, 82, 101n.4, 113, 147
Ghaut, 64, 75, 76, 85
Auckland, Earl of, (Governor General), 100, 100n.24, 114, 119–22, 130, 133–36, 138, 141, 143

Baboo Ghaut, 56
   see also Gundicha Mundeep
Bagdee(s), 46
Bahar Dewul Shewuck, 41
Balabhadra Bhanja, 28
Balasore, 55, 105
Bampton, Rev., 96
Barlow, G.H. (Governor General), 13, 60, 86, 113

Bastah, 105
Basu, 59
Batpeada(s), 74n.2, 76, 148
Batwas, 59
Baugdee, 74
Bawree(s), 46
Bayley, W.B., Secretary to Government in Judicial Department, 15
Bengal, 30, 39, 56, 105, 133
   Board of Revenue, 13, 15, 63–66, 70n.6, 71, 72, 75, 76, 83n.3, 84n.4, 87, 88, 113, 125n.3, 128n.6, 135, 135
   Hours, 45
   Regulation XII 1805, 108–10, 115–16, 119–20, 124–25, 126n.4, 131–32, 134–35, 137
   Regulation IV 1806, 13, 63–65, 68, 89, 120
   Regulation V 1806, 73, 89, 127
   Regulation IV 1809, 14, 72–75, 77–78, 85–86, 88–89, 103, 110, 117, 120, 125, 127
   Regulation XI 1810, 72, 110, 117
   Regulation XIX 1810, 110, 115, 125, 125n.3
   Regulation VII 1819, 126
   Revenue Department, 13n.2, 14n.7, 15n.10, 67–68, 71, 88, 140
   Revenue Despatch 20 February 1833, 101–104
   see also 'Christian epistle'
Bentinck, Lord William (Governor General), 97, 97n.12, 98, 98n.16, 101n.2, 102
Beopari (Bepari), 39
Berar, Raja of, 109, 143
Bettia (Betiah) Kalla, 129, 129n.7, 133, 150
Bhairava, 70n.6
Bhandara, 50n.31

Bharati, Ram Shankar, 70n.6
Bheturchoo Mahapatra (Beetur Choo), 43, 43n.20, 45
Bhitara, 43n.20
Bhog(e) (Bhoga), 39n.10, 40–41, 42n.15, 43n.22–23, 45, 47, 48, 51, 54, 60, 79–80, 127, 132,148
    Bhogapoota, 124
    Gopaul Bullub, 45
    Kote, 47, 51
    Mohun, 60, 72, 111 111n.2, 115
    Mundup 45, (gate) 124
Bhonsla (Bhowsla) Ragojee, 40, 48, 60, 84n.5, 111, 129
Bhubaneswar (Bhobanissar), 124
Bhurrung, *see* Jatri
Bimlakhya, Goddess, 61
Bishy (Bishie, Bisoyee), 51, 51n.33, 52, 148
Bitul Moal, 51
Bograe, 109
Brahma (Burma) 49, 134
Brahmacharies (Burmacharies), 44, 50, 54, 58
    Mohooree, 54n.35
Bramins (Brahmins), 17–20, 22–23, 31, 33–34, 39–42, 43n.18, 50, 59, 61, 65, 77, 85, 93, 100, 101n.26, 120, 137, 68–69, 80, 82–85. 95–97, 139, 141, 144
Buchanan, Claudius, 31, 95, 95n.2 & 4, 96–97,144
    An Apology for Promoting Chistianity in India, 96n.6
Buller, Charles, Settlement Commissioner of Cuttack, 63, 63n.7, 67
Bulpoor, 113
Bundar (Bhandar) Mehkap, 50, 50n.31
Burkandaz (Barkandaz), 48, 111, 126–27, 148
Busby, Samuel, Collector of Pilgrim Tax, 66, 76
Byragee, 58, 70n.6
    see also Jatri
Byturnee Nullah, 66

Calcutta, 93, 119
    Calcutta Review, 94, 109
    Calcutta Christian Observer, 118, 145

Campbell, Lt. Col., 17, 20, 23, 137n.5
Canning, Lord (Governor General), 131n.3
Cassels, Nancy G., *Religion and Pilgrim Tax* ... 67n.9, 68n.3, 99n.18, 122n.6, 138n.7
Chabiskud, 27
Chakra Tirtha, 74n.2
Chamar, 74
Chandradhaja, Raja of Kujang, 29
Chatree, 77–78, 82
Chattah(s), 45
Chela, 58, 148
Chhatisa Nijoga Nayaka (Chatisaniyoga Nayak, Chutees Neejog), 23, 41, 43, 58, 148
Chilka
    Coast, 95
    Lake, 137n.5
Chooly, 44
Chowdree, Bydenath, 128
    Chowries (chamaras, chourees), 77, 81
    Christian, 98, 106, 108, 133–34, 136, 143
        'Epistle', 104
        Government, 13–14, 17, 23, 26, 63, 68–69, 80, 82–85, 95–97
Christianity, 69, 71, 96, 99–100, 102
Chundal(s), 46
Cockburn, G.F., Commissioner of Cuttack, 99n.21, 131n.3
Colebrooke, H.T., 15, 66, 88, 90
Cullal (soonree), 74
Cuttack, 11, 17, 18n.2, 20–27, 31, 74, 78, 82, 84, 99, 105, 109, 114, 121, 131, 131n.3, 135, 137, 139, 144
    Board of Revenue, 106, 108–109
    Collector of, 72–74, 100, 103, 120
    Commissioner(s), 20–32, 34–35, 57–58, 60–61, 67, 131, 144
    Hospital, 101n.4, 116, 118, 129, 129n.8
    Road from, to Puri, 116, 118
    Settlement Commissioner, 63

Dalhousie, Marquis of (Governor General), 105, 138–139

Daroga, 30, 55–56, 85, 111, 126–27, 148
Darsan (Darsun, Darshan), 76–82, 84n.4, 148
Daru, Brahma, 66
Das
 Debraj, Mohunt, 111n.2
 Gooroo Mookh, 53–54
 Jyeram (Jyram), Mohunt, 48, 60, 111n.2
 Mahadeb, 50n.32
 Monohur, 53–54
Davidson, T.R., Secretary to Government of India, 18, 26, 30
Deb, Mukunda, see Khurda, Raja
Deccan, 17
Deo, Padmanabh, see Kimedi, Raja of
Desee, see Jatri
Dewan (of Raja of Khurda), 26
Dewul Kurn (Kurun, Curn), 25, 38–39, 42, 47, 49, 149
Dewul Purcha (Parichha), 24–25, 47, 51–53, 58, 63, 72–74, 79, 103, 110, 120, 149
 Bada Dewul Purcha, 37n.3, 149
Dhamra, River, 28
Dhenkanal, Raja, 78, 82
Dhome (Dhobe), 74
Dhukkoree Gate, 124
Dhurma se, 55
Dhwaja (Dhaja, Dhuja) Pandika (Pindika), 118, 140, 145, 149
Doab, Gangetic, 17
Dolgobind (Dol Govind), Rath Purcha, 32, 40
Doolia, 74
Dowdeswell, G., Secretary to Government in the Revenue Department, 13n.2, 14n.7, 15n.10, 67, 71, 86–88, 88n.4, 90–93, 92n.2, 97, 99n.22
Drummond, E., Collector of Cuttack, 30
Dundas, Robert, 11, 67–69, 68n.3
Dundee Sunnaissees, 38, 58
Durban(s), 46
Dvara Fita, 43n.24
Dyarchy, 72
Dytahs, 43n.17, 49, 51, 58
Dwarees, 58

East India Company, 11, 18, 30–31, 57, 63, 65, 67, 70–73, 70n.7, 75, 96–97, 104, 109, 135, 144
 Board of Control, 67–72, 69n.4, 98
 Court of Directors, 63, 65, 67–73, 75, 95–99, 96n.5, 99n.18, 101, 104, 106, 114, 119, 122, 130, 130n.1, 131n.3, 134, 138, 140–44
Edmonstone, N.B., Secretary to Government, 20–21, 23–26, 28, 30
Ellenborough, Lord (Governor General), 136n.2
Elphinstone, General William G.K., 136, 136n.2, 138
'Established Donation', 108–10, 113, 115, 119–21, 129, 131, 133–35, 137–40, 142, 144
Evangelical(s), 67–69, 95–96, 99n.18, 104, 122, 132n.4, 134

Faruk (Pharuk), 48, 50, 58
Friend of India, 105, 143
Fortescue, T., Secretary to Commissioners of Cuttack, 13n.1, 27n.3&4, 32, 35, 46n.27, 60–61, 97n.14, 139

Gajapati Kings, 80
Ganges
 Water, 75
Ganjam, 54, 95n.2
Garrett, R.B., 118, 140, 140n.1
Gazur, 74
Ghooskee, 74
Gobinda Rai Mahasoy, 131
Gomastah (Gumashta), 47, 59, 124, 149
Gosseins, 58
Grant, Charles
 Chairman, Court of Directors, 67n.2, 68n.3, 102n.6
 President, Board of Control, 98
Grant, J.P., 19, 32, 104, 106
Groeme, Charles, 13, 27n.4, 32, 35, 46n.27, 57, 60, 139
 Report by, 10, 13, 32, 35–57, 67, 132
Gundicha Mundeep (Goondeecha Mundup), 27
Gurjauts, 56
Gurrooro Gate, 124
Gyah (Gaya), 92, 94, 106, 119

Haddee, 74
Halliday, F.J., Secretary to Government of Bengal in Revenue Department, 18, 25–26, 30, 59, 109, 136, 138–40
Hamilton, Walter, *Geographical, Stastical and Historical Description of Hindostan*, 21
Harcourt, G., Col. 18–19, 21–29, 100, 131, 137, 137n.5, 139
Hardinge, Lord (Governor General), 142–43
Harington, J.H., 96–97, 97n.9
Hastings, Marquis of (Governor General), 14, 82, 85, 88, 89
Hindoostan, 38, 83, 108
Hjejle, Benedicte, "The Social Policy of the East India Company...", 104n.10
Hobhouse, Sir John, President of Board of Control, 98–99, 99n.18, 100n.24, 122
Hullolkore(s), 46
Hunter, James Collector of Pilgrim Tax, 13–14, 32, 46n.27, 57–61, 63, 66, 75–76
Assistant to J. Melvill, 20, 23, 27n.3, 131
Hunter, R., Commissioner of Cuttack, 108–10
Hunter, William, *Orissa*, 22, 59

Imambarah (Emambarrah) of Hooghly, 125
Indradumnya Tank, 74n.2
Isser
    Markund, 53
    Neelkaunt, 53

Jagannath, 10
    Lord (Sri Jeeo, Jew), 11, 17, 21–22, 15, 17, 39–41, 43, 43n.18, 46–50, 52–54, 57–58, 61, 67, 70n.6, 75–77, 80, 82, 84–86, 84n.4, 95–100, 102, 105, 113, 124, 132, 134
    Mahatmya, 50n.32
    Math (Muth), 53, 109, 111n.1&2, 150
        Ballabh (Bullubh), 53, 53n.34, 72, 111
        see also Sadabrut Road, 100, 116
    Temple, 11, 13–14, 17–34, 36, 38–39, 41, 46n.26, 51–53, 55, 57–61, 63–64, 66–79, 81–83, 84n.4&5, 86–89, 91–98, 101–103,101n.3, 105–106, 108–10, 113, 115–21, 123–25, 127–28, 128n.6, 131–36, 137n.5, 139–44
    of Terveni, 20
    Town, 29, 35
Jaleswar, 105
Jamadar (Jemadar), 111, 126, 149
Jama (Jamma, Jumma), 40, 53, 149
Jamabandi (Jummabundee), 132, 149
Jama Kharch (Jumma Khurch), 13, 131, 149
Jatra (Jattra), 37, 39, 53, 149
    Chundun (Chandan), 53, 148
    Dole (Dool, Dol), 37, 53, 62, 65, 149
    Rath (Ruth), 37, 43n.17&18, 53, 65–66, 76, 85, 95, 105, 113, 126, 132n.4, 133, 151
    Snan, 37, 42n.15, 43n.17&18,53, 65
Jatri (Jattree, Jaytrie), 149
    Bhurrung, 30, 59, 64, 74–76, 85, 127
    Byragee, 30, 58, 63, 80
    Desee (Dasaee), 30, 63, 66, 73, 85
    Kangal, 30, 59, 63, 65–66, 65n.8, 76, 80, 85, 150
    Lal (Laal, Lall), 25–26, 30, 37–38, 59, 64, 74–75, 84, 127
    Nimm Laul (Nimlal), 74–76
    Punjkosee, 30, 40–41, 63, 66
    Punjtirthee (Pancha Tirtha), 74–76, Punjtirthee Certificate, 74n.2
Jogee (Noorbauf), 74
Joobra (Jobra) Ghaut, 37, 37n.5, 55, 56
Jugmohun Gate, 124
Jumissur, 53
Jyebeejye Gate, 124

Kabul, 136
Kahalee, 77–78
Kangal, *see* Jatri
Kanika, Raja of, 27–28
Kapilendra, 21
Kaujbunsee, 74
Kaye, J.W., 94, 104, 106
    Christianity in India, 95n.3, 104n.10, 106, 124

Index   443

Ker, Robert, Magistrate of Cuttack, 67
Khairat (Khyrat, Khyraut), 40, 60, 63, 150
Khandpara (Kundeeparah), Raja of, 78, 81, 84, 84n.4, 87
  Brahmaravara Ray, 84n.4
Khanja (Khunja), 53, 132, 136, 142, 145, 150
Khas, 133, 150
Khee (Kekee), 39, 43, 54, 150
Khodar (Kodhar) Purgunnah, 48, 60, 111
Khomatees, 58, 66
Khumb Gate, 124
Khurda (Koordah, Khourdah), 56, 63
  Estate, 13, 35n.1, 78n.7, 84n.5, 114n.2
  Gopinath Deva (Deb), 61
  Mukunda Deb, 14, 26–28, 78, 81, 84, 93
  Raja, 11, 14, 26–27, 29–30, 39–42, 44–45, 47, 57, 61, 63, 65, 67, 82, 119–20, 128–29, 128n.6, 133, 137n.5, 142
  Ramchandar Deo (Deb), 111, 114, 116
  Rebellion, 100, 101n.2
  Superintendent of Jagannath Temple, 14–15, 63, 67, 67n.9, 72–73, 75, 77–82, 84–91, 84n.4&5, 93, 108, 111, 114–18, 120–23, 125, 126n.4, 127–30, 128n.6, 133–34, 142,144
Kimedy (Keemundy), 78n.7
  Raja Buddohlaub (Padmanabh) Narayan Deo, 14, 78–80, 78n.7, 84
  Raja Jagannath Narayan Deo, 78n.7
Kojung, 56
Komarpara, 40
Konarak, 17n.1
Kopaul Mochun, 53
Kote
  Kote Bhoge, 47, 150
  Kote Khunja (Khanja), 39, 48, 132
Kova Chukla, 118
  Kujang, Raja of, 27–28
Kulke, Hermann
  "Kings without a Kingdom...", 80
Kummardichour, 109
Kunka, 56
Kunnumbarrah, 129
Kurmunnee Putters, 42

Kurn (Kurun, Curn)
  see Dewul Kurn
  Handee, 47
Kurrow(s), 45

Lall Jatri, see Jatri
Lakeraj (Lakheraj, Lakhraj, Lakhiraj), 49, 100–101, 113, 150
Laurie, William F.B.,
  Orissa, The Garden of Superstition and Idolatry, 22, 184
Lokenath (Lokenauth), 51, 53
  Ghaut, 56, 64, 75–76
  Image, 75
Lolee (Kusbee), 74
Ludhiana, 119, 122

Machoowa (Machua), 74
Madala Bahi, 77
Madala Panji (Madlah Panjee), 77–81
Madras Government, 70, 70n.7
Mahadeb, 53
Mahanadi (Mahanuddee), 37n.5, 57
Mahant (Mohunt), 58, 111n.2, 150
Mahapatra, Krishnachandra (Kishen Chunder), Chief Hereditary Priest, 14, 24, 35, 41n.14, 46, 46n.27, 53, 57, 60
  Chhatisa Nijoga Nayaka, 23, 41n.14
  Padmanabha, 46n.27
  see Puttee, Tullechoo
Mahaprasad (Mahapershaud), 39, 41, 43, 47, 48, 80, 118, 140, 145, 150
Mahaswar, 58
Malikana, 28, 30, 150
Malud, Thanadar of, 137n.5
Manikpatam, 137n.5, 139
Mansingh, Raja, 77
Maratha (Marhatta, Mahratta), 17, 23, 27–29, 46, 77, 78n.7, 114, 134, 137, 137n.5, 139
  Government, 13, 18, 23–25, 28, 30–33, 38n.6, 41, 60, 64, 67, 70n.6, 72, 74, 79–81, 83, 86, 91–92, 130–32, 136–37, 137n.5, 139, 141
Math (Muth), see Jagannath
Mathdhari (Muthdhari), 39, 40–41, 46–48, 80, 85, 132
Meerdun(s), 45

Melvill(e) (Milivili), J., Commissioner for Affairs of Cuttack, 20–21, 23–25, 28–29, 31n.1, 78, 131
Midnapore, 26, 28, 109
Mill, James, 97n.14
Mills, A.J. Moffatt, Commissioner of Revenue, 18–19, 22, 34, 81, 83n.3, 100, 113, 118, 123–34, 126n.4, 136–37, 140, 140n.1, 141
Minto, Lord (Governor General), 63–64, 64n.7, 82, 87, 95–96, 95n.4, 96n.5
Missionaries, 95–99, 99n.18, 105, 136, 143
General Baptist, 98
Mohanty, A.B., 78
Moira (Marquis Hastings) (Governor General), 14, 82, 85, 88
Moloch, 98, 98n.17
Mookhtyar (Mukhtyar), 28, 150
Morar Pundit, 27, 35, 35n.1, 37
Chief Parichha, 35n.1, 37, 37n.3
Morebhung, 37
Muddian Dhoop, 45
Mudiratha (Mudrahasta, Moodeerut), 42n.15
Muhammad, Fateh, 137n.5
Muhooree, 53n.34
Mukunda Deb, *see* Khurda
Mundup
Gundeecha (Gundicha), 56
Mukti (Mokti) 49n.30, 50
Murpooly Parichha, 45
Musalman Government (Moguls), 84, 130
Mussol (Mashal, Masala), 45, 77, 81
Myoor Chittree, 42, 50
Mysore Wars, 11

Naba Kalebra, 128n.5
Nagas, 58
Nakara, 53
Neeladree Mahaduddhee (Niladri Mahodaya), 42, 50, 50n.32
Neelkaunt Isser, 53
Nepal, 46n.26
Nila Madhava, 43n.18
Nimakharam Taluk, 137n.5
Nirsingnath, 51, 53
Nirsingpoor Ghaut, 55
Niti (Nitty), 42n.15, 79

Sewa, 79
Nott, General, 136n.2
Numosooder (Chanda), 74
Nuzar (Nasr, Nuzur), 27, 82

Orissa, 11, 17, 26, 28, 30, 59, 65, 72, 77–78, 80, 96, 99, 114, 119, 134, 136, 137n.5
Oriya
Brahmans, 27
New Year, 27

Paeks, 58
Pagoda, *see* Jagannath Temple
Pahada, 43n.19 & 24
Paik Rebellion, 14–15, 151
Pakenham, T., Collector of Cuttack, 57–58, 81, 129n.8
Pargana (Pergunnah), 39, 48, 56, 84n.5, 109, 111, 151
Panchgarh, 84n.5
Khodar, 48
Parichha (Purcha), 13–14, 23, 38, 40, 43–54, 57, 61, 73, 77, 80, 113, 128
Dewul, *see* Dewul Purcha
Murpooly, 45
Second, 35n.1
Third, *see* Sewajee
Third, Suttaishuzarry Purcha, 74
Bada Deul, 37n.3, 148
Bur Dewul, 45
Chief, 27, 35, 35n.1, 81
Parry, Edward, 67n.2, 68n.3
Pasupalakas, 42n.16
Patita Pabana, 74n.2
Pautdoreea(s), 38
Peer Alee(s) (Peerally), 46, 74
Peggs, James, 97, 99n.18, 143
India's Cries to British Humanity, 95n.1, 96, 96n.8, 99n.20
Pilgrim Tax in India, 96, 96n.7, 99n.19, 105
Pershaud (Prasad), 44, 51, 151
Pilgrims, 24–25, 30, 33, 38–39, 41,43, 45–46,48–50, 53–59, 63, 65, 72–75, 79– 80, 89, 91–92, 96, 101, 101n.4, 104–106, 113, 116–17, 119, 121, 123, 125–29, 129n.7, 133–34, 141–42, 144–45

Collector of Pilgrim Tax, 74–75, 74n.2, 79, 82, 103, 128n.6, 142
Tax, 24–26, 28, 30–33, 37–38, 54–57, 63–65, 68, 70, 70n.7, 73–74, 79, 82–86, 88–89, 91–94, 96–106, 102n.6, 108–10, 113–22, 125, 127–31, 133–34, 136, 138, 140–45
Piply, 27
Pollock, General, 136
Pooja (Puja), 44, 50n.32, 151
Poojaree, 44
see also Mudiratha Poojarees
Potdar, 59
Poynder, John, 97, 97n.13, 105
Pratihari(s) (Purharrees, Purriarees, Padiaris), 38n.6, 43. 46n.27, 48–49, 57–60, 64, 72, 75, 80, 119, 124, 127–28, 132–33, 132n.4, 151
Priests, 13, 18–19, 21–22, 25–26, 28–29, 41n.4, 46n.26, 57–58, 61, 65–66, 69–70, 72–73, 77, 80–81, 86, 95, 102–104, 114, 119–21, 123, 125, 131n.3, 133–34, 136, 141–42, 144–45
Parichha, 139
Puan, 74
Puanda, Niladri, 50n.32
Pundahs (Pundits), 20, 38, 44, 46, 50, 55, 57–58, 60, 64–65, 72, 74n.2, 75, 80, 127–28, 133, 145
Assembly of, 13, 46n.27, 63, 65, 120
Punjkosee, see Jatri
Punjtirthee, see Jatri
Puntee, 44
Aughore (Bhooinmalee), 46, 74
Booroos, 43n.23
Puri (Pooree), 11, 15, 18n.2, 21–22, 28, 30, 51, 57–58, 63, 65n.8, 75, 78, 80–82, 84n.4, 87, 95–99, 101n.4, 108, 117, 119, 123. 125, 133, 144–45
Collector of, 126–27
Dharamsala, 101n.4
Government Dispensary, 122
Hospital, 116, 118, 129
Raja, 51n.33, 77, 80, 114
Purushottoma (Poorshootum), 21, 27, 37, 39, 40–41, 48–50, 52–53, 56, 59
Chutter (Kshetra), 37n.3

Putta (Pattee, Putna), 40n.13
Puttee, 43n.18, 49, 51, 58
Puttespore, 109
Putul, 54

Raghunathjee Temple, 131n.3
see also Seetaram Thakoo Baree
Rahang, 27
Rajabhoga Itihasa, 77–78
see also Madala Panji
Rajghat, 105
Rajguru, Jagannatha, Pundit (second parichha), 35, 35n.1, 37n.3, 78, 81, 101n.26
Rajguru, Jayi, Mookhtyar of Mukunda Deb, 28
Ramcaund, 20, 23
Ram Pundit, Raja (Subahdar), 50
Rath (Ruth), 32, 37–38, 66, 97, 103, 105, 107, 118, 131, 133, 140, 151
Khunja, 123, 53–54, 59, 78–81, 151–52
see also Rath Jatra
Reyshucooli Nullah, 66
Richardson, J., Settlement Commissioner, 14–15, 67,, 67n.9, 75, 78, 80–83, 84n.4, 85–88, 88n.22&4, 91–94, 92n.2, 97, 99n.22
Rickett, H., Commissioner of Cuttack, 57–58, 100n.23, 105, 109–10, 114–18, 124, 128
Rosom (Rusoom), 38n.6, 45, 151
Rowanna, 59,151

Sadabrut (Suddaburt, Sadabarat) Juggunnauth Bullubh, 113, 115–16, 151
Saes, 57
Sambalpur (Sumbulpore)
Mukta Dei, Rani, 84, 84n.5
Samuells, E.A., Commissioner of Cuttack, 30
Sankaracharya, 70n.6
Sarbarakar(s) of Khurda, 35n.1, 151
Sasun, 50
Sathiva, 59
Sattais Hazari Mahal (Suttaees Huzarree, Sauteeshazaree), 39, 74, 105, 111, 111n.3, 113, 115, 120–22, 126, 132–33, 140, 145, 151

Sayer, 87, 142–43,151
Seetaram Thakoo (Takoo, Tawkwur) Baree, 109, 131, 131n.3, 135
Sehan Gate, 124
Sepoys (Sepahees), 72, 103
see also Vellore
Serain, 27
Serampore, 95
Seringapatam, 11, 18n.2
Sewajee (Shivajee) Ungtis, Pundit, 14, 23–25, 32, 35, 37, 52–53
Chief Parichha, 37n.3
Parichha of Sauteeshazaree Mahal, 39
Third Dewul Parichha, 24–25, 37n.3, 39–40, 46, 52
Shaster, 44, 49, 79, 85, 93
Shelokes, 66
Shewuck (Sebaka), 10, 25, 41–44, 49–51
First Sevaka, *see* Khurda, Superintendent of Jagannath Temple
See also Bahar Dewul Shewuk
Shood, 77–78, 81, 152
Poora Shood, 78
Shoomaree, 59
Singharee(s), 42, 42n.16, 46, 46n.27, 53, 60
Singhason, 38
Snan, 49
Maha Snana, 124
Munch, 47
See also, Snan Jatra
Soophul, 49
Sooree(s), 46
Stirling, A., 35n.1, 57, 78, 81, 101, 101n.26, 103, 112
Account ... of Orissa, 107, 147
Subahdar (Soobahdar), 45, 50–51, 53–54, 79, 113, 152
Sudder Board of Revenue, 19, 22, 59, 100n.23, 105, 109–10, 114–15, 124, 126n.4, 130, 136–38, 140–42
Sunnad (Sunud), 39, 152
Sunnaissees (Sannyassees), 38, 40, 44, 50, 58, 151
Sunts, 58
Suthooas, 38, 38n.7, 55
Suttee, 141

Sveta Ganga, 74n.2
Swanlo, 53n.34
Swar (Suara, Supakar), 44, 58, 80
Booroos, 43, 43n.22
Swargadwar, 74n.2

Tadau Karana(s), 77–78
Taluk, 152
Nimakharam, 137n.5
Tarkapanchanan,Jagannath, Pundit, 23
Telegu, 66
Teor, 74
Thakur (Takhoor), 51, 53, 82, 152
Thakoo Baree (Tawkwur Baree), 109
see also Seetaram Thakoo Baree
Thanee Lands, 100
Tirupati (Tripetty) Temple
Tax, 70n.7, 94
Toynbee, G.
Sketch of the History of Orissa, 65, 105
Trower, W.,
Collector of Cuttack, 14–15, 46n.27 57–58, 60, 66, 75–76, 78, 80, 82, 84n.4, 85, 88, 101n.26
Draught Regulation, 89–90
Tucker, Henry St. George, 143
Tuhseeldar (Tahsildar, Tehsildar), 27, 37, 87, 110, 152
Tullechoo Mahapatra(s), 43, 43n.19
Turrow, 48

Udney, George, 63, 63n.7, 66, 95
Umrutmonohee Lands, 145
Utkala Khanda, 50n.32

Vakeel (Vakil), 141
of Khurda Raja, 29
Vellore
Sepoy Mutiny, 69, 69n.5, 70n.7
Venkatesvara, Balaji, 70n.7
Vidyadharpur, 53n.34
Vishnu, 59
Chalanti Vishnu, 77

Watson, Eric, Judge of Calcutta Court of Circuit, 15, 15n.8
Webb, G., Collector of Cuttack, 60, 66, 83n.3, 132

Report, 86–87, 113, 128–29, 132
Wellesley, Arthur (General), 141
Wellesley, Richard, Marquis (Governor General), 17–19, 23, 27, 29–32, 136–37, 143

Wilkinson, W., Collector of Puri, 57–58, 101n.3, 106, 108–11, 113–15, 117–18, 122, 124, 126n,4, 128

Zemindars, 132

About the Author

Nancy Gardner Cassels formerly taught in the Department of History, McMaster University, Ontario, Canada. She has also been a visiting lecturer at the University of Waterloo and a visiting assistant professor at the University of Toronto.

She has been the recipient of a Carnegie Teaching Fellowship from 1959 to 1961, a Canada Council Research Grant in 1968, a Shastri Indo-Canadian Institute Senior Fellowship from 1988 to 1989 and Social Sciences and Humanities Research Council of Canada Research Grants from 1980 to 1981 and from 1987 to 1988.

She is also the author of *Religion and Pilgrim Tax under the Company Raj*, published in 1987.

61/2